AMARNA STUDIES

HARVARD SEMITIC STUDIES

Jo Ann Hackett and John Huehnergard, editors

Syriac Manuscripts: A Catalogue	Moshe H. Goshen-Gottstein
Introduction to Classical Ethiopic	Thomas O. Lambdin
The Poet and the Historian: Essays in Literary and Historical Biblical Criticism	Richard Elliott Friedman, Editor
The Songs of the Sabbath Sacrifice	Carol Newsom
Non-Canonical Psalms from Qumran: A Pseudepigraphic Collection	Eileen M. Schuller
The Hebrew of the Dead Sea Scrolls	Elisha Qimron
An Exodus Scroll from Qumran	Judith E. Sanderson
You Shall Have No Other Gods	Jeffrey H. Tigay
Ugaritic Vocabulary in Syllabic Transcription	John Huehnergard
The Scholarship of William Foxwell Albright	Gus Van Beek
The Akkadian of Ugarit	John Huehnergard
Features of the Eschatology of IV Ezra	Michael E. Stone
Studies in Neo-Aramaic	Wolfhart Heinrichs, Editor
Lingering over Words: Studies in Ancient Near Eastern Literature in Honor of William L. Moran	Tzvi Abusch, John Huehnergard, Piotr Steinkeller, Editors
A Grammar of the Palestinian Targum Fragments from the Cairo Genizah	Steven E. Fassberg
The Origins and Development of the Waw-Consecutive: Northwest Semitic Evidence from Ugaritic to Qumran	Mark S. Smith
Amurru Akkadian: A Linguistic Study, Volume I	Shlomo Izre'el
Amurru Akkadian: A Linguistic Study, Volume II	Shlomo Izre'el
The Installation of Baal's High Priestess at Emar	Daniel E. Fleming
The Development of the Arabic Scripts	Beatrice Gruendler
The Archaeology of Israelite Samaria: Early Iron Age through the Ninth Century BCE	Ron Tappy
A Grammar of Akkadian	John Huehnergard
Key to A Grammar of Akkadian	John Huehnergard
Akkadian Loanwords in Biblical Hebrew	Paul V. Mankowski
Adam in Myth and History: Ancient Israelite Perspectives on the Primal Human	Dexter E. Callender Jr.
West Semitic Vocabulary in the Akkadian Texts from Emar	Eugen J. Pentiuc
The Archaeology of Israelite Samaria, vol. II: The Eighth Century BCE	Ron E. Tappy
Leaves from an Epigrapher's Notebook: Collected Papers in Hebrew and West Semitic Palaeography and Epigraphy	Frank Moore Cross
Semitic Noun Patterns	Joshua Fox
Eighth-Century Iraqi Grammar: A Critical Exploration of pre-Ḫalīlian Arabic Linguistics	Rafael Talmon

AMARNA STUDIES

Collected Writings

by

William L. Moran

Edited by
John Huehnergard and Shlomo Izre'el

EISENBRAUNS
Winona Lake, Indiana
2003

AMARNA STUDIES
Collected Writings

by
William L. Moran

Edited by
John Huehnergard and Shlomo Izre'el

Printed in the United States of America

Library of Congress Cataloging-in-Publication Data

Moran, William L.
Amarna studies : collected writings / by William L. Moran ; edited by John Huehnergard and Shlomo Izre'el.
p. cm. — (Harvard Semitic Museum publications) (Harvard Semitic Studies ; no. 54)
Includes the author's thesis (Ph.D.—Johns Hopkins, 1950) under the title : A syntactical study of the dialect of Byblos as reflected in the Amarna tablets.
Includes bibliographical references and index.
ISBN 1-57506-906-7 (hardcover : alk. paper)
1. Tell el-Amarna tablets. 2. Canaanite language—Dialects—Lebanon—Jubayl. I. Huehnergard, John. II. Izre'el, Shlomo. III. Moran, William L. Syntactical study of the dialect of Byblos as reflected in the Amarna tablets. 2003. IV. Title. V. Series. VI. Series: Harvard Semitic studies ; no. 54
PJ3887.M67 2003
492′.6—dc21
2003001734

The paper used in this publication meets the minimum requirements of the American National Standard for Information Sciences—Permanence of Paper for Printed Library Materials, ANSI Z39.48-1984.⊗™

Contents

Preface

For many decades, William L. Moran was widely recognized as the leading scholar of the Amarna letters, the archive of international and vassal correspondence from Egypt of the fourteenth century BCE. The grammar of the largest group of these letters, those written in Byblos, formed the topic of his 1950 doctoral dissertation at the Johns Hopkins University, and over the years he wrote many articles on both the grammar and the content of these fascinating texts, culminating in a magisterial new translation of the entire corpus, issued first in French in 1987 and subsequently in English in 1992.

In his dissertation Moran discovered the key to the grammar of the Amarna letters written in Byblos, showing that, although the lexicon was Akkadian, the syntax, the morphosyntax, and the tense-and-aspect system were almost wholly Northwest Semitic and thus closely related to that of the nearly contemporary Ugaritic language and of enormous significance for understanding the prehistory and early history of Hebrew. By doing this, he showed that the language used by Canaanite scribes as manifested in the Amarna letters was not an unordered mixture of linguistic features, but instead that it has a system; in other words, that it is a language. Later, Moran and others, especially Anson F. Rainey, demonstrated that the grammar of nearly all of the letters written in Syria-Palestine was essentially the same as that of the Byblos letters. Although Moran published many of the conclusions of his dissertation in a number of articles, he did not publish the dissertation itself, which instead became one of the most oft-cited unpublished works in the field of Near Eastern studies. Even after half a century it still offers valuable insights, and so we are pleased to include it in the present volume, along with all of the articles and notes on the Amarna letters that Moran did publish. An index of textual citations is appended to make Moran's writings as accessible to readers as possible.

In the following pages the dissertation precedes the published papers, which appear in chronological order of publication. In order to keep the form of the articles close to the original publications, we have not attempted to harmonize the citation and reference styles across this volume. We have corrected, usually silently, the few typographical and other errors that we noted in the original publications, and for ease of reference we have made a small number of other changes (e.g., replacing Moran's "ThD" in the dissertation to "*EA* 362"), but we have made no changes of substance in the content of the dissertation or the articles.

We are very grateful to Eugene McGarry, who typed the dissertation and all of the articles onto disk, providing us with an initial draft of the volume. His careful work and excellent judgment made our task of editing the papers a great deal easier and saved us from many errors. We are also indebted to him for the preparation of the text citation index.

Bill Moran died on December 19, 2000, at his home in Brunswick, Maine. On a visit to see him earlier in the year the two of us had asked him about publishing his Amarna studies, including the dissertation, and he was enthusiastic about the idea. A month before his death, we were able to show him an early draft. We are very pleased to be able to make available in one volume all of Bill's great wisdom on Amarna.

JH
ShI

Acknowledgments

We gratefully acknowledge the editors and institutions who kindly granted permission to reproduce the studies included in this volume.

"A Note on igi-kár, 'provisions, supplies,'" from *Acta Sumerologica Japonensia*, volume 5, ©1983 by The Middle East Culture in Japan. Reprinted courtesy of Motoko Sasase, The Middle East Culture in Japan.

"A Re-interpretation of an Amarna Letter from Byblos (*EA* 82)," from *Journal of Cuneiform Studies*, volume 2; "Rib-Adda of Byblos and the Affairs of Tyre (*EA* 89)," from *Journal of Cuneiform Studies*, volume 4; "The Use of the Canaanite Infinitive Absolute as a Finite Verb in the Amarna Letters from Byblos," from *Journal of Cuneiform Studies*, volume 4; "New Evidence on Canaanite *taqtulū(na)*," from *Journal of Cuneiform Studies*, volume 5; "'Does Amarna Bear on Karatepe?'—An Answer," from *Journal of Cuneiform Studies*, volume 6; "Amarna *šumma* in Main Clauses," from *Journal of Cuneiform Studies*, volume 7; "Putative Akkadian *šukammu*," from *Journal of Cuneiform Studies*, volume 31; "*duppuru* (*dubburu*)—*ṭuppuru*, too?," from *Journal of Cuneiform Studies*, volume 33. Reprinted courtesy of Piotr Michalowski, editor, *Journal of Cuneiform Studies*.

"Additions to the Amarna Lexicon," from *Orientalia*, volume 53, copyright ©1984 by Editrice Pontificio Istituto Biblico. Reprinted courtesy of Editrice Pontificio Istituto Biblico.

"Amarna Glosses," from *Revue d'Assyriologie*, volume 69. Reprinted courtesy of Dominique Charpin, Secrétaire de rédaction.

"Amarna Letters," from *The New Catholic Encyclopedia*, edited by William J. McDonald et al., Volume 1, published by McGraw-Hill, 1969. ©1969 by The Gale Group. Reprinted by permission of The Gale Group.

"Amarna Letters," from *The Oxford Encyclopedia of Ancient Egypt*, edited by Donald B. Redford, ©2001 by Oxford University Press, Inc. Used by permission of Oxford University Press, Inc.

"Amarna Texts in the Metropolitan Museum of Art," from *Cuneiform Texts in the Metropolitan Museum of Art*, I: *Tablets, Cones, and Bricks of the Third and Second Millennia B.C.*, edited by Ira Spar, copyright ©1988 by The Metropolitan Museum of Art. Reprinted courtesy of The Metropolitan Museum of Art.

"An Unexplained Passage in an Amarna Letter from Byblos," from

Journal of Near Eastern Studies, volume 8, copyright ©1949 by The University of Chicago Press. Reprinted courtesy of The University of Chicago Press.

"Early Canaanite *yaqtula*," from *Orientalia*, volume 29, copyright ©1960 by Editrice Pontificio Istituto Biblico. Reprinted courtesy of Editrice Pontificio Istituto Biblico.

"Join the ᶜApiru or Become One?," from *"Working with No Data": Semitic and Egyptian Studies Presented to Thomas O. Lambdin*, edited by David M. Golomb, copyright ©1987 by Eisenbrauns. Reprinted courtesy of James E. Eisenbraun, publisher.

"Rib-Hadda: Job at Byblos?," from *Biblical and Related Studies Presented to Samuel Iwry*, edited by Ann Kort and Scott Morschauser, copyright ©1985 by Eisenbrauns. Reprinted courtesy of James E. Eisenbraun, publisher.

"Some Reflections on Amarna Politics," from *Solving Riddles and Untying Knots: Biblical, Epigraphic, and Semitic Studies in Honor of Jonas C. Greenfield*, edited by Ziony Zevit, Seymour Gitin, and Michael Sokoloff, copyright ©1993 by Eisenbrauns. Reprinted courtesy of James E. Eisenbraun, publisher.

"*taqtul*—Third Masculine Singular?," from *Biblica*, volume 45, copyright ©1964 by The Pontifical Biblical Institute. Reprinted courtesy of The Pontifical Biblical Institute.

"Tell el-Amarna Letters," from *Encyclopedia Judaica*, ©1972 by Keter Publishing House. Reprinted courtesy of Keter Publishing House.

"The Death of ᶜAbdi-Aširta," from *Eretz-Israel*, volume 9, copyright ©1969 by the Israel Exploration Society. Reprinted courtesy of the Israel Exploration Society.

"The Dual Personal Pronouns in Western Peripheral Akkadian," from *Bulletin of the American Schools of Oriental Research*, volume 211, copyright ©1973 by the American Schools of Oriental Research. Reprinted courtesy of the American Schools of Oriental Research.

"The Hebrew Language in its Northwest Semitic Background," from *The Bible and the Ancient Near East: Essays in Honor of William Foxwell Albright*, edited by G. Ernest Wright. Reprinted courtesy of The Biblical Colloquium, Herbert B. Huffmon, Secretary-Treasurer.

"The Scandal of the 'Great Sin' at Ugarit," from *Journal of Near Eastern Studies*, volume 18, copyright ©1959 by The University of Chicago Press. Reprinted courtesy of The University of Chicago Press.

"The Syrian Scribe of the Jerusalem Amarna Letters," from *Unity and Diversity*, edited by Hans Goedicke and J. J. M. Roberts, copyright ©1975 by The Johns Hopkins University Press. Reprinted courtesy of The Johns Hopkins University Press.

Vita

William Lambert Moran was born in Chicago on August 11, 1921. The family moved to Columbus, Ohio, in 1935, where Bill was enrolled in St. Charles, a rigorous Roman Catholic preparatory school. Students were required to study Latin throughout high school and Greek during their last two years. Moran delighted in languages, writing long Latin letters during the summer between his sophomore and junior years. In his junior year, 1937, the family moved back to Chicago, and while he was able to continue his Latin and French studies, he was unable to begin Greek. Thus, when the family moved back to Columbus in 1938, Moran was required to teach himself elementary Greek during the summer so that he could enter the senior year at St. Charles. This experience proved paradigmatic, for he discovered his ability to learn independently. At age eighteen, Moran entered the Jesuit order, attracted to it because of its commitment to scholarship. After the novitiate (1939–1941), Moran received an intensive literary training in the Latin and Greek classics as well as in English literature and pursued studies in classical and scholastic philosophy, receiving his B.A. in Classics in 1944 from Loyola University in Chicago. Then, for a few years, he taught Latin and Greek in a Cincinnati high school.

Encouraged by his order to pursue biblical studies, in 1947 Moran enrolled in a doctoral program under the legendary William Foxwell Albright at Johns Hopkins, and received the Ph.D. in 1950. With prescience, Albright elected to tutor him during his second year, reading Old Babylonian and Amarna letters, and suggested that he seek out Canaanite influences in the Byblos letters, the largest subcorpus of the Amarna letters. Moran's dissertation was a syntactical study of that corpus. In a brilliant analysis, Moran elucidated the grammar of these difficult texts, showing that, although the vocabulary of the texts was Akkadian, the grammar, notably the verbal system, was actually that of the Canaanite spoken by the writers of the letters, a language very much like a precursor to Biblical Hebrew. While of interest linguistically as revealing the earliest known mixed language, Moran's discoveries also had a great impact on the study of Biblical Hebrew. In a flurry of articles in the 1950s, Moran helped revolutionize the study of Biblical Hebrew by showing how the study of these arcane cuneiform texts could explain obscure features in the grammar of the earliest biblical texts.

In the summer of 1950, Moran studied Hittite with A. Goetze at the Summer Institute of Linguistics in Ann Arbor. Having completed his doctorate, Moran also continued his theological education in Indiana and in Rome, receiving the Master of Theology degree in 1954, and the Master of Sacred Scripture degree in 1958. These studies were interrupted by summers at the Oriental Institute of the University of Chicago, where he studied Assyriology and Semitic linguistics with T. Jacobsen and B. Landsberger. He also spent the academic year 1955–1956 at the Institute working on volume I/J of the *Chicago Assyrian Dictionary*. He was then invited to remain in Chicago as a member of the *Dictionary* staff and as a research associate of Jacobsen, but instead he accepted his order's decision that he proceed to Rome, where, in 1958, he was appointed Professor of Old Testament Exegesis at the Pontifical Biblical Institute.

For the next eight years Moran lectured on biblical Hebrew and on Exodus, Deuteronomy, and Isaiah—all in Latin, as was the rule at the time. This was not a great burden for him; during the several years of his theological training in Rome, all conversation, except for one hour a day, had been conducted in Latin. One year, Moran characteristically organized a conversational classical Greek table for the remaining hour each day. While on the faculty of the Institute, Moran served as the editor of the series *Materialien zum Sumerischen Lexikon* and *Analecta Orientalia* (1961–1964) and as the associate editor of the journal *Biblica*, for which he would annually write up to a dozen book reviews. From 1963 to 1966, he was Dean of the Oriental Faculty at the Institute. During this period, in addition to further studies on the early Canaanite language and its relationship to Hebrew, Moran also found time to publish important articles in the fields of Old Testament studies and Assyriology.

In 1966 Moran was invited to Harvard as Professor of Assyriology and as the eventual successor to Thorkild Jacobsen. He taught all levels of Akkadian language and texts, mostly to graduate students, but occasionally to an intrepid undergraduate or two. He was also an enthralling lecturer, and taught a popular undergraduate course on ancient Mesopotamian history and culture. Moran was an inspiring teacher. In first-year Akkadian, to be sure, what he mostly inspired was anxiety, as he would stand behind students, Jesuit-high-school-teacher-style, as they nervously read their cuneiform signs. But in seminars and in undergraduate courses, what he inspired was a passion to understand the text, the literature, the culture, and the spirit of the language as deeply as possible.

Moran was a superb and exacting philologist. For nearly half a century he was recognized as the leading authority on the language and interpretation of the Canaanite Akkadian texts, and toward the end of his career he published a magisterial translation of the entire corpus that immediately became the standard (*Les lettres d'el-Amarna: Correspondance diplomatique du pharaon* [1987]; English version: *The Amarna Letters* [1992]). But his greatest intellectual love was literature, especially poetry, from classical to modern. When at length he turned with his vast reading to the literature of ancient Mesopotamia, he saw depth that few others had seen before. He wrote insightfully and eloquently about the Epic of Gilgamesh and its view of the human condition; he called it "a document of ancient humanism." He also wrote knowingly about the poetics of Mesopotamian texts: about how they worked as literature. Besides the present volume of Moran's Amarna studies, another posthumous collection of his articles on literary topics is also being published (*The Most Magic Word: Essays in Babylonian and Biblical Literature*, edited by Ronald S. Hendel).

For many years Moran was an active associate of Leverett House, one of Harvard's undergraduate residence houses. His keen interest in seeking the company of other scholars, especially in the Classics and the history of religion, were an important part of his intellectual life. In recognition of his wide-ranging scholarship, in 1985 Moran was appointed the Andrew W. Mellon Professor of the Humanities. In 1996 he was made a Fellow of the American Academy of Arts and Sciences.

By the time of his arrival in Cambridge (Mass.), Moran had begun to distance himself from his religious order. Not long afterwards, he met and fell in love with Suzanne Drinker Funkhouser. They were married in 1970, beginning a wonderful partnership for the next three decades. To his five stepchildren Bill became a devoted father. After his retirement from Harvard in 1990, Bill and Suzie moved to an ancient, welcoming house outside of Brunswick, Maine, where he continued his work on the literature of Mesopotamia. He also returned eagerly to the study of the Classics and of literature, immersing himself in Homer, Horace, Dante, and Virginia Woolf.

As a human being Bill Moran was simply one of the best. A wonderful friend, he was a modest, self-deprecating man of many and great passions, who loved to talk about literature, politics, dogs, and above all, sports; sidelined by an early football injury, he was one of the great fans of college and professional football and basketball, who could recall entire games he had seen decades earlier.

Moran's last years were difficult. He suffered from an illness that over the course of time gradually made it more and more difficult for him to move. But his mind remained clear and engaged; on the table beside the chair to which he had become confined one would find, for example, his beloved Horace's *Eclogues*, Seamus Heaney's *Beowulf*, the Greek New Testament, and the *Oxford Book of English Verse*.

Bill Moran died at home on December 19, 2000. He is survived by his beloved wife, Suzie, and by his five stepchildren and their families, and remembered fondly by his many students, colleagues, and friends all over the world.

Publications of William L. Moran

Items marked * are included in the present volume.

Dissertation

* 1950 *A Syntactical Study of the Dialect of Byblos as Reflected in the Amarna Tablets*. Ph.D. dissertation, Johns Hopkins University.

Books

1960 *The Assyrian Dictionary of the Oriental Institute of the University of Chicago*, Volume 7, I and J. Chicago: The Oriental Institute—Glückstadt: Augustin.

1987 *Les lettres d'el-Amarna: Correspondance diplomatique du pharaon*, avec la collaboration de V. Haas et G. Wilhelm. Traduction française de Dominique Collon et Henri Cazelles. Littératures Anciennes du Proche-Orient, 13. Paris: Cerf.

1992 *The Amarna Letters*. Baltimore/London: Johns Hopkins University Press.

2002 *The Most Magic Word: Essays in Babylonian and Biblical Literature*, edited by Ronald S. Hendel. Catholic Biblical Quarterly Monograph Series, 35. Washington: The Catholic Biblical Association of America.

Articles

* 1948 An Unexplained Passage in an Amarna Letter from Byblos. *JNES* 8: 124–25.

* 1949 A Re-interpretation of an Amarna Letter from Byblos (*EA* 82). *JCS* 2: 239–48 (with W. F. Albright).

1950 The Putative Root ^{c}*tm* in Is 9:18. *CBQ* 12: 153–54.

* Rib-Adda of Byblos and the Affairs of Tyre (*EA* 89). *JCS* 4: 163–68 (with W. F. Albright).

* The Use of the Canaanite Infinitive Absolute as a Finite Verb in the Amarna Letters from Byblos. *JCS* 4: 169–72.

* 1951 New Evidence on Canaanite *taqtulū(na)*. *JCS* 5: 33–35.

* 1952 "Does Amarna Bear on Karatepe?"—An Answer. *JCS* 6: 76–80.

* 1953 Amarna *šumma* in Main Clauses. *JCS* 7: 78–80.

A Note on Ps 119:28. *CBQ* 15: 10.

1957 Mari Notes on the Execration Texts. *Or. NS* 26: 339–45.

1958 Ugaritic *ṣîṣûma* and Hebrew *ṣîṣ*. *Biblica* 39: 69–71.

Gen 39,10 and its Use in Ez 21,32. *Biblica* 39: 405–23.

1959 Notes on the New Nabonidus Inscriptions. *Or. NS* 28: 130–40.

A New Fragment of DIN.TIR.KI = *Bābilu* and *Enūma eliš* vi 61–66. *Analecta Biblica* 12 (*Studia Biblica et Orientalia* III; Rome): 257–65.

* The Scandal of the "Great Sin" at Ugarit. *JNES* 18: 280–81.

* 1960 Early Canaanite *yaqtula*. *Or. NS* 29: 1–19.

PAR-*sa-a*. *Or. NS* 29: 103–4.

* 1961 The Hebrew Language in its Northwest Semitic Background. Pp. 53–72 in *The Bible and the Ancient Near East: Essays in Honor of William Foxwell Albright*, ed. G. Ernest Wright. Garden City, N.Y.: Doubleday.

1962 Some Remarks on the Song of Moses. *Biblica* 43: 317–27.

Moses und der Bundesschluss am Sinai. *Stimmen der Zeit* 170: 120–33 (= De foederis mosaici traditione. *Verbum Domini* 40: 3–17).

"A Kingdom of Priests." Pp. 7–20 in *The Bible in Current Catholic Thought*, Gruenthaner Memorial Volume, ed. John L. McKenzie. New York.

1963 The Ancient Near Eastern Background of the Love of God in Deuteronomy. *CBQ* 25: 77–87.

A Note on the Treaty Terminology of the Sefire Stelas. *JNES* 22: 173–76.

The End of the Unholy War and the Anti-Exodus. *Biblica* 44: 333–42.

* 1964 **taqtul*—Third Masculine Singular? *Biblica* 45: 80–82.

1965 XXVI International Congress of Orientalists. *Or. NS* 35: 141–43.

1966 The Literary Connection between Lv 11,13–19 and Dt 14,12–18. *CBQ* 28: 271–77.

1967 The Conclusion of the Decalogue (Ex 20,17 = Dt 5,21). *CBQ* 29: 543–54.

The Repose of Rahab's Israelite Guests. *Studi sull'Oriente e la Bibbia* (Milano): 273–84.

1969 New Evidence from Mari on the History of Israelite Prophecy. *Biblica* 51: 15–56.

Some Akkadian Names of the Stomachs of Ruminants. *JCS* 21: 178–82.

* The Death of ᶜAbdi-Aširta. *Eretz-Israel* 9 (Albright Volume): 94–99.

1970 The Creation of Man in Atrahasis I 192–248. *BASOR* 200: 48–56.

1971 Atrahasis. The Babylonian Story of the Flood. *Biblica* 52: 51–61.

* 1973 The Dual Personal Pronouns in Western Peripheral Akkadian. *BASOR* 211: 50–53.

1974 An Apotropaic Formula in KUB 30 6. *JCS* 26: 55–58.

* 1975 The Syrian Scribe of the Jerusalem Amarna Letters. Pp. 146–68 in *Unity and Diversity*, ed. Hans Goedicke and J. J. M. Roberts. Baltimore: Johns Hopkins University Press.

* Amarna Glosses. *RA* 69: 147–58.

Notes brèves. *RA* 69: 191.

1976 The Kesh Temple Hymn and the Canonical Temple List. Pp. 335–42 in *Kramer Anniversary Volume*, AOAT 25.

1977 Notes brèves. *RA* 71: 190–91.

1978 An Assyriological Gloss to the New Archilochus Fragment. *Harvard Studies in Classical Philology* 82: 17–19.

Puppies in Proverbs—From Šamši-Adad I to Archilochus? *Eretz-Israel* 14 (Ginsberg Volume): 32–37.

1979 The First Tablet of the Standard Babylonian Recension of the Anzu-Myth. *JCS* 31: 65–115 (with W. W. Hallo).

1980 Rilke and the Gilgamesh Epic. *JCS* 32: 208–10.

* 1981 *duppuru (dubburu)—ṭuppuru*, too? *JCS* 33: 44–47.

1983 Notes on the Hymn to Marduk in *Ludlul bēl nēmeqi*. *JAOS* 103: 255–60.

* A Note on igi-kár, "provisions, supplies." *Acta Sumerologica Japonensia* 5: 175–77.

Notes brèves. *RA* 77: 93–94; 189.

* 1984 Additions to the Amarna Lexicon. *Or. NS* 53: 297–302.

1985 Notes brèves. *RA* 79: 90.

* 1986 Rib-Hadda: Job at Byblos? Pp. 173–81 in *Biblical and Related Studies Presented to Samuel Iwry*, ed. Ann Kort and Scott Morschauser. Winona Lake, Ind.: Eisenbrauns.

1987 Some Considerations of Form and Interpretation in *Atra-ḫasīs*. Pp. 245–55 in *Language, Literature, and History: Philological and Historical Studies Presented to Erica Reiner*, ed. Francesca Rochberg-Halton. New Haven: American Oriental Society.

* Join the ^{c}Apiru or Become One? Pp. 209–12 in *"Working with No Data": Semitic and Egyptian Studies Presented to Thomas O. Lambdin*, ed. David M. Golomb. Winona Lake, Ind.: Eisenbrauns.

1988 *Nouvelles Assyriologiques Brèves et Utilitaires* Nos. 21, 36.

Notes on Anzu. *AfO* 35: 24–29 (appeared in 1990).

1991 Ovid's *Blanda voluptas* and the Humanization of Enkidu. *JNES* 50: 121–27.

Assurbanipal's Message to the Babylonians (*ABL* 301), with an Excursus on Figurative *biltu*. Pp. 320–31 in *Ah, Assyria ...: Studies in Assyrian History and Ancient Near Eastern Historiography Presented to Hayim Tadmor*, ed. Mordechai Cogan and Israel Eph'al. Scripta Hierosolymitana, 33. Jerusalem: Magnes.

The Epic of Gilgamesh: A Document of Ancient Humanism. *Bulletin of the Canadian Society for Mesopotamian Studies* 22: 15–22.

A Bowl of *alallu*-stone. *ZA* 81: 268–73 (with George F. Dole).

1993 An Ancient Prophetic Oracle. Pp. 252–58 in *Biblische Theologie und gesellschaftliche Wandel. Für Norbert Lohfink SJ.* Ed. Georg Braulik, Walter Gross, and Sean McEvenue. Freiburg/Basel/Wien: Herder.

UET 6 402: Persuasion in the Plain Style. Pp. 113–20 in *Comparative Studies in Honor of Yochanan Muffs*, ed. Edward L. Greenstein and David Marcus. New York: Ancient Near Eastern Society (*JANES* 22).

* 1995 Some Reflections on Amarna Politics. Pp. 559–72 in *Solving Riddles and Untying Knots: Biblical, Epigraphic, and Semitic Studies in Honor of Jonas C. Greenfield*, ed. Ziony Zevit, Seymour Gitin, and Michael Sokoloff. Winona Lake, Ind.: Eisenbrauns.

Contributions to Encyclopedias, Commentaries, Anthologies

* 1967 *Amarna Letters; Apiru; Hittites; Hurrians; Mesopotamian Religion. *The New Catholic Encyclopedia*, ed. William J. McDonald et al. New York: McGraw-Hill.

1969 Akkadian Letters. Pp. 623–32 in *Ancient Near Eastern Texts Relating to the Old Testament*, 3rd ed., ed. James B. Pritchard. Princeton: Princeton University Press.

Deuteronomy. Pp. 256–76 in *A New Catholic Commentary on Holy Scripture*, rev. ed., general ed. Reginald C. Fuller. London: Nelson.

* 1972 Phoenicians; *Tell el-Amarna Letters. *Encyclopedia Judaica*. Jerusalem: Keter.

1987 Gilgamesh. *The Encyclopedia of Religion*, ed. M. Eliade et al. New York: Macmillan.

* 1988 Amarna Texts (Nos. 102, 103). Pp. 149–51 in *Cuneiform Texts in the Metropolitan Museum of Art*, I: *Tablets, Cones, and Bricks of the Third and Second Millennia B.C.*, ed. Ira Spar. New York: Metropolitan Museum of Art.

1992 The Gilgamesh Epic: A Masterpiece from Ancient Mesopotamia. Pp. 2327–36 in *Civilizations of the Ancient Near East*, ed. Jack M. Sasson. New York: Scribners.

Introduction. Pp. ix–xi in *Gilgamesh: A New Rendering in English Verse*, by David Ferry. New York: Farrar, Straus and Giroux.

* 2001 Amarna Letters. *The Oxford Encyclopedia of Ancient Egypt*, ed. Donald B. Redford. Oxford/New York: Oxford University Press.

Reviews

1952 Segundo Miguel Rodriguez, C.S.S.R. *Diccionario hebreo-español y arameo-biblico español*, segunda edición. *CBQ* 14: 202–3.

Nabih Amin Faris. *The Book of Idols: A Translation from the Arabic of the Kitāb-al-Aṣnām by Hishām ibn-al-Kalbi*. *CBQ* 14: 298.

1953 Alexander Scharff und Anton Moortgat. *Ägypten und Vorderasien im Altertum*. *CBQ* 15: 118–22.

Frank Moore Cross, Jr. and David Noel Freedman. *Early Hebrew Orthography: A Study of the Epigraphic Evidence. CBQ* 15: 364–67.

1954 Hubert Junker. *Genesis. CBQ* 16: 232–34.

R. de Vaux, O.P. *Les Livres de Samuel. CBQ* 16: 236–38.

1956 Sabatino Moscati. *Oriente in nuova luce. CBQ* 18: 84–85.

1957 G. R. Driver and John C. Miles. *The Babylonian Laws*, vol. II. *CBQ* 19: 398–401.

Albrecht Goetze. *The Laws of Eshnunna. Biblica* 38: 216–21.

1958 E. L. Ehrlich. *Geschichte Israels von den Anfängen bis zur Zerstörung des Tempels (70 n. Chr.). Or. NS* 27: 221–22.

Cl. Schedl. *Geschichte des Alten Testaments. Biblica* 39: 97–100.

M. Reisel. *The Mysterious Name of Y.H.W.H. Biblica* 39: 232–33.

G. Rinaldi. *Secoli sul Mondo. Biblica* 39: 360.

J.-R. Kupper. *Les nomades en Mésopotamie. Biblica* 39: 373–75.

1959 J. Laloup. *Bible et classicisme. Biblica* 40: 124.

S. H. Hooke. *Myth, Ritual, Kingship. Biblica* 40: 126–28.

H. H. Rowley, *Prophecy and Religion in Ancient China and Israel. Biblica* 40: 128–29.

1960 Divo Barsotti. *Spiritualité de l'Exode. Verbum Domini* 38: 314-15.

John Bright. *A History of Israel. Biblica* 41: 88–90.

R. de Vaux, O.P. *Les institutions de l'Ancien Testament. Biblica* 41: 90–91.

W. Zimmerli. *Das Alte Testament als Anrede. Biblica* 41: 198–99.

N. K. Gottwald. *A Light to the Nations: An Introduction to the Old Testament. Biblica* 41: 293–95.

L. Pirot, A. Robert, H. Cazelles, ed. *Dictionnaire de la Bible, Supplément.* Fasc. xxxi-xxxii. *Biblica* 41: 295–97.

G. E. Mendenhall. *Law and Covenant in Israel and the Ancient Near East. Biblica* 41: 297–99.

R. Hentschke. *Die Stellung der vorexilischen Schriftpropheten zum Kultus. Biblica* 41: 419–22.

H. Gross. *Die Idee des ewigen und allgemeinen Weltfriedens im Alter Orient und im Alten Testament. Biblica* 41: 423–24.

R. Reymond. *L'eau, sa vie, et sa signification dans l'Ancien Testament. Biblica* 41: 426.

H. van Vliet. *No Single Testimony: A Study on the Adoption of the Law Deut. 19:15 Par. into the New Testament. Biblica* 41: 427–28.

1961 G. Ahlström. *Psalm 89, eine Liturgie aus dem Ritual des leidenden Königs. Biblica* 42: 237–39.

L. Pirot, A. Robert, H. Cazelles, ed. *Dictionnaire de la Bible, Supplément.* Fasc. xxxiii. *Biblica* 42: 371–72.

E. Mørstad. *Wenn du der Stimme des Herrn, deines Gottes, gehorchen wirst. Biblica* 42: 372.

G. Auzou. *De la servitude au service. Biblica* 42: 477.

S. Goldman. *From Slavery to Freedom. Biblica* 42: 478.

J. J. Petuchouski. *Ever since Sinai. Biblica* 42: 482–83.

1962 K. Baltzer. *Das Bundesformular. Biblica* 43: 100–6.

U. Cassuto. *The Documentary Hypothesis and the Composition of the Pentateuch. Biblica* 43: 242–43.

J. de Fraine. *Adam et son lignage. Biblica* 43: 534–35.

1963 A. Weiser. *Glaube und Geschichte im Alten Testament und andere ausgewählte Schriften. Biblica* 44: 100–1.

P. Morant. *Die Anfänge der Menschheit. Biblica* 44: 101–2.

W. Beyerlin. *Herkunft und Geschichte der ältesten Sinaitraditionen. Biblica* 44: 102–4.

H. W. Wolff. *Dodekapropheton,* 1: *Hosea. Biblica* 44: 217–19.

H. Gross und F. Mussner, ed. *Lex Tua Veritas.* Festschrift H. Junker. *Biblica* 44: 219–21.

M. Weise. *Kultzeiten und kultisches Bundesschluss in der "Ordensregel" vom Toten Meer. Biblica* 44: 229–30.

John Bright. *Altisrael in der neueren Geschichtsschreibung. Biblica* 44: 250.

O. Bächli. *Israel und die Völker: Eine Studie zum Deuteronomium. Biblica* 44: 375–77.

H. W. F. Saggs. *The Greatness That Was Babylon. Biblica* 44: 557.

S. H. Hooke. *Babylonian and Assyrian Religion. Biblica* 44: 558.

E. Zehren. *The Crescent and the Bull. Biblica* 44: 569.

1964 E. R. Dalglish. *Psalm Fifty-one in the Light of Ancient Near Eastern Patternism. Biblica* 45: 111–13.

D. Winton Thomas and W. D. McHardy, ed. *Hebrew and Semitic Studies.* Festschrift G. R. Driver. *Biblica* 45: 127–29.

U. Cassuto. *From Adam to Noah. A Commentary on the Book of Genesis. Biblica* 45: 283–84.

H. Lubsczyk. *Der Auszug Israels aus Ägypten: Seine theologische Bedeutung in prophetischer und priestlicher Überlieferung. Biblica* 45: 284–85.

E. von Waldow. *Die traditionsgeschichtliche Hintergrund der prophetischen Gerichtsreden. Biblica* 45: 288–90.

R. Fey. *Amos und Jesaya. Biblica* 45: 290–91.

R. Gradwohl. *Die Farben im Alten Testament. Biblica* 45: 312.

1965 A. Malamat. *Mari Documents Selected and Translated into Hebrew. Biblica* 46: 109–10.

W. Richter. *Die Bearbeitungen des "Retterbuches" in der deuteronomischen Epoche. Biblica* 46: 223–28.

H. W. Wolff. *Amos' geistige Heimat. Biblica* 46: 231–32.

M. Noth. *Könige.* 1. Lieferung. *Biblica* 46: 384–85.

S. Mowinckel. *Tetrateuch-Pentateuch-Hexateuch: Die Berichte über die Landnahme in den drei altisraelitischen Geschichtswerken. Biblica* 46: 481–82.

1966 G. Fohrer, *Überlieferung und Geschichte des Exodus: Eine Analyse von Ex 1–15. Biblica* 47: 131–33.

E. Würthwein und Otto Kaiser, ed. *Tradition und Situation. Studien zur alttestamentlichen Prophetie.* Festschrift A. Weiser. *Biblica* 47: 133–35.

Z. W. Falk. *Hebrew Law in Biblical Times. An Introduction. Biblica* 47: 155.

J. Jeremias. *Theophanie: Die Geschichte einer alttestamentlichen Gattung. Biblica* 47: 597–99.

1967 Manfred Weippert. *Die Landnahme der israelitischen Stämme in der neueren wissenschaftlichen Diskussion: Ein kritischer Bericht. CBQ* 30: 644–45.

Sigrid Loersch. *Das Deuteronomium und seine Deutungen. Ein forschungsgeschichtlicher Überblick. CBQ* 30: 646–47.

1969 James Barr. *Comparative Philology and the Text of the Old Testament. CBQ* 31: 238–43.

1970 Giorgio Buccellati. *The Amorites of the Ur III Period. JAOS* 90: 529–31.

1972 Walter Mayer. *Untersuchungen zur Grammatik des Mittelassyrischen. CBQ* 34: 516–18.

1976 Morton Cogan. *Imperialism and Religion: Assyria, Judah and Israel in the Eighth and Seventh Centuries B.C.E. CBQ* 38: 222–24.

1977 Angel Marzal. *Gleanings from the Wisdom of Mari. CBQ* 39: 264–65.

1978 Karl Jaros. *Ägypten und Vorderasien: Eine kleine Chronographie bis zum Auftreten Alexander des Grossen. CBQ* 40: 242–43.

Denise Schmandt-Besserat, ed. *The Legacy of Sumer. CBQ* 40: 651.

1979 Sabatino Moscati, ed. *L'alba della civiltà*, volumes I–III. *JBL* 98: 411–14.

1980 G. Dossin. *Archives royales de Mari X: Correspondance féminine. JAOS* 100: 186–89.

Wolfgang Röllig et al. *Altorientalische Literaturen. JAOS* 100: 189–90.

H. W. F. Saggs. *The Encounter with the Divine in Mesopotamia and Israel. CBQ* 42: 109–10.

1981 J. H. Hospers, ed. *General Linguistics and the Teaching of Dead Hamito-Semitic Languages. CBQ* 43: 427–28.

1982 Lennart Hellbing. *Alasia Problems. Or. NS* 51: 143–45.

Mark E. Cohen. *Sumerian Hymnology: The Eršemma. CBQ* 44: 478–79.

1984 Jean-Georges Heintz. *Index documentaire d'el Amarna—I.D.E.A.* 1: *Liste/Codage des textes. Indes des ouvrages de reférence. AfO* 31: 90.

John Gardner and John Maier with Richard A. Henshaw. *Gilgamesh;* Robert Silverberg. *Gilgamesh the King. New York Times Book Review*, November 11, 13–14.

L. Cagni. *Briefe aus dem Iraq Museum (TIM II). Altbabylonische Briefe*, 8; M. Stol. *Letters from Yale. Altbabylonische Briefe*, 9. *JAOS* 104: 573–75.

1985 Jerrold S. Cooper. *The Curse of Agade. CBQ* 47: 114–15.

1987 F. R. Kraus. *Briefe aus kleineren westeuropäischen Sammlungen. Altbabylonische Briefe,* 10. *JAOS* 107: 134–35.

1988 G. E. Mendenhall. *The Syllabic Inscriptions from Byblos. CBQ* 50: 508–10.

M. Stol. *Letters from Collections in Philadelphia, Chicago and Berkeley. Altbabylonische Briefe,* 11. *JAOS* 108: 307–9.

1990 Brigitte R. M. Groneberg. *Syntax, Morphologie und Stil der jungbabylonischen "hymnischen" Literatur*. Freiburger Altorientalische Studien 14/1–2. *JAOS* 110: 568–71.

Neil Forsyth. *The Old Enemy: Satan and the Combat Myth. Comparative Literature Studies* 27: 169–72.

1992 Samuel Noah Kramer and John Maier. *Myths of Enki, The Crafty God. CBQ* 54: 114–15.

1993 Francesco Pomponio, ed. *Formule di maledizione della Mesopotamia preclassica*. Testi del Vicino Oriente antico, 2: Letterature mesopotamiche. *CBQ* 55: 348.

1996 Raymond Jacques Tournay and Aaron Shaffer. *L'épopée de Gilgamesh: Introduction, traduction et notes*. Littératures Anciennes du Proche-Orient, 15. *CBQ* 58: 336–37.

Abbreviations

1. Literature

AASOR	Annual of the American Schools of Oriental Research
AB	A. Ungnad, *Altbabylonische Briefe aus dem Museum zu Philadelphia* (Stuttgart, 1920)
AfO	*Archiv für Orientforschung*
AHw	W. von Soden, *Akkadisches Handwörterbuch* (Wiesbaden, 1965–81)
AMT	R. C. Thompson, *Assyrian Medical Texts* (London, 1923)
ANET	J. Pritchard, *Ancient Near Eastern Texts Relating to the Old Testament* (Princeton, 1950, ^{2}1955, ^{3}1969)
AOAT	Alter Orient und Altes Testament
AOS	American Oriental Series
ARI	W. F. Albright, *Archaeology and the Religion of Israel* (Baltimore, 1942, ^{2}1946, ^{3}1953)
ARM(T)	*Archives Royales de Mari (Textes)*
ArOr	*Archiv Orientální*
AS^{2}	W. von Soden and W. Röllig, *Das akkadische Syllabar*, 2nd ed. (Rome, 1967)
AT	D. J. Wiseman, *The Alalakh Tablets* (London, 1953)
BA	*Beiträge zur Assyriologie*
BAM	F. Köcher, *Die babylonisch-assyrische Medizin in Texten und Untersuchungen* (Berlin, 1963–71)
BASOR	*Bulletin of the American Schools of Oriental Research*
BB	C. Bezold and E. A. W. Budge, *The Tell el-Amarna Letters in the British Museum* (London, 1892)
BB	A. Ungnad, *Babylonische Briefe aus der Zeit der Ḫammurapi-Dynastie* (Leipzig, 1914)
BE	*The Babylonian Expedition of the University of Pennsylvania*, Series A: *Cuneiform Texts*
BG	C. Bezold and A. Goetze, *Babylonisch-Assyrisches Glossar* (Heidelberg, 1926)
BHT	S. Smith, *Babylonian Historical Texts Relating to the Capture and Downfall of Babylon* (London, 1924)
BiOr	*Bibliotheca Orientalis*

BL	H. Bauer and P. Leander, *Historische Grammatik der hebräischen Sprache des Alten Testaments* (Halle, 1922)
BM	British Museum tablet number
BoTU	E. Forrer, *Die Boghazköi-Texte in Umschrift* (WVDOG 41/42; Leipzig, 1922–26)
BWL	W. Lambert, *Babylonian Wisdom Literature* (Oxford, 1960)
CAD	*The Assyrian Dictionary of the University of Chicago* (Chicago, 1956–)
*CAH*²	*The Cambridge Ancient History*, revised edition (Cambridge, 1961–)
CAT	M. Dietrich, O. Loretz, and J. Sanmartín, *The Cuneiform Alphabetic Texts from Ugarit, Ras Ibn Hani and Other Places* (Münster: Ugarit Verlag, 1995)
CBQ	*Catholic Biblical Quarterly*
CH	E. Bergmann, *Codex Ḫammurabi textus primigenius*, 3rd ed. (Rome, 1953)
DBSuppl	H. Cazelles and A. Feuillet, eds., *Dictionnaire de la Bible—Supplément* (Paris)
DCD	Z. Harris, *Development of the Canaanite Dialects* (New Haven, 1939)
EA	J. A. Knudtzon, *Die El-Amarna-Tafeln* (Leipzig, 1907–15)
FSAC	W. F. Albright, *From the Stone Age to Christianity* (Baltimore, 1941, ²1946)
GA	A. Ungnad, *Grammatik des Akkadischen* (Munich, 1906, ²1926, ³1949, ⁴1964, ⁵1968 [4th and 5th editions by L. Matouš])
GAG	W. von Soden, *Grundriss der akkadischen Grammatik* (Rome, 1952, ²1969, ³1995)
Ges.-Buhl¹³	W. Gesenius, *Hebräisches und aramäisches Handwörterbuch über das Alte Testament*, revised by F. Buhl, 13th ed. (Leipzig, 1899)
GHB	P. Joüon, *Grammaire de l'hébreu biblique* (Rome, 1923, ²1947)
GKC	*Gesenius' Hebrew Grammar*, edited and enlarged by E. Kautzsch, 28th ed., translated by A. E. Cowley, 2nd ed. (Oxford, 1910)
GLECS	*Comptes rendus du Groupe Linguistique d'Études Chamito-Sémitiques*

GP	Z. Harris, *A Grammar of the Phoenician Language* (New Haven, 1936)
HSM	Harvard Semitic Monographs
HSS	Harvard Semitic Studies
HUCA	*Hebrew Union College Annual*
HWB	F. Delitzsch, *Assyrisches Handwörterbuch* (Leipzig, 1896)
IEJ	*Israel Exploration Journal*
Iraq	*Iraq. Journal of the British School of Archaeology in Iraq*
JANES	*Journal of the Ancient Near Eastern Society of Columbia University*
JAOS	*Journal of the American Oriental Society*
JBL	*Journal of Biblical Literature and Exegesis*
JCS	*Journal of Cuneiform Studies*
JEA	*Journal of Egyptian Archaeology*
JEN	*Joint Expedition with the Iraq Museum at Nuzi* (= American Schools of Oriental Research, Publications of the Baghdad School, Texts, vol. 1–6)
JNES	*Journal of Near Eastern Studies*
JPOS	*Journal of the Palestine Oriental Society*
JQR	*Jewish Quarterly Review*
KAV	O. Schroeder, *Keilschrifttexte aus Assur verschiedenen Inhalts* (WVDOG, 35; Leipzig, 1920)
KBo	*Keilschrifttexte aus Boghazköi*
KUB	*Keilschrifturkunden aus Boghazköi*
LSS	Leipziger Semitische Studien
MAD	I. J. Gelb, *Materials for the Assyrian Dictionary*
MDOG	Mitteilungen der Deutschen Orient-Gesellschaft
MIO	Mitteilungen des Instituts für Orientforschung
MSL	B. Landsberger et al., *Materialien zum sumerischen Lexikon / Materials for the Sumerian Lexicon*
OA	*Oriens Antiquus*
OLZ	*Orientalistische Literaturzeitung*
Or. (*NS*)	*Orientalia* (*Nova Series*)
PEQ	*Palestine Exploration Quarterly*
PRU	J. Nougayrol and Ch. Virolleaud, eds., *Le Palais royal d'Ugarit*
RA	*Revue d'Assyriologie et d'archéologie orientale*
RB	*Revue Biblique*
RÉS	*Revue des Études Semitiques*

RLA	E. Ebeling et al., eds., *Reallexikon der Assyriologie*
RS	Ras Shamra excavation/tablet number
SLB	Studia ad tabulas cuneiformes collectas a F. M. Th. de Liagre Böhl pertinentia
StBoT	Studien zu den Boğazköy Texten
TIM	*Texts in the Iraq Museum*
UET	*Ur Excavations, Texts*
UF	*Ugarit-Forschungen*
Ugar.	C. Schaeffer, ed., *Ugaritica*
UH	C. H. Gordon, *Ugaritic Handbook* (Rome, 1947)
UT	C. H. Gordon, *Ugaritic Textbook* (Rome, 1965)
VAB	Vorderasiatische Bibliothek
VAS, VS	*Vorderasiatische Schriftdenkmäler der königlichen Museen zu Berlin*
VT	*Vetus Testamentum*
WA	H. Winckler and L. Abel, *Der Thontafelfund von El Amarna* (Berlin, 1889–90)
Waterman	L. Waterman, *Business Documents of the Ḫammurapi Period from the British Museum* (London, 1916)
WO	*Die Welt des Orients*
WVDOG	Wissenschaftliche Veröffentlichungen der deutschen Orient-Gesellschaft
ZA	*Zeitschrift für Assyriologie*
ZAW	*Zeitschrift für die alttestamentliche Wissenschaft*
ZDMG	*Zeitschrift der deutschen morgenländischen Gesellschaft*
ZDPV	*Zeitschrift des deutschen Palästina-Vereins*

II. Other

acc.	accusative
Acc., Akk.	Accadian, Akkadian
cf.	confer (compare)
col(s).	column(s)
DN	divine name
du.	dual
e.g.	exempli gratia (for example)
esp.	especially
et al.	et alii/alia (and others)
etc.	et cetera (and the rest)
f., fem.	feminine
fut.	future
gen.	genitive
i.e.	id est (that is)
ibid.	ibidem (in the same place)

impf.	imperfect
Lo. E.	lower edge
loc. cit.	loco citato (in the place cited)
m., masc.	masculine
MA	Middle Assyrian
MB	Middle Babylonian
n.	note, footnote
NA	Neo-Assyrian
neg.	negative
nom.	nominative
OA	Old Assyrian
OAkk.	Old Akkadian
OB	Old Babylonian
obv.	obverse
op. cit.	opere citato (in the work cited)
p.	page, plural
pass.	passive
pers.	personal
pl.	plural
PN	personal name
prep.	preposition
pres.	present
pro(n).	pronoun
r., rev.	reverse
RN	royal name
s., sg.	singular
Sum.	Sumerian
Ugar.	Ugaritic
v.g.	verbi gratia (as a specific example)
WPA	Western Peripheral Akkadian

x	illegible sign
1	first person
2	second person
3	third person
>	becomes, goes to
<	develops, comes from
< >	omitted by scribal error
<< >>	scribal plus, to be omitted
*	reconstructed form

A Syntactical Study of the Dialect of Byblos As Reflected in the Amarna Tablets

by

WILLIAM L. MORAN, S.J.

A dissertation submitted to the Board of University Studies
of the Johns Hopkins University in conformity
with the requirement for the degree
of Doctor of Philosophy
Baltimore
1950

Preface

Within the last two decades the Canaanite language of the Late Bronze Age has assumed an importance in Near Eastern studies that it had never enjoyed before. For with the decipherment of Ugaritic by Hans Bauer and Edouard Dhorme it immediately became apparent that the alphabetic cuneiform tablets of Ugarit were to be for many years to come a fruitful field of labor for the philologian, the historian, the student of comparative religion, and perhaps chiefly, the Biblical scholar.

Nor have these high expectations proved illusory. However, many many problems remain unsolved and many obstacles beset the path of the interpreter of the Ugaritic tablets. Not the least of them is his meager knowledge of the syntax of Ugaritic. For with the texts almost completely without vocalization it is occasionally extremely difficult, sometimes impossible, to determine the syntax of a passage. Usually the interpreter must resort, where possible, to the later Phoenician inscriptions—though the difficulty of vocalization still remains—, to Biblical Hebrew, to North and South Arabic (again no vocalization), or finally to Amorite.

The shortcomings of such a method are obvious. Arabic is a different, though related, language; Amorite, though virtually a dialect of Canaanite, is lacking material; Phoenician is a direct descendant of early Canaanite, Biblical Hebrew is a closely related dialect, but both represent a considerably later stage of Canaanite. Hence an obvious desideratum is a clear picture of the syntax of a closely related and *contemporary* Canaanite dialect.

The following study of the syntax of the dialect of Byblos as reflected in the Amarna Tablets fulfills, I believe, this desideratum to some extent. The Amarna Tablets were written in approximately the second quarter of the fourteenth century B.C., and hence in the same period from which date our copies of the Ugaritic epics. Moreover, the dialects of Byblos and Ugarit were very closely related (for further discussion, see the Introduction). Therefore, it is to be hoped that our study will prove of value not only to the philologian interested in the historical development of Canaanite, but also to the interpreter of the Ugaritic tablets.

I wish here to express my gratitude to Prof. Blake for his patient and thorough instruction in Semitic grammar, without which this study could not have been attempted; to Prof. Rosenblatt for his invaluable training in Arabic; and finally, to Prof. Albright who trained me for the specific task of this dissertation, guided and encouraged me in its progress, and gave so many hours of his time for discussion of difficulties until its completion.

Introduction

Over half a century ago, in 1887 to be exact, an Egyptian peasant woman discovered a large collection of clay tablets written in syllabic cuneiform.[1] The site of the discovery was modern Tell el-Amarna in Middle Egypt, ancient Akhetaten, the capital of Egypt in the XVIII Dynasty during the reign of the heretic king, Amenophis IV. The vast majority of the tablets (after the site was dug out, some 350) were letters from the royal archives of Amenophis IV and his predecessor, Amenophis III.[2]

Almost 250 of these letters are written either from or to Palestine and Canaan. Their singular importance for the philologian, immediately recognized, derives from the fact that the scribes had a very poor command of Accadian, the language in which the letters were written. The result was that they often substituted their native Canaanite for the none too familiar Accadian. Hence we have in these letters important evidence for the phonology, morphology and syntax of early Canaanite.

Following upon the publication of the autographs of the tablets many studies of the new material appeared. From the viewpoint of Canaanite, the three most important were Böhl's *Die Sprache der Amarnabriefe* (Leipzig, 1909), Dhorme's "La Langue de Canaan,"[3] and Ebeling's "Das Verbum der El-Amarna-Briefe."[4] All three were thorough studies by competent scholars, and the results achieved represented a great advance over previous knowledge of early Canaanite.

However, much of the evidence was either left untouched or misinterpreted. This was due to two causes: 1) the scholars treating the material knew almost nothing of virtually contemporaneous peripheral

[1]For the discovery of the tablets and their subsequent history until they found their way to various museums, see J. A. Knudtzon, *Die El-Amarna-Tafeln* (Leipzig, 1915), I, pp. 1–15.

[2]For the chronology of the tablets and their historical contexts, see W. F. Albright's forthcoming chapter "Palestine under the Late Eighteenth Dynasty" in the *Cambridge Ancient History*.

[3]In *Revue Biblique* 10, pp. 369–393; 11, pp. 37–59, 344–372.

[4]In *Beiträge zur Assyriologie* 8, pp. 39–79.

Accadian; 2) they knew absolutely nothing of contemporary Canaanite from other native Canaanite documents, and thus lacked a safe norm of Canaanitisms.

The Boğazköy and Nuzi texts have filled the first gap in our knowledge.[5] These texts correct earlier efforts in many important details and remove many supposed Canaanitisms from the Amarna Letters. Many of the peculiar forms which had been interpreted as Canaanitisms in the Amarna Letters appear in the Boğazköy texts.[6]

But, above all, it has been the decipherment and study of Ugaritic which has made renewed study of the Amarna Letters not only profitable but imperative. For though many problems remain unsolved in Ugaritic, still it has shown us clearly the essential phonological, morphological and syntactical structure of Canaanite in the Late Bronze Age.[7] With this new and invaluable knowledge, the Amarna Letters can now be attacked anew and with their indication of vowels due to the syllabic cuneiform be allowed to make their full contribution to our knowledge of early Canaanite.

Facile princeps, indeed virtually alone, in applying this new knowledge gained from the Boğazköy, Nuzi and Ugaritic texts to the

[5]René Labat's *L'Akkadien de Boghaz-Koi* (Bordeaux, 1932) has supplied us with a detailed study of Boğazköy Accadian. Gordon's "The Dialect of the Nuzi Tablets," *Orientalia* NS 7, pp. 32–63, 215–32, has done the same with Nuzi Accadian.

[6]We shall give one illustration: a form such as *ti-pa-li-ḫu-na* was considered (Dhorme, *RB* 11, p. 40) a *piel* with *ti* (for Acc. *tu*) reflecting the *shewa* in Heb. *tĕqattel*. However, Boğazköy shows us the same type of error was very frequent farther north; cf. Labat, pp. 66–67. In other words, we can draw no conclusions for Canaanite from *tipal(l)iḫūna*. The easiest explanation is that it was a type of error perpetuated in the scribal schools. On these schools, see Albright, *loc. cit.*

[7]It should be mentioned that there is not complete unanimity among scholars on the place to be assigned Ugaritic in the Semitic languages. One group of scholars, led by Albrecht Goetze (see "Is Ugaritic a Canaanite Dialect?," *Language* 17, pp. 127–138), maintains Ugaritic has a much closer affinity with East Semitic (Accadian) and is not a Canaanite dialect. The opposition to this view, led by Albright, maintains that the phonology, morphology and syntax of Ugaritic place it definitely in the Northwest Semitic group of languages, and specifically, the Canaanite group. The differences, they maintain, from the other Canaanite dialects are merely dialectal and have good parallels in other Semitic languages. The long list of characteristics of Canaanite given by Goetze, upon which he builds his case, completely ignores the historical development of the language, the evidence of dialect geography and the evidence of early Hebrew poetry. Albright has tersely remarked that the list is 40% correct, 25% partly correct, 35% quite wrong; *BASOR* 89, p. 8, n. 5. The writer is definitely on the side that considers Ugaritic a Canaanite dialect. In defense of using Ugaritic in Amarna studies, see Albright-Moran, *JCS* 2, n. b [below, Paper 2, pp. 131–132, n. b].

interpretation of the Amarna Letters is W. F. Albright. In a series of articles in recent years he has revolutionized Amarna studies.[8] His success is a patent demonstration of the correctness of his method.

The study that follows is merely an application in detail and to a larger body of texts of the method followed by Albright in his smaller studies. We have concentrated on the letters written from Byblos, since comprising some 66 letters they are the largest single corpus deriving from one Canaanite town.[9] Rather than open ourselves to the objection that we did not allow for dialectal differences, we have confined our study to the Byblian letters alone.

Moreover, we have restricted our study to the syntax of the letters. For aside from occasional remarks, earlier scholars neglected syntax and concentrated on phonology and morphology. Moreover, although, as we mentioned above, important details must be corrected in the earlier studies of the phonology and morphology of the Canaanite in the Amarna Letters, still it would remain a matter of detail, not meriting a special study in itself. Indeed, many of these morphological details, and by far the most important ones, do receive consideration in this study since they have important bearing on syntax.[10]

Our method has already been briefly indicated. All the so-called parts of speech were carefully analyzed in their respective usages. Each usage was compared first with standard Accadian (the native Accadian of Babylonia and Assyria), then with the Accadian of Boğazköy and Nuzi. If the usage was not attested in these sources or did not find an explanation in these sources,[11] the hypothesis was that the usage was

[8]See Bibliography. As Albright pointed out at the time, there had been no real progress in Amarna studies since Knudtzon's publication in 1915; *BASOR* 89, pp. 8–9.

[9]The Amarna Letters from Byblos are as follows: *EA* 68–95, 101–135, 139–140, 362; *EA* 362 = AO 7093, published by F. Thureau-Dangin, "Nouvelles Lettres d'El-Amarna," *RA* 19, pp. 91–94 (autograph pp. 102–103). I have purposely omitted *EA* 136–138, since, though they are Rib-Adda letters, they were written from Berytus.

[*Editors' note*: In the original dissertation, *EA* 362, which had not yet received a "canonical" number, was referred to by the siglum "ThD" after its original editor; for ease of reference we have changed "ThD" throughout to "*EA* 362."]

[10]For instance, *yaqtulu*, which previous scholars denied to be the equivalent of the same form in Arabic. Ugaritic has made this position untenable.

[11]We refer here to the Accadian of Nuzi and especially of Boğazköy. As we shall see, several points of syntax in the Boğazköy documents have no parallel in standard Accadian, but excellent parallels in Canaanite. In these cases we have felt

Canaanite. This hypothesis was then tested by known Canaanite usage, primarily that of Ugaritic, and then that of Biblical Hebrew. If the hypothetical usage could be shown to exist in these two sources or to be in accord with their idiom, then we considered our hypothesis confirmed and no longer an hypothesis but an established fact. Occasionally, in the syntax of the noun, for instance, we found virtually nothing specifically Canaanite. In many cases, however, our method resulted not merely in a confirmation of previous knowledge but in a genuine advance. Our discovery of the volitive *yaqtula* is a case in point.

Our chief sources have been the cuneiform texts published by Bezold-Budge,[12] Winckler-Abel,[13] and Schroeder;[14] Knudtzon's transliteration and translation of the texts (always referred to as *EA*);[15] the Ugaritic texts and Gordon's grammar in his *Ugaritic Handbook*;[16] a Byblian Amarna Letter published by F. Thureau-Dangin (*EA* 362);[17] Albright's studies of the Canaanite Amarna Letters and of the Taanach Tablets.[18] For other sources, see Bibliography; for other abbreviations, see Abbreviations.

---

justified in referring the Boğazköy usage to Canaanite or at least to Northwest Semitic (if not Canaanite, probably Amorite) influence.

[12]Carl Bezold and E. A. Wallis Budge, *The Tell el-Amarna Tablets in the British Museum*, London, 1892.

[13]Hugo Winckler, *Der Thontafelfund von El Amarna*, Heft I, *Mittheilungen aus den orientalischen Sammlungen*, Berlin, 1889. Autograph by Ludwig Abel.

[14]Otto Schroeder, *Die Tontafeln von El-Amarna*, Hefte XI–XII, *Vorderasiatische Schriftdenkmäler*, Leipzig, 1915.

[15]See n. 1.

[16]Cyrus H. Gordon, *Ugaritic Handbook*, Rome, 1947. All references to the Ugaritic texts follow Gordon's enumeration with the exception of Keret, in which we follow Ginsberg's Keret A, B, C (*The Legend of King Keret, BASOR* Supplementary Studies Nos. 2–3, New Haven, 1946).

[17]See n. 9.

[18]See Bibliography. The study of the Taanach Tablets is entitled "A Prince of Taanach in the Fifteenth Century B.C."

Byblian Syntax

I. Particles

A. *adi* = Can. *ᶜôd*

1) *again*: *inan(n)a adi yupaḫ(ḫ)iru kalī ālāni*, "now he is again gathering together all the cities" (124.14–15).[1]

2) *still* (*amplius*): *šumma awātēya tušmuna adi yulḳu* ᵐ·*azaru kīma abišu*, "if my words are heeded, Aziru, like his father, will still be taken" (117.32–33); *šumma kīʾama ḳalāta adi tilḳūna ṣumura*, "if thou art thus negligent, they will take Simyra besides" (104.31–33).[2]

3) *still* (temporal): *adi mūša šūrib ana āl ṣumura*, "while it was still night he brought (the tablet) into Simyra (112.48–50). We have a striking parallel in Jer. 15.9: *bĕᶜôd yômam*, "while it was still day."

B. *išū* = Byblian *yiš* or *ʾiš*

In its two occurrences *išū* is not used with the Accadian meaning "to have" but like Heb. *yēš*, Ug. *ʾiṯ*[3] in the sense of "(there) is": *rābiṣ šarri ša išu ina āl ṣumur*, "the commissioner of the king who is in Simyra" (68.19–20); ... *šumma išu erū ... ana yāši*, "... if there is any copper ... in my possession" (77.9–11). It is impossible to tell whether Byblian had *yiš* (Heb. *yēš*) or *ʾiš* (Ugar. *ʾiṯ*).[4] At any rate, Byblian had a similar particle for the affirmation of concrete existence.

[1]Cf. Ges.-Buhl[13], p. 592a, I 1 a. Böhl's *malaise* when treating *adi* is typical of previous attempts to explain its use in Amarna; p. 73, §34k. Albright was the first to recognize the frequent equation in Can. Amarna of Acc. *adi* = Can. *ᶜôd*; *BASOR* 87, p. 35, n. 17; 89, p. 12, n. 28. It should be remarked here that we have included some material in this section which is rather lexicographical than syntactical. We have done so to bring together all possible material on the particles, etc., including much that is new from Ugaritic.

[2]Cf. *ibid.*, I 1 c.

[3]Cf. *UH*, p. 94, §13.3

[4]There is some evidence that Hebrew also had *ʾiš* as well as *yēš*; cf. II Sam. 14.19, Mi. 6.10, and the personal name *ʾišbaᶜal*, meaning "Baal is present" (*ARI*, p. 207, n. 62). Albright's warning against rendering *ʾ/yiš* as "exist" is in place; it means "be (concretely) present"; *BASOR* 94, p. 31, n. 12.

C. *-ma/mi*

It is impossible to find any rule based on phonetics or usage which determines the use of one of these two particles to the exclusion of the other. Thus we have *attama* (73.36, 117.8) and *attami* (83.36), *yānuma* (107.43) and *yānumi* (94.6); with the same preceding vowels, *pānūya-ma* (118.39, 119.38) and *miyami* (84.6, etc.), *taškarinnima* (126.4) and *kit(t)imi* (127.25), *tulḳūma* (362.13) and *iltiḳūmi* (69.10). Judging solely from the evidence of the Byblian letters,[5] we regard *-mi* as the specifically Byblian particle in the usages attested in these letters (enclitic attached to pronouns, nouns, verbs, etc.). The reasons are: 1) *-mi* has a very restricted use both in standard Accadian[6] and the Accadian of Boğazköy,[7] whereas in these letters *-mi* has the widest possible usage; 2) the parallel usage of *-ma* and *-mi*, with only the former good Accadian, indicates *-mi* is the Byblian counterpart of Accadian *-ma*; 3) *-mi* is more frequent than *-ma*, a large number of the occurrences of the latter being found in cliché greetings such as *mārukama* (73.2, 82.2), *ardukama* (87.3, 103.3, 104.3, 118.3, 130.3, 132.3), *ḳibīma* (95.1, 102.2, 104.2, 118.2, 120.2, 132.2); 4) the substitution of *ḳibīmi* (362.1) for the cliché *ḳibīma* indicates that at least in this usage the Byblian particle was *-mi*, not *-ma*; 5) the use of *-mi*, not *-ma*, in the specifically Canaanite construction discussed in the next paragraph indicates not only one usage where we have *-mi* and not *-ma*, but since syntactically it functions merely as an enclitic particle, it would seem probable that in analogous usages we should likewise have *-mi*.

The specifically Canaanite construction just referred to is the insertion of the particle *-mi* in the construct chain between the *nomen regens* and *nomen rectum*: *tišmuna aṣīmi ṣābi piṭati*, "it hears the coming forth of the archer-host" (73.12–13).[8] Cf. also 127.33 and the discussion of this line in the Appendix.

[5]The gloss *baṭnum(m)a* (232.10, a letter from Accho) and phrases like *kabattumma u zuḫrum(m)a* (306.10) may indicate that Can. had a particle *-ma* which was used in such adverbial expressions. However the evidence is not decisive. South Arabic used a particle *mw* (*maw*); cf. Höfner, pp. 56–57, §48.

[6]*GA*, p. 80, §58b.

[7]Labat, p. 168.

[8]This is the only specifically Canaanite noun syntax in our letters.—To examples of enclitic *-mi* already discovered in Biblical Hebrew, the writer would add: 1) *naᶜatm(i)* (rt. *nwᶜ*; MT *neᶜtam*, which has hitherto remained an insoluble difficulty) in Is. 9.18 and render "at the wrath of Yahweh of hosts the earth trembled"; 2) likewise, *harĕrêm(i) śēᶜîr* in Gen. 14.6 for MT *harĕrām śēᶜîr* and

D. *-na*

This particle is affixed to the indicative *yaqtulu*, to the imperative, and to the volitive *yaqtula*. Indicative: *īpušuna* (74.63, 90.22, 91.26, etc.), *inaṣ(ṣ)aruna* (112.10, 125.12), *tiliʾuna* (82.6), *tištapruna* (117.8), etc.[9] Imperative: *liḳūna*, "take ye" (117.63); *ušširūnanī*, "send ye to me" (71.23).[10] Volitive: *ul timaḫ(ḫ)aṣananī*, "lest they strike me down" (77.37: 3rd. sg. fem. *timaḫḫaṣa* used with a plural subject taken as a collective).[11] Note that pronominal verbal suffixes are affixed to this particle in the imperfect, the imperative, and the volitive *yaqtula*.

The evidence from Ugaritic justifies our considering it the same particle with all three verbal forms. For in Ugaritic we find *yrʾaʾun* (*yîraʾuna*, "he fears"),[12] *ʾiqrʾan* (*ʾiqraʾana*, "let me invoke"),[13] and *šrn* (*šurna*, "harass!").[14]

---

render "the mountains of Seir"—another example of *-mi* in a construct chain. See the writer's forthcoming article in the *Catholic Biblical Quarterly*, "The Putative √ᶜ*tm* in Is. 9.18" [*CBQ* 12 (1950), pp. 153–154—*Eds.*].

[9]For a more detailed discussion of *yaqtuluna*, see the study of the Energic.

[10]The energic *-an(na)* is also used with the imperative in Arabic; Wright-de Goeje, p. 44, §20.

[11]For a possible correspondence to this usage in the Arabic energic, see the study of the Energic.

[12]67.ii.6. The writing is admittedly peculiar, for we would expect *yrʾun*. However, I agree with Goetze (*JAOS* 58, p. 291, n. 129) that in view of the parallel *yrʾu* (49.vi.30) there can be no doubt as to the verb and that *ʾun* cannot be a separate word. Goetze also reads *ytrʾun* (*yittariʾuna*) in 67.ii.22. In view of the Amarna parallels, Goetze should have had no trouble in explaining the affixed *-n*.

[13]*UH* 52.23. Since, as will follow from our study of *yaqtula*, the cohortative in Hebrew is a survival of the older *yaqtula* (Ar. subjunctive), we feel justified in considering *ʾiqraʾana* an instance in the 1st person of *yaqtulana*. It should be remarked here that it is difficult to separate the Heb. particle *-naʾ*, which is used primarily with cohortatives, jussives, and imperatives (*GKC*, §105b), from our *-na* with the imperative and volitive. Nor is the final aleph of *-naʾ* an insuperable difficulty. The name שֶׁבְנָא (MT; LXX Σοβνα) has long been explained by Albright as a misvocalization for *Šubnaʾ*, a hypocoristicon for שבניהו, "turn, pray, O Yahweh!"; *BASOR* 79, p. 28, n. 1. This has recently been confirmed one hundred percent by the Dead Sea Scrolls reading שובנא. To be noted is that *-naʾ* loses its *aleph* when it is not final. It is quite possible that *-na* in final position developed a strong *aleph* (glottal catch), and then became an enclitic particle that could be attached to other particles like *ʾim* and *ʾal*. For the development of a final strong *aleph*, cf. *paʾ* (Ar. *fa*, Ugar. *pa*) in Zendjirli—I am indebted to Dr. Frank M. Cross, Jr. for this parallel. Albright has already compared energic *-na* with Heb. *-naʾ*; *BASOR* 82, p. 17, n. 1; 89, p. 15, n. 47. However, if he is correct in relating Proto-Sinaitic *mʾ* with Heb *naʾ*, then the *aleph* cannot be secondary; *BASOR* 110, p. 16, n. 50. The use of *naʾ* with the jussive (*yiqtōl-naʾ*), which is common in Heb., but is

The force of the particle, both in Byblian and Ugaritic, was to give emphasis. For a more detailed study of its usage, see the study of the Energic.

E. *šumma*, "if, behold"

The first meaning is of course merely Accadian, the second is not Accadian but Canaanite. *šumma* = "behold" in 74.13, 74.32, 103.36, 108.34, 109.54, 112.25. *šumma ennabtū kalī* lú.pl.*maṣ(ṣ)arti*, "Behold, all the garrison has fled" (103.36–38). In this regard compare Ugar. *hm* which means both "if" and "behold."[15]

In 89.43 *šumma* introduces a single direct question: *šumma ana ḫāzāni āl ṣurri lā yišaʾilu šarru*, "Will the king not make inquiry concerning the governor of Tyre?" In Hebrew, *ʾim* is used more often to introduce the second member of a disjunctive question, but it is also occasionally employed like *šumma* in 89.43.[16] The development "if" > "whether" > introductory particle indicating a question is easy and natural. Compare Lat. *an*: *nescio utrum ad me venturus sit an domi mansurus*, "I do not know whether he is going to come to me or stay at home"; *an ad me veniet*, "Will he come to me?"

F. *umma*

Albright was the first to recognize that the Accadian of the west, contrary to normal Acc. usage, employed the genitive after *umma* (thus *umma* m.*ribaddi*, 84.3).[17] He compared Heb. *nĕʾum*, so frequent in the prophets, and Ugar. *tḥm*, "word," which functions in Ugaritic epistolary style like *umma* in the Taanach and Can. Amarna letters.

Marcus, following Albright's lead, has recently made a more detailed study of *umma* in Can. Amarna and has found about a 10% variation in the endings of nouns in apposition to a proper name follow-

---

ruled out absolutely in Byblian, may derive from the use, attested in Byblian and Ugaritic, of *na(ʾ)* with the volitive *yaqtula*, which, as we shall see, is virtually identical in use with the jussive. When *yaqtula* was lost, the atypical use of *na(ʾ)* with the jussive may have taken its place.

[14] Keret A, 110.

[15] *UH*, p. 91, §12.3; p. 94, §12.7. For the bearing of this discovery on the nature and syntax of conditional clauses, see Conditional Sentences.

[16] Cf. I Ki. 1.27; *JCS* 4, p. 167 [see below, Paper 4, p. 149].

[17] *BASOR* 87, p. 33, n. 7.

ing *umma* (cf. *umma* $^{\mathrm{m}\cdot}$*ribadda*, 73.2).[18] To this short study Goetze added a very valuable note in which he points out that in Hittite texts *umma* is interchangeable with the construct *awat*, which necessarily requires a following genitive.[19]

In view of the excellent parallels to such usage in Can., we are almost certainly correct in seeing, if not specifically Canaanite, at least Northwest Semitic influence as the explanation of this peculiarity of Northwest Accadian. Moreover, in view of Ugar. usage of *tḥm*, it is probable that the Byblian scribes considered *umma* as the Acc. counterpart of their own Byblian *tḥm* or the like.

G. The Negatives

a. *ul, lā*

In general, there is no distinction made in the usage of *ul* and *lā*. Thus as the negative of a protasis, *ul* (77.26) and *lā* (83.45); as negative of an independent clause, *ul* (82.10) and *lā* (32.21), etc.

There is a pleonastic use of the negative which must be noted: *ul tišmūna mimma u šaprū ana šāšu*, "as soon as they hear anything, they write to him" (82.10–12); *u lā kašid irīšu u ušširtīšu*, "as soon as the request arrives, then I shall send him" (82.16–17). For this construction we have two excellent parallels in Hebrew: *ʾap bal niṭṭāʿû ʾap bal zōrāʿû ʾap bal šôrēš bāʾāreṣ gizʿām wĕgam nāšap bāhem wayyîbāšû usĕʿārāh kaqqaš tiśśāʾēm*, "hardly have they been sown, hardly has their stock taken root in the earth, and He blows upon them and they wither, and a whirlwind like stubble carries them away" (Is. 40.24); *wayhî yĕšaʿyāhû loʾ yāṣāʾ hāʿîr hattîkônāh udĕbar YHWH hāyāh ʾēlāw*, "and it happened, hardly had Isaias gone out of the middle city and the word of Yahweh came to him" (II Ki. 20.4). Note that in the first example the negative is *bal*, the standard negative in Ugaritic and Phoenician.

The force of the negative is clear: it is hyperbolic, used to emphasize the immediate connection between the action expressed in its own clause and that expressed in the following clause. Thus literally, *u lā kašid* ..., "He will not have arrived and I will send him back ..." Perhaps "hardly," "immediately" (as a conjunction), or "as soon as" are the

[18]Ralph Marcus, "On the Genitive after *umma* in the Amarna Tablets," *JCS* 2, pp. 223–224.
[19]*Ibid.*, p. 224.

best English renderings of the Canaanite idiom. As is clear from the Byblian examples and the passage from *Kings*, this idiom, though not common, was used in narrative prose.[20]

b. *bali*

1) *not* = Canaanite *bal*: *šumma libbi šarri bali uššar ṣābi piṭati yašpur ana* m.*yanḫame*, "if the king does not wish to send an archer-host, let him write to Yanḫamu" (117.59–61); *bali aṣī ṣābi piṭati ina šanti annīti u ilḳūmi ālāni gubla*, "if the archer-host does not come forth this year, then they will take the cities of Byblos" (129.40–42). In the first example we have *bali* used as the negative of a nominal sentence, for which we have an excellent parallel in Prov. 23.7: *wĕlibbô bal ᶜimmāk*, "but his heart is not with thee" (cf. also 24.23). In the second it is the negative of the infinitive *aṣī*. Both usages can only reflect Byblian *bal*; Acc. *balum* is never so used.

2) *aššum bali*, "for lack of" = Heb. *mibbĕlî* and the Byblian equivalent of the Heb. expression: *eḳliya aššata ša lā mūta mašil aššum bali irēšim*, "my field for lack of cultivation is like a woman without a husband" (74.17–19, etc.). Note the use of the expression with the infinitive. Neither Acc. *balu* (older *balum*) nor Boğazköy *balu(m)*[21] is ever so used. Indeed when used as a preposition, the form is regularly *balu*—thus even *ina balu*.

c. *yānu*

The syntax of *yānu* is not that of Acc., according to which the predicate noun is in the nominative case. Rather it is consistently in the accusative—a fact we shall establish—, leaving as the only possible conclusion that Byblian *ʾēn* or *ʾēna* took the acc.[22]

Together with many examples like *yānu limna* (94.6), *yānu ḫāzāna* (117.9–10), *yānu miamma* (85.74), *yānu mimma* (92.21, 112.25,

[20]As Albright and the writer have noted elsewhere (*JCS* 2, p. 241, n. e [see below, Paper 2, p. 132, n. e]), the same idiom is found in the Agushaya epic, written in the archaizing hymnal-epic dialect: *išātu ul tamḫat atelī (a-eteli) / itarrū (a-)dašni*, "Scarcely has the kindled fire flamed up, They are reduced to ashes" (Zimmern, *VS* X 214, obv. III 9ff., 13ff.). However, this is not against considering the Byblian use as reflecting native idiom, since this idiom, so far as the writer knows, never became part of Acc. prose idiom, as it clearly did in Byblian and Hebrew.

[21]Cf. *HWB* p. 174a; Labat, p. 110.

[22]Properly, an accusative of specification. Böhl, p. 72, §34f, has noted that *yānu* is followed by the acc., but has failed to note that this must reflect Canaanite idiom.

116.41, 117.74), *yānu* $^{\text{lú.pl.}}$*tillata(m)* (92.22), the most convincing evidence comes from a comparison of the syntax of the same phrase in the same letter when found with or without *yānu*—case endings then are really significant. Thus in 129.33–34 *minā tīpušu ṣābu piṭatu*, "what will the archer-host do?"; but in 129.30,49 we twice have *šumma yānu ṣāba piṭata(m)*, "if there is no archer-host ..." So too in 362.19,56 we twice have *tūṣu ṣābu piṭatu*, "the archer host will come forth"; but as the object of a verb (*yišaru*, line 10) and after *yānumi* (line 17) we have *ṣāba piṭata(m)*. Compare too: *mūtumi ana mātāti*, "the lands are plague-stricken" (362.47); *yānumi mūtāna ana mātāti*, "there is no plague in the lands" (362.49-50).

Final proof that the word *yānu* is the decisive factor in this use of the accusative, and that there is no more general rule according to which any expression of non-existence has the predicate in the accusative, is furnished by the contrast of 122.28–31 and 112.54–56: *annū anāku ul maṣṣartu u ul balāṭ šarri ana yāši*, "behold as for me, I have no garrison nor royal provisions"; *annū inan(n)a yānu balāṭ šarri u yānu maṣṣarta*, "behold now, there are no royal provisions and there is no garrison."[23]

H. The Conjunction

The conjunction *u*, so much more frequent in the Byblian letters than in standard Accadian, is used exactly like Heb. *wa*. Besides its ordinary function of joining coordinate clauses and of introducing virtually subordinate clauses (for which see the various types of clauses), there is one use meriting special note, paralleled in Hebrew, where it is happily called by Joüon the *waw de sentiment*.[24] In this idiom the conjunction indicates less a logical connection—what there is is always illative—with what precedes than a certain nuance of emotion. Thus *u ušširūnanī*, "so send me ..." (71.22–23); *u ḳibāmi awata annīta ana pāni šarri*, "come, inform the king of this matter" (73.33–35); *u nudabbir*

[23]The restoration *u yānu* is certain from context and the parallel in 122.16–19.—Exceptions to the rule of the acc. after *yānu* are confined to ideograms with phonetic complements: *awīlu(m)*$^{\text{lu(m)}}$ (69.23), *awīli(m)*$^{\text{li(m)}}$ (74.33), *bīti*^{ti} (89.49), *mū*^{u} (85.54), *šeʾi(m)*$^{\text{i(m)}}$ (105.85). However, little importance can be attached to these forms, since the phonetic complements tended to be stereotyped. The only real exception, *yānu* LÚ$^{\text{pl.}}$*maṣ(ṣ)arti* in 122.18, is most probably to be explained as *maṣ(ṣ)arti* being a genitive dependent on LÚ$^{\text{pl.}}$, here to be read *awīlūt* and not as a determinative.

[24]*GHB*, §177m.

$^{\text{lú.pl.}}$*ḫāzānūta*, "so come, let's drive out the governors" (74.34). Note also the phrase *u inanna* in 102.24–28 and compare Heb. *wĕᶜattāh*, where "and now" is not temporal but interjectional.

The conjunction also has a slightly adversative force ("but," "however"): *u annūš inanna innipšat māt šarri u āl ṣumura āl maṣ(ṣ)artikunu ana* ^{m}GAZ$^{\text{pl.}}$ *u ḳalāta*, "... but thou art negligent" (76.33–37; cf. also 71.21, 74.8, 104.26). Heb. has the same usage.[25]

Finally, the ubiquitous conjunction *u* in these letters reflects the same idiom we find in Hebrew: parataxis of clauses with a predilection for syndeton. One example will illustrate sufficiently: *yišmē šarru bēlī awātē arad kit(t)išu u yiz(z)iz* $^{\text{m.}}$*iḫripita ina āl ṣumura u liḳī* $^{\text{m.}}$*ḫaʾip ana muḫ(ḫ)ika u dagalšu u limad awātēšu u šumma damiḳ ina pānika u šukun ina* ^{lú}*rābiṣi šemīrum ina pāni* $^{\text{lú.pl.}}$*ḫāzānūti šarri u yišmē bēlī awātēya*, "Let the king my lord hear the words of his loyal servant, and let Iḫripita stay in Simyra and take Ḫaʾip to thyself and investigate him and learn his deeds and if it is good in thy sight, then place a ring on the commissioner in the presence of the governors, and let my lord heed my words" (107.11–25). By rendering each *u* literally one gets a very clear idea of the sentence structure. How different it is from Accadian is immediately apparent.

On the *waw of succession*, cf. The Nature of the Perfect [pp. 33–38 in the present volume].

[25]*GHB*, §172.

II. PREPOSITIONS[26]

A. *ana*

1) *from*: this meaning follows from the parallel usage of *ḳālu* with *ištu* (68.14,31) and *ana* (74.13,48). Ugar. *la* and Heb. *lĕ* have the same meaning.[27]

2) *according to*: so in the phrase *ana pī*, "according to the command of" (79.12,22). Cf. Heb. and Punic *lĕpî*.[28]

3) *(up)on*: so in the phrase *ašābu ana kussī*, "to sit upon the throne" (cf. 116.66). Cf. Ugar. *yaṯibu lakaḥṯi*;[29] standard Acc. idiom is *ina kussī*.[30]

4) *ana pāni* = *before*: *passim*; cf. especially in the phrase *damiḳ ana pāni*, "it seems good before, in the eyes of" (84.6–7). Cf. Heb. *lipnê* and *ṭôb lipnê*.[31]

Cf. also the Canaanite idiom *nadānu pānī ana*, used both in a hostile sense, "to set oneself against" (79.10–11) and in the sense of "to direct the face to (beseechingly)" (73.38). Cf. Heb. *nātan pānîm ʾel* (hostile sense) and *nātan pānîm bĕ* (second sense);[32] also Ugar. *ytn pnm ʿm*.[33] This also shows us *la* was used in Byblian in the sense of "against."

5) *ana īdīniya*, "by myself" (91.26); cf. Heb. *lĕbaddî*.[34]

[26]Many uses of the prepositions are of course common both to Acc. and Can. Only those which are specifically Can. or are frequent in Can. but quite rare in Acc. will be listed. For example, *ana ṣīriya* (92.24, etc.) is paralleled by Ugar. *lẓry* and may well reflect Byblian idiom, but since it is also good Old Babylonian (cf. Ungnad, *Babylonische Briefe*, 132.7) we do not list it.—Some merely lexicographical material is included under the prepositions.

[27]*UH*, p. 81, §10.1; p. 86, §10.11.

[28]Ges.-Buhl[13] 656a; *GP*, 136. Also in South Arabic (*wbf krbʾl*, at the order of KRBʾL); cf. Höfner, p. 141, §123.

[29]*UH* 49.i.30.

[30]*HWB*, p. 244a. The idiom occurs also in a Cyprus letter (34.52).

[31]Ges.-Buhl[13], p. 293.

[32]Ges.-Buhl[13], p. 552b.

[33]*UH*, p. 237, §18.929.

[34]*ēdēnum* in Acc. is used as an adverb; cf. *HWB*, p. 20b, where all examples are adverbial (old adverbial *-um*), though Delitzsch is correct in considering *ēdēnum* as basically a noun; cf. *qirbum*, *līṭum*, etc., with the same usage. Its proper use as a noun, however, is not attested.

Note finally the idiom *šemū ana*, "hearken to" (86.17, 103.22, 126.62, 131.34–35, 132.53). The idiom is not Acc. but Canaanite; cf. Heb. *šāmaᶜ lĕ* and Ugar. *šmᶜ l*.[35]

B. *ina*

1) *from*: like *ana* (see above), also used with *ḳālu* (139.10, 140.6). Cf. Heb. *bĕ*, Ugar. *ba*.[36]

2) *as*: *ištaparka šarru ina rābiṣi*, "the king has sent thee as commissioner" (71.9–10); *luwaš(š)ira* ᵐ·*yanḫama ina rābiṣi*, "let him send Yanḥamu as commissioner" (106.36–37). This use of *ina* is identical with the so-called *beth essentiae* of the older Hebrew grammarians;[37] cf. Ex. 18.4 *ᵓĕlôhê ᵓabî bĕᶜezrî*, "the god of my father is my help." The idiom is not only West Semitic,[38] but Hamito-Semitic (cf. in Egyptian the so-called "*m* of equivalence").[39]

3) *according to*: so in *ina pīšu*, "according to his command" (81.18); cf. Heb. *bidĕbar*, *baᶜăṣat*.[40]

4) *(in exchange) for*: *gamrū mārēnū u mārātu ḳadunū ina nadānim ina māt yarimuta ina balāṭa* (error for *balāṭ*, cf. 75.14, 81.41, 85.15) *napištinū*, "besides ourselves our sons and daughters are lost by selling (them) in Yarimuta for provisions" (74.15–17; cf. also 75.11–14, 85.12–15). The identical use of *bĕ* after *nātan* is found in Heb.; cf. Jo. 4.3, Deut. 14.25, and especially Lam. 1.11 where we have a most interesting parallel—*nātĕnû maḥămawddêhem bĕᵓōkel lĕhāšîb nāpeš*, "they give of their treasures for food to keep themselves alive." Cf. also 107.3.

5) *ina pāni*, with virtually the same meaning as *ana pāni*, and indeed used in identical expressions. Thus *damāḳu ina pāni* (85.33, 107.20, 108.8) and *damāḳu ana pāni* (see above), *nazāzu ina pāni* (71.25, 94.12) and *nazāzu ana pāni* (362.65). With the latter idiom we find the same fluctuation in Heb.: *ᶜāmad lipnê* and *ᶜāmad bipnê*.[41]

[35]Ges.-Buhl[13], p. 858a; *UH*, p. 86, §10.10.

[36]*UH*, p. 81, §10.1; p. 83, §10.5.

[37]For a discussion of this use of *ba* in Heb. and many more examples, cf. *GHB*, §133c. Böhl (p. 69, §33d) has already noted the idiom in Amarna.

[38]Cf. Qoran 68.2 for one of many examples in Arabic.

[39]Cf. Gardiner, *Egyptian Grammar*, p. 110, §38.

[40]Ges.-Buhl[13], p. 86b.

[41]Ges.-Buhl[13], p. 621a.—The parallelism of *ana pāni* and *ina pāni* as well as the parallelism of *ana* / / *ina* (cf. *pānu ina* [90.21–22] and *pānu ana* [117.12]; *ana īdīniya* [91.26] and *ina īdīniya* [74.64, 81.51, 90.23, 122.20, 134.16]) should be

C. *ištu*

1) *more than*: *kabit ištu mār šipriya*, "he was honored more than my messenger" (88.47; cf. also 106.15, 362.50). The idiom is pure Canaanite; cf. Heb. *min*.[41a]

2) *ištu pāni* = *because of*: so in *ištu pāni kalbi*, "because of the dog" (108.56). Cf. Heb. *mippĕnê*.

D. *itti*

1) *to*: *ušširami awīlaka ittiya*, "send thy man to me" (82.15; cf. also 87.10). Cf. Ugar. *ᶜm*[42] and the Canaanitism in the Taanach Letters, *ittiya* = "to me."[43]

---

noted, especially since it has been misunderstood by Ebeling (*EA* II, 1374, "*ana* fälschlich gebraucht"). The same apparent confusion of *ana* for *ina* exists at Boğazköy (Labat, p. 100). Some cases such as *ana idi* = *ina idi*, *ana ḳāti* = *ina ḳāti* may be paralleled in Amarna texts of Accadian origin, but such phrases as *ašābu ana kussī*, *ašābu ana āli*, *ana ūmi*, etc. are not standard Acc. idiom. On the other hand, *every case* of the so-called erroneous use of *ana* for *ina* may be paralleled by *lĕ* in Heb. (cf. Ges.-Buhl[13], pp. 394–395), most cases by *la* in Ugar. (cf. *UH*, pp. 85–86, §10.10–11). In other words, Northwest Semitic idiom is at work, not only in Canaanite Amarna where it would be expected, but at Boğazköy. Thus it is wrong to refer to such uses of *ana* as erroneous, though they are not normal Accadian. Abnormal in East Semitic, they are not so in Northwest Semitic. In short, the use of the prepositions in these letters is Canaanite, and hence we may safely include in our list the use of *ana* / *ina* in the sense of *from*, even though such a use is not unknown in good Accadian texts (cf. J. Kohler-A. Ungnad, *Hammurabi's Gesetz*, II, p. 119; *Glossary* under *ina*).

[41a]Already noted by Böhl, p. 70, §33 l.

[42]*UH*, p. 87, §10.14.

[43]Cf. *BASOR* 94, p. 17, n. 27.

III. PRONOUNS

A. Interrogative

1) A frequent idiom of the Byblos letters is the use of "what" (not "who") in expressions like "what is he that ...": *minū* $^{\text{m}\cdot}$*abdaširta ardu kalbu u yilḳu māt šarri ana šāšu*, "what is ʿAbd-Ashirta, the slave (and) dog, that he takes the land of the king for himself?" (71.16–19); cf. also 76.11–14, 88.9, 92.41, etc. Compare in Hebrew: "And we, what (are we) that you murmur against us" (Ex. 16.7; cf. Nu. 16.11).

2) Twice *minū(mi)* is used in the sense of "why": *minūmi lā yūdanu mimmu ištu ēkalli ana yāši*, "why is nothing given to me from the palace" (126.49–51; also l. 14). Cf. Ex. 14.15: *mah tiṣʿaq ʾēlay*, "why dost thou cry to me?". We should expect the accusative *minā* in this adverbial use. It is probably only a scribal error—note that both occurrences are in the same letter.

3) An idiom, completely unrecognized in the Byblian letters and only partially understood in the Bible, is the use of *ana manni* (Heb. *lāmāh*) as a negative.[44] If one examines 125.37ff. very closely, one will see that to render *ana manni* in l. 39 by "why" is meaningless: "My cities belong to Aziru, and he is seeking me (my death). *Why* shall I make an alliance with him? What are the dogs, the sons of ʿAbd-Ashirta, that they do as they please and set the king's cities on fire?" It is obvious that Rib-Adda has every reason in the world to make an alliance with Aziru. On the other hand, in view of his dire situation, to say "I shall not make an alliance with him" is a strong protest of loyalty and makes excellent sense.

The same idiom has been only partially recognized in Biblical Hebrew. The negative sense of *lāmāh* = "lest" has been recognized and correctly explained as a development from a rhetorical question.[45] However, there are at least two very clear examples of *lāmāh* used as a simple negative. The first is in I Sam. 20.8, where David and Jonathan are planning to test Saul's feelings towards David. Considering the pos-

[44]Acc. *mannu* is frequently used in the sense of "what"; v.g., *muḫḫi ša manni*, "for what reason" (114.41–42). Note also the idiom *manni ūmī, manni ūmāti* below. Cf. *man hûʾ* in Ex. 16.15. It would seem that Canaanite had an interrogative *man(nu)* = "what."

[45]Cf. Ges.-Buhl^{13}, p. 424a–b.

sibility that they are unfavorable, David tells Jonathan: *wĕʾim yēš bî ʿāwôn hămîtēnî ʾattāh wĕʿad ʾābîkā lāmmāh zeh tĕbîʾēnî*, "But if there is any guilt in me, kill me thyself. But to thy father thou shalt not bring me." The second is in I Sam. 27.5 where David has gone to Gath and is requesting that he and his men be allowed to live in some outlying town. He goes on: *wĕlāmmāh yēšēb ʿabdĕkā bĕʿîr hammamlākāh ʿimmāk*, "For thy servant cannot dwell in the royal city with thee."—It is clear that in neither of these passages does the meaning "lest" make sense. Nor would it be correct to analyze them as really affirmative statements—"otherwise I will ..."[46] In the first it is clear that David wishes Jonathan to kill him rather than be brought to Saul; in the second, David would hardly tell Achish that unless he was granted an outlying city he would simply settle down in Gath, *rege volente nolente*. In short, the Byblian passage in Amarna and the two passages in Samuel mutually confirm each other.

4) Another idiom to be noted is the phrase *man(n)i ūmī* (114.35, 119.39, 122.38) and *man(n)i ūmāti* (88.19) meaning "how long, how often." Compare Keret C, 81–82: *mn yrḫ km*[*rṣ*] / *mn kdw kr*[*t*], "how many moons hath he been sick, how many hath Keret been ill?" Böhl correctly saw that this use of *mannu* belonged under the interrogative pronouns, not, as Winckler wished, under the preposition מִן.[47] However, he lacked the Ugaritic parallel as his final confirmation.

B. Personal

The independent pronoun is used in apposition to a pronominal verbal suffix: *u ušširašu šūta(m)*, "so send him back (even him)" (83.37). Compare in Heb.: *bārăkēnî gam ʾănî*, "bless me too" (Gen. 27.34); in Ugaritic *šmk ʾat*, "thy very name" (*UH* 68.11).

šunu yubaʾu laḳā (78.12) seems to reflect an emphatic personal pronoun **himat*. For *šunu* cannot be a *casus pendens*, or we would have *laḳāšunu*. If this analysis be correct, then the emphatic pronoun could be placed in the emphatic position, the beginning of the sentence, and, as in Ugaritic,[48] be the object of a verbal form.

[46]"Of very frequent occurrence also are questions introduced by לָמָּה which really contain an affirmation and are used to state the reason for a request or warning ..." (*GKC*, §150e). The example from Gen. 27.45 cited by *GKC* would, I believe, be better classified with my two examples of the simple negative.

[47]Böhl, p. 30, §18e.

[48]*UH*, p. 26, §6.13.

The independent pronoun *anāku* is also used as a *casus pendens*. It seems most probable that we may regard this usage as reflecting Byblian idiom, for: 1) the Old Babylonian idiom usually employed the oblique cases of the pronoun if the retrospective pronoun referring to it were in an oblique case;[49] 2) this same usage was in force at Boğazköy;[50] 3) of the particular idiom we find in these letters (with *anāku* resumed by a pronominal suffix of the noun) I cannot find an example in some 270 Old Babylonian letters;[51] nor does it seem to have been found at Boğazköy.[52] In late Assyrian the construction is attested,[53] but in Old Babylonian, which Northwest Accadian reflects, the construction must have been rare, and if used, would generally (and more correctly) have the genitive *yāši* rather than the nominative *anāku*. Hence when we find the construction with *anāku* fairly common in the Byblian letters, it seems most probable to consider it as a reflection of native idiom, especially since the construction is well attested in Heb.[54]

Examples: *amur anāku nukurtum muḫḫiya 5 šanāti*, "behold, as for me, for 5 years there has been enmity against me" (106.16–17); *u anāku ālāniya ana* ᵐ·*aziri*, "and as for me, my cities belong to Aziru" (125.36–37); cf. also 106.6–7, 117.9–11, 118.39–40, 122.27–31, etc.[55] Cf.

[49]Cf. Poebel, *Das appositionell bestimmte Pronomen*, p. 7, n. 1 and p. 85, n. 5—the latter example being undoubtedly an archaism. Poebel has a very penetrating study of the use of *anāku* as a *casus pendens* in Northwest Semitic. His work merits closer study than I have been able to give it, but it seems that though his evidence from Accadian is convincing, his treatment of Biblical material is a bit arbitrary with the evidence being forced to fit the theory; cf. for example, his treatment of Gen. 15.7 on pp. 70–71. Moreover, Blake has brought forward evidence from South Arabic which almost certainly disproves Poebel's thesis; cf. *JAOS* 62, p.117. —Cf. the use of *yāti* in Ungnad, *Babylonische Briefe*, 17.14, 53.9, 143.17, 215.16. Once (171.7) in this selection of letters *anāku* is resumed by a verbal pronominal suffix: *anāku u šībūt ālim tukab(b)itanniʾāti*, "as for me and the elders of the city, thou didst honor us."

[50]Labat, p. 134 (under *yāši*).

[51]Ungnad's *Babylonische Briefe*.

[52]Labat makes no reference in his grammar to such a usage, which would surely have been noted if it existed.

[53]Cf. Waterman, *Royal Correspondence of the Assyrian Empire*, I 2. rev. 4.

[54]*GHB*, §156b.

[55]We do not include here examples where *anāku* (or any other personal pronoun) precedes the verb, since it is impossible to determine in this hybrid Accadian so fine a point as the word-order of the verbal sentence.

the perfect parallel in Ugaritic: *ʾank . ʾin . bt ly kʾilm*, "and as for me, I have no house like the other gods."[56]

The personal pronoun may be used to express the subject of an infinitive functioning as a finite verb. Thus, *u tiḳbūna ṣabātmi nīnū ālāni gubli u minā tīpušu ṣābu piṭatu*, "and they say, 'If we take the cities of Byblos, what will the archer-host do?' " (129.32–34); *paṭārima šūta(m) u yānu ša yūbalu ṭuppīya*, "if he leaves, then there will be no one to carry my tablets" (113.40–41). As will be pointed out in our discussion of the infinitive, this construction has good parallels in later Phoenician inscriptions, and at least one parallel in Biblical Hebrew.

C. Objective verbal suffixes

As in Ugaritic,[57] the verbal suffix, usually the direct object of the verb, may also express the indirect object: *ušširūnanī 50 tapal sisī*, "send (ye) to me 50 teams of horses" (71.23–24).

[56] *UH* 129.19.
[57] *UH*, p. 97, §13.43.

IV. The Finite Verbal Forms

Few problems of Semitic grammar have tasked the ingenuity of scholars more than that of the nature of the finite verbal forms. The large number of studies on the subject from the early nineteenth century up to the present testifies to the failure of every theory so far offered to explain *all* the facts.

We are not guilty here of the fatuous presumption that the limited evidence of the Byblos letters, or indeed of all Canaanite Amarna, can supply us with the solution of this perplexing problem. However, our source does have one advantage: it derives from one Canaanite city—and hence reflects only one dialect—and from one short period of thirty years.

It is, we believe, only by careful analysis of material of this sort that a solution to the problem of the Semitic verb will, if ever, be reached. The actual use of the verb forms is thus established in a given historical period. One then has a firm basis for concluding from its use to the nature of the form in *that particular period*. Given enough studies of this sort, one can attempt an *inductive* historical treatment of the verb. But once we begin our analysis with, say, *yaqtul* as the original verb form,[58] then we are so far back in the prehistorical period and so far beyond the evidence we can control that we have entered the realm of pure theory. The conclusions derived from this theoretical basis are as valid as the initial theory.

[58]So, for example, H. Bauer, "Die Tempora im Semitischen," *BA* 8, p. 8: "Es spricht also alles für, nichts gegen die Annahme einer Ursprünglichkeit des Imperfekts, so dass wir mit ihr als einer feststehenden Tatsache rechnen dürfen." With this I agree, but when one realizes that the perfect goes back to the time when Hamitic and Semitic were closely related languages or families of languages, and that the earliest Semitic evidence we can *control* dates from the Dynasty of Accad, it becomes clear that theory, and theory alone, bridges the gap of millenia for which we have no evidence at all. Aside from our tremendous ignorance is the complexity of the problem. Thus in Egyptian the active-transitive use of the old perfective (pseudo-participle) is in Middle Egyptian merely a survival in a few narrative forms of the 1st person, but in Old Egyptian more common, though already rare. See Gardiner, *Egyptian Grammar*, p. 238, §312. This would indicate that the active-transitive use goes back into the prehistoric period and is perhaps as old as the stative-intransitive use. Yet in Semitic the usual view is that the active use of the perfect is a later development and perhaps confined to West Semitic. This one example is a good warning against speculation and an indication of its futility without solid evidence.

Hence, though we have consulted the more important studies of the Semitic verb forms, particularly the studies of the Hebrew verb, we have proceeded quite independently in our analysis of the Byblian material. Only where our problems coincide are these studies referred to for further illustrations, or as agreeing to or dissenting from the solution proposed by us. Likewise, our references to Hebrew are meant to be merely illustrative where the same problems exist in Hebrew and Byblian. Thus whatever validity our conclusions as to the nature of the verb forms may have is restricted to Amarna Byblian. That they may apply elsewhere, either completely or with modification, depends upon further investigation.

In the analysis of the verb that follows we shall proceed inductively without any presuppositions as to the nature of *qatala (qatila)* or *yaqtulu(na) (yiqtaluna)*. The two tables on the *Use of the Perfect* and the *Use of the Imperfect* are merely descriptive, intended to give an over-all picture of verb usage with the "tense" derived solely from context. Only after a careful analysis of verb usage shall we attempt to determine the nature of the verb form.

The Use of the Perfect[59]

Verb	Present	Future	Past
aḫāru			1
*alāku**			2–1
aṣū			5–7
*ašābu**	5		1
ašāru		1	3–10
*balāṭu**	1	5	1

59* = stative verb; # = passive (or permansive); under Past, first column = present perfect, second column = simple past narrative (Greek aorist). Here of course there is often much room for argument, since it is often extremely difficult, if not impossible, to decide between the two possibilities. However, results are not seriously affected by doubts as to the exact interpretation, since the usage in either case is specifically Canaanite, not Accadian.—The tabulation of *ašābu* and *nazāzu* (with *ᶜāmad* its probable Canaanite equivalent) as stative verbs is admittedly open to doubt; cf. Blake, *JAOS* 24, p. 191. I have done so because their meaning is stative and their usage more in accord with that of stative verbs. However, again results are not seriously affected one way or the other.

*bašū**	7[60]	2	2
gamāru	9#		
dabāru			1
dāku			11–2
*damāḳu**	8		
*danānu**	6	3	2
epēšu		5	15–2
erēbu			6
ḫabātu			1
*ḫadū**	1		
ḫatū	1#[61]		
*kabāṭu**			1–1
*kānu**	1		
*kašādu**[62]	1	1	1–1
lamādu			1
leḳū		1	18–10
*maʾādu**	6		
magāgu (*maḳāḳu*?)	2#[63]		
*marāṣu**	8		
mašālu	4		
*mātu**	1	2	1
nadānu			14–5
*nakāru**			2
naṣāru		1	1
nazāzu	1		
paḫāru			2–1
*paṭāru**			3

[60]The forms here tabulated are the blends of the present *ibaššī* and the perfect afformatives.

[61]Ebeling was the first to recognize that *tiḫtātī* (102.13) is most probably to be explained as a *tifʿel* (Ebeling, p. 69). However, Albright's derivation from *ḫatū*, with its perfect parallel in Ugaritic, makes better sense than Ebeling's derivation from *ḫaṭaʾ*; *BASOR* 82, p. 48.

[62]The writer has elsewhere offered evidence that *kašādu* was used by the Byblian scribes as the Acc. equivalent of their own *b(w)ʾ*; see *JCS* 2, p. 245, comm. no. 13 [below, Paper 2, p. 137].

[63]As F. Thureau-Dangin has shown, *manga* (*manḳa*) is the permansive of *magāgu* (*maḳāḳu*?), which having the same ideogram as *sanāḳu* and *ḫanāḳu* probably means "to squeeze, to press"; *RA* 19, p. 92, n. 3.

*palāḫu**	12		
palāšu			2
pašāḫu	5		2
ṣabātu		1	8
ṣwr	1#[64]		
ḳabū		1	3–3
*ḳālu**	12[65]	2	2
*ḳṣp**	2#		
*ḳarābu**			1
*raʾāmu**	1		
rakāšu			1–1
*rāḫu**	9[66]		
šaḫātu	1#		
šaṭāru			1
šakānu	6#		4
*šalāmu**	8		
šapāru	1		9
*šemū**		1	1–1
tarāṣu	2[66a]		
tāru			2–1
Total	122	33	100–75

[64] I follow Ebeling (p. 59) and interpret the *zi-ir-ti* in 127.34 as the passive of *ṣ(w)r*.

[65] The etymology of forms like *ḳalāta*, etc., has so far been unknown. Böhl, p. 67, §32n, has rightly insisted that the verb is hollow and not to be derived from the root *qll* (so Müller). On the other hand, his proposal to derive it from Acc. *q(w)l*, "to look at, give attention to," is highly questionable, since he can cite no parallels for the idiom. Ugaritic, we believe, gives the key to the solution. There we have a root either *q(w)l* (so Albright) or *qll* (so Gordon) meaning "to fall." Now an attested idiom in Heb. is *rāpā min*, "to neglect" (cf. Ex. 4.26; Ju. 8.3; Neh. 6.9), *rāpā* properly meaning "to sink." Hence we conclude: 1) that *ḳālu ištu* (or *ana, ina*), "to fall from" = "to neglect," in the Byblos letters is a Canaanite idiom; 2) that the Ugaritic verb is definitely *q(w)l*. This is a pretty example of Amarna and Ugaritic mutually complementing each other.

[66] The forms enumerated under *rāḫu* are the blends of the I_2 *irtīḫ* and the perfect afformatives.

[66a] The permansive *tarāṣu* with *ana pāni* in the sense of "to act (fairly) towards someone" is attested also at Boğazköy; cf. Labat, p. 218.

A. The Use of the Perfect

We need not give a long justification of what at first may seem a gratuitous assumption, namely, our treatment of *qatala*, etc. as Canaanite perfects. It is generally admitted that the perfect active *qatala* is in full use in Canaanite Amarna and the distinction between active and stative forms generally observed.[67]

1. *With present meaning*: Of the 122 occurrences of the perfect with present meaning, 95 are forms of a stative verb, 22 are forms of a passive (permansive), only one a form of an active verb, while the four occurrences of *mašil* with present meaning are difficult to classify since it is uncertain whether we should consider this form an Acc. permansive or a Can. *piᶜel*.

Stative verbs: The present meaning of the stative perfect has of course its parallel in Biblical Hebrew.[68] It is instructive to note that *yqtl* of the stative verb is ordinarily not employed for the present. Note the glosses *naqṣapū* in 82.51 (gloss to *tāšaš*) and *naqṣaptī* in 93.5 (gloss to *attašaš*), both with present meaning, where after Acc. *iqtul*, which clearly does not have its proper preterite meaning in these passages, we might expect *tiqaṣṣipu* and *ʾiqaṣṣipu* or the like. Thus the Can. perfect stative is the rule for expressing the present of intransitive verbs, whereas, as we shall see below, *yaqtulu* is the rule in transitive verbs.

The following examples will illustrate the use of the perfect stative with present meaning: *šalmat āl gubla*, "Byblos is flourishing" (68.10); *awīlu rabū u bēlī ālim šalmū itti mārī ᵐ·abdašrata*, "the commissioner and the nobles of the city are at peace with the sons of ᶜAbd-Ashrata" (102.22–23); *mit rābiṣši*, "its commissioner is dead" (106.22); *pašiḫ ana šunu*, "they enjoy peace" (362.57); *palḫātī*, "I am afraid" (74.43); *ibaš-(š)atmi al ṣumura ana šarri*, "Simyra belongs to the king" (116.9–10).

Many of the stative verbs in our list have exact parallels in Hebrew. Thus *ul kinā*, "they (their words) are not true" (89.14)—cf. Heb. *kēn*; *mǐt*, cf. Heb. *mēt*; *šalim*, cf. Heb. verbal adj. *šālēm*. Most striking, however, of the parallels and most instructive for early Canaanite usage are: 1) the perfect stative *ašābu*, as, for example, in *ašbāta ana kussī bīt abika*, "thou sittest upon the throne of thy father's house" (116.65–66). In Ez. 28.2 and Lam. 1.1 the perfect *yāšab* is used with present mean-

67 *DCD*, p. 45, no. 18; Dhorme, *RB* 10, p. 385.

68 *GKC*, §106g. For a detailed analysis of the stative in Hebrew, see F. R. Blake, "The So-called Intransitive Verbal Forms in Hebrew," *JAOS* 24, pp. 145–204.

ing. 2) in 103.13–14 the perfect of *nazāzu* is used as a stative: *ina āl ṣumura iz(z)izātī*, "I am (lit., "I stand") in Simyra." Heb. *ᶜāmad* is also employed as a stative in I Ki. 17.1, 18.15; II Ki. 3.14, 5.16.[69]

So closely related to the genuine stative verbs that we may call them quasi-statives are the passives of several active verbs. Though all of these passives, with the exception of *tiḫtātī* (102.13), could be explained as permansives, we may be certain that their usage is Canaanite since the high frequency of the perfect and the over-all syntax is undoubtedly Canaanite.[70]

Now in these passives the action received results in a present state or quality, that is, of a stative. Thus *gamir gabbu*, "everything is used up" (102.12); *šiḫtat āl ṣumur*, "Simyra is laid waste" (106.10-11); *tiḫtātī gabba*, "I am wholly ruined" (102.13).

The glosses *naqṣapū* and *naqṣaptī* have been mentioned above. These Nifᶜal glosses are interesting in that they are a phenomenon paralleled in Hebrew: a stative verb with the reflexive Nifᶜal. In Heb., for instance, the statives *šāʾar* (originally *šaʾira*; cf. Arabic *saʾira*) and **maruṣ* are both used in the Nifᶜal, the latter exclusively.

Active verbs: *ul tišmūna mimma u šaprū*, "they do not hear a thing but they write" (82.10–12). This is the only example of an active verb with a present meaning in the perfect. Since this sentence expresses a general truth and hence implies repetition, this example should be noted carefully, for it is of importance in our analysis of the perfect.

[69]See however n. 59.

[70]The evidence on the morphology of the perfect passive in our letters is too meager to draw any certain conclusions, but two facts are worth notice: 1) there is no evidence whatever for a passive perfect *qutila* (like Arabic) or *qutala*. This is significant in view of so much evidence for the imperfect passive *yuqtal(u)*. If *qutila* or *qutala* were the passive perfect in the Canaanite of this period, one would certainly expect one occurrence in all the Can. Amarna letters; 2) on the other hand, the stative and the passive both have the form *qatila*. The most striking example is *apiš* (81.18, 108.19, 122.42,43, 123.10,12) which is always passive, while the active is always *apaš* (113.10, 122.32, 139.13—note the shift from *apiš* to *apaš* in 122). Now the Acc. permansive is neither *apaš* or *apiš*, but *ipuš*. It is possible that *apiš* is merely an error due to the fact that *qatil* is usually the form of the permansive—hence the form, and hence the passive meaning. But it is also possible that *apiš* is formed on the analogy of Byblian usage and that *qatila* was not only the form of the stative but also of the passive.—Note too the passive *laḳī* (105.20, possibly 108.32, 132.17), *ḳabī* (119.18), *dik(i)* (131.22—the active is always *daka*, etc.), *dika* (132.45), *dikū* (131.9). With these hollow verbs, cf. the statives *mit* and *kina*. Finally, note the non-Byblian passive of *lakada*, "to capture": *lakida*! (274.15).

2. *With past meaning*: The perfect-pres. perf. or past narrative is restricted largely to active verbs (151 occurrences), being relatively rare with stative verbs (24). Too much importance should not be attached to the infrequency of the stative perfect since the circumstances of the correspondence may be the explanation; more important is the fact that the stative perfect was a narrative form. The importance of the 151 occurrences of the active perfect is that they show that the ordinary form for narration of the past was *qatala*, not *yaqtulu*.

With stative verbs: *2 arḫē ašib ittiya*, "for two months he has encamped against me" (114.41); *inūma ibaš(š)āta ina āl ṣumura*, "when thou wast in Simyra" (73.40–41); *mār šipri šar āl akka kabit ištu mār šipriya*, "the messenger of the king of Accho was more honored than my messenger" (86.46–47). This narrative use of stative verbs is pure Canaanite.[71]

With active verbs: *ušširtī awīla annū*, "I have sent this man" (117.52); *ipšu ša lā apiš ištu dārīti apiš ana āl gubla*, "a deed which had not been done from (all) ages has been done to Byblos" (123.9–12); *laḳū sisē šarri*, "they have taken the horses of the king" (109.13–14); *inūma ušširtī 2 mār šipri*, "when I sent the two messengers" (108.46–47); *laḳū 3 awīlī*, "they took three men" (123.16).[72]

[71]Contrast the use in Acc. of intransitive verbs in the permansive; cf. A. Goetze, "The So-Called Intensive of the Semitic Languages," *JAOS* 62, p. 5.

[72]It should be remarked here that the same narrative use of the perfect is found in Ugaritic. It is true that *yaqtulu* is used frequently in narrative passages, but when we allow for poetic usage and *vivid* narrative—Hammershaimb, *Das Verbum im Dialekt von Ras Schamra*, p. 62ff., also lays stress on the use of the Ugaritic texts in ritual—the importance of this fact for the analysis of tenses—as well as for deciding whether or not Ugaritic is a Canaanite dialect—diminishes. Much more significant is the clear use of the active perfect as a narrative preterite. The numerous instances of this are explained by Goetze as a "continuous state which a person has effected by his action with regard to another person or an object" (*JAOS* 58, p. 228). Thus *qatala ʾaṯṯata* is to be rendered "he had a woman killed." Goetze (p. 279, n. 81) lays stress on the fact that those perfects are common in narrative in which the actions described correspond to previous commands to perform the actions. I simply do not see the force of this argument. Another argument on which he lays stress is the use of *bnt* in *UH* 51.vi.36: *šmḫ ʾalʾiyn bʿl <b>hty bnt dt ksp hkly dtm ḫrṣ*. This he claims cannot be rendered "Aliyan Baal rejoiced, 'My houses I have built of silver, my palace of gold'." Reason: Baal was not the architect, but Kauthar! By the same argument Solomon (I Ki. 8.20) could not have said "I built," since Hiram was the architect of the Temple. This argument is little short of absurd.—In short, every example offered by Goetze (pp. 278–282) is a Canaanite perfect, reflecting the same usage of *qatala* as we find in Byblian Amarna.

3. *With future meaning*: We are here faced with perhaps the most difficult of the many problems centered around the verbal forms. In spite of the fact that the usage of the perfect in Can. Amarna reflects Can. idiom rather than Acc. (v.g., the narrative use of *qatala*), Amarna has not been allowed to make its contribution to the problem of how a form that is regularly past in meaning can at times have just as clearly a future meaning.

In the Byblos letters we have 33 cases of a perfect with future meaning. 32 of the 33 fall into two groups: 1) those preceeded by *u* ("and")—24 occurrences—2) those not preceded by *u*, but functioning as the verb of a protasis of a conditional clause—8 occurrences. The other example falls into neither of these categories.

With stative verbs: *dūkūmi eṭlakunu u ibaš(š)ātunu kīma yātinu u pašḫ̮ātunu*, "kill your lord, and then you will be like us and will have peace" (74.25–27); *šumma ṣābu piṭati ibaš(š)at kalī mātāti nilkū ana šarri*, "if there will be an archer-host, all lands shall we take for the king" (103.55–57). It should be remarked here that all the examples of the perfect with future meaning in the protasis of a conditional sentence are stative verbs (83.27–30, 104.31–32, 104.43–51, 107.20–24, 119.17–18, 119.18–23, 132.46–48). This is purely fortuitous, since there is no reason why *qatala* could not be used the same way. Our analysis will bear this out.

With active verbs: *allū paṭārima awīlūt ḫ̮upšī u ṣabtū* lú.pl.GAZ *āla*, "behold if the serfs desert, then the Ḫ̮apiru will capture the city" (118.36–38). Cf. also 77.28, 79.42, 88.31, 104.51. The cases of *qatala* with future meaning (9) are considerably fewer than those of stative verbs (24). However, this again is fortuitous since the construction is the same, be the verb stative or active.

The example that fits into neither of the above categories is *u lā kašid irīšu u ušširtīšu*, "as soon as the request arrives, I will send him" (82.16–17). The future meaning of *kašid* is certain, though neither preceded by *u* nor the verb of a protasis.

With regard to the 24 cases preceded by *u* we seem to have clear examples of the so-called inversion of tenses with *waw conversive*, so familiar from Hebrew. However, we have on the other hand very many examples of a perfect preceded by *u* where there is clearly no inversion of tenses. Thus *u palḫ̮ātī anāku*, "and I am afraid" (75.34); *u laḳū ālānišu*, "and they have taken his cities" (104.28–29). Cf. also 83. 11, 84.10, 84.24, 85.54, 101.5,9, 105.15,17, 106.24, 108.15, 109.13, 109.26,

113.31–32, 116.12, etc. How explain this anomaly? We are directly confronted with the nature of the perfect. However, before attempting to determine the nature of the perfect, its use as a future should be analyzed a little more in detail.

The first fact to be grasped is that in 18 cases the verb functions as the predicate of an apodosis,[73] in 4 cases it follows an imperative.[74] Now, both a conditional sentence and an imperative refer to the future. This is obviously true of an imperative and need not be stressed. Of a conditional sentence it is equally true with the one qualification that the context is required. But in any given context it will be clear if the condition refers to the past (contrary-to-fact) or the present-future. This being true, it follows that the verb of the apodosis or a verb logically connected with an imperative in order to express future meaning need not of itself express the future. The tense may derive from the context. On the other hand, it also follows that the perfect cannot have an intrinsic time-determination, say a past, else it would of its nature be repugnant to a use other than past.

The one fact of the irregularity in the inversion of tenses after *u* makes such a view probable. That the apparent inversion of tenses is chiefly confined to the apodosis of conditional sentences and "imperative sentences" makes it even more probable. Examination of the remaining cases will make this view peremptory.

With the 8[75] cases of the future meaning of the perfect in the protasis of conditional sentences, we have but the reverse of the coin we have been examining. The future meaning in these instances can only derive from the context.

The same explanation holds true in 362.62–64: *ana ūmi tūṣu u in(n)ipušat gabbi mātāti ana šarri bēliya*, "when thou dost come forth, all lands will be made thine." This sentence, apart from context, could

[73]*balāṭu*, 82.45, 88.39 (cf. the Appendix for the possibility of reading *u bal-<ṭá>-ti*), 112.23; *danānu*, 93.27, 362.27,29; *epēšu*, 77.28, 104.51 (on 104.43–52 as a conditional sentence, cf. the Appendix), 88.31, 79.42 (in view of 114.23–24 and the context, Knudtzon's restoration of 79.38ff. is virtually certain; *leḳū*, 132.35 (on the meaning of this line and the following, cf. the Appendix); *naṣāru*, 127.29; *paṭāru*, 73.14, 82.44, 83.47,50; *pašāḫu*, 74.37 (if our interpretation of *šumma* = "behold" in 74.32 is correct, then more properly *pašḫū* follows the volitives *nudab(b)ir* and *tin(n)ipuš* and belongs rather with the examples of the perfect after imperatives; on this passage cf. Appendix); *ṣabātu*, 118.38.

[74]*balāṭu*, 82.37, 123.35; *bašū*, 74.26; *pašaḫu*, 74.27.

[75]*bašū*, 103.56; *mātu*, 87.31, 119.17; *paṭāru*, 83.28; *ḳabū*, 119.18; *ḳālu*, 104.31, 132.47; *šemū*, 104.43.

equally well be rendered, "when(ever) thou camest forth, all lands became thine." Context, and context alone, gives a future meaning to *in(n)ipušat*.

The next example is particularly convincing: *ušširami awīlaka ittiya ana ēkalli u lā kašid irīšu u ušširtīšu ḳadu ṣābi tillati ana kāta(m)*, "send thy man to me at the palace, and as soon as the request arrives, then I will send him back to thee along with an auxiliary force" (82.15–18). Only on the supposition that the futurity of the perfect depends on the context can this example be explained. If we prescind from the imperative and its dependents, then we could as well render "and the request did not arrive and (so) I sent him ...," or "as soon as the request arrived, I sent him." Whereas in the previous example it might be argued that *tūṣu* indicates the tense, here it cannot be argued that *kašid* indicates the future. Only because of the preceding imperative do we know that *kašid* and *u ušširtī* are future in meaning.[76]

B. The Nature of the Perfect

We have seen that with stative verbs the perfect may have present, past, or, as in the cases just examined, future meaning. With active verbs we have seen its use restricted chiefly to the past, though with future meaning as above, and even in one case with present meaning.

First, it seems clear from these facts that the perfect cannot be a tense in the true sense of the word.[77] No form that expresses past, present and future has an intrinsic time determination. This is not to say that the Byblians were completely oblivious of time distinctions. *A priori* it is virtually incredible that they should be unaware of so obvious a distinction.[78] Moreover, the consistent use of the perfect to describe what is clearly a past event and of the imperfect to describe what is just as clearly present–future points to a time distinction. However, it is one thing to say that the Byblians were aware of time distinctions, another to say that the verb forms employed were intrinsically tenses. Rather, the intrinsic nature of the form may have been such that it

[76]Blake calls attention to Chinese, Siamese, Malay and other languages in which a single verb form is used unchanged in all tense relations; *JBL* 63, pp. 275–276.

[77]That the Semitic verb forms are properly tenses is held by H. Bauer (*BA* 8, pp. 1–53), who made the most devastating attack on the opposed aspect theory of the verb forms, followed by Brockelmann (*Grundriss*, II, pp. 144–159, §§74–79) and for all practical puposes by G. R. Driver (*Problems of the Hebrew Verbal System*).

[78]Cf. Blake, *JBL* 68, p. 273.

would naturally be used for the expression of one tense rather than another. This we believe to have been the case at Byblos.

Secondly, it also seems clear from these facts that the perfect does not express of itself the completion of an action or a state.[79] A form that expresses completed action is not suited to express general truths or describe repeated or customary action. Nor is it exact to compare in this regard the so-called gnomic aorist in Greek. The Greek aorist does not express completed action: "The aorist takes its name ... from its denoting a simple past *occurrence*, with none of the limitations ... as to *completion, continuance, repetition*, etc."[80]

Moreover, it appears impossible to explain perfect statives with present meaning on the basis of the perfect stative = completed state. To explain such forms as *ḫādī* (362.6), *kašdātī* (93.7), *balṭat* (68.21), etc., as meaning "has rejoiced" > "is rejoicing," "have come" > "am coming," "has been alive" > "is alive," etc., is not only forced but is often contradictory to the obviously intended meaning of a passage.[81]

Many other illustrations could be presented from Hebrew of the difficulty this view of the perfect meets when encountered with all the facts.[82] However, our Byblian material is sufficient to indicate the basic weakness.

The view of the perfect we here offer has, we believe, a twofold advantage: 1) it accords better with the most probable explanation of

[79]It is this view of the perfect which more or less dominates among Semitists. It was given its first complete and systematic exposition by S. R. Driver in his *A Treatise on the Use of the Tenses in Hebrew*, first published in 1874. Since that time it has received so many adherents that it would be folly to attempt a list of them. Note only most recently Maria Höfner in her *Altsüdarabische Grammatik* and E. Hammershaimb in his *Das Verbum im Dialekt von Ras Schamra*. For a good summary of the various positions taken by scholars, on one side or the other, see G. R. Driver, pp. 9–31.

[80]Goodwin-Gulick, *Greek Grammar*, p. 269, §1261. Bauer has correctly stressed the impossibility of explaining the frequentative use of the perfect on the supposition that perfect = completed action or state; see Bauer, pp. 31–33. However, his equation of the perfect with the Acc. present (*ikaššad*) is absolutely false, and hence his own solution cannot stand.

[81]Knudtzon (*ZA* 7, p. 35) has collected some excellent Biblical examples illustrating the same contradiction.

[82]See the list of perfect = present-future in Brockelmann, *Grundriss* II, pp. 149–150, §76b.

the genesis of the form;[83] 2) it can explain its apparently contradictory uses.

Probably the perfect was originally a nominal sentence with personal pronominal elements affixed to a stem *qatal / qatil / qatul*.[84] Whether the entire formation is secondary or not need not concern us.[85] Nor need we be concerned whether *qatal* with transitive force is in Semitic a peculiarly West-Semitic development.[86] What is of importance is the origin in a nominal sentence. For a nominal sentence is tenseless, the tense deriving from the context in any given case. The essence therefore of the perfect is to predicate of the pronominal afformative the state (usually *qatil, qatul*) or the action (*qatal*) expressed by the respective stem.

The perfect then says nothing of present, past, or future. It does not say whether the action or state be completed or not completed. It merely states the fact of the occurrence of the action or the existence of the state.[87] We might call it a tenseless aorist. The question now remains to

[83]It may seem that in basing our view on the probable origin of the perfect we are falling into the same error we have attacked above, viz., substituting theory for controllable evidence. Actually our view is not based on any view of the origin of the perfect. The hypothesis that we set up can easily prescind from origin and previous development. Since the two views of the perfect that we have rejected plus the one we propose seem to exhaust the possibilities, the use of the third regardless of origin is methodologically defensible. However, since the view taken of the origin of the perfect is that most widely accepted, it seemed convenient to use it as a *point de depart* in our exposition.

[84]Cf. *DCD*, p. 46, no. 18; Blake, *JBL* 63, p. 276.

[85]For the variety of views on this subject, see G. R. Driver, pp. 9–31.

[86]This much may be said: G. R. Driver's position (pp. 81–82) that *qatal* replaced the older *qatil* because the loss of case-endings made a distinction between transitive and intransitive verbs necessary cannot stand. In Amarna case-endings are certainly still in use, while *qatala* most definitely has its place in the language.

[87]This view of the perfect was arrived at independently and presented in a seminar early in the Fall of 1949. Only in the course of further reading on the subject did I discover that Knudtzon had arrived at the same conclusion in 1892 (*ZA* 7, 33–63). I mention this to show the striking coincidence of the lines of evidence, one line from the small Byblian correspondence, the other from the Semitic perfect in general. What is even more striking is that both Knudtzon and myself should have struck upon the *same word* for a succint statement of our position. "... das assyrische Permansiv ist durch alle Konjugg. mit dem Perfektum zusammenstellen. So sollten wir auch für beide einen gemeinschaftlichen Namen haben. Zu einem solchen eignet sich weder 'Perfekt' noch 'Permansiv'; denn keiner dieser beiden Namen ist schon auf dem Gebiete, auf dem er jetzt verwandt wird, befriedigend; 'Faktum' dagegen dürfte ein dem Wesen beider Verbalformen entsprechender sein" (p. 48).

see whether this hypothetical view of the perfect fits the facts, or what modification of the view, if it be true at all, the facts force upon us.

It fits the use of the perfect with present meaning, be it the expression of general truths and the description of an action which is *de facto* repeated or customary, or be it with ordinary present meaning. In the former the perfect expresses the *fact*, leaving the idea of repetition, etc., to be derived from context.[88] Thus *ul tišmūna mimma u šaprū*, "hearing anything (circumstantial *yaqtulu*, on which see below), they write" (82.10–12). The perfect with its achronic-punctual character, though incapable of expressing the repetition of the action, gives a certain immediacy and absoluteness to the statement. Thus though the perfect does not *express* the repetition, neither does it deny it. It *prescinds* from it.

This view of the perfect accords with the fact that the perfect with present meaning is almost completely confined to stative verbs. A state or quality of being is of its essence an enduring thing, so that the affirmation of the existence of such a state or quality implicitly carries with it the affirmation of duration. Duration, however, "going on-ness," is essentially a thing of the present. Hence it is most natural that the stative verbs be frequently employed with present meaning.

The difference then between *palḫūni* (89.43) and *tipal(l)iḫuna* (105.22) is not that in the former "the state ... is regarded ... as already completed" while in the latter it is regarded "as still continuing or just taking place."[89] Such a distinction makes no sense, for both are definitely continuing. Rather, all that *tipalliḫūna* adds to *palḫūni* is an explicit affirmation of duration. To use a trite comparison, it turns a movie camera on the subject and shows it *fearing*, while *palḫuni* takes a snapshot of the subject, freezes it, as it were, in the state of fear, but by affirming the state of fear implicitly affirms a duration.

An action, however, in contrast to a state, is not of its essence an enduring thing—it may be continuous, it may be instantaneous. Of a present action one may merely wish to assert the fact of its existence, and then the perfect is used.[90] If, however, one wishes to affirm the

[88]Knudtzon: "In solchen Fällen bezeichnet das Perf. einfach etwas Geschehenes, etwas Eingetretenes, das vorliegt; es wird ein vorliegender Faktum konstatiert" (*ibid.*, p. 37).

[89]*GKC*, §106 l.

[90]This would apply to the cases in Hebrew noted by Brockelmann, *Grundriss* II, p. 149, §76bβ-γ.

duration of a present action, one cannot do so by the perfect. And since a present action, in contra-distinction to the nature of the action itself, is peculiar in its duration, this is the aspect of a present action which is usually affirmed. Hence the relative infrequency of the perfect active with present meaning.

Our view that the perfect merely states the *fact* of an action or state fits the use of the perfect with future meaning. For a future event is not, like a present or past event, a *fact*. Now this fits perfectly the usage we have seen of the perfect with future meaning. Not once did the perfect have future meaning except in contexts which were clearly future (in a conditional sentence, after an imperative). The nature, therefore, of the perfect precludes the possibility of its use to express the future except in contexts where there can be no doubt of the time in question.

Turning to the use of the perfect with present perfect and preterite meaning, we can readily see that the perfect is here most suited. For whether the verb be stative ("he has been sick," "he was sick") or active ("he has killed," "he killed"), we ordinarily view the past as so many individual facts or static events. To express such a view of the past the perfect is obviously the form. It is most significant in this regard to note that whenever in the Byblian letters actions prevailing in the past over a period of time are described, the form used is not the perfect, but *yaqtulu(na)*.

Before concluding, two remarks are in place. First, on the function of the conjunction *u* before the perfect with future meaning. We have seen that it does not invert the tenses, a past becoming a future. On the other hand, its almost universal presence when the perfect does have future meaning cannot be mere coincidence, especially in view of the Hebrew idiom with the so-called *waw conversive*.

We shall meet this conjunction again in conditional clauses, where in the parlance of Hebrew grammarians it is called the *waw of apodosis*. In conditional sentences the force of the conjunction is clearly "and then," like Arabic *fa*.[91] When used before a perfect with future meaning, its force, we believe, is the same, empasizing that the following perfect is *successive* to the previous action, and hence in a future context also a future. It is significant that of the ten examples of an apodosis not introduced by the conjunction, not one is a perfect. Hence, a better

[91]See Ges.-Buhl[13], p. 207b.

name for the conjunction in this usage would be, in Hebrew grammar terms, *waw of succession.*[92]

Secondly, it may appear that we have done nothing more than give another name to the theory that the perfect expresses completed action or state. The difference, it is true, between the affirmation of the *fact* of an action or state and the affirmation of their completion is at times slight. Actually, however, the basic differences are great. In the one, the perfect says nothing about whether the action be completed or not; in the other, it must be completed. It is when confronted with *all* the facts that the theory of completed action meets one impasse after another. Only the view we have here but briefly developed, by which the perfect, stating merely the fact of the action or state, is tenseless, aoristic, and *prescinds* from the fact whether the action be instantaneous, continuous or completed, customary, repeated, etc., can explain, we believe, all the facts in the Byblian use of the perfect.

C. The Existence of *yaqtulu* (= Imperfect)

Before examining the use and nature of *yaqtulu* we must establish that the form exists in our letters. For, even subsequent to the discovery of Ugaritic, Harris has maintained that "the difference in form between *yaqtulu* and *yaqtul* cannot be adduced from these letters ..."[93] The partial reason he offers in defense of his position—what other reason or reasons he has he does not say—is the nature of syllabic cuneiform writing which often necessitates final vowels even when they do not exist in speech.[94]

This reason is not valid: 1) because, though Accadian syllabic cuneiform is incapable of reflecting a final two-consonant cluster, this does not affect the writing of *yaqtul* or *yaqtulu*; 2) *yaqtulu* is used too often and too rigidly according to rule not to reflect actual Canaanite usage.

[92]So *GHB*, §117a. Since "and then" is the meaning of *fa* in Arabic, and since we find *pa* in Ugaritic and *paʾ* at Zendjirli, it seems probable that in early Northwest Semitic there were both *wa* and *pa*. When *pa* dropped out of most dialects, *wa* presumably took over the meaning of *pa* in addition to its own proper meaning of "and." Blake (*JAOS* 62, p. 117) suggests that Heb. *ʾap* is connected with *pa*.

[93]*DCD*, p. 48, no. 21.

[94]*Ibid.*

The position of Böhl[95] and Dhorme,[96] who likewise denied that Canaanite Amarna *yaqtulu* can be compared with the same form in Arabic, is somewhat understandable. They were denied the evidence of Ugaritic. However, with the existence of the form in Ugaritic in the writer's opinion indisputable,[97] there can be now no reason whatever for doubting the existence of the form in virtually contemporary Canaanite dialects.[98]

Moreover, even apart from the Ugaritic evidence, close analysis of *yaqtulu* (and *yaqtul*) shows conclusively that *yaqtulu* is an "imperfect" form, virtually identical with its Arabic counterpart. This will become perfectly clear in the analysis that follows where *all* occurrences are examined. There is really no need, then, to refute in detail the old position that *yaqtulu* was significant only syntactically, not morphologically. Sufficient to remark that the syntactical reasons adduced are valid neither in Accadian nor in Canaanite.

[95]Böhl, pp. 74–75, §34p–q.

[96]*RB* 10, p. 379. Dhorme warns us to have care "de noter que la voyelle *u* ... est introduite non pas d'après la morphologie, mais d'après la syntaxe." Again, "on doit résister à la tentation d'assimiler la voyelle *u* finale à la terminaison *u* de l'imparfait arabe"; *RB* 10, p. 383, n. 1.

[97]*UH*, p. 60, §9.7. Harris's position on Amarna *yaqtulu* is undoubtedly influenced by his position that there is a present (*yaqattalu*) in Ugaritic; *DCD*, p. 49, no. 22. However, no real evidence for this form has yet been adduced, despite Goetze's detailed study (*JAOS* 58, pp. 266–309). George E. Mendenhall has proved to the writer's satisfaction that the Amarna evidence is decidedly against the existence of a present in the Canaanite dialects reflected in the Amarna letters; see the unpublished Johns Hopkins University dissertation, *The Verb in Early Northwest Semitic Dialects*, pp. 5–7. On the Ugaritic evidence, see Hammershaimb, pp. 105–110. Additional arguments could be given against Goetze's evidence.

[98]In view of the use of *iqtulu* several times in the new Idri-mi inscription, and S. Smith's approbation of Böhl's analysis of the Amarna evidence (*The Statue of Idri-mi*, p. 37), it is necessary to survey the use of this form in the peripheral Acc. of the 15th–14th centuries B.C. At Boğazköy there are three instances of *iqtulu* in a main clause (Labat, p. 67); at Nuzi *iqtulu* is quite exceptional in a main clause (see S. N. Kramer, "The Verb in the Kirkuk Tablets," *AASOR* XI, p. 84; C. H. Gordon, "The Dialect of the Nuzu Tablets," *Orientalia* NS 7, p. 37). If we contrast Boğazköy and Nuzi practice with the 250 instances of *(y)iqtulu* in the relatively small Byblian material, it is immediately obvious that the Byblian situation is entirely different. The Boğazköy and Nuzi instances are probably just errors; the Byblian reflects *usage*. Hence perhaps the explanation of *iqtulu* in the Idri-mi inscription is that it is due to Canaanite influence—Alalaḫ is about 60 miles from Ugarit as the crow flies. Perhaps, however, they too are simply errors.

The Use of the Imperfect

Verb	Yaqtulu(na)[99]		(Y)iqtul	
	Pres.-Fut.	Past	Pres.-Fut.	Past
abālu	4	1		
abātu		1		2
alāku	3	1	1	
amāru			1	
aṣū	4		1	
arādu	1		1	
ašāru	10	3		3
ašāšu	2		2	
balāṭu		1	1	
buʾū	24	1	1	
dabāru			1	
dāku	4	1		1
dālu	2			
ezēbu	1		7	3
elū	1		1	2
epēšu	27	2	7	3
erēbu	3		1	2
etēḳu			1	
idū	3		25	1
kalū				1
kašādu	2		1	
leʾū	19	1	4	
leḳū	21	3	6	7
maḳātu				1
marāru	1			
mašāḫu		1		1
mātu	1		2	
nadānu	11	3	1	3
nakāru			1	

[99]*Yaqtulu* is meant only as a type-form, i.e., an indicative form of the imperfect. Thus the forms tabulated are both stative and active, of the *Qal* and derived conjugations.

naṣāru	5		1	
nazāzu	2		6	3
paḫāru	1			
paṭāru	1			
palāḫu	1		1	
parāšu		1		
pašāḫu	1			
petū			1	
ṣabātu			1	2
ḳabū	17		5	7
ḳālu	1		3	
raʾāmu	1		2	
rāḫu	1			
rāṣu	1		1	
šaʾālu	7			
šaḫātu			1	1
šakānu	1		2	
šanū			2	5
šapāru	24	5	9	16
šemū	18	2	2	5
tāru	5			
Total	231	27	103	69

D. The Use of *yaqtulu(na)*

As with the table on the Use of the Perfect, we would emphasize again that the table on the Use of the Imperfect is purely descriptive. Again, as with the perfect, our approach is purely inductive, taking the forms as they occur, putting them in categories according to their use in context, and only after a careful study of usage attempting any conclusions as to the nature of the form.

With present-future meaning: As the preceding table shows conclusively, *yaqtulu(na)* was employed primarily to express the present or the future.[100] To illustrate: *awīlūt ḫupšīya paṭārama tubaʾūna*, "my

[100] My results differ somewhat from those that would be reached by tabulating under *pres.-fut.* and *past* according to Knudtzon's translations. Following

serfs wish to desert" (114.21–22); *kalī ḫ̮āzānīka tudākūna*, "all thy governors will be killed" (132.49–50); *mūša tūbalūna u mūša tutērūna mārū šipri ša šarri*, "by night the king's messengers carry (tablets) and by night they bring (tablets) back" (108.52–55).

With past meaning: As the table shows, the use of *yaqtulu(na)* with past meaning is relatively rare. Since the use of *yaqtulu(na)* with present-future meaning is not surprising but in view of the use of Heb. *yiqtōl* expected, this rarer use merits close analysis as perhaps providing a clue to the nature of the form.

Knudtzon one would have many more cases of *yaqtulu(na)* as a past. Important individual differences will be commented on in the Appendix. Here we offer typical cases. 1) The tense of *aḳbu* in 107.10 (*u pūya awātē aḳbu ana šarri kittama*) or *ašpuru* in 108.24 (*u awata ša īdī u ša estemē ašpuru*)—as F. Thureau-Dangin has recognized (*RA* 19, p. 93, n. 6), these are general protestations of loyalty and are to be rendered by the present. 2) The tense of *yaḳbu* in 117.7 (*yaḳbu šarru bēlī ana minī attama tištapruna ana yāši*)—parallel passages in 106.30 and 117.30 have the present and show *yaḳbu* is to be rendered as a present. 3) The tense of *tištapruna* in the very common phrase just cited—the parallel passage 124.36–40, misunderstood by Knudtzon, proves the verb is present: *tištapru ana yāši ištu kalī ḫ̮āzānūti ana minīm tištap(p)arūna šunu ana kāta(m) ālānu ana šāšunu ālāniya laḳī* ^{m}*·aziru*, " 'thou dost write to me more than all the (other) governors'; why should they write to thee? The(ir) cities are in their possession, (but) my cities Aziru has taken." This parallel passage makes it clear that the Pharaoh's complaint is not that Rib-Adda *has written* to him, but that he *writes* (repeatedly) to him. 4) The tense of *yištap(p)aru* in 119.8 (*inūma yištap(p)aru šarru bēlī uṣur ramānka*)—the fact that several parallel passages have the present indicates the tense of *yištap(p)aru*: *yiḳab(b)u* (117.83), *išap(p)aru* (123.29), *iḳab(b)u* (125.8). 5) The tense of *yadinu* (126.14,18) and *ašpuru* (126.24): *minūm yadinu mimma u balāṭa(m) šarru ana ḫ̮āzānūti ibrīya u ana yāši lāmi yadinu mimma anum(m)a anāku ašpuru ana ṣābi*. If one carefully studies this passage, one will see that ll. 14–18, 23–28 describe the prevailing situation at the *present* and are in contrast to ll. 18–23 where "the good old days" of Rib-Adda's predecessors are described. 6) The tense of *ašpuru* and *tušmuna* in *anum(m)a kīʾama ašpuru ana ṣābi piṭati u ana tillati u ul tušmuna awātūya* (91.27–30). First to be noted is that in 92.12–15, a virtually parallel passage, we have the present *yišim(m)e* (1.15). This indicates that *tušmuna* is to be rendered by a present. Moreover, if one examines the contexts in which this cliché constantly occurs, one will see that the content of Rib-Adda's letters to the court concerns two or three standard complaints and oft repeated counsels: I am out of food, send some quickly or my serfs will revolt; I am all alone and helpless, so send troops, etc. This indicates that *ašpuru* at least describes a repeated action on the part of Rib-Adda and *lā tušmuna* the repeated response he gets. It is not impossible that *ašpuru* and its parallels are past ("I wrote again and again"). Be it past or present, our over-all analysis of *yaqtulu(na)* remains unaffected, the only difference being that, if it be a past iterative, we would have about ten less examples of *pres.-fut.* and ten more cases of past iteratives.

Of the 27 cases of the form with past meaning, 10 occur after *pānānu* in contexts describing the prevailing state of affairs in the past, "the good old days." Thus: *yūdanam šeʾim mūṣa ša māt yarimuta ša yūdanu pānānu ina āl ṣumura / yūdanam inan(n)a ina āl gubla,* "let be sold the grain, the product of the land of Yarimuta, which was formerly sold in Simyra, let it now be sold in Byblos" (85.34–37); *pānānu balāṭ* (written *ba-lu-aṭ*) *šarri ibaš(š)i eliya u nidinu ag<rū>ta(m) awīli ša nišpuru u annū inan(n)a yānu balāṭ ...,* "formerly the provisions of the king were in my possession, and we would give (it) as the wage of the man whom we sent. But behold now there are no provisions, etc." (112.50–53); *pānānu ištu māt yarimuta tubal(l)iṭūna awīlūt ḫupšīya u annū annū lā yadinušunu* ^{m}·*yappada alāka(m),* "previously my serfs secured provisions from the land of Yarimuta, but behold Yapadda does not allow them (now) to go ..." (114.54–59); *pānānu awīlūt maṣ(ṣ)arti šarri ittiya u šarru yadinu šeʾim ištu māt yarimuta ana akālišunu u annū inanna ištaḫatnī* ^{m}·*aziru u ištanī,* "formerly the king's garrison was with me and the king gave grain from the land of Yarimuta for their food, but behold now Aziru has repeatedly attacked me" (125.14–21); cf. also *yūšaru* and *yūširu* in 126.18–23; *ennabtū* in 109.44–46; *tupar(r)išū* in 118.50–53.[101]

In all of the above examples *yaqtulu(na)* expresses repeated or customary action. That the use of *yaqtulu(na)* in these passages is not a matter of chance nor due to the caprice of a scribe, but significant and reflecting Canaanite idiom, is shown by the following example which describes not a repeated, but a *single* past action: *pānānu yiz(z)izmi* ^{m}·*abdaširta muḫḫiya u aštapar ana abika ušširami ṣāba piṭati šarri u tulḳu kalī māti ina ūmi ul laḳī* ^{m}·*abdaṣirta ḳadu mimmišu ana šāšu u annū inan(n)a puḫ(ḫ)ir* ^{m}·*aziru kalī awīlūti* GAZ, "Previously ^{c}Abd-Ashirta attacked me and I wrote to thy father, 'Send the archer-host of the king and the entire land will be taken in a day'; did he not take for himself ^{c}Abd-Ashirta along with his property? And behold, now Aziru has gathered all the Ḫapiru" (132.10–21). Cardinal in this discussion is the fact that we have in this passage *yiz(z)iz*, not *yiz(z)izu*, *aštapar*, not *aštaparu*.

The next example is quite long, but it must be quoted in its entirety, since it is particulary instructive on the use of tenses. *miyami mārū* ^{m}·*abdaširta ardi kalbi šar māt kašši u šar māt mitan(n)i šunu u*

[101]Because of the other examples with *yaqtulu(na)* after *pānānu*, it is certain that the plurals *ennabtū* and *tuparrišū* derive from a sg. *ennabitū, yupar(r)išū.*

tilḳūna māt šarri ana šāšum pānānu tilḳūna ālāni ḫāzānīka u ḳalāta annū inan(n)a dub(b)irū rābiṣaka u laḳū ālānišu ana šāšunu anum(m)a laḳū āl ullaza šumma kīʾama ḳalāta adi tilḳūna āl ṣumura u u tidūkūna rābiṣa u ṣāb bilati (error for *tillati*) *ša ina ṣumura,* "Who are the sons of ᶜAbd-Ashirta, the slave (and) dog? Are they the king of the Cossaeans or the king of the Mitanni that they take the land of the king for themselves? Previously they used to take the cities of thy governors, and thou wast negligent. Behold, now they have driven out thy commissioner and have taken his cities for themselves. Behold, they have taken Ullaza. If thou wilt thus be negligent, they will take Simyra besides and will kill the commissioner and the auxiliary force which is in Simyra" (104.17–36).—Three facts are to be noted: 1) *tilḳūna* is used in contexts of present (22), past (25), and future (32); 2) *tilḳūna* as a past is used to describe repeated action—Aziru and his brothers had previously made a practice of taking only cities ruled by a royal governor, keeping hands off of a city ruled by a royal commissioner; 3) when the latest *single* enormity of ᶜAbd-Ashirta's sons is contrasted with the customary action of capturing cities belonging to a governor, the scribe shifts from *tilḳūna* to *laḳū*.

Other examples of *yaqtuluna* as a past: *tūbalūna* (117.18), describes a customary action—"they used to carry"; *uwaš(š)iru* (114.35), describes a repeated action, as is clear from the introductory *mani ūmī* "how often"; *yīpušu* (119.40), describes repeated action, as is again clear from the introductory *man(n)i ūmī*; *yīpušu* (131.36), almost certainly describes repeated action in view of the plural object *ipšāta(m) šārūta(m)*—thus "he repeatedly acted treacherously"; *yiliʾu* (114.36), describes a repeated action, as is clear from the introductory *man(n)i ūmī* (114.35); *tulḳuna* (90.18) and *tušmuna* (90.17) most probably describe continuous actions since this same cliché (*awātūya ul tušmuna*, etc.) is very frequently used in the same sense in the present;[102] *ammašaḫu* (85.9) describes a continuous state, as is clear from the adverbial phrase *2 šanāti*—this is to be contrasted with *šeʾimya ammašaḫ*, "as for my grain, I have been plundered" (91.16), where the adverbial phrase is missing; *yašpuru* (89.36) is probably descriptive of a repeated action—the same argument as for *tulḳuna* (90.18) above applies here; *ašpuru* (89.66) is probably used as an iterative but broken context makes it impossible to decide its exact meaning; *aštap(p)aru* (117.29) is of course in itself an iterative form in Accadian (I_3), but as has been pointed out

[102]See n. 100, above.

elsewhere,[103] the iterative force of the I_3 form was not felt by the Byblian scribes—rather here the iterative force is to be proved from the parallel *tištap(p)aru* (117.31) which is certainly to be rendered "(why) dost thou keep on writing"; *tušmuna* (89.37), cf. *yašpuru* (89.36) above; *yišmu* (131.34), cf. *yīpušu* (131.36)[104] above.

Some of the examples above are admittedly open to dispute in so far as their expressing some form of continued action is concerned. However, in all cases our interpretation has seemed the most probable. Admitting that a few of the examples are not beyond cavil, still we must emphasize the fact that 16 of the 23 examples examined are *certainly* descriptive of past *continuous* action.

The remaining 4 cases of *yaqtulu(na)* with past meaning fall into a category which we might call subordinate–circumstantial use.[105] For all four are verbs of subordinate clauses (virtual or formal), and all are circumstantial to the main clause. Thus: *kīma ištapru*, "just as (when?) I wrote" (114.27—circumstantial); m.*aduna šar āl irḳata idūkūna* lú.pl.GAZ *u yānu ša ḳabī mimma ana* m.*abdaširta* ..., "although the Ḫapiru killed Adona, the king of Irqata, still there was no one who said a thing to ᶜAbd-Aširta" (75.25–29—circumstantial);[106] *inūma yilakuna* m.*amanappa*, "when Amanappa came ..." (117.23—circumstantial); *šar māt mitan(n)a aṣī adi āl ṣumura u yubaʾu alāka(m) adi āl gubla u yānu mū*u *ana šatēšu u tāra ana mātišu*, "the king of the Mitanni went forth as far as Simyra, and when he desired to come as far as Byblos, there was no water for him to drink, and so he returned to his own land" (85.51–54—circumstantial); *yūdanu* in 85.36 and *nišpuru* in 112.53, both

103*JCS* 2 comm. no. 3 [below, Paper 2, pp. 134–135].

104In 117.43 we should certainly read after *pānānu ubaʾ[u]*, but the uncertain context prevents its inclusion under the iteratives. In 127.31 we have *ītilu* after *pānānum*, but again difficulties of interpretation make it impossible to list *ītilu* as an iterative. We should also note here the present *yinam(m)ušūna* in 109.7 following *pānānu* (l. 5) and describing past durative action; the same remark on the present *ibaššu* in 81.48. Finally, be it noted that the perfect *dan(n)ū* in 130.22 and *ḳalāta* in 104.26, both after *pānānu*, are not difficulties against our insistence on the necessity for *yaqtulu(na)* to express past continued action. As stative verbs they implicitly express the enduring possession of some quality or state; an active perfect does not have this implicit nuance of duration.

105Cf. Albright's view on *yaqtulu* in Ugaritic: "The *yaqtulu* form was used, he believes (against the author [Z. Harris]) mainly as a narrative, *circumstantial*, and *subordinating* (italics mine) tense (in this respect like the Accadian "subjunctive," *ikšudu*, properly subordinative) ..."; *JAOS* 60, p. 419.

106On *ḳabī*, see Appendix.

dependent on *ša*, we have included under the examples of *yaqtulu* following *pānānu*, since their iterative force was clear.

To be noted about all these examples is the fact that, though in none of them can there be any question of continued action—and they are the only cases of *yaqtulu(na)* with past meaning of which this can be said—, still they are all verbs of subordinate-circumstantial clauses. This is important for the problem to which we shall now attempt an answer: what is the nature of *yaqtulu(na)*? For further and confirmatory evidence on circumstantial *yaqtulu*, see the analysis of its use in the protasis of conditional sentences.

E. The Nature of *yaqtulu(na)*

We have seen: 1) that the form is used primarily in present-future contexts; 2) that where it is used in past contexts it is chiefly iterative; 3) that in past contexts, if not iterative, then circumstantial. To be noted further is the fact that though in present contexts the form, as is natural, carries a durative force, still this is not true of its use in future contexts where it expresses the simple fact of the occurrence of an action in the future. Moreover, it is quite significant that after *pānānu* describing a past general situation not once was the perfect used, even though, as we have seen, the perfect is the regular form for narrative descriptions of the past.

Hence, I believe we may conclude: 1) *yaqtulu* is not primarily or essentially a tense. The argument is the same as that with regard to the perfect: no form that expresses present, future, and past action possesses an intrinsic time-determination; 2) Its use to express some type of continued action in the past indicates that the essence of the form consists in the expression of continued action, the time and particular nuance of continued action (incipiency, repetition, custom, duration) deriving from the context.

This view fits not only its use to express past repeated action, but also its use as a present and as a circumstantial form. For the present is *par excellence* the tense of duration, and an action which is subordinate to another action as an attendant circumstance is best expressed by a form which, expressing continuity, brings out the fact that the one action parallels the other.[107]

[107]Cf. the Latin idiom which uses the present for past circumstantial action: *in hortum veni dum ille servum suum percutit*, "I came into the garden as he *was striking* his slave."

As for the use in future contexts as merely expressing a future fact, we can do no better here than to quote S. R. Driver: "The same form [the imperfect] is further employed to describe events belonging to the *future*: for the future is emphatically τὸ μέλλον and this is just the attribute specially expressed by the imperfect. ... that which is in the process of coming to pass is also that which is *destined* or *must* come to pass (τὸ μέλλον) ..."[108]

F. The Modal Use of *yaqtulu(na)*

As in Arabic,[109] and like Heb. *yiqtōl,*[110] *yaqtulu(na)* is often used where an accurate translation would seem to call for the expression of certain modal nuances such as "should," "can," etc. Thus *minā īpušuna anāku ina īdīniya,* "what can I do by myself?" (74.63, *passim*); *u īdī ipša ša īpušu,* "in order that I may know what I should do" (83.8–9, *passim*);[111] *ana minī tištaparūna šunu ana kāta(m),* "why should they write to thee?" (124.37–39). However, these modalities are not of the nature of the form *yaqtulu(na),* and were left unexpressed, though perhaps implied, where our own idiom is more explicit. *Indicative* remains an adequate and accurate designation of the form in so far as its modality is concerned.

G. The Existence of *yaqtul*

With *yaqtulu* established for Amarna Byblian, the question of *yaqtul* immediately arises: what was its usage? Howver, before attempting an answer to this question, we must first establish its existence in Byblian. This we shall do by establishing one clear usage of the form which clearly sets it apart from *yaqtulu,* that is, the jussive usage.[112]

[108]S. R. Driver, *The Use of the Tenses in Hebrew,* pp. 25–26. Bauer, p. 39, points to the interesting parallel of Old German, in which a future had not been developed and the present was used to express both the present and the future.

[109]Reckendorf, *Die syntaktischen Verhältnisse des Arabischen,* p. 60, §33.

[110]*GHB,* §113 l.

[111]Knudtzon consistently failed to understand this phrase. The parallel 85.59–63 proves conclusively the correctness of our interpretation: *u īdī ipša ša īpušu adi yiktašduna šarru u yidag(g)alu šarru arad kit(t)išu,* "in order that I may know what I should do until the king comes and sees his loyal servant."

[112]Though Harris (*DCD,* p. 7) admits a jussive *yaqtul* throughout all the Semitic languages of Syria and Palestine and even quotes Amarna examples as illustrations (p. 7, n. 8), still he does not believe, as we have already seen, we can distinguish between *yaqtulu* and *yaqtul* in Amarna (p. 48, no. 21). We have

As has been recognized by all translators, there are many examples of *yaqtul* as a jussive: *yaškun* (108.59), *yadin* (113.32), *yašpur* (117.60), *yišmī* (78.17, 79.13, etc.). These are significant in that *yaqtul* or, more properly, *iqtul* is not a jussive in Acc., but the jussive must be expressed by the so-called precative, *liqtul*. This is used in our letters, but only very sporadically: *liṣṣur* (84.28), *lišmē* (88.23), etc. Hence it would seem that the Byblian scribes were familiar with *yaqtul* as a jussive.

This is proved conclusively by the fact that only *yaqtul* is used as a jussive, never *yaqtulu*. There are three apparent exceptions to this rule, possibly one real one. In 95.31 *yuwaš(š)iru*, in 116.31 *yuwaš(š)iruna*, and in 140.5 *yaḳūlu* are in contexts where we would expect a jussive. However, since this usage of *yaqtulu* as a virtual command has good parallels in Arabic,[113] it is really no difficulty at all.

The one real exception may be in 92.47 where we perhaps should read *lu<waš(š)i>ru*, the precative *lu* with a singular ending in *u*. However, allowing for scribal errors and considering the very bad state of the text where this exception seems to occur, one cannot lay much stress on this one word.

The really significant facts are these: 1) not one of over 250 examples of *yaqtulu* can be interpreted as jussives; 2) aside from the doubtful 92.47 instance, no form with precative *lu* ever has the indicative ending; 3) when the same verb is employed both in the *yaqtulu* and *yaqtul* forms, the former never has jussive force: *yadinu* (105.85, 114.58, 119.51, etc.) but jussive *yadin* (101.28, 113.32), *yilḳu* (71.18, 91.4, 124.15, etc.) but jussive *yilḳī* (117.70, etc.), *yaḳbu*, *yuḳbu*, *taḳbu*, *tiḳbu*, *aḳab(b)u*, etc., but jussive *yaḳbī* (83.34, 101.32, 116.32), *yišmu*, *yušmu*, *ešmu*, etc., but jussive *yišmī* (85.16,75, 107.35, etc.) or *lišmē* (88.23), *yašpuru* and *ašpuru* but jussive *yašpur* (117.60), *yimal(l)iku* (114.48) but jussive *yamlik* (105.6, 114.20) or *limal(l)ik* (94.72), etc.

H. The Use of *yaqtul*

When we attempt to analyze the use of *yaqtul* in these letters beyond the jussive usage, we are confronted with the ambiguity of our evidence. However, a few facts are significant and deserve attention:

---

already replied to the reason he gives for this position; the material on *yaqtul* will only serve to confirm our stand on *yaqtulu*.

[113]Wright-de Goeje II, p. 19, §8.

1) With the exception of *akḅī* (82.21) and *ītelam* (88.14), not one of the 69 examples of *yaqtul* with past meaning refers to continued action. This is significant as a confirmation of our analysis of *yaqtulu(na)*.

2) The use of *yaqtul* referring to the past (pres. perf. or historical perf.) is relatively rare, due consideration being given to the fact that these letters are written in a language whose idiom calls for the past meaning of the form. It is very significant that the instances of the perfect (175) with the same meaning greatly outnumber those of *yaqtul*. Almost every example of a past *yaqtul* can be paralleled by perfects either in parallel passages or in similar contexts. All of which indicates that in Byblian the perfect was *normally* used to express a present or historical perfect, though it is impossible to say that *yaqtul* could not, at least in certain circumstances, have a similar use.[114]

More we cannot say—unfortunately so, for Amarna Canaanite with its vocalization of verb forms is the key to Canaanite verbal syntax.

I. Summary of Tense Usage

In the dialect of Byblos in the middle of the fourteenth century B.C. the usual form for past narrative was the perfect (*qatala*, etc.). Only in the case of a repeated or customary past action, or a simple past action circumstantial to another past action, was the imperfect *yaqtulu* used. The latter was the form generally employed to express the present or future. However, with stative verbs the perfect was usual to express the present, and in certain contexts the perfect active could be used both to express the present (very rare) or the future (less rare).

The relation of the perfect to the imperfect seems to have been neither that of tense to tense, nor that of completed to incomplete, but that of static fact (or point) to moving progression (or continuum). Whatever the previous history of the forms—whether they had been previously objective (i.e., tenses) or subjective (i.e., aspectual), their usage in the fourteenth century B.C. was aspectual in the sense just given.[115]

[114]Hence I cannot agree with Harris, who says "the Amarna letters provide no evidence" (*DCD*, p. 47, no. 20). It is true that they do not rule out a preterite use of *yaqtul*, but they do show what was normal, that is, the perfect.

[115]Harris believes that the aspect-system of Canaanite is secondary and after the development of *qatala*; *DCD*, p. 84.

V. THE USE OF THE ENERGIC[116]

Ebeling's thorough study of the energic in the Amarna letters still stands in its essentials. The following remarks are mainly refinements of his basic work.[117]

First, the form of the energic. This is consistently *yaqtuluna*. There is no real evidence for an energic *yaqtulana* which could be used in emphatic indicative uses.[118] Once *yaqtulu* is recognized as the normal indicative form in Byblian of the 14th century B.C., then there can be no reason for rejecting *yaqtuluna* as the indicative-energic in Byblian of the same time.[119] This is confirmed by evidence from Ugaritic that in this Canaanite dialect there was likewise an energic *yaqtuluna*.[120]

As to usage, the first fact to be noted is that the energic is not confined to one type of clause.[121] Usually it is found with the verb of the main clause, but we also have examples of the energic in temporal, substantival, conditional, and relative clauses. Thus *inūma yilakuna*, "when he came" (117.23); *inūma ašar danni tilakuna*, "... that it follows the stronger party" (73.15–16); *šumma tišmuna*, "if it hears" (73.11–12); *kalī mimme ša yulḳuna*, "with regard to all the property that is taken" (117.67–68).

Secondly, the energic is never used with the jussive. Thus never *yaqtulna*, "let him kill."

Thirdly, of the 38 examples of *yaqtuluna*, 22 are the verbs of an interrogative sentence. Here we probably get our clearest idea of the nature of the energic in Byblian, and see that the name energic is well chosen. For most of the questions are either dubitative, in which Rib-Adda stresses his perplexity as to his course of action, or querulous, in

[116]I confine my remarks here to *yaqtuluna*, though *yaqtulana* and its possible counterpart in Arabic is discussed at the end of this section. On *qutulna*, cf. the section on Particles (I D) [pp. 11–12 in the present volume].

[117] Ebeling, pp. 69–73. Brockelmann (*Grundriss* I, §259 *Bf*) treats the energic as an Accadian phenomenon in the Amarna tablets, "wo sie allerdings gegen den Verdacht kanaanäischer Herkunft nicht geschützt sind."

[118]A few forms like *yūṣana* (74.39, 77.27), *tūṣana* (73.9) and *timaḫ(ḫ)aṣananī* (77.37) are no evidence at all. The last is really a subjunctive plus the energic. However we explain the others, they are obviously not the rule.

[119]Albright has long recognized *yaqtuluna* as the Can. energic-indicative; *BASOR* 87, p. 15, n. 47; p. 33, n. 8; p. 34, n. 15.

[120]See above under the Particles (I D) [pp. 11–12 in the present volume].

[121]Cf. Goetze, *JAOS* 58, p. 293, n. 144, for the same use of the energic in Ugaritic.

which he complains of the king's treatment, etc. E.g., *minā īpušuna anāku*, "what can I do?" (122.49, etc.); *ana minī lā tutēruna awata(m) ana yāši*, "why dost thou not reply to me?" (83.7–8); *minā aḳab(b)una ana awīlūt ḫupšīya*, "what can I say to my serfs?" (85.11–12); *ul tiliʾuna laḳāya ištu ḳāt* m·*abdaširta*, "art thou unable to rescue me from the power of ᶜAbd-Ashirta?" (82.6–8), etc. Particulary significant are *innaṣ(ṣ)aruna* (112.10) and *inaṣ(ṣ)iruna* (123.32), both in slightly ironic questions and the only examples of the energic of this rather common form. Elsewhere we have *inaṣ(ṣ)ar* (122.21), *inaṣ(ṣ)iru* (119.15, 130.49), *anaṣ(ṣ)ar* (119.13, 127.37), but always in declarative sentences.

Other examples of the energic are hard to put under one or several categories. Thus while we have *adi yiktašduna* (85.61), we also have other examples of *adi* without the energic (85.38, 96.21–22, 104.16). In exact parallels we have *yištaparu* (119.8) and *yištapruna* (121.7), *tišmuna* (74.50) and *tišmē* (90.13), *yišmuna* (85.7) and *yušmu* (132.52). Indeed, we might add that in many questions, where, in view of the usage seen above, we might expect the energic, we do not have it. Thus *ana minī lā taḳbu ana šarri* (73.6–8).

Hence we see that no hard and fast rules govern the use of the energic in Byblian either as to the type of clause in which it may be used, or as to its use or non-use in any given syntactical situation. Only its use with the jussive is ruled out absolutely. Essentially it is an emphatic form of *yaqtulu*, with the precise nuance of emphasis determined by the context.

Excursus

Adopting the view that *yaqtuluna* is the normal energic in Byblian raises a problem: what view shall we adopt of the Arabic energic *yaqtulan(na)*? Is *yaqtulan(na)* merely the Arabic counterpart of Byblian *yaqtuluna*?

The usual view of the energic in Arabic has been stated very succinctly by Höfner: "Alles, was hervorgehoben und besonders betont werden soll, wird durch den Energicus wiedergegeben."[122] However, in South Arabic this view encounters serious difficulties of which Miss Höfner is not unaware. For it is often used where there can be no ques-

[122]Höfner, p. 73, §60.

tion of emphasis: it is regularly used to express purpose in Minaean and Sabaean.[123]

Höfner's explanation is based on the analogy of Mehri. In Mehri the indicative and subjunctive fell together, the only distinction being in accent. However, the energic is a regular substitute for the indicative. In South Arabic, analogously, she maintains, the indicative and subjunctive fell together, and then the energic was substituted for the subjunctive.[124]

This explanation is not satisfactory. For, what is the evidence that the indicative and the subjunctive fell together so early as the time of the Minaean and Sabaean inscriptions? The fact that from all indications case-endings are in full usage in the same inscriptions is strong evidence to the contrary.[125]

We would propose a hypothesis and only indicate briefly the facts which seem to confirm it. A detailed study of the matter is not in place in this paper.

The hypothesis is: *yaqtulan(na)* is another form of the subjunctive, i.e., the subjunctive plus the energic ending *-na*. This of course explains perfectly the use of *yqtln* to express purpose in Minaean and Sabaean.[126] Moreover, it fits remarkably well with the use of *yaqtulan(na)* in North Arabic. For as we shall see in more detail in our study of *yaqtula*, the most probable view of *yaqtula* is that it was originally an emphatic volitive form. Moreover, as we shall also see, *yaqtula* and *yaqtul* have many parallel uses in Arabic. Now, it is most striking that the use of *yaqtulan(na)* in North Arabic is again paralleled by the jussive: in protases and apodoses of conditional sentences, in wishes, commands, prohibitions.[127] If we add its emphatic usage,[128] paralleled by the cohortative in Hebrew, which as we shall see is a survival of the subjunctive, then the view that *yaqtulan(na)* is an emphatic/volitive form is seen to be quite reasonable.

[123]Note too its clear use as a virtual jussive (in an independent clause); cf. Brockelmann, *Grundriss* I, §259*b*.

[124]Höfner, p. 74, §60.

[125]*Ibid.*, pp. 123–124, §104.

[126]Since *yaqtula* is used like a jussive in Amarna, it would also explain its quasi jussive use noted above.

[127]Wright-de Goeje, pp. 42–43, §19.

[128]*Ibid.*, pp. 41–42.

Turning to Amarna and Hebrew, the hypothesis is again confirmed. For there we find the energic with a form which, as we shall see, must certainly be subjunctive: *timaḫ(ḫ)aṣana* (77.37). In Hebrew the cohortative, the survival of the subjunctive, is frequently followed by *-naʾ*.[129]

In short, all of the evidence seems to converge on the probability of *yaqtulan(na)* being the subjunctive-energic, though a far more detailed study of the matter is necessary before this can become anything more than an interesting hypothesis. This much, however, seems certain: the Amarna evidence from which we establish with certainty an indicative-energic *yaqtuluna* and a volitive *yaqtula* in early Canaanite that may be used in dependent or independent clauses, and from which it follows that the Heb. cohortative is a survival of *yaqtula* in the 1st person—this evidence must be taken into consideration in the study of the problems of Arabic grammar. Arabic grammarians have worked in the narrow confines of Arabic and have been too often slavishly dependent on Arab grammarians of the Middle Ages. Their treatment of the subjunctive is typical: it is stated categorically that the subjunctive is confined to subordinate clauses[130] and almost always has purposive force, then everything possible is forced into this mould, and the rest—and this not a little—is left without explanation.[131]

[129]On the relation of *-naʾ* to the energic, see above n. 13.

[130]Wright-de Goeje, p. 24, §15.

[131]For example, the use of the subjunctive in protases and apodoses of conditional sentences; cf. Wright-de Goeje, p. 40, Rem. *c*.

VI. The Infinitive

As in all Semitic languages, including Accadian, the infinitive is used in these letters to emphasize the finite form of the verb. However, unlike Accadian, the infinitive is never in the nominative in these letters: *šamā ul tušmuna*, "my words are not heeded at all" (89.9–10); *ašāba lā ašib*, "he does not sit" (92.10); *laḳīmi tilḳūnaše*, "they will certainly take it" (131.17). The first two examples are clearly in the accusative, the latter perhaps is since there is a fluctuation in the scribes' use of *-i* or *-a* as the ending of infinitives *tertiae infirmae* as an accusative construct; cf. *laḳī* (114.44), *laḳā* (124.54), *aṣī* (69.32, 127.39), *aṣā(m)* (79.17, 87.26).[132] Hence *laḳī* may be on the analogy of this good Accadian acc.-construct form. In this construction then the infinitive functions in Byblian as a kind of cognate accusative.[133] It will be noted that the infinitive precedes the finite verb as regularly in Hebrew.

There is another use of the infinitive, well established in Canaanite but not found in Accadian: the infinitive used as a finite verb.[134] Thus: *pānānu dagālima awīl māt miṣri u ennabtū šarrāni māt kinaḫni ištu pānišu*, "previously if they saw an Egyptian, then the kings of Canaan would flee before him" (109.44–46); *kašādima awīliya u rakšašu*, "when my man arrived, he bound him" (116.27–28); *paṭārima awīlūt ḫupšī u ṣabtū* ^{lú}GAZ$^{pl.}$ *āla*, "if the serfs desert, then the Hapiru will take the city" (118.37-38); cf. also 116.11, 129.40.

More striking than these examples is the use of the infinitive as a finite verb with the independent personal pronoun functioning as subject:[135] *ṣabātmi nīnū ālāni āl gubla u minā tīpušu ṣābu piṭatu*, "if we

[132]For *aṣā(m)* in 87.26, see the writer's article in *JNES* 8, pp. 124–125 [below, Paper 3, pp. 141–142].

[133]In Ugaritic, however, the infinitive in this usage is in the nominative; *UH*, p. 68, §9.23.

[134]Already recognized by Brockelmann as a Canaanitism; *Grundriss* II, p. 168, §88b. He failed, however, to note the use of the infinitive with the independent pronoun.—The infinitive is also used as a finite verb in South Arabic; Höfner, p. 64, §54. Höfner explains this usage as a survival from the time when grammatical categories of verb and noun had not been fixed, and hence the infinitive was either verbal or nominal.

[135]This construction is found later at Byblos in the Yehawmilk inscription, is common in the new inscriptions from Karatepe, and there is one good example in Biblical Hebrew, *wĕšabbē(a)ḥ ʾănî*, "and I praised" (Eccles. 4.2). No one has noted

take the cities of Byblos, then what will the archer-host do?" (129.32–34; 362.25–26); *paṭārima šūta(m) u yānu ša yūbalu ṭuppīya*, "if he leaves, then there will be no one to carry my tablets" (113.40–41); *apāši atta kit(t)a itti mārī* ^{m}*·abdaširta u laḳūka*, "if thou makest an alliance with the sons of ᶜAbd-Ashirta, then they will take thee" (132.32–35);[136] also 362.28–29, 89.38–39.[137]

Several problems, however, are immediately apparent: 1) are these infinitives to be called absolute or construct; 2) how explain the case-ending in forms like *paṭārima* etc.; 3) what is the difference between the construction with an apparent genitive like *paṭārima* and that with no case-ending like *ṣabātmi*?

The ambiguity of our evidence prevents an answer to the first problem. Since Accadian made no distinction between the so-called infinitives absolute and construct of Hebrew but employed *qatālu(m)* for both, the Canaanite scribes had at their disposal only one infinitive form for all the uses of their native infinitive. Moreover, O'Callaghan on the basis of the new Karatepe inscriptions has recently raised again the question whether the distinction of the two infinitives is characteristic of Canaanite in general or whether it is not rather an inner Hebrew development.[138] Hence with the evidence now at our disposal, we must transmit the first question.

As to the second, the use of the genitive is strange, lacking any known Canaanite parallel. However, again our meager knowledge of early Canaanite case-syntax will not allow us to dispose of the construction as due merely to scribal error. It is too regular to permit of such a facile solution.

---

in his treatment of the Karatepe inscriptions the evidence in Amarna Byblian. Honeyman (*Muséon* 61, p. 50), who refers to Amarna, is content with citing Brockelmann and believes the Karatepe inscriptions the first certain evidence of this construction in Canaanite. It should be remarked here that the parallels from the later inscriptions point to our infinitives being infinitives absolute. However, for the difficulties, see below.—The contention of Obermann (*JBL* 68, p. 303) and Sidney Smith (*The Statue of Idri-mi*, p. 38) that Karatepe may be using a participle rather than an infinitive is absolutely groundless.

136On this passage, see the Appendix.

137On 89.38–39, see *JCS* 4 [below, Paper 4, pp. 148–149].

138O'Callaghan, *Orientalia* NS 18, p. 184. The big difficulty in the Karatepe inscriptions is the use of pronominal objective suffixes with what seems to be an infinitive absolute. This is never found in Biblical Hebrew with the infinitive absolute, though it is common with infinitives construct.

Attention should be called to the use of the genitive at Boğazköy as "le complément circonstanciel du verbe."[139] Analysis of the Boğazköy construction shows that *ina* or *ana* has been omitted, or better, would be expected.

If we look again at our examples of the genitive-infinitive, we shall see that *ina* or *ana* could very well be expressed in any of them with no change of meaning. Thus we can attest the construction elsewhere so far as the genitival use is concerned. The problem remains however whether there has merely been an ellipsis of *ina* or *ana* or whether this is a true circumstantial genitive; whether, moreover, the idiom derives from Canaanite or has another source.[140]

As to the independent pronoun, we can here definitely state that it is to be construed as nominative. There are excellent parallels in Hebrew with the so-called infinitive construct construed with a clear nominative as its subject.[141] This is true even where the infinitive stands in a genitival relationship after a preposition: *bišlō(a)ḥ ʾōtô sargōn*, "when Sargon sent him" (Is. 20.1). Thus *paṭārima šūta(m)* causes no difficulty so far as the pronoun is concerned.[142]

As to the third problem, there are two possibilities: 1) *ṣabātmi* is only apparently different from *paṭārima* due to syncope of the short vowel: *ṣabātĭmi* > *ṣabātmi*; 2) we have an entirely different construction in which the independent pronoun functions as subject of an infinitive construct, that is, an infinitive without case-ending. If the latter be the case, then an explanation of the syntax escapes me.[143]

[139]Labat, p. 73.

[140]Labat, p. 73, n. 14, suggests that the idiom reflects Hittite rather than Semitic.

[141]*GKC*, §115g, k.

[142]It follows therefore that the noun-subjects with the infinitive (examples quoted above) are most probably nominatives also.

[143]It should be noted that the syntax (and the morphology) of the infinitive is still quite obscure in Ugaritic. Thus *bnšʾi ʿênêha*, "on lifting her eyes" (*UH* 51. ii.12) where we seem to have the *qatālu* form of the infinitive with a preposition, though in the same verb we have the short imperative *šaʾa* (Keret A, 75), and hence on the analogy of Hebrew would expect something like *bšiʾt* = *bašiʾti* (Heb. שְׂאֵת). Also *wʿn rbt ʾaṯrt ym*, "and the lady, Asherah of the Sea, replied" (*UH* 49.i.25). Ginsberg explains the form as an infinitive absolute *ʿanâwu* > *ʿanô*, Hammershaimb as an infinitive construct but with no attempt at vocalization (Hammershaimb, p. 131, and n.1 for Ginsberg references), Gordon as an infinitive absolute *ʿanâ* but with no explanation of the morphology (*UH*, p. 68, §9.25). In short, Ugaritic raises much the same problems as does Byblian Amarna, and so while we may have no solution as yet for the difficulties in

VII. Agreement of Verb with Subject

It is to be remarked at the beginning that in many respects the agreement of the verb with the subject in the Byblian letters is paralleled at Boğazköy. The reason for including these constructions here is that they are more probably reflections of Canaanite usage. For several important idioms are either extremely rare or unparalleled at Boğazköy, indicating that the Canaanite scribes went their own way in the syntax of agreement. This is confirmed by the fact that the syntax of agreement in the Byblian letters is paralleled almost in detail in Biblical Hebrew.

Feminine sg. subject: 1) the verb is regularly fem. sg.: g·*bēlit ša āl gubla tid(d)in dunna ana šarri*, "may Baᶜalat of Byblos grant strength to the king" (118.6–8); *taḳbu ālu*, "the city will say" (89.40–41), etc. This rule is rarely observed in the Hittite Boğazköy texts.[144] 2) A masc. sg. verb precedes a fem. sg. subject: *lā yatūruna awatu an yāši*, "a reply does not come back to me" (126.53–55). This construction is well known in Hebrew. However, *nukurtum ... ennipuš* (92.11) with the noun preceding reflects more Boğazköy practice;[145] note too at Boğazköy *nukurtu dannu*.[146]

Masculine plural subject: 1) may be taken as a collective and construed with a 3rd sg. *feminine—palḫātī* lú.pl.*ḫupšī ul timaḫ(ḫ)aṣananī*, "I fear the serfs lest they strike me down" (77.36–37). 2) Twice we have the 3rd sg. masc. of the verb[147]—*awīlūt māt miṣri ša aṣa ...*, "the Egyptians who came forth" (105.83–84); lú.pl.*ḫāzānūtu ul tarṣa ittiya*, "the governors are not just to me" (109.60–61). Since the use of the sg. with a plural subject is extremely rare at Boğazköy and rather common in these letters (we shall see many more examples), we must consider this usage as Byblian. The general rule of course is 3rd pl. masc. of the verb.

Amarna, we can be sure that the difficulties we have isolated are the difficulties belonging to the syntax of the Canaanite infinitive.

144 Labat, p. 69.

145 *Ibid.*

146 *Ibid.*, p. 70.

147 The construction is attested at Boğazköy; *ibid.*, p. 72.

Feminine plural subject: we do not have one clear instance of a fem. plural form of the verb. The rule is either masc. pl.[148] or fem. sg., in the latter case the plural subject being construed as a collective. Thus *ālāniya dannū*, "my cities are strong" (69.16);[149] *awātūya ul tulḳuna u šamā ul tušmuna*, "my words are not received and they are utterly unheeded" (89.8–10; 89.37; 90.16–18; 91.29–30; 108.20–21; 117.32; 362. 12–13); *ennipšat mātātu ana* ˡᵘ́GAZᵖˡ·, "the lands are joined to the Ḫapiru" (85.72–73); *tinipuš mātātu ana šarri*, "that the lands may be joined to the king" (129.80). In 105.20–21 *elippētīšunu aṣa* we have possibly a fem. pl. form of the verb; if not, a masc. sg. with a fem. pl. subj. The former seems preferable.

Fem. and masc. subject: always masc. plural[150]—*pānānu āl ṣumura u awīlūtuši dannūtum ibaššū*, "previously Simyra and its men were strong" (81.48–49; 74.38; 85.5–7; 95.3–5).

Collective subject: the verb may be either sg. or plural,[151] in one striking instance a plural serving as a gloss to a sg. *māt amurri* ... *tubā*, "the land of the Amorite desires" (70.25–26); *māt amurri* ... *ul tāšaš\naḳṣapū*, "the land of the Amorite ... is not embittered\angry" (82.48–51). Other examples: with a sg., 73.12,16; with a plural, 73.13,14.

kalū or gabbu as subject: the Byblian scribes had a predilection for *kalū*. Of the 54 occurrences listed in Knudtzon's glossary, all but 6 are Byblian! At Boğazköy *kalū* is used only once![152] These facts, together with the syntax of *kalū*, which is virtually identical with that of Hebrew *kōl*, make it certain that the syntax underlying the use of *kalū* is that of Byblian **kullu* = Heb. *kōl*.

The usage is as follows: 1) if the *nomen rectum* is a masc. pl., then usually the verb is masc. plural[153]—*kalī* ˡᵘ́·ᵖˡ·GAZᵖˡ· *nadnū pānīšunu ana yāši*, "all of the Hapiru have turned against me" (79.10–11; 73.24; 103.49; 106.40, *gabbu*; 132.50); 2) once the verb is masc. sg. with a

[148]So at Boğazköy; *ibid.*, p. 69.

[149]In Canaanite Amarna *ālu* is regularly construed as a feminine. Thus *balṭat āl gubla* (68.21), *ennipšat āl ṣumur* (84.12), *taḳbu ālu* (89.40–41), *milik ana ālika ul yilḳīši* (90.11–12; *-ši*, not *-šu*), etc. This reflects the gender of Can. *ᶜîr*. In Acc. *ālu* is masc.

[150]Also at Boğazköy; Labat, p. 69.

[151]Also at Boğazköy; *ibid.*, p. 69, 71. The idiom with *mātu* is identical with that of Heb.; cf. I Sam. 17.46 *wĕyēdĕᶜû kōl hāʾāreṣ*. Gesenius explains such usage as a collective term denoting masculine persons; *GKC*, §145e.

[152]Labat, p. 143.

[153]Same construction in Biblical Heb.; *GHB*, §150c.

masc. pl. *nomen rectum—kalī* $^{\text{lú.pl.}}$*maṣṣarti ša irtīḫū marṣa,* "all of the garrison that remains is sick" (103.47–49);[154] 3) if the *nomen rectum* is a fem. plural the verb may be either fem. sg. or masc. pl.:[155] *u tinnipuš kalī mātāti ana* $^{\text{lú.pl.}}$GAZ, "that all lands may be joined to the Ḫapiru" (74.35; for other fem. sg. cf. 73.32, 84.9, 77.28, 79.42, 88.32–33 with *gabbu*, 362.63–64); *kalī ālāniya ennipšū ana* $^{\text{lú.pl.}}$GAZ$^{\text{pl.}}$, "all of my cities have gone over to the Ḫapiru" (116.37–38; for other masc. pl. cf. 74.21 with *gabbu*, 76.42–43, 79.19–20). Thus the syntax of Byblian **kullu* is very similar to that of Heb. *kōl*. Like it the verb is usually determined by the *nomen rectum*. Unlike it, however, is the use of the fem. sg. form of the verb with a fem. pl. *nomen rectum*.

Dual subject: the writing 2 URU-*ni-šu* (79.31) makes it very doubtful if nouns preceded by "2" are to be considered duals. Hence it is difficult to determine the rules of agreement. In 103.22 *tišmana* seems more probably a dual than a sg.[156] In 117.18 *tūbaluna* may be a sg. or it may be a pl. (subj. 2 LÚ, l. 17); *aṣa* in line 19 may be masc. sg. or a dual. The evidence is too meager to draw any conclusions.

Plural of majesty: in 71.5 and 86.4 we have the jussive plural *tid(d)inū* with a sg. subject, ^{g}*amana*. On *tiddinū* as a plural, see Resumé below. Note also *ennipšat ... āl ṣumura āl maṣ(ṣ)artikunu ana* ^{lú}GAZ$^{\text{pl.}}$ *u ḳalāta*, "Simyra, your garrison city, is joined to the Ḫapiru, for *thou* art negligent" (76.34–37). We have a plural of majesty in the suffix *-kunu*, but in the verb we immediately shift to the singular. Both constructions are attested in Hebrew.[157]

Resumé: there is little in the syntax of verbal agreement in these letters that cannot be paralleled in Biblical Hebrew. One exception is

[154] Just as rare in Biblical Hebrew; *GHB, ibid.*

[155] F. Thureau-Dangin interprets *ālānu gubli* (la ville de Gubla; *RA* 19, p. 92, 362.12,24,26,32) and *mātāti* (362.34,36,47,50) as singulars. As for *mātāti*, the examples already cited prove him wrong, for it is certainly often construed with a pl. As for *ālānu gubli*, first, this does not affect the rule that a fem. sg. may be construed with a fem. pl. subject; secondly, *ālānu gubli* in this letter refers to the villages clustered around Byblos, the metropolis (*ʾēm*, cf. II Sam. 20.19). Compare I Sam. 2.3: *wayyēšĕbû bĕʿārê ḥebrôn*, "and they dwelt in the villages of Hebron." This seems the more probable explanation and in accord with Canaanite idiom. The *āl gubli* of l. 28 is either an error of the scribe who forgot to add MEŠ, or due to the fact that the capture of the surrounding villages and of Byblos itself was regarded as virtually one and the same thing.

[156] I have previously considered it as 3rd fem. singular; *JCS* 2, comm. no. 6 [below, Paper 2, pp. 135–136].

[157] *GKC*, §145h.

the frequent use of the fem. sg. with a plural construed as a collective. This idiom, familiar from Arabic, may have had a larger place in early Hebrew.

However, this is not to say that all *taqtulu* forms with a plural subject are to be considered as 3rd fem. sg.[158] There is considerable evidence against this view. 1) The form is used as a jussive. Now the jussive form of the 3rd fem. sg. must be *taqtul*, not *taqtulu*.[159] Thus ᵍ·*amana u* ᵍ·*bēlit ša āl gubla tid(d)inū baštaka ina pāni šarri*, "may Amun and Baᶜalat of Byblos grant thee favor before the king" (95.3–5; see also 71.5, 86.4). Compare ᵍ·*bēlit ša āl gubla ilat šarri lid(d)in baštaka*, "may Baᶜalat of Byblos, the goddess of the king, grant thee favor" (102.5–7). Therefore, because of the jussive force of the verb in the first example the form must be plural, *tid(d)inū*.

2) In our study of purpose clauses we shall establish a principle of modal sequence: if the governing verb is indicative, then the verb of the purpose clause is indicative; if the governing verb is a volitive (*qutul, yaqtul, yaqtula*), then the verb of the purpose clause is also a volitive. Now very frequently *taqtulu* occurs in the volitive sequence. This being true, then the same argument as above is again in place: if the form were sg., then it should appear as *taqtul*. Its consistent occurence in the form *taqtulu* establishes the length of the *u*-vowel.[160]

3) The form *taqtuluna* is used almost exclusively with plural subjects. Of 110 occurrences of *-na* affixed to some form of *yaqtulu*, 70 are

[158]This represents a modification of my former view in *JCS* 2, comm. no. 6 [below, Paper 2, pp. 135–136]. Of course I speak here for myself and not for Dr. Albright with whom I collaborated on the article referred to.—This has been a much disputed point ever since the discovery of the Amarna letters, and interest in a solution has been increased by the discovery of Ugaritic. For in the latter we also find the apparent plural *tqtl(n)*. Andrée Herdner has most recently given a detailed defense of the position that the form is a plural in Ugaritic; *RÉS* 1938, pp. 76–83. This has also been the position of the majority of scholars with regard to Amarna; cf. Böhl, pp. 52–53, §28i–m, Dhorme, *RB* 10, p. 379, Brockelmann, *Grundriss* I, p. 567, §260f. Brockelmann, however, admitted the possibility that *taqtulū(na)* was a blend of Can. 3rd fem. sg. and an Acc. pl. No one, however, has examined the evidence from the viewpoint of syntax. Yet it is only syntax that can yield a decisive answer, since the evidence from morphology alone must remain ambiguous. Indeed, on the basis of morphology alone the view that *taqtulu* is always 3rd fem. sg. is more probable. Hence in the arguments that follow we would lay stress most of all on our second argument from the syntax of purpose clauses. This evidence, we believe, is decisive.

[159]See above under IV G.

[160]This argument is presented in detail in our study of purpose clauses.

with *taqtulu* (rarely *yaqtulu*) construed with a plural subject. This points to a regular 3rd masc. pl. ind. *taqtulūna* corresponding to Arabic *yaqtulûna*, Aramaic *yiqtĕlûn*. Note too that the energic ending, apart from verbal suffixes, is preserved in Hebrew chiefly in the plural.[161]

4) Finally, the fluctuation between *taqtuluna* and *taqtulūni* should be noted. The latter is the allative ending of Accadian, restricted to plurals; otherwise it is *-am* or with the second sg. fem. *-m*.[162] This fact is not too impressive when the occurrences are in different letters, since blend formulations are common in Amarna. But it is impressive when the fluctuation occurs in the same letter: *tiḳbūni* (362.17,25), *tiḳbūna* (362. 21), *teba'ūna* (362.24), *tamūtūna* (362.44). Since there is not a single case where *-ūni(m)* is used with a sg. subject, it is difficult to escape the conclusion that the scribe who wrote 362 considered *tiḳbūna* / *tiḳbūni* as plurals.—Thus, from these four lines of evidence, we conclude that there was a masc. pl. form of the imperfect with a *t*-preformative.[163]

Impersonal Expressions

There are a number of impersonal expressions in the Byblian letters unparalleled in both standard Accadian and the Accadian of Boğazköy.

[161]*GKC*, §47m.

[162]*GA*, §31e.

[163]There is a bewildering fluctuation in the verbal agreement of ERÍN.MEŠ, and until a satisfactory explanation is found we cannot use this material for determining the rules of verbal agreement. ERÍN.MEŠ is often treated as a masc. sg.: *ina* ERÍN.MEŠ *ṣeḫri* (117.24), *ītilī* ERÍN.MEŠ (124.12), ERÍN.MEŠ *piṭati rabā* (76. 38–39), *yīṣana* ERÍN.MEŠ *piṭati* (77.27), *yimaḳ(ḳ)uta* ERÍN.MEŠ *karaši* (83.43). On the other hand, it is frequently treated as a fem. sg.: ERÍN.MEŠ *aṣat* (129.36), ERÍN.MEŠ *piṭati ibaš(š)at* (103.55–56), ERÍN.MEŠ *piṭati rabīti* (127.38–39), *tīpušu* ERÍN.MEŠ *piṭatu* (129.33–34), *tūṣu* (ERÍN.MEŠ) (129.38–39), ERÍN.MEŠ *piṭata(m) rabītam* (131.40). Twice the ideogram seems to be construed as a plural, though it is possible here to have a *constructio ad sensum*: *puḫurūnimmi* (an imperative addressed to ERÍN.MEŠ; 74.31), ERÍN.MEŠ *dikū* (131.9). At Boğazköy there is a parallel situation with ERÍN.MEŠ construed with a sg. or a pl. verb (Labat, p. 72).—Knudtzon (*EA* II, p. 1590) and Weber (*EA* II, p. 1538) offer the solution that ERÍN.MEŠ = *ummānu*, thus getting rid of the difficulty of the fluctuation in gender. However, the gloss *ṣa-bi pí-ṭá-te* after ERÍN.MEŠ in 166.4 indicates that the ideogram was interpreted as *ṣābu* (cf. *RA* 19, p. 91, n. 2. Nor is there any basis in Canaanite for *ṣaba'(u)* being feminine; cf. *JCS* 2, comm. no. 14 [below, Paper 2, p. 137]. One possibility, hitherto not considered, is that *piṭa-tu* / *i* / *a* may be responsible for the fem. agreement, for Egyptian *pḏtyw*, "archers" is often Accadianized as a fem. sg.: *piṭatu* (nom.), *piṭati* (gen.), *piṭata(m)* (acc.). However, we cannot be certain.

Hence they must reflect Byblian idiom, though it is often difficult to determine exactly the underlying Canaanite.

damiḳ ana, damiḳ ana pāni (*ina pāni*), "it is pleasing to." The idiom is the same as Heb. *ṭôb lĕ, ṭôb lipnê.*[164] *damiḳ ana yāši*, "it is pleasing to me" (116.48, 117.71); *šumma damiḳ ina pānika*, "if it is pleasing in thy sight" (107.20). In 84.6–7 *epēš* is the subject of *damiḳ ana pāni*, but undoubtedly the phrase could also be used impersonally. Cf. also *lidmiḳ ina pāni šarri*, "may it be pleasing in the sight of the king" (85.33–34) and Heb. *yîṭab lĕ / lipnê*, also used impersonally.[165]

mariṣ ana, "it goes ill with, x is in bad straits." *mariṣ ana yāši*, "it goes ill with me" (103.7–8; 114.50; 116.54–55; 362.59); *mariṣ danniš ana mātāti*, "it goes ill with the lands" (84.24–25). Also *mariṣ ana īnē*: *mariṣ ana īnēnū*, "it is displeasing in our sight" (131.26). Compare *raʿ lĕ* and *raʿ bĕʿênê* in Hebrew.[166]

mangammi, "there is distress" (362.15). Thureau-Dangin's rendering "elle (Gubla) est dans l'angoisse" overlooks the fact that names of towns (and *ālu*) are regularly feminine in the Canaanite Amarna letters.[167] Hence an impersonal rendering is much more probable.

pašiḫ ana šunu, "they are well off, they have peace." Compare in Heb. *yanû(a)ḥ lĕ* (Is. 23.12; Job 3.13; Neh. 9.28).

šalim ištu pānā<nu>m, "health conditions are better than before" (362.50).

To be included under impersonal expressions is the impersonal use of the Qal passive: *lā yušmu ana yāši*, "no heed is given me" (132.52);[168] cf. also 119.18–19 below. Perhaps too 3-*tan iz(z)iz muḫḫiya šatta annīta*, "three times this year there has been an attack against me" (85.8–9). Since *izziz* is not a passive this example properly speaking does not belong here. Moreover, in this example the scribe may merely have failed to indicate the subject (ʿAbd-Ashirta?).

[164] Ges.-Buhl[13], p. 293b.

[165] *Ibid.*, p. 320b.

[166] *Ibid.*, p. 780b.

[167] See n. 149.

[168] Compare *yuggad* in Gen. 27.42 with an object! I agree with Joüon that the reason for the object (with *ʾet*) is that the passive is here equivalent to a vague personal subject and hence the verb is implicitly active; *GHB*, §128b. He happily compares classical *legitur Vergilius* with medieval *legitur Vergilium* (on lit Virgile). The impersonal use of the passive has many parallels in Heb.; cf. *GKC*, §121a.

To be noted concerning all the impersonal expressions is that the 3rd sg. *masculine* is employed, as is the general rule in Hebrew.[169]

As in Hebrew,[170] an indefinite subject may be expressed by the 3rd pl. masc.: *anumma inanna inam(m)ušū urra mūša*, "behold, now they are deserting day (and) night" (69.12–13); *tiqbūni*, "they say, it is being said" (362.17,21,25); *inūma yiḳabūna ina pānika*, "if they say in thy presence" (116.8–9). With the latter compare *inūma ḳabī ana pāni šarri*, "if it is said in the presence of the king" (119.18–19).

[169] *GHB*, §152d.
[170] *Ibid*., §155b.

VIII. SUBSTANTIVAL CLAUSES

By a substantival clause I understand any clause which has the same function as that of a noun such as subject of a sentence, object of a verb, etc.

As the object of a verb there are three types of clauses:

1) an asyndetic union of two clauses, the first containing a *verbum sentiendi vel declarandi,* the second the object of this verb:[171] *ešmī puḫ(ḫ)irmi kalī* $^{lú.pl.}$GAZ$^{pl.}$, "I hear (that) he has gathered all the Ḫapiru" (91.23–24); *išim(m)ī ištu pī awīlūtum*$^{tu(m)}$ *awīlu emḳu šūta(m),* "I hear men say (that) he is a wise man" (106.38–39); *yīdī šarru bēlī anāku arad kit(t)i,* "the king, my lord, knows (that) I am a loyal servant" (139.29–30); cf. also 69.15–16, 82.47–50.

2) The substantival clause is introduced by the coordinating conjunction *u*:[172] *u išim(m)ī u yānum mimma u inūma yānum tillatam ša aṣat ana yāši* ..., "if he hears that there is absolutely nothing (for me) and that there is no rescue-force which has come forth for me ..." (92.21–23; a very important example because of the parallelism of *u* and *inūma*).

3) The third, and most frequent, type is introduce by *inūma* (= Byblian *kī*):[173] *īdū inūma tamūtūna,* "they know that they are to die" (362.44); cf. 68.9–10, 73.15–16, 74.5–6, 104.6–9, 119.24, 114.6, 116.6–8, 116.10–14, 362.51–52, etc.

With an impersonal expression like *damiḳ* "it is good" any of the three constructions just noted may function as subject:[174] *damiḳ ittaka*

[171]Same idiom in Hebrew; *GHB,* §157b.

[172]Same idiom in Hebrew; *ibid.,* §177h.

[173]Same idiom in Hebrew; *ibid.,* §157c. The same use of *inūma* is found in line 25 of the Idri-mi inscription. Sidney Smith (*The Statue of Idri-mi,* p. 98) would read *inu-ma,* comparing Heb. *hēn, hinnēh,* and render "behold." The Amarna use of *inūma* is, he says, the same. This does not, however, explain the construction, for it is unknown in Accadian. Since the uses of *inūma* in our letters parallel those of Can. *kī,* and since the construction is hitherto known only in Amarna, we must certainly consider this use of *inūma* as a Canaanitism both in Amarna and in the Idri-mi inscription. Albright has long recognized that the use of *inūma* throughout Can. Amarna is identical with that of Can. *kī; BASOR* 89, p. 30, n.7; 94, p. 23, n. 64.

[174]Same idiom in Hebrew, though the use of the conjunction in this particular construction is not attested in Biblical Hebrew; *GHB,* §157a.

ayābu šarri nakrū itya, "is it pleasing to thee that the enemies of the king are hostile to me?" (114.46–47); *damiḳ ina pāni šarri ... u tīpušūna mārū* $^{m.}$*abdaširta kīma libbišunu*, "is it pleasing in the sight of the king ... that sons of ᶜAbd-Ashirta do as they please?" (108.8–13); *damiḳmi inūma iṣbat āl gubla*, "is it pleasing that he should capture Byblos?" (84.36); cf. also 114.46, 116.48–50.

To be especially noted among the examples of substantival clauses are the following: *inūma iḳab(b)u šarru bēliya uṣurme ramānka ... ištu man(n)i inaṣ(ṣ)aruna ramāniya*, "the king says, 'guard thyself ...'; (but) with what shall I guard myself?" (125.7–13); *inūma taštapra ana yāši alikmi iziz ina āl ṣumur adi kašādiya tīdī inūma nukurtum*$^{pl.}$ *dannat danniš muḫḫiya*, "thou writest to me, 'go, stay in Simyra until I arrive'; (but) thou knowest that the hostility against me is very great" (102.14–18); *inūma yištappara šarru*^{ru} *ana yāši anum(m)a* $^{m.}$*irimayašša yakšuduna ana muḫ(ḫ)ika ul kašid ana muḫ(ḫ)iya*, "the king wrote to me, 'behold, Irimayashsha will come to thee'; (but) he has not come to me" (130.9–14); cf. also 77.6–7, 126.4–8; *ul inūma ušširtī awīliya ana ēkalli*, "is it not a fact that I sent my man to the palace?" (82.35–36).

The last example is almost certainly elliptical, as the translation indicates, with *tīdī*—then the substantival clause is the object—or *ibašši*—then the clause is the subject—understood as the main verb. Cf. the perfect parallel in II Sam. 13.28: *hălôʾ kî ʾānôkî ṣiwwîtî ʾetkem*, "is it not a fact that I ordered you?" For the other examples we have an excellent Heb. parallel in Ruth 2.21: *gam kî ʾāmar ʾēlay ᶜim hannĕᶜārîm ʾăšer lî tidbaqîn*, "moreover, he said to me, 'thou shalt stay close to my servants.' " The question remains, however, whether the use of *inūma* (or *kī*) in these examples is also elliptical in origin with a verb "to be" understood as the main verb; thus "(it is the case, it is) that ..."[175]

We do not think it is necessary to adopt this explanation, but rather see here a use of Can. *kī* analogous to its use in the protases of conditional sentences, in concessive clauses, and in the so-called *kī of affirmation*.[176] All of these derive from the original deictic force of the particle: in protases pointing to and emphasizing the hypothesis (compare the use of *šumma* = "behold"), in concessive clauses with almost the same function, in its asseverative use almost with its original deictic force. So

[175]So *GHB*, p. 479, n. 2; cf. also §164.

[176]We are thus in agreement with Brockelmann; cf. *Grundriss* II, p. 111, §56d, p. 606, §397.

here in our examples we have the particle merely reinforcing the affirmation. In the Amarna examples the deictic force of the particle can perhaps be best brought out by some rendering such as "as to the fact that ..."[177]

A substantival clause may also stand in apposition to a noun: *tīdī parṣaya inūma ibaš(š)āta ina āl ṣumura inūma arad kit(t)ika anāku,* "thou knowest my way of acting when thou wast in Simyra, (namely,) that I am thy loyal servant" (73.39–42); *damiḳmi epēš šarri bēliya inu šapar šarru ana šar āl bērūta,* "the deed of the king is pleasing, (namely,) that he wrote to the king of Berytus" (92.30–32). Hebrew is lacking examples of this use.[178]

Finally, to be noted is the idiom, so familiar from Hebrew,[179] by which the subject of the object-clause is anticipated in the governing clause as the object of the verb: *tīdī māt amurri inūma ašar danni tilakuna,* "thou knowest the land of Amurru, that it follows the stronger party" (73.15–16); *ul tīdī māt amurri urra mūša tubaʾuna ṣāba piṭati,* "dost thou not know the land of Amurru (that) day (and) night it longs for an archer-host?" (82.47–50).

[177]Cf. Lachish III, 8: *wky ʾmr ʾdny,* "and as for what my lord hath said ..." (Albright's translation; *BASOR* 73, p. 18). Note that *kī* introduces the body of the letter in Lachish just as *inūma* does in our instances.

[178]Cf. *GHB*, §157a.

[179]*GHB*, §157d.

IX. Causal Clauses

There are three specifically Canaanite types of causal clauses in the Byblian letters:

1) Introduced by the conjunction *u*:[180] *minā īpušuna u anāku lā ili*ᵓ*u alāka(m) ana āl ṣumura*, "what shall I do since I cannot go to Simyra?" (104.36–39); *lā tīrubūna* ᵍⁱˢ*elippēti awīlūt* MIŠI *ana māt amurri u dakū* ᵐ·*abdaširta*, "the ships of the MIŠI shall not enter Amurru, for they have killed ᶜAbd-Aširta" (101.3–6; also 101.29–30).

2) Introduced by *inūma* (= *kī*):[181] *u milik inūma arad kit(t)ika anāku*, "so take concern, for I am thy loyal servant" (116.14–15); *yīpušu dumḳa ana yāši inūma yānu libbi*ᵇⁱ *šanā ana yāši*, "he performed kindness(es) for me because there is no duplicity about me" (119.40–42); cf. 73.26,35–37; 94.67; 103.15–17; 126.9–11; 132.43–46; 362.57,59.

3) Introduced by *muḫḫi* (= ᶜ*al*):[182] *muḫḫi ma*ᵓ*id mimmiya ittašu kinan(n)a ītipuš nukurta ana yāši*, "because my property with him is great, thus he is displaying hostility to me" (105.38–40). Compare in Hebrew, Ps. 119.136: *palgê mayim yārĕdû* ᶜ*ênay* ᶜ*al lô*ᵓ *šāmĕrû tôrātékā*, "streams (lit. canals) of water run down (from) my eyes, because they do not keep thy law."

[180]Same idiom in Hebrew; *GKC*, §158a.

[181]Same idiom in Hebrew; *GKC*, §158b.

[182]Same idiom in Hebrew; *GKC*, §158b–c.

X. CONDITIONAL SENTENCES

As in Hebrew, there are three ways of expressing a conditional sentence in the Byblian letters, all specifically Canaanite: 1) simple juxtaposition of two clauses;[183] 2) two clauses coordinated by *u*;[184] 3) introduction of a protasis by *šumma*[185] or *inūma* (= *kī*).[186]

Simple juxtaposition: *yānum awīla lā tīṣa ana šāšunu*, "there is no one if thou comest not forth to them" (362.29–30).

Coordinated clauses: *ālānu ana šāšunu u pašḫū*, "if they have (their) cities, then they will be at peace" (118.45–46).

Introduction of protasis by *šumma* or *inūma*:[187] *šumma ana aḫiya tišaʾilu u taḳbu ālu*, "if thou makest inquiry concerning my brother, then the city will say ..." (89.39–41); *inūma* 1 *ḫāzānu libbušu itti libbiya u udabbira* ...," if there were one governor whose heart were (one) with my heart, then I would drive out ..." (85.66-69).

There are only eleven exceptions, aside from 362.29–30 noted above, to the general rule that the apodosis of the conditional sentence is introduced by *u*. One apodosis is introduced by *šanīta(m)* (93.21), but in view of *šanīta(m)* introducing the protasis in lines 18–19, it seems the scribe was confused and we may discount the use of *šanīta(m)* as significant. The other ten merely join the apodosis immediately to the protasis: *šumma libbi šarri bali uššar ṣābi piṭati yašpur* ..., "if the mind of the king is not to send an archer-host, let him write ..." (117.59–60); cf. also 83.27–30, 103.55–57, 104.31–32, 108.56–58, 112.16–18, 112.30–39, 117.32–33, 119.17–18, 130.44–46. The *u* introducing the apodosis is, of course, the so called *waw of apodosis* of the Hebrew grammarians.[188] The exact significane of this conjunction will be noted shortly.

[183] *GKC*, §159b.

[184] *Ibid.*

[185] The use of *šumma*, of course, is Accadian, but the syntax of *šumma* clauses is Canaanite, as will be clear from the following analysis.

[186] Cf. *GKC*, §159 L.

[187] As is often the case in Hebrew (*GKC*, *ibid.*), it is virtually impossible to point to any real difference of meaning in the use of *šumma* or *inūma*; "supposing that" might be the best translation of the latter in its three occurrences (85.66–69, 119.18–23, 362.33–37).

[188] Cf. *GHB*, §176. The fact that the conjunction is so used at Boğazköy (Labat, p. 78) and Nuzi (C. H. Gordon, "The Dialect of the Nuzu Tablets," *Orientalia* NS 7,

The verb of the protasis may be:

1) *yaqtulu* (15 examples). *šumma lā tutēruna awata(m)* ..., "if thou dost not send back word ..." (83.47–48); cf. also 73.11–14, 89.15–17, 89. 39–41, 93.19–23, 103.51–54, 112.14–15, 112.16–18, 112.18–24, 114.23–25, 114.44–46, 116.34–35, 117.32–33, 131.15–17, 362.9–11. That *yaqtulu* is not due to tense considerations, although all our examples are conditions referring to the present or future, is clear from two facts: 1) the use of perfects in the protasis, again with present or future meaning; 2) the use of the infinitive absolute, of itself timeless, but again when functioning as the verb of a protasis a present or a future. What then is the force of *yaqtulu* in the protasis?

To answer this question we must remember what is the nature and use of *yaqtulu*, that is, that it is essentially a form expressing continued action with a derived use we have called circumstantial. Now many of the examples of *yaqtulu* in the protasis (93.19–23, 116.34–35, 117.32–33, etc.) *in themselves* do not call for any idea of continued or repeated action. It follows that *yaqtulu* is used in a protasis, not to express continued action independently of the apodosis, but *precisely in relation to the apodosis*. In other words, its function in a protasis is to express action circumstantial or attendant to the action of the apodosis. Hence it is very similar to our use of the participle in English in a sentence like "Sitting there, he is/will be/would have been cold," in which "sitting" = "if he sits, will sit, had sat." As we have already seen, such a circumstantial usage accords perfectly with the nature of the form, and, incidentally, these additional examples confirm our analysis of *yaqtulu* as a form expressing circumstantial or attendant action.

2) *qata/i,ula* (7 examples). *šumma kīʾama ḳalāta adi tilḳūna āl ṣumura*, "if thou art thus negligent, they will take Simyra besides" (104.31–32); cf. also 83.27–30, 103.55–57, 104.43–51, 107.32–34, 119.17–18, 119.18–23, 132.46–48. It is purely fortuitous that we have no example of a *qatala* as the verb of a protasis.

When the perfect is employed in the protasis, the latter is not viewed, as is the case with *yaqtulu* in the protasis, as circumstantial to

---

p. 47) is here no argument against considering this idiom as native Byblian. The idiom is too well attested in, and in its frequency, peculiarly (Brockelmann, *Grundriss* II, p. 634, §432) Northwest Semitic not to reflect in the Byblian letters local practice. The Boğazköy and Nuzi usage (which is contrary to that of standard Acc.) merely shows how profoundly Northwest Semitic influenced the *lingua franca* of the Near East.

the apodosis, but rather as a *datum*, a *fact*, consequent upon which the apodosis follows. This alternate view of the protasis is easily understood if one remembers that essentially the conditional sentence consists of two coordinate clauses (see below).

This explains the illusion of the perfect's being used like the Lat. future perfect, that is, with the aspect of completion.[189] Thus one might be tempted to explain *ḳalāta* in the example above as a perfect to express the anteriority of the negligence to the taking of the cities. Many examples, however, prove this wrong: *šumma šarru bēlī lā yušaru ṣāba piṭata(m) u nīnū nimut*, "if the king, my lord, does not send an archer-host, then we will die" (362.9–11). On the hypothesis of the perfect = Lat. future perfect we should have here *uššir* (Lat. *miserit*). Compare too *ibaš(š)at* (103.56) where the perfect is *contemporaneous* (!) with the verb of the apodosis. The Canaanite use of the "tenses" simply does not fit into such a framework. In the first example (*šumma kīʾama ḳalāta adi tilḳūna* ...), we could just as well have had *taḳulu*.

3) *yaqtula* (4 examples). *inūma imūta minū yinaṣ(ṣ)aruše*, "if I die, what/who will guard it (Byblos)?" (130.50–52); cf. also 88.34–35, 114.67–68, 362.33–37. The use of the volitive in conditional sentences will be commented on at more length in our discussion of the Subjunctive. Suffice it here to point to the excellent parallels in Hebrew for the use of a volitive both in protasis and apodosis of conditional sentences.[190]

4) The infinitive (8 examples). *paṭārima šūta(m) u yānu ša yūbalu*, "if he leaves, then there will be no one to carry ..." (113.40–41; for the other examples, see the section on the infinitive). The use of the infinitive is analogous to that of the perfect, both merely stating the fact of the action; cf. *paṭārima* above with *paṭra* (83.28).[191]

5) A participle (1 example). *šumma šarru zāʾir ālišu u īzibaši*, "if the king hates his city, then I will abandon it" (126.44–45). The use of the participle is analogous to that of *yaqtulu*, both expressing action circumstantial to the apodosis.

[189]*GKC*'s *futurum exactum*; cf. §159n.

[190]Cf. *GKC*, §159d–e. *yīṣana* (77.27), *tiḳbī* (83.45), *irām* (123.23) are probably neither *yaqtula* nor *yaqtul*, but Acc. for *yaqtulu*. These are the only three forms not accounted for in our treatment of the protasis—we must allow for the influence of Accadian in these letters.

[191]Compare the use of the infinitive absolute in the Karatepe inscriptions as a narrative form for the past; cf. Gordon, *JNES* 8, p. 112, comment. on line 3.

6) An impersonal expression like *damiḳ*, "it is good" (107.20–24), or *yānu* (79.18–19, 82.41–45, 93.25–28, etc.), or a phrase like *libbi šarri*, "it is the desire of the king" (85.66–69, 108.56–58, 112.30–39, etc.).

As in Hebrew, there is a large variety of verbal forms possible in the apodosis: 1) an imperative—*šumma damiḳ ina pānika u šukun ...*, "if it is pleasing in thy sight, then place ..." (107.20–22; cf. also 112.30–39, 114.23–25, 114.44–46, 116.34–35, 123.23–26, 129.49–50, 130.44–46); 2) a jussive—*šumma libbi šarri bēlī bali uššar ṣābi piṭati yašpur*, "if the mind of the king is not to send an archer-host, let him write ..." (117.59–60; cf. also 83.27–30); 3) *yaqtula*—*inūma* 1 *ḫāzānu libbušu itti libbiya u udabbira*, "if there were one governor whose heart was (one) with my heart, then I would drive out ..." (85.66–69); 4) a perfect—*šumma ... ul yīṣana ṣābu piṭati u innipšat kalī mātāti ...*, "if ... the archer-host does not come forth, then all lands will be joined ..." (77.26–29; cf. also 82.41–45, 83.45–47, 83.47–50, 88.29–32, 112.18–24);[192] 5) *yaqtulu*—*šumma awātēya tušmu adi yulḳu* m·*azaru*, "if my words are heeded, Aziru will yet be taken" (117.32–33, *passim*). The use of "tenses" here follows the general principles already set down.

The conditional sentence is essentially two independent clauses. This follows from our discovery that *šumma* means both "if" and "behold" in the Byblian letters.[193] Not that the nature of the conditional sentence had not long been suspected by scholars.[194] As most recently pointed out by E. A. Speiser,[195] the close connection between Arabic *ʾin* and *ʾinna*, Aramaic *hen*, Syriac *ʾen*, Hebrew *hēn* and *hinnēh* is obvious. Moreover, in Ugaritic *hm* pretty clearly means "if" and "behold," though the evidence has not been accepted by all as conclusive.[196] But with *šumma* having the two meanings in the Byblian letters, there can

[192]Albright has identified the sequence *yaqtulu* (protasis)/*qatala* (apodosis) as Canaanite; *BASOR* 87, p. 34, n.16.

[193]For references, see Particles I E.

[194]Reckendorf, p. 353, §128; p. 682, §227; Brockelmann, *Grundriss* II, p. 635, §419.

[195]*JCS* 1, p. 324. Speiser overlooked South Arabic where *hn* is both a particle meaning "behold" and introductory of protases; Höfner, p. 173, §229 and p. 185, §142. At Goetze's suggestion, he explains Acc. *šumma* as original *šuʾ-ma* > *šumma* (with assimilation of the aleph), that is, a demonstrative particle plus the enclitic particle *-ma*.

[196]*UH*, p. 91, §12.3; p. 94, §12.7.

be no reason for hesitating to ascribe both meanings to Ugaritic *hm*.[197] Moreover, the syntactical relationship of protasis and apodosis in early Canaanite is now certain.

With the nature of the conditional sentence understood,[198] two facts about conditional sentences become clear: 1) the so-called *waw of apodosis*—the conditional sentence consisting essentially of two independent clauses, the use of the conjunction between them was natural;[199] 2) the omission of the conditional particle—since it basically meant only "behold," and did not formally subordinate the first member to the second, it could be omitted without any appreciable change of meaning.

[197]Correct therefore Brockelmann, *Grundriss* II, p. 635, §419, where he says interjections of the *m* stem (like Heb. *ʾim*) have been completely lost in West Semitic, retaining only conditional meaning. This is not true of Ugaritic, and almost certainly not of Byblian, though we cannot be certain just what particle was being used in the 14th century.

[198]Correct *GKC*, §159w, therefore, where *hēn* with the meaning "if" is considered to be probably a pure Aramaism.

[199]See n. 92. In South Arabic *f(a)* regularly introduces the apodosis if the verb is an imperfect; Höfner, p. 185, §142. The same is true in classical Arabic, regardless of the verb form of the apodosis, as already noted by medieval Hebrew grammarians; cf. S. R. Driver, p. 248. However, Driver did not understand the function of either *fa* in Arabic or *wĕ* in Hebrew, as he shows by his statement (p. 224) that, though the use of the jussive in protases of conditional sentences is intelligible if there is no introductory particle, its use in the same clause, if introduced by a particle, rules out the genuine volitive sense of the verb. In other words, he believed that the introductory particle formally subordinated its clause.

XI. Temporal Clauses

There are only 31 examples of clauses that we can with confidence interpret as temporal. Most of these conform to ordinary Acc. idiom, and hence cannot be of use in determining the idiom of Byblos. For example, the use of *ina* with an infinitive (69.25, 112.41, 119.15, 130.49–50), though excellent Canaanite,[200] is likewise good Accadian.[201] However, there are several types of temporal clause which either are specifically Canaanite or which we may interpret as reflecting Can. idiom, even though the idiom is known in Acc.

1) Introduction of temporal clauses by *inūma*: *tīdī parṣaya inūma ibaš(š)āta ina āl ṣumura,* "thou knowest my way of acting when thou wast in Simyra" (73.39–41); *inūma ušširti* 2 [lú]*mār šipri ana āl ṣumura u ukal(l)ī awīli(m)*[li(m)] *annū,* "when I sent the two messengers to Simyra, I detained this man" (108.46–49); *awīla šaprātī ... ana abika inūma yilakuna* [m.]*amanappa ina sābi*[pl.] *ṣiḫri,* "I sent a man ... to thy father when Amanappa came with a small force" (117.21–24); cf. also 119.20–22, 362.42–44. Though *inūma* in a temporal sense is good Accadian, still in view of the definitely Canaanite treatment of *inūma* (= *kī*) throughout these letters, we cannot be wrong in considering *inūma* as again the equivalent of Can. *kī* in its temporal use. Cf. Ugar. *k*,[202] Heb. *kî*.[203]

2) Almost certainly reflecting Can. idiom is the use of *adi* in the sense of "while" in 82.45; cf. the use of *ᶜad* in II Sam. 14.19. *u ītizib āla u paṭrātī u balṭat napištiya adi īpišu*[204] *ipēš libbiya,* "I will abandon the city and depart, and my life will be safe while I do what I want to do" (82.43–46).

3) The temporal clause may be expressed by the infinitive used as a finite verb: *kašādima awīliya u rakšašu,* "when my man arrived, then he bound him" (116.27–28).[205]

[200] Cf. *UH*, p. 68, §9.22; p. 83, §10.4. In Hebrew, cf. Ex. 3.12, 16.13; Lev. 23.43; Deut. 23.5, 24.9, 25.17; Jos. 2.10, 5.13; Ju. 5.2,4.

[201] Cf., e.g., *Gilg.*, XI, 97: *mimmū šēri ina namāri,* "at the break of dawn."

[202] *UH*, pp. 91–92, §12.3.

[203] *GKC*, §164d.

[204] On *īpišu* as 1st sg. impf., cf. *JCS* 2, Comm. no. 31 [below, Paper 2, p. 139].

[205] For this use of the infinitive and further analysis, see section on Infinitive [pp. 54–56 in the present volume].

4) The temporal clause may be expressed by a coordinate clause: *miya irāmu u amūta*, "who will be loyal when I die" (114.68). The same idiom is common in Hebrew.[206] Contrast *inūma imūta minū yinaṣ(ṣ)aruše*, "when I die, what (who?) will guard it?" (130.50–52).—To be included here are the two examples of a coordinate clause with a pleonastic negative in 82.10–12,16–17, both best translated by "as soon as": *u* lú.pl.*ḫāzānūtu ul tišmūna mimma u šaprū*, "and as for the governors, as soon as they hear anything, they write to him"; *u lā kašid irēšu u ušširtīšu*, "as soon as the request arrives, I will send him ..." The same idiom is found in Heb.[207]

5) Undoubtedly Canaanite is the use of *ina ūmi* and *ana ūmi*, not in the literal sense of "on the day," but in the sense of "when." With *ina ūmi*, like *bĕyôm* in Hebrew,[208] we probably have[209] the infinitive: *ina ūmi*kam[210] *paṭār ṣābi* KI.KAL.KIB *bēliya nakrū gabbu*, "when the KI.KAL.KIB force departed, all became hostile" (106.47–49). With *ana ūmi* we have the indicative: *ana ūmi tūṣu u in(n)ipušat gabbi mātāti ana šarri bēliya*, "when thou comest forth, then all lands will be joined to the king, my lord" (362.62–64). Cf. the use of *bĕyôm* with the perf. in Lev. 7.35.

As for the use of "tenses," they are in general accord with our analysis of *qatala* and *yaqtulu*. The use of the volitive *yaqtula* in 114.68 and 130.50–52 should be noted. The construction is that of a protasis in a conditional sentence, and hence the clause might best be termed "temporal-conditional." The difference in meaning between "when I die, who will ..." and "if I die, who will ..." is of course slight, and in many languages the construction of temporal clauses is largely based on that of conditional sentences. Compare the use of *ʾim* in Heb. with the meaning of "when,"[211] the construction of temporal clauses in Greek (ὅταν,

[206] *GKC*, §164a.

[207] The idiom with the pleonastic negative and the Heb. parallels have already been discussed under the Particles. It should be remarked that Heb. syntacticians have failed to note this construction and its clear temporal force.

[208] Cf. Ges.-Buhl[13], p. 315b. Though noted in the lexicon, this use of *bĕyôm* is not treated in the grammar. In Ugar. *b-ym* also means "when." Failure to recognize this has led astray interpreters of several Ugaritic passages; cf. *BASOR* 94, p. 35, n. 39.

[209] "Probably," in view of Heb. idiom; but *paṭar* may be a perfect.

[210] On the use of *kam* as a time-determinative, cf. Böhl, p. 10, §4d.

[211] *GHB*, §166p.

ἐπειδάν, etc.), etc. The use of *yaqtula* in conditional clauses is discussed under the subjunctive.

Finally, as in Hebrew, note the general, though not universal, use of the so-called *waw of apodosis* in the examples above, introducing the main clause. Our preference for the term *waw of succession* is confirmed by this usage in temporal clauses.[212]

[212]Cf. discussion of the Nature of the Perfect, *ad fin.* [pp. 37–38 in the present volume].

XII. RESULT CLAUSES

Consequence or result of one action upon another is expressed in two ways: 1) by means of the conjunction *u* (= *wa*), formally coordinating two clauses but of which the second is a result of and logically subordinate to the first; 2) by means of *inūma* (= *kī*). Both are paralleled in Hebrew and Ugaritic.[213] The verb is either *yaqtulu* (continued action) or *qatala* (fact, narrative present perfect or historical perfect).[214]

As in Hebrew and Ugaritic, such clauses are especially frequent after (rhetorical or indignant) questions.

Examples with u: *minū* m·*abdaširta ardu kalbu u yilḳu māt šarri ana šāšu*, "what is ᶜAbd-Ashirta, the slave (and) dog, that he is taking the land of the king for himself" (71.16–19); *ana minī ḳalāta u tulḳu mātka*, "why art thou negligent so that thy land is being taken" (83.15–16); *minū šūta(m)* m·*abdaširta kalbu u yubaᵓu laḳā ālāni šarri šamši ana šāšu*, "what is he, ᶜAbd-Ashirta the dog, that he (should) desire to take the cities of the king, the Sun, for himself?" (76.11–14); cf. also 79. 45–46, 85.63–65, 88.10, 91.4, 104.17–24, 116.67–69, 122.38–40, 125.40–45).

Examples with inūma: *šar māt mitan(n)a u šar māt kašše šūta(m) inūma yubaᵓu laḳā māt šarri ana šāšu*, "is he the king of the Mitanni or the king of the Cassians that he (should) desire to take the land of the king for himself" (76.14–16; compare 76.11–14 cited above); *atta ḳalāta ana ālānika inūma yiltiḳūšunu* lúGAZpl., "thou art negligent of thy cities so that the Ḫapiru are taking them" (90.23–25); *miya šunu inūma īpušū arna u dakū rābiṣa zūkina* m·*puwura*, "who are they that they (can) commit crime—for they have killed the commissioner (*sōkinu*) Puwuru" (362.68–69); cf. also 84.7–10, 92.41, 129.7–8.

213*GKC*, §166a–b; *UH*, p. 98, §13.54,58.

214The *yaqtul* in 88.10 (*ippuš*), also expressing continued action, is isolated and may safely be regarded as a pure Acc. form for a Can. *ippušu*.—*GKC*, §166, fail to distinguish between *intended* result and pure result clauses. The former are virtually the same as purpose clauses and take the same construction; see the examples of *yaqtula* expressing intended result under the Subjunctive. The latter are result clauses *stricto sensu*. Note that in South Arabic the energic, which is normal in final clauses (Höfner, p. 76, §62), is never used in result clauses (*ibid*., p. 75, §61). This agrees strikingly with our analysis of result clauses in Byblian in which a volitive never expresses result.

XIII. The Expression of Purpose

There are two ways of expressing purpose found in the Byblian letters. The first is to use *ana* (twice *aššum*) with the infinitive. Thus: *ana naṣār āl šarri* (79.15–16, etc.); *ana šutēr awati* (108.49–50), *ana ṣabātišu* (108.64), etc.; *aššum ṣabāt elippētīya* (114.19–20), *aššum abāli* (113.38). Since, however, such usage is good Accadian, no certain conclusions can be drawn for Byblian usage.

The second is specifically Canaanite, though similar to Acc. In Acc., besides *ana* or *aššum* with the infinitive, one may use the precative. This is much like the Can. use of a volitive, but three facts, apart from detailed analysis, show us that the syntax of purpose clauses in these letters is Byblian, not Accadian: 1) the use of the indicative according to definite rules; 2) the extremely rare use of *lu*; 3) the use of the allative as a subjunctive.[215]

The first rule of purpose clauses is that an indicative *never* expresses purpose except when virtually dependent on another indicative, so that if the governing verb is a volitive, purpose in a following clause can only be expressed by another volitive, never by an indicative.[216] Since this involves us in the problem of the nature of the form *taqtulu* when used with plural subjects—that is, is it sg. or pl.?—we will first confine our analysis to verbs with a singular subject. Their number is sufficiently great that with them as a basis we may safely induce to the fundamental principle underlying the syntax of purpose clauses.

First, singular indicatives used to express purpose: *ana minīm ḳalāta u lā tiḳbu ana šarri u yuwaš(š)iruna ṣāba piṭati u tiltiḳuna āl ṣumura*, "why are thou negligent and dost thou not speak to the king that he may send an archer-host and that it may take Simyra" (71.10–16);[217] *ana minīm ḳalāta u lā taḳbu ana šarri bēlika u tūṣana ḳadu*

[215]The subjunctive will be analyzed in detail in the following section.

[216]Joüon, *GHB*, §116, has established the existence of the same law in Biblical Hebrew. Orlinsky, who seems to have been unaware of Joüon's work, has made a more detailed study; *JQR* NS 31, pp. 371–382; 32, pp. 191–205, 273, 277. In view of the evidence from Amarna on purpose clauses and its use of *yaqtula*, I believe he is correct in using textual criticism to explain away the apparent exceptions to the rule. Blake, however, does not agree; *JBL* 65, p. 53, n. 8.

[217]That *ḳabū* is followed by a purpose clause will be shown at the end of this section.

ṣābi piṭati u timaḳ(ḳ)utu muḫḫi māt amurri, "why art thou negligent and dost thou not speak to the king, thy lord, in order that thou mayest come forth along with an archer-host and fall upon the land of the Amorites" (73.6–11); *ul taḳbī ana bēlika u yuwaš(š)irunaka ina pāni ṣābi piṭati u tušamriru* $^{\text{lú.pl.}}$GAZ *ištu* $^{\text{lú.pl.}}$*ḥāzānūti,* "wilt thou not speak to thy lord in order that he send thee at the head of an archer-host and in order that thou mayest drive the Ḫapiru away from the governors" (77.21–25); *adi yupaḫ(ḫ)iru kalī ālāni u yilḳuše,* "he is again gathering together all the cities that he may capture it" (124.14–15); *ḳabītī kinan(n)a ana* $^{\text{m.}}$*pawura u lā yišmu ina awātē* $^{\text{m.}}$*ḫa*ᵓ*ip,* "I spoke thus to Pawura lest he heed the words of Haᵓip" (132.37–40); *inūma šapar bēlī ana taškarinnima ištu māt a<l>alḫi u ištu āl ugarite tulḳuna lāmi ili*ᵓ*u uššar* ^{giš}*elippētīya ana ašrānu,* "as to my lord's writing for beechwood (that) it be taken from Alalaḫ and Ugarit, I am not able to send my ships there" (126.4–8).[218]—It is to be noted that in each of these examples the indicative expressing purpose follows another indicative.

Secondly, examples of non-indicative singulars expressing purpose. The examples are too many to quote; we will give a few typical examples and only references to the rest. *yuḫam(m)iṭa uššar ṣābi piṭati ṣarru u yilḳīšunu u tin(n)ipuš mātātu ana šarri bēliya,* "let the king hasten the despatching of the archer-host that he may capture them and the lands be joined to the king, my lord" (129.78–80); *uššira ṣāba piṭati u tilḳīšu u tapšuḫ māt šarri,* "send an archer-host that it may capture him and the land of the king be at peace" (107.29–31); *yuwaš(š)ira šarru* ^{lú}*rābiṣašu u yupar(r)aš bērikuni,* "let the king send his commissioner to decide between us" (113.17–18). Cf. also *ennipuš* (68.17), *yiz(z)iz* (74.61), *tudab(b)ir* (76.39), *īdī* (83.8, 85.59, etc.), *nuballiṭ* (85.38), *tuṣabat* (85. 46), *yilḳīši* (90.12), *nidag(g)al* (93.12), *īrub* (102.31), *yušamrir* (103.30), *yupar(r)iš* (117.67), *tilḳīnī* (114.46), *tin(n)ipuš* (117.94), *yušapšiḫ* (118. 44), *tīpuš* (122.47), *yinaṣ(ṣ)arši* (126.48).[219]

Analysis of all these examples shows that all of them are dependent on volitives. It is interesting to compare the indic. *timaḳ(ḳ)utu* which

[218]In view of the fact that *yaqtula* is used three times after *šapāru,* this construction is almost certainly that of a purpose clause.

[219]We have not included here all the examples of *yaqtula* expressing purpose. These will be studied in the following section. Suffice it here to say that they offer the strongest confirmation possible of the rule indicative-indicative/volitive-volitive.

depends on *tiḳbu* (73.6ff.) with *yadina* (93.11) which depends upon the imperative *ḳibāmi*; or the ind. *tiltiḳuna* which depends on *taḳbu* (71. 10ff.) with *tilḳī* dependent upon the imperative *uššira* (107.29ff.); or the ind. *ilḳu* dependent on *yupaḫ(ḫ)iru* (124.14ff.) with *yilḳī* dependent upon the imperative *milik* (90.11ff.). This shift from *yaqtulu* to *yaqtul(a)* when the governing verb is a volitive is a strong indication that the dependent verb is also volitive.

Another indication is the fact that twice after volitives we find the verb form with *lu*: *ušširammi* [lú]*mār šiprika ittiya ana maḫar šarri bēlika u lū lid(d)inaku ṣāba u narkabāti izirtam ana kāta(m)*, "send thy messenger to me in the presence of the king, thy lord, that he may give thee an army and chariots as help for thee" (87.9–13); *lid(d)inam bēliya ... u lū anaṣ(ṣ)ar māt bēliya adi aṣī ṣābi piṭati rabīti*, "let my lord give me ... that I may guard the land of my lord until the coming forth of the mighty archer-host" (127.35–39).

Finally, the fact, already noted, that we *never* have *yaqtulu* expressing purpose if the governing verb is a volitive, is conclusive evidence that verbs expressing purpose, dependent on volitives, are likewise volitive.

It is in the light of this conclusion that we must examine apparent exceptions to this rule. First, verbs with sg. subjects; secondly, verbs with plural subjects.

uššira ṣāba piṭati rabā u tudab(b)ir ayābī šarri ištu libbi mātišu u tin(n)ipšū kalī mātāti ana šarri (76.38–43). As has been shown in our treatment of verbal agreement, the phrase *kalī mātāti* may be construed as a singular or a plural. Hence *tin(n)ipšū* in this case is a plural, and therefore belongs in the second category. In 92.47 we may have [*lu-wa*]-*ši-ru* after the volitive *litriṣ*, but since the whole context is badly damaged we cannot be certain, and perhaps we should read [*ú-wa*]-*ši-ru*. In 94.11 Knudtzon reads *ti-el-ḳú*, which is dependent on the imperative *ušširami*. However, the autograph has *ti-el*-X. Moreover, in 107.30 and 114.46, both dependent on *uššira*, we have *tilḳī*; the indicative occurs only after another indicative in 71.10ff. In 132.15 *tulḳu* might at first sight be interpreted as dependent on *ušširami* (l. 13). However, as Knudtzon recognized and the phrase "in a day" shows, *tulḳu* is in an independent clause: thus, "Send a royal archer-host. In a day the entire land will be taken" (132.13–16). Finally, in 112.33–35 (also 130.46–48) we read: *uššira maṣ(ṣ)arta u tinaṣ(ṣ)arū ālaka*, "send a garrison that it may guard thy city." This certainly looks like an ind. (3rd fem. sg.) dependent on a volitive. However, *maṣ(ṣ)artu* is always construed as a plural in these letters, and hence the suffix *-šunu* referring to a *maṣṣartu* in 79.33 and 117.81. Note too 136.17–20: *uššira* UN/*maṣ(ṣ)arta ana ardika u lū tinaṣ(ṣ)arū āla*. The particle *lū* clearly shows the form *tinaṣ(ṣ)arū* must be a volitive, which it cannot be if the form is singular, in which case the short vowel would drop. Note too 263.24 *awīlūta / maṣṣarta*. Hence *tinaṣ(ṣ)arū* of 112.35 belongs below with verbs with plural subjects.

1) *luwaš(š)ira bēliya awīlūta u tilḳū mimmi*$^{\text{pl. g.}}$DA.MU-*ya ana maḫar bēliya u ul iltiḳa mimma*$^{\text{pl.}}$ *ša ilānika kalbu šūta(m)*, "may my lord send men in order to take the possessions of my Adonis to the king lest that dog take the possessions of thy god" (84.31–35); 2) *yadina* 4 *mē awīlūti* 30 *tapal sisē kīma nadāni ana* $^{\text{m.}}$*zurata u tinaṣ(ṣ)arū āla ana kāta(m)*, "let him give 400 men and 30 teams of horses, as are given to Zurata, in order that they may guard the city for thee" (85.19–22); 3) *ušširammi* ^{lú}*mār šiprika ittiya ana maḫar bēlika u lū lid(d)inaku ṣāba u narkabāti izirtam ana kāta(m) u tiṣ(ṣ)urū āla*, " ... that they may guard the city" (87.9–14; cf. also 88.40–42); 4) *yaḳbī šarru ana* 3 *ālāni u* ^{giš}*elippi awīlūt* MIŠI *u lā tilakū ana māt amurri*, "may the king give orders to the three cities and the ship of the MIŠI men lest they go to the land of the Amorites" (101.32–35); 5) *yaḳbī šarru ana šāšunu u tupar(r)išū bērikuni*, "let the king give orders to them that they may decide between us" (116.32–33); 6) *yūšira bēlī* 3 *mē ṣābi* 30 *narkabāti* ... *u tinaṣ(ṣ)arū āl gubli*, "let my lord send 300 soldiers, 30 chariots ... that they may guard the city of Byblos" (131.12–14); 7) for 76.38–43, 112.33–36 and 130.46–48, see above.

Concerning these examples note: 1) forms with a final *u* after a volitive are confined to verbs with plural subject; 2) in the first example, when the shift is to the singular subject (*kalbu šūta*[*m*]), then the verb is *iltiḳa*,[220] not *iltiḳū*; 3) in the two parallels to the 5th example where the subject is singular (113.18, 117.67) the form is *yupar(r)a / iš*, not *yupar(r)a / išū*; 4) the ending *-na* is never attached to these forms, though, as we have seen in our study of verbal agreement, it is most common with plural subjects. This reflects the same usage as Arabic where the jussive and subj. pl. never have the ending *-na* in the plural.[221] These facts, coupled with the evidence already gathered in

[220]As will be shown in the following section, *yiltiḳa* is a volitive.

[221]Thus I find it difficult to agree with Albright's rendering of *tūdanūna* as "let them be given" in Taanach II, 20; *BASOR* 94, p. 23. Whether it be singular or

connection with purpose clauses and the other evidence for a plural *taqtulū(na)* brought forward in our treatment of verbal agreement, make it certain that these forms are plural and not singular.

Negative purpose clauses are introduced by *u lā* and (*u*) *ul*: *šupšiḫ māta u lā yinam(m)ušū ištu muḫḫika*, "pacify the land lest they fall away from thee" (113.33–35); *yaḳbi šarru ... u lā tilakū*, "let the king order ... lest they go" (101.32–34); *ḳabītī ... u lā yišmu*, "I ordered lest he heed" (132.37–39); *palḫātī* $^{\text{lú.pl.}}$*ḫupšī ul timaḫ(ḫ)aṣananī*, "I fear (my) serfs lest they strike me down" (77.36–37); *lā iliʾu uššar<šu> ul yišma* $^{\text{m.}}$*abdaširta*, "I cannot send him lest ᶜAbd-Aširta hear (of it)" (82.21–23); *uššira* $^{\text{lú.pl.}}$*maṣ(ṣ)arta ana mātika ul tuṣabat ālka*, "send a garrison to thy land lest thy city be taken" (85.45–46).

It is impossible to determine if *u lā* = Byblian **walôʾ*, *ul* = Byblian **ʾal*. If they do, then in Byblian, as in Hebrew,[222] **walôʾ* with the indicative has invaded the proper sphere of **ʾal* with the volitive. Hence we would have to consider *yinam(m)ušū* and *tilakū* above as indicative plural rather than jussive plural. However, since *ul* is often construed in the Byblian letters with the indicative and *lā* with the jussive,[223] and since there is really nothing in the above examples to support such a stand, it is much more probable that these forms are jussives. Hence the rule of ind.-ind./vol.-vol. holds in negative purpose clauses with the one exception of *yišma* in 82.21–23, which is to be explained immediately.

Secondly, though there is not one exception to the rule that an indicative expresses purpose only if dependent upon another indicative, rarely a volitive expresses purpose though dependent on a preceding indicative. This is the rule after verbs of fearing, but since these are implicit volitives, there is nothing unusual in a volitive following them. However, note in addition the following: *aštappar ana ēkalli u yuwaš(š)ara šarru ṣāba rabā*, "I wrote to the palace that the king might send a large host" (117.24–27); *ašpuru ana ēkalli ana maṣ(ṣ)ar u awīlūt māt miluḫ(ḫ)a u lā ibluṭa* $^{\text{m.}}$*danuna*, "I write to the palace for a garrison and men from Miluhha that Danuna may not be saved" (117.90–92);

---

plural the jussive form could not be *tuqtaluna*. If singular, it would be *tuqtal* (not *tuqtalna*); if plural, *tuqtalu*. Render perhaps, "they should be given," *yaqtulu* being used where we would render by a slight modal nuance; see *The Use of Yaqtulu(na)* (§IV D, above) [pp. 41–46 in the present volume].

[222] *GHB*, §116j.

[223] In the same letter *ul* and *lā* with the jussive (68.30,14). For *ul* with the indicative, cf. 73.18, 74.50, etc.

ašpur u tūṣa ṣābu piṭatu u tilḳī ᵐ·*abašunu*, "I wrote to the palace that an archer-host come forth and take Abashunu" (362.18–20); add *yišma* in 82.21–23 quoted above.—The first two examples have the volitive *yaqtula* form, the latter two may be *yaqtula* or *yaqtul*—in my opinion, more probably *yaqtula*. The use of a volitive to express purpose after an indicative is just as rare in Hebrew.[224]

Thirdly, we should note the idiom which has a purpose clause as the object of a verb of commanding where Accadian (and English) has an infinitive.[225] That the construction is one of purpose is clear from the fact that we have the same rule of modal congruence (ind.-ind./vol.-vol.) that is characteristic of the purpose construction. To quote only two examples—almost all have been quoted in the course of this analysis—*ḳibāmi ana šarri u yadina ana kāta(m)* ..., "urge upon the king to give thee ..." (93.10–13); *ḳabītī* ... *u lā yišmu*, "I ordered (him) not to heed ..." (132.37–39). Cf. in Hebrew *ʾĕmōr ʾel ʾelʿāzār* ... *wĕyārēm*, "tell Eleazar ... to lift up" (Nu. 17.2); *dabbēr ʾel ʾahărôn* ... *wĕʾal yābōʾ*, "tell Aaron ... not to enter" (Lev. 16.2).[226]

Fourthly, as in Hebrew,[227] we may have subordination without the use of the conjunction. Thus compare *uššira ṣāba piṭati u tilḳīšu* (117.29–30) and *luwaš(š)ira bēliya awīlūta u tilḳū* (84.31–32) with *uššira ṣāba piṭati tilḳīnī* (114.45–46).

Finally, it follows from the principle of modal congruence that subordination is really an inexact term to apply to the purpose clause. For the principle indicates that the second member is essentially paratactic

[224]*GHB*, §116c,e,g. However, for the possibility that *šapāru* is implicitly volitive, see following section.

[225]Cf. Latin *mando ut, mando ne*. Note that in South Arabic *nlk* and *nl*, both ordinarily used to introduce purpose clauses, also introduce indirect commands; Höfner, pp. 169–170, §127. "Die Grenze zwischen Final- und indirektem Befehlsatz ist ja oft fliessend."

[226]In view of the Amarna evidence, I am highly sceptical of the idiom pointed out by various Hebrew grammarians (*GKC*, §120f, §165a; *GHB*, §177j) according to which an historical statement is dependent on a verb of commanding. Though the MT pointing is in their favor, I believe the Masoretes were in error. The examples just cited (*wĕʾal yābōʾ*, etc.) are clearly not historical statements. Moreover, the parallelism in Gen. 42.25 (*wayṣaw yôsēp waymalĕʾû ʾet kĕlêhem bar ulĕhāšîb* ...) of *waymalĕʾû* and the infinitive *lĕhāšîb* is very suspicious. In all such cases I believe the correct pointing would be with *wĕ*; thus *wîmalĕʾû*, etc. As for examples like Am. 9.3 (*ʾăṣawwēh ʾet hannāḥāš unĕšākām*), I believe we should render "I will command the serpent, and it will bite them," not "to bite them" (Joüon).

[227]Cf. *GKC*, §120c, §165a.

to the first and not hypotactic. If the opposite were true, we should find *yaqtula*, a volitive and the Canaanite counterpart of the Arabic subjunctive, quite frequently after an indicative. The few cases we have seen of this indicate that virtually hypotactic structure was not unknown in Byblian, but at the same time their rarity shows that it was foreign to the common idiom. The possibility of expressing purpose by an asyndetic second member confirms this.

It is possible that, as in Hebrew, there were particles in Byblian which formally subordinated one member to another but which could not be used in the medium of Accadian. However, if this is true, it is most likely that they were rare, for as will be clear again and again in our study, Byblian syntax was essentially paratactic.[228]

[228]One apparent purpose construction calls for comment. For example, 123.33–35, 3 *awīlī ša šūrib* ᵐ·*piẖura uššira u balṭātī*, which one is tempted to translate, "send ... that I may be safe." Cf. also 83.27, 74.26, 74.27. In all of these examples the perfect seems to express purpose. For a similar difficulty cf. II Sam. 24.2 where *wĕyādaᶜtî* is paralleled in I Chron. 21.2 by *wĕʾēdĕᶜāh*. Joüon's position that *wĕqātaltî* is occasionally employed after a volitive to emphasize the fact of succession and that its purpose meaning is left implicit and to be derived from context seems the soundest; cf. *GHB*, §119i.

XIV. The Subjunctive

The question as to whether Northwest Semitic had a subjunctive corresponding to Arabic *yaqtula* is so far a mooted one. Ugaritic, with its clear distinction of *yaqtulu* and *yaqtul* forms, might have been expected to solve the problem but as yet the evidence is inconclusive.[229] Moreover, because of our dependence in this case on verbs *tertiae aleph* it is virtually certain that even if the form be attested with certainty, still the paucity of examples will preclude the possibility of a detailed syntactical analysis of its usage.

The Hebrew cohortative has also been compared to the Arabic subjunctive.[230] The Hebrew evidence alone does favor the possibility of the cohortative being a survival of the old subjunctive.[231] However, other and clearer evidence is required before the existence of a subjunctive in Northwest Semitic can become probable or certain.

The method followed by the writer in attacking this problem in the Byblian letters was to collect all instances of *yaqtula* and then, after careful analysis, to form as many categories of usage as the facts demanded. The outcome—to anticipate a bit—was a suprisingly small number of categories, with by far the largest being that of a volitive usage. It was only then that he approached the use of the subjunctive in Arabic, the cohortative in Hebrew, and, allowing for different dialectal developments, the use of the volitive in general in both Arabic and Hebrew.

We mention our method of handling the material, for we shall reverse this order in our presentation, beginning with the use of the subjunctive and jussive (in so far as it concerns us) in Arabic. Without

[229] *UH*, p. 61, §9.7; *DCD*, p. 8, n. 9.

[230] *B-L*, p. 273, §36d; *GHB*, p. 315, §116b, n. 1.

[231] As early as the late 18th century the cohortative was compared with the Latin subjunctive (Driver, p. 63, Obs. 1), but strangely enough the possibility of its connection with the Arabic subjunctive does not seem to have occurred to anyone. Driver, for instance, admits there is no vestige of the subjunctive in Hebrew; p. 49, §44. He relates the cohortative to the Arabic energic; p. 247. G. Driver, following Haupt, considers the Acc. allative ending *-a(m)* as the East Semitic counterpart of the Heb. cohortative; p. 77. It will follow as a necessary corollary of our analysis of *yaqtula* that Bauer, followed by Joüon, was correct in relating the cohortative to the Arabic subjunctive.

this explanation of method many points stressed by us might at first seem irrelevant.

Originally, according to Reckendorf, the use of the subjunctive was quite free.[232] Survivals of such usage are seen in poetry and in the frequent use of the subjunctive after *fa*, *wa*, and *ʾau*.[233] The development of the subjunctive, however, led to its general restriction to subordinate clauses introduced by a subordinating conjunction (*li*, *liʾan*, *kamā*, *ḥattā*, *likā*, *ʾan*, etc.).[234] In the vast majority of cases there is purposive force to the use of the subjunctive.[235]

To be noted under the use of the subjunctive with *ʾan* is that it is regular after expressions of desire, resolve, refusing, emotion, etc.; in short, after verbs which are, implicitly at least, volitive in character.[236]

The subjunctive may be used with *fa* (or *wa*, though more rarely) with purposive force[237] after 1) a negative proposition, 2) an imperative, 3) a negative command, 4) an interrogative clause, 5) particles of exhortation or reproach, 6) a wish, 7) an expression of hope.[238] It should be noted that nos. 2, 3, 5, 6, 7 are volitives.

The subjunctive is also used with *fa*, *wa*, or *ʾau* in the second member of a double protasis or apodosis. Note that the jussive has the same use.[239]

[232]Reckendorf, pp. 59–60, §32.

[233]*Ibid.*, p. 61, §34.

[234]*Ibid.*, pp. 730–745, §237–242.

[235]*Ibid.*, p. 730, §237.

[236]*Ibid.*, p. 740, §242. It is also used with verbs like *ḫāna*, *qalla*, etc., though there is no volitive force to such words. This represents, perhaps, a secondary development of *ʾan* with the subjunctive.

[237]By purposive force is to be understood not only clauses that we would render by "in order that ...," but also clauses of intended result. The same distinction is found in the use of the cohortative in Hebrew; cf. *GKC*, §108d. See Reckendorf's penetrating remarks on the use of the subjunctive after *ḥattā* (*op. cit.*, p. 734, §241) and *fa* (*ibid.*, p. 747, §244).

[238]Vernier, *Grammaire Arabe*, Tome II, p. 501, #1049; Wright-de Goeje II, p. 30, §15d. To be noted in connection with no. 4 (interrogative clause) is the use of the cohortative and jussive in Hebrew after questions; *GHB*, §116c,e.

[239]Vernier, *op. cit.*, p. 428, #983, no. 2–3; Wright-de Goeje II, p. 40, §17, Rem. c. Note also that after *ʾau* the subjunctive need not be in the second member of a protasis or an apodosis. Thus *laʾarḥalanna biġazwatin taḥwī lġanāʾima ʾau yamūta karīmun*, "I am going on a predatory expedition which will bring in booty, or a nobleman will die" (quoted by Reckendorf, pp. 750–751, §246). Reckendorf's long explanation of this use of the subjunctive is far from clear and it would seem to be purely *ad hoc*. Note that the jussive is used the same way, in

The use of the subjunctive, therefore, in Arabic indicates 1) that the subjunctive need not be confined to subordinate clauses, the evidence from the poets and the use of the subjunctive after *fa, wa, ʾau,* and in conditional sentences indicating that the general restriction to subordinate clauses is a specifically Arabic development; 2) the subjunctive is basically a volitive—hence used to express purpose—and in the vestiges of its earlier free use after *fa, wa,* and *ʾau* employed primarily in a volitive sequence.

Turning to the other Arabic volitive, the jussive, two facts are germane to the issue at hand: 1) not only the subjunctive expresses purpose, but the jussive also;[240] 2) the jussive is used both in protases and apodoses of conditional sentences, not only of the purely hypothetical type, but in those cases whose actuation is considered probable or possible.[241]

The Hebrew cohortative is striking not only by its similarity in form with the Arabic subjunctive—the *-a* ending could have another explanation—but especially by its usage, so similar to that of the Arabic subjunctive. It may be used as a volitive in the main clause expressing self-encouragement,[242] a wish, a request, etc.[243] It may express purpose in a virtually subordinate clause with or without *waw* as the introductory particle, especially when dependent on another volitive (an imperative, a jussive, another cohortative).[244] It is also used in conditional sentences, both in the protasis and the apodosis.[245] Its use to express purpose is identical with the use of the subjunctive in Arabic, and its use in conditional clauses is similar to the use of the subjunctive and jussive in Arabic. More important, however, for our present purpose than these striking parallels with the Arabic subjunctive is the amazing parallel

---

which case, says Reckendorf, the construction is that of a conditional sentence. There is absolutely no reason for considering this use of the subjunctive as different from that of the jussive.

[240]Reckendorf, p. 680, §226. The construction is limited to jussives joined asyndetically to a preceding imperative, but the purposive force of the jussive is clear ("... der Nachsatz stellt dann, wenn auch nicht der Form, so doch der Sache nach, den Endzweck dar"). S. R. Driver has pointed out the similarity of the Hebrew and Arabic idioms in this respect; p. 195.

[241]*Ibid.*, p. 686, §287.

[242]*GKC*, §108b.

[243]*Ibid.*, §108c.

[244]*Ibid.*, §108d.

[245]*Ibid.*, §108e–f.

between the use of the volitive *ʾeqtĕlāh* (*niqtĕlāh*) in Hebrew[246] and the use of *yaqtula* in the Byblian letters.

Turning, then, to the Byblos letters we are at once confronted with a problem: how distinguish the hypothetical Can. subjunctive from the Acc. allative or ventive? Morphologically there can be no distinction except that the allative may occasionally show the older form *yaqtulam*. It is clear, then, that usage, not form, must be our norm.

To prove that there is a subjunctive in these letters, we must show: 1) that *yaqtula* is reserved for the expression of a certain type of idea or for a certain syntactical situation, and this is in general accord with the use of the subjunctive in Arabic; 2) that *yaqtulu* and *yaqtula* are not used indiscriminately but that a shift from one to the other is significant.

Without tipping the scales in favor of the subjunctive I believe we may demand two concessions. First, if there are cases (and there are) where *yaqtula* is clearly only the Acc. allative, this in itself is not evidence against a subjunctive. The allative being peculiar to Acc. and of common usage, we must expect examples of it, and it is only if such examples are sufficiently numerous that they become significant in this study. Secondly, we consider it *legitimate* to include a few examples of *yaqtulam*, since, first, final *m* is often otiose in Amarna,[247] and secondly, we are primarily interested in usage. *Yaqtula(m)* would not be used so regularly if it did not have some basis in Accadian. What we wish to see is exactly *how* the scribes used it.

The overall statistics on the *yaqtula* forms in the Byblos letters are the following: out of 75 occurrences, 18 are used as jussives, 30 are used to express purpose, or intended result, 14 are verbs of an apodosis or a protasis in a conditional sentence, 5 are doubtful because of a damaged context, 8 can only be called allatives.

In themselves, apart from detailed analysis, these facts are significant, for they show that *yaqtula* found favor with the Byblian scribes only in a very restricted usage, that of a volitive. 48, almost 5/7 of all the examples, are clear volitives. Its use in conditional sentences may be paralleled by the use of the subjunctive and jussive in Arabic and by the use of the cohortative and jussive in Hebrew. Hence 62 of the 70

[246]The non-emphatic, non-volitive use of the cohortative with *waw conversive* is probably a later development; see Blake, *JBL* 63, p. 284. The plethora of cohortatives in the new Isaiah Scrolls (see Millar Burrows, *JBL* 68, p. 207) not found in the MT deserves close analysis.

[247]As for example, *awata(m)*, *nimūtu(m)*, *kāta(m)*, etc.

cases, that is, over 6/7 of the examples that can be interpreted, have excellent volitive parallels in Hebrew and Arabic. In the light of these facts it is difficult to avoid the conclusion that Byblian had a *yaqtula* volitive. The following detailed analysis, with its comparison of the use of *yaqtulu*, will bear this conclusion out and make it imperative.

NAṢĀRU

Purpose: *yubal(l)iṭ (šarru) ardašu u anṣ(ṣ)ara āl kit(t)išu*, "let the king give life to his servant that I may guard his loyal city" (74.55–56). *tadinnī ina ḳāt* $^{\text{m.}}$*yanḫami u yatina šeʾi(m) ana akāli yāši anaṣ(ṣ)ara āl šarri ana šāšu*, "put me under the charge of Yanḫamu that he may give me grain for food so I can guard the king's city for him" (83.30–33). *yuwaš(š)ira šarru sisī ana ana ardišu u anaṣ(ṣ)ara āl ṣarri*, "let the king send horses to his servant that I may guard the city of the king" (117.72–74). *šumma irām šarru bēli arad kit(t)išu u uššira* 3 *awīla u ibluṭa u inaṣ(ṣ)ira āla ana šarri*, "if the king, my lord, loves his loyal servant, then send the 3 men that I may live and guard the city for the king" (123.23–28).

With the use of *anaṣṣara*, etc., above contrast the use of the indicative *inaṣṣiru* as a simple statement of act or as the verb of an interrogative sentence in 119.15–16, 130.50, 112.10, 125.12, and especially in 123.32 with its shift from the volitive in line 27 (quoted above) to the indicative: *inūma išap(p)aru šarru uṣurmi ramānka ištu man(n)i inaṣ(ṣ)iruna*, "as to the king's writing, 'guard thyself,' with what shall I guard?" (123.29–32).—It should be noted that all the examples of *yaqtula* depend on volitives, the general rule in Hebrew for the use of the cohortative to express purpose and in Arabic for the subjunctive after *fa*.

PAḪĀRU

Purpose: *ušširūnanī* 50 *tapal sisī* ... *u iz(z)iza ina āl šigata ina pānišu adi aṣī ṣābi piṭati ul yupaḫ(ḫ)ira kalī* $^{\text{lú.pl.}}$GAZ$^{\text{pl.}}$, "send me 50 teams of horses ... that I may resist him in Shigata until the coming forth of the archer-host, lest he gather all the Ḫapiru" (71.23–28).

Intended Result: *yišmī šarru awātē ardišu yadina awīlūta ana naṣār ālišu ul yupaḫ(ḫ)ira kalī* $^{\text{lú.pl.}}$GAZ$^{\text{pl.}}$, "let the king hear the words of his servant so that he gives men to guard his city lest he gather all the Ḫapiru" (85.75–78).

Contrast *inan(n)a adi yupaḫ(ḫ)iru kalī ālāni u yilkuše*, "now he is again gathering all the cities that he may take it (Byblos)" (124.14–15). Here an indicative followed by an indicative to express purpose; above a jussive followed by two *yaqtula* forms, one expressing affirmative purpose, the other negative purpose. This accords perfectly with the hypothesis that *yaqtula* is a volitive, since we have already established on independent grounds that there is a principle of modal sequence underlying the purpose construction in these letters.

LAḲŪ

Purpose: *ul yupaḫ(ḫ)ira kalī* lú.pl.GAZpl. *u yilḳa āl šigata*, "... lest he gather all the Ḫapiru in order to take Shigata" (71.28–30). *lūwaš(š)ira bēliya awīlūta ... u ul iltiḳa mimma ša ilānika kalbu šut*, "let my lord send men ... lest that dog take anything belonging to thy god" (84.31–35). *tilḳa* (86.43) and *yilḳa* (91.6), both uncertain; tablets damaged.

Contrast *minū* m.*abdaširta ... u yilḳu māt šarri*, "what is ᶜAbd-Ashirta that he takes the land of the king" (71.16–19) with *yilḳa* in 71.30 quoted above, an especially significant shift since they both occur in the same letter; also 124.14–15, quoted above, with 71.28–30. The difference in the first is that it expresses simple consequence; in the second, that it expresses purpose dependent upon an indicative.

NADĀNU

Intended Result: *lišmī šarru awātē ardišu u yadina balāṭa ardišu*, "let the king hear the words of his servant so that he will give his servant's means of subsistence" (74.53–54). *lidmiḳ ina pāni šarri bēliya u yūdana(m)*[248] *šeʾi(m) mūṣa māt yarimuta ša yūdanu pānānu ina āl ṣumura yūdana(m) inan(n)a ina āl gubla*, "may it seem good to the king, my lord, so that the grain, the product of Yarimuta, be sold which was formerly sold in Simyra—that it be sold now in Byblos" (85.33–37). This latter example is very important, for in the same sentence we see the scribe shifting between *yaqtulu* and *yaqtula* as regularly as if he were writing Arabic! For other examples cf. 85.19–20, 85.76 (quoted above; see 1st example of purpose under *paḫāru*).

Purpose: *ḳibāmi ana šarri u yadina ana kāta(m)* 3 *mē awīlūti*, "speak to the king that he may give thee 300 men" (93.10–11). *uššira rābiṣa*

[248]*yūdana(m)* with a long *ū* on the analogy of the Qal passive of *Pe Waw* verbs in Arabic. See following note.

yišmē awātēya u yadina kit(t)iya ina ḳātiya, "send a commissioner to hear my words and give me my due" (118.14–17). *ḳibāmi ana bēlika u yūdana ana ardišu mūṣa ša māt yarimuta*, "speak to thy lord that the product of Yarimuta be given to his servant" (86.31–33). *tadinnī ina ḳāt* $^{\text{m.}}$*yanḫami u yatina šeʾi(m) ana akāli*, "put me under the charge of Yanḥamu that he may give grain to eat" (83.30–32).

Jussive: *yadina* $^{\text{lú.pl.}}$*maṣ(ṣ)ara ana naṣār arad kittišu*, "let him give a garrison to guard his loyal servant" (117.78–80). For other examples with jussive meaning, cf. 86.47, 118.11, 127.27.

For the real significance of all these examples, compare the following examples of the indicative. It will be noted that the same, or virtually the same, phrases are used (thus ruling out as significant the specifically Accadian force of the allative), the sole difference being that which exists between a volitive and a statement of fact. *šumma yadinu šarru ana ardišu u idin*, "if the king will give to his servant, then give!" (116.34–35). *pānānu awīlūtu maṣ(ṣ)arti šarri ittiya u šarru yadinu šeʾi(m) ištu māt yarimuta*, "previously a royal garrison was with me and the king would give grain from Yarimuta" (125.14–17). *u (šarru) ana yāši lāmi yadinu mimma*, "and the king gives nothing to me" (126.17–18); cf. also 105.85, 110.50.

Conditional: *šumma šarru yišaʾilu u nadna pānīnū ana arādika*, "if the king makes a request, then we will be devoted to thy service" (89. 15–17).[249] For a fuller discussion of a volitive in conditional sentences, see below.

(W)AŠĀRU

Purpose: *yaḳbī šarru u yuwaš(š)ira awīliya*, "let the king command that he send my man" (83.34–35).

Intended result: *litriṣ ina pāni bēlīya yuwaš(š)ira awīlašu*, "may it please the king so that he send his man" (74.59–61). *yišmī šarru*^{ru} *bēlī*^{li}

[249]The form *nadna* merits comment. Knudtzon by his translation shows that he considers the form 3rd sg. masc. perfect; Ebeling lists it in the Glossary (***EA*** II, p. 1478) as 3rd pl.! On Ebeling's side is the fact that the putative subject *pānīnū* is plural. Against it is the wrong case-ending; we should have *pānūnū*. The same objection must be made against Knudtzon's interpretation as 3rd sg. with a pl. subject. Actually we have here clear evidence that in Byblian the perfect *yatana* had already developed. Significant is the fact that nowhere is there any evidence of doubling in specifically Canaanite forms like *yadinu*, *yadina*, etc. Our form *nadna* seems decisive. It is 1st pl. impf., as the context, morphology and syntax demand, with syncope of the short second vowel: thus *nadina* > *nadna*.

*arad kit(t)išu u yuwaš(š)ira šeʾi(m)*ḫá *ina libbi* gišelippētipl., "let the king, my lord, hear the words of his loyal servant so that he send grain in ships" (85.16–18); cf. also 89.53, 121.47, 122.44.

Jussive: *yuwaš(š)ira bēlī*li lú.pl.*maṣ(ṣ)arta ana* 2 *ālānišu*, "let my lord send a garrison to his two cities" (79.29–31); cf. also 104.14, 116.72, 117.66, 117.92, 118.42, 123.41, 131.12, 139.30.

Purpose: *aštapar ana ēkalli u yuwaš(š)ara*[250] *šarru ṣāba rabā*, "I wrote to the palace that the king might send a large host" (117.24–27). It should be noted that this is a rare example of the subjunctive dependent on a declarative clause; the cohortative is equally rare in such a context.[251]

Contrast the indicatives in *uššira maṣ(ṣ)arta u tinaṣ(ṣ)arū ālaka u ardaka adi yīdu šarru ana mātātišu u yuwaš(š)iru ṣāba piṭatišu u yušapšiḫu mātātišu*, "send a garrison to guard thy city and thy servant until the king takes concern for his lands and sends his archer-host and pacifies his lands" (112.33–39; note the use of the indicative in the temporal clause, especially significant in view of the volitive *uššira* which precedes, showing that the use of *yaqtulu* or *yaqtula* was not merely formulaic, that is, that automatically *yaqtula* followed a volitive). *yiššira maṣ(ṣ)arta ina ālišu ... a yaškunnū šarru libbašu ina mimmi ša yišširu* m.*aziru ana šāšu ... mim* m.*ḫāzāni šarri ša dak yišširu*, "let him send a garrison to his city ... let not the king pay attention to anything that Aziru sends ... he sends the property of the governor he has killed" (139.30–38); note the *yaqtula*/*yaqtul* volitives, the *yaqtulu* statements of fact. *šumma libbi šarri bēliya ana āl gubla u yūšira bēlī*, "if the heart of the king, my lord, is (well-disposed) towards Byblos, then let my lord send" (131.10–12); but in line 15, *šumma ... lā yūširu ...*, "but if he does not send ..."—again a shift from a volitive *yaqtula* to an indicative *yaqtulu*. Cf. also 71.10–14, 95.31–32, 112.18, 114.61, 116.31.

ḲABŪ

Jussive: *ul yuḳba ina ūmī rābiṣūti laḳū* lú.pl.GAZpl. *kalī mātāti, ul kāma yuḳbu ina ūmī*[252] *u lā tiliʾu laḳāši*, "let it not be said, 'In the time of the commissioners the Ḫapiru took all the lands'; not thus shall it be said and they shall not take it" (83.16–20). *aḳba* (121.25), no context; *yiḳba* (129.52), probably a negative jussive, but context partly destroyed.

[250]There is almost certainly a dittography in this passage, *u yuwaš(š)ara* being repeated.

[251]*GHB*, §116c.

[252]*ina ūmī* is almost certainly a dittography; cf. *ul yuḳba ina* in 83.16–17.

BALĀṬU

Purpose: *uššira* 3 *awīlī u ibluṭa*, "send the three men that I may be safe" (123.25–26). *ašpuru ana ēkalli ana maṣ(ṣ)ar u awīlūt māt miluḫ(ḫ)a u lā ibluṭa* ᵐ·*danuna*, "I write to the palace for a garrison and men from Miluḫḫa so that Danuna will not be safe" (117.90–92). The latter is another example of the volitive following an indicative; cf. 117.24–27 under *(w)ašāru*.

NAZĀZU

Purpose: *ušširūnanī* 50 *tapal sisī ... u iz(z)iza ina āl šigata ina pānišu*, "send me 50 teams of horses ... that I may resist him in Shigata" (71.23–26).

Conditional: *šumma inan(n)a ḳalāta u* ᵐ·*piḫura lā yiz(z)iza ina āl kumedi*, "if now thou art negligent, then Piḫura cannot stay in Kumedi" (132.46–49). *šumma kiʾama ibaš(š)ū u lā tiz(z)iza āl ṣumura*, "if matters continue thus, then Simyra cannot stand" (107.32–34). *miyami yimal(l)ik iz(z)iza ina pāni ṣāb piṭat šarri*, "who would counsel (that) he would resist (successfully) the archer-host of the king?" (94.12–13). This last example is really only the verb of an apodosis, the protasis being suppressed. Contrast *miya yiz(z)izu ana pāni ṣābi šarri*, "who will resist the host of the king?" (362.65).

DABĀRU

Conditional: *inūma* 1 *ḫāzānu libbušu itti libbiya u udab(b)ira* ᵐ·*abdaširta ištu māt amurri*, "if there were one governor whose heart were one with my heart, then I would drive ᶜAbd-Ashirta out of the land of the Amorite" (85.66–69). The use of *udab(b)ira* has exact parallels in the Hebrew cohortative.[253]

(W)ABĀLU

šá-ni-tam a-wa-[*te*] *la yu-si-bi-la be-li* "if my lord does not send word to me ..." (88.34–35); dubious.

MĀTU

Conditional: *inaṣ(ṣ)iru (āla) ina balāṭiya inūma imūta minū yinaṣ(ṣ)aruše*, "I will guard (the city) while I am alive. (But) if I die, what (who?) will guard it?" (130.49–52). *milik ana yāši miya irāmu u*

[253]Cf. Jer. 9.1, Ju. 9.29; *GKC*, §108f.

amūta, "take care of me. (For) who will be loyal (to thee) if I die" (114.67–68).—It is difficult to determine in these two instances whether we should translate the subordinate clauses as temporal or conditional. Since either way the meaning is virtually the same, the essentially conditional character of such a temporal clause would allow a use of the volitive as in other conditional sentences.

ŠAPĀRU

tašpura (95.7), no context; *yišpura(m)* (362.22), *tašpura* (77.7), *taštapra* (102.14), *yištappara* (130.9), *yištapara* (130.15) are all Accadian allatives—at least I can find no other satisfactory explanation for *yaqtula* in these instances.

MAḲĀTU

Jussive: *ul yimaḳ(ḳ)uta ṣāb karaši muḫḫiya*, "let not the soldiers of the camp fall upon me" (83.43–44); in 81.31 the same form is either jussive or intended result, a damaged context making it impossible to decide.

ELŪ

Conditional: *šumma 2 arḫē lā tūṣana ṣābu piṭati u ītila* ᵐ·*abdaširta*, "if within two months the archer-host does not come forth, then ᶜAbd-Aširta will attack" (81.45–47).—*ītilām* in 88.14,17 is an allative.

EPĒŠU

Conditional: *šutēra awata(m) ana yāši u īpuša anāku kit(t)a itti* ᵐ·*abdaširta*, "send back word to me or I will make an alliance with ᶜAbd-Ashirta" (83.23–25). This is another example of a suppressed protasis, and is exactly like the use of the subjunctive in Arabic after *ʾau* with a suppressed protasis.[254]

DABĀBU

Conditional: *inūma ḳabī ana pāni šarri* ᵐ·*ribadda šumīt ṣāb piṭat šarri inūma balṭū* ˡᵘ́·ᵖˡ·*rābiṣūtu u adab(b)uba kalī ipšīšunu*, "if it is said in the presence of the king, 'Rib-Adda put to death the archer-host of the king when the commissioners were alive,' then let me tell all their deeds" (119.18–23).[255]

[254]Cf. n. 239 above.
[255]Cf. Job 31.7ff.; *GKC*, §108f.

DĀKU

Purpose: *palḫātī anāku lāmi udāka,* "I am afraid lest I be killed" (131.27–28).[256] The volitive after a verb of fearing, as in Arabic.

MAḪĀṢU

Purpose: *palḫātī awīlūt ḫupšī ul timaḫ(ḫ)aṣananī,* "I fear my serfs lest they strike me down" (77.36–37). Again the volitive (*timaḫḫaṣa,* plus energic *-na*) after a verb of fearing.

KAŠĀDU

Conditional: *inūma ikaššada(m) mātāti u tepaṭ(ṭ)erūna awīlūtu ana laḳī mātātimi ana šāšunu,* "should I enter the lands, then the men will desert to take the lands for themselves" (362.33–37).

ḪAMĀṬU

Jussive: *yuḫam(m)iṭa bēlī ṣāba(m) piṭata(m) u nimut,* "let my lord hasten the archer-host or we die" (362.40–41); also 129.78.

AṢŪ

Jussive: *yīṣa(m) šarru bēliya,* "let the king my lord come forth ..." (362.60).

Purpose: *ašpur u tūṣa ṣābu piṭatu u tilḳī* m·*abašunu,* "I wrote that an archer-host might come forth and take Abashunu" (362.18–20). The volitive after a non-volitive, as already noted above, is rare; note the following *tilḳī,* not *tilḳu*. It should be noted that the three examples we have follow some form of *šapāru*. Perhaps we should see in *šapāru* an implicit volitive, that is, "to write requesting" or the like.

Conditional: *iānuammi awīla lā tīṣa ana šāšunu,* "they would have no one shouldst thou not come forth to them" (362.29–30). *u uṣṣa(m) riḳūtam u išim(m)ē enu yānum ṣāba ittišu u ten(n)ipuš āl baṭrūna ana šāšu,*[257] "should he return empty-handed and he (ᶜAbd-Ashirta) hear that there is no host with him, then Baṭrūna will be joined to him" (87.17–20).

Contrast the first three examples with the use of *tūṣu* in the same letter: *lā raʾimū inūma tūṣu ṣābu piṭatu,* "they do not like the fact that

[256] KA in *udāka* is not certain; from the traces in BB 24 and from context Knudtzon's conjecture seems quite probable.

[257] On the reading of line 18, see the Appendix [p. 110 in the present volume].

the archer-host is coming forth" (362.55–56); *ana ūmi tūṣu u innipušat gabbi mātāti ana šarri*, "when thou comest forth, then all lands will be joined to the king" (362.62–64).

ŠANŪ

taštanā (82.14) is an Accadian allative.

Excursus

I *The Use of Volitives in Conditional Sentences*[258]

Since we are confronted in this analysis of *yaqtula* with the nature of a volitive as nowhere else in our syntactical studies, we have postponed the analysis of its use in conditional sentences to this point. The use of a volitive to express purpose, intended result, exhortation (in the first person), jussive (in the third person), presents no problem. All of these uses are of their nature volitives. But the use of a volitive in a conditional sentence is often quite a problem.

It is not, of course, a problem where the idea to be expressed is of itself volitive, be it in protasis or apodosis. *adabbuba* ("then let me speak") in 119.23 is an example. In fact, in any protasis the use of a volitive is understandable, for the protasis sets up the hypothesis. Compare our own volitive expression, "suppose a man does so and so, ...," the equivalent of "if a man does so and so, ..." This becomes very clear when we remember that the protasis is originally an independent sentence, so that to express something like "if he goes to war, he will die" a volitive "let him go to war" is most natural in the protasis.

In the apodosis it is not quite so simple. The Arabic use of the jussive (sometimes the subjunctive under certain conditions, on which see introduction to the study of *yaqtula*) and the Hebrew jussive and cohortative are understandable in apodoses of so-called ideal or should-would conditional sentences. This is especially true if the jussive (on *yaqtula* having the same meaning, see part II of this *excursus*), which seems the most probable view, includes not only the jussive meaning, properly

[258]The view of Brockelmann (*Grundriss* II, p. 636, §420) and others that *yaqtul* in a conditional sentence is not a volitive but the proto-Semitic omnitemporal, omnimodal form of the verb is proved wrong, I believe, by the parallel use of the subjunctive in Arabic (Wright-de Goeje II, p. 40, Rem. c), of the cohortative in Hebrew (*GKC*, §108e–g), and of *yaqtula* in our letters. Brockelmann's failure even to mention the use of the subjunctive in conditional sentences, both in protasis and apodosis, is typical of the treatment of the subjunctive by grammarians.

speaking, but also the modal meanings of the Greek optative.[259] But if this not be true, Reckendorf's suggestion that the jussive urges one to draw the conclusion from the hypothetical case (expressed by another jussive) set up in the protasis is a satisfactory explanation in conditional sentences of the ideal type.[260] The use of *udabbira* in 85.68 is a perfect example.

However, there are many examples in Arabic and some in our letters in which the conditional sentence is not of the ideal type and yet we have the volitive in the apodosis. Thus the common construction in Arabic, recognized even by Arab grammarians as a conditional sentence, in which the protasis is expressed by an imperative, the apodosis by a jussive. Thus *ʾarfiq bī waʾadullika ʿalay ʿadiyyin* "Übe Gnade an mir, und ich werde dir den Adī zeigen" (Reckendorf's translation).[261] Note also *tizziza* (107.32–34) quoted above.

Reckendorf's second suggestion—he makes no distinction between ideal conditions and probable or possible ones in his attempt to explain the use of the jussive in apodoses—might be here adduced: the volitive in the apodosis is due to a kind of mood-agreement (*Moduskongruenz*).[262] However, this fits neither the evidence of the Byblian letters nor Arabic usage, for in the latter we not rarely have the perfect in the protasis with a jussive in the apodosis.[263]

The only view that seems to fit all the evidence is that the volitive form in Arabic and Canaanite had the following meanings: 1) strictly volitive; 2) those of the Greek optative; 3) emphatic asseverative. The first needs no comment. The second is admitted by many authorities, and the evidence is all in its favor. The third is not purely *ad hoc*. The Heb. cohortative, clearly a volitive, is just as clearly an emphatic asseverative.[264] If our view of Ar. *yaqtulan(na)* as a subjunctive-energic be correct, we have additional corroboratory evidence.[265] Even if it be incorrect, it is certainly significant that in South Arabic *yqtln* is not only

[259]This is Albright's view; *JAOS* 60, p. 419. *GKC* have a similar view, but with this difference that they consider it a weakening of the original volitive meaning; §109i.

[260]Reckendorf, p. 62, §35.

[261]*Ibid.*, p. 680, §226.

[262]*Ibid.*, p. 62, §35.

[263]*Ibid.*, p. 688, §227, A.1.

[264]*GKC*, §108a–b.

[265]See above under the Energic, Excursus [pp. 51–53 in the present volume].

an emphatic form but is the form used in purpose clauses.[266] The difference between an emphatic asseverative and a volitive is slight.

With the volitive form possessing these meanings, all difficulties disappear: in a conditional sentence any of these three meanings may belong to the volitive, the context making clear which one is found in any given instance. The chief source of difficulty lies in the fact that Arabic and Canaanite frequently use a volitive where our own idiom employs an indicative.[267]

II *The Difference between the Volitive* yaqtula *and Jussive* yaqtul

With *yaqtula* functioning in the Byblian letters not only as the verb of purpose and intended result clauses but also with jussive meaning, the question naturally arises as to the difference between *yaqtula* and *yaqtul*. One explanation might be that *yaqtula* with jussive meaning represents a secondary development, an invasion of *yaqtula* into the proper sphere of *yaqtul*. This could be the analysis. Thus with *yaqtul* practically functioning as a verb of a purpose clause in sentences like, "Do this and let him recover" (= "Do this that he may recover"), *yaqtula*, which properly belongs in such clauses, analogically took over jussive meaning.

However, there are two serious objections to this explanation: 1) the evidence from Arabic indicates that the subjunctive is not necessarily a mood of subordination; 2) the principle of modal sequence we have seen in our study of purpose clauses and throughout our study of *yaqtula* indicates that the structure of a sentence with a purpose clause is essentially paratactic with two parallel members, the subordination of one to another deriving from the context. Were the structure not essentially paratactic, then there is no reason why *yaqtula* should not consis-

[266] *Ibid.*

[267] Actually, in literary English we have an analogous usage, though it is lost in ordinary speech. Polotsky in his analysis of the so-called *final form* in Coptic, which in many usages is the counterpary of Byblian *yaqtula*, calls attention to the English literary idiom in which the future auxiliaries (*I shall, thou wilt, he will*) are reversed in clauses dependent upon an imperative or following a hypothetical clause, becoming *I will, thou shalt, he shall*; H. J. Polotsky, *Études de Syntaxe copte*, pp. 15–17. *I will* he considers a future volitive, *he shall* a virtual promise. The Coptic counterpart to Byblian *yaqtula* in its conditional usage derives from Egy. *dỉ.ỉ* "I will make, effect," and hence is also a future volitive; Polotsky, pp. 12–14. Thus we do have parallels for a volitive in the apodosis of conditional sentences, however obscured its original force may have become through constant usage.

tently follow verbs in the indicative—we have noted only three *possible* exceptions to the rule that *yaqtula* follows another volitive. For these two reasons it is difficult to consider the use of *yaqtula* in independent clauses as secondary and analogical.

Rather we would view *yaqtul* and *yaqtula* as essentially the same with the accidental difference of emphasis, the latter probably the more emphatic form. This view is confirmed by the parallel of the subjunctive and jussive in Arabic both in purpose clauses and conditional sentences. It is confirmed by the parallel use of the cohortative and jussive in Hebrew, their uses being identical in the 1st and 3rd persons respectively. It is further confirmed by the sequence *yaqtul-yaqtula* or *yaqtula-yaqtul* in the Byblian letters: thus *yišmī-yadina* (85.75–78), *yuballiṭ-anaṣṣara* (74.55–56), *tadin-yatina, anaṣṣara* (83.30–33), *yuḫammiṭa-yilḳī, tinnipuš* (129.78–80), *yuwaššira-yuparraš* (113.17–18), *tūṣa* / / *tilḳī* (in parallelism, both expressing purpose; 362.19-20), etc. In other words, the Byblian scribes used interchangeably *yaqtul* and *yaqtula*, though undoubtedly with some slight difference of meaning which escapes us.

Conclusion

Whatever be the solution to the use of a volitive in conditional sentences and whatever the precise difference be between *yaqtul* and *yaqtula*, it suffices for our purpose to call attention to the *use* of the volitive in Arabic and Hebrew paralleling the use of *yaqtula* in Byblian Amarna. We must emphasize again that every example of *yaqtula* in the Byblian letters, with the exception of 8 (hence 62 out of the 70 cases that can be interpreted), has a good parallel volitive in Hebrew and Arabic. Moreover, we have seen clear evidence that the shift from *yaqtulu* to *yaqtula* and *vice versa* is significant, that is, determined by the idea to be expressed and the syntactical situation. Hence, the conclusion is inescapable that *yaqtula* functioned in 14th century Byblian as a volitive in the usages we have just examined. We may say that Byblian had a subjunctive, though the term should not be interpreted as the exact equivalent of the Arabic subjunctive. We prefer the term *volitive*, for this covers both its so-called dependent (purpose, intended result) and independent uses.

Appendix: Improved Translations and Readings

The title of this appendix indicates clearly its purpose. The new readings are for the most part dependent on a careful study of the autographs and parallel passages. In a few cases, for which I am indebted to Dr. Albright and his recent study (July, 1949) of the Amarna tablets in the British Museum, they depend on a study of the tablets themselves.

The improved translations have a threefold source: 1) the grammatical study of the Byblos letters which precedes; 2) our knowledge of virtually contemporary Canaanite, denied our predecessors, which we now have thanks to Ugaritic; 3) a simple common-sense understanding of the situation in Canaan at the time the letters were written, of the purpose of the correspondence, and finally of the nature of the relations between the various local governors (*ḫāzānūti*) and their relations in turn with the Egyptian court.

This last source may at first sight seem a doubtful one and highly subjective. The best proof of its validity will be the translations themselves. However, this may be said briefly in its defense. "Common-sense"—the governors were neither demented nor prone to the esoteric. Reading and re-reading of their letters make this perfectly clear. "The situation in Canaan at the time"—a time when the Egyptian hegemony was weakening, excessive governmental exactions were arousing the greatest possible hostility and unrest, and political intrigue was rife. "The purpose of the correspondence, etc."—to allay any suspicions of personal disloyalty, to put oneself in the best possible light and usually one's fellow governors in the worst, *never in any way* to prejudice one's own position and security.

EA 68; *VS* XI, 32

Line 10: *šalmat* is to be rendered "is well" or the like, not "sich woll befunden hat" (Knudtzon). The verb is regularly treated as a Canaanite stative. Besides, the verb is still part of a cliché greeting, not narrative or factual; cf. the greetings in the Mari Letters, ... *a-lum ḳa-at-tu-na-an*^{ki} *ù ḫa-al-ṣú-um ša-lim.*[1]

Line 14: I follow Knudtzon's reading despite the rather unusual writing of ḲÚL. The autograph, which shows a horizontal wedge under the *a*

[1]C.-F. Jean, *Archives Royales de Mari* II, 80.5, 82.4, etc.

(*a-ḳúl-me*), indicates that before the erasure the scribe has written *i-ḳúl*, then either intending to write *ia-ḳúl* or by a simple error (note the sequence *la-a a-ḳúl*) produced the anomalous 3rd sg. *aḳul*. Cf. line 31.

Line 22: ᵐ·*pa-ḫa-am-*[*n*]*a-ta* = *Pꜣ-ḥm-nṯr*, "The Priest"; cf. Albright, *JNES* 5, p. 17.

Line 25: Von Soden has failed to note that ḲÁM occurs in Amarna as well as at Nuzi; Wolfram von Soden, *Das akkadische Syllabar*, p. 72, no. 235.

Line 25: Read *pu-uš-ḳám* MA.GAL(!). I follow Albright's unpublished emendation of *EA*'s *ma-na-aš*. The reading is not certain since the autograph certainly has NA, and the last horizontal wedge in the series is set apart about 1/8 in. (about average distance separating signs in the tablet), whereas GAL in lines 12 and 29 has it pressed close to the vertical wedge at the left. However, since *manaš* makes no sense whatever (if it were a noun, it should have a case-ending), and since a slight error caused by the scribe's forgetting to add a longer horizontal wedge at the top of what looks like NA easily accounts for the mysterious *manaš* (note that GAL in lines 12 and 29 is written with four horizontal wedges to the left of the vertical, not three), we prefer at present to read MA.GAL.

Line 31: [*i*]*(!)-ḳúl*, not [*ia*]-*ḳúl*. There is not enough room for IA. Knudtzon was aware of this[2] but lacking parallels for *iḳul* in the Rib-Adda letters he restored *IA*. However, note that *iḳul* is at least probable in line 14 before the erasure.

EA 69; *BB* 73

Line 10: [*a*]-*ḳa-bu ìl-ti-ḳú-mi ga*[*b-bu a-wa-ta*] *i-na bi-ri-šu-nu muḫḫi-*[*ia*], "I say, 'They have all made an agreement among themselves against me.'" Cf. 116.50–52: ᵐ·*aziru ù* ᵐ·*yapa-adda laḳū awata bērišunu muḫḫiya*. This parallel is my justification for reading *awata*, not *awati* (Knudtzon), and *muḫḫiya* with virtual certainty as to the suffix. As for *gabbu* rather than *gabbi*, it makes sense which Knudtzon's "Genommen haben sie sämtliche Wörte" fails to do.

Line 21: *àl ma*(!)-*aṣ-pát*^{ki}. Dr. Albright's recent collation of the Amarna Tablets in the British Museum removes the strange Kuaṣpat; cf. Biblical *Miṣpāh* (Mizpah). Though in view of *ḥōmītu*, "wall" (cf. the gloss *ḫu-*

[2]*EA* I, p. 362, n. a.

mi-tu, 141.44), for later *ḥômāh*, and *manḥītu*, "offering," for later *minḥāh*,[3] we should prefer to read PÍT (not PÁT), still the value PÍT of the BAD sign is attested only from Neo-Babylonian and subsequently; cf. von Soden, *Das akkadische Syllabar*, p. 36, no. 42.

Line 27: read *ti-ul*$_{11}$*-ḳí*. Though this writing lacks parallels, it is not an unparalled phenomenon in these letters—cf. *ni-ub-lu-uṭ* in 86.36, *ba-lu-aṭ* in 112.51, etc. Only on the supposition that the form is passive is the syntax satisfactory, since the case-ending of *nuḫuštum* in line 28 shows it to be the subject. Render therefore lines 26–28: "and as for all my city-gates, the bronze was seized."

Line 30: Correct my *ku-ru-u*[*b*](!) here and in 87.25.[4] Dr. Albright informs me that the last sign is definitely UD, as Knudtzon read it. I failed to realize that the lower oblique wedge on which I based my emendation belonged to the ID-sign in 87.26. Dr. Albright suggests reading *ṭúr-ru-ud* in the sense of "press upon, urge"; whether however the verb can have such a meaning is not certain.

EA 71; *VS* XI, 33

Line 1: On the possibility of reading *pa-zi-*[*te*] cf. Albright, *JNES* 5, pp. 12–13. TE is conjectured on the basis of Winckler's copy as corrected by Knudtzon (cf. *EA* I, p. 366, n. c). If the conjectured reading be correct, then *pazite* = New Kingdom *pꜣ-ṯꜣty*, "the vizier."

Lines 4–9: Knudtzon renders, "Siehe, du bist ein weiser Mann zur Seite des Königs, und wegen deiner Zuverlässigkeit hat dich geschickt der König als Vorsteher." Albright (*ibid.*) renders "Behold, thou art a wise man who dost know the king and because of thy wisdom(!) the king sent thee as commissioner." I follow Albright's (*ibid.*, n. 8) probable restoration *im-<qú>-ti-ka*. As he points out, the supposed equivalence of *imtu* with Hebr. *ʾĕmet* postulates an unparalleled phonetic development. However, I find it difficult to interpret *i-di* as a participle, for *īdī* elsewhere is always 3rd sg. masc. pret. Besides, I think the interpretation of the form as 3rd sg. gives slightly better sense in the context. Therefore I render these lines: "Behold, thou art a wise man. The king knows (it) and because of thy wisdom the king has sent thee as commissioner."[5]

[3]Albright, *The Vocalization of the Egyptian Syllabic Orthography*, XII B.2.

[4]*JNES* 8, p. 124 [see below, Paper 3, pp. 141–142] .

[5]Dr. Albright informs me that Prof. Goetze in a private communication accepted *im<ḳū>tu* but also proposed the same explanation of *īdī* as I have.

Lines 20–22: *mi-nu ti-la-at-šu u dannat i-na* lúGAZ *danni til-la-at-šu*, "What is his own force? But his force is strong through the mighty Ḫapiru." This rendering seems to fit the context best. *tillatu* is not, of course, "Erhebung" but "force, body of troops"; cf. Ebeling, *EA* II, p. 1591.

Lines 23–31: "So send (ye) to me 50 teams of horses and 200 foot-soldiers that I may resist him in (the environs of?) Shigata until the coming forth of the archer-host, lest he gather all the Ḫapiru and take Shigata and Ampi." The phrase *iz(z)iza (ina āl šigata) ina pānišu* corresponds to Hebr. *ᶜāmad bipnê*; cf. Ges.-Buhl[13], p. 668a. On the verb forms *iz(z)iza*, *yupaḫ(ḫ)ira*, *yilḳa*, cf. section on the Subjunctive.

Line 32: *y*[*i-za(!)*]*-az*. This is based on the parallel passage in 76.23. Knudtzon's *yi-bar-za* is not only obscure but very doubtful. The traces in the autograph of EA 76 indicate ZA rather than BAR—hence the present of *nazāzu*. However, this form is unparalleled in the Byblos letters (cf. line 25). Until we can find out what the ideogram is at the beginning of the line conjecture is useless.

EA 73; *BB* 15

Lines 11–14: "If it hears of the coming forth of the archer-host, then they will abandon their cities and desert." This is one of those places where common-sense is decisive. Contrast Knudtzon's translation: "Wenn es doch erführe, dass Feldtruppen auszögen! Haben sie ja ihre Städte verlassen und sind abgezogen." Our rendering fits the context perfectly, and the construction is well-attested; cf. Conditional Sentences.

Lines 18–19: "They will not be loyal to ᶜAbd-Ashirta! What will he do to them?" Again context and common-sense make our rendering imperative. Rib-Adda has just pointed out in the previous lines that the Amorites follow the stronger party, and hence when the Egyptian archer-troops show themselves they will desert ᶜAbd-Ashirta. He goes on with the lines just rendered. For an exact parallel to line 19 with *yīpušu* functioning as a future, cf. 74.41 *u minā yīpušu ana yāšinū*, "and what will he do to us?"; cf. also 73.31.

Lines 22–23: "... that we might be joined to it." Knudtzon's interpretation of this clause as a direct quotation is unnecessary and is unparalleled. Our rendering makes perfect sense; the Amurru wanted Rib-Adda to join forces with the longed for archer-troops. It is possible that *šāše* in line 23 refers to *māt amurri* and we should render "joined to them." In any case, there is no foundation for interpreting the clause as a direct quotation.

Lines 27–29: "Kill your lord and join the Ḫapiru." I interpret *innipšū* as an imperative since it fits the context a little better and does away with an otherwise extremely choppy and unparalleled construction. *innipšū* would then be the equivalent of a Can. nifᶜal imperative *hiqqatlū*.

Line 29: "They say," not "sagten."

Line 35: " ..., for thou art father and master to me." There is no reason for making this a direct quotation with Knudtzon. Render lines 33–38: "So mention this matter in the presence of the king, thy lord, for thou art father and master to me, and to thee have I directed my face (beseechingly)." Compare the interesting parallel passage in a Ugaritic letter: *wht . ᵓaḫy / bny . yšᵓal / ṯryl . prgm / lmlk . šmy*, "And now as for my brother, my son, let him ask Ṯryl; and mention my name to the king."[6]

Lines 39–42: "Thou knowest my way of acting when thou wast in Simyra, that I am thy loyal servant." *parṣu* (39) is the equivalent in the Byblian letters of Can. *mišpaṭ*, as is clear from 117.82 and 118.40 where *kīma parṣi* = Can. *kamišpaṭi*, "according to the custom"—cf. I Ki. 18.28, etc. For the meaning "way of acting" for *mišpaṭ(u)*, cf. II Ki. 17.26.

EA 74; *BB* 12

Lines 10–15: "Let the king examine closely the royal archives, for is not the man who is in Byblos a loyal servant? (Therefore) do not neglect thy servant. Behold, the hostility of the Ḫapiru against me is great, and as the gods of thy land live, lost are our sons (and) daughters ..." For *šumma* = "behold," see section on Particles [p. 12 in the present volume]. Knudtzon correctly interpreted TI (15) as an ideogram for *balāṭu*, but he failed to see the obvious fact that it is an oath. However, Knudtzon may be correct in interpreting *inūma ul* (11) as "whether not." If so, then this represents a use of *kī* in Canaanite so far unattested outside of Amarna.[7]

[6] 138.10–13.

[7] Sidney Smith (*The Statue of Idri-mi*, p. 34) has recently offered a new translation of 74.14ff. "If the war by the Khapiru against me has been dire, verily the gods of your land preserved alive all our sons and daughters with us in our life when there was a delivering up in the land Yarimuta." This is far worse than Knudtzon's rendering. Smith has simply ignored Knudtzon's reference (*EA* I, p. 347, n. 6) to all the parallels which show TI cannot be joined with what follows. He also shows he has misunderstood the phrase *ina nadānim ina māt yarimuta*

Lines 31–41: Dr. George E. Mendenhall was the first to recognize that these lines comprise ^{c}Abd-Ashirta's message to the army.[8] His translation stands except in the following points:

1) render lines 32–33, "behold, there is no one who can save it (Byblos) from our hand(s)." To render *šumma* by "behold" makes much better sense than by a conditional clause (protasis). Read *ḳa-ti-n*[*u*], not *ḳa-ti* ^{n}[^{u}*nukurti*] in line 33. The reasons are: 1) there is almost no room for the conjectured KÚR; 2) if *nukurti* were correct, we would expect *ḳāt*, not *ḳāti*, which is never used as a construct in the Byblian letters; 3) who is the "enemy"? In context it could only be ^{c}Abd-Ashirta and his cohorts, and it seems most unlikely that he would refer to himself as "the enemy." Note also *šūzubu ištu ḳāti* plus pronominal suffix in lines 44–45.

2) Mendenhall's rendering of *u pašḫū mārē* (37) by a purpose clause, if he meant it to reflect the Canaanite construction and not the sense, is wrong. The perfect is never used to express purpose in these letters, or, as a matter of fact, in Canaanite. For a discussion of the use of tenses here, cf. above n. 228 [p. 83 in the present volume].

Line 42: *tiškunū* NAM.ŠUB *ana bērišunu*. Knudtzon did not recognize NAM.ŠUB as an ideogram; he read *nam-ru* and did not attempt a translation. Until the new Idri-mi inscription I had read NAM.ŠUB = *šiptu*, "incantation," and translated according to context, "they took an oath among themselves." However, lines 50–51 of the Idri-mi inscription read *ana bērišunu* NAM.ERÍM *danna iškunūnim*. Once we see the idiom *šakānu* NAM.ERÍM in use in the West, it immediately becomes apparent that our ŠUB is merely a scribal error, the scribe leaving off the first half of ERÍM (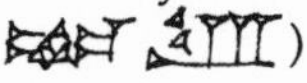) either by a mere oversight or through ignorance of the ideogram. For NAM.ERÍM = *māmītu*, "oath," cf. Labat, *Manuel d'Épigraphie akkadienne*, p. 75, no. 79.

Line 52: Render *yatamar* more probably by "he will tell" rather than "(er) hat gesehen." In 138.36 *amāru* certainly means "to say" rather than "to see." This of course reflects the Canaanite meaning of the root.

---

ina balāṭ napištinū. Render: "by selling (them) in Yarimuta for provisions to keep alive."

[8] *JNES* 6, pp. 123–124.

***EA* 75; *WA* 79**

Line 27: Knudtzon's [lú.p]l.*šimi* (= *Šam*) is without parallel, and the autograph (*EA* I, p. 1003, no. 73) is completely unconvincing. Heavily hatched, the sign could just as well be GAZ, and in view of the innumerable parallels this reading is virtually certain.

Line 28: *ḳà*(!)-*bi*. The traces in WA show the sign could just as well be ḲÀ as AK, and since this makes sense (which *aḳbī* does not), we prefer this reading. One fact against it is that nowhere else in the Byblos letters do we have ḲÀ, though it is attested in Amarna.[9]

Line 29: *ù* TI *ili-ka*(!), "and as thy god lives, ..." *WA* shows only TI.DINGIR. Knudtzon at first read *ti-il-m*[*a-n*]*a*, but offered no translation.[10] Later he read *ti-il-m*[*a-t*]*ú*, and offered with hesitation "*obwohl du (es) erfahren hast*."[11] Against this are two facts: 1) the use of *lamādu* is very suspicious; 2) there is not a valid instance of UD = TÚ in the entire Byblos correspondence, if indeed in all Amarna. In favor of my reading and rendering is that my reading is paralleled in 74.14–15 *u ilāni mātika* TI, likewise used as an oath. As for interpreting the traces of the supposed MA-NA/UD as KA, there is no difficulty at all: the beginning of MA and KA are virtually identical; Knudtzon's fluctuation between NA and UD prove that all he saw was the end of the two horizontal shafts followed by a vertical. Unfortunately I have neither autograph nor tablet to support this reading, but since it is perfectly possible and the resulting sense is paralleled and excellent, I consider it quite probable. The following will illustrate what I believe Knudtzon saw:

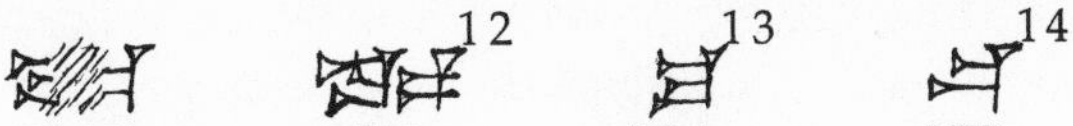

75.29 KA[12] MA[13] UD[14]

Line 37: *ka-li mātāti tuklātī(!) šar māt mitta<na>*, "all lands, the allies of the king of the Mitanni." Thus I interpret KU.TI.TI as KU= *tukultu*, with TI.TI repeated to indicate the plural. Though I have no parallel for such a writing of the plural, the repetition of a sign to indi-

[9]Von Soden, *Das akkadische Syllabar*, p. 32, no. 15.

[10]*BA* 4, p. 117.

[11]*EA* I, pp. 377–378.

[12]Traced from sign-list in *VS* XII, p. 76.

[13]*Ibid.*, p. 87.

[14]Traced from Albright's autograph of 88.18.

cate the plural is standard Accadian practice. In view of the scribes' cavalier treatment of Accadian orthographic practices, the repetition of a phonetic complement to express the plural would not be surprising.

EA 76; VS XI, 35

Lines 27–29: ... [*a*]-*nu-ma* [*ki-a-ma*] / [*aš-pu-ru a-na ēka*]*lli ù* [*la-a*] / [*yi-iš-mi šarru a*]-⌜*wa*⌝-*ta(m)*. The restoration is based on many parallels. [*a*]-*nu-ma* is virtually certain, and Knudtzon would undoubtedly have it if he had seen, as Schroeder did, the NU. *kīama* is based on the stereotyped phrase *anuma kīʾama* found in 74.49,64, 91.27, 103.20, 118.8, 119.11, 122.53–54, 132.51 (cf. also 85.6); it also fits the space perfectly. *ašpuru ana* is based on the fact that GAL is clear, and É is fairly certain from the two vertical wedges seen by Schroeder. Granted *ēkallu*, we are virtually certain in restoring *ašpuru ana* or the like in view of the parallels 74.49, 89.7–8,[15] 91.27, 118.9, 119.11, 122.54, 132.51. Examination of these passages will show that *anuma kīʾama ašpuru* (or the like) *ana ēkalli* is a stereotyped phrase in the Byblos letters.—LA fits the space well, and usually follows the above formula.

EA 77; VS XI, 36

Line 8: *lit*-⌜*i*⌝-*di*. Knudtzon's *lit*-[*ti*]-*i-di* is impossible, to judge from the size of the break in the autograph. I would interpret the preformative as asseverative and render lines 6–11: "As for thy writing for copper and for ivory, verily Baᶜalat of Byblos knows whether I have any copper or ivory."—The traces in the autograph support [*a-n*]*a* at the end of line 10 rather than Knudtzon's [*e*]*rī*. Besides, what does *erū* mean here after its appearance at the beginning of the line? Our *ana* satisfies the requirements of the space and the traces, only presupposing a common dittography in these letters (cf. 107.45–46, 108.15–16, 112.49–50, 114.57–58).

Line 28: *in-ni*-[*ip-š*]*a*. There simply is not enough room for Knudtzon's *innipšat*, even though it is expected from the parallels. Moreover, the traces of the last sign are almost certainly *ša*. Perhaps *at* was left out by mistake, perhaps *innipša* is a feminine plural.

EA 79; VS XI, 38

Line 33: *yu(!)-da-na-ni*, not *yi-da-na-ni* with Knudtzon. The form must be passive in view of the characteristic *a* vowel; cf. *yu-da-na* in 86.32,

[15] See *JCS* 4, note on line 8 [below, Paper 4, p. 146].

47, *yu-da-na(m)* in 85.34,37. *mimma,* which undoubtedly caused Knudtzon to interpret the form actively, may be indeclinable.[16] Therefore render lines 32–33, "... and so let something be given me for their food."

EA 81; VS XI, 40

Line 15: [*i*]-*zi-i*[*z*] BAR.KA.BAR.G⌜ÍR⌝ / *p*⌜*aṭ*⌝*(!)-*[*r*]*a(!) muḫḫi-ia,* "he drew a bronze-dagger (*paṭru*) against me." GÍR, about which Knudtzon is in doubt (*EA* I, p. 394, n. b), is certain since Schroeder's autograph shows the gloss to be *paṭru.*—BAR.KA.BAR represents the confusion of some scribe, who tripped over the ideograms. He meant, as is clear from the parallel in 82.38, to write GÍR.UD.KA.BAR. For the translation of *izziz* we argue from context. Presumably some Canaanite word meaning "to draw" which is similar in form to *izziz* underlies the *izziz* of the text. However, we must not rule out the possibility of *paṭar siparri* being an acc. of instrument (cf. Jos. 7.25 *ʾeben,* Prov. 10.4 *kap*?), and perhaps translate "he attacked me with a dagger." We would then have normal Accadian in *nazāzu muḫḫi.*

Line 20: "I dwell and lie (helpless) in my city." It seems most improbable that *ḳa-la-ti* is to be derived from *kalū*: 1) *tertiae infirmae* verbs in the perfect have *-ītī* (*ḳabītī,* etc.); 2) the use of the ḲA-sign with one exception (*ka₄-bi-it,* 88.47) always reflects a *qoph*; 3) *ḳalātī* (or the like) never has the meaning "I am held back," but rather "I am negligent." This points to *ḳālu* = Ugar. *qwl,* "to fall," see above, n. 65 [above, p. 27]. For the meaning "to lie," cf. *npl* in Ges.-Buhl[13], p. 535a.

Line 22: [*a-nu-ma ki-a-ma*] *aš-ta-par* ... For this restoration rather than Knudtzon's cf. note on 76.27–28.

Line 23: [*ù la-a ta*]*-te-ru-na a-wa-tu*. In view of the nom. *awatu* Knudtzon's *TUtēruna* is very doubtful. *ta-te-ru-na* = *tattēruna,* IV_1. Cf. *tu-te-ru-na a-wa-ta(m)* in 83.7–8.

Line 33: *mi-na* <*a-ḳa-bu*> *a-na* ... The omission seems certain from the parallel in 85.11–12, *minā aḳabuna ana awīlūt ḫupšīya*. Following the parallel in detail, we should perhaps restore *aḳabuna*.

EA 82

For a full discussion and a new translation of this letter, see Albright-Moran, *JCS* 2 [below, Paper 2, pp. 131–139] .

[16]Cf. von Soden, *ZA* NF 6, p. 205.

EA 83; *BB* 14

Lines 7–9: "Why dost thou not send back word to me that I may know what I should do?" On the quasi-modal force of *īpušu* (9) and the purpose force of *īdī* ..., see above IV F [p. 47 in the present volume].

Lines 16–20: "Let it not be said, 'In the days of the commissioners the Ḫapiru took all the lands.' Not thus shall it be said and they will not be able to take it!" *ina ūmē* (19) is almost certainly a dittography. With line 20 (*lā tiliʾu laḳāši*) compare 108.45 *allū lā tiliʾūna*, "behold, they shall not prevail." My rendering, based on the syntax of *yuḳba* and *yuḳbu* (on which see the section on the Subjunctive, above [pp. 84–98 in the present volume]), gives much better sense than Knudtzon's.

Line 30: [*t*]*a(!)-din-ni*, not [*t*]*u-din-ni* (Knudtzon). As already mentioned, there is not a valid instance of UD = TÚ in the Byblos letters, if indeed in all Amarna. *tadin* is attested in 91.17. Render lines 30–31: "place me under the charge of Yanḥamu."

Line 37: *ušširašu šūta(m)*, "send him back, even him." Knudtzon was led astray in his translation by failing to recognize the Canaanitism of the independent pronoun in apposition with a verbal suffix, on which see above III B [p. 18 in the present volume].

Line 43: "... soldiers of the camp (garrison)." ERÍN.MEŠ *ka-ra-š*[*i*] cannot be separated from ERÍN.MEŠ KI.KAL.KIB (106.48) and ERÍN.MEŠ. KAL.BAD.KIB (92.48), nor the latter from the frequent KI.KAL.BAD = *karāšu* at Boğazköy.[17] The KI.KAL.KIB cannot be different from the KAL.BAD.KIB. We seem to have a confusion in the ideogram, though a satisfactory explanation for KIB is wanting.

EA 84; *VS* XI, 41

Line 15: *i-pí-ti*, "I opened."

Line 17: *šūta(m)* lúšaḫū(!) *u kalbu*, "he, the swine and dog." The sign in question, heretofore unidentified, is GIR; cf. the Middle Babylonian forms of the sign in Labat, *Manuel d'Épigraphie akkadienne*, p. 158, no. 346. On GIR = *šaḫū*, cf. Chicago Syllabary, p. 19, no. 113. For the pejorative use of "swine" in Canaanite, cf. Prov. 11.22. (Dr. Albright identified this sign after a guess on my part that it was an ideogram for "swine"; I had erroneously tried to identify it with ŠAḪ.)

[17]Cf. Labat, p. 145.

Line 21: Knudtzon reads *b*[*e*]-*l*[*i*]. Correct to *be-lí(!)-ia(!)*. There simply is no LI in this place. LÍ is identical in form with its occurrences (as NI) in lines 18 and 38. IA is just a bit different from its form elsewhere; note also that IA of line 7 is also a bit unusual.

Line 24: *ma-ri-iṣ ma-g*[*al*]*(!)*. Knudtzon reads *mariṣma*, but the autograph shows traces of another wedge following. Though it appears to be a vertical, one cannot be sure because the tablet is broken at this point. In view of the parallels in 95.41, 103.7, 114.50, and 116.54 GAL is virtually certain.

Line 33: g·DA.MU-*ia*, "my Adonis." For DA.MU = *Tammuz*, see Otto Schroeder, *OLZ* 1915, cols. 291–293.

***EA* 85; *VS* XI, 42**

Line 9: "For two years have I been continually plundered of grain." For *mašāʾu*, *mašāḫu*, see BG, p. 182b.

Line 19: *arda-šu a(!)-na(!) ia(!)-šu*, "his servant for himself" (IA being an error for ŠA). Knudtzon reads *ardašu u āla-šu*, yet the traces in Schroeder are absolutely clear and URU is simply impossible. The scribal error noted above may be the reason for this lapse on the part of the amazingly accurate Knudtzon.

Line 26: The gloss *ḫu-ta-ri-ma* is possibly to be related with Ugar. *ʿtrṭm*, parallel with *ksmm* (Hebr. *kussĕmîm*; cf. *UH*, p. 256, no. 1473).

Line 38: *ti-š*[*a-i-l*]*u(!)*, not *ti*-m[a-la-k]u (Knudtzon). The latter fits neither the traces (compare LU in line 62 and KU in line 85 with the traces here) nor morphology, which demands *timaliku* (cf. *yimallik*, 94.12; *yimaliku*, 104.16, 114.48). The Glossary corrects this error (EA II, p. 1461) to *timaliku*. This however is impossible because there is not enough room for LI.—For the form and meaning of our restoration cf. 89.40.

Line 58: *mārē-ia*. The autograph shows conclusively that the sign is TUR, not I (Knudtzon).

Line 81: [*tu*]-*da-bi-ra-šu*, not [*ù ú*]-*da-bi-ra-šu*. There is little space at the beginning of this line, certainly not enough for Ù.Ú. Knudtzon also neglected the parallel (76.39) and the fact that ERÍN.MEŠ *piṭatu* is regularly construed as fem. sg.[18] The asyndetic structure is not without parallel (cf. Purpose Clauses).

[18]Cf. n. 163 [p. 61 in the present volume].

EA 87; BB 22

Line 8: "Why dost thou put me off (saying): ..." For this rendering, which makes perfect sense in the context, cf. BG p. 81a.

Line 10, "to me." Knudtzon missed this Canaanitism, for which cf. Prepositions II D above [p. 19 in the present volume].

Lines 15–20: "And behold, I shall heed thy words and will send (a man). But if he returns empty-handed, and he (ᶜAbd-Ashirta) hears that there are no troops with him, then Batruna will be joined to him." In line 16 read most probably *u-wa-si*[r_4]*(!)*, following Albright's autograph. For ŠIR$_4$, cf. 84.39. In line 18 read *ù i-ši-me e-nu(!)-ú ia-nu-um*. I am indebted to Dr. Albright for this reading which is completely confirmed by *e-nu-ú* in 92.31. Cf. BB, pl. 6, where the NU is quite clear.

Line 23: Knudtzon read AT and explained it as an error for LA which the sense demands. However, Dr. Albright informs me that the sign really is LA, though written a bit unusually: the very small initial lower horizontal wedge seems to be a peculiarity of the scribe who wrote this letter, for we find it again in 88.19, undoubtedly written by the same scribe; he also overlays his first vertical with a second, thus leading Knudtzon to read the sign as SI in 88.19. Cf. note *ad loc*.

Line 25: For the correction here, cf. note on 69.30.

Line 26: [*a-ṣa-a*]*m*; cf. *JNES* 8, 124–125 [below, Paper 3, pp. 141–142].

Line 26: The doubt I expressed in the above article on *ša damḳat* (not *ša damḳi* with Knudzton; *ṣābu* is regularly *feminine*), I retract. Knudtzon's certainty about the sign and the parallels now appears convincing.[19]

EA 88; BB 17

Line 19: *ma-ni ūmāti*^{ti} *la(!) yi-na-mu-uš*, "how long will he not budge ..." Cf. the parallel 87.23–24. On LA, cf. note on 87.23. The TI phonetic complement is not surprising since the fem. pl. form of *yôm* is attested in Heb. (Deut. 32.7) and in later Byblian Phoenician.[20] On the idiom *man(n)i ūmāti*, lit. "what of days," cf. III A [above, p. 21].

Lines 37–39: "and I will request a city from him for my dwelling-place and I will be safe." This rendering is not certain but does seem an im-

[19] *EA* I, p. 417, n. h.
[20] *GP*, p. 106.

provement over Knudtzon's. As for *ir-r*[*i*]*-iš* = "I will request," cf. *i-ri-šu*, "request" in 82.17. In line 39 I read *u bal-*<*ṭá*>*-ti*. This is of course not certain, but in its favor are several parallels (83.27, 123.35, 82.45). As for Ú = "and," cf. line 10 above, and Knudtzon's note (*EA* I, p. 418, n. f); also 84.32.—De facto, Rib-Adda later carried out this threat and did name a city he wanted to live in once Byblos was lost; cf. 137.64.

EA 89; VS XI, 43

For a discussion and translation of this letter see the forthcoming article, "Rib-Adda and the Affairs of Tyre," by Albright-Moran, *JCS* 4 [below, Paper 4, pp. 143–150].

EA 90; VS XI 44

Line 6: *muḫḫi-*[*ia il-ḳí*]. In view of the exact parallel in 91.18–20 *ilḳī* rather than *laḳū* (Knudtzon).

Line 17: *tu-uš-mu-na* ⸢*ù*⸣, not [*ù la-ḳ*]*a* (Knudtzon). Cf. *JCS* 4, note on line 9 [below, Paper 4, p. 146].

Line 21: [*kalb*]*u*. Knudtzon reads [*m*]*a*. The traces in the autograph could very well be that of KU. Since it is certainly ᶜAbd-Ashirta to whom Rib-Adda is referring, we need not hesitate to give him his usual epithet, especially in view of the parallels in 79.45 and 84.35.

Line 47: *u* [*ti*]*-na-ṣa-ru*, not [*a*]*-na-ṣa-ru*, with Knudtzon. This is certain both from parallels (85.19–22, 131.12–14) and from our study of purpose clauses according to which an indicative never expresses purpose if dependent upon a volitive.

EA 92; VS XI, 46

Line 10: *a-ši-ib ù*(!). The autograph shows a vertical wedge not noted by Knudtzon. It is certainly the end of Ù.

Line 11: *maš-ši-ik-tum*. The MAŠ is clear in the autograph. Cf. Idri-mi, line 4, where *mašiktu* occurs in a similar context. Render in line 11: "An evil war has been made against me."

Lines 18–23: "And if ᶜAbd-Ashrati hears that my man has arrived from the presence of the king and he hears that there is nothing (with him) and that there is no force which has come forth to me, then behold, he will *attack*."

Line 35: [*al*]-⸢*lu*⸣-⸢*mi*⸣. There is a clear LU in the autograph.

EA 93; VS XI, 47

Line 12: *nidag(g)al āla*, "that we may care for the city." "To inspect the city" makes little sense. For the idiom, cf. *rāʾāh* (Ges.-Buhl[13], 75a).

Line 24: "Things are not as they were before." I believe this line is to be connected with what follows rather than, as Knudtzon interprets it, with the preceding lines. Thus, "Things are not as they were before. If this year there is no archer-host, then he will be powerful forever."

EA 94; WA 78

Lines 7–13: "I do not speak any treacherous word to the king, my lord, I consider my word and my word is good, o king, my lord! I said to the king, my lord: 'Send an archer-host that it may take ᶜAbd-Ashrata.' Who would advise (that) he would resist the archer-host of the king, my lord?" For *a-wa-te* = "my word," note *ḳa-be-te* in line 10. For *da-mi-iḳ* in spite of Knudtzon's *iš*(!)-*mi-ig*, the traces in WA are certainly those of DA—and *damiḳ* makes sense! For the correct rendering of *nazāzu ina pāni*, cf. 71.25–26, 108.26–27, 362.65. Our rendering is virtually certain, at least in its understanding of the situation and the import of the letter. We have striking confirmation in 108.20–28, the burden of which is virtually the same as that of 94.7–13. In 108 Rib-Adda complains of slanders against him. He affirms that he tells the king everything exactly as he sees and hears it. He goes on (25–28): "But who are they, the dogs, that they can resist the archer-host of the king, the Sun?" From this it is clear that the slanderers claimed Rib-Adda was leading the Egyptians into a trap by asking for troops to be sent to them to capture ᶜAbd-Ashirta—ᶜAbd-Ashirta was too powerful to be overcome by a casual detachment. Which interpretation is confirmed by lines 51–58 of the same letter, of which 51–52 were completely misunderstood by Knudtzon. For a fuller analysis of these lines, cf. note *ad loc.*; suffice it now to say that Rib-Adda hearkens back to the idea that the king should not believe what others tell him—he can take ᶜAbd-Ashirta's sons in a couple of days!—For Weber's views, cf. *EA* II, pl. 1186, 1592; for Ebeling's, cf. *BA* 8, p. 77.

EA 101; BB 44

Lines 3–9: "Behold, the ships of the MIŠI men are not to enter the land of the Amorites. For they (the Amorites) have killed ᶜAbd-Ashirta, since they had no wool and he no purple linen ... to sell (to give?)."

Lines 3–6 have been interpreted by Weber (cf. *EA* II, p. 1197–1198) and Knudtzon to mean that the *awīlu miši* killed ᶜAbd-Ashirta. However, if one compares lines 28–30, one sees that *dakū* can here refer only to *māt Amurri* (taken as a plural). Rib-Adda's indignation at the assassination of ᶜAbd-Ashirta is, of course, feigned. What he is clearly attempting to do is to have the Amorites boycotted, and so remove their threat to himself. Men appointed by the king are to see that no Amorite ship enters Sidon or Beirut (24–29), and the three cities (also Arvad?) and the MIŠI men are to be ordered not to send ships to Amurru (32–35).—In line 7 read *ia-nu šipāta*(!). The sign, read by Knudtzon as KIN but not translated, is clearly SÍG. The same sign occurs in *EA* 22 I.46, II.38. As Knudtzon himself noted (*BA* IV, p. 413), the lower oblique wedge in this sign is further to the left than in the Amarna writing of KIN. While KIN and SÍG are virtually identical in Old and Middle Babylonian, a consistent difference is exactly that noted by Knudtzon in the Amarna writings. Moreover, the writing of the sign at Ugarit is identical with the writing here; *Syria* 15, p. 140, ll. 1–4. Confirming SÍG is the fact that in *EA* 22 II.38 the sign occurs in a list of garments.—The use of ZA.GÌN in the meaning of "purple" is found in an Accadian text at Ugarit: SÍG.ZA.GÌN = *uknātum*, "purple wool"; *Syria, ibid.* Perhaps we should interpret GAD.ZA.GÌN as *uknātum*. The meaning, however, whether we take GAD = *kitū* or as part of an ideogram, remains the same.

EA 102; *BB* 23

Line 10: Should we interpret *tašapparta* as passive: "Why wast thou (hast thou been) sent?"

Lines 11–13: For the correct translation, see Albright, *BASOR* 82, p. 48.

Lines 25–27: "Thou knowest that all of them are slanderers, and therefore thou shalt not make inquiry concerning me from my enemies." Knudtzon missed the meaning of *tišalunī*, for which cf. 82.12. *šāru* is not so much "feindlich" as "treacherous, slanderous"; cf. the various contexts of *awīlūtu šārūtu*, v.g., in 94.15 and the context discussed above.

EA 103; *VS* XI 52

Line 36: *šumma* = "behold"; cf. Particles.

EA 104; WA 60

Lines 19–24: From 76.14–16 it is clear that Knudtzon misinterprets these lines (also 116.70–71) when he makes them an affirmative statement. It is obvious too from the context that they are rather a sarcastic question. "Are they the king of the Cossaeans, etc.?"

Lines 34–39: "... and they will kill the commissioner and the auxiliary force which is in Simyra. What can I do, for I am not able to go to Simyra?" Knudtzon interprets *ṣāb tillati* (35; BI is an error for TIL) as the subject of *īpušuna* in line 37. Against this are three facts: 1) the word order would be quite unusual; 2) *ṣābu* is usually feminine, and so we should have most probably *tīpušuna*; 3) *minā īpušuna*, though usually with *anāku*, is a stock phrase of the 1st person (cf. 74.63, 90.22, 117.92, 119.14, etc.). Note that in the Glossary (*EA* II, p. 1402) *īpušuna* is listed under the 1st person.

Lines 40–52: "The cities of Ampi, Shigata, Ullaza, Arvad are hostile to me. Should they hear that I have entered Simyra, these cities, the ships and the sons of ᶜAbd-Ashirta will follow(?) me and attack me and I will be unable to get out and Byblos will be joined to the Ḫapiru." I thus interpret *ša-ma-ma* as 3rd pl. fem. with enclitic *-ma*. This accords perfectly with the pl. "cities" as the implied subject, for *ālu* is regularly feminine in these letters. The syntax is also good, for we have good parallels for the interpretation of *šamā* as the verb of a virtual protasis of a conditional sentence (cf. Conditional Sentences). And the resulting meaning is perfect, fitting the context in every respect. Note that unless we interpret lines 43–52 as we have, then 50–52 are unintelligible: Byblos's falling does not depend on Rib-Adda's going to Simyra—as Knudtzon would have it—but it would depend on his getting back there once it was under attack. For the dittography of *šunu* (43–44), see the parallels in the note on 77.10. *ina ṣēri*, lit. "at the back." I think it better to interpret this as "follow" than "against," which idea is expressed in the next line.

EA 105; VS XI 53

Lines 18–20: "... when the archer-host came forth all the property of ᶜAbd-Ashirta in their possession was not taken away." Knudtzon renders "... haben sie nicht ... alles ... mit sich genommen?" I object to this because *laḳī* is taken as a sg. agreeing with a plural subject, a construction which, though attested, is very rare in these letters; moreover, because we would expect a question to be introduced by the negative and the verb.

Line 34: Albright reads ${}^{\text{m.}}$*a-ma-an-*⸢*ma-ša*⸣; *JNES* 5, p. 10.

EA 106; VS XI 54

Line 15: Following Thureau-Dangin[21] read *ēkalli ma-an-ga(qa?),* "... He is distressed ..."

Line 30: "And how can the king say ..." *kī* = "how," not "wenn" (Knudtzon).

Lines 30–34: " 'Why does Rib-Adda send a tablet to his lord concerning a crime which was committed (much) earlier?' And behold, now, lest it be done so now to me!" Line 32 is obviously part of Pharaoh's question, not of Rib-Adda's reply (Knudtzon).

Line 38: "the fan-bearer of the king, my lord." For this title, see *JNES* 5, p. 13 and references there given.

Lines 45–49: "Moreover, as for all my cities which I speak of in the presence of my lord, my lord knows whether they have returned. When the troops of the camp departed, all were alienated." For the use of *tāru* referring to cities, cf. the interesting parallel in I Sam. 7.14: *wat-tāšōbnāh heʿārîm ʾăšer lāqĕḥû pĕlištîm.*

EA 107; VS XI, 55

Lines 10–11: "And with my mouth I speak words to the king which are true." Knudtzon renders: "und (was betrifft) meinen Mund, (meine) Worte, so habe ich zum König Wahrheit gesprochen." Obviously this is clumsy, postulating two accusatives of specification. I consider *kitta* as an acc., predicative to *awātē*.—As for *pūya,* either the scribe started out with this as his subject and slipped into the first person because of the sense, or it is an error either for *pāya* (acc. of specification) or for *pīya* (with *ina* omitted on the analogy of the Can. practice of omitting the labial *ba* before a following labial).

Line 14: ${}^{\text{m.}}$*iḫ-ri-pí-ta,* not ${}^{\text{m.}}$*aḫ-ri-bi-ta* (Knudtzon); *JNES* 5, p. 14.

Line 16: ${}^{\text{m.}}$*ḫa-ip,* not ${}^{\text{m.}}$*ḫa-ib; ibid.,* p. 10.

Line 42: As Knudtzon recognized (*EA* I, p. 474, n. b), this is the same sign as in 108.15, and probably in 124.51. In 108.15 we have the gloss

[21] *RA* 19, p. 92, n. 3.

ši-ir-ma. This has always been baffling, for it has been considered a word, whereas in fact it is the phonetic spelling or the ideogram plus enclitic *-ma* (note *wi-i-ma* in 108.16). The sign is KEŠDA, the writing being almost identical with an attested writing in Old Babylonian.[22] Their connection with horses and chariots here and in 108 points to "chariot-drivers" or the like.

EA 108, VS XI, 56

Line 15: See 107.42 above.

Line 16: On this Egyptian word (*wᶜw*), cf. Albright *JEA* 23, p. 96 and references there given.

Lines 20–28: For a discussion of these lines, cf. note on 94.8.

Lines 32–33: "Did he not take ᶜAbd-Ashirta for himself(!)?" Knudtzon mistranslated this passage and 117.27–33. See the discussion of the parallel in 117.

Line 37: *ki-na-na da-an-n*⸢*u*⸣(!). Knudtzon is correct (*EA* I, p. 108, n. d) that the traces are against NU and are more like PAP. However, since *kinanna dannū* or the like has perfect parallels (cf. 82.13, 109.60, 126.66), and since in 122.15 the traces of an indisputable NU are identical with our NU (note that, as in 108, NU in 122 extends its cross wedge far below the horizontal), the reading is virtually certain. Note too that in view of *šunu* in line 28 *da-an-X* must be an adjective or a permansive of which *šunu* is the subject.

Lines 34–38: "Moreover, behold the governors have not set their faces against them, and so they are powerful." For *šumma* = "behold," cf. Particles above [p. 12 in the present volume].

Line 45: "Behold, they shall not prevail!"

Lines 51–52: "Why dost thou listen to other men?" Knudtzon's rendering is completely wrong. Rib-Adda wants to point out to the king that there is no need of listening to others, for the king's messengers still can keep up contact with the court even though, due to that dog, Aziru, they must travel at night. Just what *awīlū šanūtu* are saying is clear from 56–58: they deny Aziru can be taken, but Rib-Adda says he and his brothers could be taken in a few days.

[22]Cf. Labat, *Manuel d'Épigraphie akkadienne*, p. 104, no. 99.

_EA_ 109; _VS_ XI, 57

Lines 16–19: [*šum-ma ū*]*ma*$^{pl.}$ *yi-iš-mu šarru*^{ru}
[*ù i-na ū*]*mī*$^{pl.}$ *yi-ìl-ti-ḳú šu-nu*
[*ù šum*]-*ma mu-ša yi-iš-mu ù*
[*mu-š*]*a yi-ìl-ti-ḳú šu-nu*

"If the king takes heed for a day,
then in a day he will capture them;
and if he takes heed for a night, then
in a night he will capture them."

The restoration in line 16 fits perfectly the broken space. There is some confirmation from the parallel in lines 18–19, which probably begin as indicated (cf. *EA* I, p. 482, n. b). I restore *ù i-na* in line 17 because it fits the space better, *ù* itself being too small, despite the *mūša / mūša* parallelism in lines 18–19. For *ina* UD.KAM.MEŠ cf. 108.57–58. I consider UD.KAM.MEŠ as singular because of the *mūša / mūša* parallelism. For otiose MEŠ, cf. ERÍN.MEŠ = *ṣābu*. Against Knudtzon I regard *šunu* in lines 17,19 as the object of the verb, not the subject. *šunūti* is unknown in these letters.

Lines 48–49: [*ti*]-*da-lu-na awīlūt māt mi-iṣ-ri* [*ki-ma*]
[*ka*]*lbē da-mi-iḳ mu-tu a*-[*na ia*]-*ši*

"They drive out the Egyptians like dogs. Death is sweet to me. (And line 50.) May they not rejoice over my lord!" In line 49 Knudtzon reads [^{iṣu}]*kakkē*$^{pl.}$, declaring there is not enough room for Ù, though admitting GIŠ does not fit the space satisfactorily (*EA* I, p. 484, n.b). I read UR.KU, a well-attested ideogram (cf. Glossary, *EA* II, p. 1432). *kīma* is only conjectured then from context. We must of course read *damik mūtu ana iāši*, not *dami iḳmutu*, which has no meaning. In line 50 Knudtzon leaves *išmuḫū(m)* untranslated; Ebeling and Weber derive it from *šm*ᶜ. Against this is the fact that *šm*ᶜ is never so written in the Byblos letters, and the characteristic vowel is inexplicable on the supposition that the root is *šm*ᶜ. On the other hand, *išmuḫū* is a good Acc. form of *šamāḫu*. Ps. 35.19: *ʾal yiśmĕḥû lî ʾôyĕbê šeqer*, "Let not my lying enemies rejoice over me."

_EA_ 112; _VS_ XI 61

Line 10: Here, as in 125.11–12, it has been taken for granted that *ištu manni* means "from whom." However, closer analysis shows that such a rendering has little meaning. It is certainly quite clear against whom

Rib-Adda is to guard the city and himself, but it is not clear, at least not to Rib-Adda, what means he is to use in guarding himself, etc. This is perfectly clear in 125.14ff. where Rib-Adda points out that *formerly* there was a garrison in Byblos, and besides there was food; the same is true in 122.11ff. Note also 121.10 *minū yinaṣ(ṣ)irannī*, "What will protect me?" followed likewise by a description of his former strength. Note too 126.33 where instead of *ištu manni* we have *kī*. As for 112.11–12 (*ištu nakrīya u ištu* $^{\text{lú.pl.}}$*ḫupšīya*), this is an ironical question—Rib-Adda asks if he is to use his enemies or his serfs to protect himself. Hence we must translate *ištu manni* by "with what."—As for the meaning *ištu* = "with," there are several possibilities. One: *ištu* = Can. *ba*, "from, with," used analogically with the meaning "with" because of its proper meaning "from." For the same possibility in 82.30, cf. *JCS* 2 [see below, Paper 2, p. 138]. Two: this meaning of *ištu* reflects an instrumental meaning of Can. *min* though this preposition is not attested with certainty in later Phoenician. Third: *ištu* reflects *išti / u* of Old Accadian, Assyrian, and the Hymnal Epic Dialect with the meaning "along side of, with."[23] In view of the use of the rare *inu* in 87.18 and 92.31 for *inūma* this possibility is not as remote as it might at first seem.[24]

Line 49: *šūrib* is more probably passive, "he was brought in."

EA 113; *WA* 63

Line 6: *ia-aš-ku-u*[*n*] according to the autograph.

Line 15:

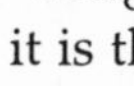
161.21 (BB, pl. 22)

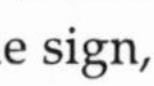
Mari II, 140.31

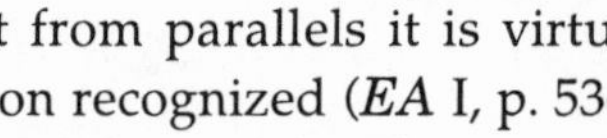
Labat, *Manuel d'Épigraphie akkadienne*, p. 72.

The sign in question is MÁŠ (= *urīṣu*), hitherto unidentified here and in 55.12, 124.50, 125.22, 161.21, 324.14, 325.16. In 125.22 the sign is lacking the oblique wedge found elsewhere, but from parallels it is virtually certain that it is the same sign, as Knudtzon recognized (*EA* I, p. 536, n. d). Above I give the sign as it appears in Amarna (the only occurrence for which there is a photo), in Mari—this occurrence has not hitherto been noted, wrongly read as SÍG by Jean[25]—and in Middle Babylonian. It will be noted that there is considerable fluctuation in the writing. Our Amarna MÁŠ preserves the essentials of the sign. Moreover, it

[23] Von Soden, *ZA* NF 7, pp. 138–139.

[24] On *inu*, see von Soden, *ibid.*, p. 98, n. 2.

[25] *RÉS*, "Autres Lettres de Mari," p. 30 (reprint of articles appearing 1942–1945).

fits every context perfectly. However, until we find a closer parallel for the Amarna writing, some doubt must remain as to the correctness of the identification. MÁŠ is certainly the most probable.

EA 114; *BB* 13

Line 23: From the parallel in 79.40 I suspect that we should read neither *la-ḳa-t*[*um*] (Knudtzon) nor *la-ḳa-am* (*BB*), but *la-ḳa-ia*(!). However, lacking both photograph and a good autograph, we cannot be sure.

Line 27: We should probably read *ki-*⌜*a*⌝*-ma*, *kīma* not being used elsewhere as a subordinating conjunction. For the *cliché*, *anum(m)a kīʾama ištapru* (or the like), cf. *JCS* 4, note on line 7 [below, Paper 4, p. 146].

Lines 46–49: "Is it pleasing to thee (that) the king's enemies are hostile to me, and his governors for whom he takes concern are on their side?" For the construction, cf. VIII Substantival Clauses [above, pp. 64–66]. Contrast Knudtzon's translation (italics indicate a doubtful rendering): "Ist (doch dies) bei dir gut? Ein Gegner des Königs übt Feindschaft mit mir, und seine Regenten (*sind wohl die*), für welche er sorgen *sollte*."

EA 116; *WA* 61

Line 61: Knudzton's translation of lines 61ff. as a declarative sentence and Weber's note (*EA* II, p. 1214) stressing the contradiction between these lines and what we read elsewhere of the previous Pharaoh's action as described by Rib-Adda are almost incredible. As if Rib-Adda would admit the predecessor of the Pharaoh had not been ever ready to send help! Moreover, the implicit argument of these lines is missed: your father (Amenophis III) aided us, now you are the successor not only to his throne, but to his policy! Render therefore "Behold thy father, did he not come forth and did he not care for the lands of his governor?" For *dagālu* in the sense of "care for," cf. note on 93.12.

EA 117; *VS* XI, 62

Line 11: I render *eštu āl ṣumura*, "because of Simyra." This makes better sense in the context. Moreover, "a governor from Simyra" would be expressed *ḫāzān(u) (ša) āl ṣumura*.

Line 12: "the face of everyone is against me." Strike off the two supposed occurrences (here and 134.30) of *panū*, "to turn." *pānu* (**pănyu*) is a noun; cf. 90.21–22 and II Chron. 32.2 *pānāu lammilhāmāh*.

Line 26: The second *u yuwaš(š)ara* is certainly a dittography.

Lines 27–34: "Did he not capture ᶜAbd-Ashirta together with his property just as I said? Did I write lying words (then) to my lord? Yet thou sayest: 'Why dost thou write lying words?' If my words are heeded, Azaru like his father will still be taken. Behold I am the courageous one of the king, my lord!"—Knudtzon mistranslated and misunderstood these lines: 1) He makes the first two sentences declarative—certainly an ignorance of psychology; 2) He restores at the end of line 33 *abišu*, and has therefore Rib-Adda promise the Pharaoh the same success—or lack of it—with Aziru as his father had with ᶜAbd-Ashirta! Note that in line 29 the question is rhetorical—ᶜAbd-Ashirta was certainly taken by Amenophis III. Lines 30–31 refer to Rib-Adda's present advice to capture Aziru, which thing Amenophis IV seems to think beyond his power. In lines 33–34 Rib-Adda reaffirms his advice. In line 34 Knudtzon leaves KAL.GA untranslated. My rendering is based on the probable equation of Acc. *dannu* and Can. *ḥazaq(u)*. I do not know whether to render "the courageous one" (cf. II Sam. 10.12) or "the loyal one" (cf. I Chron. 11.10).

Line 55: *ša-ri a-na ia-ši*. I follow Dr. Albright's rendering "I am lied to." The case ending of *šāri* is a problem. Perhaps it is an acc. pl. (of exclamation) or a verb like *taḳbu* is understood.

Line 83: Restore *l*[*u n*]*a-ṣa-ra-*[*ta*]; cf. F. Thureau-Dangin, *Recueil d'Études égyptologiques dédiées à la mémoire de Jean-François Champollion*, "Une lettre d'Amenophis (III ou IV)," p. 380–381.

EA 118; *BB* 25 and *VS* XI, 63

Lines 16–17: "let him give me my due." Knudtzon renders "und gibt mein Recht in meine Hand." This is too vague and sins by literalism. The same idiom is found in Job 36.3 (*ulĕpôᶜălî ᵓettēn ṣedeq*) with the same meaning, though *ṣedeq* is usually rendered by "righteousness" or the like. For *nadānu ina ḳāti*, cf. I Chron. 16.7. Note: "my due" does not mean Rib-Adda is to get something out of this suit, but he wants the credit due to him for his share in the property taken by Yapa-Adda for the king.

Line 50: "There is hostility against him." We take the enigmatical ḪAR as UR_5 = *šūᵓatu*. The construction is frequent in these letters (cf. lines 21–22, 29–30) and the resulting meaning fits the context perfectly. However, since this ideogram is unparalleled (so far) in the Amarna letters, it must remain only a plausible suggestion. Note, however, the rather recherché MU = *yāši* in Taanach I, 14; cf. *BASOR* 94, p. 17, n. 25. This lends probability to our UR_5.

_EA_ 119; _VS_ XI, 64

Lines 18–23: "If it is said in the presence of the king, 'Rib-Adda put to death the archer-host of the king when the commissioners were alive,' then let me tell (thee) all their deeds." Knudtzon leaves *adab(b)uba* untranslated. I follow Ebeling (*EA* II, p. 1593), with the slight difference that I consider *adabbuba* a cohortative, on which see the discussion of the Subjunctive above [pp. 84–98 in the present volume].

_EA_ 120; _VS_ XI, 65

Line 11: *ma-ḳí-bu* = Can. **maqqibu* = Heb. *maqqébet*, "hammer." First recognized by Dr. Albright.

Line 18: *ka-aḫ-šu* = Ugar. *kaḥṯu* "chair throne." First recognized by Gordon.[26]

_EA_ 121; _VS_ XI, 66

Line 15: Restore [*ú-ul*]. This restoration rather than *iānu* (Knudtzon) follows both from the fact that *iānu* takes the acc. and the parallel in 122.28.

Line 51: *i-na mātāti*, not *ina šeē* (Knudtzon); cf. F. Thureau-Dangin, *RA* 19, p. 93, n. 1.

_EA_ 122; _VS_ XI, 67

Line 21: Restore ⸢*i*⸣*-na-ṣa-r*[*u ra-m*]*a-ni-ia*. Knudtzon's restoration of *diniya* is unparalleled and does not fill the space of the break. For a parallel to my restoration, cf. 125.12–13.

_EA_ 124; _WA_ 62, 64d, 65

Lines 35–40: "Thus thou dost say, 'Thou writest to me more than all the (other) governors.' Why should they write to thee? Their cities belong to them, my cities Aziru has taken." In line 35 I suspect that we should read *at-t*[*a*](!) and ignore the middle wedge which led Knudtzon to read *ma*. There are many cases where a scribe has written over another wedge, erasing or covering it only imperfectly; cf. note on 87.23. In line

[26] *UH* p. 238, no. 962.

39 at the end, read *š*[*a-šu-nu*]. Knudtzon's rendering of these lines makes no sense whatever.

EA 126; *VS* XI, 68

Line 4: ^giš^*taš*[*karinni-m*]*a*. For ^giš^KU = *taškarinnu*, not *urkarinnu*, I am indebted ultimately to Prof. Benno Landsberger, who has informed Prof. Albright privately that a vocabulary makes this reading certain. The reading of KU, however, is here a bit doubtful; cf. *EA* I, p. 538, n. d.

Lines 4–8: "As for my lord's writing for beechwood(?) that it be taken from Alalḫi[27] and from Ugarit, I am not able to send my ships there." On the use of *inūma*, see Substantival Clauses [above, pp. 64–66]; on the asyndetic subordinate clause, see Purpose Clauses [pp. 77–83].

Lines 14–18: "Moreover, why does the king give everything possible and provisions to the governors, my friends, and to me he does not give anything?" Knudtzon completes the first sentence with *mimma* in line 15. This results in a very unusual word order in the following sentence. Besides the first sentence as a result is not very meaningful. I consider *mimma u balāṭa(m)* a kind of hendiadys; cf. *mimmū ana balāṭišu* in line 21. For *minūm*, "why," cf. line 49.

Line 26: *tu-*[*ša-ru*]. Knudtzon's *tu-*[*ši-ra*] cannot be right: 1) *ši-ra* does not fill the break; 2) the form must be passive with ERÍN.MEŠ *maṣ(ṣ)artu* in line 25 the subject.

Line 33: *a-na-ṣa-r*[*u ra-ma-ni-ia*]. For this restoration, cf. note on 122.21 and 125.12–13.

Lines 44–47: "If the king hates his city, then I will abandon it. But if me (he hates), then let him set me free." At the end of line 46 Knudtzon reads doubtfully *ši-b*[*a*]. Read Ù which fits the traces perfectly and makes the passage perfectly clear. For *paṭāru* in line 47 as active, cf. II Chron. 23.8 where the same verb means "to free from service."

EA 127; *VS* XI, 69

Line 33: *riḫiṣmi awīlūtiya*, "sind meine Leute niedergeschmettert" (Knudtzon). This translation rests on the assumption that *rḫṣ* = Can. *r*^c^*ṣ*,

[27]For Alalḫi instead of Zalḫi, see Albright, *BASOR* 63, p. 25. Sidney Smith, following Badawi, identifies *t*ʾ*rḫ*ʾ of the Karnak stele of Amenhotep II with Zalḫi of *EA* 126.5; *Statue of Idri-mi*, p. 53. There is no basis, as far as I can discover, for Egy. *ṯ*ʾ = cuneiform ZA (*sa*, *ṣa*, *za*). Dussaud's attempt to equate Ugar. *Ṯlḫn* with Zalḫi is, as Maisler remarks, not too happy; *JPOS* 16, p. 157.

first proposed by Winckler (Glossary, p. 29*). It is based principally on 141.31, hitherto read *ti-ra-ḫa-aṣ*. However, Prof. Albright's recent collation of the Amarna Tablets in the British Museum shows that we are to read here *ti-ma*(!)-*aḫ*(!)-*aṣ*.—Though we must therefore retain Acc. *riḫṣu*, we may have a parallel for the idiom in Dan. 11.22 where *šāṭap* is used in the sense of overwhelming armed forces. Hence here we would render, "Behold, there has been an overwhelming of my men."

EA 129; *VS* XI, 70

Line 32: *ṣa-bat-mi ni-*[*nu*]. The restoration is certain from the parallel in 362.25–26. Render lines 32–34: "And they say, 'If we take the cities of Byblos, then what will the archer-host do?"

EA 130; *VS* XI, 72

Lines 21–24: "Behold, formerly my fathers were strong. Though there was hostility against them, still the royal garrison was with them, the provisions of the king in their possession." I here follow Ebeling (*BA* 8, p. 77) and take *dan(n)u* with *abūtiya*.

Lines 31–35: "Behold the governors are hostile. They decimate our city. They are like a dog, and there is no one who desires to follow them." In line 31, following the autograph, read *a-nu-ma* [*nu*]-*kúr*(!). In line 32 read *ti-du-ku-*[*na*], and omit Knudtzon's [*ia*]-*nu*. The autograph definitely puts the sign Knudtzon read as NU on the line above, and it is definitely KÚR. In line 38 *ālu*^{la}*-nū* is sg. acc., not nom. pl. It is the object of *tidūkūna*. For *dāku* with an impersonal object, cf. 140.25–26. Our rendering and readings thus remove the logical and grammatical inconcinnities of Knudtzon's interpretation.

EA 131; *BB* 24

Line 16: Read ERÍN.MEŠ *pí-ṭá-ta(m)* with BB. Though Prof. Albright copied line 15 this past summer in the British Museum, neither of us can solve it. Knudtzon's *šeē gi-e-zi* is almost certainly wrong.

EA 132; *BB* 18

Lines 30–41: "So ask him if I did not say to him, 'If thou makest an alliance with the sons of ᶜAbd-Ashirta, then they will take thee prisoner.' He heeded me and guarded the cities of the king, his lord. I spoke thus to Pawuru lest he heed the words of Ḫaʾip, whose father alienated the cities." In line 30 I follow Knudtzon's very probable restoration. In line

32 I follow Ebeling[28] and read the MEŠ of line 32 as really belonging to line 33, and restore TUR. This is forced on us because there is not enough room between *apāši* and the MEŠ to allow for an object of *apāši* and a verb for *atta*; in fact, there is very little room. The resulting good sense with the construction (cf. section on Infinitive, above [pp. 54–56 in the present volume]) well attested speaks strongly for the corrections of our interpretation. In line 35 I read *la-ḳú-ka ša-ma a-n*[*a ia-ši*]. Knudtzon reads *la-ḳú ka-ša-ma*. In favor of my reading and interpretation are several facts: 1) *kāša* is unattested in the Byblos letters, *kāta(m)* being used; 2) *naṣar* of line 36 is almost certainly not the object of *ḳabītī* (line 37) since this would be contrary to the usual word-order and since *ḳabū* never takes an infinitive in these letters; 3) line 39 must depend on *ḳabītī*, a fact which Knudtzon missed and doing so had to violate rules of syntax in line 41. In line 41 Albright[29] was the first to recognize that we have a virtual relative clause. However, since *dika rābiṣu* (lines 45–46) in all probability refers to *Pawuru* (cf. 131.22–23), I cannot follow his rendering of line 39, "and he must not hearken ..."

Line 57: Read [*ù ti-n*]*a-ṣí-r*[*u*]. For the restoration, cf. *JCS* 4, note on line 15 [below, Paper 4, p. 147].

EA 134; *WA* 83

Line 5: *i-ti-li-y*[*u*]. The reading YU is virtually certain from the traces in WA which show, besides the two oblique wedges noted by Knudtzon (*EA* I, p. 565, n. d), a horizontal wedge to the right with just enough room for a vertical wedge in between.

Line 13: Read perhaps [*mārē*] UR^{ri} *lim-n*[*i*], and render lines 12–13, "to kill the sons of the wicked dog." For *ur-ri* = *kalbi*, note first UR = *kalbu* (129.7, 137.26), also UR.KI = *kalbi* (138.96). Since the ideograms were pronounced, RI is merely a phonetic complement. Dr. Albright suggests *n*]*ak-ri lim-n*[*i*], "wicked foe."

EA 139; *BB* 45

Line 10: The photograph (BB pl. 4) rules out Knudtzon's ZU. The sign is almost certainly BA. The last sign cannot be seen on the plate; BB reads SU(?), Knudzton *ardu*(?).

[28]*BA* 8, p. 77.
[29]*JNES* 5, p. 18.

Line 13: Read *a-⌜pa⌝(!)-aš*. The plate shows at the left the head of one horizontal, and at the right the head of one vertical. For the form, cf. 113.10; 122.42,43.

Line 17: I agree with Ebeling (*EA* II, p. 1595) in his identification of *pa-la-ša* as 3rd sg. m. of *palāšu*. A different rendering than "einbrechen" however is required. If you burglarize a house (*bītam palāšu*; cf. *CH*, IX 16), you *plunder* a city.

Line 33: The plate makes NU quite probable. If the reading is correct, then we have a Canaanitism *yaškunhū* > *yaškunnū*, with the pron. anticipating the object *libba*; cf. Lev. 13.57.

_EA_ 362 (AO 7093; Thureau-Dangin, _RA_ 19, p. 102–103)

Lines 18–23: "So I wrote that an archer-host be sent forth and that it capture Abashunu. Behold now they say, 'He did not write, and we will be captured!' " Thureau-Dangin goes astray here precisely because of the Canaanite idiom (introduction of a purpose clause by a coordinating conjunction; on which see Purpose Clauses and Subjunctive). His translation of lines 18–19 makes little sense in context: "(Une fois) j'écrivis et (alors) des troupes se mirent en route et firent prisonnier Abašunu." It makes no sense to suppose that any troops were sent by the Pharaoh, not only because of every other letter in Rib-Adda's correspondence, but because the people would not claim Rib-Adda had failed to write if troops actually had arrived on the scene.

Lines 33–37: "If I should go to the lands, then the men would desert in order to capture the lands for themselves." In favor of this rendering of *inūma* ... rather than Thureau-Dangin's rendering of it as a present general temporal clause is the fact that we are nowhere else informed of Rib-Adda's carrying the attack himself. The construction is perfect Canaanite; for the volitive *ikaššadam*, see section on the Subjunctive.

Bibliography

Albright, W. F., "An Archaic Hebrew Proverb in an Amarna Letter from Central Palestine," *BASOR* 89, pp. 29–32.

——, *Archaeology and the Religion of Israel*, Baltimore, 1946.

——, "A Case of Lèse-Majesté in Pre-Israelite Lachish," *BASOR* 87, pp. 32–38.

——, "Cuneiform Material for Egyptian Prosopography 1500–1200 B.C.," *JNES* 5, pp. 7–25.

——, "The Early Alphabetic Inscriptions from Sinai and Their Decipherment," *BASOR* 110, pp. 6–22.

——, "The Egyptian Correspondence of Abimilki, Prince of Tyre," *JEA* 23, pp. 190–203.

——, "A Hebrew Seal from the Reign of Ahaz," by C. C. Torrey, with a note by W. F. Albright, *BASOR* 79, pp. 27–28.

——, "The 'Natural Force' of Moses in the Light of Ugaritic," *BASOR* 94, pp. 32–35.

——, "New Canaanite Historical and Mythological Data," *BASOR* 63, pp. 23–32.

——, "Palestine under the Late Eighteenth Dynasty," *Cambridge Ancient History* (forthcoming).

——, "A Prince of Taanach in the Fifteenth Century B.C.," *BASOR* 94, pp. 12–27.

——, "A Reexamination of the Lachish Letters," *BASOR* 73, pp. 16–21.

——, and Moran, W. L., "A Re-interpretation of an Amarna Letter from Byblos," *JCS* 2, pp. 239–248.

——, Review of Zellig Harris' *Development of the Canaanite Dialects*, *JAOS* 60, pp. 414–422.

——, and Moran, W. L., "Rib-Adda and the Affairs of Tyre," *JCS* 4 (forthcoming).

——, "The Seal from the Reign of Ahaz Again," by C. C. Torrey, with a note by W. F. Albright, *BASOR* 82, pp. 16–17.

——, "A Teacher to a Man of Shechem about 1400 B.C.," *BASOR* 86, pp. 28–31.

——, "Two Letters from Ugarit (Ras Shamrah)," *BASOR* 82, pp. 43–49.

——, "Two Little Understood Amarna Letters from the Middle Jordan Valley," *BASOR* 89, pp. 7–17.

——, *The Vocalization of the Egyptian Syllabic Orthography*, New Haven, 1934.

——, "A Vow to Asherah in the Keret Epic," *BASOR* 94, pp. 30–31.

Bauer, Hans and Leander, Pontus, *Historische Grammatik der hebräischen Sprache des alten Testamentes*, Halle, 1922.

——, "Die Tempora im Semitischen," *BA* 8, pp. 1–53.

Bergsträsser, G., *Hebräische Grammatik*, II Teil: Verbum, Leipzig, 1929.

Bezold, Carl, *Babylonisch-Assyrisches Glossar*, ed. by A. Goetze, Heidelberg, 1926.

——, and E. A. Wallis Budge, *The Tell el-Amarna Tablets in the British Museum*, London, 1892.

Blake, Frank R., "The Form of Verbs after *Waw* in Hebrew," *JBL* 65, pp. 51–57.

——, "The Hebrew Waw Conversive," *JBL* 63, pp. 271–295.

——, "The So-called Intransitive Verbal Forms in Hebrew," *JAOS* 24, pp. 145–204.

——, "Studies in Semitic Grammar II," *JAOS* 62, pp. 109–118.

Böhl, Franz M. Th., *Die Sprache der Amarnabriefe*, Leipzig, 1909.

Brockelmann, Carl, *Grundriss der vergleichenden Grammatik der semitischen Sprachen*, Zwei Hefte, Berlin, 1908 (Heft I) and 1913 (Heft II).

Burrows, Millar, "Orthography, Morphology, and Syntax of the St. Mark's Manuscript," *JBL* 68, pp. 195–212.

Delitzsch, Friedrich, *Assyrisches Handwörterbuch*, Leipzig, 1896.

Dhorme, Paul (Edouard), "La Langue de Canaan," *RB* 10, pp. 369–393; 11, pp. 37–59, 344–372.

Driver, G. R., *Problems of the Hebrew Verbal System*, Edinburgh, 1936.

Driver, S. R., *A Treatise on the Use of the Tenses in Hebrew*, Oxford, 1874.

Ebeling, Erich, "Das Verbum der El-Amarna-Briefe," *BA* 8, pp. 39–79.

Gardiner, Alan H., *Egyptian Grammar*, Oxford, 1927.

Gesenius, Wilhelm, *Hebräisches und aramäisches Handwörterbuch über das alte Testament*, revised by Frants Buhl, 13. Auflage, Leipzig, 1899.

——, *Hebrew Grammar*, revised by M. Kautzsch and translated by A. E. Cowley, Oxford, 1946.

Ginsberg, H. L., *The Legend of King Keret, Bulletin of the American Schools of Oriental Research*, Supplementary Studies Nos. 2–3, New Haven, 1946.

Goetze, Albrecht, "Is Ugaritic a Canaanite Dialect?" *Language* 17, pp. 127–138.

——, "The So-called Intensive of the Semitic Languages," *JAOS* 62, pp. 1–8.

——, "The Tenses in Ugaritic," *JAOS* 58, pp. 266–309.

Goodwin, William Watson, *Greek Grammar*, rev. by Charles B. Gulick, New York, 1930.

Gordon, Cyrus H., "Azitawadd's Phoenician Inscription," *JNES* 8, pp. 108–115.

——, "The Dialect of the Nuzu Tablets," *Orientalia* NS 7, pp. 32–63, 215–232.

——, *Ugaritic Handbook, Analecta Orientalia* 25, Rome, 1947.

Hallock, Richard T. *The Chicago Syllabary and the Louvre Syllabary AO 7661*, Chicago, 1940.

Hammershaimb, Erling, *Das Verbum im Dialekt von Ras Schamra*, Kopenhagen, 1941.

Harris, Zellig S., *Development of the Canaanite Dialects*, New Haven, 1939.

——, *A Grammar of the Phoenician Language*, New Haven, 1936.

Herdner, Andrée, "Une Particularité grammaticale commune aux textes d'El-Amarna et de Ras-Shamra," *RÉS*, 1938, pp. 76–83.

Höfner, Maria, *Altsüdarabische Grammatik*, Leipzig, 1943.

Honeyman, A. M., "Phoenician Inscriptions from Karatepe," *Le Muséon* 61, pp. 43–57.

Joüon, Paul, *Grammaire de l'Hébreu Biblique*, Rome, 1947.

Knudtzon, J. A., *Die El-Amarna-Tafeln*, Anmerkungen und Register bearbeitet von Otto Weber und Erich Ebeling, Zwei Hefte, Leipzig, 1915.

——, "Zur assyrischen und allgemein semitischen Grammatik," *ZA* 7, pp. 33–63.

——, "Ergebnisse einer Collation der El-Amarna-Tafeln," *BA* 4, pp. 101–154.

——, "Weitere Studien zu den El-Amarna-Tafeln," *BA* 4, pp. 279–337.

——, "Nachträge und Berichtigungen zu 'Weitere Studien zu den El-Amarna-Tafeln,' " *BA* 4, pp. 410–417.

Kramer, S. N., "The Verb in the Kirkuk Tablets," *AASOR* XI, pp. 62–119.

Labat, René, *L'Akkadien de Boghaz-Koi*, Bordeaux, 1932.

——, *Manuel d'Épigraphie akkadienne*, Paris, 1948.

Leander, Pontus, Hans Bauer and ——, *Historische Grammatik der hebräischen Sprache des Alten Testamentes*, Halle, 1922.

Maisler, B., "A Genealogical List from Ras Shamra," *JPOS* 16, pp. 150–157.

Marcus, Ralph, "On the Genitive after *umma* in the Amarna Tablets," *JCS* 2, pp. 223-224.

Mendenhall, George E., "The Message of Abdi-Ashirta to the Warriors," *JNES* 6, pp. 123–124.

——, *The Verb in Early Northwest Semitic Dialects*, unpublished Johns Hopkins University dissertation, Baltimore, 1947.

Moran, William L., "The Putative √ᶜ*tm* in Is. 9.18," *CBQ* 12, pp. 153–154.

——, W. F. Albright and ——, "A Re-interpretation of an Amarna Letter from Byblos," *JCS* 2, pp. 239–248.

——, W. F. Albright and ——, "Rib-Adda and the Affairs of Tyre," *JCS* 4 (forthcoming).

——, "An Unexplained Passage in an Amarna Letter from Byblos," *JNES* 8, pp. 124–125.

Obermann, Julian, "The Divine Name *YHWH* in the Light of Recent Discoveries," *JBL* 68, pp. 301–323.

O'Callaghan, Roger T., "The Great Phoenician Portal Inscription from Karatepe," *Orientalia* NS 18, pp. 173–205.

Orlinsky, Harry, "On the Cohortative and Jussive After an Imperative or Interjection in Biblical Hebrew," *JQR* NS 31, pp. 371–382; pp. 191–205, 273–277.

Poebel, Arno, *Das appositionell bestimmte Pronomen*, etc., Chicago, 1932.

Polotsky, H. J., *Études de Syntaxe copte*, Cairo, 1944.

Reckendorf, H., *Die syntaktischen Verhältnisse des Arabischen*, Leiden, 1895.

Schroeder, Otto, *Die Tontafeln von El-Amarna*, Hefte XI–XII, *Vorderasiatische Schriftdenkmäler der königlichen Museen zu Berlin*, Leipzig, 1915.

——, "Ueber den Namen des Tamuz von Byblos in der Amarnazeit," *OLZ* 1915, cols. 291–293.

Smith, Sidney, *The Statue of Idri-mi*, London, 1949.

Speiser, E. A., "A Note on the Derivation of *šumma*," *JCS* 1, pp. 321–328.

Thureau-Dangin, F., "Nouvelles Lettres d'El-Amarna," *RA* 19, pp. 91–108.

——, "Une lettre d'Amenophis (III ou IV)," *Recueil d'Études égyptologiques dediées à la mémoire de Jean-François Champollion*, pp. 377–382, Paris, 1922.

——, "Un Comptoir de pourpre à Ugarit, d'après une tablette de Ras-Shamra," *Syria* 15, pp. 137–146.

Torrey, C. C., "A Hebrew Seal from the Reign of Ahaz," *BASOR* 79, pp. 27–28.

——, "The Seal from the Reign of Ahaz Again," *BASOR* 82, pp. 16–17.

Ungnad, Arthur, *Babylonische Briefe*, Leipzig, 1914.

——, *Hammurabi's Gesetz II*, Leipzig, 1909.

——, *Grammatik des Akkadischen*, München, 1949.

Vernier, Donat, *Grammaire Arabe*, 2 tomes, Beirut, 1891 (Tome I), 1892 (Tome II).

von Soden, Wolfram, *Das akkadische Syllabar*, *Analecta Orientalia* 27, Rome, 1948.

——, "Der hymnisch-epische Dialekt des Akkadischen," *ZA* NF 6, pp. 163–227; 7, pp. 90–183.

Waterman, Leroy, *The Royal Correspondence of the Assyrian Empire*, Four Vols., Ann Arbor, 1930 (Vols. I-II), 1931 (Vol. III), 1936 (Vol. IV).

Winckler, Hugo, *The Tell-El-Amarna Letters*, New York, 1896.

——, *Der Thontafelfund von El Amarna*, Heft I, *Mittheilungen aus den Orientalischen Sammlungen*, Berlin, 1889.

Wright, W., *A Grammar of the Arabic Language*, revised by W. Robertson Smith and M. J. de Goeje, Two Vols., Cambridge, 1896 (Vol. I) and 1898 (Vol. II).

Zimmern, Heinrich, *Sumerische Kultlieder aus altbabylonischen Zeit*, Heft X, *Vorderasiatische Schriftdenkmäler der königlichen Museen zu Berlin*, Leipzig, 1913.

2. A Re-interpretation of an Amarna Letter from Byblos (*EA* 82)

W. F. ALBRIGHT and WILLIAM L. MORAN, S.J.

We are now in a much better position than were our predecessors to interpret the cuneiform tablets of the Late Bronze Age in Palestine.[a] From the Nuzu and Boğazköy texts we have a much clearer idea of contemporary peripheral Accadian as written by non-Accadian peoples. Even more important, Ugaritic has immeasurably advanced our knowledge of contemporary Canaanite, enabling us to clarify many heretofore obscure passages.[b]

[a]Cf. *BASOR* 86 28–31; 87 32–38; 89 7–17; 92 28–30; 94 12–27; *Journal of Egyptian Archaeology* 23 (1937) 190–203; *JNES* 6 (1947) 123–124; 8 (1949) 124–125.

[b]Though it is objected by some scholars that Ugaritic is a different language from Canaanite and hence should not be used comparatively until the two have been worked out independently, the authors believe that Ugaritic and the Canaanite of Byblos are only dialectal variants of one Northwest-Semitic speech. Though there is ample evidence that the Canaanite of Byblos was more closely related to the Canaanite of other Phoenician and Palestinian towns than it was to Ugaritic, it is already clear that there was so much dialectal variation between different local forms of South Canaanite that we are not justified in treating Ugaritic as a distinct language. Proto-Hebrew, the parent of Biblical Hebrew, is different from both, though more akin to South Canaanite than to Ugaritic. The Ugaritic epics originated in Phoenicia proper, as shown by their place names, and it is probably not accidental that the deities mentioned in the epics are more characteristically South Canaanite than those listed in the ritual texts from Ugarit. The language of the epics is probably, therefore, even more closely related to Byblian Canaanite of the early fourteenth century B.C. than would be true of the ordinary speech of Ugarit. In the writers' opinion, the correct approach is thus through the linguistic methods familiar to us from modern dialect geography (presented in an extreme form by the exponents of neo-linguistics), which supplement the neogrammatical approach and correct its one-sided isolationism (which worked very well with the major divisions of the widely separated Indo-European family, but has worked badly in the case of Romance philology, where we must deal with a great many neighboring dialects; cf. Albright, *CBQ* 7 14–18). For the writers' point of view in more detail see *BASOR* 89 8, n. 5 (in reply to Goetze, *Language*, 17 127ff.) and *JAOS* 67 155ff. (for the close relation between Byblian and Ugaritic even in the tenth century B.C.). The standpoint of dialect geography has been very effectively presented by Zellig S. Harris in his *Development of the Canaanite Dialects* (1939); cf. the review in *JAOS* 60 414–422. In other words, research on

The study of *EA* 82 which follows is an illustration of this fact. One will note by comparing, for example, Knudtzon's translation with that of the writers, that in many places there is complete divergence, a fact the more striking in that the divergence never rests on different readings.[c] The reason, in short, is that Knudtzon failed, quite understandably, to see the underlying Canaanite idiom, which once detected solves almost every problem of a hitherto enigmatic letter.

Meriting special note is the syntactical peculiarity in the use of the negatives in lines 10 and 16, heretofore quite baffling to interpreters of the letter. The negative is used pleonastically, in a typically Canaanite parataxis of clauses, and is best translated by "as soon as," "scarcely," or the like. This same usage is found occasionally in Biblical Hebrew, though it has been neglected by Hebrew syntacticians.[d] Thus II Ki. 20 4: *wayhî yĕšaᶜyāhû lôʾ yāṣāʾ hāᶜîr hattîḵônāh ūḏĕḇar Yhwh hāyāh ʾēlāw*, "And it came to pass as soon as Isaiah had gone out of the middle city that the word of Yahweh came to him." And Is. 40 24: *ʾap̱ bal niṭṭā́ᶜû ʾap̱ bal zôrā́ᶜû ʾap̱ bal šôrēš bāʾāreṣ gizᶜām wĕgam nāšáp̱ bāhem wayyîḇā́šû ūsĕᶜārāh kaqqaš tiśśāʾēm*, "Scarcely have they been planted, scarcely have they been sown, scarcely has their stock struck root in the earth, than He blows upon them and they wither, and a whirlwind sweeps them away like stubble." Cf. also Zeph. 2 2.—To be noted is that *bl* is the regular negative in Ugaritic and Phoenician.—Another good parallel, this time in the archaizing "hymnal-epic dialect," is found in the Agushaya Epic:[e] *išātu ul tamḫat áteli (a-ételi) /*

---

each dialect must take constant stock of pertinent phenomena in all the other dialects, without reading interpretations valid for one dialect into another unless these interpretations fit the facts of the case in question. There is nothing wrong with comparative method when it is properly employed and does not violate the canons of sound scientific and logical method. In other words, comparative method as we apply it to adjacent Northwest-Semitic dialects in the present essay cannot be used for the interpretation of—say—Elamite by drawing on heterogeneous languages of ancient Western Asia such as Sumerian, Hurrian, Cossaean, and Urartian. On the other hand it can be used—if employed critically—in the comparative study of new or rare Sumerian or Accadian dialects by reference to other better known Sumerian or Accadian dialects.

[c]The autograph may be found in Scheil, *Mémoires publiés par les membres de la Mission archéologique française au Caire*, vol. 6 298ff. We follow throughout Knudtzon's revised text.

[d]However, already noted by Gesenius-Buhl; cf. *bal* 99b (17th ed.).

[e]Zimmern, VS X 214 obv. III 9ff. 13ff. Prof Goetze has called our attention to von Soden's reading *a-li-li* rather than *a-te-li* (cf. *ZA* NF 7 165 note 4), but since the middle sign occurs twice and *alili* is very obscure at best, we follow Zimmern.

itarrū (a-)dašni, "Scarcely has the kindled fire flamed up, They are reduced to ashes."

TEXT AND TRANSLATION[f]

a-na ^{m}*a-m[a-a]n-ap-pa*[1] *a-bi-ia*	To Amanappa, my father,
ḳí -bí -ma	speak:
um-ma ^{m}*ri-ib-addi māru-ka-ma*	Thus Rib-Addi, thy son:
a-na šēpē a-bi-ia am-ḳú-ut	I fall down at the feet of my father.
aḳ-ta-bi ù aš-ta-ni	I have repeatedly said
a-na ka-ta(m)[2] *ú-ul ti-li-ú-na*[3]	to thee: "Art thou not able
la-ḳa-ia[4] *iš-tu ka-at*	to rescue me from the hand
^{m}*abdi-a-ši-ir-ta ka-li*	of ᶜAbdi-Ashirta? All
LÚ ^{pl}GAZ^{pl} *it-ti-šu*	of the Khapiru are on his side;
ù ^{LÚ}*ḫa-za-nu-tu*[5] *ú-ul*	and as for the governors, as soon as
ti-eš-mu-na[6] *mi-im-ma*	they hear anything,
ù šap-ru a-na ša-a-šu	they communicate (it) to him,[7]
u ki-na-na dan[8] *ù*	and therefore he is powerful." And
ta-aš-ta-na a-wa-ta(m) a-na ia-ši	thou hast repeatedly commanded me
uš-ši-ra-mi awīla-ka it-ti-ia	"Send thy man to me[9]
a-na ēkalli ù la-a[10] *ka-ši-id*	at the palace, and as soon as the request[11]
i-re-šu ù uš-ši-ir-ti-šu[12]	is granted,[13] I will send him
ḳa-du ṣābi[14] *til-la-ti*[15] *a-na ka-ta(m)*	along with auxiliary forces to thee—
a-di a-ṣí ṣābi pi-ṭá-ti[16]	until the time when the archers come forth—
a-na na-ṣa-ar napišti-ka ù	in order to protect thy life." But
aḳ-bi a-na ka-ta(m) la-a	I have said to thee:
i-li-ú uš-ša-ar-‹šu›[17]	"I am not able to send him.
ú-ul yi-eš-ma ^{m}*abdi-a-ši-i[r-ta]*	Let[18] not ᶜAbdi-Ashirta hear (of it),
ù ma-an-nu ìl-ti-ḳa-ni	for then[19] who will rescue me
e[š]-tu ḳa-ti-šu ù ta-a[ḳ-bi]	from his hand?" And thou sayest
a-na ia-ši ú-ul ta-pa-la-[aḫ]	to me: "Do not fear!"
ù ta-aš-ta-ni a-wa-ta(m) a-na ia-ši	And thou tellest me again and again:
uš-ši-ir-mi ^{GIŠ}*eleppa a-na*	"Send a ship to
māt ia-ri-mu-ta[20] *ù ú-ṣa-ka*[21]	the land of Iarimuta that I may send thee
kaspī lu-bu-ši eš-tu ša-šu-nu	money (and) clothing from them."[22]

[f]Notes to the text and translation follow in the form of a commentary.

a-nu-ma awīlūtu ša na-ad-na-ta	Behold, the men whom thou hast given
a-na ia-ši en-na-ab-tu gab-bu	to me have fled, all of them.
ḫa-ba-li-ia muḫḫi-ka šum-ma	Thou art accountable for injury to me if
ta-[ḳ]ú-u-ul a-na ia-ši a-nu-[m]a	thou art negligent in my regard. See,
eš-ti-mi ú-ul i-nu-ma[23]	I did obey. Is it not (a fact) that
uš-ši-ir-ti awīli-ia a-na ēkalli	I sent my man to the palace,
ù iḳ-bi a-na awīli ù iz-zi-iz	and he (ᶜAbdi-Ashirta) commanded a man and he drew
paṭar siparri muḫḫi-ia[24] *ù am-ma-ḫa-aṣ-ni*[25]	a bronze dagger against me, and I was stabbed
9-ta-an a-nu-ma dan i-na	many times?[26] Behold, he was able to commit[27]
ar-ni an-nu-ú ù i-na ar-ni	this crime, so from another
ša-ni mi-nu ìl-ti-ḳa-ni šum-ma	crime what will save me? If
2 *arḫē ia-nu ṣāba*[28] *pí-ṭá-ti*	within two months there are no archers,
ù i-ti-zi-ib āla^{KI}	then I will abandon the city
ù pa-aṭ-ra-ti[29]	and depart, and
bal-ṭa-at napišti-ia a-di	my life will be safe while[30]
i-pí-šu[31] *i-pé-eš libbi*^{bi}*-ia*	I do what I wish to do.
ša-ni-ta(m) ú-ul ti-i-di	Besides, art thou not aware
at-ta māt a-mur-ri ur-ra	thyself (that) the land of the Amorite day
mu-ša tu-ba-ú-na	(and) night longs for
ṣāba pí-ṭá-ti ú-ul ta-ša-aš	the archers? They have not become bitter
\ *na-aḳ-ṣa-pu ù ḳí-bi a-na šarri*	(angry).[32] And so say to the king:
ku-uš-da ki-ma ar-ḫi-eš	"Come with all haste."

COMMENTARY

(1) On the name and identity of this Egyptian official, cf. *JNES* 5 (1946) 9 and references there given.

(2) In the letters from Byblos, *kāta(m)* is the regular form of the second sg. independent pronoun in the oblique cases. *Kāša*, frequent elsewhere in Amarna as in the Acc. of Boğazköy (cf. Labat, *L'Akkadien de Boghaz-Köi* 56), is found only once in the Byblian letters, and then as an accusative (132 35).

(3) *Yaqtulu*, used in Acc. only in subordinate clauses (the so-called "subjunctive"), is in Amarna Can., as in Ugaritic, the normal form of the indicative (cf. *aštaparu*, 89 7; 117 29; *yištapparu* 103 20; *ašpuru* 83 44; *niliʾu* 88 20,

etc.). Frequently the energetic *-na* is suffixed (cf. *inaṣarŭna*, 112 10; *tištaprŭna*, 117 8, etc.). In this, as in so many other points, the verbal syntax is pure Canaanite.

(4) In the Byblos letters, as often in Accadian (cf. Ungnad, *Altbabylonische Briefe*, 176 9, etc.; see glossary 323 under *leʾū*), the infinitive with *leʾū* is in the acc. case (88 20–21; 102 19, 24–25; 104 38, 50–51; 114 35–36; 137 27), or if followed by an object, in the construct state (109 56; 113 29; 126 7–8, etc.). There is this difference however, reflecting probably the Can. idiom, that whereas in Acc. the infinitive regularly precedes *leʾū*, in Byblian usage it follows.

(5) The plural *ḫāzānūtu* is formed on the analogy of abstract collectives like *awīlūtu*. The sg. *ḫāzānu* is derived from old *ḫāziʾānu*, a form like Old Babylonian *dāʾikānu*, "murderer," etc., where *-ānu* is added to the participle to indicate professional status (cf. Albright, *Vocalization of the Egyptian Syllabic Orthography* 61 above; also Goetze, *Language*, 22 [1946] 128 for a slightly different position).

(6) Frequently in the Byblos letters (105 36; 108 11; 118 47, etc.) a fem. sg. verb is construed with a masc. pl. subject taken as a collective. As is well known, the construction is common Can. idiom, found in the Can. Amarna letters, Ugaritic I AB ii 35, 36; iii 6–7; Keret B iii 18; vi 2, etc.), and in Biblical Hebrew (cf. *CBQ* 7 [1945] 22–23). Some scholars, however, maintain that the form is a 3rd pl. with a preformative *t* (A. Herdner, *RES* 1938 76–83; *UH* I 9 10). It is true that there are cases in the Amarna letters where the preformative *t* is found with a plural ending, such as *tadinūni* and *tubaʾūni(m)* (cf. Ebeling, *Beiträge zur Assyriologie* 8 50), but since conflate Can.-Acc. formations are so common in the Amarna letters, such evidence cannot be conclusive. It is also true that the majority of cases are not decisive, supporting either view. On the supposition, however, that the form in question is a plural, the following facts cannot be explained:—1) The form, both in Amarna and in Ugaritic, appears constantly in the indicative without the ending *-na*, whereas if the form were plural, the reverse should be true. 2) Forms like *timaḫasanan*[*i*] (77 37; cf. Schroeder's copy) and *tišmana* (103 22) cannot be plurals either in Acc. or in Can., or by a conflation of the two. The former must be 3rd sg. *timaḫaṣa* (with subjunctive force?; cf. note 21 below), with energic *-na* plus the verbal suffix (for the energic plus verbal suffix, cf. 77 22; 143 16; 251 11–12, etc.; judging from Amarna, we should vocalize *yqtlnh* in Ugaritic *yaqtulŭnahū*).—*Tišmana* may represent either Can. *tišmaᶜna* or *tišmaᶜ(ă,ŭ)na*, since the laryngeals produced irregularities in the orthography. It is difficult to find in the form any support for a supposed underlying *tišmaᶜūna*, according to which the scribe would have failed to represent a long vowel in an accented syllable. 3) The form is construed with a dual subject as in 117 17–18. That the subject was considered a dual is indicated by the dual perfect *aṣā* in 14 and 19. Since the verb in question, *tubaluna*, cannot be a dual, it must be, as in Arabic, a 3rd fem. sg. (cf. also 117 54–56). The same construction is found in Biblical Hebrew, and the form is 3rd fem. sg. (cf. Mi. 4 2; Hab. 3 4). In view of the Arabic and

Hebrew idiom, together with the evidence from Amarna, *ttb*ᶜ in Keret A 300, which is construed with the dual *mlʾakm* (note the dual in 303, *tšʾan*), is to be taken as 3rd fem. sg. There is no reason to conjecture with Gordon that the dual also could have a preformative *t* in the third person (cf. *UH* I 9 10, note 1). 4) The gloss *naḳṣapū* (plural) in line 51 of this letter shows that *tašaš* (50) is not a jussive sg. but an indicative sg. construed with the subject *māt Amurri* taken as a collective (cf. 73 12–14 for the same construction). The form cannot be plural either in Can. or Acc.; it can only be an Acc. 3rd fem. sg., the Canaanized form of which we find in 83 35 (*tišašuna*). We conclude, then, that the form must be, as in Arabic and Hebrew, a fem. sg., and where we do find it with *-na*, that this can only be the energic.—Dt. 5 20–21, then, which Gordon cites for his position, merely preserves the *nun* of the old Can. energic (for other examples in Biblical Hebrew, cf. *JBL* 63 [1944] 212 note 3); Dt. 33 3, also cited by him (*Orientalia* 16 [1947] 10) is a case of *obscurum per obscurius* and of no use whatever in deciding this problem (for a recent discussion of this obscure form, MT *tukkû*, cf. Cross and Freedman, *JBL* 67 [1948] 200 note 16).

(7) The construction of lines 10–12 is basically the same as that of lines 16–17. The pleonastic negative *ul* has been discussed above. The imperfect-perfect sequence of tenses in the two clauses is pure Canaanite, and is frequently employed in Hebrew to express a general truth; cf. G-K-C 112m.

(8) At Prof. Goetze's suggestion we use the *status indeterminatus* according to normal Acc. syntax. Since there is so little evidence one way or the other in Can. Amarna, this does seem preferable. One may doubt, however, since the construction is foreign to Canaanite, whether the Can. scribes observed such niceties of Acc. syntax.

(9) "To me," and not "mit mir" with Knudtzon. Acc. *itti* is here used like Can. ᶜ*m* (cf. *UH* III 18 1940), as elsewhere in the Byblos letters (87 10).

(10) On the pleonastic negative *lā*, cf. note 7 above. The construction, as already noted, is basically that of lines 10–12, but with this difference, that *kašid* is a *futurum exactum* (cf. G-K-C 106o) and *ušširtī* has a future meaning, on which see note 12 below. Cf. G-K-C 159o for an exact parallel in conditional clauses.

(11) The word in question is certainly Can. ʾ*rš* (cf. *UH* III 18 302; Hebrew ʾ*ăréšeṯ*), as already noted by Winckler (*The Tell-El-Amarna-Letters* 59 page 134). One of the writers has also identified the root in *EA* 285, where, as he will show in a forthcoming study of the ᶜAbdu-Kheba letters, in line 11 we are to read [*a-ta*]*r-šu*, and in line 25 [*a*]-*ra-šu*.

(12) One of several certain occurrences in the Byblos letters of the so-called *waw*-consecutive with the perfect, two of which occur in this letter (lines 12 and 44; cf. also 73 14; 75 42; 83 27, 47, 50; 118 46; 137 47). This is clear proof of the antiquity of the construction in Can. For the evidence from inscriptions, cf. Zellig Harris, *A Grammar of the Phoenician Language* 1936 39–40; to the three examples cited there from Punic should be added two more from the Nora stone (cf. *BASOR* 83 19).

(13) This rendering is based on the Hebrew idiom found in Prov. 13 12 (*wĕᶜēṣ ḥayyîm taʾăwāh ba̱ʾāh*, "... and a tree of life is a desire fulfilled.") and Job 6 8 (*mî yittēn tāḇôʾ šeʾĕlāṯî*, "Would that my request were granted ..."). In the mind of the scribe, then, ***kašādu*** was equal to *bôʾ*, which equation is confirmed by a comparison of the use of ***kašādu*** in 93 7 with the use of *bôʾ* in Gen. 37 23 and I Sam. 9 12; cf. also Jer. 32 24 where *bôʾ* means "to reach."

(14) Prof. Goetze has called the writers' attention to the fact that ERÍN.MEŠ is the ideogram of a singular in Amarna. Besides 76 38–39 (*uš-ši-ra* ERÍN.MEŠ *pí-ṭá-ti / ra-ba*) and 129 36 (*a-nu-ma* ERÍN.MEŠ *a-ṣa-at*), which he has indicated, cf. also 117 27, 137 42, and 138 98. We have an almost exact parallel to our passage in a recently published letter of Hammurabi where we read *ṣa-ba-am til-la-tam* (cf. Kupper, *Revue d'Assyriologie* 42 [1948] page 46 line 18′).—Apparently, to judge from 129 36 and 138 98, the scribes were familiar with Old Babylonian *ṣābu*, which is feminine (cf. Jean, *Archives Royales de Mari*, II 22 lines 6 and 13: *ṣa-bu-um ki-bi-it-tum* and *ṣa-bu-um ḳa-al-la-tum*). They lapsed, however, into their native Canaanite, in which, as in Hebrew, *ṣaba(u)* was masc. (cf. 76 39; 117 27; 137 42). To be noted is that the apparently one clear instance in Hebrew of *ṣābāʾ* as fem. (Is. 40 2b) is made extremely doubtful by the new Isaiah scroll, where we read *mlʾ* and not *mlʾh*.

(15) Not *bilati* (Knudtzon); cf. Ebeling, *EA* II 1591.

(16) Egyptian *pḏtyw*, "archers," a nisbe-formation (vocalize: *piṭátyĕ*) of *pḏt*, "bow" (Coptic: *pīte*); cf. *JNES* 5 (1946) 14. Old Egyptian *ḏ* (pronounced *ğ*, i.e., *dj*) split into two sounds, *ğ* and *d*, both pronounced as voiceless unaspirated stops (W. H. Worrell, *Coptic Sounds* 14ff.; J. Vergote, *Phonétique historique de l'Egyptien: Les Consonnes* 11 ff.), before the end of the third millennium. The former sound was regularly transcribed as *ṣ* in Semitic and served to transcribe Semitic *s*; the latter sound was regularly transcribed (whether original *d* or *ḏ*) by *ṭ* in Semitic and served to render Semitic *t* (and *d*) in Egyptian. Examples are numerous; restricting ourselves to a few good examples of original Egyptian *ḏ* in Semitic transcription we have: Eg. *ḏbᶜ.t*, "finger-ring," whence Amarna plural *timbuʾēti* and Heb. *ṭabbáᶜat*; Eg. *dnʾ*, "basket," from older Eg. *ḏnʾ* in *ḏn-ʾb*, etc., whence Heb. *ṭéneʾ*; *(Pr)-bꜣ-nb-ḏd*, "Mendes," whence Assyr. (7th century) *Binṭeṭe*.

(17) Since ***uššar*** in its six other occurrences in the Byblos letters is always found with an object expressed, and since the context demands it, we add ‹*šu*›. Knudtzon (*EA* I 398 note e) has already noted the possibility of a small sign following.

(18) Can. *ʾal yišmaᶜ*. To be noted is that there is considerable evidence in the Byblos letters that the vowel of the native Byblian preformative followed the Barth-Ginsberg law of dissimilation (cf. *UH* I 9 6; *EA* 73 16, *tilakŭna* for Acc. *tallik* or *tallak*; 83 14, *yakbī* for Acc. *iḳbī*; 83 31, *yatina* for Acc. *iddina*; 117 60, *yašpur* for Acc. *išpur*, etc.).

(19) The construction is that of a conditional sentence with the protasis suppressed, to be supplied from context. "For, (if he does hear) who ..."; cf. G-K-

C 159dd. On the introduction of a causal clause by the simple conjunction, cf. G-K-C 158a.

(20) Though the identification of Iarimuta still eludes us, still we may rule out with certainty Biblical Jarmuth (cf. *BASOR* 87 13 note 30).—The evidence from the Amarna letters makes it virtually certain that very many place-names ended in all cases in *-a* (cf. *UH* I 8 9). The Egyptian *Execration Texts*, though indicating mimation in many Can. place-names and personal names, never do so in the case of those ending in *-ānu* (cf. Goetze, *Language* 22 [1946] 129 note 43). This points to their being diptotes, which is confirmed by the presence in Ugaritic of the archaic feminine ending in *-y*, corresponding to the masc. *-ānu* (cf. Arabic *sakrān*, fem. *sakrā* for older **sakray*; Wright-Smith-de Goeje, *A Grammar of the Arabic Language* I 309 241; on the Ugar. evidence cf. *UH* I 8 38).—Goetze has argued convincingly for the existence in Proto-Semitic of a feminine *-ayu* that corresponded to masc. *-ānu* (cf. *Language*, ibid., 130).—By law in South Canaanite, *-ānu* > *-ōnu* and by dissimilation > *-ōna*; hence the nominative and oblique cases fell together. Thus *Aškalūna* (287 14, etc.), *Baṭrūna* (78 19, etc.), *Šarūna* (241 4), *Ṣidūna* (85 71, etc.). The development is parallel in place-names ending in *-ūtu* (South Can. *ōtu* < *ātu*); hence *Iarimūta* and *Bērūta* (a gen. in 101 25; 114 13; 118 28).

(21) Ebeling (*Beiträge zur Assyriologie* 8 64) has probably identified the form correctly as a Can. *hifʿil*, i.e., *ʾauṣiʾ* > *ʾōṣiʾ*, with a pronominal suffix. The vocalization need cause no difficulty, since verbs *tertiae infirmae* receive very irregular treatment from the Can. scribes. Thus we find for the 3rd sg. masc. *yilḳi*, *yilḳa*, *yilḳu* (cf. 91 4 and 6 where the scribe shifts from *yilḳu* to *yilḳa* with no apparent syntactical reason). If there is a *yaqtula* form in Byblian Can. with subjunctive force—the writers have reached no definite conclusion on the matter, which is extremely elusive; cf. 85 34, 36 and 83 16, 19 where the shift from *yaqtula* seems significant, but also contrast 85 68, 81 (on the same problem in Ugar. cf. *UH* I 9 7 note 1)—then we have a perfect parallel in 138 68 where *ū yilḳanū* clearly has purposive force.

(22) Perhaps equals Can. *bhm*, "through their intermediation." If so, then from the fact that Can. *ba* = "from" = *ištu*, *ištu* took on analogically another meaning of Can. *ba*, "by means of, through." Cf. the similar treatment of *inūma*, which is employed with the various meanings of Can. *kī*.

(23) Again Can. idiom; cf. II Sam. 13 28: *hălôʾ kî ʾānôḵî ṣiwwîṯî ʾeṯkem*, "... is it not true that it is I who have ordered you?" The phrase is certainly elliptical in origin, with *tīdī* or the like understood (cf. 73 14–15).

(24) The phrase *izziz muḫḫiya* is here a bit obscure. In 85 8 it seems to correspond to Hebrew *ʿmd ʿl* (cf. Dan. 8 25; 11 14) or *qwm ʿl*, "to attack," and Ugar. *qm*, "adversary." Here, however, we probably have some Can. word meaning "to draw" or the like, similar in form to Acc. *izziz*; though we should perhaps not rule out the possibility of an acc. of instrument (cf. *ʾeḇen*, Jos. 7 25; *ḵap*, Prov. 10 4?) and translate "and he attacked me with a bronze dagger." The same expression is found in 81 15, though the scribe tripped over the ideograms. GÍR, about which Knudtzon seems to have some doubt,

is certain, since it is clear from Schroeder's copy that the gloss is to be read ⌜*paṭ*⌝-[*r*]*a*.

(25) The form is a blend of *ammaḫaṣ* and *imḫaṣnī*. For the suffix -*nī* added directly to the verb (not -*annī*), cf. 87 8, 125 20, 137 24.

(26) The formula "nine times" to express frequent repetition is often found in the date-lists of Ur III; cf. Kugler, *Sternkunde* II 194; *Reallexikon der Assyriologie* II 142.

(27) The translation follows from the context, where Rib-Addi would seem to stress the impunity ᶜAbdi-Ashirta enjoyed in the first crime, and hence the imminence of another crime against himself, should he send a man to the Egyptian court; cf. lines 22–25.

(28) The evidence from Byblos points to an accusative specification after *iānu*. Thus *mimma* or *miamma* (79 34; 85 74; 92 21; 112 25; 116 42; 117 74); *ḫāzāna* (117 10; 138 26); *limna* (94 6); *libbi*^{bi} *šanā* (119 42) and *libba(m) šanā(m)* (136 41); ERÍN.MEŠ *maṣarta* (137 22) and *maṣarata* (138 31); ERÍN.MEŠ *piṭata* (93 26?; 129 38, 49). The only evidence against this is *šari* in 137 71; other exceptions such as *še*$^{\text{im.ḪA}}$ (85 10; 125 25, etc.), *mū*^{u} (85 54) etc., are all written ideographically and no importance can be attached to the phonetic complements, which are stereotyped and considered by the scribes part of the ideogram (cf. above *libbi*^{bi} *šanā*[*m*] in 119 42).

(29) Cf. note 12 above.

(30) Probably a Canaanitism reflecting Can. ᶜ*d*; cf. I Sam. 14 19.

(31) Probably a scribal error for *i-pu-šu*, because of following *i*-PÉ-*eš*. Prof. Goetze has suggested Old Babylonian *ippeš*, but since there is no evidence in Amarna of a knowledge of this form, our explanation seems to us preferable.

(32) On the interpretation of *tašaš* and its gloss, cf. note 6 above. In 93 4 [*na*]*kṣaptī* appears as the gloss of [*at*]*tašaš*.

3. An Unexplained Passage in an Amarna Letter from Byblos

In *EA* 87.25–26 Knudtzon reads: [a-mu]r *ḳú-ru-ud-mi a-na šarri bēli-ia* / [ti-iṭ-]ḫi *it-ti-ka ṣābē ša damḳi*.[1] We propose the reading: [a-mu]r *ku-ru-ub-mi a-na šarri bēli-ia* / [a-ṣa-a]m, etc. Likewise, in *EA* 69.30, we read *ku-ru-ub-mi* instead of *ḳú-ru*-u[d-mi], and also omit the conjectural ù at the end of 69.31.

That we must read the imperative of *karābu* instead of the imperative of *ḳarādu* is absolutely certain. A careful examination of the published photograph of *EA* 87.25 shows that Knudtzon, like his predecessors, failed to see the two small oblique wedges above and below the horizontal wedges.[2] The horizontal wedges are quite short, and this is probably the reason for Knudtzon's reading *ud* and his overlooking the lower oblique wedge, which is just below the head of the lower horizontal and quite clear. The upper oblique wedge is not so clear and is pressed very close to the head of the vertical wedge.

We are thus rid of the putative verb *ḳarādu*, which appears in neither Accadian nor Canaanite, and have a construction attested in Old Babylonian correspondence and exceedingly common in Assyrian correspondence. The ordinary meaning of *karābu* with *ana* or the dative is either "to bless"—superior to inferior—or "to pay homage"—inferior to superior.[3] In the Amarna occurrences, however, it must mean "to make entreaty," "beseech," or the like, which apart from the poor Acca-

[1]All conjectural additions, whether of Knudtzon or the writer, will be in roman type.

[2]Bezold and Budge, *The Tell El-Amarna Tablets in the British Museum*, L 29804; BU 88–10–13, 31; Pl. 6. These small oblique or corner wedges are often very hard to recognize; cf. Ungnad, *Keilschrifttexte der Gesetze Hammurapis*, XXVIIIr 85, where we must read not *da-ni-a-tim* but *á-lí-a-tim*, and translate *errētim á-lí-a-tim Enlil ... līruršuma*, "with loud curses may Enlil ... curse him." This reading is certain from XXVr 39, where the original actually has *á* but is wrongly changed to *da* by Ungnad in his transliteration; cf. Albright, *JBL* 54 (1935), 201, n. 96. I am indebted to Dr. Albright for pointing this out to me.

[3]Delitzsch, *Assyrisches Handwörterbuch*, p. 350a. For *karābu* in the sense of "to pay homage" or the like, cf. Leroy Waterman, *Royal Correspondence of the Assyrian Empire*, 2. r.13; 10.4; 418. r.7; 435.11; 1384. 3, etc. The Old Babylonian occurrences (cf. Ungnad, *Altbabylonische Briefe*, 238.71; 180.21; 219.22; 181.23; 240.35) are doubtful in the sense of "to pay homage"; however, see n. 4 below.

dian of the Canaanite scribes, is not a strange development in view of the close connection between "to pay homage" to a superior and "to pray to" or "to beseech" him.[4]

[A-ṣa-a]m, if not certain, is preferable to Knudtzon's conjecture, [ti-iṭ-]ẖi. *Ṭeẖū* is never used elsewhere in the Byblos letters, whereas *aṣū* is not only common, but frequently joined with *ṣābē* or *ṣābē pí-ta-ti* as its subject.[5] The request that Egyptian troops "go forth" to the aid of Byblos is one of the main themes of Rib-Addi's correspondence with the Egyptian court. The accusative of the infinitive is paralleled in 70.26 *tu-ba a-ṣa pí-ta-ti*, 79.14–17 [*uš-ši-r*]*a-ni* / awēlūta*ma-ṣa-ar-ta a-n*[*a*] / *na-ṣa-ar āl šarri a-*[*di*] / [*a-*]*ṣa ṣābē pí-ta-ti*, and 93.16. Mimation with the accusative is found in 88.20–21 *ú-ul ni-li-ú* / *a-ṣa-am*, and fluctuation in the use of mimation in 81.21 *la-a i-li-e a-ṣa*, 104.50–51 *la-a i-li-ú* / *a-ṣa*.

In 69.30–32 *ku-ru-u*[*b-mi*] / *a-na šarri bē-l*[*i-ia*] / *a-ṣí* ..., *a-ṣí* is paralleled by 73.12 *ti-eš-mu-na a-ṣí-mi ṣābē*, 137.49 *a-ṣí-mi ṣābē pí-ta-tu ù ša-mu*.[6] The fluctuation we find here between the infinitive construct in 69.32 and the accusative of the infinitive in 87.26 is paralleled by 127. 38–39 *a-di a-ṣí* / [*ṣāb*]*ē pí-ta-ti*, 79.16–17 *a-*[*di*] / [*a-*]*ṣa ṣābē*, and 70.26 quoted above.[7]

Therefore, we render 87.21–26: "And he (Abdi-Ashirta) has placed[8] therein the Hapiru-warriors and chariots, and they do not budge from the entrance to the city-gate of Gub(la). Come, make entreaty to the king, my lord, for the coming forth with you of the warriors *ša damḳi*."[9]

[4]For a possible parallel in Old Babylonian, cf. Ungnad, *op. cit.*, 116.17. In this letter one Aštamar-Adad writes on behalf of certain gardeners. The latter wish to reclaim their assistants who had escaped but had later been recaptured. He goes on (12–17): *a-we-li-e šu-nu-ti at-ṭar-da-kum* ri-*ig-mi-šu-nu* (reading Albright's emendation of Ungnad's meaningless si-*ik-mi-šu-nu*) *mu-ẖu-ur-ma ma-ẖa-ar* il*Šamaš li-ik-ru-bu-ni-kum*, "... and may they in the presence of Shamash address their pleas to you"—which seems to make better sense in the context of a juridical procedure than Ungnad's "dass sie vor Samaš für dich beten mögen."

[5]Cf. *EA* 70.23,26; 71.27; 76.31; 77.27; 127.12; 129.40, etc.

[6]Dr. Albright has pointed out to me that the scribe must have transposed in this line, and we should read *ù ša-mu a-ṣí-mi ṣābē pí-ta-tu*.

[7]The writer hopes to treat in detail at a later date the employment of case endings in the Byblos letters.

[8]Not "sind gelegt" with Knudtzon. The permansive *šakin* is also used as a Canaanite perfect; for a similar use of the permansive, cf. 73.14, 38; 82.16; 83.28, 36, etc.

[9]*Ša damḳi* is doubtful, and so we refrain from a translation.

4. Rib-Adda of Byblos and the Affairs of Tyre (*EA* 89)

W. F. ALBRIGHT AND WILLIAM L. MORAN, S.J.

The present paper continues the series begun with the writers' study of *EA*[1] 82 in this Journal.[2] In dealing with that letter, the writers were fortunate in being able to follow Knudtzon's readings throughout in a virtually intact document. The radical changes in interpretation were invariably due to the tremendous improvement in our knowledge of Northwest-Semitic dialects of the Late Bronze Age during the past twenty years. The letter with which we are dealing here, *EA* 89, is not so complete, the last lines of both obverse and reverse being badly damaged. Where the breaks are relatively minor, as in lines 7–9, it is possible, by exhaustive use of parallels, to fill them. The real difficulty lies in the inability of previous students to grasp the peculiar hybrid Accadian-Canaanite idiom of the letters from Phoenicia and Palestine.

For example, by neglecting the fact that *ālu*, in accordance with Canaanite treatment of words for "town," is regularly construed as feminine in these letters, Knudtzon entirely missed the true interpretation of lines 40–41. Inability to understand lines 14, 18, 47, etc., spoiled his interpretation of the following passages having to do with the relations between Byblos and Tyre. Yet it is only by reckoning at all times both with the Canaanite usage of that age and with the peculiarities of the Byblos and related letters that progress in interpretation becomes possible. Our advance in understanding this letter, which has hitherto remained so obscure, is derived almost entirely from these two chief sources.

Thanks to our revised translation of lines 7ff. and 36ff., the historical situation of the letter becomes very much clearer, as will become evident on comparing Weber's discussion of this letter in the commentary to Knudtzon's edition with the following paragraphs in the present

[1]*EA* refers to J. A. Knudtzon, *Die El-Amarna-Tafeln*, 1915. For the autograph see Schroeder, *VS* XI no. 43.

[2]*JCS* 2 239–248 [above, Paper 2].

paper. We now see that Rib-Adda had tried to bind the princely house of Tyre to his interests by marrying his sister to the prince of Tyre, following time-honored practice in both ancient and modern worlds. The move ended, however, in failure when an opposing faction, probably in league with ^{c}Abd-Ashirta of Amurru (cf. line 24), murdered the prince of Tyre (called "governor" in the usual parlance when addressing the Egyptian court), together with Rib-Adda's sister and their sons; the daughters were valuable property and hence presumably escaped the massacre. At the time of this letter the prince of Byblos was at odds with the ruling faction of Tyre, and he is therefore anxious to warn the king against accepting the version of events emanating from the usurper and his followers. He alleges that the latter faction feigns a loyalty which it does not in fact cherish (14–17), and that it is not actually popular with the people of Tyre, as it claims (40–45).

Even more interesting than this new, though one-sided, picture of Canaanite political manipulations, is the attitude expressed in lines 46–53. The Byblian prince says that the real ground for the Tyrians' fear of their present chief is that the princely house of Tyre is very rich, providing the basis for further aggrandizement. For Tyre is no ordinary residence of a prince-governor, but is exceedingly wealthy—in fact, it is in a class with Ugarit itself. This is an invaluable insight, furnished by a most competent source, into the place occupied by Ugarit in the age of Niqmadda, about 1375 B.C. The Ugarit of the decades immediately preceding the great earthquake was thus regarded by its South-Phoenician contemporaries as the wealthiest of the Canaanite seaports.

TEXT AND TRANSLATION[3]

1–6 [Rib]-Adda say[s to] / [his lord], king of the universe, migh[ty] king: / [May Ba^{c}alat o]f Byb[los grant] / [strength t]o the king, [my] lo[rd]. / [At the fee]t of my lord, [m]y S[un] / [seven times sev]en I f[a]ll.

7	*[a-nu-ma] k⸢i⸣-a-ma aš-ta-pa-ru*	[See], thus have I written
	[a-na ēkal]li a-wa-tu-ia ú-ul	[to the pal]ace. (However), my words are not
	[tu-ul$_{11}$*-ḳú]-na ù ša-ma ú-ul*	[taken to hea]rt, but are completely
10	*[tu-u]š-mu-na a-mur i-pé-eš*	[un]heeded. Behold what is being done
	ā[l] ṣur-ri ki-na-na pal-ḫ̮a-ti	by Tyre. On this account I am afraid.
	i-na-na la-a yi-ša-a-lu šarru^{ru}	Now the king does not inquire

[3]The formulaic introduction of lines 1–6 we merely translate, following Knudtzon's additions.

a-na ḫa-za-ni-šu a-na a-ḫi-ia yi‹-iš-me› šarru	about his governor, about my brother. Let the king hear my words!
ú-ul k⸢i⸣(!)-n⸢a⸣ a-na-ti-šu-nu\ a-wa-te-ia	Their words(!) are not true:
šum-ma šarru^{ru} *yi-ša-i-lu*	"If the king makes inquiry,
ù na-ad-na pa-ni-nu a-na	we will devote ourselves to
a-ra-di-ka a-na-ku-me ip-ša-ti	thy service." I made
i-mu(!)-t⸢a⸣ a-n⸢a⸣ āl ṣur-ri	connubium wit[h] Tyre,
i-ba-šu i-na pa-ni-ia	while they were on good terms with me.
al-lu-ú ḫa-za-na-šu-nu da-ku	Behold, they have killed their governor
ka-du a-ḫa-ti-ia ù mārī$^{pl.}$*-še*	along with my sister and her sons.
$^{f.}$*mārāti*$^{pl.}$ *a-ḫa-‹ti›-ia uš-š⸢i⸣-ir-ti*	My sister's daughters I had sent
a-na āl [ṣu]r-[ri] ⸢iš⸣-tu pa-ni	to [Ty]r[e] away from
$^{m.}$*abd-⸢a⸣-[ši-ir-ta da(?)-k]u(?)-šu*	ᶜAbd-[Ashirta. They kill]ed(?) him
ḳa-[du(?) .... -a]d	al[ong with(?) ....].
Rev.	
31 *⸢ša⸣rru*^{ru} *[ù ti-ni-ip-šu]*	the king, then all lands
ka-li mātāti$^{p[l.}$ *a-na* ^{LÚ}SA.GAZ$^{pl.]}$	[will be attached to the Ḫapiru].
šum-ma a-na a-ḫi-i[a la(?)-a(?)]	If regarding m[y] brother
yi-ša-i-lu šarru^{ru} *[ù(?)]*	the king does [not(?)] inquire, [then(?)]
GUR *i-na ba-li i[d-..........]*	... without ..[..........]
ia-aš-pu-ru a-na šarri$^{r[i]}$ *⸢ù⸣*	He wrote to the king, but
la-a tu-uš-mu-na a-wa-tu-š[u]	hi[s] words were not heeded.
ù ma-ti-ma šu-ut a-nu	And when he died, truly
i-di-šu ù šum-ma a-na a-ḫi-ia	I learned of it. And if concerning my brother
ti-ša-i-lu ù ta-aḳ-bu	thou dost inquire, then the city
ālu an-nu-ú la-a ḫa-za-nu ša-al	will say: "This (man) is not the governor. Investigate,
šarru^{ru} *muḫḫi-šu ú-ul ni-li-ú*	o king, concerning him. We are unable
i-pé-eš mi-im-mi ù pal-ḫu-ni	to do anything." And they are afraid!
šum-ma a-na ḫa-za-ni āl ṣur-ri	Will the king not inquire
la-a yi-ša-i-lu šarru^{ru}	concerning the governor of Tyre, —
i-nu-ma ma-id mi-mu-šu ki-ma	for his property is as great
a-ia-ab a-na-ku i-di-šu	as the sea—I know it!
a-mur bīt āl ṣur-ri	Behold, the house of Tyre —
ia-nu bīti^{ti} *ḫa-za-ni*	there is no governor's house
ki-ma šu-a-ta ki-ma bīt	like it. It is
[ā]l ú-ga-ri-ta i-ba-ši	like the house of Ugarit!
[ma]-id danniš mi-mu	Exceedingly great is the wealth
[i-na] libbi^{bi}*-šu yi-eš-me šarru*^{ru}	[wi]thin it. Let the king hear
[a-wa-t]e ardi yu-wa-ši-ra	[the word]s of (his) servant. Let him send
[....... u]š(?)-da ù yi-zi-iz	[......] ... that he may stay
[....... e]r-ṣé-ti ù	[......] of the land and

[.......] *a-na ḫa-za-nu-ti ù*	[......] to the governors and
[..... *y*]*u(?)-da-an m*⌜*i*⌝-[*m*]*u*	[.....] let their prop[er]ty be [gi]ven(?)
[.......]-*šu-nu* ⌜*ù*⌝ [...]	[......] their [...] and [...]
[......] *rābiṣ šarri*^{ri} *i*[...]	[......] the king's commissioner .[....]
[......] *ḳa-ti šarri*^{ri} .[...]	[......] the hands(?) of the king .[....]
mātāti$^{pl.}$	lands
[.....] *i-di i-ra-am šarru*^{ru} [.....]	[......] the king loves [.....]
[$^{m.}$*abd*]-⌜*a*⌝-*ši-ir-ta la-ḳa a-ia-ab* [....]	[ᶜAbd]-Aširta. He has taken control of the sea(?) [.....]
[*i-n*]*a pa-ni-šu-nu ù pa-aš-ḫu*	[be]fore them and they are at peace.
[.......]. *-šu-nu šarru*^{ru} *ú-ul aš-pu-r*[*u*]	Let(?) the king [.....] them. Have I not describ[ed]
ar-na-nu a-na šarri	our crime to the king?

COMMENTARY

1.7 For *a-nu-ma*, cf. *a-nu-ma ki-a-ma* in 74.49,64, 91.27, 103.20, 118.8, 119.10–11, 122.53–54, 132.51; also 85.6 (*a-nu-ma ki-a-ma-am*). On the form of the verb (Can. indicative), see *JCS* 2, p. 243, Comm. no. 3 [above, Paper 2, pp. 134–135].

1.8 Against Knudtzon (*EA* I 422 n. a), Schroeder's autograph shows that the first sign after the break is certainly GAL. It is identical with the GAL of line 52, except that the scribe extended the shaft of the middle horizontal wedge through the vertical to indicate the horizontal on the right. Moreover, 74.49, 118.9, 119.11, 122.54 show that *anumma kīʾama aštapparu* (or the like) *ana ēkalli* is a stereotyped phrase in the Byblos letters, and confirm completely the reading GAL.

1.9 For the restoration cf. *EA* 90.16–18: *a-wa-t*[*u-ia*] / [*ú*]-⌜*ul*⌝ *tu-uš-mu-na* ⌜*ù*⌝ / [*ú*]-⌜*ul*⌝ *tu-ul-ḳú-na*. (Knudtzon's conjectural addition of *laḳā* at the end of line 17 is impossible; there is only room for *ù*.) We read UL_{11}, found in this same form in 126.6, since it fits the space better than *UL*. It is to be admitted that even this supposes the signs were rather crowded. It is not impossible that one of the signs was omitted, an error of which we have at least two examples in this letter (lines 13 and 22).

1.10 *i-pé-eš āl ṣur-ri*, lit. "the doing (inf.) of Tyre."

1.11 It appears virtually certain that the determinatives URU and KUR were pronounced as construct nouns in most places where they occur in Amarna; for a classic illustration see *EA* 256 and the transcription in *BASOR* 89.10 ff., where the names of towns are nearly always in the genitive, just as in Hebrew. Old Assyrian and Mari *ālum Aššūr*, *ālum Qaṭṭunān*, etc., reflect a different grammatical tradition. That KUR was generally pronounced *māt* in this age in the West is shown clearly by the Idrimi inscription, passim (Sidney Smith, The Statue of Idrimi, 1949).

1.13 We interpret *ana aḫiya* as appositional to *ana ḫāzānišu*. The appositional phrase was probably employed to distinguish the *ḫāzānu* who was Rib-Adda's brother-in-law from the usurper in Tyre.—The use of *šaʾālu* elsewhere in the letter rules out the possibility of supplying it here with Knudtzon (*EA* I 422, n. e). On the other hand, *yišmē awāte* or its practical equivalent is found frequently (see lines 53–54; also 107.25, 108.30, 118.15, 131.39, etc.).

1.14 Ebeling also reads KI but interprets the line differently (*EA* II 1591). The traces in Schroeder could support either DI or KI. *Dīna*, however, makes no sense in the context.—We also presuppose in this line a simple scribal error of NA for WA, occasioned perhaps by the *a-na* of the previous line (vertical dittography). One difficulty is that the plural of *awătu* is not written elsewhere with TI in the Byblos letters. However, in view of the almost exact parallel in 162.19–20 (*ú-ul ki-i-na / gab-bi a-wa-te*^{pl}), the error is virtually certain. Note that this passage also confirms the reading *ki-na*.

1.15 The form *yišaʾil*, occurring only in this letter (also lines 34, 40, 45), is of course not Accadian. Nor is the problem confined to this verb. Cf. the bewildering fluctuation between *a* and *i* in *EA* 112: *inaṣ(ṣ)arŭna* (10), *yinaṣ(ṣ)irannī* (13), *yinaṣ(ṣ)irŭ* (14), *yinaṣ(ṣ)arŭnī* (17), *yinaṣ(ṣ)irŭnī* (18). The most probable explanation of the forms with *i* is that the Can. scribes treated the unfamiliar Acc. *iqattal* as a Can. *piʾel*, and hence the form *(y)iqattil* with the characteristic vowel of the imperfect.

1.16 The form *nadna* merits comment. Ebeling lists it in the Glossary (*EA* II 1478) as 3rd pl. with *pa-ni-nu* taken as subject; Knudtzon's rendering ("... unsere Antlitze sind darauf gerichtet") seems to show him in agreement. However, the form cannot be 3rd pl. fem., since *pānu* is masc. Moreover, it is most unlikely that it is 3rd sg. masc. with *pa-ni-nu* as the subject. If this were the case we should have *pa-nu-nu* (cf. *pa-nu-ia-ma* in 118.39, 119.43, *pa-nu-ia-ma a-na a-ra-ad šarri*^{ri}); there is not a single instance of *pa-ni*, with or without a pronominal suffix, functioning as a nom. in Can. Amarna. It follows that *pa-ni-nu* must be the object of *nadna*; cf. *pa-ni-ia na-ad-na-ti* (73.38), *na-ad-nu pa-ni-šu-nu* (79.10–11), etc. This being true, the only way to construe *nadna* that makes sense is to take it as 1st pl. imperfect. This is the earliest evidence in South Canaanite of the secondary *yatana* (Phoen.-Ugar. *ytn*): *nadina* > *nadna* (by syncope of the short vowel); *nadna* could hardly represent *naddina*. It is significant in this regard that nowhere in the Byblos letters is there any evidence of doubling in specifically Canaanite forms like *yadinu*, *yadina*, *yadin*, etc.

1.18 Several facts support MU rather than Knudtzon's ZIR: 1) the autograph shows a fourth oblique wedge, though it is smaller than the other three; 2) the value ZIR for NUMUN in Middle Babylonian is extremely doubtful (cf. von Soden, *Das akkadische Syllabar*, 37); 3) *epēšu izirta* is an unnatural expression, and we would expect rather *nadānu* or *uššuru* (cf. 87.13). *Imūtu* = *emūtu*, "connubium"; cf. *bīt emūtišu*, "house into which he has married." For the idiom cf. *ḫatnūta epēšu*, lit. "make betrothal" (Taanach Letter No. 2: 24, for which see *BASOR* 94, 23).

1.20 Can. *dakū* for Acc. *dēkū* (Dhorme, *Revue Biblique* 11 [1914] 56).

1.21 The use of the verbal suffix *-še* (*mārī-še*) with a noun is to be explained by the fact that a distinction between verbal and nominal suffixes was unknown in Canaanite in the 3rd person.

1.22 Scribal error for *a-ḫa-TI-ia*, most likely through vertical haplography (note *a-ḫa-ti-ia* in line 21). Rib-Adda explains the presence in Tyre of his nieces, who were presumably either sold into slavery or made members of the usurper's harem. They had most likely been in Byblos, the metropolis and a far greater city than Tyre at the time, for their education and training at the court of Rib-Adda. Fearing for them because of the threat of ᶜAbd-Ashirta, Rib-Adda sent them back to Tyre, only to involve them in the calamity which there befell the royal house.

1.24 For the doubtful restoration here and in the next line, cf. the end of line 20 and the beginning of line 21.

ll.31f. For the restorations cf. *ù ti-ni-pu-šu ka-li mātāti*$^{\text{pl.}}$ / *a-na* $^{\text{LÚ.pl.}}$GAZ (73.32–33), *en-ni-ip-ša-at* / *māt*^{ki} *šarri ù āl ṣu-mu-ra āl ma-ṣa-ar-ti-ku-nu* / *a-na* ^{LÚ}GAZ$^{\text{pl.}}$ (76.34–37), *ù ti-ni-ip-šu ka-li* / *mātāti*$^{\text{pl.}}$ *a-na šarri*^{ri} (76.41–43), *ù en-ni-i*[*p*]*-šu ka-*[*li*] [*māt*]*āti*$^{\text{pl.}}$ *a-na* $^{\text{LÚ.p[l.}}$ G]AZ$^{\text{pl.}}$ (79.19–20; 79.25–26), *ù gab-bi mātāt*^{ḫá} *š*[*arri*] / *a-di māt mi-iṣ-ri ti-ni-ip-šu* / *a-na* $^{\text{LÚ.pl.}}$SA.GAZ$^{\text{pl.}}$ (88.32–34), *ka-li ālāni*$^{\text{pl.}}$*-ia* / [*e*]*n-ni-ip-šu a-na* $^{\text{LÚ.pl.}}$G[AZ$^{\text{pl.}}$] (116.37–38). These parallels make our restorations possible, though we cannot be sure whether to restore *ti-ni-ip-šu* or *en-ni-ip-šu*, etc. In fact, lack of context prevents our being sure that the passages cited really are parallel.

1.33 Our restoration fits the break well—lines 33–35 are perhaps in contrast to lines 39–43.

1.34 Our restoration again fits the break well, and since with but ten exceptions every apodosis of a conditional sentence in the Byblian letters is introduced by *ù* at the end of the line, *ù* is quite probable.

1.35 An explanation of GUR escapes us. It seems best to isolate *i-na ba-li*, but lack of parallels renders the whole line quite uncertain.

1.38 *ma-ti-ma*: Schroeder's autograph has only *ma-ti*, but in view of Knudtzon's *ma-ti-MA*, confirmed by Winckler-Abel, the omission of the final syllable must be due to an oversight on Schroeder's part. The form is an infinitive absolute and it is followed by the independent personal pronoun. Since its use in the Amarna letters has an important bearing on the correct interpretation of the new Karatepe inscriptions, it has been made the subject of a separate article which is published in the same issue of this Journal.—It follows from lines 38–43 that the Egyptian court had not yet been informed of the palace revolution at Tyre (cf. also lines 20 ff.), but Rib-Adda claims he is certain that the legitimate ruler, his brother-in-law, is dead and that upon investigation the whole city of Tyre will confirm him. Probably the usurper had previously either denied that there had been a revolution—perhaps writing to the Pharaoh in his formal rival's name—or had maintained a prudent silence, hoping thus to gain time to establish himself firmly in power so that eventually the Pharaoh would be forced or at least content to accept the *status quo*.

l.38 *šu-ut*: This reading, for Knudtzon's *šu-tú*, is much preferable to a possible *šu-ta(m)*, since it is obviously intended for the Accadian status absolutus (indeterminatus) of the personal pronoun (masculine *šūt*, feminine *šīt* in Old Assyrian and Hittite Accadian), though in over a dozen occurrences in Byblos it reflects the independent personal pronoun ending in *t* (cf. note on line 50). In Hittite Accadian and in two Amarna letters written by Hurrian scribes we have the spelling *šu-ú-ut* for the status indeterminatus.

l.43 Schroeder's autograph has only *pal-ḫu*, but Winckler-Abel read *pal-ḫu-NI*, as did Knudtzon.

l.44 From the meaning "whether, (German) ob" it is only a step to the indication of a following question. We have not been able to find any other clear indication of this use of *šumma* elsewhere in *EA*, but in view of the fact that Heb. *ʾim*, "if, whether," is often used to introduce a disjunctive question ("whether ... or") and appears a number of times (e.g., I Ki. 1.27; Isa. 29.16; cf. Ges.-Buhl[16] 46b B 1) as introduction to a simple direct question, this rendering of the Canaanite particle underlying *šumma* is natural. In Ugaritic the particle *hm* is also used both as conditional (like *ʾim* and *šumma*) and as interrogative; see *UH* 91 (12.3) and 93 (12.5).

l.46 *ma-id*: a Can. stative (for *maʾida*); cf. Ugar. *maʾâdu* (*ʾamʾidu*, Keret A 58).

l.47 From 74.20 (*a-ia-ab*), 105.13 and 114.19 (*a-ia-ba*) which certainly mean "sea," it is clear that the ideogram A.AB.BA was pronounced, hence the spelling with IA. Cf. also 138.96 where UR.KU (*kalbu*) is written UR.KI (as though it were genitive) after the preposition *kī*!—In line 64 we propose the rendering, "... has taken control of the sea." The one horizontal wedge following AB is no justification for Knudtzon's conjectured *š*[*unu*].

l.48 The use of *bītu* here as "family, clan, dynasty," is very common in Semitic, especially in West-Semitic documents. In Mari, for instance, we read: *ṣuḫārtam mārat Išḫi-Adad akkāšim eleqqē—bīt Mari šumam išū u bīt Qaṭanim šumam išū* (Dossin, Archives royales de Mari I No. 77: 8–10), "The maiden daughter of Yišᶜi-Hadad (king of Qaṭna) I will take for thee (Yasmaᶜ-Hadad), for the house of Mari is renowned and the house of Qaṭna is renowned." In Amarna we find the same use of *bītu*, e.g., in *EA* 256.20, on which see ***BASOR*** 89 12 nn. 30–32. In Biblical Hebrew cf. such expressions as *bêt Dāwîd*, "dynasty of David" (cf. Ges.-Buhl[16] 96a). Parallel usage in Phoenician of the eighth century B.C. is illustrated by the Karatepe inscriptions, where *bt Mpš* means "dynasty of Mopsus." This interpretation, which now appears so obvious, has been overlooked in the past. Weber's labored explanation of *bītu* in this letter as "citadel" (*EA* II 1180) is opposed to all Semitic usage and may be definitively abandoned.

l.50 The Accadian pronoun *šūata* is employed here like Ugaritic *hwt*, the emphatic pronoun corresponding to simple *hw*; for the use of *hwt* as a genitive see Gordon, *Ugaritic Handbook* I 26 (§6.14). In the Canaanizing spelling *šu-wa-at* the same form appears, again probably in the genitive, in *EA* 85.72; we may render the passage in lines 69–73 as "Since thy father returned from Sidon (to Egypt)—since his time (lit.: the days of him) the lands have joined the Ḫapiru." In the Phoenician of Byblos in the tenth century B.C. this emphatic pronoun appears as *hʾt* (*JAOS* 67 156 n. 31). It is to be noted that the plural emphatic pronoun *hmt* appears in Ugaritic, Phoenician and Biblical Hebrew (*hēmāh*), and that the survival of the emphatic *hūʾat* in Hebrew as *hūʾāh* is now attested by the frequent spelling *hwʾh* of the new cave scroll of Isaiah. Cf. note on line 38.[4]

[4]We wish to thank Professor Goetze for valuable criticisms of this paper, all of which have been carefully considered in writing the present draft.

5. The Use of the Canaanite Infinitive Absolute as a Finite Verb in the Amarna Letters from Byblos

Attention was called in the preceding article to the Amarna construction *qatāli* + independent personal pronoun and its bearing on the Karatepe construction *qtl*/*yqtl* *ʾnk*.[1] A more detailed study is in place. A new entry in Canaanite and Phoenician grammar, the construction merits close analysis, especially in view of the conflicting interpretations hitherto offered.

Of the various interpretations of the Karatepe construction only two merit serious consideration.[2] The one maintains that *qtl* and *yqtl* are respectively Qal and Yifʿil participles construed with the personal pronoun in a narrative sense;[3] the other, that *qtl* and *yqtl* are rather infinitives absolute used with the force of finite verbs, the personal pronoun functioning as agent/subject of the infinitive.[4] Since Amarna offers irrefutable evidence on the side of the latter, there would be little purpose in subjecting the arguments for the first view to a detailed criticism. However, this much should be said: while the attempt, which they represent, to put a puzzling construction into a more familiar

[1]W. F. Albright and William L. Moran, S.J., "Rib-Adda of Byblos and the Affairs of Tyre," p. 167, Commentary on line 38 [above, Paper 4, page 148].—I wish here to thank Profs. Albright and Goetze, who kindly read my manuscript, discussed with me the various problems involved, and made many valuable suggestions.

[2]For the interpretations so far offered see Julian Obermann, "Phoenician YQTL ʾNK," *JNES* 9 (1950), pp. 95–96, fns. 4–6. Add Albrecht Alt, "Die phönikischen Inschriften von Karatepe," *Die Welt des Orients*, 1949, pp. 272–287. He agrees (pp. 279–280) with Friedrich in believing that *yqtl* is Yifʿil 3rd sg. perfect, employed for the 1st sg. *yqtlt*.

[3]So Obermann, *JBL* 68 (1950), p. 303, and especially *JNES* 9 (1950), pp. 94–100 (see fn. 2). Sidney Smith has also recently admitted the possibility of considering Karatepe *qtl* and *yqtl* as participles; *The Statue of Idri-mi*, p. 38.

[4]So Cyrus H. Gordon, "Azitawadd's Phoenician Inscription," *JNES* 8 (1949), pp. 112–113; A. M. Honeyman, "Phoenician Inscriptions from Karatepe," *Le Muséon* 61 (1948), p. 50; Roger T. O'Callaghan, "The Great Phoenician Portal Inscription from Karatepe," *Orientalia* NS 18 (1949), p. 184; A. Dupont-Sommer, *Oriens* 1 (1948) 195; 2 (1949) 122.

grammatical category is understandable, still the weight of the evidence, even apart from Amarna, is decidedly against them.[5]

The pertinent Amarna passages are the following:

A. *qatāli(-ma / mi)* + noun-subject[6]—

1. *EA* 116.27–28 (WA 61), *kašādi-ma*: *ka-š[a-d]i-ma awīli-ia*[7] *ù / ra-ak-[š]a-šu*, "When my man arrived, he bound him."
2. *EA* 118.36–39 (VS XI 63), *paṭāri-ma*: *al-lu / pa-ṭá-ri-ma awīlūt ḫu-up-ši*[8] *ù / ṣa-ab-tu* $^{\textit{LÚ.pl.}}$GAZ$^{\text{pl.}}$ / *āla*, "Behold, if the serfs desert, then the Ḫapiru will capture the city."
3. *EA* 129.40–42 (VS XI 70), *aṣī*: ... *ba-li a-ṣí ṣābu*$^{\text{pl.}}$ *pi-ṭ[á-tu]*[9] / *[i-na*^{MU}*]*[10] *ša-an-ti an-ni-ti* / *[ù la]-ḳú-mi*[11] *ālānī*$^{\text{[k]i.[pl.]}}$[12] *gub*^{ub}*-la*, "If an archer-host

[5]See the evidence briefly summarized below (pp. 154–156). Particularly pertinent is the biblical evidence, e.g., Eccl. 4.2, *wĕšabbē(a)ḥ ʾănî*, "And I praised." Obermann offers no explanation.

[6]We give the instances of *qatāli* + noun-subject since the construction is the same as that with the independent personal pronoun. Ebeling was perhaps the first to note the construction (see Glossary, *EA* II, p. 1436 and the example from 116.27). Brockelmann, *Grundriss* II, §88b, p. 168, has already collected all the examples we have under A, and considered them Canaanitisms; however, he has none of the examples under B. In support of his position on the Karatepe construction Honeyman merely refers to Brockelmann.—In the following passages the autographs are indicated in parentheses. Note the abbreviations: BB: Carl Bezold and E. A. Wallis Budge, *The Tell el-Amarna Tablets in the British Museum*, 1892; VS: Otto Schroeder, *Die Tontafeln von El-Amarna*, Vorderasiatische Schriftdenkmäler der königlichen Museen zu Berlin, Heft XI, 1915; WA: Hugo Winckler and Ludwig Abel, *Der Thontafelfund von El Amarna*, Mittheilungen aus den orientalischen Sammlungen, Hefte I-III, 1889.

[7]LÚ-*ia*, in form a genitive, but in view of the use of the independent pronoun (see examples under B) and *pi-ṭá-tu* in 137.49 (see A 4) it must stand for the nominative. The confusion between *-ia* and *-ī* in the nominative is frequent. Note the following nominatives: LÚ-*ia* (92.20, 117.76 [?]), *eḳ-li-ia* (74.17, passim), *ḫa-ba-li-ia* (82.33), EN-*ia* (68.9, 15, 84.26, 114.6, etc.), *be-lí-ia* (84.21), etc.

[8]Since LÚ.MEŠ *ḫu-up-ši* serves elsewhere as a nominative (114.21–22, 56–57, 125.27), it may do so here. This is forced on us by the rest of the evidence; see fn. 7. The Amarna usage (always LÚ.MEŠ *ḫu-up-ši*[*-ia*]) seems to indicate that *ḫupšu* is an abstract standing in a genitival relation after LÚ.MEŠ, which accordingly is not a determinative.

[9]Restoration from 137.49 (A 4). The interpretation of *aṣī* here and in 137.49 is not beyond dispute, due to the fluctuation in the gender of ERÍN.MEŠ; see *JCS* 2, Comm. no. 14, p. 45 [above, Paper 2, page 137]. Thus one could argue that *aṣī* is 3rd sg. m. of the permansive. However, since in the same letter we find the 3rd sg. fem. *tīpušu* (129.34) and *tūṣu* (129.39) agreeing with ERÍN.MEŠ *piṭatu*, and *aṣat* (129.36) agreeing with ERÍN.MEŠ, it is virtually certain that *aṣī* is an infinitive.

[10]Following Knudtzon's probable restoration.

[11]*la-ḳú*, which is rather common in the Byblian letters (see Glossary, *EA* II, p.

does not come forth this year, then they will seize the towns of Byblos."

4. *EA* 137.49 (WA 71), *aṣī-mi*: *a-ṣí-mi ṣābu*$^{pl.}$ *pi-ṭá-tu ù ša-mu*, "If an archer-host comes forth, then they will hear (of it)."[13]

B. *qatāli(-ma / mi)* + independent pronoun-subject (+ object)—

1. *EA* 89.38–39 (VS XI 43), *māti-ma*: *ù ma-ti-ma šu-ut a-nu / i-di-šu*, "And when he died, truly I learned of it."
2. *EA* 113.40–42 (WA 63), *paṭāri-ma*: *pa-ṭá-ri-ma šu-ut* [*ù*] / *ia-nu ša-a yu-ba-lu* [*ṭuppi*^{pí}*-ia*] / *a-na mu-ḫi-ka*, "If he leaves, then there will be no one to carry my letter(s) to thee."
3. *EA* 129.32–34 (VS XI 70), *ṣabāt-mi*: *ù ti-*⌜*i*⌝*-ḳ-bu-na ṣa-bat-mi n*[*i-nu*][14] *ālānī*$^{ki.pl.}$ *gub*^{ub}*-li ù mi-*[*na*] / [*t*]*i-p*[*u*]*-šu ṣābu*$^{pl.}$ *pí-ṭá-tu*, "And they say, 'If we capture the towns of Byblos, then what will the archer-host do?'."
4. *EA* 362.25–29 (AO 7093; F. Thureau-Dangin, "Nouvelles Lettres d'El-Amarna," *RA* 19 [1922], p. 102), *ṣabāt-mi*: *ù te-eḳ-bu-ni ṣa-bat-mi / ni-nu-um ālānī*$^{pl.}$ *gub*^{ub}*-li / ù da-na-nu-um a-mur-mi / ṣa-bat-mi šu-nu āl*^{ki} *gub-li / ù da-an-nu*, "And they say, 'If we capture the towns of Byblos, then shall we be powerful.' Behold, if they capture Byblos, then they will be powerful."
5. *EA* 132.30–35 (BB 18), *apāši*: ... *ù š*[*a-al-šu*][15] / *šum-ma la-a ḳa-bi-ti / a-na ša-a-šu a-pa-ši / at-ta ki-ta it-*[*ti*] [*mārī*^{p}]$^{l.}$ / ^{m}*·abd-a-ši-ir-ta* ⌜*ù*⌝ / *la-ḳú-ka*, "Ask him if I did not say to him, 'If thou makest an alliance with the sons of ᶜAbd-Ashirta, then they will seize thee.' "
6. *EA* 109.44–46 (VS XI 57), *dagāli-ma*:[16] *pa-na-nu da-ga-li-ma /* [*a*]*wīl māt mi-iṣ-ri ù en-ab-tu /* [*šar*]*rānī*$^{pl.}$ *māt ki-na-aḫ-ni iš-tu pa-n*[*i-šu*],

1453), rather than *il-ḳú* (Knudtzon), which is unattested.

12 Restoration on the basis of URU$^{ki.pl.}$ in line 33 of the same letter.

13 On *aṣī-mi* as an infinitive see fn. 9. Brockelmann has an additional example from 129.4, but the badly damaged text makes it extremely doubtful.

14 So, and not *ṣa-bat mi ni*—(Knudtzon). The virtual parallel (see following example), denied Knudtzon, makes the restoration certain [see below, Paper 7, p. 170, n. 23].

15 In line 30 we follow Knudtzon's restoration. In line 32 we follow Ebeling and read the MEŠ of line 32 as really belonging to line 33, restoring DUMU; "Das Verbum der El-Amarna Briefe," *BA* 8, p. 77. This is forced on us because there is not enough room between *apāši* and the MEŠ to allow for an object of *apāši* and a verb for *atta*. The resulting good sense speaks for the correctness of our interpretation.—On lines 35 ff. see the forthcoming article of the writer, in which many new readings and translations of the Amarna Byblos correspondence will be suggested.

16 This example is placed here rather than under A because I believe the subject (*šunu*) is to be understood with *dagāli-ma*. This makes better sense than the interpretation of Brockelmann and Knudtzon, according to which the subject is *awīl māt miṣri*. Note that the subject of the following clause is the same. The subject of the infinitive absolute is regularly omitted in biblical Hebrew.

"Previously if they saw an Egyptian, the kings of the land of Canaan would flee from him."

It is immediately evident from these passages that forms like *ka-ša-di-ma*, etc., can only be infinitives on the pattern *qatāl*. It is too obvious to need proof that they cannot possibly be participles. Nor, as might perhaps be suggested, can they be permansives. Orthographically, morphologically, and syntactically this is impossible. With the exception of *di-ki* = *dēk* (*EA* 131.22), there is not a single instance of an overhanging final vowel in the entire corpus of the letters from Byblos.[17] Moreover, the permansive of *mātu* could only be *mīt*, not *māt*, for the distinction in hollow verbs between *qīl* (stative-passive) and *qāl* (active) is rigorously observed.[18] And syntactically, it is impossible in *EA* 129.32 and *EA* 362.25–26, 28 to construe *ṣabat-mi* taken as a permansive with *nīnu* or *šunu*.

There can then be no question of the form involved. As for the syntax, though our parallels in the other languages are not as close as we might wish, still they do throw some light on the construction, enough at least to show that the construction is in accord with Semitic idiom. In fact, as we shall see immediately, the Amarna construction, if it does not clarify, at least focuses in truer perspective what had been heretofore an isolated phenomenon in Arabic.

The use of the infinitive absolute as a finite verb is familiar enough from Hebrew. Though in Hebrew the subject is not as a rule expressed, still a noun or independent pronoun may serve as subject, especially where clarity requires it.[19] This usage reflects the earlier Amarna construction.

Similar evidence is not lacking elsewhere. In the Ugaritic ex-

[17]Forms like *di-ka* (132.45) are of course Canaanitisms, reflecting the Can. stative-passive (*qīla*) of hollow verbs.

[18]The distinction is another Canaanitism. It is worth noting that there is no evidence in Amarna Canaanite for a perfect passive of the type *qutila* found in Arabic. In view of so much evidence for the imperfect passive *yuqtalu* this is very significant. Cf. the use of *apiš* always in a passive sense (81.18, 108.19, 122.42, 43, 123.10, 12) with that of *apaš* always in an active sense (113.10, 122.32, 139. 13—note the shift from *apiš* to *apaš* in 122). The same distinction of *qatil(a)* and *qatal(a)* obtains in hollow verbs: *dīk(i)* (131.22), *dīka* (132.45), *dīkū* (131.9)—all passives—, *mīt* (106.22) and *kīnā* (89.14)—both statives—, but *dāk* (139.14, 38, 140.11, 13, 26) and *dākū* (89.20, 101.5, 29, 122.35, etc.)—all actives. All of which seems to point to *qatila* (*qīla*) as the normal stative and passive perfect in Canaanite of the Amarna period.

[19]Gesenius-Kautzsch-Cowley, §113gg, p. 347.

pression *ʿn* + noun-subject, the element *ʿn* is probably an infinitive absolute.[20] In Syriac the use of the independent personal pronoun + infinitive with the force of a finite verb is attested.[21] In Old South Arabic the infinitive is quite commonly used in place of a finite verb.[22] In Ethiopic the so-called gerund may take the place of a finite verb in a subordinate adverbial clause, under certain conditions being construed with the primary form of the independent pronoun.[23]

Thus the Amarna construction, which is unknown in Accadian and therefore must reflect the scribes' Canaanite, has more or less close parallels in Northwest and South Semitic. It raises, however, a new problem. I refer to the use of *qatāli*. This apparent genitive is at first quite enigmatic. There is nothing in the use of the genitive in Accadian or Arabic that remotely resembles it. And while a novel dialectal usage is not an impossibility, especially in view of our ignorance of the use of case-endings in Canaanite, still any explanation starting with the assumption that the form is a genitive raises as many problems as it solves.

A non-genitival, indeclinable *qatāli* in Arabic provides the solution. This form is used in Arabic either to express a command or to emphasize in some way the idea of the finite verbal form.[24] This usage is identical with that of the so-called infinitive absolute in biblical Hebrew,

[20]Gordon, *Ugaritic Handbook*, §9.25, p. 68.

[21]Brockelmann, *Grundriss* II, §88c, pp. 168–169. Brockelmann agrees with Nöldeke in explaining the construction as due to an ellipsis of the finite verb.

[22]Maria Höfner, *Altsüdarabische Grammatik*, §54, p. 64. Miss Höfner considers this use of the infinitive as perhaps the most striking feature of Old South Arabic syntax; see her article, "Die Kultur des vorislamischen Südarabien," *ZDMG* 99 (NF 24, 1945–1949), p. 27.

[23]A. Dillmann, *Ethiopic Grammar* (trans. by J. A. Crichton), §181, pp. 450–451. The parallel in Ethiopic is weakened by the fact that the suffixed form of the pronoun is always attached to the gerund even when the independent pronoun is employed.—The use in Egyptian of the independent pronouns with the infinitive in place of a finite verb should also be mentioned; Gardiner, *Egyptian Grammar*, §300, p. 225, §306.6, p. 230.

[24]Wright-De Goeje, I, §98, p. 62. There are a few other uses of the form in Arabic but they are not pertinent to our discussion; see Reckendorf, *Die syntaktischen Verhältnisse des Arabischen*, §121, pp. 329–330, and Barth, *Nominalbildung*, p. 58.—The form *na-pa-ḫi* in Enūma Eliš (V 15) is hardly sufficient evidence for ascribing with Brockelmann (*Grundriss* I, §131c, p. 345; II, §10a, p. 15) an imperatival *qatāli* to Accadian: the passage is difficult, other interpretations are possible, and the text is late, so that nothing can be concluded from the *i*-ending. See Langdon, *The Babylonian Epic of Creation*, p. 159, fn. 8.

and the parallel has long been recognized by grammarians.[25]

In Arabic, it is true, *qatāli* is never used in place of a narrative finite verbal form. However, in view of the consistent use of the form *qatāli* in the Amarna passages we have examined, the two exceptions being only apparent,[26] and in view of the parallel use of Arabic *qatāli* and the Hebrew infinitive absolute, the conclusion is inescapable that we are dealing in Amarna with the same form that we find in Arabic, though in a use not attested in the latter.[27]

The origin of the *i*-ending escapes us.[28] One is inclined to see in it a fossil of an older and more complex case-system lost to us in prehistory. This possibility does not appear as remote as it might seem at first when one compares the Ugaritic construction *qatālu(-mi) qatala*[29] and the Accadian construction *parāsum(-ma) iprus*.[30] The latter shows the old adverbial ending *-um* found in expressions like *qerbum Bābili* and *lītum Dagan*, and therefore literally means, "with deciding he decided." In the Ugaritic construction it is virtually certain that *qatālu* is not a nominative. The final *-u* may reflect the *-u* in expressions like *ina libbu* found in Accadian,[31] or, as seems more probable, the adverbial *-um* noted above, the final *m* (not mimation) disappearing at the same time as the mimation, just as it did in Old Babylonian.[32]

[25]Brockelmann, *Grundriss* II, §10a, p. 15; König, *Lehrgebäude* II 2, §217*a*, p. 114; Praetorius, "Über den sogen. Infinitiv absolutus des Hebräischen," *ZDMG* 56 (1902), p. 547.

[26]*ṣabāt-mi* in 129.32 and AO 7093.25 is the result of syncope of the short vowel after the accent: *ṣabā́ti-mi* > *ṣabā́t-mi*. Cf. *nádina* > *nadna* in 89.16; for a discussion of the form see above, Albright-Moran, p. 167, Comm. on line 16 [above, Paper 4, page 147].

[27]For an additional parallel between the use of *qatāli* in Arabic and Amarna see below.

[28]Another problem is why *qatāli* is restricted in Arabic, and perhaps also in Canaanite, to the form *qatāl*.

[29]*Ugaritic Handbook*, §9.23, p. 68.

[30]For the most recent discussion see Julius Lewy, "Studies in Akkadian Grammar and Onomatology," *Orientalia* NS 15 (1946), pp. 410–415. The construction is well known in Old Assyrian (see Lewy, ibid.), in the Mari letters (see C.-F. Jean, "Lettres de Mari," *RA* 39 1942–1944, p. 64, fn. 2). Prof. Goetze makes the important observation that the construction, although known in southern Babylonian, becomes rather frequent in the north, that is, as one approaches the West Semitic area of influence.

[31]W. von Soden, *ZA* NF 7 (1933), pp. 93–94. Fr. Rosenthal has already suggested this possibility; *Orientalia* NS 11 (1942), p. 175.

[32]W. von Soden, *op. cit.*, p. 92, fn. 2.

Under the hypothesis, then, of an old *-i* ending, similar to Accadian *-um* and Ugaritic *-u*, we should see the origin of the Amarna construction in a nominal sentence: *qatāli anāku*, "I am (engaged) in killing." This hypothetical adverbial *-i* receives additional support from Amarna *la-ḳ[í]-m[i] ti-ìl-ḳú-na-ši* (131.17), "They will surely take it (i.e. Byblos)," lit., "in taking they will take it."[33] The parallel with the paronomastic infinitives *parāsum(-ma)* in Accadian and *qatālu(-mi)* in Ugaritic is evident.

Finally, the use of the enclitic particles *-ma* and *-mi* with the infinitive should also be noted.[34] From their use in nine out of eleven examples, it seems that the enclitic was the rule, at least in the Byblian dialect. In this regard one should compare the similar use of the enclitic with the infinitive in Ugaritic and Accadian.[35]

Thus the Amarna letters from Byblos, while raising a new problem for grammarians with their use of *qatāli*, relieve them of another. Other, and perhaps better, explanations of the final *-i* will undoubtedly be offered in the future, but the fact at least is clear that we are dealing both in Amarna and in the Karatepe inscriptions with the same construction: the infinitive absolute + independent personal pronoun.[36]

[33]Rosenthal (ibid., fn. 1) cites this example as uncertain. The traces, however, make it probable (Knudtzon, *EA* I, p. 537, fn. k), and in view of the parallel construction in Arabic we may regard it as virtually certain. Though on the basis of Arabic this adverbial use might have been assumed for Amarna Canaanite once the existence of *qatāli* in Canaanite could be shown, still the example is important in that it shows the Arabic construction is not an independent development.

[34]In this usage *-mi* probably reflects more accurately the scribes' native Canaanite, *-ma* reflecting rather Accadian usage; see Moran, *CBQ* 12 (1950), p. 153, fn. 4.—I agree with Gordon (*JNES* 8 [1949], p. 114) in regarding the *m* of the Karatepe Yifᶜil infinitives absolute *yrdm* (I 20) and *yšbm* (ibid.) as this same enclitic particle rather than as a pronominal objective suffix.

[35]*Ugaritic Handbook*, §9.23, p. 68; C.-F. Jean, *Archives Royales de Mari* II, 22.11 (*sa-da-ru-um-ma sa-di-ir*), 101.17 (*ba-la-ṭú-um-ma ba-li-iṭ*), etc.

[36]It hardly need be added that even in the Amarna period the South Canaanite form was actually not *qatāli*, but *qatôli*, and with the loss of final short vowels about a century and a half later became *qatôl*. The vocalization therefore of Phoenician *qtlm* (*qatôl-m*) is uncertain, though there must have been an anaptyctic vowel between *l* and *m*. Moreover, though the date of the change *ô* > *û* in Phoenician is uncertain, still *qatôl* must have already become *qatûl* by the time of the Karatepe inscriptions.

6. New Evidence on Canaanite *taqtulū(na)*

In a recent study of EA 82 in this Journal Prof. Albright and the writer had occasion to discuss briefly the form *taqtulū(na)* construed with a plural subject both in the Canaanite Amarna letters and in Ugaritic.[1] The view there expressed was that the form is to be taken as third feminine singular, the plural subject being construed as a collective. This was in opposition to the majority of scholars who had studied the problem, but the writers were loathe to admit an anomalous masculine plural *taqtulūna* with a *t*-preformative, assumed by others, especially in view of the fact that the construction with the third feminine singular had support in biblical Hebrew and Arabic. Until clear evidence to the contrary was presented, their view seemed the safer.

The abrupt *volte face* the writer makes in this article is due to the fact that in his opinion he has found such evidence in the syntax of purpose clauses in the Amarna letters from Byblos.[2] Setting aside a detailed analysis of purpose clauses for a future study, we shall here present merely the pertinent conclusions and their bearing on the question of *taqtulū(na)*. The writer's desire to correct as soon as possible an earlier published view will, he trusts, excuse this summary treatment of the evidence.

If in the analysis of purpose clauses in the Byblian Amarna letters *taqtulū(na)* is left aside for the moment, a very clear rule emerges, without exception in almost sixty examples: wherever the verb of the main clause is an indicative, the verb of the purpose clause is likewise

[1] *JCS* 2, pp. 243–244, Comm. no. 6 [above, Paper 2, pp. 135–136]. The use of the macron with *taqtulū(na)* throughout this paper, which anticipates our conclusion, is not meant to prejudge the question, but is merely an attempt to avoid a bewildering fluctuation between *taqtulū(na)* with and without the macron. The form *taqtulūna* can, of course, only be plural.

[2] See the writer's Johns Hopkins University dissertation, A Syntactical Study of the Dialect of Byblos as Reflected in the Amarna Tablets, 1950 [pp. 77–83 in the present volume].—Needless to say, the writer alone is responsible for the views expressed in this article, which are not meant to reflect those of Prof. Albright.

an indicative; wherever the verb of the main clause is a volitive,[3] the verb of the purpose clause is likewise a volitive. To illustrate: (indicative-indicative) *i-na-na a-di yu-pa-ḫi-ru ka-*[*l*]*i* / *ālānī*pl. *ù yi-ìl-ḳú-še*, "Now he is again gathering together (the forces of) all the cities that he may capture it (Byblos)" (124.14–15); (volitive-volitive) *ù uš-ši-ra ṣāb*pl. / *pí-ṭá-ti ù ti-ìl-ḳí-šu* / *ù ta-ap-šu-uḫ māt šarri*, "So send an archer-host in order that it may capture him and the land of the king be at peace" (107.29–31). The sequence of indicative, *yupaḫ(ḫ)iru* and *yilḳuše*, will be noted in the first example, whereas in the second after the imperative *uššira* we have *tilḳīšu* (not *tilḳušu*) and *tapšuḫ* (not *tapšuḫu*) in the two clauses expressing purpose.[4]

This rule of what we may call modal congruence[5] in purpose clauses is, as we said above, without exception in almost sixty instances. However, once we turn to cases where *taqtulū(na)* occurs with a plural subject, we are immediately confronted with a number of exceptions provided we consider the form as third fem. sg. This is not true, however, if the form is masculine plural. It was this fact that made it clear to the writer that he must abandon his earlier attempt to explain all occurrences of *taqtulū(na)* with a plural subject as third fem. sg.

The following are the apparent exceptions:

1. *ù lu-wa-ši-ra*[6] *be-li-ia* / *awīlūti ú*[7] *ti-ìl-ḳú mi-im-mi*pl. / d.*DA.MU-ia*[8] *a-na ma-ḫar bēli-ia* / *ù ú-ul ìl-ti-ḳa mi-im-ma*pl. / *ša ilānī-ka* LÚ*kalbu šu-ut*, "May my lord send men to take the possessions of my Adonis to my lord lest that dog take anything belonging to thy god(s)" (84.31–35). Exception: *ti-ìl-ḳú*.

[3]By a volitive is to be understood not only an imperative or a jussive, but also *yaqtula*. The use of *yaqtula* in the Byblos letters is almost without exception that of a volitive, that is, in a main clause it is virtually equivalent to a jussive; in a subordinate clause dependent on a volitive it expresses purpose or intended result. Other uses can be paralleled by the use of the subjunctive in Arabic. The writer will publish a complete study in the future. This discovery of an early Canaanite *yaqtula* throws considerable light not only on the Hebrew cohortative, but also on several uses of the subjunctive in Arabic, besides opening up new possibilities for the study of the form in Ugaritic.

[4]It might be objected that the use of the indicative in these letters is not rigid, so that *tapšuḫ* might stand for *tapšuḫu*. However, it suffices for our purpose here that the indicative is never used to express purpose after a volitive.

[5]Reckendorf, *Die syntaktischen Verhältnisse des Arabischen*, p. 62, §35, uses this term (Moduskongruenz) in a different connection.

[6]On *luwaš(š)ira*, *yadina* (second example), etc., see fn. 3.

[7]*Ú* here is strange, but not without parallel; cf. 88.10, 39 (reading *ú bal-<ṭá>-ti*).

[8]For DA.MU = Tammuz (Adonis), Otto Schroeder, *OLZ* 1915, cols. 291–293.

2. *ya-di-na / 4 mētim awīlūta 30 ta-pa[l sī]sē / ki-ma na-da-ni a-na* $^{m\cdot}$*zu-[r]a-[t]a / ù ti-na-ṣa-ru āla a-na ka-ta(m)*, "Let him give 400 men and 30 teams of horses, as are given to Zurata, that they may guard the city for thee" (85.19–22). Exception: *ti-na-ṣa-ru*.
3. *uš-ši-ra-am-mi* ^{LÚ}*mār šipri-ka / it-ti-ia a-na ma-ḫar / šarri bēli-ka ù lu-ú / li-di-na-ku šāba*$^{pl.}$ *ù* ^{GIŠ}*narkabāti / i-zi-ir-ta(m) a-na ka-ta(m) / ù ti-ṣú-ru āla*, "Send thy messenger to me to present himself before thy lord that he may give thee soldiers and chariots to aid thee and that they may guard the city." (87.9–14; also 88.40–42). Exception: *ti-ṣú-ru*.
4. *ia-aḳ-bi šarru a-na 3 ālānī / ù* ^{GIŠ}*eleppi* LÚ.MEŠ.MI.ŠI / *ù la-a ti-la-ku a-na / māt a-mur-ri*, "Let the king give orders to the three cities and the ship of the MI.ŠI that they are not to go to Amurru" (101.32–35). Exception: *ti-la-ku*.[9]
5. *ia-aḳ-bi šarru*^{ru} *a-na ša-šu-nu / ù tu-pa-ri-šu be-ri-ku-ni*,[10] "Let the king give orders to them to decide between us" (116.32–33). Exception: *tu-pa-ri-šu*.
6. *yi-ši-ra be-li 3 mētim sāba*$^{pl.}$ *30* ^{GIŠ}*narkabāti / ... ù ti-na-ṣa-ru / āl*^{KI} *gub*^{ub}*-li āl be-li-ia*, "Let my lord send 300 soldiers, 30 chariots ... to guard Byblos, my lord's city" (131.12–14). Exception: *ti-na-ṣa-ru*.[11]

[9]The construction after *ḳabū* in these letters is always that of a purpose clause; the infinitive never follows.

[10]An explanation of the form *bēriku-ni* escapes me, though the meaning is clear from context; cf. *bēri-nu* (116.67).

[11]Though it might be urged as a difficulty against the rule of modal congruence, 76.38–43 belongs among these examples: *uš-ši-ra ṣāb*$^{pl.}$ *pi-ṭá-ti / ra-ba ù tu-da-bi-ir / a-ia-bi šarri ištu / lìb-bi māti-šu ù / ti-ni-ip-šu ka-li / mātāti*$^{pl.}$ *a-na šarri*^{ri}, "Send an archer-host ... that all lands may be united to the king." In view of *tin(n)ipuš* construed with *kalī mātāti* in 74.35, *tin(n)ipšu* seems both to violate the rule of modal congruence and to be a clear case of the third fem. sg. with a plural subject (in these letters the nomen rectum after *kalū* usually determines the gender and number of the verb). However *kāli* + fem. pl. noun is also construed with a masc. pl. verb. (116.37–38, 79.19–20), and this is the case with *ti-ni-ip-šu*. Two other exceptions are *ti-na-ṣa-ru* (112.35) and *ti-na-ṣi-ru* (130.48) with *maṣṣartu* as subject. However, *constructio ad sensum* is the rule with *maṣṣartu* in Amarna; note the suffix *-šunu* referring to *maṣṣartu* in 79.33 and 117.81, LÚ.MEŠ*ma-ṣa-ar-ta* in 263.24, and *lu-ú ti-na-ṣa-ru āla*^{KI} (subject *maṣṣartu*) in 136.19–20. (In these letters *lu* is never used with an indicative.) Hence, like *ti-ni-ip-šu, ti-na-ṣa-ru* and *ti-na-ṣi-ru* are not exceptions to the rule of modal sequence with singular subjects, but rather are volitive plurals with a plural subject dependent on governing volitives.—It should be noted that in every example the form is *taqtulū*, never *taqtulūna*. This is in accord with Arabic *yaqtulû* in the jussive and subjunctive (*yaqtulûna* in the indicative) and Aramaic *yiqṭĕlû* in the jussive (*yiqṭĕlûn* in the indicative). This perfect agreement with known Semitic usage plus the fact that *taqtulūna* is frequent elsewhere with plural subjects (see below), confirms our view that we are dealing here with volitive plurals.

Concerning these apparent exceptions several facts are to be noted. In the first example where there is a shift to a singular subject (*kalbu šūt*) in the parallel purpose clause, the form is *iltiḳa*,[12] not *iltiḳu*, though the latter is what we should expect if *tilḳu* in the first clause is third fem. sg. indicative.

Moreover, there are two important parallels to our fifth example in which the subject is singular: [*yu-wa*]-*ši-ra šarru*^ru ^LÚ*rābiṣa-šu* / [*ù yu*]-*pa-ra-aš be-ri-ku-ni*, "Let the king send his commissioner to decide between us" (113.17–18); *y*[*u*]-*wa-ši-ra šarru* ⌜LÚ⌝*rābiṣa* / [*ù*] *y*[*u-p*]*a-r*[*i-ì*]*š* [*b*]*e-ri-nu*, "Let the king send the commissioner to decide between us" (117.66–67). Note that the verbs are *yupar(r)aš*/*yupar(r)iš*, not *yupar(r)a*/*išu*. In other words, in both cases where the subject is singular our rule of modal congruence is observed, whereas in the case of *tupar(r)išu* with a plural subject we must postulate an exception to the rule if we consider the form third fem. sg.

In short, sound methodology leads us ineluctably to the conclusion that everyone of these apparent exceptions is no exception at all, but that all of them contain true plural forms. Only the long -*ū* of the plural explains the final -*u* in these instances. If the forms were really third fem. sg., then in none of them should there appear a final -*u*, for the indicative is out of place in a purpose clause dependent on a volitive main clause.

Other and confirmatory evidence in the Byblian Amarna letters for a masc. pl. *taqtulūna* is not lacking, some of which has already been urged by others who argued for the existence of such a form. However, in itself it was too meager to prove the case.

First, *taqtulū* is used as a jussive: ^d.*a-ma-na ù* / *ù*[13] ^d.*bēlet ša āl gub-la* / *ti-di-nu bāšta-ka i-na pa-ni* / *šarri*^ri *bēli*^li-*ka-ma*, "May Amun and Ba^c^alat of Byblos grant thee favor before the king, thy lord" (95.3–6); ^d.*a-ma-na ilu ša šar*[*r*]*i* [*be-li-k*]*a* / *ti-di-nu bāšta-ka* ..., "May Amun, the god of the king, thy lord, grant thee favor ..." (71.4–6; also 86.3ff.).[14]

Whether *taqtulū* in these cases is to be considered as jussive or subjunctive plural is hard to say. We shall confront this problem in our study of *yaqtula*.

[12]See fn. 3.

[13]Dittography.

[14]In the latter example we must be dealing with a case of plural of majesty; cf. *maṣ(ṣ)artikunu* in 76.36. At any rate it is difficult to see how the form could be third fem. sg. without having recourse to the questionable assumption that both in 71.4 ff. and 86.3 ff. *bēlet ša āl gubla* was omitted. However, even if this be

The argument here is virtually the same as that given above: since the form is clearly a jussive, it must be a plural form, for the third fem. sg. jussive would necessarily be *tid(d)in*. Cf. [d.]*bēlet ša āl gub-la / il šarri bēli-ia li-din / bāšta*[ba]*-ka* ... (102.5–7).

Secondly, the form *taqtulūna* is used almost exclusively with plural subjects. Of 110 occurrences of *-na* affixed to some form of *yaqtulu*, 70 are with *taqtulū* (rarely *yaqtulū*) construed with a plural subject. This points to a regular third masc. pl. indicative *taqtulūna* in Byblian corresponding to Arabic *yaqtulûna* and Aramaic *yiqṭĕlûn*.

Thirdly, the fluctuation between *taqtulūna* and *taqtulūni* should be noted. Now in Old Babylonian, the usage of which Amarna Accadian reflects, the terminative ending *-ni(m)* is restricted to plural forms with a final long vowel. The use of *taqtulūni(m)*, therefore, with a plural subject points to a *t*-preformative with the masc. pl. Though recourse might be had here to a blend formation,[15] a common enough feature of Amarna Accadian, so that *taqtulūni(m)* would be a blend of Canaanite third fem. sg. *taqtulŭ* and Accadian *iqtulūni(m)*, still this is extremely difficult when we find a fluctuation between *taqtulūna* and *taqtulūni* in the same letter: *tiḳbūni* (362.17, 25), *tiḳbūna* (362.21), *teba*ʾ*ūna* (362.24), *tamūtūna* (362.44). Since there is not a single case where *-ūni(m)* is attached to a verb construed with a singular subject, it is difficult to escape the conclusion that the scribe who wrote 362 considered *tiḳbūna / tiḳbūni* as plurals.

As for a *t*-preformative with the dual (*taqtulāna / i*), the Amarna evidence is too meager to permit any definite conclusions. The writing 2 URU-*ni-šu* (79.31) makes it very doubtful whether nouns preceded by 2 are to be considered duals. Hence it is difficult to determine the rules of agreement. In 103.22 *ti-iš-ma-na* may be a dual (for *tišma*ʿ*āna*).[16] Apart from this one instance, there is nothing in Byblian Amarna either for or against a *t*-preformative with the dual.

One remark in conclusion. The writer's opinion that there now can be no doubt of the existence of *taqtulūna* in early Canaanite is not to be taken to mean that he therefore denies the existence of the construction

---

conceded, an explanation is still required why the form is not *tid(d)in* rather than *tid(d)inu*.

[15]This was the explanation offered in *JCS* 2 [above, Paper 2], but due consideration was not given to *EA* 362 (= AO 7093, published by F. Thureau-Dangin, *RA* 19, pp. 102–103).

[16]In *JCS* 2 [Paper 2, above] this possibility was not considered.

in which the third fem. sg. is construed with a plural subject taken as a collective.[17] In fact, he is inclined to accept the suggestion that the explanation of the *t*-preformative with the masculine plural is to be found in the analogical change of the prefix *y*- > *t*- on the basis of the idiomatic use of the 3rd feminine singular indicative *taqtulu* with a plural subject.[18]

[17]*timaḫaṣanan*[ī] in 77.37 is an example.
[18]Cross and Freedman, *JBL* 67 (1948), p. 201, fn. 16.

7. "Does Amarna Bear on Karatepe?"— An Answer

In *JCS* 5 (1951), pp. 58–61 Prof. Julian Obermann has raised the question, "Does Amarna Bear on Karatepe?" His answer, an emphatic negative, is by way of reply to an article in which the writer, in view of the evidence of some ten passages, came to the conclusion: (1) that Amarna presents us with the idiom of an infinitive absolute plus nominative nominal/pronominal subject (plus object), the infinitive substituting for a finite verb; (2) that this idiom was the clear Canaanite parallel we had been looking for in our efforts to solve the *qtl*/*yqtl* *ʾnk* construction in the Karatepe inscriptions.[1] Prof. Obermann, however, not only denies the relevance of the Amarna evidence for the Karatepe problem, but also maintains that the writer failed to give the correct analysis of the Amarna passages. In short, the Amarna evidence is at best irrelevant, but is probably non-existent.

Its irrelevance is shown, he thinks, because the construction "is employed to define the time when, or the condition under which, an action has taken or will take place, while the action itself is described by a finite verb ..."[2] The construction is really that of a subordinate clause, or more accurately, a prepositional phrase of temporal or conditional character. Hence, whatever its correct analysis, it cannot possibly bear on the Karatepe inscriptions, in which the problem, the construction of independent sentences in Phoenician, is totally different.[3]

This abrupt dismissal of the Amarna evidence rests on the not only unproved but false assumption that if a speech-unit "is employed to define the time when, or the condition under which, an action has taken or will take place," *therefore* it is subordinate or hypotactic. In a translation we may, or at times even be forced to, subordinate such a unit; but the speech categories of one language are no norm for the categories of another language. And to add one more banality, where we subordi-

[1] *JCS* 4 (1950), pp. 169–172 [above, Paper 5].

[2] Obermann, p. 58b.

[3] The preceding lines are a brief summary, more or less in his own words, of Obermann, *ibid.*

nate one clause to another, Canaanite for the most part coordinates.[4] If, for example, in Ruth 2.9 (*wĕṣāmît wĕhālakt*) it is permissible to translate the first member "when you are thirsty," and even to describe it as a temporal clause, the fact remains that this "time when" determination of the following clause is itself an independent clause. In itself such a determination does not indicate grammatical structure.

Even granting then that the Amarna construction "is employed to define the time when, etc.," we cannot immediately infer its subordination. In fact, in at least two of the Amarna passages quoted in the writer's previous article even our own speech categories permit us to translate the infinitive member as an independent clause: A1 (116.27–28), "My man arrived and he bound him" (for "When my man ..."); B1 (89.38–39), "He died; truly I learned of it" (for "When he died ...").[5] Which translation is more accurate depends entirely on the syntax of the original. How, therefore, Prof. Obermann, without first having determined the syntax of the passages, can go so far as to say that the Amarna construction may be rendered even "more accurately as a prepositional phrase of temporal or conditional character,"[6] is difficult to explain.

Testing the several hypotheses of prepositional phrase, hypotaxis, or parataxis as the correct analysis of the Amarna construction, we must rule out the first, as we shall see, on the basis of syntax. On the same grounds we must likewise rule out the second, there being not the slightest indication of the subordination of the first clause to the second. This lack of subordination accords perfectly with Canaanite sentence structure in general, and the burden of proof is certainly on those who would consider the clause as subordinate.

Before considering Prof. Obermann's analysis of the Amarna passages, the writer would call attention to another instance of *qatāli* in Amarna, unfortunately discovered too late for use in his first paper. In the writer's opinion it is the *coup de grâce* to any equivocations about subordinate clauses, etc. It occurs in a Jerusalem letter, *EA* 287.45–48: ^{45}*a-di e-tel-li* ^{m}*Pa-ú-ru* ^{LÚ}*rābiṣ šarri*^{ri} ^{46}*a-na māt āl Ú-ru-sa-lim*^{KI} *pa-ṭa-a(!)-ri(!)* ^{47}[^{m}*A*]*d-da-ya a-di* $^{\text{LÚ.pl}}$*ma-ṣar-ti* ^{LÚ}*ú-e-*⌜*e*⌝ ^{48}[*ša i*]*-din šarrī*^{ri}. Knudtzon, it is true, read *pa-ṭa-ar(!)*, but Schroeder's autograph is very

4Examples in Hebrew are legion; Gesenius-Kautzsch-Cowley, §§156a, 158a, 159b–k, etc. Cf. also Gordon's remarks, *UH*, p. 98, 13.54.

5A1, etc., in this paper refer to the enumeration of the Amarna passages in the writer's paper cited in fn. 1; here see p. 169b, 170a [above, Paper 5, pp. 152–154].

6Obermann, *ibid.*

clear, Schroeder himself adding the marginal note that the last sign is "eher *ri* als *ar*."[7]

On details of the translation there is room for disagreement. Prof. Albright's recent translation[8] agrees with Knudtzon's in joining the clause *a-di* ... *Ú-ru-sa-lim*^{KI} to what precedes, and in taking ^{m}*Ad-da-ya* as subject of *pa-ṭa-ar/a-ri*. If this be correct, then we have an exact parallel to the examples A1–B5 from Byblos: *qatāli* plus nominative subject. However, Prof. Albright and the writer now translate: "Even before Pewure, the royal commissioner, came up [46]to the land of Jerusalem, he removed [47]Addaya together with the garrison (and) the Egyptian officer [48]which my king had given (me)."[9] If this be correct, then we have an additional parallel to the subjectless *dagāli-ma* in B6 (*EA* 109.44–46).[10] In either case *qatāli* is now unequivocally attested as describing a definite, past action in an independent clause.[11]

Prof. Obermann's view is that the Amarna construction does not involve an infinitive absolute at all, but rather is identical with the con-

[7]VS XI 163.

[8]In Pritchard, ed., *Ancient Near Eastern Texts*, p. 489b.

[9]*adi* = before, 245.13, 256.32. There is no reason for taking *e-tel-li* as an infinitive (so Ebeling, *EA* II, p. 1401), unattested in Amarna, rather than the attested preterite (cf. *ibid.*); *adi* as a conjunction causes no difficulty (*ibid.*, p. 1362; and note that Ebeling lists 287.45 under the use of *adi* as a conjunction despite his classifying *e-tel-li* as an infinitive), and the nominative ^{m}*Pa-ú-ru* definitely favors the preterite.

[10]See the remarks below on B6.

[11]The solution of *EA* 116.10ff. is, in the opinion of the writer, to be found in a similar past narrative use of *maqāti-ma*: [10]*yi-di* [11][*šar*]*ru i-nu-ma ma-qa-ti-ma a maṣṣarti(UN)-nu* [12]*ù ṣa-ab-tu-še mārū*^{pl} ^{m}*Abd-a-ši-ir-*[*t*]*a*, "Let the king know that the sons of ʿAbd-Ashirta fell upon our garrison and captured it." Knudtzon's "dass ich *verzweifelt* bin und *klage*" is only a guess. Kootz's (see *EA* II, p. 1461 s.v. *maḳû*) *ma-qa-ti ma-a-un-nu*, "dass gefallen ist die Aussenstadt," is much better. However, aside from the difficulty of the writing *ma-a-un-nu* for the assumed Can. *maʿôn(u)*—we would rather expect *ma-ḫu-(ú)-nu*—the fem. suffix in *ṣabtū-še* remains to be explained. It cannot refer to Simyra in line 10, for it is clear from the rest of the letter that Simyra itself had not yet been captured. The writer proposes that UN is the ideogram for *maṣṣartu*: in 136.18 *ma-ṣa-ar-ta* is found as a gloss of UN, and it is quite likely, as Knudtzon noted (*EA* I, p. 498, fn. c), that in 114.31 UN = *maṣṣartu*. This reading would give some explanation of the fem. suffix *-še*, though *maṣṣartu* is usually treated *ad sensum* as a masc. pl. (see *JCS* 5 [1951], p. 34, fn. 11 [above, Paper 6, pp. 161–162]). For *a* = *ana*, cf. *a da-ri-ti* (74.13), *a ša-šu-nu* (103.10), *a mi-ni* (125.31), and perhaps *a i*[*a*]*-ši* (138.135)—all from Byblos. For *ana* rather than *ina*, cf. *EA* II, p. 1374 ("*ana* fälschlich gebraucht"—*idiomatisch* would be more exact; cf. *ašābu ana kussī* in the same letter, 116.66, and Ugar. *yṯb lkḥṯ*, *UH* 49.I.30).

struction, common in Amarna as elsewhere in Semitic, in which an infinitive is introduced by a preposition and followed by its subject in the genitive.[12] The one difference is, he thinks, that in the ten passages studied by the writer there is an ellipsis of the preposition; the ellipsis is to be explained by the assumption that the Amarna writers felt free to omit the preposition when the infinitive was qualified by *-ma*.

To support this view Prof. Obermann attempts to prove that the subjects of the infinitive are in the genitive, the writer's attempt to prove they are in the nominative being characterized as "arbitrary postulation." This he does in a long footnote,[13] the substance of which—together with the writer's criticism—is as follows:

A1 (116.27–28): "*awīli-ia*, a plain genitive ..."—In view of the evidence presented by the writer that *awīli-ia, bēli-ia*, etc., are very often clear nominatives, this apodictic "plain genitive" is at least surprising.[14] The fact is that such forms in Amarna are not "plainly" any case, but one must, as the writer did,[15] determine the case by analysis of parallel constructions.

A2 (118.36–39): according to Prof. Obermann, *awīlūt ḫu-up-ši* is either another genitive or a non liquet. The writer again had recourse to parallels, that is, A3–B5.[16]

A3 (129.40–42): Prof. Obermann rejects the writer's restoration *ṣābu*^{pl} *pí-ṭ[á-tu]* as irrelevant, since it is based on the equally irrelevant parallel in A4 (137.49). The latter's irrelevance is shown, he says, by quoting an erroneous use of TU in *EA* 202.18, a letter which does not come from Byblos, and by confusing TU with TÚ when citing the Byblian letter 137.39; the confusion of TU and TÚ is, it would seem, the basis for Prof. Obermann's "and frequently passim."—In 137.39 we should of course read *pí-ṭá-ta(m)*, or more exactly, *pí-ṭá-ta*$_5$. A study,

[12] Obermann, p. 59b. Prof. Obermann complains (pp. 58–59) that the writer failed to state "the plain fact, highly pertinent to any appraisal of those passages, that their use is rather rare and exceptional, while actual prepositional phrases designed to take the place of temporal and conditional clauses are the rule and norm in Amarna as well as elsewhere in Semitic, being particularly well known to us from Hebrew." That *qatāli-ma* plus subject is rare the writer considered obvious from the fact that he could cite at the time only ten passages; that "actual prep. phrases ... are the rule, etc." is highly pertinent to any appraisal of the construction only when one overlooks the facts that rule out the comparison.

[13] P. 60, fn. 10.

[14] *JCS* 5 (1950), p. 169, fn. 7 [above, Paper 5, p. 152].

[15] *Ibid.*

[16] *Ibid.*, fn. 8.

moreover, of the writings of this Egyptian word in 129 and 137 discloses that *pí-ṭá-tu* in the latter and its restoration in the former are far from irrelevant. In 129 *pí-ṭá-tu* occurs once and is the subject of *tīpušŭ* (34); *pí-ṭá-ta*₅ occurs four times, in each case after *iānu* (30, 38, 49, 95), and the accusative is according to rule[17]; *pí-ṭá-ti* occurs once and is an objective genitive after *uššar* (78).[18] In 137 *pí-ṭá-tu* occurs once, the supposedly irrelevant case; *pí-ṭá-at* occurs once and is a clear construct (45), though the case is uncertain because of the dubious verb in the preceding line; *pí-ṭá-ta*₅ occurs twice, once as the subject of *yadina* (40), the second time as the object of *yarḫiša* (98); *pí-ṭá-tu* of line 49 is referred to in line 50 by the suffix *-ši* (*ka-ša-di-ši*). It is obvious therefore that both in 129 and 137 ERÍN.MEŠ *piṭatu / i,a* is treated by the scribes like a Canaanite feminine singular noun, and that the use of the case-endings is flawless—hence the significance of *pí-ṭá-tu* in 137.49. Two other occurrences of *pí-ṭá-tu* in the Byblos letters should be mentioned: 362[AO 7093].19,[19] subject of *tūṣă*, and *ibid.*, 56, subject of *tūṣŭ*. In the same letter occur: *pí-ṭá-te* (8), a genitive dependent on *uššar* as in 129.78 above; *pí-ṭá-ta*₅ three times, object of *yišaru* (10), after *iānu-mi* (18), object of *yiḫammiṭa* (41); it is also referred to by the suffix *-ši* (*a-ṣí-ši*, 58). Again the same fem. sg. treatment, the same flawless use of case-endings. In short, wherever we find *pí-ṭá-tu* in the Byblos letters, it is a clear nominative. Hence only by the most arbitrary methods can one reject as meaningless its occurrence in 137.49 and the restoration *pí-ṭ[á-tu]* in 129.40, the obvious parallel to 137.49.[20]

B1 (89.38–39) and B2 (113.40–42): Prof. Obermann accepts as likely the suggestion of Prof. Albright and the writer that the use of *šūt* in the Byblos letters reflects Canaanite *hwt*.[21] Thus, comparing the use of *hwt*

[17] JCS 2 (1948), p. 248, Comm. no. 28 [above, Paper 2, p. 139].

[18] For an objective genitive after an infinitive, cf. *uš-ša-ar awīli*^{li} (113.29), *a-na šu-te-er / a-wa-ti* (108.49–50).

[19] *RA* 19 (1922), p. 102.

[20] The above remarks are not meant to deny that Egy. *piṭátye* (*pḏtyw*) gave rise to some confusion among the Canaanite scribes. Besides treating it as a declinable f. sg., they also employed *pí-ṭá-ti* more or less consistently, regardless of case. No fixed rules, therefore, are possible, but the usage of each letter must be examined.

[21] *JCS* 4 (1950), p. 167 (on l. 38) and p. 168 (on l. 50) [above, Paper 4, pp. 149–150]. The comparison of *šūt* with *hwt* was made in order to offer some explanation of the fact that *šūt* in Amarna is virtually confined to the Byblos letters; for though Accadian in form, it is Canaanite in syntax. As far as the evidence of actual usage goes, the reference to the Yeḥimilk inscription is more pertinent, since a genitival use of *šūt*, parallel to the use of Ugar, *hwt*, is unattested; see fn. 22.

as a genitive in Ugaritic, he feels free to dismiss the *šūt* after *māti-ma* and *paṭārī-ma* as a genitive.—The use of *šūt*, however, in the Byblos letters merited closer attention, for it is used exclusively either as a demonstrative adjective or as a personal/demonstrative pronoun in the nominative, the latter being the much commoner.[22] Unless, therefore, we are to postulate two exceptions—the only two—, we must consider *šūt* both in B1 and B2 as nominatives.

B3 (129.32–34): rejecting the writer's restoration, Prof. Obermann seems to suggest *ṣabāt-mi-ni*, *-ni* being "very possibly the normal Akkadian pronominal suffix ... and perhaps even intended as an enclitic."[23]—The pronominal suffix in the Byblos letters is *never -ni;* it is *-nu*.[24] Moreover, *-mi never* separates a noun and its pronominal suffix, nor do the examples cited by Prof. Obermann (*ana-me šarri* [197.6], *ištu-mi pa-ni* [161. 31], etc.) prove it did or could do so. What is meant by enclitic *-ni* is not clear to the writer, unless it is the *-ni* in forms like *tadinū-ni* (126.64,65). If such forms are referred to, one asks for a parallel; if not, one asks for an example.

B4 (362.25–29): Prof. Obermann considers *ni-nu-um* an error for the non-existent *-ni* (see above). He considers *šu-nu* of course as the pronominal suffix, but *-mi never* separates a noun and its suffix (see above).

B5 (132.30–35): the writer accepts Prof. Obermann's criticism and admits that he should not have used a passage the reading of which is doubtful. Rather the other examples should have been used to confirm the correctness of Ebeling's view, which was arrived at independently of any concern for the form involved in *a-pa-ši*.

[22]*šūt* = pers. pro. in nominative; 74.52, 76.11, 15, 20, 79.45, 84.17, [88.9], 92.41, 94.64, 66, 69, 72, 95.21 (?), 106.39, 119.58, 128.26 (?), 132.24 (?), 138.6; *šūt* = demonst. adj.: 84.35, 90.21 (?). In 83.37 (*uš-ši-ra-šu šu-ut*) the writer believes that *šūt* is not the object of the verb, but rather is to be compared to the use of the personal pron. in Hebrew and Ugaritic to emphasize the pronominal suffix; thus, render "Send him back, him!" The reading *ana šūt* in 85.84 and 94.76 is extremely doubtful, and the badly damaged context is of no help; elsewhere we find *ana šāšu*.

[23]Obermann's remarks here might be misunderstood to mean that Knudtzon in some way supported either of Obermann's suggestions. Actually Knudtzon separates *mi-ni* from *ṣa-bat*, and in simple despair renders, "*Was sind* ..." (Correct the writer's article, p. 170, fn. 14, "denied *by* Knudtzon," to "denied Knudtzon" [corrected in the present volume (p. 153, fn. 14)—*Eds.*]; the latter is the reading of the manuscript. When Knudtzon published *EA* he did not have the parallel of 362 [AO 7093], which, the writer is sure, would have guided his restoration and interpretation of 129.32–34.)

[24]Böhl, *Die Sprache der Amarnabriefe*, p. 27, §15.

B6 (109.44–46): Prof. Obermann and the writer agree at least on the fact that *da-ga-li-ma* is grammatically subjectless. The former, however, would compare the use of the infinitive in Gen. 25.26; the writer insists that the use of *qatāli-ma* / *-mi* in the other Amarna passages must guide our interpretation here, and he would compare the use of the subjectless infinitive absolute in Hebrew, in which, as in this case, the subject is determined by the context. For a parallel to the use of *dagāli-ma*, cf. Hag. 1.9.

In short, Prof. Obermann's attempt to explain the subjects of the infinitives as genitives appears to the writer unsuccessful. Most of his explanations simply collapse when confronted with the established facts. It is these same facts which make imperative the explanation of the infinitive-subjects as nominatives.[25]

Other difficulties with Prof. Obermann's analysis are not lacking. To mention only one, there is the consistent use of the conjunction *u* between the two members of the sentence. Prof. Obermann tries to minimize the importance of this fact by referring to Ugaritic and Hebrew parallels, in which such a syndetic element is found even after prepositional phrases.[26] He fails to cite an Amarna parallel, though at least two are to be found.[27] However, there is not one indisputable case in the Byblos letters.[28] And even if we admit that the conjunction was so used

[25]It seems to the writer that Prof. Obermann could have saved himself the effort of trying to get around the clear evidence for the nominative subjects, and yet still maintained the parallel with the prepositional phrases in Hebrew. A nominative subject of an infinitive governed by a preposition is well attested (GKC, §115g–k). This, in fact, was the very tentative position that the writer took in his dissertation [see in the present volume pp. 54–56] before he saw that Arabic *qatāli* was the obvious solution of his difficulties. The difficulties, which could not be minimized, were: (1) the assumption of an ellipsis in every case without a single parallel in the letters to support it (Obermann's appeal to *-ma* is also unsupported); (2) contrary to the evidence on the use of *u* (on which see below), the assumption that the infinitive member is subordinate to the following clause; (3) the fact that, when the preposition is used, there is no evidence for the use of the nominative.

[26]P. 59, fn. 9.

[27]*EA* 245 ^{13}*ù a-di ka-ša-di-ia* ^{14}*ù da-ku-šu*; 256 ^{32}*a-di ka-ša-di-ka* ^{33}*iš-tu ḫarrāni*$^{\text{ra-ni}}$*-ka ù an-nu-*[*ú*] ^{34}*ka-ši-id*.

[28]There are only two instances where such a use of *u* may be found: 79 ^{21}[*eš*]*-tu ṣa-ba-at āl Bīt-A*[*r-ḫa*] ^{22}[*a-na*] *pí-i* ^{m}*Abd-a-ši-ir-ta* ^{23}[*ù*] *ki-na-na tu-ba-ú-na* ^{24}[*i-p*]*é-ša āl Gub-la*; 137 ^{50}*a-na ú-mi ka-ša-di-ši ù* ^{51}*ta-ra-at ālu*^{KI} *a-na šarri be-li-ia*. As to the first, Knudtzon considers the restoration of *ù* in line 23 doubtful because of lack of room; see *EA* I, p. 390, fn. d. The writer would readily admit the second example, though Prof. Albright joins *ana ūmi* to *šamū* of the previous line

occasionally in the Byblos letters, the absolute consistency with which the conjunction is used after the type infinitive plus subject is in striking contrast with the almost equal consistency with which it is omitted after the type preposition plus infinitive plus subjective genitive.[29] This is but one more indication that the infinitive construction is a clause, not a prepositional phrase.

In conclusion, one more point: it struck the writer as curious that, searching as Prof. Obermann's criticism is, he passes over in complete silence the writer's emphasis on the parallel between Amarna and Arabic *qatāli*. He merely mentions in passing the writer's professed inability to explain the origin of the *i*-ending and arbitrary appeal to "another and more complex case-system lost to us in prehistory."[30] But neither Prof. Obermann's silence nor the writer's inability to explain origins can obscure the obvious parallel between an adverbial *qatāli* in Arabic and the use of *qatāli* in Amarna.[31]

Prof. Obermann's detailed criticism of the writer's first presentation of the Amarna evidence and his own attempt at a solution along other lines have provided the writer with an opportunity to clarify and expand many features of the Amarna material which really deserved more detailed treatment. For this the writer can only be grateful.

(*ANET*, p. 483b). Cf. also 362 (AO 7093) [43]*ù a-nu-mi* [44]*ù i-du.*—Knudtzon's restoration of 115.19–20 is mere guesswork and need not be taken seriously.

[29]Cf. the asyndetic union in the following: *ištu*, 79.8ff., 138.75ff.; *ina*, 69.25ff., 70.27ff., 77.13ff., 105.18ff., 112.41, 119.15, 130.29ff.; *adi*, 70.23, 71.26ff., 79.17, 31ff., 82.19, 88.27, 102.16, 113.28, 127.38ff. This list is not exhaustive, containing only the examples where on the analogy of the hypothetical prepositionless infinitive we would most expect to find *u* between the prepositional phrase and the clause.

[30]Obermann (quoting the writer), p. 59b.

[31]The writer sees no reason for a detailed reply to Prof. Obermann's remarks on the extra-Amarna evidence. Note, however, the following: (1) in order to isolate the testimony of Eccl. 4.2 he must reject *tāmôḵ* in Ps. 17.5, accepted by Briggs (ICC, p. 134), Buttenwieser (The Psalms, p. 484), probably Ehrlich (Die Psalmen, p. 30), and rejected by some on other than grammatical grounds (e.g., H. Schmidt, Die Psalmen, p. 25); (2) he must likewise offer a new grammatical analysis of Est. 3.13 and 9.1, which the writer doubts anyone will accept—neither the commentators (Holler, Paton, Schildenberger, Wildeboer) nor Streidl, who has studied the syntax and style of Esther most closely (*ZAW* 55 [1937], pp. 73–108; cf. especially p. 75), offer any support to Obermann's original view; (3) if the Syriac examples are to be taken as due to ellipsis of the finite verb, we should perhaps be as generous with ellipses in the Karatepe inscriptions. On further parallels to Amarna and Karatepe in Ugaritic, see Herdner, *GLECS* V, p. 62, and Wevers, *ZAW* 62 (1949–50), pp. 316–317.

8. Amarna *šumma* in Main Clauses

There is a use of *šumma* in the Amarna letters which, even if it reflects Canaanite rather than Accadian speech—a point to which we shall return—, is not irrelevant, at least from the viewpoint of comparative grammar, to the discussion in this Journal on the etymology of Accadian *šumma*.[1] As Knudtzon recognized, in a number of passages (*EA* 35.13, 74.13, 103.36, 109.54, 112.25, 137.60) *šumma* cannot mean "if": no apodosis follows (or precedes), and recourse to an ellipsis would be forced, in some cases (e.g., 112.25) virtually impossible. Accordingly, guided by context, Knudtzon rendered *šumma* by "denn,"[2] which, it is to be admitted, makes sense in the passages where he recognized this anomalous use of the article.

However, this rendering, it seems to me, should be abandoned. In two of the additional occurrences of this use of *šumma* which we propose below, it will not fit. This is clearly true of 108.34ff., and hardly less so of 244.30–38. In the latter passage, if one consults the entire context, it seems fairly clear that the *šumma* clause in lines 30–33 is the basis of the request for troops in lines 34ff., rather than the reason for the demand that the king save Megiddo from falling into the hands of Labʾaya (lines 25–29). Abandoning "denn," in view of the comparative evidence (Hebrew, South Arabic, Ugaritic, etc.)[3] we retain the more original deictic force of the particle, conventionally rendered by "lo, behold."

To the six occurrences noted by Knudtzon four more should be added:

1. *ina Bīt*-NIN.URTA *pu-ḫu-ru-nim-mi ù / ni-ma-qú-ut muḫḫi āl Gub-la šum-ma ia-*[*nu*] / *awīli*^{li} *ša ú-ši-zi-bu-*[*š*]*e iš-tu qa-ti-n*[*u*] / *ù nu-da-bir*$_5$ $^{LÚ.pl}$*ḫa-za-nu-ta* ..., "Assemble in Bīt-?, and let us fall upon Byblos—behold! there is no one who will save it from our hand—, and let us drive out the governors ..." (74.31–34).[4]—Against understanding

[1]Speiser, *JCS* 1, pp. 321–327; Haldar, *JCS* 4, pp. 63–64. See also Schoneveld, *Bibliotheca Orientalis* 8 (1951), p. 112, and Speiser's remarks, *JCS* 6, p. 81, fn. 5.

[2]Indicated as doubtful in 35.13, 109.54, 137.60. Knudtzon may also have been led to "denn" by the parallelism of *šumma* in 35.13 and *aššum* in 35.37. Though we reject this meaning for the participle, the parallelism of *šumma* (74.32, 137.60) and *inūma* (74.43, 89.46) might also be urged in its favor.

[3]See the articles of Speiser and Haldar.

[4]For the readings *ú-ši-zi-bu-*[*š*]*e* and *nu-da-bir*$_5$, plus the fact that ʿAbd-Ashirta's

šumma as introductory of a conditional protasis are these reasons: (1) If you consider the preceding clause as the apodosis, then not only is the position of the protasis most unusual, but a cautionary "if" in a summons to arms and rebellion is most unlikely. The entire context demands that we understand the call to fall upon Byblos was just as absolute as the advice to the men of Ammia (lines 25ff.) to kill their ruler. (2) If you take the following clause as the apodosis, the objection on the grounds of an unlikely caution still obtains. Further, the connection between there not being anyone to save Byblos from ᶜAbd-Ashirta's forces and the exhortation to drive out the rest of the governors is not too clear. One might maintain that the implicit argument is that, if Byblos falls, so will all the other towns. However, there is no evidence that Byblos was considered so strong that it could be advanced as a test case. On the other hand, all these difficulties disappear once we recognize that *šumma* may mean "behold" or the like, already used with this meaning in line 13 (see above). The *šumma* clause is introduced parenthetically to give the grounds for assured success in the initial venture, the attack on Byblos, but the *nimaqqut* and *nudabbir* clauses are parallel, the conquest of Byblos being only one step in a large campaign, though of course the one mentioned by Rib-Adda.[5]

2. *ša-ni-ta*$_5$ *šum-ma* $^{\text{LÚ.pl}}$ / *ḫa-za-nu-tu*$_4$ *la-a na-a*[*d-nu*] / *pa-ni-šu-nu a-na mu-ḫi-šu*-[*nu*] / *ù ki-na-na da-an-n*[*u*(!)] / *šu-nu*,[6] "Moreover,

---

speech includes lines 31–41, see Mendenhall, *JNES* 6, pp. 123–124. Against Knudtzon and Mendenhall, in line 33 we must read *qa-ti-n*[*u*], not *qa-ti* $^{n[u}$*nukurti*]: (1) there is almost no room for the conjectured KÚR, to judge from the plate; (2) if *nukurti* were correct, we would expect *qa-at*, not *qa-ti*, which in the Byblos letters is never used as a construct before a nomen rectum; (3) cf. *ia-nu awīla ša ú-še-zi-ba-an-ni* / [*iš*]-*tu qa-ti-šu-nu* below in lines 44–45, a clear reference to lines 32–33.

[5]To remove the last difficulty in this entire passage, read in line 42: *ki-na-na ti-iš-ku-nu mamīta*(!) *a-na be-ri-šu-nu*, "Thus they exchanged oaths." Knudtzon read *nam-ru*, but offered no explanation. While NAM.ŠUB might be read, as I had done previously, interpreting *šiptu* in the context as virtually equivalent to "oath," still in the light of the Idri-mi inscription, lines 50–51 (*ana bērišunu* NAM.ERÍM *danna iškunūnim*), attesting *šakānu* NAM.ERÍM *ana bēri*-X in the West, it is apparent that our ŠUB is only a scribal error, the scribe omitting the first half of ERÍM either by an oversight or through a faulty recollection of the ideogram.

[6]Knudtzon (*EA* I, p. 108, fn. d) is correct in saying that in *da-an*-X the traces are against NU and are more like PAP. However, since *ki-na-na da-an-nu* has excellent parallels (82.13, 109.60, 126.66—note that in 109.54 *šumma* means "behold"), and since in 122.15 the traces of an indisputable NU are identical with the traces here, our reading seems certain.—It should be noted that there is a dif-

behold! the governors have not given them resistance, and thus they are strong" (108.34–38).—Here *šumma* in the sense of "if" is, in context, almost meaningless. Further, the immediately following lines (38–41), which are clearly parallel in sense to lines 34–38, omit *šumma*; the construction is paratactic and the sense of the first clause is obviously affirmative, not conditional.[7] Note finally that in the parallels cited in fn. 6 for the reading *da-an-n[u]*, the enemies' strength is in each case explained in the previous clause.

3 and 4. *šum-ma-me ga-am-ra-at-me / ālu*^{KI} *i-na mūti / i-na mu-ta-a-an / i-na u[b]-ri*[8] *ù lu-ú li-di-nam-mi šarru*^{ru} */ 1 metim awīlūta ma-an-ṣa-ar-ta*$_5$ */ a-na na-ṣa-ri āla*^{KI}*-šu / la-a-me yi-iṣ-bat-ši /* ^{m}*La-ab-a-ya šum-ma-me / i-ia-nu pa-ni-ma / ša-nu-ta*$_5$ *i-na /* ^{m}*La-ab-a-ya / a-ba-at-me āl Ma-gid*$_6$*-da*$^{[KI]}$ */ yu-ba-áʾ-ú*, "Behold! the city is destroyed by pestilence (and) by ... So may the king give a hundred men as a garrison to guard his city, lest Labʾaya seize it. Lo! Labʾaya has no other purpose; he desires the destruction of Megiddo" (244.30–43).—Mercer[9] recognized that Knudtzon's interpretation of the first *šumma* clause, joining it with the preceding clause, is to be rejected. This position of the protasis is, as we have already noted, extremely rare, and here yields little sense. However, there is hardly more sense in having Biridiya ask for troops if Megiddo is consumed by pestilence. It is explicitly stated (lines 21–24) that Labʾaya is determined to capture Megiddo. In fact, at the time of writing the town is under siege or at least sorely harassed (lines 11–17). Hence Biridiya's demand for troops can hardly be subject to the condition that pestilence first have destroyed the populace. Again *šumma* in the sense of "behold" removes the difficulties. Moreover,

---

ference of opinion on whom *šu-nu* in line 38 refers to. I take it as referring to the sons of ᶜAbd-Ashirta, as do De Koning (*Studien over de El-Amarnabrieven*, p. 215, §473) and, with hesitation, Säve-Söderbergh (*The Navy of the Eighteenth Egyptian Dynasty*, p. 64, fn. 4), whereas Weber (*EA* II, p. 1197) understands it of the governors. The question does not really affect the interpretation of *šumma*, since the subject, expressed or not, of *dannū* must be the sons of ᶜAbd-Ashirta.

[7] *ù* $^{LÚ.pl}$*mi-ši / tu-ba-lu-na ḫi-ši-iḫ-t[a ù] / ki-na-na la-a pal-ḫ[u]* / LÚ.GAL. On the *mi-ši* see the article of Thomas O. Lambdin in this issue of *JCS* [*JCS* 7 (1953), pp. 75–77—*Eds.*].

[8] Ebeling (*EA* II, p. 1540) recognized that this word can hardly mean "dust" (*upru*), but probably refers to a kind of pestilence. De Koning's attempt (op. cit., p. 501, §1086) to reconcile both meanings is quite unconvincing. Prof. Goetze suggests the possibility of *ubru*, comparing the proper name *Ubburum* (Holma, *quttulu*, 23f.), apparently meaning "paralyzed" or the like.

[9] *Tell el-Amarna Tablets* II, p. 641.

once the import of lines 30–37 is clear, the meaning of *šumma* in line 37 is also evident. Besides, to have Biridiya question at all Labʾaya's sinister designs on Megiddo fails to take account of the constant cry of these native princes: each is, allegedly, a sorry *solus contra mundum*.

One question, alluded to in the beginning of this paper, remains: does this use of *šumma* reflect Canaanite or Accadian idiom? Against the almost natural assumption in favor of Canaanite it may be urged that the non-Canaanite provenience of one occurrence (35.13, from Alashia) argues to a common Accadian source, especially since in the same letter there are no other demonstrable Canaanitisms.[10] Moreover, there is the group of proper names like *Šumma*-AN, *Šumma-ibaššī*-AN.MEŠ. Prof. Goetze, who kindly reminded me of them, would render, "it is indeed AN," "god indeed exists." If this be their correct interpretation, as it certainly is the first satisfactory one,[11] then we would seem forced to admit the possibility that the Amarna use of *šumma* is genuinely Accadian.

However, on the other side of the ledger we must note that Canaanite influence on non-Canaanite scribes must be reckoned with. Thus, the scribe of *EA* 34, also from Alashia, uses at least two forms that betray Canaanite influence, *yūbal* (19) and *ušširtī* (52). That he was a Canaanite himself is doubtful. Again, the Egyptian scribe of the Abimilki letters uses *ušširtī* (151.26) and *yiṣa* (151.70).[12] The use of *šumma*, therefore, in *EA* 35.13 may be a similar sporadic Canaanitism. Further, the proper names just mentioned are, grammatically, unparalleled in Accadian in the sense that, with the possible exception of these names, a similar use of *šumma* is unattested. In view, therefore, of the fact that nine of the ten occurrences are found in Canaanite letters, Amarna *šumma* in main clauses is with the evidence at hand more probably explained by the native idiom of the Canaanite scribes. But we leave the question open, hoping that new evidence will throw further light on this interesting feature of Amarna syntax.[13]

[10]The use of *u* in lines 22, 48, 52, comparable to the so-called *waw* of apodosis, is also found at Boğazköy, Mari, Nuzi; see Finet, *RA* 46 pp. 23f. The use of the so-called subjunctive (*ú-te-er-ru*, 53) in a main clause is equally inconclusive, again paralleled in Nuzi documents and most recently in the Idri-mi inscription.

[11]Cf. Stamm's (*Die akkadische Namengebung*, p. 135) efforts.

[12]On the scribe of these letters see Albright's article, *JEA* 23, pp. 190–203.

[13]Prof. Goetze notes that in EA *šumma* is almost always followed by a statement referring to the degree to which something exists, extending from "zero" to "complete."

9. The Scandal of the "Great Sin" at Ugarit

In *JNES*, 18 (1959), 73, Professor Jacob J. Rabinowitz drew our attention to an interesting parallel to the biblical expression "great sin" (Gen. 20:9; Exod. 32:21,30,31; II Kings 17:21). It occurs in four Egyptian marriage contracts, is also called a "great sin," and the context identifies it as adultery. This is clearly the sense of the biblical expression in Gen. 20:9 (Abimelek and Sarah), and, aware of the biblical view of idolatry as adultery, we should not hesitate to identify similarly the "great sin" where it is the question of the golden calf or its later counterpart under Jeroboam.

We would suggest that the "great sin" is to be found also in the Akkadian documents of Ugarit. The texts (Jean Nougayrol, *Le Palais Royal d'Ugarit*, IV [Paris, 1956], pp. 132–48) concern the wife of the king of Ugarit, Ammištamru. In the words of the editor, she is guilty of a "faute mystérieuse," which forces her to flee Ugarit and take refuge in her native land of Amurru. To Ammištamru's request for her deportation the incumbent of the Amurru throne, Šaušgamuwa, refuses to accede, at first gently in the language of diplomacy, but this failing, subsequently with a show of force such as to constrain Ammištamru to agree to let the matter drop. Despite his written promise, however, the king of Ugarit had recourse to the Hittite king, Tudḫaliya IV, who thereupon ordered Šaušgamuwa to return the woman. This he did, but for reasons which are not clear was also compensated for her life (*mullâ ša dami*) with a quite substantial sum. Thus, eventually Ammištamru, though it hurt his purse, had his revenge for his wife's "faute mystérieuse."

All of this M. Nougayrol has presented admirably and in much greater detail (pp. 129–31). Much remains obscure about this scandal in high places, but we believe that in view of the biblical and Egyptian references cited above there should be little doubt about the nature of the lady's sin; it was the "great sin," adultery. It is consistently designated as such throughout this diplomatic imbroglio. Thus, *šinništum šīt ana kāša ḫiṭṭa rabâ tiḫteṭi*, "That woman has sinned a great sin against you" (pp. 139–40:5–6); *anumma mārat rabīti ša ḫiṭṭa rabâ ana kāša tētepaš liqiši*, "Now, as for the daughter of the 'Great-Lady' who has committed a great sin against you, take her" (p. 140:11–13). The same expression, *ḫiṭṭa rabâ epēšu*, also occurs p. 141:6. Once the lady is said simply to have sinned against Ammištamru (p. 132:10, *ana kāša tiḫtaṭi*), another time to have committed a sin (p. 142:22, *ḫiṭṭa tēt*[*a*]*paš*.[1] Once too we apparently have a plural: [*ša ḫi*]*ṭâte r*[*abâte tētapaš ana kāša*] (p. 144:1′), but it is quite doubtful that we are to attach any special significance to the plural, not only because of the consistent use of the singular elsewhere, but also because of *ḫiṭṭa* GAL.MEŠ in *Le Palais Royal d'Ugarit*, III, 97:15.

The comparative evidence, especially the biblical, which even extends to the expression "to sin a great sin" (Exod. 32:30,31; cf. also II Kings 17:21), certainly urges us to identify the "great sin" at Ugarit as adultery. It accounts for Ammištamru's obvious rage, it accounts for the punishment of death. Of course we are not suggesting that every "great sin" is adultery (see the end of the last paragraph), but in the present context it is difficult to see why we should look for another, if less banal, solution.

[1]In this text, however, in line 6 the sin has already been identified as great (*rabâ*). *Mutatis mutandis*, the same observation is to be made with regard to *bēl ḫiṭṭika* (140:10; 142:8; 145:4′) and *bēltu ḫiṭṭika* (145:15′).

10. Early Canaanite *yaqtula*

Despite great advances in our knowledge of early Northwest Semitic dialects a still mooted point is the existence in any of these dialects of the morpheme *-a* which is found in the Arabic subjunctive. Sources such as Alalakh and Mari have yielded nothing relevant for the problem, and Ugarit has been hardly less disappointing. The little it offers is quite ambiguous,[1] and even if one accepts the existence of *yaqtula* in Ugaritic, its function and distribution remain completely obscure. In the present state of the question, therefore, *yaqtula* in early Northwest Semitic is still little more than the hypothesis of some grammarians to explain the origin of the Hebrew cohortative.[2]

In this article we hope to present evidence which not only demonstrates the existence of *yaqtula*, but also gives us a fairly good idea of its range of usage in one Canaanite dialect in the early 14th century B.C.[3] Our source is the sixty-six Amarna letters written from Byblos.[4] Restricting ourselves to this small corpus we thus have for our study the language of a small number of scribes within rather narrow limits of time and place. This reduces to a minimum the margin of error due to other and conflicting scribal traditions.

In view of the verbal prefixes *ya-*, *yi-*, *yu-*, the suffixes *-a* (3rd sg. perf.) and *-tî* (1st sg. perf.), etc., the presence of a Canaanite morpheme in these letters is in itself not surprising. Our problem is one of identification, for in Akkadian we have the homophonous morpheme known as the ventive, and a large number of the relevant occurrences of *-a* are readily explained, at least at first sight, as examples of the ventive. What we shall try to show is that in the vast majority of instances they

[1]For the material see Cyrus H. Gordon, *Ugaritic Manual*, 57, §9.7.

[2]Bauer-Leander, *Historische Grammatik*, 273, §36d; Joüon, *Grammaire de l'hébreu biblique*[2], 315, n. 1.

[3]The writer first presented this evidence in his dissertation [see pp. 84–99 in the present volume]; see also *JCS* 5 (1951) 33, n. 3 [above, Paper 6, p. 160, n. 3]. Though we have reworked the material completely for this study, our conclusions remain substantially the same.

[4]We therefore omit from consideration *EA* 136–138, which were not written from Byblos, though the use of *yaqtula* in these three letters is virtually identical with its use in Byblos letters. *EA* 103 seems to have been written from Simyra, but *yaqtula* does not occur in this letter.

are really not ventives, but ventives which have been equated with a formally identical morpheme in a completely different speech pattern.[5] And this speech can only be the scribes' native Canaanite.

We begin with a description of the two most common uses of *yaqtula*:

A) To express wish, request, command—

1. *aṣû*: a. *ù yi-ṣa-am*[6] LUGAL *be-li-ia yi-*⌜*mur*⌝ [K]UR.MEŠ-*šu ù yi-ìl-qí gab-ba*, "And so may the king my lord come forth, look upon his lands and take possession of everything" (*EA* 362:60–61). b. *yi-ṣa* LUGAL, "May the king come forth" (*EA* 124:46, broken context).

2. *ḫummuṭu*: a. *ù yu-ḫa-mi-ṭá be-li* ERÍN.MEŠ *pí-ṭá-tam ù ni-*$UŠ_x$(BAD), "And so may my lord hastily despatch the archers or we die" (*EA* 362:40–41). b. *ki-na-*[*na*] *yu-ḫa-mi-ṭá uš-šar* ERÍN.MEŠ *p*[*í-ṭá*]*-t*[*i*] LUGAL *ù yi-ìl-qí-šu-nu ù ti-ni-pu-uš* KUR.MEŠ *a-na* LUGAL BE-*i*[*a*], "Accordingly may the king speed the sending of the archers so he may capture them (the sons of ᶜAbdi-Aširta) and the lands be joined to the king my lord" (*EA* 129:77–80).

3. *maqātu*: a. *ú-ul yi-ma-qú-ta* ERÍN.MEŠ *ka-ra-*[š]i UGU-*ia*, "Let not the men of the camp (?) fall upon me" (*EA* 83:43–44). b. *ú-ul yi-ma-qú-ta* x-[x-x] [UGU]-*ia ù yi-ìl-qa-ni*, "Let not the ... fall upon me to take me captive" (*EA* 81:31–32).

4. *nadānu*: a. *ù ia-di-na* LUGAL LÚ.MEŠ *ma-ṣa-ar-ta a-na* ARAD-*šu*, "And so may the king give his servant a garrison" (*EA* 118:11–13). b. *ù* LÚ-*ia an-nu-ú yu-wa-ši-ra-šu* LUGAL-*ru ki-ma ar-ḫi-eš ù ia-di-na* LÚ.MEŠ *ma-ṣa-ar-ra a-na na-ṣa-ar* ARAD *ki-ti-šu ù* URU-*šu*, "And as for this man of mine, may the king send him with all haste and grant a garrison to protect his loyal servant and his city" (*EA* 117:76–80). c. *li-eš-mi* LUGAL-*ru a-wa-te* ARAD-*šu ù ia-di-na ba-la-ṭá* ARAD-*šu ù a-na-ṣa-r*[*a* URU *k*]*i-it-ti-šu*, "May the king heed his servant's words and grant his servant's means of sustenance, and keep his servant alive that I may guard his loyal city" (*EA* 74:53–56). d. *š*[*u*]*m-ma lìb-bi* LUGAL *be-li-ia a-*[*n*]*a na-ṣa-*[*a*]*r* URU-*šu ù ya-*[*d*]*i-n*[*a*]*m* BE-*ia* L[Ú].MEŠ *ma-*

[5]Because of this equation (*yaqtula* = *iprusa*) we have included the occurrences (9) of the ventive in the form *-am*. Moreover, final *-m* is often otiose in these letters: *ka-ta, ka-tam, mi-ni, mi-nim, ni-nu-um* (for *nīnu*), etc.

[6]Or *yu-ṣa-am* in view of *tu-ṣa* (line 19), *tu-ṣú* (lines 56,62). For the copy of *EA* 362 see Thureau-Dangin, *RA* 19 (1922) 102–103.—With regard to the interpretation of verbs *tertiae infirmae*, the rule is this: jussive (or preterite) forms end in *-i* (*yiqbi, yišmi*/*yišme, yilqi*, etc.), indicative in *-u* (*yiqbu, yišmu, yilqu*, etc.), *yaqtula* in *-a* (*yiqba, yilqa*, etc.).

ṣa-ar x-x *ù na-aṣ-ra-at*, "If the intention of the king my lord is to protect his city, then let my lord give a garrison ... and then it will be protected" (*EA* 127:26–29). e. *yi-eš-mi* LUGAL-*ru a-wa-te* ARAD-*šu* [*i*]*a-di-na* LÚ.MEŠ *a-na na-ṣa-ar* [UR]U-*šu ú-ul yu-pa-ḫi-ra ka-li* [LÚ].MEŠ. GAZ.MEŠ *ù* DI.AB-t[u][7] [URU], "May the king heed his servant's words, may he give men to guard his city lest he collect all the ᶜApiru and take the city" (*EA* 85:75–79). f. *ia-di-na* 4 ME LÚ.MEŠ ... *ù ti-na-ṣa-ru*[8] URU *a-na ka-tam*, "May he give 400 men ... so they may protect the city for you" (*EA* 85:19–22). g. [*š*]*a-ni-tam li-*[*i*]*d-me-iq i-na pa-ni* LUGAL-*ri* EN-*ia ù yu-da-nam še-im*$^{\text{HI.A}}$ *mu-*[*ú-ṣ*]*a* KUR *Ia-ri-mu-ta ša-a yu-da-*⸢*nu*⸣ *pa-na-nu i-na* URU *Ṣu-mu-ra* [*y*]*u-da-nam* [*i*]*-na-na i-na* URU *Gub-la*, "Moreover, may it seem good to the king my lord and may the grain, the product of Yarimuta, be given; what was formerly given in Simyra, may it now be given in Byblos" (*EA* 85:33–37). h. *ù iš-tu* KUR *I*[*a-ri-mu-ta*] *yu-da-na* [*š*]*e-*[*im*$^{\text{HI.A}}$] [*a-n*]*a a-ka-li-*[*nu* ...] (*EA* 86:46–48).

5. *puḫḫuru*: *ú-ul yu-pa-ḫi-ra ka-li* LÚ.MEŠ.GAZ.MEŠ *ù yi-ìl-qa* URU *Ši-ga-t*[*a*] *ù* URU *Am-pí*, "Let him not gather together all the ᶜApiru that he may take Šigata and Ampi" (*EA* 71:28–31).

6. *qabû*: a. *ú-ul yu-uq-ba i-na* UD.KÁM.MEŠ LÚ.MEŠ.MAŠKIM *la-qú* LÚ.MEŠ.GAZ.MEŠ *ka-li* KUR.KUR.ḪI.A *ú-ul ka-a-ma yu-uq-bu i-na* UD.KÁM.MEŠ *ù la-a ti-li-ú la-qa-ši*, "May it not be said in the days of the (royal) commissioners, 'The ᶜApiru seized all the lands.' Not thus will it be said in the days (of the commissioners)[9] and they will not be able to take it" (*EA* 83:16–20).[10] b. *ù uš-ši-ra* GIŠ.MÁ.MEŠ *ti-ìl-qú-ni qa-du* DINGIR.MEŠ *ba-al-ṭì a-na* BE-*ia la-a-mi yi-iq-ba* LUGAL *be-lí-*[ia], "And send ships that they may take me together with the living god[11] to my lord. May the king my lord not say ..." (*EA* 129:50–52).

[7]See Knudtzon, *EA* I 411, note i.

[8]On this form as a plural see *JCS* 5 (1951) 33–35 [above, no. 6].

[9]This phrase seems to have been omitted by vertical haplography.

[10]Our version differs somewhat from that of Knudtzon. First, the indicative *yuqbu* should not be translated as if we again had *yuqba*; the shift from wish to emphatic assertion makes perfect sense. Second, we take *ti-li-ú* as a plural because of the context: Rib-Adda has chided the king for his neglect, which has resulted in the latter's land being taken (lines 15–16); then he makes the wish, "May it not be said, 'They have taken' "; finally he makes the bold assertion, "It will not be said and they will not be able to take it (i.e., the land [sg.] referred to in line 16)."

[11]Both grammar and word-order indicate that *ba-al-ṭì* modifies *ilāni*; if Knudt-

7. *šemû*: *ú-ul yi-iš-ma* ^{m}ARAD-*a-ši-i*[*r-ta*] *ù ma-an-nu ìl-ti-qa-n*[*i*] *e*[*š*]-*tu qa-ti-šu*, "Let not ᶜAbdi-Aširta hear (about it) or who could rescue me from him?" (*EA* 82:23–24).[12]

8. *šapāru*: *i-na-an-na tu-ma-al ša-al-ša-mi te-eq-bu-ni ia-nu-mi* ERÍN.MEŠ *pí-ṭá-tam ù aš-pu-ur ù tu-ṣa* ERÍN.MEŠ *pí-ṭá-tu ù te-ìl-qí* ^{m}*a-ba-šu-nu a-nu-ma i-na-an-na te-iq-bu-na la yi-iš-pu-ra-am ù nu-ul*$_{11}$-*qa-am-mi*, "Now formerly they were saying, 'There are no archers,' and so I wrote and archers came forth and captured their father. See, now they are saying, 'May he not write or we (too) will be captured' " (*EA* 362:15–23).[13]

9. *(w)uššuru*: a. *a-mur a-n*[*a*]-*ku pa-nu-ia-ma a-*[*n*]*a a-ra-ad* LUGAL *ki-a par-ṣí ša a-bu-ti-*[*i*]*a ù yu-wa-ši-ra* LUGAL-*ru* E[R]ÍN.MEŠ-*šu pí-ṭá-ti-*[*š*]*u ù yu-ša-ap-ši-iḫ* KUR-*šu*, "See, as for me, my sole purpose is to serve the king in accordance with[14] the practice of my fathers,

---

zon were right in referring it to Rib-Adda (that is, to the verbal suffix -*ni*), then we should have the acc. *balṭa(m)*. *ilāni* (cf. Heb. *ʾelôhîm*) is singular in meaning as in *EA* 84:35, where it is obvious that *ilāni* refers to ^{d}DA,MU in line 33 (see below Usage B 2,b).

[12]On the syntax of this sentence see *JCS* 2 (1948) 246 [above, no. 2]. However, contrary to the view there proposed that *yi-iš-ma* reflects Can. *yišmaᶜ*, the final vowel must be considered an addition to the verbal stem; see above, n. 6.

[13]This translation differs considerably from that of Thureau-Dangin. The correct understanding of the passage depends on recognizing that *EA* 129 and *EA* 362 are written in the same period, probably by the same scribe, and describe the same peril for Byblos, which in *EA* 129 is explicitly attributed to Aziru and his brothers (see Dhorme, *RB* 33 [1924] 5–8 = *Recueil Édouard Dhorme*, Paris, 1951, 489–492). The speakers therefore in our passage are Aziru and his brothers, and the person captured is unquestionably their father, not an otherwise unknown Abašunu (for the use of the determinative see Böhl, *Die Sprache der Amarnabriefe*, 9, §4b; also J. Nougayrol, *Le palais royal d'Ugarit* III 38, 15.41:4 and note 2). This is proved by *EA* 108:28ff. and *EA* 117:24ff. (cf. also *EA* 138:31ff.), both of which passages Knudtzon misunderstood. For the former see below Usage E 1; for the latter see Usage E 2, which in a revised translation goes on to say: "Did he not take ᶜAbdi-Aširta together with his possessions just as I had said? Was I writing lies (at that time)? And yet you say, 'Why do you keep on writing lies?' If my words are heeded, Azaru like his father will still be taken!" In all of these passages Rib-Adda exploits the fact that he persuaded Amenophis III to take action against ᶜAbdi-Aširta and it was eminently successful; a prophet of success in the past, he should be listened to now. — We cannot discuss here the interpretation of *EA* 101 and M. Cavaignac's view (*Journal asiatique* 243 [1955] 135–138) that ᶜAbdi-Aširta was not killed; in our opinion his interpretation of *dakū* in lines 5 and 29 is on grammatical grounds impossible, for if "il s'agit de l'intention de tuer, non pas du fait accompli" (p. 136), then grammar rules out *dakū* (see below on modal congruence).

[14]The orthography *ki-a* indicates *kiya* instead of *kī*; cf. Ugar. *kī* as a conjunction

and so may the king send his archers that he may pacify his land" (*EA* 118:39–44). b. [*yu-wa*]-*ši-ra* LUGAL-*ru* LÚ.MAŠKIM-*šu* [*ù yu*]-*pa-ra-aš be-ri-ku*-[*n*]*i*, "May the king send his commissioner that he may decide between us" (*EA* 113:17–18). c. *y*[*u*]-*wa-ši-ra* LUGAL LÚ.M[AŠ]K[IM] [*ù*] *y*[*u-p*]*a-r*[*i-e*]*š* [*b*]*e-ri-nu* (*EA* 117:66–67). d. *ia-aq-bi* LUGAL *ù yu-wa-ši-ra* LÚ-*ia*, "Let the king command and send my man" (*EA* 83:34–35). e. See also *EA* 74:59–61; 79:29–33; 85:16–18; 89:53–55; 116:72–73; 117:71–74; 117:92–94 (*yu-wa-*‹*ši*›*-ra*); 121:45–48; 122:44–48; 123:41–42. f. *ù yu-ši-ra* LUGAL-*ru til-la-ta a-na* URU *Ṣu-mu-ra*, "And may the king send an auxiliary force to Simyra" (*EA* 104:14–15). g. *šum-ma lìb-bi* LUGAL *be-li-ia a-na* URU.KI *Gub*^{ub}*-la ù yu-ši-ra be-li* 3 ME ERÍN.MEŠ … *ù ti-na-ṣa-ru* URU.[K]I *Gub*^{ub}*-li*, "If the king my lord really wants Byblos, then let my lord send 300 men … to guard Byblos" (*EA* 131:10–14). h. See also *EA* 139:29–31.

B) In clauses of purpose (or intended result)[15]**—**

1. *balāṭu*: [*šum*]-*ma i-ra-am* LUG[AL-*ru*] [*b*]*e-li* ARAD *ki-t*[*i-šu*] [*ù*] *uš-ši-ra* [3] LÚ *ù ib-lu-ṭá ù i-na-ṣí-ra* URU *a-na* LUGAL-*ri*, "If the king my lord loves his loyal servant, then send the three men that I may live and guard the city for the king" (*EA* 123:23–28).

2. *leqû*: a. *yi-ìl-qa EA* 71:30 (see A 5). b. *ù lu-wa-ši-ra be-li-ia* LÚ.MEŠ *ú ti-ìl-qú mi-im-mi*^{MEŠ} ^{d}DA.MU-*ia a-na ma-ḫar* BE-*ia ù ú-ul ìl-ti-qa mi-im-ma*^{MEŠ} *ša* DINGIR.MEŠ-*ka* LÚ UR.KU[16] *šu-ut*, "And may my lord send men that they may take the possessions of my Adonis to my lord's presence, lest that dog of a man take anything belonging to your god" (*EA* 84:31–35).

3. *nadānu*: a. [*t*]*a-din-ni*[17] *i-na qa-at* ^{m}*Ia-an-ḫa-mi ù ia-ti-na še-im*$^{\text{ḪI.A}}$ *a-na a-ka-li ia-ši a-na-ṣa-ra* URU LUGAL *a-na ša-a-šu*, "Put me in the charge of Yanḫamu that he may give me grain for food (and) I

(C. Virolleaud, *Le palais royal d'Ugarit* II 31:7 and possibly 42:13).

[15]Because of the paratactic sentence structure it is often difficult, not to say impossible, to distinguish between Usages A and B; hence, the classification of some examples under A rather than under B, and vice versa, is at times somewhat arbitrary. Although *EA* 132:37–40 seems to indicate that the second clause is subordinate to the first (see below, n. 27), the bulk of the evidence speaks for simple coordination of the two clauses.

[16]This is the Amarna reading of the logogram; cf. the "genitive" *ur-ki* in *EA* 138:96.

[17]Knudtzon's [t]ú-*din-ni* is impossible, TÚ being unknown in the Byblos syllabary.

may guard the king's city for him" (*EA* 83:30–33). b. *qí-ba-mi a-na* LUGAL-*ri ù ya-di-na a-na ka-tam* 3 ME LÚ.MEŠ *ù ni-[d]a-gal* URU *ù ni-pu-uš* ..., "Speak to the king that he may give you 300 men and we may take concern for[18] the city and do ..." (*EA* 93:10–13). c. *uš-ši-ra* LÚ.MAŠKIM *yi-eš-me a-wa-te-ia ù ia-di-na ki-ti-[i]a i-na qa-ti-ia*, "Send the commissioner that he may hear my case and give me my due" (*EA* 118:14–17). d. [*š*]*a-ni-tam qí-ba-mi a-na* [EN-*ka*] *ù yu-da-na a-n*[*a* ARAD-*šu*] *mu-ú-ṣa ša* KUR *Ia-a*[*r-mu-ta*] *ki-ma na-da-ni-šu* [*pa-na-nu*] *a-na* URU *Ṣu-mu-ra* [*ù*] *ni-ub-lu-uṭ*, "Moreover, speak to your lord that the product of Yarimuta be given his servant, as it was given previously to Simyra, in order that we may live" (*EA* 86:31–36).

4. *naṣāru*: a. *a-na-ṣa-r*[*a*] *EA* 74:56 (see A 4, c).[19] b. *i-na-ṣí-ra EA* 123:27 (see B 1). c. *ša-ni-tam yu-wa-ši-ra* LUGAL-*ru* ANŠE.KUR.RA *a-na* ‹‹*a*-[*n*]*a*›› ARAD-*šu ù a-na-ṣa-ra* URU.KI LUGAL, "Moreover, may the king send horse(s) to his servant that I may protect the royal city" (*EA* 117:71–74).

5. *puḫḫuru*: *ú-ul yu-pa-ḫi-ra EA* 85:77 (see A 4, e).

6. *(w)uššuru*: *ù qí-bi a-na* LUGAL *be-li-*[*ka*] *ù* [*t*]*u-wa-ša-*‹*ra*›[20] *til-la-tu a-*[*na*] *ia-ši*, "And speak to the king your lord that an auxiliary force be sent to me" (*EA* 73:43–45).

7. *uzuzzu*: *uš-ši-ru-na-ni* 50 *ta-pal* ANŠE.KUR.RA *ù* 2 ME ERÍN.MEŠ GÌR.MEŠ *ù i-zi-za i-na* URU *Ši-ga-ta i-na pa-ni-šu*, "Send me fifty teams of horses and two hundred infantry(?)-men in order that I may resist him in Šigata" (*EA* 71:23–26).

The thirty-six occurrences in clauses expressing wish, etc., and the thirteen occurrences in the closely related use in purpose clauses comprise almost two-thirds of the examples of *yaqtula* in these letters. It is therefore within this small and well-defined pattern that we must seek an understanding of the *-a* morpheme, especially since the remaining occurrences are too few and too diversified in use to provide a solid basis for interpretation.

Now the pattern itself is important, for as such it is without foun-

[18]Context suggests this meaning of *dagālu*, which also appears in *EA* 76:32; 85: 62; 107:18; 116:42; see also *Le palais royal d'Ugarit* III 16, 15.33:29, IV 197:18.

[19]For the problem at hand it is immaterial whether the Canaanite scribes thought of such forms as Akk. *iparras* or, as has been suggested (*JCS* 4 [1950] 165 [= p. 147 in the present volume]), as Can. piᶜel.

[20]The rule of modal congruence (see below) demands that we restore either <*ar*> or <*ra*>, certainly not <*ru*>. Since jussive *yuwaššar* appears only in *EA* 362:66, <*ra*> is much more probable.

dation in Akkadian. However, as we have already admitted, most of the occurrences can at first sight be explained as ventives, and it could therefore be argued that the pattern is fortuitous and results from the peculiar circumstances in which these letters with their never ending requests for troops, food, etc. were written. That this is not the explanation follows from two considerations.

First, there is the use of the indicative *yaqtulu*, another Canaanite feature of these letters.[21] In view of Arabic, the Amarna verbal scheme of *qatala* (perf.)—*yaqtul* (jussive)—*yaqtulu* (indicative) is highly suggestive once one has any indication of the existence of *yaqtula*. This however is not our argument, which rests rather on a comparison of the same verb in similar or identical contexts in which *yaqtula* expresses wish, etc., but *yaqtulu* states a simple fact. Thus: 1. with *yadina* (*yatina*) in A 4, a–f compare *pa-na-nu* LÚ.MEŠ *ma-ṣa-ar-ti* LUGAL-*ri it-ti-ia ù* LUGAL-*ru ia-di-nu še-im*$^{\text{HI.A}}$ *iš-tu* KUR *Ia-ri-mu-ta*, "Previously a royal garrison was with me and the king used to give grain from Yarimuta" (*EA* 125:14–17); *ša-ni-tam mi-nu-um ia-di-nu mi-im-ma ù ba-la-ṭám* LUGAL *a-na* $^{\text{LÚ.MEŠ}}$*ḫa-za-nu-ti ib-ri-ia ù a-na ia-ši la-a-mi ia-di-nu mi-im-ma*, "Moreover, why[22] does the king give whatever is necessary for sustenance to the governors, my associates, but to me he gives nothing?" (*EA* 126:14–18). Here we have a simple statement of fact and a simple question; in both cases *ia-di-nu*. If in the examples above where *ia-di-na* expresses a request the *-a* morpheme were really a ventive, then we should also expect *ia-di-na* in these two examples. 2. The same

[21]We leave to another study a detailed description of the use of *yaqtulu*. In summary form it is as follows (the numbers are subject to slight revision): 231x = present-future; 28x = past, usually iterative (24x). A good indication of its use is found in *EA* 104:17–34: *mi-ia-mi* DUMU.MEŠ ^{m}ARAD-*a-ši-ir-ta* ARAD UR.KU LUGAL KUR *Ka-aš-ši ù* LUGAL KUR *Mi-ta-ni šu-nu ù ti-il-qú-na* KUR LUGAL-*ri a-na ša-šu-nu pa-na-nu ti-ì*[*l-q*]*ú-*[*n*]*a* URU.MEŠ *ḫa-za-ni-ka ù qa-la-ta an-nu-ú i-na-na du-bi-r*[*u*] LÚ.MAŠKIM-*ka ù la-qú* URU.MEŠ-*šu a-na ša-šu-nu a-nu-ma la-qú* URU *Ul-la-za šum-ma ki-a-ma qa-la-ta a-di ti-ìl-qú-na* URU *Ṣu-mu-ra ù* ‹‹*ù*›› *ti-du-ku-na* LÚ.MAŠKIM, "Who are the sons of ᶜAbdi-Aširta, the slave and dog? Are they the king of the Kassites or the king of the Mitanni that they seize the land of the king for themselves? Previously they used to take the cities of your governors, and you were negligent. Behold, now they ha-ve driven out your commissioner and have seized his cities for themselves. Behold, they have taken Ullaza. If you remain so negligent, they will take Simyra and will kill the commissioner." Cf. *tilqūna* in 22 (present), in 25 (past iterative), in 32 (future), and *laqū* in 28 and 30 (present perfect).

[22]Here, as in line 49 of the same letter, only "why" makes sense; cf. *mā* in Ex 14: 15.

argument obtains with regard to A 4, g–h when compared with *ù mi-im-mu* [*la-a*]*-mi yu-da-nu* [*a-na i*]*a-a-ši*, "And nothing whatever is given to me" (*EA* 126:26–28). Again, if *yu-da-nam* / *yu-da-na* contain genuine ventives, why is it that when we again turn to a simple statement of fact we find *yu-da-nu*, not *yu-da-na(m)*? If, however, what we really have is a contrast of *-a*: request and *-u*: indicative, then we also have a simple explanation of the shift between *yu-da-nam* and *yu-da-nu* in A 4, g, the former twice expressing a request, the latter describing customary action in the past. 3. With B 4, a–c all the instances of the indicative (*EA* 112:10; 119:15; 125:12; 130:49) should be compared, but especially *EA* 123:32 where we have the indicative *i-na-ṣí-ru-na* in a simple question,[23] but *i-na-ṣí-ra* in line 27 (B 4, b) according to rule (for which see below). When (after an imperative) the scribe wishes to express "that I may guard" he uses the *-a* suffix; when he wishes to express "with what shall I guard," he shifts to the indicative. 4. Similarly, with B 2, a compare *mi-nu* ᵐARAD-*a-ši-ir-ta* ARAD UR.KU *ù* [*y*]*i-ìl-qú* KUR LUGAL *a-na ša-a-šu*, "What is ᶜAbdi-Aširta, slave and dog, that he takes the land of the king for himself?" (*EA* 71:16–19). Within the same letter, with regard to the same person, and in virtually identical contexts the scribe shifts between *yi-ìl-qú* and *yi-ìl-qa*: it is certainly not mere chance that explains the scribe's shift to *yilqa* when he wishes to express purpose. The distinction of *yilqu* and *yilqa* cannot be explained by recourse to the ventive, which would leave *yilqu* unexplained; besides, there is no reason for a ventive in either passage. 5. In the light of these examples one understands the shift from *yi-*[*i*]*š-ši-ra*, "May he send," in *EA* 139:30–31 (A 9, h) to *yi-iš-ši-ru* a few lines later (*mi-im-mi ša yi-iš-ši-ru* ᵐ*A-zi-ru*, "whatever Aziru sends," lines 34–35.[24]

The clear contrast between *yaqtulu* and *yaqtula* in these passages[25] makes it evident that the function of the *-a* suffix is not that of the Akkadian ventive. This is borne out by a further consideration in connection with the use of *yaqtula* in purpose clauses. The syntax of purpose clauses in these letters is governed by a rule which we call modal con-

[23]There are 38 cases of the energic form of the indicative (*yaqtuluna*), the majority (22) as here occurring in questions.

[24]As countless examples demonstrate, *yišširu* is not to be explained as an Akk. subjunctive.

[25]Cf. also the sequence *yuwaššira-yušapšiḫ* in *EA* 118:42–44 and *yuwašširu-yušapšiḫu* in *EA* 112:37–38.

gruence:[26] if the verb of the first clause states a fact (perfect, indicative), then in the purpose clause the verb is in the indicative; if the verb of the first clause is an imperative, a jussive or *yaqtula* expressing wish, etc., then in the purpose clause the verb is a jussive—or *yaqtula*.

Examples of the indicative: 1. *i-na-na a-di yu-pa-ḫi-ru ka-[l]i* URU.MEŠ *ù yi-ìl-qú-še*, "Now he is again gathering together all the cities in order to take it (Byblos)" (*EA* 124:14–15). 2. *a-na mi-nim qa-la-ta ù la-a ti-iq-bu a-na* LUGAL-*ri ù yu-wa-ši-ru-na* ERÍN.MEŠ *pí-ṭá-ti ù ti-ìl-ti-qú-na* URU *Ṣu-mu-ra*, "Why are you negligent and do you not speak to the king so he will send archers to take Simyra?" (*EA* 71:10–16). 3. *qa-bi-ti ki-na-na a-na* ᵐ*Pa-wu-[ri] ù la-a yi-iš-mu i-na a-wa-te*ᴹᴱŠ ᵐ*Ḫa-i[p]*, "I spoke thus to Pawuru lest he heed the words of Ḫaʾip" (*EA* 132:37–40).[27] See also *EA* 73:6–11;[28] 77:21–25.[29]

Examples of the volitive sequence: *ù uš-ši-ra* ERÍN.MEŠ *pí-ṭá-ti ù ti-ìl-qí-šu ù ta-ap-šu-uḫ* KUR LUGAL, "And so send archers that they

[26]Briefly described in *JCS* 5 (1951) 33 [above, Paper 6, p. 160].

[27]This translation differs considerably from Knudtzon's and rests on a completely different understanding of the passage: *[a]l-lu-mi* ᵐ*Ia-an-ḫ[a-mu] it-ti-ka ù š[a-al-šu] šum-ma la-a qa-bi-ti a-na ša-a-šu a-pa-ši at-ta ki-ta it-[ti* DUMU.M]EŠ ᵐARAD-a-*ši-ir-ta ù la-qú-ka ša-ma a-n[a ia-ši] ù na-ṣa-ar* UR[U.MEŠ] LUGAL EN-*šu qa-bi-ti ki-na-na*, etc., "Behold, Yanḫamu is with you, so ask him if I did not say to him, 'If you make an alliance with the sons of ᶜAbdi-Aširta, then they will take you prisoner.' He heeded me and guarded the cities of the king his lord. I spoke thus to Pawuru lest he heed the words of Ḫaʾip, (whose) father had alienated the cities. Behold, Ḫaʾip has handed over Simyra. Let not the king be negligent about this deed, for a commissioner has been killed!" On the text of 32–34 see *JCS* 4 (1950) 170, n. 15 [above, Paper 5, p. 153] and *JCS* 6 (1952) 79 [above, Paper 7, pp. 171f.]; in line 35 the restoration *n[a ia-ši]* is on the basis of context, and in line 41 with Albright (*JNES* 5 [1946] 18) we see a virtual relative clause. However, we cannot accept Albright's version of *u la yišmu*, "and he must not hearken," since the commissioner whose death is mentioned in lines 45–46 is certainly Pawuru (see also *EA* 131:22–23; 362:69). Against Knudtzon's interpretation are the following: 1. against *la-qú ka-ša-ma* is the fact that *ka-ša* is unattested in the Byblos letters, *kâta(m)* being used; 2. *na-ṣa-ar* in line 36 cannot be the object of *qabīti* in line 37, not only because of the word-order, but because *qabû* is never followed by the infinitive in these letters. The point Rib-Adda wishes to make is that he is loyal and has a deep knowledge of the forces at work in Canaan; Yanḫamu can attest to his advice against any alliance with Aziru and to its wisdom, while events have shown that Pawuru should have listened to Rib-Adda's warnings about Ḫaʾip, obviously an Aziru sympathizer.

[28]In the sequence *taqbu–tu-ṣa-na–timaqqutu* I cannot explain the second satisfactorily; it also appears in *EA* 76:31 as 3rd fem. sg., and is probable in *EA* 81:45 (in *EA* 117:55 it is perhaps a dual). I would expect *tu-ṣú-na*.

[29]Restore *ta-aq-[bu a-n]a* in line 21 on the basis of parallels.

may capture him and the land of the king be at peace" (*EA* 107:29–31). It will be noted that whereas in the examples of the indicative (no. 1) after the indicative *yupaḫḫiru* we have the indicative *yilqu*, here after the imperative *uššira* we have the jussive *tilqi*. See also *EA* 68:14–17 (*la yaqu*[*l*]*me*[30] ... *la ennipuš*, "let not the king be negligent lest everything be united ..."); 74:60–61 (*yuwaššira* ... *u yizziz u akšu*[*d*], "let him send ... that he may stay and I come"); 76:38–39 (*uššira* ... *u tudabbir*, "send ... that you[31] may drive out"); 85:37–38 (*yūdanam* ... [*ù*] *nuballiṭ*, "may it be given ... that we may have means of sustenance"); 85:45–46 ([*uš*]*šira* ... *ul tuṣabbat*, "send ... lest be taken"); 86:31–36 (*qibami* ... *yūdana* ... *nibluṭ*, "Speak ... that it may be given ... that we may live"); 90:11–12 (*milik* ... [*u*]*l yilqiši*, "take concern ... lest he seize it"); 93:10–13 (*qibami* ... *yadina* ... *ni*[*d*]*aggal* ... *nīpuš*; see B 3, b); 101: 36–37 (*ya-di-en* ... *limad*, "may it grant ... to take heed");[32] 102:29–31 (*ḫummiṭam* ... *īrub*, "send quickly ... that I may enter"); 103:25–30 (*uššira* ... *yušamrir*, "send ... that he may drive out");[33] 114:45–46 (*uššira* ... *tilqini*, "send ... to take me"); 117:92–94 (*yuwaš‹ši›ra* ... *ul tinnipuš*, "may he send ... lest it be joined"); 118:42–44 (*yuwaššira* ... *yušapšiḫ*; see A 9, a); 122:46–47 (*yuwaššira* ... *ul tīpuš*, "may he send ... lest it commit"); 126:48 (*uššira* ... *yi*[*naṣṣa*]*rši*, "send ... so he may guard it").

It should be noted, first, that the rule of modal congruence is established quite independently of the occurrences of *yaqtula*, and secondly, that it is a rigorously observed rule.[34] Therefore, unless the thirteen

[30]The *a-qúl* of the text is obviously a mistake for *ia-qúl*; cf. line 31 and Knudtzon's note.

[31]ERÍN.MEŠ *pí-ṭá-tu*, etc., is often treated as a fem. sg. (*JCS* 2 [1948] 245 [above, Paper 2, p. 137] and *JCS* 6 [1952] 78 and n. 20 [above, Paper 7, p. 169]), but in view of *rabâ* it seems to be treated here as masc., and hence *tudabbir* is better taken as 2nd sg. than as 3rd fem. (like *tilqišu EA* 107:30, etc.).

[32]The passage is difficult: *ù ṣa-bat* ᵐARAD-*a*-<*ši*>-*ir*-[*t*]*a ù ya-di-en a-na katam ù li-ma-ad a-wa-te* ARAD *ki-ti-ka*, "And as for the seizure of ᶜAbdi-Aširta, well, may it cause you to heed (in the future) the words of your loyal servant" (*EA* 101:35–38). For the reading ᶜAbdi-Aširta we follow Bezold–Budge, *The Tell-El-Amarna Tablets in the British Museum*, no. 44. The grammar and idiom then become pure Canaanite: *ya-di-en* is from *nadānu* (cf. the same orthography in line 28), and the volitive sequence of jussive-imperative to express intended result or purpose is well known from Hebrew (see especially Ruth 1:9: *yittēn YHWH lākem umᵉṣeʾnā*, "May Yahweh grant you to find ...").

[33]Cf. the sequence in *EA* 77:21–25: *yaqbu–yuwašširunaka–tušamriru*.

[34]On some apparent exceptions to this rule see *JCS* 5 (1951) 34, n. 11 [above, Paper 6, pp. 161–162]. Passages like *EA* 123:33–35 (2 LÚ *ša-a šu-ri-ib* ᵐ*Pí-ḫu-ra uš-š*[*i*]*-ra ù bal-ṭá-ti*; cf. also *EA* 74:25–27, 83:27), in which one is inclined to

examples of *yaqtula* in purpose clauses are to be considered so many exceptions to the rule, we must conclude that, like the jussive, *yaqtula* is also a volitive.[35] And again we can contrast *yaqtulu* and *yaqtula*. The most striking example is that of *yupaḫḫiru–yilqu*, "he is gathering–that he may take" (*EA* 124:14–15) and *ul yupaḫḫira–yilqa*, "let him not gather–that he may take" (*EA* 71:28–30). Identical verbs, identical contexts, referring to the same person: *yupaḫḫiru* states a fact, *ul yupaḫḫira* a negative wish; *yilqu* and *yilqa* both express purpose, the former after another indicative, the latter after *yaqtula*. For such shifts between *yaqtulu* and *yaqtula* within a rigid scheme the Akk. ventive offers no explanation whatever.[36]

We have, therefore, in these forty-nine examples of *yaqtula* a closely coherent pattern, and the ventive does not explain it. As a pattern, however, it demands explanation, and we should hardly look for it elsewhere than in the scribes' native speech. This solution is confirmed by the evidence of a closely related Canaanite dialect, biblical Hebrew. In Hebrew also there exists an *-a* morpheme which yields the verbal form called the cohortative. Its principal uses are two, those we have seen in our description so far of Byblian *yaqtula*.[37] In independent clauses in the rare third person it expresses a wish,[38] in the first person determination, exhortation, self-encouragement, etc.; in purpose clauses it is governed by the rule of modal congruence. Its third most common use is in conditional sentences, both in protasis and apodosis;[39] this, as we shall see, is the third most common use of *yaqtula* in the Byblos letters. A neater correspondence could hardly be asked for, and

---

translate, " … that I may live," are not genuine exceptions; the perfect emphasizes the fact of succession and is thus equivalent to the apodosis of a conditional sentence (Joüon, *Grammaire de l'hébreu biblique*^{2}, 329, §119i). Cf. 2 Sam 24:2 where *w*^{e}*yāda*^{c}*tî* is paralleled in 1 Chron 21:2 by *w*^{eʾ}*ēdē*^{c}*ā*. An exception does seem to occur in *EA* 92:46–47 in the sequence *li-it-ri-iṣ* … [*lu* / *yu-wa*]-*ši-r*[*u*]; *uš-ši-ram-mi* … *ti-el-qú* in *EA* 94:10–11 is also difficult, but the autograph in Winckler–Abel, *Der Thontafelfund von El Amarna*, no. 78:28, which offers *ti-el-*[*x*], suggests that Knudtzon failed to indicate that his reading is actually a restoration. See also n. 28 above.

[35]The term "volitive" we borrow from Joüon as the most general designation of those forms which indicate command, wish, request, etc.

[36]Compare also *tiqbu–yuwašširuna–tiltiquna* (*EA* 71:12–15) and *qibi–tuwaš-ša‹ra›* (*EA* 73:43–44).

[37]Gesenius-Kautzsch-Cowley, *Hebrew Grammar*, §108a–d.

[38]So *yāḥîšā* and *w*^{e}*tābôʾā* in Is 5:19.

[39]Gesenius-Kautzsch-Cowley, *op. cit.*, §108e–f.

in our opinion it proves conclusively that in the evidence so far examined we are dealing with a specifically Canaanite morpheme.

Before considering the remaining occurrences of *yaqtula*, we must take brief notice of the subjunctive in Arabic. From the viewpoint of Arabic the use of *yaqtula* in purpose clauses is only to be expected; in fact, in the general restriction of the subjunctive after *fa* to clauses after an imperative, a negative command, a wish, particles of exhortation or reproach, etc., one seems to discern the older rule of modal congruence. But, accustomed as we are to thinking of *yaqtula* in terms of the subjunctive, its independent usage in Amarna may seem a difficulty. It could not, however, be seriously urged by anyone aware of the two millennia which separate the two bodies of evidence and of far more divergent developments of identical morphemes (for example, *-u* in Akk. *iprusu*, and in Can. and Arabic *yaqtulu*). Furthermore, one should note the uses of the subjunctive in Arabic which point to an earlier paratactic stage:[40] 1. The subjunctive after *fa, wa*, and *ʾau*;[41] 2. the subjunctive in clauses with no introductory conjunctions;[42] 3. the subjunctive in the protasis or apodosis of conditional sentences, etc.[43] These indications counsel a more flexible notion of the subjunctive and allow for the independent Amarna usage, whether it be original or due to secondary development within Canaanite.

As we remarked earlier, because of their paucity and diversity the remaining twenty-five examples of *yaqtula* are impossible to test for their specifically Canaanite character; we can do little more than examine them for consistency with the results which we have established.

C) After a verb of fearing —

1. *ù pa*[*l-ḫ*]*a-ti a-n*[*a-k*]*u la-a-mi ú-da-a-*k[a],[44] "And I am afraid that I shall be killed" (*EA* 131:27–28). This is quite consistent with the volitive character of *yaqtula*: "I am afraid, may I not be killed." Whether the *yaqtula*-clause is really subordinate to the previous clause is impossible to say; cf. also the use of the subjunctive in Arabic after

[40]See Reckendorf, *Die syntaktischen Verhältnisse des Arabischen*, 59–60, §32.

[41]*Ibid.*, 61, §34. Reckendorf also refers to the use of the subjunctive in the poets.

[42]Wright–de Goeje, *Arabic Grammar*[3] II 26, rem. b.

[43]*Ibid.*, 40, rem. c.

[44]The final sign is not absolutely certain, but the syntactical correspondence which this reading yields with Usage A and B as well as with Arabic usage increases its probability.

verbs of fearing.[45]

D) In conditional sentences —

1. in the protasis: a. *i-nu-ma i-ka-ša-da-am* KUR.KUR. MEŠ.KI *ù te-pa-ṭe$_4$-ru-na* LÚ.MEŠ-*tu a-na la-qí* KUR.KUR.MEŠ-*i-mi a-na ša-šu-nu ù ia-nu-am-mi* LÚ.MEŠ-*li a-na na-ṣa-ri* URU.KI *Gub-li* URI.KI LUGAL *be-li-ia,* "If I (attempt to) conquer the lands, then the men will desert in order to take the lands for themselves, and there will be no men to guard Byblos the city of the king my lord" (*EA* 362:33–39).[46] b. *i-nu-ma* [*i*]-*mu-ta mi-nu* [*y*]*i-na-ṣa-ru-še,* "If I die, who will guard it (Byblos)?" (*EA* 130:50–52).[47] c. *ia-nu-am-mi* LÚ *la te-i-ṣa a-na ša-šu-*[*nu*], "There is no one (to oppose them) if you do not come forth against them" (*EA* 362:29–30). d. [m]i-*ia i-ra-mu ù a-mu-*[t]a, "Who will be loyal if I die?" (*EA* 114:68).[48]

2. in the apodosis: a. *šum-ma i-na-na qa-la-ta ù* ^{m}*Pí-ḫu-ra la-a yi-zi-za i-na* URU *Ku-me-di,* "If now you are negligent, then Piḫura will not remain in Kumedi" (*EA* 132:46–49). b. *šum-ma ki-a-ma i-ba-šu* [*ù l*]*a-a ti-zi-za* URU *Ṣu-mu-ra,* "If the situation remains like this, then Simyra will not stand" (*EA* 107:32–34). c. *šum-ma* LUGAL-*ru yi-ša-i-lu ù na-*[*a*]*d-na pa-ni-nu a-na a-ra-di-ka,* "If the king will investigate, then we will devote[49] ourselves to your service" (*EA* 89:15–17). d. *šu*[*m*]-*ma* 2 ITI *la-a tu-*[*ṣa-na*] [ERÍ]N.MEŠ *pí-ṭá-ti ù i-ti-la* [^{m}A]RAD-*a-ši-ir-ta ù ìl-ti-qí* 2 U[RU], "If within two months the archers do not come forth, then ^{c}Abdi-Aširta will come up and take the two cities" (*EA* 81: 45–47). e. *i-nu-ma qa-bi a-na pa-ni* LUGAL-*ri* ^{m}*Ri-ib-*^{d}IM *šu-mi-it* ERÍN.MEŠ *pí-ṭá-at* LUGAL-*ri i-nu-ma ba-al-ṭú* LÚ.MEŠ.MAŠKIM *ù a-da-bu-ba ka-li ip-ši-šu-nu,* "If it is said in the king's presence, 'Rib-Adda killed the royal archers (even) when the commissioners were alive,' then I will calumniate[50] all their deeds" (*EA* 119:18–23). f. *i-nu-*

45 Wright–de Goeje, *op. cit.*, 25.

46 Context seems to indicate that Rib-Adda here envisages only the possibility of his taking action here and now against Aziru, not a more general truth (Thureau-Dangin: "Lorsque je vais à la conquête du pays, les gens font défection ...").

47 "When I die" is equally probable; this would not however change the syntactical analysis (Joüon, *op. cit.*, 506, §166a).

48 [t]a is uncertain, but cf. Usage D 1, b.

49 On *na-ad-na* as first plural see *JCS* 4 (1950) 166 [above, Paper 4, p. 147].

50 Since it does not seem likely that Rib-Adda would let the charge of disloyalty go by without some sort of a denial, in view of Heb. *dibbā* we suggest that

ma 1 *ḫa-za-nu lìb-bu-šu it-ti lìb-bi-ia ù ú-da-bi-ra* ^{m}ARAD-*a-ši-ir-ta iš-tu* KUR *A-mur-ri*, "If there were one governor of the same mind as I, then I would drive ^{c}Abdi-Aširta from Amurru" (*EA* 85:66–69). g. *šu-te-ra a-wa-tam a-na ia-ši ù i-pu-ša ki-ta it-ti* ^{m}ARAD-*a-ši-ir-ta*, "Send back word to me or (if you do not) I will make an alliance with ^{c}Abdi-Aširta" (*EA* 83:23–25). h. *la-a yi-iš-pu-ra-am ù nu-*ul_{11}*-qa-am-mi*, "May he not write or (if he does) we will be taken" (*EA* 362:22–23). i. *mi-ia-mi yi-ma-lik i-zi-za* [*i*]*-na pa-ni* ERÍN.MEŠ *pí-ṭá-at* LUGAL *be-lí-ia*, "Who indeed would counsel, '(If the king sent them) he would resist successfully the archers of the king my lord'?" (*EA* 94:12–13).

The use of *yaqtula* in protases of conditional sentences is paralleled by the similar use of volitives both in Hebrew and in Arabic. In the former, exactly as in Amarna, cohortative and jussive are frequently employed in conditional sentences of the real type;[51] in the latter, the jussive is regular in the same type, and the subjunctive is also possible, though with the restriction that it appears only in the second member of a compound protasis, the first member containing a jussive.[52]

As for *yaqtula* in apodoses of conditional sentences, we again have in Hebrew and in Arabic, *mutatis mutandis*, the same parallels.[53] Two points of inner consistency should be noted: first, it is only in the context of a conditional sentence that we find *yaqtula* with the force of a future asseverative (2 a–e, g–h);[54] second, in 2, d after *i-ti-la* the jussive form *ìl-ti-qí* (not *iltiqu*) follows, an additional indication that the syntactical situation has determined the use of *yaqtula*.—In brief, the use of *yaqtula* in conditional sentences squares with the other uses we have seen so far.

E) In past narrative —

1. *aš-at-par a-*[*na*] ‹‹*a-na*›› *a-bi-ka ù yi-*[*eš-me*] *a-w*[*a-t*]*e-ia ù yu-*[*wa-ši* / *ša*]*-ra* [E]RÍN.MEŠ *pí-ṭ*[*á-t*]*i ú-ul la-qi* [^{m}]ARAD-*a-ši-ir-ta a-na*

---

dabābu here has the sense of calumniate.

[51] Gesenius-Kautzsch-Cowley, *op. cit.*, §108e, §109h.

[52] Wright-de Goeje, *op. cit.*, 36ff.

[53] Gesenius-Kautzsch-Cowley, *op. cit.*, §108f, §109h, Wright–de Goeje, *op. cit.*

[54] Usage D 2, f has perfect parallels in the Heb. cohortative (Gesenius-Kautzsch-Cowley, *op. cit.*, §108f). It is quite possible that in Usage D 2, a–b we should render " ... cannot remain," " ... cannot stand" (cf. Knudtzon's translation), and if so the Heb. jussive provides excellent parallels (Gesenius-Kautzsch-Cowley, *op. cit.*, §109e; Gesenius-Bergsträsser, *Das Verbum*, 50, §10k).

š[a-šu],[55] "I wrote to your father and he heeded my words and sent archers. Did he not take ᶜAbdi-Aširta for himself?" (*EA* 108:28–33). 2. *aš-ta-par a-na* É.GAL *ù yu-w*[*a-ša*]*-ra* ‹‹*ù yu-wa-ša-ra*›› LU[GA]L-*ru* ERÍN.MEŠ *ra-ba*, "I wrote to the palace and the king sent a large force" (*EA* 117:24–27). 3. *tu-ṣa EA* 362:19 (see A 8). 4. *ù ta-aš-ta-na a-wa-tam a-na ia-ši*, "And you repeatedly said to me" (*EA* 82:14). 5. *ù uṣ-ṣa-am ri-qú-tám*, "But he came forth empty-handed" (*EA* 87:17). 6. [*ù*] *i-te-la-am a-na ṣi-ri-ia*, "And he has come up against me" (*EA* 88:17; also 88:14).

F) In clauses introduced by *inūma*, "as to (the fact)" —

1. *i-nu-ma ta-aš-pu-ra a-*[*na*] URUDU *ù a-na si-en-ni*, "As to your writing for copper and ivory" (*EA* 77:6–8). 2. Similarly *t*⌜*a*⌝*-aš-pu-*⌜*r*⌝*a* (*EA* 95:7),[56] *ta-aš-tap-ra* (*EA* 102:14), *yi-iš-tap-pa-ra* (*EA* 130:9), *yi-eš-ta-pa-ra* (*EA* 130:15).

Here one is admittedly tempted to interpret these last two uses in some way consistent with the volitive character of *yaqtula* in its other occurrences. Undoubtedly one could excogitate some arguments, but not only would they be quite unconvincing; they would also betray a misconception of the nature of our source, which is sixty-six letters written not in Canaanite but in Akkadian, however wretched it may be. Hence we should not be surprised if the misunderstanding which led to the equation of *iprusa(m)* and *yaqtula* did not issue in a completely consistent pattern of usage. The scribes inherited stock expressions, and this we believe is the explanation of Usage F.[57] The practice too of individual scribes certainly differed, and it is probably not an accident that the three examples in E 5–6 come from the same scribe.[58] We are

[55]For the suggested restoration cf. *EA* 71:19; 104:23–24,29. For a discussion of this and the following passage (*EA* 117:24–27) see above n. 13.

[56]Instead of *inūma* in this case Knudtzon reads [*a*]-*nu-ma;* the traces in Schroeder's copy (*VAS* 11, 48) favor this reading, while parallels support [*i*]-*nu-ma*.

[57]We find *inūma taštapra* in a letter from Alašia (*EA* 34:8), *enūma iltapra* (*Le palais royal d'Ugarit* III, p. 5:9) and *enūma ... taltapra* (*Le palais royal d'Ugarit* IV, p. 217:9–11) at Ugarit (on the latter letter see Goetze, *BASOR* 147, 25–26). The usage of *inūma* seems to reflect Can. *kî*; cf. Lachish III 8 *wky ʾmr ʾdny*. In all of the passages referred to, with the exception of *EA* 77:6–8, the words of the addressee are then cited. Basically this is the deictic *kî* which underlies the use of *kî* in the protases of conditional sentences, in concessive clauses, and the *kî* of affirmation (cf. Brockelmann, *Grundriss* II, 111, §56d; 606, §397).

[58]Characteristic of the scribe of *EA* 87 and 88 is the LA which appears in 87:23 (*ù*

therefore quite willing to admit a dozen examples of the *-a* suffix which do not reflect Canaanite usage.

However, we should perhaps hesitate with regard to E 1–3 for the following reasons: 1. elsewhere the use of *yuwaššira* always reflects Canaanite usage, 2. it does so in the same letter in which E 2 occurs (*EA* 117:66,72,92), 3. in the same letter in which E 3 occurs *yi-ṣa-am* (A 1, a) is Canaanite, as are *te-i-ṣa* (D 1, c) and the indicatives *tu-ṣu* (*EA* 362: 56,62), 4. following *tu-ṣa* in this letter is the jussive form *te-ìl-qí* (line 10, and note Knudtzon's restoration, which we have followed, *yi-*[*eš-me*] in E 1). These considerations suggest strongly that we should seek a solution of these three anomalies within Canaanite.

Unfortunately a convincing solution escapes us. We can only suggest that in clauses of intended result the idea of actual accomplishment has begun to supersede that of intention, not completely however, and thus *(u) yaqtula,* still felt as indicating a willed result, expresses actual result only after a clause in the first person. This suggestion is prompted by a comparison of *EA* 138:31ff.,42ff. In the first we have *ašpur ana šarri bēliya u tuṣa ṣābu u tilqi āl Ṣumuri,* whereas in the second passage we have *ašpur ana ekalli ana ṣābi u ul tū*[*d*]*anu ṣābu ana iaši.* The change from *yaqtula* (*yaqtul*) to *yaqtulu* is perhaps to be understood as based on the distinction between willed and simple result: "I wrote with the result (intended) that the troops came forth," "I have written with the result (not intended) that troops have not been given to me." This may be the explanation of E 1–3. However, with the little evidence available this is much too speculative, and for this reason, as our translations in E 1–3 indicate, we classify, though not without reluctance, these occurrences as non-Canaanite.

To conclude our study we should consider briefly the evidence for the use of *yaqtula* with verbal suffixes. In general it fits into the pattern which we have seen so far. Thus, 1. to express wish, etc.: *yu-da-na-ni,* "may there be given me" (*EA* 79:33); *yu-wa-ši-ra-šu,* "may he send him" (*EA* 117:77); 2. in clauses of purpose: *yi-ìl-qa-ni,* "that he may take me captive" (*EA* 81:32); *ú-ṣa-ka,* "that I may bring out to you" (*EA* 82: 29);[59] [*ú*]*-da-bi-ra-šu,* "that I may drive him out" (*EA* 85:81); *yi-ìl-qa-šu-*

la(!) *i-nam-mu-šu-nim;* Knudtzon here assumes AD is a mistake for LA) and 88: 19 (*ma-ni* UD.KÁM.MEŠ*-ti la(!) yi-na-mu-uš,* "How long will he not budge?"; for the expression *man(n)i ūmāti* see also *EA* 114:35, 119:39, 122:38, 292:44–45 (here with the phonetic complement *-ti*) and cf. Ugar. *mn yrḫ* in Keret C 81).—I owe the reading in 88:19 to Prof. Albright.

[59]On the form see *JCS* 2 (1948) 247 [above, Paper 2, p. 138].

nu, "that he may seize them" (*EA* 118:33); 3. after a verb of fearing: (*palḫātī awīlūt ḫu*[*pši*]) *ú-ul ti-ma-ḫa-ṣa-na-n*[*i*], "that they will smite me" (*EA* 77:37);[60] 4. in conditional sentences: *šum-ma* LUGAL *za-ir* URU.K[I]-*šu ù i-zi-ba-ši ù šum-ma ia-ti-ia* ⌜*ù*⌝*(!) i-pa-ṭá-ra-ni-mi*, "If the king hates his city, then let him abandon it, and if (he hates) me, then let him desert me" (*EA* 126:44–47); 5. finally a number of occurrences which perhaps without exception may reflect nothing specifically Canaanite, though it should be noted that with the exception of the first all occur in questions: *ú-še-zi-ba-an-ni* (*EA* 74:44), *ìl-ti-qa-ni* (*EA* 82:24, 41), *yi-na-ṣí-ra-an-ni* (*EA* 112:13), *yi-na-ṣa-ra-ni* (*EA* 119:10), *i-ri-ṣ*[*a*]-*an-ni* (*EA* 127:16), *yi-na-ṣí-ra-ni* (*EA* 130:20).[61]

Such is the use of *yaqtula* in the Amarna letters from Byblos, and in our opinion it provides us with the hitherto elusive evidence for the existence of *yaqtula* in early Canaanite. It also establishes the origin of the Hebrew cohortative; the virtually perfect correspondence between Byblian *yaqtula* and the cohortative leaves little room for doubt on this score. In conclusion, we would note one problem which our material raises: the distinction between jussive *yaqtul* and *yaqtula*. To judge from attested usage one would conclude that in the Amarna period there was little or no distinction, but whether this was actually the case and the earlier distinctions, which certainly existed, had broken down by the 14th century, or whether the apparent lack of distinction derives from the special conditions which gave rise to the use of *yaqtula* in these letters,[62] the evidence at our disposal makes it impossible to decide.

[60]The form is 3rd fem. sg. plus energic -*na* (plus obj. suffix), the plural subject being construed as a collective. See *JCS* 5 (1951) 35 and n. 17 [above, no. 6].

[61]In all of these occurrences a potential meaning would fit perfectly; see above n. 54.

[62]Since it seems most likely that the Can. use of *yaqtula* found its way into accepted scribal usage through a misunderstanding of expressions like *lu-wa-(aš)-ši-ra šarru*, "May the king send to me," etc., there was perhaps a limited number of verbs in which a specifically Can. *yaqtula* could be used, with the result that the use of *yaqtula* could not accurately represent actual Can. usage.—Because of lack of context, uncertainty of readings, etc., the following examples of *yaqtula* have not been considered in this study: [*yi*]-*na-mu-ša* (*EA* 77:20), [t]u-*da-na* (*EA* 86:29), *ti-ìl-qa* (*EA* 86:43), [ú]-ṣ[a] (*EA* 86:50), [ú]-*ṣa-am* (*EA* 87:29), *yu-si-bi-la* (*EA* 88:35), *uṣ-ṣa-am* (*EA* 88:51), *yi-ìl-qa* (*EA* 91:6), [*y*]*i-k*[*u*]-*u*[*š-d*]*a* (*EA* 95:17), *ú-ṣa* (*EA* 101:10), [*ib*]-*lu-ṭá* (*EA* 117:92), *yu-n*[*a-d*]*a* (*EA* 131:29).

11. The Hebrew Language in its Northwest Semitic Background

The last three decades may justly be called a new epoch in the study of the Hebrew language. What sets this period apart in the history of Hebrew studies is the great increase it has brought to our knowledge of earlier and related dialects. The history of any language is always illuminating; obscurities can become luminous when seen in the light of their historical development. For the student of an ancient language, however, whose only source material is the written word, and this in a relatively small body of material, such an historical perspective is often indispensable. The limitations of his material and the lack of native informants force him to the comparison of related, especially earlier, dialects. Only thus can he hope to grasp with greater precision the structure of the language, or to isolate and understand the function of those archaic speech forms which are so frequent in literary texts, especially in poetry. For the Hebraist, besides, such a procedure is the more necessary in that his texts have been the object of a long tradition, in the course of which dialectal and archaic elements have necessarily been obscured.

It is in the light of these problems that the importance of the new sources for the Northwest Semitic background of Hebrew is easily understood. Writing in 1822, Wilhelm Gesenius, "the father of modern Hebrew grammar," was confronted with "a total lack of historical data for the earlier (pre-Biblical) history of the origin and development of Hebrew."[1] A century later, in 1922, in the historical grammar of Hebrew published by H. Bauer and P. Leander,[2] of pre-Biblical Hebrew one still finds little history and much reconstruction. However, apart from the justifiable criticisms of both their reconstruction and their method, the task these scholars set themselves is to be appreciated in the light of the material available to them. Through the discoveries of the intervening century, among which was Gesenius's revolutionary

[1]Wilhelm Gesenius, *Hebräische Grammatik*[5], Halle, 1822.

[2]Hans Bauer und Pontus Leander, *Historische Grammatik der Hebräischen Sprache* I, Halle, 1922.

decipherment of the Phoenician inscriptions, they were in an incomparably better position than Gesenius to write a history of the Hebrew language. Nevertheless, with the notable exception of the Amarna letters, there had occurred no significant break in the darkness which hung over Hebrew and related dialects in the second millennium.

The Amarna letters, it is true, had made a considerable contribution. Over two hundred of these letters were sent by vassal Canaanite kings to the Egyptian court in the early 14th century B.C. Composed by Canaanite scribes little conversant with the Babylonian language they were employing, besides containing numerous Canaanite glosses to Babylonian words, they constantly betray in form and idiom the native Canaanite speech of their writers. Discovered in 1887 at Tell el-Amarna in Egypt, and given a first-rate edition in 1907,[3] they advanced greatly our understanding of the early history of Hebrew, thanks especially to the studies of Böhl, Dhorme, and Ebeling.[4]

However, for the period of pre-Biblical Hebrew, there was still, for purposes of linguistic analysis, the same total lack of genuinely Canaanite texts which had confronted Gesenius.[5] The Amarna letters, moreover, instructive as they are, do attempt to pass as Babylonian, so that one cannot accept uncritically every feature of the language as genuinely Canaanite. The possibility must be left open for barbarisms inherited from other, both non-Babylonian and non-Canaanite, traditions. Besides, in order fully to exploit the indications of the vowels in the syllabic cuneiform, one ordinarily needs the guidance of some fairly comprehensive conception of what Canaanite speech was in this period.[6]

The last three decades or so have seen the situation changed profoundly. Owing especially to the great increase in archaeological activity between the two wars, many new sources of the greatest importance

[3]J. A. Knudtzon, *Die El-Amarna Tafeln* I, Leipzig, 1907 (abbreviation *EA*); II (Glossary and remarks with collaboration of O. Weber and E. Ebeling), 1915.

[4]Böhl, *Die Sprache der Amarna Briefe*, Leipzig, 1909; Dhorme, *RB* 10 (1913), pp. 369–93; 11 (1914), pp. 37–59, 344–72 (reprinted in *Recueil Édouard Dhorme*, Paris, 1951, pp. 405–87); Ebeling, *Beiträge zur Assyriologie* 8, 39–79.

[5]The proto-Sinaitic inscriptions had not been deciphered, and the valuable material in Max Burchardt, *Die altkanaanäischen Fremdworte und Eigennamen im Aegyptischen* (Leipzig, 1910), could not be fully exploited until the orthographic principles governing Egyptian transcriptions were determined; this was Albright's contribution in *The Vocalization of the Egyptian Syllabic Orthography*, New Haven, 1934.

[6]Albright and Moran, *JCS* 2 (1948), pp. 239–40 [above, Paper 2, pp. 131–32].

for Hebrew began to appear. They were to throw special light on two periods in the development of Hebrew, the first *ca.* 1900–1700 B.C., the second the Amarna period in the 14th century B.C.

For the earlier period mention should first be made of the publication in 1926 of *Die Ostkanaanäer* by the German Assyriologist, Theo Bauer.[7] Under the direction of B. Landsberger, he collected all of the personal and geographical names scattered through the Old Babylonian documents which had previously been recognized to reflect a West Semitic speech, and therefore of some relevance for early Hebrew.[8] Bauer's collection alone was an invaluable service, and to this he added the first systematic grammatical analysis of the names.

Also in 1926, Kurt Sethe published his decipherment of the execration texts.[9] Written in Egyptian, and dating from *ca.* 1925–1875 B.C., these texts were inscribed on vases with the names of potential rebel vassals, who, in the conceptions of sympathetic magic, were to be smashed with the smashing of the vases. Among these names were those of some thirty Palestinian and Syrian chieftains, together with their respective localities. All were clearly of the same type and reflected the same language, with possible minor dialectal variations, which Bauer had studied in the cuneiform sources.

Complementing and doubling Sethe's material were the Brussels statuettes published by Posener in 1940.[10] Written on small figurines instead of vases, and of a later date (second half of the 19th century B.C.), they were likewise execration texts and, from a linguistic viewpoint, identical with the earlier texts. Finally, from Egyptian sources, an important contribution is an 18th-century list of Egyptian slaves (the Hayes list), recently published by Albright, in which are found over thirty Northwest Semitic names, mostly of women.[11]

[7]*Die Ostkanaanäer, Eine philologisch-historische Untersuchung über die Wanderschicht der sogenannten "Amoriter" in Babylonien*, Leipzig, 1926.

[8]Dhorme, *RB* 5 (1908), p. 216.

[9]*Die Ächtung feindlicher Fürsten, Völker und Dinge auf altägyptischen Tongefäss-scherben des mittleren Reiches*, Berlin, 1926.

[10]*Princes et Pays d'Asie et de Nubie*, Bruxelles, 1940. On the personal names of the execration texts, see Albright, *JPOS* 8 (1928), pp. 223–56; *BASOR* 81, pp. 16–21; 83, pp. 30–36; Noth, *ZPDV* 65 (1942), pp. 9–34; Moran, *Orientalia*, NS 26 (1957), pp. 339–45.

[11]*JAOS* 74 (1954), pp. 222–33. The dates for the Egyptian texts given here follow those of Albright in this article.

We thus have from Egyptian sources around one hundred fifty personal and geographical names from Syria and Palestine between *ca.* 1900–1750 B.C. While in itself this is a meager source for purposes of linguistic analysis, still from the substantial identity of these names with those found in the incomparably richer cuneiform sources, we can safely project, with minor differences, the more detailed Mesopotamian picture into Syria and Palestine, while the Egyptian material, with its more accurate representation of the consonants, can at times be of great help in resolving the ambiguities of the cuneiform script.

Since Bauer's *Die Ostkanaanäer* in 1926, further publication of Old Babylonian letters and economic documents has added not a little to the stock of relevant personal names, but this contribution appears insignificant when compared with the results of excavations at Mari, Alalakh, and Chagar Bazar. Since 1933 ancient Mari, modern Tell Harîri, on the middle Euphrates, has been, and will continue to be for many years, the principal source for early Northwest Semitic.[12] Because of its position, Mari was, by the standards of the time, a rich and powerful city, which, before its destruction by Hammurapi of Babylon, was coveted and ruled by two rival dynasties, whose native speech was close to, but not identical with, the Hebrew of the Patriarchal Age. A. Parrot and his staff have unearthed at this site over twenty thousand tablets, of which so far, apart from scattered publications in various journals, seven volumes with approximately eight hundred texts have been published.[13] From these documents, both letters and economic texts, we have over five hundred personal and geographical names pertinent to a reconstruction of early Northwest Semitic.[14] Moreover, though not to the extent found in the Amarna letters, the lexicon and idiom of the Mari letters are at times non-Babylonian, so that through them we gain further insights into the Northwest Semitic speech of this period.[14a] With but a small part of the Mari texts available, further publication can

[12]Bibliography up to 1950, *Studia Mariana*, Leiden, 1950, pp. 127–38.

[13]Translations and transliterations in *Archives royales de Mari* (*ARM*), I–VI, Paris, 1950–54 (at the time of writing *ARM* VII has not appeared); cuneiform texts, *Textes cunéiformes de Louvre*, XXII–XXVIII; *Répertoire analytique des tomes I–V* (*ARM* XV), Paris, 1954.

[14]The names occurring in *ARM* I–V are to be found in *ARM* XV, 120–60; for a study of these names, see especially Noth "Mari und Israel," *BHT* 16, pp. 127–52.

[14a]Much of this material, with references to earlier studies, may be found in A. Finet, *L'accadien des lettres de Mari*, Bruxelles, 1956.

only increase the already tremendous importance of Mari for Northwest Semitic studies.

In ancient Alalakh of northern Syria, which was excavated between 1936–49 under the direction of Woolley, we have another important source.[15] Aside from an occasional interesting lexical item such as LÚ (.MEŠ) *ma-si/zi*, "men of the corvée" (Heb. *mas*),[16] Alalakh's contribution is also one of personal names, about a hundred from a period contemporary with the First Dynasty of Babylon, with a smaller number from the 15th century.[17] Another roughly contemporary onomasticon is revealed in the Chaga Bazar texts from northwestern Mesopotamia.[18]

Our primary need now is a study like Theo Bauer's which, utilizing all the new material, will present us with a complete grammatical analysis of the language.[19] Only thus shall we be able to see what is involved in the discussion, if not to agree on the solution, of the problem of naming this language. Bauer called the language East Canaanite, here following Landsberger, who still, "*faute de mieux*," retains this designation.[20] At first M. Noth preferred proto-Aramaic and, though he has subsequently abandoned the term itself, he has continued to urge

[15]Sir Charles Leonard Woolley, *Alalakh*, Oxford, 1955; for a popular account by the same author, *A Forgotten Kingdom*, Penguin Books, 1953.

[16]D. J. Wiseman, *The Alalakh Tablets*, London, 1953, 246:6,13 (autograph *JCS* 8 [1954], p. 16), 259:15 (autograph ibid., 19), 265:7 (autograph ibid., 21), 269:18,19. Cf. also [LÚ]*za-ki-ni* (all references in Wiseman, *The Alalakh Tablets*, p. 159; correct references in 256 to lines 19 and 27), which is Amarna *zu-ki-ni* (*EA* 256:9), *zu-ki-na* (*RA* 19 [1922], 103 [=*EA* 362]:69), and Heb. *sôkēn* (cf. Dhorme, *RB* 33 [1924], pp. 16–17).

[17]Index of personal names, Wiseman, op. cit., pp. 125–53. (This index must be used with caution, being incomplete and not free from error in readings and datings; for corrections of dating, see Oppenheim, *JNES* 14 [1955], p. 197, n.1, and Wiseman, *JCS* 8 [1954], p. 3.)

[18]C. J. Gadd, *Iraq* 7 (1940), pp. 35–42.

[19]We may expect this in a forthcoming monograph by I. Gelb. The writer would acknowledge his indebtedness to Professor Gelb for many discussions of the Amorite language, and in particular for the observation of the extent of the *me-* preformative in the causative participle (see below).

[20]Landsberger, *ZA*, NF 1 (1926), p. 238; *JCS* 8 (1954), p. 56, n. 103. Recently, Dietz Otto Edzard, *Die "Zweite Zwischenzeit" Babyloniens*, Wiesbaden, 1957, p. 43, has given a qualified acceptance of Landsberger's view, though more from the historical than the linguistic viewpoint. Kupper, *Les nomades en Mésopotamie au temps des rois de Mari*, Paris, 1957, pp. 243–44, sees the problem as one remaining to be solved, and an important problem "car l'insuffisance de la terminologie ne peut que nuire à la rigueur et à la clarté de la synthèse historique."

connections with later Aramaic.[21] This is the linguistic relationship also stressed by J. Lewy, though he would insist that the speakers of the language be called Amorites.[22] By distinguishing Arabic and Canaanite theophorous elements in the onomasticon, E. Dhorme distinguished two linguistic groups.[23] Albright's position is more nuanced. Though he has frequently used Bauer's term, often with a parenthetical addition, "East Canaanite (Amorite)," still he does not agree with Bauer, as is clear from his review of *Die Ostkanaanäer*.[24] For him the language is one of five principal dialects distinguishable in the second millennium, identical with neither (South-) Canaanite nor proto-Aramaic.[25] Yet he can also write that "the Aramean language sprang from a West Semitic dialect spoken in northwestern Mesopotamia in the early second millennium B.C., a dialect which seems to have left clear traces in the Mari documents,"[26] thus drawing our language closer to Aramaic than to Canaanite. Most recently A. Caquot has cut the Gordian knot by refusing to call the language anything more than early West Semitic.[27] In his opinion the language evidences a stage of early development to which the later divisions of West Semitic cannot be applied.[28]

The answer to this problem is obviously of importance to the Hebraist. If Bauer's "East Canaanite" is justified, then the Mari and related material is of greater immediate relevance for the history of Hebrew than if, as the writer believes, we should avoid both "Canaanite" and "Aramaic" as misleading and see rather in this language an ancient and venerable uncle of both Canaanite and Aramaic, who was, it should be stressed, a colorful personality with an individuality bordering on eccentricity.[29] In this case we should adopt, as henceforth in this

[21]*Die israelitischen Personennamen im Rahmen der gemeinsemitischen Namengebung*, Stuttgart, 1928, pp. 41–49; *ZDPV* 65 (1942), p. 34, n. 2; *BHT* 16, op. cit., p. 152.

[22]*ZA*, NF 4 (1929), pp. 243–72.

[23]*Recueil*, pp. 82–165, especially 104.

[24]*AfO* 3 (1926), pp. 124–26.

[25]*Atti del XIX Congresso Internazionale degli Orientalisti*, pp. 448–50.

[26]*FSAC*², p. 182 (Anchor ed., p. 239); cf. also *CBQ* 7 (1945), p. 18.

[27]A. Caquot, *Annales archéologiques de Syrie* 1 (1951), p. 216.

[28]Goetze's view, which connects the language with Ugaritic especially, should also be noted (cf. *Language* 17 [1941], pp. 134–37). This scholar would call the language Amorite.

[29]Note that there is evidence of at least two dialects in this period, the distinguishing feature being a different scheme of sibilants. In cuneiform sources, with

paper, one of several candidates, all with historical credentials, such as "Amorite" or "Khanean."

Turning to the second period illumined by the discoveries of the last thirty years, that of the 14th century B.C., we come to the revolutionary aspect of our topic—the discoveries at ancient Ugarit. As at Amarna forty years earlier, it was the chance discovery of an Arab peasant which led to the excavation of this site on the northern Syrian coast.[30] But excavations here by French archaeologists revealed cuneiform tablets written, not only in Babylonian[31] but also in an alphabet which, on decipherment by H. Bauer, Dhorme, and Virolleaud, disclosed a hitherto completely unknown Northwest Semitic dialect. More important, the contents of the tablets were principally epic literature. Contacts with Biblical literature were immediately apparent, and today there are few areas of Biblical studies unaffected by the discoveries at Ugarit. Prosody, textual criticism, literary history, Biblical theology—all have a pre- and post-Ugaritic date.

Not the least affected was Hebrew grammar. While the relationship of Ugaritic with Canaanite and, therefore, with Hebrew is a matter of increasing discussion,[32] no one denies its invaluable contribution, both directly and indirectly, to our understanding of the Hebrew language. Since it could be overlooked, the indirect contribution should be stressed. For it is because of Ugaritic that we have returned to earlier known material, and to new discoveries. It was Albright who, in a series of articles, indicated the new possibilities, especially in the Amarna

---

the exception of Alalakh, etymological *ŧ* is represented by *š̆*, *ś* and *š̆* by *s*; in Egyptian sources, etymological *ŧ* is represented by *s*, *ś* by *s* (at least probably, on the evidence of the Hayes List and later material), *š̆* by *š̆*; cf. Albright, *BASOR* 110, p. 15, n. 42. This is the general scheme, but there are many complicating factors in assessing the Egyptian evidence and, above all, that of Alalakh, where the confusion of the sibilants may reflect either actual differences of dialect, or simply the practice of the *Hurrian* scribes. Note also *ARM* II, 57:9, *sa-al-gu*$_5$ (etymological *ŧ*!). The problem is not merely philological, but has important historical aspects, far beyond the scope of this paper.

[30] For a brief review of the discoveries, translations, and bibliography, cf. G. R. Driver, *Canaanite Myths and Legends*, Edinburgh, 1956; also H. L. Ginsberg, *ANET*^{2}, pp. 129–55.

[31] For the Akkadian texts, cf. J. Nougayrol, *Le palais royal d'Ugarit*, III, Paris, 1955; IV, 1956.

[32] Literature reviewed by Moscati, "Il semitico di nord-ovest," *Studi Orientalistici in onore di Giorgio Levi della Vida*, II, pp. 203–6.

letters, that Ugaritic had opened up.[33] The significance of Ugarit can be justly estimated only if this further contribution is also recognized.

In what follows we present a summary of the discoveries of the last thirty years which we owe to the sources described above. Unsatisfactory as this is from the viewpoint of linguistic description, it has the merit of avoiding, so far as possible, undue and unproved assumptions in the very complicated problem of Northwest Semitic relationships. At the same time, it should, we believe, show how few areas of Hebrew grammar have remained unaffected by the discoveries of these three decades.

Behind the phonemic structure of the Hebrew transmitted to us in the Biblical text there is a long history, of which we mention here only the more important developments in the earlier stages. Proto-Hebrew and related Northwest Semitic dialects possessed at one time, allowing for dialectal divergences, about twenty-five to twenty-seven consonants. Though the evidence for the period *ca.* 1900–1700 B.C. is not without its gaps and ambiguities,[34] later evidence indicates that *ca.* 1400 B.C. is a *terminus post quem* for the developments which resulted in the twenty-two consonant Hebrew alphabet. This date follows from the now famous ABC tablet at Ugarit.[35] If we bracket both those consonants which later coalesced with other consonants and the demonstrable Ugaritic additions at the end, this tablet gives us the Hebrew alphabet of later centuries in exactly the same order: *ᵓa*, *b*, *g*, [*ḫ*], *d*, *h*, *w*, *z*, *ḥ*, *ṭ*, *y*, *k*, [*š*], *l*, *m*, [*đ*], *n*, [*ẓ*], *s*, *ᶜ*, *p*, *ṣ*, *q*, *r*, *ŧ*, [*ǵ*], *t*, [*ᵓi*, *ᵓu*, *s̀*]. Since the Ugarit additions are placed at the end of this alphabet, it is clear that the order of the

[33]*BASOR* 86, pp. 28–31; 87, pp. 32–38; 89, pp. 7–17, 29–32; cf. also Albright and Moran, *JCS* 2 (1948), pp. 239–48 [above, Paper 2]; ibid., 4 (1950), pp. 163–68 [above, Paper 4].

[34]Noth, *ZA*, NF 5 (1930), pp. 219ff., questioned Bauer's assumption that the phonetic shifts producing the consonantal scheme of Hebrew had actually occurred in Amorite. Goetze, *Language* 17 (1941), p. 134, n. 60, equating *Ia-ás-ku-ur* with *Iađkur*, would find evidence for the preservation of *đ*. We would point rather to *A-ad-ku-ur* (*JCS* 9 [1955], p. 47) and *Ia-ad-kur*-DINGIR (*Sumer* 5 [1949], p. 143, no. 8), whereas we would relate *Ia-ás-ku-ur* to a stem *śkr* (cf. Albright, *JAOS* 74 [1954], p. 228, n. 38), with which cf. also *Sa-ki-ra-am*, *Sa-ku-ra-nu*, *Sa-ki-ru* (*ARM* XV, p. 154) and *Sa-ki-rum* (*RA* 49 [1955], p. 16, i, 14, and note that the *đkr* stem in the last mentioned tablet is written *Za-ku-ra-a-bu*, *Zi-ik-ra*-^{d}ES$_4$.DAR, etc. [ibid., pp. 30–31]). Kupper's (op. cit., p. 73, n. 2) comparison with *škr*, "intoxicated," seems highly improbable to the writer. For etymological *đ*, cf. also *Da-ki-ru-um* (Bauer, *Die Ostkanaanäer*, p. 16) and *Za-ki-ru-um* (ibid., p. 41).

[35]Virolleaud, *Syria* 28 (1951), pp. 21–23.

other consonants must be borrowed from elsewhere. Were the other bracketed consonants also Ugaritic additions, some principle governing their place of insertion should be observable; as Gordon has rightly stressed,[36] there is no such principle. The source, therefore, of this alphabet must be sought elsewhere, which, in view both of the general historical and cultural situation, as well as of known prior alphabetic activities, must be in the Canaanite-speaking area to the south.[37] This only confirms what Albright has maintained for years on the evidence of the Egyptian transcriptions: before the earliest Phoenician and Biblical texts, Canaanite possessed a larger number of consonants than the later Phoenician alphabet indicated.[38]

In Hebrew, as elsewhere in Canaanite, *ḫ* coalesced with *ḥ*, *ṯ* with *š*, *ḏ* with *z*, *ẓ* with *ṣ*, *ǵ* with *ᶜ*; the period of these shifts probably began in the 14th century.[39] However, diverging from the rest of Canaanite, Hebrew went its own way in preserving proto-Semitic *ś*. While the Jerusalem Amarna evidence on etymological *ṯ*, *ś*, and *š* is not without its difficulties, the writer agrees with Goetze,[40] against Harris,[41] that the apparent anomalies are to be explained as due to the syllabary which the Jerusalem scribe employed, rather than as reflecting a complicated and unparalleled development. Goetze's view receives confirmation from several other peculiarities of the Jerusalem Amarna texts which set the Jerusalem scribe in another scribal tradition than that found in the other Canaanite Amarna letters.[42]

We have already seen dialectal divergences in the earliest attested evidence for Northwest Semitic. The picture after that is one of increasing variation and the gradual emergence of more dialects.[43] In addition

[36]*Orientalia* NS 19 (1950), p. 375; for problems raised by the ABC tablet, see Speiser, *BASOR* 121, pp. 17–21.

[37]Albright, *BASOR* 119, p. 24, and Speiser, op. cit., pp. 20–21.

[38]*BASOR* 118, pp. 12–13.

[39]Z. Harris, *Development of the Canaanite Dialects*, pp. 35–36, 40–41, 62–63.

[40]Goetze, *Language* 17 (1941), p. 128, n. 15 (however, *a-si-ru/ri* in *EA* 287:54, 288:21, has nothing to do with a stem *ʾṯr*); p. 129, n. 19.

[41]Op. cit., pp. 33–34, 62–63.

[42]Thus the Jerusalem scribe (1) never employs the *y*-preformative in the verb; (2) uses *muššuru*, as in letters of Hurrian provenience, instead of *wuššuru* with the Canaanite scribes; (3) Ass. *lamnu* rather than Baby. *lemnu*, another Hurrian text feature; (4) Ass. *ezābu* rather than Baby. *ezēbu*. Note also KUR.URU (Urusalim), found in Hittite texts, occasionally at Ugarit.

[43]For the phonetic changes, cf. Harris, op. cit.

to the consonantal differences just noted, vocalic changes took place. While the originally long vowels were in general stable, *â* became *ô* in most of the Canaanite-speaking groups south of Ugarit in the period between 1700–1375 B.C. Short vowels were much more susceptible of mutation, and after the Amarna period final short vowels were generally lost, including the case endings of the noun (*-u*, *-i*, *-a*), The diphthongs were contracted (*au* > *ô*, *ai* > *ê*) before the Amarna period from Ugarit as far as Jerusalem. In the early period *au* still existed,[44] whereas for *ai* there is no clear evidence.[45] The Jerusalem dialect of Hebrew, however, retained the diphthongs and thus diverged dialectically from the Hebrew of the northern kingdom. There, as we know from the Samaria ostraca, Hebrew followed the pattern of Phoenicia, which in view of Israel's geographical position is understandable. In general, Palestine repeatedly appears as a linguistic "backwoods" in the development of Canaanite. Many changes occurred in Canaanite which either never reached Palestine, or only after a considerable interval.[46]

The loss of case endings in the noun, just mentioned above, is nothing new, but what is new is that there are not nearly so many remnants of the early case endings as had been previously thought. One established view was that the so-called *he locale* in expressions like *šamaima*, "heavenwards," preserved the earlier accusative ending *a*. This has been conclusively disproved by Ugaritic, where we also find, for example, *šmmh*. In the purely consonantal script of Ugarit the final

[44]Cf. the Causatives *Ia-ú-ṣí* (Bauer, op. cit., p. 31), *Ia-au*$_x$(PI)-*ṣí* (*ARM* XV, p. 147; VII, 189:6; *RA* 49 [1955], p. 26; for *au*$_x$, see now Kupper, op. cit., p. 73, n. 1, but, in our opinion, he goes beyond the evidence in concluding to *yô*) and possibly *Ia-ú-ḫi* (Bauer, op. cit.). The writer agrees with Bauer, ibid., p. 66, that these are causatives of *Primae-Waw* verbs, and cannot accept Goetze's (op. cit., p. 135, n. 167) *Yūṣi* and *Yūḫi*—nor is *Ia-ṣi*/*ṣí* a perfect, since it always occupies the initial position in a name.

[45]*Skmimi* of the execration texts is probably a dual, but does it stand for *sakmaimi* or *sakmêmi*?

[46]See Harris's remarks, op. cit., p. 98. If Noth, *BHT* 16, p. 139, were correct in explaining Mari elements like *Itar* and *Išar* as deriving from *Yitar* and *Yišar*, we would have some evidence for the Barth-Ginsberg law as early as Mari. However, in the writer's opinion, there is so far no clear evidence for a preformative *yi* in any of the Amorite material. Writings like *Ia-e-im-ṣí*, *Ia-e-šu-bi*, *Ia-en-ḫi-mu-um*, etc. (Bauer, op. cit., pp. 25–26) show the existence of *ye*, which is either dialectal for *ya*, or an intermediate stage in the *ya-e* development. Nowhere do we find *Ia-i-* or *Yi-i*.

h cannot be a *mater lectionis* indicating the vowel *a*, but must also be consonantal.[47]

Another remnant of the case endings has been thought to be the explanation of the *i* ending called the *hireq compaginis*; this, too, at least in the majority of cases, must be seriously questioned. In Exodus 15:6, "Thy right hand, O Yahweh, is fearful [*neʾdārî*] in strength," in *neʾdārî* we must deny at least any immediate connection with the genitive, for, as has been pointed out,[48] the grammatical difficulties which have led scholars to prefer the easier reading, *neʾdārā*, admit of an easy solution if we revocalize the consonantal text as *neʾdôrî*, that is, as an infinitive absolute. The basis for such a revocalization is to be found in similar infinitives, also with a similar *i* ending, in both the Jerusalem and the Byblos Amarna letters.[49] So, too, in Genesis 49:11, "He tethers [*ʾôsᵉrî*] his ass to the vine," we would revocalize the apparent participle as an infinitive absolute (*ʾāsôrî*).[50] Not only is the participle with the *hireq compaginis* almost exclusively confined to appellatives,[51] which does not fit here, but an infinitive absolute used in narrative with subject unexpressed is quite normal, which is not true of the participle.

The presence in Amarna, moreover, of three participles with an *i* ending suggests that the *hireq compaginis* with participles in Hebrew is also not a remnant of the older genitive.[52] Speculation as to the precise function of this final vowel is, of course, impossible on the basis of three examples, but some connection with the *hireq compaginis* is hard to avoid. Since, whatever its function, the vowel in Amarna cannot be a remnant of the genitive in a period when case endings are still in use, the archaizing participles in Hebrew are not to be considered differently.

Ugaritic, with corroboration from Amorite and Amarna, has clarified or revealed several particles in Hebrew, the existence of some of

[47]For a fuller discussion and the possible origin of the morpheme, see Speiser, *Israel Exploration Quarterly* 4 (1954), pp. 108–15.

[48]Cross and Freedman, *JNES* 14 (1955), p. 245; Huesman, *Biblica* 37 (1956), p. 293.

[49]*JCS* 4 (1950), pp. 169–72 [above, Paper 5].

[50]Cross and Freedman, op. cit.

[51]First properly stressed by Barth, *ZDMG* 53 (1899), p. 593.

[52]The participles are *di-ki* (*EA* 131:23), *ḫa-zi-ri* (*EA* 138:80,130). They are not finite forms, or we should have *di-ka* (cf. *EA* 132:45) and *ḫa-zi-ra*. They can, therefore, only be participles, and probably passive: this is certain for the first, virtually so for the first instance of *ḫa-zi-ri* (*ʿaṣîri*, "held back, detained"), probable for the second (with same meaning).

which had been forgotten in later centuries. The most important of these is enclitic *mem*, which has cleared up scores of grammatical and logical inconcinnities of the Hebrew text. It is found in Mari names like *ᶜAbdu-ma-Dagan*, "Servant of Dagan,"[53] and in a variety of uses in Amarna as well as in Ugaritic. After H. D. Hummel's completely convincing study on the subject,[54] a skepticism which prefers to suspect the text rather than accept a linguistic feature attested in Amorite, Ugaritic, and Amarna (Jerusalem!) should be virtually impossible.[55] The *motnê-m qāmau* of Deuteronomy 33:11 clearly belongs with Ugaritic *ṯakmê-mi/ma ḥâmîti*, "the top of the wall,"[56] and Jerusalem Amarna's *ûbilī-mi ḫarrānāt šarri*, "the porters of the royal caravans."[57]

From Ugaritic, too, we learn of the particle *l* (vocalization uncertain) with different uses. The first and commonest is the asseverative *l* (probably *la*), found also in Amorite, as, for example, in *Sumī-la-ᶜammu (Su-mi-lam-mu)*,[58] *ᶜAmmī-la-ᵓaddu (Am-mi-la-du)*,[59] *La-ᵓaḫī-ṣaduq (La-ḫi-ṣa-du-uq)*.[60] Thus in Psalms 89:19 we have "For truly is Yahweh (*l-YHWH*) our shield, truly the Holy One (*l-qᵉdôš*) of Israel our king."[61] It is also found before a verb, as in Albright's ingenious solution to the hitherto hopelessly obscure Hab. 3:6, "While everlasting mountains broke up, Eternal hills collapsed, Eternal orbits were shattered (*l-tḫtᵓn*)."[62] A second use is with vocatives, pointed out by Al-

53*ARM* XV, p. 140, p. 144.

54*JBL* 76 (1957), pp. 87–103.

55So Driver, op. cit., p. 129, n. 16; p. 130, n. 2.

56*UH, Krt* 75.

57*EA* 287: 55.

58Wiseman, *The Alalakh Tablets*, p. 145.

59*JCS* 8 (1954), p. 21, 267:17 (not indexed in *The Alalakh Tablets*).

60Wiseman, op. cit., p. 141, and add 455:47 (*JCS* 8 [1954], p. 30). Cf. also *La-ki-in-a-du*, Wiseman, op. cit., p. 141, for *La-kin-ad(d)u*, "Truly trustworthy is Addu."

61See Nötscher's thorough study in *VT* 3 (1953), pp. 372–80.

62*Studies in Old Testament Prophecy*, 15, n. u. In *La-aḫ-wi-ma-li-ku* (*ARM* VII, 61:2), *La-aḫ-wi-ba-lu* (*Iraq* 7 [1940], p. 39), *La-[aḫ]-wi-*DINGIR (*RA* 49 [1955], p. 27), *La-aḫ-[wi]-a-du* (Wiseman, op, cit., p. 141, reading *La-aḫ-[mi?]*), we seem to have *La-yaḫwi* > *Laḫwi* (cf. the verbal preformative *la* of later Aramaic dialects!); note also *La-ḫu-un-ᵈDa-gan* (*ARM* XV, p. 150) and *Ia-ḫu-un-*DINGIR (*ARM* VII, 211:4). However, *E-ki-la-aḫ-wi* of *ARM* VII, 185:3′, urges caution; I cannot explain this name. The frequent *Larim* element, however, in view of *Ka-bi-la-ri-im* (*Iraq* 7 [1940], p. 39, and cf. *Ka-bi-ᵈ*IM [ibid.; Bauer, op. cit., p. 32; *ARM* VII, 106:10], *Ka-bi-e-ra-ah* [Bauer, op. cit.], *Ka-bi-ᵈDa-gan* [*ARM* VII, 180 iv 24]), seems to be a theophorous element rather than verbal *Larîm* < *La-yarîm*.

bright in Psalms 68:34, *l-rôkēb*, "O Rider," by coincidence occurring with the same word in Ugaritic.[63] A similar use of the particle is perhaps the best explanation of the *l* in the name *Remaliah*: *Rûm-l-Yāhû*, "Be exalted, O Yahu."[64]

Ugaritic has thrown light on several other particles. This is true of the particle *kî* in Genesis 18:20 (*kî rabbā, kî kābᵉdā*, "indeed great, indeed excessive") and in several other places, where, as in Ugaritic, we find the verb thrown to the end of its clause.[65] Moreover, in the light of Ugaritic,[66] now confirmed by Amarna,[67] where the conditional particle *hm* retains its original deictic force of "behold" or the like, Patton has collected a number of cases of Hebrew *hm(h)* where the apparent personal pronoun becomes intelligible when taken as a deictic particle.[68] The evidence for the conditional particle with this force confirms the earlier explanation of the so-called "*waw* of apodosis," found also at Mari[69] as well as in the Canaanite of the 14th century, as deriving from the original paratactic construction in Hebrew conditional and temporal clauses.

Examples where the Hebrew prepositions *bᵉ*, *lᵉ*, *ᶜal* have been clarified in the light of Ugaritic are now legion, and many of the old textual emendations now seen to be quite unnecessary. For it is now clear that where our idiom demands "from," Hebrew (Canaanite) and Ugaritic idiom employed "in," "in regard to," and "upon."[70]

To the Hebrew pronouns Ugaritic has added the indefinite interrogative *mn*, discovered by Albright in Deuteronomy 33:11, *umiśśônᵉʾau mn yᵉqûmun*, "and from his enemies whoever rises up."[71] It has also provided the first evidence in Northwest Semitic, outside of Hebrew, for

[63]*HUCA* 23 (1950–51), p. 35.

[64]Beegle, *BASOR* 123, p. 28.

[65]*UH*, p. 65. See also O'Callaghan, *VT* 4 (1954), p. 175, and Albright, *Mélanges bibliques rédigés en l'honneur de André Robert* (Paris, *n.d.*), pp. 22–26.

[66]For references, see *UH*, p. 226, 18:602–3.

[67]*JCS* 7 (1953), pp. 78–80 [above, Paper 8].

[68]*Canaanite Parallels in the Book of Psalms*, p. 37; cf. also M. Dahood, *CBQ* 16 (1954), p. 16.

[69]Finet, op. cit., p. 236, §84n; 240, §85g; occasionally in Ugar. Akkadian texts (Nougayrol, op. cit., III 15.89 [p. 53]:12).

[70]The writer agrees with Sutcliffe, *VT* 5 (1955), pp. 436–39, that we should not say that these prepositions *mean* "from."

[71]*CBQ* 7 (1945), p. 23, n. 64. The form *yᵉqûmun* preserves the old indicative-energic found in Amarna.

the use of *ʾăšer* as a relative pronoun: *ʾṯr ʾiṯ bqṯ wšt ly*, "Find out what there is available, and then place [it] at my disposal."[72] The archaic use of the demonstrative in expressions like *ze Sînai*, "the one of Sinai," now finds parallels both in Ugaritic *ḏ-pʾid*, "the one of mercy," an epithet of El, and in Mari names like *Zu-ḫatni(m)*,[73] *Zu-ḫadim*,[74] *Zu-sumim*,[75] and possibly *Zu-ša-abi*.[76]

However, important as these discoveries have been for our knowledge of Hebrew, the major advances have been in the area of the verb. The Hebrew verb, it is true, still remains the source of most grammatical *cruces*, but progress within the last thirty years, if not bringing definitive solutions to all the problems, has at least focused the problems more clearly.

We may mention first the discovery of the unsuspected role of the infinitive absolute in Hebrew. The largest share of the credit for this discovery must be given to the long Phoenician inscription from Karatepe in Cilicia, though Ugaritic and Amarna are not without some contribution.[77] The use of the infinitive absolute instead of a finite verb was not unknown to Hebrew grammar, but it was not given due consideration nor, as a result, brought to bear on the solution of certain problems of the Hebrew text. It was Karatepe and, in its light, Ugaritic and Amarna, which demanded a serious investigation of the infinitive absolute in Hebrew and the extent of its use. This Huesman has given

[72]Cited in *Orientalia*, NS 25 (1956), p. 417.

[73]*ARM* XV, p. 159; VII, 217:6, 271:2.

[74]*ARM* VII, 227:12′. For the theophorous element *Ḫadu*, cf. also *Su-mu-ḫa-d*[*u*]-*ú* in *ARM* VII, 217:1, and in view of these passages we should probably read *Ma-lik-ḫa(!)-du-um* for Bauer's, op. cit., p. 34, *Malik-za-du-um*.

[75]*RA* 47 (1953), p. 174. For *Sumum* as a theophorous element, cf. for the present Noth, op. cit., p. 133, and the writer's remarks, *Orientalia*, NS 26 (1957), p. 343, n. 3.

[76]*RA* 49 (1955), p. 31. This recalls Biblical *Mᵉtūšāʾēl*, but the *ša*-element is not explained. In *ARM* VII, 232:5, despite the autograph, I would read *Zu(!)-ḫa-am-mu*, "The One of *ʿAmmu*."

[77]*JCS* 4 (1950), pp. 169–72 [above, Paper 5]; ibid., 6 (1952), pp. 76–80 [above, Paper 7]. For further Ugaritic material, see A. Jirku, *Jahrbuch für kleinasiatische Forschung* 3 (1954), pp. 111–15. Driver, op. cit., denies that the Karatepe and Ugaritic passages contain infinitives, ignoring the Amarna evidence. Since what we consider infinitives absolute are occasionally found with pronominal suffixes, Driver argues "the form ceases *ipso facto* to be 'absolute' when it is thus qualified." A new term seems the solution of this difficulty.

us in two articles,[78] demonstrating that the substitution of the infinitive absolute for the finite verb was a fairly common construction.

Amarna and Ugaritic have shown the antiquity of the construction, and the relevance of the former, with its final *i* vowel added to the infinitive, for *neʾdārî* in Exodus 15:6 and *ʾôsᵉrî* in Genesis 49:11 we have already seen. The infinitive with the additional *i* vowel is also used paranomastically in Amarna,[79] and we would suggest that the same construction underlies the text of Genesis 30:8. The text *naptûlê ʾĕlôhîm niptaltî* has had different explanations, but all agree in taking *naptûlê* as a noun. Yet a *naqtûl* formation is otherwise unknown in Hebrew. It seems much simpler to revocalize, leaving the consonantal text untouched, *niptôlî ʾᵉlôhîm niptaltî*, and translate, "Greatly (lit. "with contending"), O God, have I contended," that is, to see in NPTWLY an infinitive absolute. While this has the slight difficulty of separating the infinitive from the finite verb—*ʾᵉlôhîm*, however, may be secondary—it is far easier to accept than an anomalous *naqtûl* formation.

Another feature of the verb that is now clear regards the prefix of the Piᶜel and causative conjugations. This had formerly been thought, at least in the Piᶜel, to go back to *yu* as in Arabic and Akkadian. But in Ugaritic, it is *ya* both in the Piᶜel and in the causative.[80] In the earlier material the situation is not clear with regard to the Piᶜel. The hypocoristicon *Ibassir*[81] is, on the evidence of all the Semitic languages, a Piᶜel, and since the only evidence we have is for *ya* > *i*, we would reconstruct a more original *Yabassir*. Another group of forms (*Yamatti*, etc.) that might possibly be cited in this connection will be discussed below. But in the causative the prefix is clearly *ya*: *Ia-ki-in*,[82] *Ia-ri-im*,[83] *Ia-ás-ki-in*,[84] *Ia-ú-ṣí*,[85] *Ia-au*$_x$*(PI)-ṣí*,[86] *Ia-ás-li-im*,[87] *Ia-ši-ib*,[88] possib-

78*Biblica* 37 (1956), pp. 271–95, 410–34.

79*JCS* 4 (1950), p. 172 [above, Paper 5, pp. 156–57].

80*UH*, p. 70, §9:31 and n. 3; ibid., p. 72, §9:34.

81*ARM* XV, p. 148.

82*ARM* VII, 209:4.

83*ARM* XV, p. 146.

84*ARM* VI, 79:9.

85Bauer, op. cit., p. 31.

86*ARM* XV, p. 147; *ARM* VII, 189:6; *RA* 49 (1955), p. 26.

87*ARM* VI, 22:14.

88*JCS* 8 (1954), p. 19, 258:24 (not indexed in Wiseman, *The Alalakh Tablets*), also Wiseman, ibid., p. 136 (*Ia-ši-bi-il-*[*la*]).

ly *Ia-am-li-ik*.[89] Further, in view of the participles *Me-mi-ḫi-im*[90] and *Me-bi-šum*,[91] we would take *-emiḫ* in *Mu-ti-e-mi-iḫ*[92] as deriving originally from a causative *yamiḫ*, and *Ia-bi-šum*[93] as another causative.

In connection with the causative, it is to be noted that Amorite evidences a somewhat surprising antiquity for the preformative *mē-* in the participles of the so-called hollow verbs. At Alalakh we have *Me-ki-in*,[94] and at Mari *Me-ki-nu-um*,[95] both identical with the Hebrew participle *mēkîn*. At Chagar Bazar we have *Me-mi-ḫi-im* and possibly *Me-ḫi-ri*.[96] However, it is possible that the origin of *mēkîn* in Hebrew is not the same as in this dialect, for we also find *Me-pí-ḫu-um*,[97] *Me-eḫ-ni-yu-um*,[98] *Me-ki-bu-um*,[99] *Me-ès-ki-nim* (genitive),[100] *Me-es₅-ki-ru-um*,[101] *Me-es₅-li-mu-um*,[102] *Me-en-ḫi-mu-um*,[103] as well as *Me-bi-šum* already mentioned above. These forms show us that *meqtil* was the regular form of the causative participle in Amorite, though the origin of the preformative remains obscure.[104]

[89]Bauer, op. cit., p. 28.

[90]*Iraq* 7 (1940), p. 40. The form is a genitive; cf. pl. iv r. 3 (GÌR *Me-mi-hi-im*) and 33 (GÌR *Kab-ka-bi-im*).

[91]*ARM* VII, 201 r. 9′.

[92]*RA* 49 (1955), p. 28; for the possibility of this element in the execration texts, see *Orientalia*, NS 26 (1957), p. 341.

[93]Bauer, op. cit., p. 24 (*Ia-pí-šum*).

[94]Wiseman, op. cit., p. 142.

[95]*ARM* VII, 185 ii 13′; and cf. also *A-bu-um-e-ki-in*, *ARM* XV, p. 140, and *A-bu-me-ki-*[*i*]*n*, *ARM* VI, 18 r. 1′.

[96]*Iraq* 7 (1940), p. 40. Gadd does not inform us of the case of the name, so the ending must remain unexplained. With this name cf. Amarna *Baᶜal-me-ḫír*, etc. (*EA* II, pp. 1558–1559) and perhaps Biblical *Jāᶜîr*.

[97]*RA* 47 (1953), p. 173.

[98]Ibid., 49 (1955), p. 28.

[99]*ARM* XV, p. 152.

[100]Ibid.

[101]Bauer, op. cit., p. 34; for the causative of this stem in personal names, Albright, *JAOS* 74 (1954), p. 227.

[102]*JCS* 9 (1955), p. 64, no. 18:18.

[103]Ibid., p. 91, no. 57:17.

[104]The only evidence for causative participles without *me-*, to the writer's knowledge, is *Maḫšimānum* (Bauer, op. cit., p. 46), and the place name *Mankisum* (*ARM* XV, p. 120). The evidence allows for a *Hifᶜil* causative, but does not demand it; cf. the divine name *Haddu*, which appears also as *Iandu*, *Iaddu*, and *Ed(d)a*, intervocalic *h* becoming the "gliding" *y* (see Kupper, op. cit., p. 230, n.1).

An anomaly of the Canaanite verb in the 14th century, without parallel in the other Semitic languages, is the third plural masculine form *taqtulû(na)*, along with the usual *yaqtulû(na)*. While the existence of the form in Ugaritic might be doubted if one confines himself to the obscurity of a script which generally does not indicate vowels, still in view of the clear Amarna evidence for the form we should have no indication in extending *taqtulû(na)* from Byblos to Ugarit.[105]

The relevance, however, of this form for the explanation of certain *t* preformative forms with plural subjects in the Bible is still not settled. Albright, while admitting the Amarna and Ugaritic evidence, has not extended its application to the Hebrew forms, preferring to see in them a third feminine singular with plural subject taken as a collective.[106] Since this construction is attested in Hebrew,[107] it is virtually impossible to decide the question because of the ambiguities of the Hebrew text. However, it would be most surprising if in archaic or archaizing texts the Amarna-Ugaritic form never occurred, so that in the writer's opinion the existence of the form in Hebrew must be considered highly probable, though lacking conclusive proof.[108]

Two more discoveries bring us to the central problem of the Hebrew verb.[109] The first regards the imperfect, in so far as it derives from the earlier indicative *yaqtulu*. That Hebrew one time possessed an indicative is not new, but its usage has never been determined from texts of Canaanite provenience, and the date of its appearance in Canaanite placed much too late. Usage and date can now be fixed with considerable accuracy as the result of a re-examination of the Amarna letters.

In the largest single group of texts, those from Byblos, we can establish two principal uses of the indicative in the 14th century: first, as a

---

Therefore, possibly *muhaqtil* > *muyaqtil* > *muyeqtil* > *meqtil*, but *yahaqtil* > *yayaqtil* > *yaqtil*.

[105] *JCS* 5 (1951), pp. 33–35 [above, Paper 6].

[106] Most recently *HUCA* 23 (1950–51), p. 17. This is also Driver's explanation for the Ugaritic occurrences (op. cit., p. 130), and he apparently (ibid., n. 6) rejects the writer's arguments for *taqtulû* (cf. above n. 105), accepting only *taqtulûna*; he gives no reasons.

[107] *GKC* §145k.

[108] Nah. 1:5, however, might be noted. Albright has clarified the passage (*CBQ* 7 [1945], pp. 22–23), but instead of rejecting the *waw* (*tbl W kl*), one may see here an indication that the correct reading is the plural form *têbālû*.

[109] For full references and discussion of the Byblian verb, see the writer's forthcoming article on the subject [above, Paper 10].

present-future, and second, as a past iterative. The first is found in over two hundred examples; the latter, with twenty-three examples, is much rarer, but sufficiently well attested. One passage may be quoted, since it illustrates very happily the use of the "tenses" at Byblos: *miya mārū Abd-aširta ardi kalbi šar māt Kašši u šar māt Mitanni šunu u tilqûna māt šarrri ana šāšunu panânu tilqûna ālāni ḫazānīka u qâlāta annû inanna dubbirū rābiṣaka u laqû ālānišu ana šāšunu anumma laqû āl Ullaza šumma kiʾamma qâlāta adi tilqûna āl Ṣumura u tidûkūna rābiṣa u ṣāb tillati ša ina Ṣumura,* "Who are the sons of ᶜAbd-aširta, the slave and dog? Are they the king of the Kassites or the king of the Mitanni that they take the royal land for themselves? Previously they used to take the cities of your governors, and you were negligent. Behold! now they have driven out your commissioner and have taken his cities for themselves. Indeed, they have taken Ullaza. If you are negligent this way, they will take Simyra besides, and they will kill the commissioner and the auxiliary force which is in Simyra."[110]

Especially striking here is the use of the verb *leqû* in the perfect and imperfect. Three times we have *tilqûna*, once as a present, once as a future, once as a past. In the last instance it describes repeated action: previously the sons of ᶜAbd-aširta had made a practice of capturing cities ruled by a royal governor (Canaanite king), keeping clear of a city where a royal commissioner was stationed. However, when the latest single enormity is contrasted with former practice, there is an immediate shift from the imperfect indicative *tilqûna* to the perfect *laqû*.

While, admittedly, this passage is something of a *tour de force*, it does not convey a false impression of the general picture which emerges from a careful study of every example of the indicative in the Byblos letters. Moreover, there is no reason why, allowing for minor differences, we should not consider Byblian usage as comparable with that of contemporary Hebrew. Whatever, therefore, the previous history of the Canaanite verb, we can say that by the 14th century the imperfect indicative with the above usage was not starting to develop, as Harris thought,[111] but was already well established as part of the verbal scheme.

The second discovery is that of the origin of the Hebrew cohortative. The origin of *ʾeqtᵉlā* and *niqtᵉlā* has long been a moot point of Hebrew

[110] *EA* 104:17–36.

[111] Op. cit., p. 84.

grammar. Of the many views proposed, that of H. Bauer[112] and Joüon[113] turns out to be correct: the cohortative is a remnant of the earlier "subjunctive." This follows as an obvious corollary once the use of *yaqtula* in Byblian Amarna is established, since the use of the cohortative is substantially identical with that of *yaqtula* in Byblos.

Of the seventy-nine occurrences of the subjunctive form which can be analyzed, over seventy per cent fall into a jussive-purpose use, slightly more than fifteen per cent occur in conditional sentences. The statistics in themselves are very significant. Of equal or greater importance are two other aspects of the usage. First, the scribe shifts between *yaqtulu* and *yaqtula* within the same letter, even within the same sentence, in a clearly defined pattern of usage. Thus, *yûdana šeʾim mûṣa māt Yarimuta ša yûdanu panânu ina āl Ṣumura yûdana inanna ina āl Gubla,* "Let grain, the product of Yarimuta, be given; what used to be given in Simyra, let it be given now in Byblos."[113a] Second, besides many illustrations of this sort, the syntax of purpose clauses is to be noted: after an indicative in the main clause, an indicative in the purpose clause; after a jussive or an imperative in the main clause, another jussive, imperative, or *yaqtula* in the purpose clause. This rule can be established quite independently of *yaqtula,* the use of which, therefore, in purpose clauses must be significant and reflect Canaanite idiom. In brief, the existence of a form corresponding to the Arabic subjunctive is beyond doubt for the 14th-century Canaanite of Byblos, and since the Hebrew cohortative squares with Byblian usage, its origin is now clear.

For the 14th-century Hebrew we would, therefore, reconstruct the following verbal scheme: punctual *qatala,* durative *yaqtulu,* jussive *yaqtul,* "emphatic" jussive *yaqtula*. That the Hebrew perfect goes back to the Amarna period has long been known, but what has not received due attention are the parallels to the *waw*-conversive with the perfect.[114] Yet in the Byblos letters there are thirty-three cases where the perfect is used with reference to the future. Of these, twenty-four are preceded by the conjunction *u,* "and," and are comparable, therefore, to the well-known construction of Hebrew; of the remaining nine, eight are in the protasis of a conditional sentence, the ninth in a temporal

[112]Bauer-Leander, p. 273, §36d.

[113]*Grammaire de l'Hébreu biblique*^{2}, p. 315, n. 1.

[113a]*EA* 85:34–37.

[114]Notice of the construction was taken briefly in *JCS* 2 (1948), p. 245 [above, Paper 2, p. 136].

clause. For example, *dûkūmi eṭlakunu u* IBAŠŠĀTUNU *kīma yatinu u* PAŠḪĀTUNU, "Kill your lord, and then you will be like us and have peace";[115] *šumma ṣābu piṭati* IBAŠŠAT *kali mātāti nilqu ana šarri*, "If there will be an archer-host [at our disposal], we will seize all lands for the king";[116] *allu paṭārima awīlūt ḫupši u* ṢABTŪ *Ḫapirū āla*, "Behold! if the serfs desert, then the ᶜApiru will seize the city";[117] *u la* KAŠID *irēšu u ušširtīšu*, "As soon as the request arrives, I will send him."[118]

However, besides such cases, we also have examples like *u laqû ālānišu*, "and they have taken his cities," where the underlying Canaanite *waw* does not convert the tense; above in discussing *yaqtulu*, we cited *u tidûkūna*, "and they will kill," not *u dâkū*. A clue toward resolving this apparent conflict in "tense" usage is probably to be found in the fact that, with the exception of the two perfects in the last passage cited above, all of these perfects occur in sentences which are implicitly or explicitly conditional. And the exceptions are more apparent than real, since they occur with a temporal clause, the general structure of which is identical with that of conditional sentences. This restriction to conditional sentences, where optative and precative elements are well attested, would seem to corroborate H. L. Ginsberg's insight[119] that the development of the *waw* conversive with the perfect in Hebrew was favored by one of the original functions of the perfect, namely, as an optative or precative. This much seems clear: Byblos shows us an early stage of the far more developed Hebrew usage.

The history of the Hebrew verb earlier than the Amarna period is most obscure. It has been frequently pointed out that the use of the verb in Ugaritic finds much closer parallels in Hebrew poetry, especially the earlier poetry, than in Hebrew prose.[120] Valuable as this observation is, the central problem remains of finding a clear pattern of complementary distribution for *yaqtul*, *yaqtulu*, and *qatala*—and if one holds the existence of *yaqattal(u)*, for this form too. It is clear that the Ugaritic tense system is not that of contemporary Byblian Amarna. But what is

[115] *EA* 74:25–27.
[116] *EA* 103:55–57.
[117] *EA* 118:36–38.
[118] *EA* 82:16–17.
[119] *Orientalia*, NS 5 (1936), p. 177.
[120] *UH*, p. 114, §14.3.

it?[121] The writer would make no pretensions of knowing, and so must content himself with pointing out some material from the new sources which must be taken into account by anyone attempting a solution.

First, the following names are to be considered: *Ia-ma-at-ti-*DINGIR,[122] *Ia-na-ab-bi-*DINGIR,[123] *Ia-na-bi-*DINGIR,[124] *Ia-na-bi-im*,[125] *Ia-ba-si-*ᵈ*Da-gan*,[126] *Ia-ḫa-at-ti-*DINGIR,[127] *Ia-ḫa-at-ti-*ᵈUTU,[128] *Ia-za-at-ti-*DINGIR,[129] *Ia-ba-an-ni-*DINGIR.[130] These names are extremely important because they raise anew the question of the existence of the so-called present-future in early Northwest Semitic. The only alternative explanation would be that the verbs in question are to be considered Piᶜels.[131] Arguments can be made for both views, none of which is decisive, though the writer leans to the present-future.

Along with these forms are to be taken into account the clear cases (six) in the Mari letters where we find the form *iparrasu* and *iprusu*, not in subordinate clauses as Akkadian grammar demands, but in main clauses. Finet has called them "*subjonctif d'insistance ou d'emphase*,"[132] but this is a *pis aller*, as is seen from his having recourse to the barbarous Akkadian of Idrimi for parallels. Certainly the simplest solution is to take these forms as momentary lapses of the scribes into their native idiom; if so, we would have further evidence, first, of the *yaqattal(u)* form in early Northwest Semitic, and secondly, of *yaqtulu* used in past narrative as at Ugarit.

[121]For various proposals, J. Aistleitner, *Untersuchungen zur Grammatik des Ugaritischen*, Berlin, 1954, pp. 47ff.; Goetze, *JAOS* 58 (1938), pp. 266–309; E. Hammershaimb, *Das Verbum im Dialekt von Ras Schamra*, Kopenhagen, 1941. Harris follows Goetze, whereas Albright presents a quite different view (cf. *JAOS* 60 [1940], pp. 418–19). See also Ginsberg's remarks, *Orientalia*, NS 5 (1936), p. 177.

[122]*ARM* XV, p. 146; VII, 180 iii′ 35′.

[123]*ARM* VII, 185 ii 5′; 189:2.

[124]*RA* 49 (1955), p. 26.

[125]Ibid., p. 26, n. 1.

[126]Jean, *RES* 2 (1937), p. 104.

[127]*RA* 49 (1955), p. 25; *Iraq* 7 (1940), p. 38.

[128]*University of California Publications* 10, no. 89:15.

[129]*RA* 49 (1955), p. 26, and n. 4; cf. also *ARM* VII, 180 v′ 9′.

[130]*RA* 49 (1955), p. 25; *ARM* VI, 14:10.

[131]Noth, op. cit., refers only to *Ia-ma-at-ti-*, and without hesitation identifies the form as a *Piᶜel*.

[132]Finet, op. cit., p. 262, §91f.

Finally, the very meager evidence for the perfect in the early period is to be considered. Against Noth, who has persistently argued the opposite, it should be stressed that the perfects which he alleges are all statives,[133] which is something quite different in a discussion of tense distribution. Genuine perfects are to be found only in *Da-ni-*DINGIR,[134] *Su-mi-ra-pa*,[135] and possibly in *Qa-ra-*^{d}EŠ$_4$.DAR[136] and *Ma-la-ak-ì-lí*.[137] Whether this is to be explained as due to the normal content (prayers of petition rather than statements of fact) of the names, or to the recent emergence of the perfect, must be a cardinal point in any discussion of tenses.

Rome; January, 1957; revised, April, 1958.

133Noth, *Die israelitischen Personennamen*, p. 23, and *BHT* 16, p. 140. Posener, *E* 5, cited by Noth, *ZDPV* 65 (1942), p. 24, n. 3, is much more likely to be *ʾAbi-râpiʾ* (participle) than *ʾAbi-rapaʾ* (perfect), in view of the almost innumerable *râpiʾ* names in the sources as against one *rapaʾ* name. The other name, cited ibid., may be a perfect *ʾasap* (Posener, *E* 7, *ʾčphddw*), but it is not certain and the position is against it.

134*ARM* VII, 263 iii 24′.

135Wiseman, op. cit., p. 145.

136*ARM* VII, 210:13.

137*ARM* VII, 181 r. 3′.

12. *taqtul—Third Masculine Singular?

In the *Journal of Biblical Literature* 82 (1963) 317–318, Nahum M. Sarna has discussed the difficult forms תשכון, ותצעדהו in Job 18:14–15 and תשורנו in Job 20:9. If correct, his analysis would not only remove these cruces, but also force us to make a new entry in the Hebrew verbal system, for according to Dr. Sarna these verbs are "rare masculine forms with a *t*-preformative." In support of the existence of this alleged third masculine singular **taqtul* he cites four passages from the Amarna letters.[1] In fact, I think it is fair to say that his case for the presence of comparable forms in Job stands or falls with the Amarna evidence. If **taqtul* (3 masc. sg.) is really found in the Amarna letters of Canaanite provenience, one will be ready to admit the possibility of its appearing in Job; if not, there will be an understandable reluctance to postulate it in Job.

Two of the examples cited from Amarna are *ti-di-nu* in *EA* 71:5 and 86:4, two letters from Rib-Adda of Byblos: *ᵈAmana ilu ša šarri bēlika ti-di-nu bāštaka ina panī šarri bēlika*, "May Amon, the god of the king your lord, establish your power in the presence of the king your lord." I discussed this form in the *Journal of Cuneiform Studies* 5 (1951) 35, and argued that it is a jussive third plural, *tiddinū*. That it is a jus-

[1]The same forms were cited long ago and given the same analysis by E. Ebeling, *Beiträge zur Assyriologie* 8 (1910–12) 48. P. Dhorme, *Revue biblique* 22 (1913) 375 = *Recueil Édouard Dhorme* (Paris 1951), 416, cites one of them (*EA* 323:22) and adds *tiqbi* and *tidin* with the extremely annoying *passim*! As for *tid(d)in* all occurrences are found in the greeting formula "May Baᶜalat of Byblos establish your power"; there is not one case where a masculine subject is found. The only *tiqbi* references which could make one pause at all, are *taqbi* (*EA* 138:111) and *tiqbi* (138:44) where the subject is *ālu* "city"; but the explanation is clear, and Ebeling's Glossary (*EA* II 1444) rightly classifies the forms under 3 fem. sg., for *ālu* is regularly treated as fem. in these letters (cf. *balṭat āl Gubla* 68:21; *ennipšat āl Ṣumur* 84:12; the suffix *-ši*, not *-šu*, in *yilqiši* 90:12). In *Zeitschrift für die Alttestamentliche Wissenschaft* 60 (1944) 156–159, an article to which Father M. Dahood kindly referred me, A. Alt proposes three more examples of 3 masc. sg. **taqtul* in Punic, arguing on the basis of parallels that the form of votive inscriptions requires the third person. Confirmation of his proposal he finds in the Amarna letters and refers to the studies of Ebeling and Dhorme. However, J. Friedrich, *Phönizisch-Punische Grammatik* (Analecta Orientalia, 32; Rom 1951), 57–58, still adheres to the earlier interpretation of the forms in question as second person. But even if we admit the force of Alt's argument from literary form, which is considerable, a plural of majesty is possible (cf. n. 2), or if the forms really are 3 masc. sg., we must allow for later local developments (analogy, non-Semitic substratum). Certainly without much earlier examples from Canaanite the possible occurrences of 3 masc. sg. **taqtul* in Punic may not be used for the interpretation of problematic verbal forms in biblical Hebrew.

sive is, I believe, beyond question. In such a greeting formula a jussive is required (cf. Old Babylonian *liballiṭ, liballiṭū*, etc.), and the closely parallel use of the precative *liddin* in *EA* 102:6 removes any possibility of doubt on this score. As a matter of fact, Sarna himself translates *ti-di-nu* as a jussive. But if it is a jussive, it cannot be singular; it must be plural.[2] In over 250 examples of *yaqtulu* in the Byblian Amarna letters,[3] there is not a single instance of the form with jussive force; rather, usage conforms with what we know of *yaqtulu* from Arabic and its reflexes in the distinction in Hebrew between forms like *yāqûm* and *yāqōm*. The singular form postulated by Dr. Sarna would have to appear in the Byblian dialect as *tiddin* or *tiddina*.[4]

Another example is supposed to be found in *ti-ra-am* in *EA* 323:22 (Ascalon): *mār* ᵈ*šamaš ša ti-ra-am* ᵈ*šamaš*, "the son of Šamaš, whom Šamaš loves." This seems to be clear enough evidence until we recall the fluctuation in the gender of Hebrew *šemeš* and, above all, the fact that in both the South Arabic and Ugaritic pantheons the Sun is a goddess. Of course this was not true of the Sun in the Egyptian pantheon, but a lapse here, prompted by the religious background of the Canaanite scribe, is not in itself improbable,[5] and certainly far more probable than 3 masc. sg. *taqtul* unsupported by other evidence.

Only *ta*-A[Z-*r*]*a*-*ḫi* in *EA* 143:27 (Beirut) is left: *u anâku kīma* LÚ *ta*-A[Z-*r*]*a*-*ḫi šisē ša ša*[*rri b*]*ē*[*liy*]*a ebaššâku*. Dr. Sarna translates, "I am like a man who grooms (?) the horses of the king." First of all, it must be remarked that the Akkadian text does not have a relative pronoun. Of course the omission of the pronoun does not mean that the translation is wrong; the implied construction is known in both Akkadian and Hebrew. But without the pronoun Dr. Sarna's case is weakened considerably, for there is then no compelling reason for taking *taZraḫi* as a verb. Besides, if it is a verbal form, how are we to explain the final vowel? Certainly we may not appeal in the Amarna letters to the extremely rare examples of a comparable *i* in Old Babylonian.[6] Are we then to postulate another new morpheme and add **yaqtuli* to **yaqtulu* and **yaqtula*? And finally, since we do not know

[2]Plural of majesty; cf. the pl. suffix of *maṣṣartikunu* in *EA* 76:36 (not *maṣṣartika*).

[3]For a summary of the evidence see my remarks in G. Ernest Wright (ed.), *The Bible and the Ancient Near East* (New York 1961), 63–64 [above, Paper 11, pp. 213–214].

[4]Cf. the examples of *tiddin* referred to in n. 1; for the fluctuation between **yaqtul* and **yaqtula* see *Orientalia* 29 (1960) 19 [above, Paper 10, p. 195].

[5]Cf. A. Caquot, *Syria* 36 (1959) 90, n. 1.

[6]For a recent discussion see Thorkild Jacobsen, *Journal of Near Eastern Studies* 19 (1960) 110, n. 12.

what the word means,[7] it is surely perilous to draw from it any conclusions for Canaanite morphology. However with what we do know, *taZraḫi* should be analyzed as a noun in the genitive case and the preceding LÚ as merely a determinative ("like the ... of the horses").

To sum up: of the alleged four examples of 3 masc. sg. **taqtul* in the Amarna letters only one, *tirâm* in *EA* 323:22, stands up under closer grammatical analysis, and even here, as we have seen, there are not lacking strong reasons for being skeptical. We seriously doubt therefore whether Dr. Sarna has solved the Job passages.[8]

[7]In Middle Assyrian *ṣurruḫu* is used of horses in the sense "to keep warm" (*Chicago Assyrian Dictionary* 16 [Chicago 1962], 99); if this is the stem in *EA* 147:27, then the nominal formation would have to be *taprās* as a *nomen agentis* (W. von Soden, *Grundriss der akkadischen Grammatik* [Analecta Orientalia, 33; Rom 1952], 67). But a "warmer (of horses)" has little to recommend it.

[8]A very probable solution of תשכון in Job 18:15 has been offered by M. J. Dahood in *Biblica* 38 (1957) 312–314, who revocalizes consonantal *tškn* as *toškan* and unravels the very obscure מבלי־לו into "fire" (*mbl*) with the final *l* attached to the following verb as an asseverative. In 18:14 we should perhaps revocalize, *w^e^taṣ^c^îdûhû*, "they march him," the subject being either the indefinite plural (cf. e.g. *yimṣāʾûhû* in 20:8) or understood in context as the denizens of the underworld; on *t*-preformative with the plural see *JCS* 5 (1951) 33–35 [above, Paper 6] and *The Bible and the Ancient Near East*, 71, n. 108 [above, Paper 11, p. 213]. For תשורנו in 20:9 I have no suggestion unless *māqom*, like the plural regularly, was dialectically feminine.

13. Amarna Letters

Diplomatic correspondence of the 14th century B.C. discovered in 1887 at El-Amarna, a plain on the east bank of the Nile about 190 miles south of Cairo. The place now called El-Amarna was the site of the capital of Egypt, Akhet-Aton, during most of the reign of Akhnaton (Amenhotep IV); and the letters came from the diplomatic correspondence with Mesopotamia, Syria, and Asia Minor in the last years of Amenhotep III (1413–1377 B.C.) and in the reign of Amenhotep IV (1377–1358 B.C.). Perhaps a few letters may be dated to the reign of Smenkhere (1358 B.C.). In 1907, J. A. Knudtzon collated virtually all the letters, which had been divided among various museums and private collections, and together with some scribal exercises and a few Akkadian literary texts from El-Amarna, published them in transliteration and translation (abbreviated *EA*). Later about 20 more texts were found either in museums or through excavation, so that the number of the Amarna Letters now stands at 377.

Linguistic Features. The language of the letters is Akkadian and written in syllabic cuneiform script on clay tablets; exceptions are two letters written in a Hittite dialect (*EA* 31–32) and one very long letter in Hurrian (*EA* 24). At this period Akkadian was the lingua franca of the Near East, as it had been for several centuries. From a linguistic viewpoint the letters written from Palestine and the Phoenician coast are especially important. Written by scribes with little knowledge of Akkadian, they contain many Canaanitisms reflecting the scribes' native speech: glosses (e.g., Akkadian *nīru*, "yoke," is glossed *ḫullu* representing Hebrew *ᶜol*—the *ḫ* because Akkadian had no sign for West Semitic *ᶜayin*), hybrid forms partly Akkadian, partly Canaanite (e.g., *yuwaššira*, "let him send," is Akkadian *uwaššir* with Canaanite *y*-verbal preformative and *-a* suffix indicating a wish), and Canaanite syntax in sentence structure. For this reason, though written in Akkadian, the Amarna Letters are a valuable source for the Canaanite language, of which Biblical Hebrew was a dialect, in the 14th century B.C.

Historical Background. From *c.* 1450 B.C. all of Palestine and Syria were under Egyptian hegemony, while to the east, across the

Euphrates, lay the kingdom of Mitanni. This balance of power was destroyed in the Amarna period. A new power appeared on the international scene, the Hittites, who under Suppiluliuma (*c.* 1380–46) moved east against Mitanni and south into Syria, eventually forming a string of small vassal states. Another power also began to make itself felt; led by Assur-uballit I (*c.* 1363–28), Assyria shook off the Mitanni yoke and finally held what the Hittites failed to subject.

The Amarna Letters bear witness to these events and to Egyptian inaction. Neither Amenhotep III nor his successor, who was absorbed in a religious revolution, seems to have understood the gravity of the situation. Other interests, complacency born of almost a century of unquestioned power, perhaps doubts arising from the conflicting reports of vassals and corrupt Egyptian officials—these resulted in Egypt's loss of power in Syria and along the Phoenician coast and in political chaos in Palestine.

Correspondence with Major Powers. Only a small part of the letters is from or to major powers. In *EA* 17–29 Tuishrata of Mitanni writes to Amenhotep III, his widow Teye, and Amenhotep IV; relations are cordial, and the principal topic is Tuishrata's daughter as Amenhotep III's prospective wife. Behind the cordiality loom the Hittites, though they are mentioned only once to record an early Mitanni victory, of which a part of the booty is sent to Egypt (*EA* 17). Alliance through marriage is also the subject of the correspondence of Amenhotep III with Kadashman-Enlil of Babylon (*EA* 1–5), whose successor, Burnaburiash, is eager to continue the good relations (*EA* 6–11). Significantly, the latter complains of the presence of Assyrians at the Egyptian court and wants them sent away empty-handed. However, only two of the Amarna Letters come from Assyria (*EA* 15–16); they are written by Assur-uballit I and are to be dated to the end of the reign of Amenhotep IV. In *EA* 15 announcement is made of the sending of a treaty along with gifts. This desire to be leagued with Egypt undoubtedly reflects the Hittite menace in nearby Mitanni.

Correspondence with Vassal States. The remaining Amarna Letters, more than 300, are mostly from, or to, vassals. The letters from Syria and the Phoenician coast concern chiefly the efforts of Amurru, a small state in central Syria south of Kadesh, to expand through exploitation of Egyptian weakness and Hittite support. Its rulers, ᶜAbd-Ashirta (*EA* 60–64) and ᶜAziru (*EA* 156–161, 164–168), protest their loyalty, but the letters from their neighbors, especially those from Rib-Adda of

Byblos (*EA* 68–95, 102–138, 362 [= *RA* 19 (1922) 102–103]), reveal their attacks and eventual control of the coast as far as Beirut. Pleas for help and decisive intervention go unheeded; even the murder of a high Egyptian official leaves the court unmoved. As a result of this lethargy Amurru became a vassal of the Hittites along with other states to the north. By *c.* 1350 Hittite power extended south of Byblos and inland to the Syrian desert.

Even in nearby Palestine confusion reigned: the kinglets of Jerusalem, Sichem (Shechem), Mageddo (Megiddo), Lachish, and Gazer (Gezer) were at war with each other—plundering caravans, filling their letters with recriminations—or joined in uneasy alliance by the threat of a common enemy. The Egyptian yoke weighed heavily and unrest was deep. Exactions were severe; the fertile lands of Mageddo and Sharon, worked by Canaanites under *corvée*, were crown property and their produce was stored in royal granaries. Egyptian garrisons were to be fed and clothed, and troops passing northward were also to be supplied.

The population of Palestine, confined largely to the plains and low hills—the coastal plain, the Plain of Esdraelon, and the Jordan Valley—was small. W. F. Albright estimates it at around 200,000. The central mountain range, apart from a few centers like Hebron, Jerusalem, and Sichem, was largely unoccupied. Except in the extreme north, Transjordan was the home of seminomads. Ethnically, the population was very mixed. Biridiya of Mageddo and Intaruda of Achshaph (cf. also Arzaya, Yashdata, Rusmanya, etc.) bore Indo-Aryan names, while Abdi-Kheba of Jerusalem, in name at least, was "The Servant of Kheba," a Hurrian goddess. This was the Palestine that the Israelites entered a century later, and with this background much of the Biblical narrative, especially their initial confinement to the hill country, becomes clear.

Bibliography: Pritchard *ANET*^{2} 483–490, selected letters in translation and bibliography. E. F. Campbell, "The Amarna Letters and the Amarna Period," *Biblical Archaeologist* 23 (1960) 2–22. W. L. Moran, "The Hebrew Language in its North-West Semitic Background," *The Bible and the Ancient Near East*, ed. G. E. Wright (Garden City, N.Y. 1961) 54–72 [above, Paper 11]. P. Dhorme, *DBSuppl* 1:207–225.

14. The Death of ^{c}Abdi-Aširta

After a long period of consensus on their interpretation, two passages in *EA* 101[1] have recently become the subject of quite divergent views among historians of the Amarna Age in Syro-Palestine. We cite them with a translation which we shall try to defend in the course of this article:

1. *EA* 101:3–6

[a-nu-*m*]*a la-a ti-ri-bu-na*	[*No*]*w*, the ships of the army
GIŠ.MÁ.MEŠ LÚ.MEŠ *mi-ši a-na*	are not to enter
KUR *a-mur-ri ù da-ku*	the land of Amurru, for they have killed
^{m}ÌR-*a-ši-ir-ta*	^{c}Abdi-Aširta

2. *EA* 101:27–31

šu-ku-un 1 LÚ 1 LÚ *i-na lìb-bi*	Put one man in each
URU *ù la ya-di-en* GIŠ.MÁ	city, and let him not permit a ship
KUR *a-mu-ri ù da-ku*	of the land of Amurru (to enter), for they have killed
^{m}ÍR-*a-ši-ir-ta* LUGAL *eš-ta-kán-šu*	^{c}Abdi-Aširta. The king put him
UGU-*šu-nu ú-ul šu-nu*	over them, not they.

The consensus was that from these passages we learn (1) that ^{c}Abdi-Aširta met a violent death, (2) at the hands of the LÚ.MEŠ *mi-ši*.[2] It is

[1]Though its introduction is missing, this letter is generally considered to have been written by Rib-Addi of Byblos. His authorship is supported by the external evidence of script and the tablet's color and texture, and by a number of internal indications: Only the letters from Byblos mention the LÚ.MEŠ *mi-ši*, an argument already adduced by Edward F. Campbell, Jr.: *The Chronology of the Amarna Letters*, Baltimore, 1964, p. 78; concern for the ships of the Arvadites, also expressed in *EA* 105 (see below); efforts to involve Sidon and Beirut in an anti-Amurru policy, and cf. *EA* 118:26ff. It should be noted, however, that Albright: *CAH* II^{2} (ch. XX), p. 5, does not include *EA* 101 in his two groups of Rib-Addi letters (*EA* 68–96 and 102–138).

[2]So Knudtzon in his translation; Weber: *EA* II, 1198; J. de Koning: *Studiën over de El-Amarna brieven en het Oude Testament inzonderheid uit historisch oogpunt*, Delft, 1940, pp. 131, 394f.; T. Säve-Söderbergh: *The Navy of the Eighteenth Egyptian Dynasty*, Uppsala, 1946, pp. 64–67; and most recently, K. A. Kitchen, *Suppiluliuma and the Amarna Pharaohs, A Study in Relative Chronology*,

the first point which is now challenged; the second receives at least qualified acceptance in that it is held that the subject of *dakū* is the LÚ.MEŠ *mi-ši*.[3] In 1955 Cavaignac expressed the opinion that *ù dakū ᶜAbdi-Aširta* may not be translated as a statement of fact; rather, there is question in the text only of the intention of killing: 'que les vaisseaux de débarquement n'aillent pas faire des descentes en Amurru et tuer Abdiasirta,' '... et qu'il ne donne pas de vaisseaux pour l'Amurru et pour tuer Abdiasirta.'[4] Then in 1962 Helck stated that the reason ᶜAbdi-Aširta disappears from the correspondence of Rib-Addi is not his alleged death in *EA* 101, but his being captured by the Egyptians, an event referred to in other letters of Rib-Addi.[5] The translation we have proposed above of lines 3–6 he rejects on the grounds that it does not fit the tenor of a Rib-Addi letter. He calls attention to Tadmor's article on *dâku* (not only 'to kill', but also 'to smite, defeat'), and in its light translates: 'Aber die Schiffe des Heeres sind nicht nach Amurru gekommen und haben auch Abdi-Aširta nicht geschlangen.' In other words, from *EA* 101 we really learn nothing about what happened to ᶜAbdi-Aširta, but rather what did not happen to him. And finally, in 1964, when Klengel had occasion to review the literature on this letter, he grants that from it we learn of the end of ᶜAbdi-Aširta, but denies that the evidence permits us to decide whether ᶜAbdi-Aširta was murdered, died a natural death, or was captured.[6]

It will be the contention of this paper that (1) ᶜAbdi-Aširta met a violent death (with the earlier consensus), (2) but at the hands, not of the

---

Liverpool, 1962, pp. 27f.—T. O. Lambdin: *JCS* 7 (1953), pp. 75–77, has shown that (LÚ.MEŠ) *mi-ši* reflects Egyptian *mšᶜ*, 'army'.

[3]An exception is Lambdin, *ibid.*, who accepts the views presented in this paper, which were already briefly expressed in the writer's dissertation under Professor Albright, *A Syntactical Study of the Dialect of Byblos as Reflected in the Amarna Tablets* (Johns Hopkins Univ., 1950), pp. 162–163 [= pp. 112–113 in the present volume].

[4]E. Cavaignac: *Journal asiatique* 243 (1955), pp. 135–138, especially, p. 136.

[5]W. Helck: *Die Beziehungen Ägyptens zu Vorderasien im 3. und 2. Jahrtausend v. Chr.*, Wiesbaden, 1962, pp. 178 and 193f., n. 33. In support of his position Helck refers to the present writer's article in *Orientalia* NS 29 (1960), p. 4 [= p. 182 in the present volume], but notes the translation cited by Lambdin: *JCS* 7 (1953), p. 75. Klengel (see following note) even lists the writer with Helck as holding that ᶜAbdi-Aširta was not killed; this comes from a misunderstanding of our insistence that ᶜAbdi-Aširta was at some time captured by the Egyptians. On the relation between this event and ᶜAbdi-Aširta's murder, see below.

[6]H. Klengel: *Mitteilungen des Instituts für Orientforschung* 10 (1964), p. 63 and n. 29. The disjunction, we must admit, is logically somewhat puzzling.

LÚ.MEŠ *mi-ši*, but of his own people, 'the land of the Amurru' (against the still common opinion on the subject of *dakū*).

Pace Cavaignac, *ù dakū* not only may, but must be translated as a statement of fact. It should not be necessary to prove 'they (have) killed' may be so expressed, and not only by *idūkū*.[7] From the earliest Amarna studies it has been perfectly evident and universally accepted that the suffix-conjugation in the letters of Canaanite provenance is used very much like the Hebrew perfect, and most commonly for past narrative. Moreover, in over three hundred examples of the form in the letters from Byblos it is never used to express purpose, which, if a finite form of the verb is employed, is done by using *yaqtul(a)* or *yaqtulu*, depending on the syntactical situation.[8] Lastly, *ti-ri-bu-na* may not be translated as a jussive, which would require *ti-ri-bu*.[9] Because of these objections based on grammar, which additional arguments below will only confirm, Cavaignac's interpretation of the lines in question and the speculation built on it must be rejected.[10]

Against Helck's view that *EA* 101 tells us what did not happen to ᶜAbdi-Aširta it must first be urged that this letter is clearly written at the beginning of a new period in Rib-Addi's struggle with Amurru. Not very long after it was written his enemy is no longer ᶜAbdi-Aširta, but the latter's sons. For Weber was certainly right in connecting the complaint in *EA* 105:20–21 that the ships of the Arvadites have been allowed to leave Egypt, with the request in *EA* 101:15–18 that the ships of the Arvadites be seized.[11] Since, too, the ships hardly remained in Egypt for a very extended period, and Rib-Addi in *EA* 105 seems to speak of their departure from Egypt as a fairly recent event, the interval between *EA* 101 and *EA* 105 cannot have been very great. Yet when *EA* 105 was written ᶜAbdi-Aširta has disappeared; only his sons are active, cutting off access by land to Ṣumur (line 11).

[7]Cavaignac, *op. cit.* (above, n.4), actually writes *idukku*, but this is a present, not a preterite; he must mean *idūkū*.

[8]See *JCS* 5 (1951), pp. 33–34 [above, Paper 6, p. 160] and *Orientalia* NS 29 (1960), pp. 7–9, 11–13 [above, Paper 10, pp. 184–187, 188–190]. On the use of the suffix-conjugation in *EA* 74:27; 83:27; 123:35, see *ibid.*, p. 12., n. 1 [above, pp. 188–189, n. 34].

[9]Cf. *ti-la-ku* in line 34 (on the construction, see *JCS* 5 [1951], p. 34, n. 9 [above, Paper 6, p. 161, n. 9]) and the forms cited in *ibid.*, pp. 34–35 [above, pp. 161–163].

[10]Cavaignac ignores the evidence that *EA* 101 is a Rib-Addi letter and has it written by someone in sympathy with ᶜAbdi-Aširta.

[11]*EA* II, 1203.

Furthermore, the activity of all the other people mentioned in *EA* 101 falls in this same general period. The LÚ.MEŠ *mi-ši*, who are mentioned only in letters from Byblos, are attested in *EA* 101:4, 33; 105:27; 108:38; 110:48(?), 52; 111:21(?); 126:63. We have just seen when *EA* 105 was written, and to the same general period when ᶜAbdi-Aširta's sons have replaced him are to be ascribed *EA* 108 (see lines 10ff.), 110 (see line 44), and 126 (see lines 9ff., 64f.); *EA* 111 cannot be dated. In short, the army (*mi-ši*) is a factor in the Byblian political scene only when ᶜAbdi-Aširta's sons hold the power in Amurru. The only exception would be *EA* 101, if Helck is right and the letter implies that ᶜAbdi-Aširta is still alive.

Similarly, the Arvadites are mentioned in *EA* 101:13; 104:42(?);[12] 105:12,16,18; 149:59. The last letter is from Tyre and reports on the failure of Aziru, ᶜAbdi-Aširta's son, Zimredda of Sidon and the Arvadites to capture the city; on the date of *EA* 104, if pertinent here, see lines 7ff., and on 105 see above.

Finally, there is Haya (*EA* 101:2,19), who, if Knudtzon's restoration in *EA* 109:63 is correct, is mentioned in a letter which also notes the perfidy of the sons of ᶜAbdi-Aširta (lines 9ff.). He reappears in *EA* 112: 42, 48, according to which he was slipped into Ṣumur by night, and therefore during the blockade referred to in *EA* 105.

The people, therefore, involved in the events reported in *EA* 101 are always spoken of by Rib-Addi in the period when ᶜAbdi-Aširta himself is no longer a threat. To make *EA* 101 the lone exception runs against all the evidence. Furthermore, the implication that ᶜAbdi-Aširta is still alive is read into *EA* 101 by understanding the negative of the previous clause (*lā tīribūna*) with *dakū;* such a usage is unattested in any letter from Byblos or, so far as we know, in any Amarna letter. And finally, to anticipate some of our remarks below on the immediately following clause in lines 6–7, it admittedly makes sense to say that the army did not come to Amurru and did not kill ᶜAbdi-Aširta, 'weil sie keinen Proviant (o. ä.) hatten.'[13] However, as we shall see, the text actually says nothing about provisions, but 'since they had no wool(!),' and it makes little sense to say that the army did not kill ᶜAbdi-Aširta because they had no wool. In brief, we must accept Knudtzon's placement of the letter and agree with Klengel that *EA* 101 reports the end of ᶜAbdi-Aširta.

[12]Some doubt attaches to this occurrence; see Weber: *EA* II, 1202.
[13]This is Helck's translation of *EA* 101:6–7.

That this end was violent and not to be identified with the capture of ᶜAbdi-Aširta, mentioned elsewhere, seems clear from an examination of *dâku* in the Byblos letters. The verb does mean 'to smite' or the like, and not 'to kill,' in some Amarna letters (*EA* 140:26; 149:65; possibly 185:46; 245:14), and one of these is from Byblos (*EA* 140). However, this letter is not from Rib-Addi, and the object of the verb is 'lands'. In Rib-Addi's letters, in which the verb is relatively frequent,[14] the object is always a person and the meaning is always either demonstrably (most cases) or very probably 'to kill'; there is not one bit of evidence for 'to smite'.

The lexical argument is confirmed by two additional considerations. First, it seems most unlikely that ᶜAbdi-Aširta would never again be spoken of as alive had he simply become an Egyptian prisoner. Second, as we shall show, the subject of *dakū* in line 5 is 'the land of Amurru'. This immediately rules out identifying this event with the capture of ᶜAbdi-Aširta by the Egyptians. It is hardly more favorable to the meaning 'to smite, defeat' in this passage. Popular uprisings, which ᶜAbdi-Aširta himself had been so adept in inciting, did not end simply in a ruler's defeat. In brief, the evidence converges: ᶜAbdi-Aširta was murdered.

The murderers were not the LÚ.MEŠ *mi-ši* of line 4. Certainly the writing in lines 4–5 is ambiguous and the subject could be either LÚ.MEŠ *mi-ši* or *māt Amurri*; since the former is the subject of the previous verb (*tīribūna*) it has simply been assumed to be the subject of *dakū*. However, when *dakū* reappears in line 29 the LÚ.MEŠ *mi-ši* have not been mentioned for twenty-five lines and will not be mentioned for four more. Unless one makes the quite gratuitous assumption that here the writing is utterly inept, the subject cannot be LÚ.MEŠ *mi-ši*. But in line 29, just as in line 5, we again find *māt Amurri* immediately before the *ù dakū* clause. Moreover, *māt Amurri* is construed elsewhere in the Byblos letters with a plural form of the verb (*constructio ad sensum*).[15] And lastly, in the very next clause it is said that 'the king put him over them, not they', and 'they' are certainly the subject of *dakū*. Now of whom could it have been said that ᶜAbdi-Aširta was placed over them by the Pharaoh if not of the people of Amurru

[14] *EA* 73:27; 74:25; 75:26,33; 81:12,16(?); 85:26; 89:20; 104:34; 122:35; 123:14; 131:9,18,22,28; 132:45,50; 134:12; 138:39,40–41; 139:14,38; 362:69 = *RA* 19 (1922), p. 103.

[15] *EA* 73:12–14; 82:51.

and, in all probability, of them alone?[16] The logical subject, therefore, of *dakū* in line 29 is *māt Amurri*, and this clarifies the ambiguity of line 5, where of course the subject must be the same.

This is what the text says, and therefore Helck's objection from the tenor of Rib-Addi's letters cannot stand. *Contra factum non valet illatio!* But it fails, too, we believe, to grasp the situation. If ᶜAbdi-Aširta were alive at the time of *EA* 101, it would certainly be contrary to the tenor of a Rib-Addi letter to have him demanding strong reprisals against any opposition to his arch-enemy in Amurru. But at the time of *EA* 101 ᶜAbdi-Aširta is not alive; he is dead, and a dead enemy is no enemy. The enemy now are the people of Amurru and their supporters, the Arvadites. Rib-Addi is apparently aware that he must still count on the political ambitions of Amurru and consequently on their hostility. Hence his own hostility and his efforts to denigrate them. They are presented, not as having rid him of an old nemesis, but as rebels whose insurrection is really against the Pharaoh himself, for it was he who had constituted ᶜAbdi-Aširta the legitimate ruler of Amurru. This is no *volte face*; Rib-Addi is being perfectly consistent with his policy of the past and its single goal—survival.

To punish the murderers he seems to ask that they be boycotted. Thus in lines 32–35 he writes: *ia-aq-bi* LUGAL *a-na* 3 URU.MEŠ *ù* GIŠ.MÁ LÚ.MEŠ *mi-ši ù la-a ti-la-ku a-na* KUR *a-mur-ri* 'Let the king tell the three cities and the ship(s) of the army not to go to the land of Amurru.' These lines also indicate how we are to understand *la-a ti-ri-bu-na* in line 3 (cited above). According to the general pattern of the use of the indicative (*yaqtulu*) in the Byblos letters, the phrase may mean either 'they did not enter (repeatedly),' or 'they are not entering/do not enter,' or 'they will not enter' (either as a statement of fact or as an emphatic prohibition); it should not mean 'they did not enter' (narrative punctive preterite).[17] In view of lines 32–35 it is clearly the emphatic prohibition which is to be preferred. Furthermore, just as ships are not to go to Amurru ports, so too ships from there are not to be granted entrance to Ṣumur(?),[18] Sidon and Beirut (lines 27ff., cited

[16]Helck: *Beziehungen* (above, n. 5), pp. 176, 261, sees this, but does not see the implications for the subject of *dakū*; see also Klengel, *op. cit.* (above, n. 6), p. 62.

[17]See for the present, *The Bible and the Ancient Near East* (ed. G. Ernest Wright), Garden City, 1961, p. 63 [above, Paper 11, pp. 213–214].

[18]The text seems to have *āl šarri* (on the reading see Knudtzon *ad loc.*). In context it is hard to see what 'the king's city' can be except the administrative center of Ṣumur.

above). The last two cities are probably singled out because they have been allies of ᶜAbdi-Aširta (*EA* 83: 24–26)[19] and are therefore suspected of pro-Amurru sympathies; events will soon prove how well founded these suspicions are (*EA* 118: 26ff.). Ṣumur, if it is referred to, as the most important coastal city in Amurru, would of course have a decisive role in a boycott, which is meant to keep Amurru weak economically and thereby much less dangerous politically.

We turn now to the problem of ᶜAbdi-Aširta's capture by the Egyptians, which has been considered a difficulty for our interpretation of *EA* 101.[20] We may begin by observing that within the relative chronology of events we can narrow down the time in which ᶜAbdi-Aširta was captured to a fairly short period. Rib-Addi never speaks of the incident prior to ᶜAbdi-Aširta's death. He does not mention it when his enemy is gradually moving in on Ṣumur and finally takes it, and yet under the circumstances, if the Egyptians had by this time already intervened in the past and seized the Amurru leader, the prince of Byblos would certainly not have failed to appeal to this rare example of Egyptian action in his favor and to urge, as he later did, its being imitated. The argument from silence is here a strong one, and we must put the capture of ᶜAbdi-Aširta some time after he occupied Ṣumur. But once he was taken, events seem to have moved very swiftly. This seems the only possible inference from the silence of Rib-Addi about both the prisoner, if ᶜAbdi-Aširta was in fact interned, and his subsequent release, which could hardly have failed to elicit a strong protest from Byblos if ᶜAbdi-Aširta's freedom had lasted very long. We can only conclude that it was cut short by his murder. In the Byblos correspondence we pass, somewhat abruptly and unexpectedly, from an ᶜAbdi-Aširta alive and in possession of Ṣumur to a dead ᶜAbdi-Aširta with the city once again in Egyptian control.

This of course suggests that ᶜAbdi-Aširta was taken when the city fell. A connection between the two events seems all the more likely in view of the fact that the intervention of Egyptian arms in the affairs of Syro-Palestine was at the time a very great rarity, and yet it is to such

[19]We accept Helck's identification, *Beziehungen* (above, n. 5), pp. 178 and 193, n. 29, of Yapaᶜ-Addi as the prince of Beirut; he is also followed by Campbell: *Chronology* (above, n. 1), p. 92, n. 59.

[20]The passages are *EA* 108:28ff.; 117:24ff.; 132:12ff.; 362:15ff. (*RA* 19, 102). Reconciling the capture with the murder of *EA* 101 is called 'an acute problem' by Campbell: *Chronology* (above, n. 1) p. 87, n. 50.

intervention that the capture of both ᶜAbdi-Aširta and Ṣumur (*EA* 138: 31–34) is attributed. It is easier to assume only one intervention.

There is also a very striking similarity in the phrasing and structure of the passages in which Rib-Addi recalls the two events:

a. Message sent—'I wrote' (*aštapar, EA* 108, 117, 132; *ašpur, EA* 138, 362 [on the taking of Ṣumur]);
b. Destination—'to thy father' (*EA* 108, 132), 'to the palace' (*EA* 117), 'to the king my lord' (EA 138); *EA* 362 omits;
c. Message cited—only *EA* 132;
d. Favorable hearing—only *EA* 108;
e. Troops sent—'he sent archers' (*EA* 108); 'the king sent a large host' (EA 117); 'the archers came forth' (*tu-ṣa, EA* 362); 'a host came forth' (*tu-ṣa, EA* 138);[21]
f. Success of mission—'did he not take ᶜAbdi-Aširta for [himself]?' (*EA* 108); 'did he not take ᶜAbdi-Aširta together with his possessions?' (*EA* 117, and with minor variations, *EA* 132); 'and they took their [the sons of ᶜAbdi-Aširta] father' (*EA* 362);[22] 'and it took the city of Ṣumur' (*EA* 138).

In the last part, it should be noted, the verb *leqû* is used in all five passages. Note, too, that in *EA* 132 and *EA* 362, just as in *EA* 138, transition to the present is marked by the phrase *anumma inanna*.

And finally, there is what immediately follows 'and it took the city of Ṣumur' in *EA* 138: *ù* (end of line 33) [x-x-x-(x)]-x-*ti ù a*-[*nu-m*]*a i-na-an-na*. The transition-marker *anumma inanna* shows that the first part of the line belongs with what goes before on the capture of Ṣumur. After the break at the beginning of the line, what we have transliterated by x is either *ni* or *ir*; Knudtzon opted for the former, but in view of all that we have seen, plus the fact that ᶜAbdi-Aširta has just been mentioned in line 29, we can hardly hesitate to read [ᵐÌR-*a-ši*]-*ir-ti* and translate: 'it came forth and took the city of Ṣumur and ᶜAbdi-Aširti.'[23]

So ᶜAbdi-Aširta was captured at the fall of Ṣumur. However, as we have seen, he was released either immediately or not long afterwards. That he was released follows from *EA* 101 which puts him back among

21 On ERÍN.MEŠ construed as fem. sg., see the remarks in *JCS* 2 (1948), pp. 245–246 [above, Paper 2, p. 137].

22 On this passage and the interpretation of ᵐ*a-ba-šu-nu*, see *Orientalia* NS 29 (1960), p. 4, n. 5 [above, Paper 10, p. 182, n. 13].

23 The fact that in line 29 the name is written ᵐÌR-*aš-ra-ti* (also 50,102,116) is no difficulty; the spelling ᵐÌR-*a-ši-ir-ti* is found in line 72.

his people at the time of this death (see, too, below on the immediate occasion of the murder). This inference should hardly be questioned simply because we cannot explain why the Egyptians should have freed someone whose loyalty was at best questionable. They may have felt that the popular unrest which he had so successfully exploited would be even more dangerous if he were removed from the scene.[24] Possibly, too, they thought he would prove more tractable than his sons who were waiting in the wings to succeed him. And of course he may simply have bought his freedom with a bribe.[25]

In any case, his freedom was shortlived. The fact that he was dispatched so promptly certainly argues that the loss of Ṣumur had gravely undermined his authority. Perhaps so decisive a setback to his plans and promises was taken as evidence that the charism of the past had abandoned him. The ease, too, with which his sons seem to have succeeded him makes one suspect that they too felt it was time for younger and more vigorous leadership.

A partial motive for the crime is, as a matter of fact, provided by Rib-Addi himself in *EA* 101:6–10: *i-nu-ma ia-nu* SÍG *a-na ša-šu-nu ù ia-nu* GADA ZA.GÌN NA_4.MAR\BU-BU-*mar a-na ša-šu a-na na-da-ni x-ú*-ZA *a-na* KUR *mi-ta-na*, '(they have killed ᶜAbdi-Aširta) since they had no wool, and he had no *garment(s)* of blue-purple (or) of MAR-stone (*color* called) *bubumar* (or *pupumar*) to *sell* as ? to the land of Mitanni.' The passage remains somewhat obscure, and we can offer only the following brief commentary:

Line 7, read SÍG (*šipātu*), not KIN (Knudtzon). On Knudtzon's own admission[26] the sign is indistinguishable from that in *EA* 22 i 46 and ii 38 where with Goetze[27] we must read SÍG(!) GAN.ME.TA, a Hurrianized form (TA for DA) of the logogram for *nabāsu*.

Line 8, GADA ZA.GÌN is hardly *kitû ebbu* (Knudtzon), 'pure linen', for we should not ascribe to the Byblos scribe's very limited lexical knowledge so rare a logogram as ZA.GÌN = *ebbu*. We must rather assume ZA.GÌN = *uqnû*. However, rather than GADA = *kitû* we prefer

[24] See M. Liverani: *Revista degli Studi Orientali* 40 (1965), pp. 267–277, and *Rivista Storica Italiana* 77 (1965), pp. 315–336.

[25] On the venality of Egyptian officials at the time, see Albright: *CAH* II² (ch. XX), p. 9.

[26] *Beiträge zur Assyriologie* ... 4 (1902), pp. 413–414, where he also admits the difficulty of reading KIN in our passage.

[27] A. Goetze: *JCS* 10 (1956), p. 34, n. 19; also *CAD* Ṣ, p. 250 (*ṣuppuru*).

GADA = *malbašu* (*nalbašu*), for (1) dyed linen is not attested in any Akkadian text, and (2) the second equation makes the passage more coherent: The people could not furnish wool (the dyeing of which is so frequently attested) and as a result ^{c}Abdi-Aširta could not have the finished product. GADA is glossed *malbašu* in an Amarna letter from Egypt.[28]

The MAR-stone and its gloss remain unexplained. We propose that they refer to a color (red-purple?) on the basis of context; NA_4, even though the stone as such is not meant, is not a serious difficulty for this proposal.

Line 10, Knudtzon read UŠ *ú-ṣa*, but collation does not support this reading and it yields no sense.[29] The doubtful sign we cannot identify. Since the word in question is uncertain, it cannot help in resolving the ambiguity of the infinitive *nadāni* (line 9), of which it seems to be the object. We prefer 'to sell' rather than 'to give', with the latter's implications of some sort of tribute, since inability to meet the exactions of a foreign power does not seem the sort of thing which would stir up rebellion in Amurru.[30] An economic motive seems more plausible, and would fit nicely with the boycott of the country requested by Rib-Addi.

Why were the people without wool? Had their flocks been confiscated or slaughtered by the Egyptians when Ṣumur was taken (cf. 'together with his possessions' in *EA* 117 and 132)? Was this why ^{c}Abdi-Aširta was held responsible for the shortage, which also left him without goods to market? These are some of the questions which we are still unable to answer about the death of ^{c}Abdi-Aširta. We only hope to have answered the important ones of when he was captured, how he died, and who was responsible, according to the report of Rib-Addi.

[28] G. Dossin: *RA* 31 (1934), 127:9; on GADA and TÚG.GADA at Ugarit see Dietrich-Loretz: *WO* 3/3 (1966), pp. 224–225.

[29] Dr. Edmond Sollberger kindly collated the text for us. The sign is 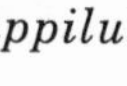 .

[30] Certainly the passage should not be cited as 'one more slight evidence in favour of a continued Egypto-Mitannian alliance' (Kitchen: *Suppiluliuma*, [above, n. 2], p. 28).

15. Tell El-Amarna Letters

TELL EL-AMARNA LETTERS, a collection of cuneiform tablets named after al-ᶜAmārna, a plain on the east bank of the Nile about 190 mi. (304 km.) S. of Cairo, in the territory of the Beni-ᶜAmrān, or ᶜAmārna, tribe. (Tell ᶜAmārna, or Tell el-ᶜAmārna, is a popular but not native designation of the ancient city mound or tell on this plain, the local people referring to it merely as et-Tell, "the tell.") This was the site of the Egyptian capital, Akhetaten, for about 15 years around the middle of the 14th century B.C.E.: here, in 1887, through the chance discovery of a peasant, a part of the diplomatic correspondence in the royal archives was unearthed. The clandestine explorations of the natives which followed, and the later scientific excavations (1889–92, 1912–14, 1921–22, 1926–36), yielded about 355 letters—some might be better classified as lists (of gifts)—besides more than 20 other cuneiform documents (scribal exercises, vocabularies, mythological and epical texts). The entire Amarna (cuneiform) corpus numbers 379 tablets. Though incomplete and lacking nos. 359–379, the standard edition, with transliteration of the cuneiform and a German translation, remains that of the Norwegian scholar J. A. Knudtzon, *Die el-Amarna Tafeln* (1915 = EA; for nos. 359–379 and other translations, see bibl.).

With only three exceptions (EA 24, Hurrian; EA 31 and 32, Hittite), the letters are all written in Akkadian, the lingua franca of the Ancient Near East in the second millennium B.C.E. In general, the language belongs to the "peripheral Akkadian" found at Nuzi, Alalakh, Ugarit, etc. Eloquent and moving as it may be at times, it lacks all elegance: it is awkward, often barbarous, betraying the scribes' ignorance not only of Akkadian but of their own native speech. This is especially true of the letters from Phoenicia and Palestine, and for this reason they are one of the most important sources for the early Canaanite language (and therefore for the background of biblical Hebrew). From the glosses to Akkadian words, the non-Akkadian morphemes, the non-Akkadian use of morphemes common to the two languages, and the syntax in these letters, it is possible to reconstruct much of the Canaanite grammar in this period.

The Amarna letters are also an invaluable historical source. Together with contemporary Ugaritic and Hittite documents and other

Egyptian records, they make the two decades or so which they cover the best known in the early history of Syria and Palestine. They span, in absolute dates, around 1385/1375–1355 B.C.E.: about the last decade of the reign of Amenophis III, the 17-year reign of Amenophis IV, and the three or four years before Tutankhaten (Tutankhamun), to whom EA 9 is addressed, abandoned the capital. (The difference of a decade in estimating the period is due to the still very mooted question of the co-regency of Amenophis IV with his father and predecessor; according as one accepts or denies a co-regency, the chronology of the Amarna letters must be lowered or raised.) Some (at least nine) of the letters, which are probably copies of the originals, have a pharaoh as author; the rest were written outside Egypt, and, with few exceptions, are addressed to the pharaoh or, less commonly, to a high Egyptian official at court. The correspondents are the kings of major states (Babylonia, Assyria, Mitanni in northern Mesopotamia, Ḫatti and Arzawa in Anatolia, Cyprus) and Egyptian vassals in Syria and Palestine. The letters (41) to and from the larger powers are in striking contrast with the vassals' correspondence, and hardly hint at the political situation which motivates so many of them. According to the custom of independent nations at peace, their majesties exchange messages of mutual friendship, which are carried by their emissaries and accompanied by gifts; often their principal concern is the discussion and working out of marriages, a conventional bond of international amity. Were it not for the vassals' letters and other contemporary sources it would be impossible to measure the real significance of the efforts of Tushratta of Mitanni to re-establish diplomatic relations with Amenophis III (EA 17) and to maintain them with his successor (EA 26); of his passing reference to a victory over the Hittites (EA 17); of the presence of Assyrians at the Egyptian court (EA 15–16), with its implications of rising Assyrian power (cf. EA 9:31–35) and Mitannian weakness: of the reported request of the Canaanites for Babylonian support in a rebellion against Egypt (EA 9), etc. The general impression these letters give is one of legendary Egyptian wealth in an era of relative peace and political stability.

This impression is dispelled by the remaining Amarna letters. The vassals from Tyre across to Damascus and northward were caught, directly or indirectly, in the struggle of the Mitannians to defend their control of northern Syria and even their own independence, and of the Egyptians to maintain their rule in the rest of Syria, against their common enemy, the resurgent Hittites under Suppiluliuma. Though their letters to the pharaoh are all filled with protests of unswerving loyalty, it is evident from the accusations against their fellow vassals that many of them were exploiting the situation to secure and expand their own power while toadying to both sides and avoiding for as long as possible an irrevocable commitment to one or the other. Most prominent in this group of letters, and most successful in this game of intrigue, sedition, and popular and palace revolts, were Abdi-ashirta and his sons, particularly Aziru, who made of Amurru an important minor state in central Syria east of the Orontes. The almost 70 letters of Rib-Adda of Byblos are a long, increasingly nervous denunciation of their advances along the coast and of Egyptian inaction. The latter is probably to be attributed, in part at least, to the tendency of the vassals' accusations to cancel each other out; but it is also likely that the court felt Egyptian interests would be safeguarded best by a strong Amurru as a buffer against the Hittite thrust. Events proved Rib-Adda right: like so many of his neighbors (Ugarit, Kadesh, etc.), Aziru became a Hittite vassal.

In Palestine the situation reflected by the vassals' letters, if less dire in its consequences for Egyptian rule, was not less chaotic. The letters reflect the same rivalries of the local rulers, the same charges against one another of perfidy, and the same signs of deep popular unrest. These petty kings are constantly at war with one another, plundering and seizing villages, at times forming small coalitions against a common enemy, which soon break up, regroup, and exchange the roles of enemies and allies. In central Palestine, in the struggles involving Gezer, Megiddo, Taanach, Acre, Jerusalem, Lachish, and (perhaps) Hebron, the main instigators were the rulers of Shechem, Labʾayu and his sons, who in a movement comparable to that in contemporary Amurru, attempted to expand their city-state into a territorial state, with one important objective being the possession of the fertile Plain of Esdraelon. The local Egyptian administration, when not corrupt and supporting treason, was apparently really concerned only with the payment of tribute and with a few other Egyptian interests like the provisions for troops moving northward, and this policy seems to have had the court's approval.

Bibliography

EXCAVATIONS: Wm. F. Petrie, *Tell el-Amarna* (1894); L. Borchardt, in: *Mitteilungen der deutschen orientalischen Gesellschaft*, 46 (1911), 1–32; 50 (1912), 1–40; 52 (1913), 1–55; 55 (1914), 3–39; 57 (1917), 1–32; T. E. Peet and C. L. Wooley, *The City of Akhenaten*, 1 (1923); D. D. S. Pendelbury et al., *The City of Akhenaten*, 1 (1923); B. Porter and L. B. Moss, *Topographical Bibliography of Ancient Egyptian Hieroglyphic Texts, Reliefs, and Paintings* ... (1934), 192–239; H. Kees, *Ancient Egypt* (1961), 288ff.

PRIMARY PUBLICATIONS AND COLLECTIONS: H. Winckler and F. M. Abel, *Der Thontafelfund von el Amarna*, 1–3 (1889–90); C. Bezold and E. A. W. Budge (eds.), *The Tell el-Amarna Tablets in the British Museum* (1892); O. Schroeder, *Die Tontafeln von El-Amarna* (1915); idem, in: *OLZ*, 20 (1917), 105–6; F. Thureau-Dangin, in: *RA*, 19 (1922), 91–108; P. Dhorme, in: *RB*, 33 (1924), 5–32; G. Dossin, in: *RA*, 31 (1934), 125–36; S. A. B. Mercer, *The Tell el-Amarna Tablets*, 1–2 (1939); C. H. Gordon, in: *Orientalia*, 16 (1947), 1–21; A. R. Millard, in: *PEQ* (1965), 140–3; A. F. Rainey, *El Amarna Tablets* (1970), 359–79; R. Borger, *Handbuch der Keilschriftliteratur* (1967), 237–40; W. Reidel, *Untersuchungen zu den Tell el-Amarna Briefen*, 1–2 (1920); F. Bilabel, *Geschichte Vorderasiens und Aegyptiens vom 16–11 Jahrhunderten* ... (1927); Maisler, *Untersuchungen zur alten Geschichte und Ethnographie Syriens und Palästinas* (1930), 43–46; idem, in: *JPOS*, 9 (1929), 80–87; W. F. Albright, in: *JEA*, 23 (1937), 190–203; idem, in: *BASOR*, 87 (1942), 32–38; 89 (1943), 7–17; 104 (1946), 25–26; idem, in: *JNES*, 5 (1946), 5–25; idem, in: Pritchard, *ANET*^{3}, 483–90; idem, in: *CAH*^{2}, 2 (1966), ch. 20 (incl. bibl.); W. von Soden, in: *Orientalia*, 21 (1952), 426–34; Y. Aharoni, in: *IEJ*, 3 (1953), 153–61; Aharoni, *Land of the Bible* (1967), 87, 157–64; idem, in: *VT*, 19 (1969), 137–45; A. Alt, *Kleine Schriften*, 3 (1959), 158–75; E. F. Campbell, in: *Biblical Archaeologist*, 23 (1960), 2–22; idem, in: G. E. Wright (ed.), *Shechem* (1965), 191–207; D. O. Edzard, in: *Journal of Economic and Social History of the Orient*, 3 (1960), 38–55; M. Liverani, *Storia di Ugarit* (1962), 18–30; idem, in: *Revista degli studi Orientali*, 40 (1965), 267–77; idem, in: *RA*, 61 (1967), 1–18; Ph. H. J. Houwink Ten Cate, in: *Babylonian and Oriental Record*, 20 (1963), 270–76; M. C. Astour, in: *For Max Weinreich* (1964), 7–17; H. Klengel, in: *MIO*, 10 (1964), 57–83; P. Artzi, in *RA*, 58 (1964), 159–66; idem, in: *JNES*, 27 (1968), 63–71; idem, in: *Bar-Ilan Decennary Volume*, 2 (1969); idem, in: *Proceedings of the 27th International Congress of Orientalists* (1969); A. Goetze, in: *CAH*^{2}, 2 (1965), ch. 17; H. Klengel, *Geschichte Syriens*, 1–2 (1965–68); A. F. Rainey, *Christian News from Israel*, 2 (1966), 30–38; 3 (1966), 23–24; idem, in *IEJ*, 18 (1968), 1–14.

LINGUISTIC STUDIES: F-M. Th. Böhl, *Die Sprache der El-Amarna Briefe* (1910); E. Ebeling, *Das Verbum der El-Amarna Briefe* (1910); E. Dhorme, in: *RB*, 10 (1913), 369–93; 11 (1914), 37–59, 344ff.; O. Schroeder, in: *OLZ*, 18 (1915), 105–6; S. Smith and C. J. Godel, in: *JEA*, 11 (1925), 230–40; J. Friedrich, *Kleinasiatische Sprachdenkmäler* (1932), 8–32; W. F. Albright, in: *BASOR*, 86 (1942), 28–31; idem and W. L. Moran, in: *JCS*, 4 (1950), 163ff. [above, Paper 4]; B. Landsberger, in: *JCS*, 8 (1954), 55–61; W. L. Moran, in: *Orientalia*, 29 (1960), 1–19 [above, Paper 10]; idem, in: G. E. Wright (ed.), *The Bible and the Ancient Near East* (1961), 54–72 [above, Paper 11]; idem, in: *Eretz Israel*, 9 (1969), 94–99 [above, Paper 14]; R. Youngblood, in: *BASOR*, 168 (1962), 24–27; E. Salonen, *Die Gruss- und Höflichkeitsformeln in babylonisch-assyrischen Briefen* (1967), 61–70; P. Artzi, in: *Bar-Ilan*, 1 (1963), 27–57; idem, in: *JNES*, 28 (1969), 261ff.

CHRONOLOGY: K. A. Kitchen, *Suppiluliuma and the Amarna Pharaohs* (1962); E. F. Campbell, Jr., *The Chronology of the Amarna Letters* (1963); D. B. Redford, *History and Chronology of the Eighteenth Dynasty of Egypt* (1967).

STUDIES ON THE HISTORICAL, POLITICAL, GEOGRAPHICAL BACKGROUND: B. Maisler, *Toledot Ereẓ Yisrael* (1938), 125–52; H. Reviv, in: *Bulletin of the Israel Exploration Society*, 27 (1963), 270–5; P. Artzi, in: *Eretz Israel*, 9 (1969), 22–28; Z. Kalai and H. Tadmor, *ibid.*, 138–47.

16. The Dual Personal Pronouns in Western Peripheral Akkadian

It has long been recognized that Western Peripheral Akkadian (WPA) is like a palimpsest, a mélange of *nova et vetera* in which the origin of some features, long abandoned in the contemporary centers of Assyria and Babylonia, must be dated as early as the Old Akkadian or Ur III periods. So far, however, the most ancient survivals have belonged to the writing-systems (sign-forms, logograms, syllabary), and nothing of comparable antiquity has been pointed out in the various dialects.[1] Here the earliest level to appear has been Old Babylonian.[2]

In the light of the important article by Robert M. Whiting, Jr., "The Dual Personal Pronouns in Akkadian," an even earlier level now emerges.[3] In this study Whiting not only demonstrates the existence in OAkk, OA, and very early OB, of dual personal pronouns,[4] he also sends anyone familiar with WPA back to his sources, for two of the ancient dual forms are well attested there:

-kunī	1.	*ana muḫḫīkunī* (*Ugar.* V No. 54:21);
	2.	*ina bi*[*rī*]*kunī* (*EA* 34:33, Alašia);
	3.	*berīkunī* (*EA* 113:18; 116:33, Byblos);
-šunī	4.	*pīšunī* (*EA* 1:86, Egypt);
	5.	*ana bītīšunī* (*EA* 245:45, Megiddo);

[1]On sign-forms and logograms, see E. Forrer, ***BoTU*** I (*WVDOG* 41); A. Goetze, *ZA* 40 (1931) 65ff. (correct according to ***MSL*** VIII/1, 21, ad 167); B. Landsberger-H. G. Güterbock, *AfO* 12 (1937–39) 55–57. On the syllabary, F. Thureau-Dangin, *Le Syllabaire Accadien*, iv-v; A. Goetze, ***Language*** 14 (1938) 134–137; ***JCS*** 4 (1950) 225ff.; E. Speiser, ***Introduction to Hurrian***, 13ff.; *AS*², xxxv–xxxvii. Th. V. Gamkrelidze's article on the origin of the Akkado-Hittite Syllabary, ***ArOr*** 29 (1961) 406–418, is also to be noted, but it must be remarked that his arguments for a North Syrian origin of the Akkado-Hittite syllabary are largely vitiated by his failure to distinguish at Alalakh between Levels IV and VII. Most of the evidence he cites is from Level IV, but he interprets it as if it came from Level VII.

[2]The existence of this level has been recognized, but its nature and extent are still not clearly defined. This we shall undertake in another study.

[3]*JNES* 31 (1972) 331–337.

[4]The forms attested are: *šunīti* (indep. oblique), *-kunī* and *-šunī* (noun suff.), *-šunīšim* and *-šunī(ti)* (vb. suff., dat. and acc., resp.).

6. *kaspīšunī* (*EA* 246 rev. 7, Megiddo);
7. *pānīšunī* (*EA* 250:6, south Palestine);
8. *abūšu*[*nī*] (ibid.:8);
9. *ana muḫḫīšunī* (ibid.:33);
10. *ina libbīšunī* (ibid.:34);
11. *i*[*t*]*t*[*īš*]*unī* (ibid.:38);
12. *ippalšunī* (ibid.:19,48);
13. *i̯addinšunī* (*EA* 197:11,12, Damascus region);

šunī 14. *šunīma* (*EA* 366:24, south Palestine—used as indep.).

Examination of the seventeen forms in context reveals that eleven have clear dual antecedents (No. 1, 5, 6, 7, 8, 9, 10, 11, 12bis, 14), four may be so interpreted (Nos. 2–3bis, 4), and only two present obvious difficulties (No. 13bis). To begin with the clearest cases:

No. 5 *ù* PN *i̯ú-ta-šar* PN_2 *ù* PN *i̯ú-ta-šar* PN_3 *a-na* É-*šu-ni*, "Surata let Labᵓayu go, and Surata let Baᶜl-*me-ḫir*[5] go, to their house(s)."

No. 6 *ù a-nu-um-ma* 2 DUMU[MEŠ] PN *te-ed-*[*di*]*-na* KÙ.BABBAR. MEŠ-*šu-ni a-na* LÚ.MEŠ.SA.GAZ, "And now the two sons of Labᵓayu have given their money to the ᶜApiru."

Nos. 7–12, all from the same letter, also have as their antecedent the two sons of Labᵓayu, No. 7 ... *tu-ur-ri-ṣú-m*[*e*] 2 DUMU LÚ *ar-ni* LUGA[L *b*]*e-lí-ia* 2 DUMU PN *pa-ni-šu-ni a-na ḫal-lí-iq* KUR LUGA[L]-*ri* EN-*ia* EGIR-*ki ša ḫu-lí-*[*iq*] ^{lú}*a-bu-šu-*[*ni*], "... the two rebels against the king, my lord, the two sons of Labᵓayu, have made their purpose the destruction of the land of the king, my lord, over and above what[6] their father destroyed."

No. 12, twice after speeches of Labᵓayu's two sons who are constantly urging the correspondent to support their rebellion, there follows: *ù ip-pal-šu-ni*, "but I answer them."

No. 11 ... *a-na ḫal-lí-i*[*q*] EGIR-*k*[*i-t*]*i* KU[R] L[UGAL E]N-[*i*]*a i*[*t*]-*t*[*i-š*]*u-ni*, "... to destroy the rest[7] of the land of my king, my lord, with

[5] On this personage, see P. Artzi, *JNES* 27 (1968) 165, n. 13.

[6] This rendering of *arki ša*, instead of "after," not only avoids having Labᵓayu's sons destroy the same territory as their father, but is supported by the use of *arki* in *EA* 99:20 ("May the king, your lord, say to you, 'This is good!'; (i.e.) what you gave as a present to the king along with your daughter" [*arki mārtīka*]). See also the following note.—To our knowledge there is no evidence to support Albright's rendering (*ANET* 485–486) of *ḫulliq* in this letter by "died."

[7] *a-ṣí-it* ^{uzu}ZI PN *a-na* [*šu*]*-ri-ib* 2 DUMU PN_2 [*i*]-*n*[*a*] GN *a-n*[*a*] *ḫal-lí-i*[*q*] EGIR-*ki-ti* KU[R] L[UGAL E]N-[*i*]*a i*[*t*]-*t*[*i-š*]*u-ni* [E]GIR-*ki ša ḫu-lí-*[*i*]*q* PN *ù* PN_2

the assistance of the two of them."

Nos. 9–10. Though the passage is damaged, there can be little doubt that reference is made to Lab^ʾayu's two sons.

No. 14 *ù* PN LÚ URU *Ak-ka ù* PN LÚ URU *Ak-ša-pa šu-ni-ma en-ni-ri-ru* / *na-aZ-a-qú i-na* 50 gišGIGIR.ḪI.A *a-na mu-ḫi-ia*, "Surata, the ruler of Akka, and Endaruta, the ruler of Akšapa, the two of them came to my help/were called to my help,[8] with fifty chariots." Whether indep. *šunī* reflects Akk. usage of any period, or is simply a provincial aberration for postulated **šunā*, is impossible to say, and in the present discussion is a question of secondary interest. If it is a solecism, it is certainly an extension of suff. *-šunī*, motivated perhaps by the analogy *-šunu* (suff.) : *šunu* (indep.) :: *-šunī* (suff.) : x = *šunī* (indep.).

No. 1 *ana* PN *bēlīi̯a ana* PN_2 *bēltii̯a qibīma um*<*ma*> PN_3 *ardi lū šulmu ana* [*mu*]*ḫ-ḫi-ku-ni*, "Say to Rap^ʾanu, my lord, (and) to Bišišaya, my lady: The wo<rd> of Patunu, (your) servant. Greetings to both of you." From *liṣṣurūkunu* two lines below one may not conclude that *-kunī* is simply a lapse for *-kunu*. Against such a view are both the other evidence for the survival of dual pers. pros. in WPA and the difficulty of assuming that the scribe lapsed precisely where the antecedent is a dual.

No. 3 is an old crux.[9] It has been taken to mean "between us," i.e., Rib-Addi and his rival litigant, Yapaᶜ-Adda. This certainly makes perfect sense in the context, but it also leaves the apparent 1 pl. suff. *-kuni* a complete enigma. The prep. is *beri*, an infix {ku} is unknown, and in the Byblos letters the 1 pl. suff. is {nu}, not {ni}.

However, if we translate "between the two of you," not only do these difficulties disappear, but the passages in question still make perfect sense. On this reading, what Rib-Addi requests is that the Pharaoh send either one (*EA* 113) or more (*EA* 116) commissioners to decide between *the Pharaoh* and Yapaᶜ-Adda. In other words, he identifies his cause with that of his master.

Nor is this tactic simply plausible in itself. The identification is almost certainly made in EA 113:7–13: *al-lu-mi* PN *i-t*[*i-p*]*u-*[*uš*] *ar-na li-*

"*Aroused* (cf. Heb. *yṣt*?) is the desire of Milkilu to get the two sons of Labʾayu into GN, in order to destroy the rest of the land of the king, my lord, with the assistance of the two of them, over and above what Milkilu and Labʾayu destroyed" (lines 35–39). Apart from the first word, the passage makes perfect sense once it is recognized that *arkītu* here has the meaning of Heb. *ʾaḥ^arīt*.

[8] On the gloss *nazᶜaqū* or *naṣᶜaqū*, see J. J. Finkelstein, ***Eretz Israel*** 9 (1969) 33.

[9] See Böhl, ***LSS*** V/2, 27.

ma-ad [mi-na] *a-pa-aš* LUGAL-*ru a-na ša-a*-[šu] *ša-ni-tam mi-na ep-ša-ti a*-[*na* (x-x)] PN *i-nu-ma* ia_8-a[š-ku-nu] *lum-na lum-na-ma a-na ia*-[*ši*], "Look, Yapa^c-Adda has committed a crime. Attention! What has the king done to him? Moreover, what have I done to (the x-x of?) Yapa^c-Adda that he commits evil upon evil against me?"[10] There is probably only one crime, which in being directed against a loyal vassal becomes a case of lèse-majesté. Certainly Rib-Addi intimately associates the king's cause with his own. It would, then, not be surprising if a few lines later, in requesting royal intervention, he should designate his side of the dispute *a parte potiori*.

No. 2 allows for a similar reinterpretation: *ù lu*-[*ú* en-ni]-*pu-uš ki-it-tu i-na bi*-[*ri*]-*ku-ni*, "And an agreement should be made between the two of you."[11] Unfortunately, the context is badly damaged, but instead of assuming that the parties in question are the kings of Alašia and Egypt ("between us"), one must also consider the possibility that the former speaks here of his agent (the merchant in line 39?) who is to conclude the necessary formalities with the Egyptian king.

No. 4, at first blush, seems a clear case of *-šunī* being simply a replacive of *-šunu*: LÚ.DUMU.MEŠ.KIN-*ka ša pí-šu-ni sà-a-ru ša ta-šap-pa-ar an-ni-ka-a šum-ma pal-ḫu-ni-ik-ku ù i-‹dab›-bu-bu sà-ra-ti aš-šum a-ṣí-e i-na* ŠU-*ti-ka*, "Your messengers, whose mouth(s) are lying (and) whom you sent here, (I swear) they have not served you and so they told lies in order to avoid your punishment" (*EA* 1:86–88). Moreover, not many lines before we find *pīšunu*: "The first time the messengers went off to *your* [*father*] *ù pí-šu-nu sà-ru-ti i-dab-bu-bu*, and their mouth(s) spoke lies" (72–73).

However, this last passage goes on to speak of a *second* and equally mendacious embassy, and lines 86–88 are a summation referring to *both*. It is here that the scribe shifts from *pīšunu* to *pīšuni*, and the reason for the shift is clear: however many the ambassadors involved, they are viewed as comprising *two* delegations "the mouth(s) of both of which are lying."

No. 13 has as its antecedent ^{giš}GIGIR.MEŠ. Here we must either admit an erroneous use of the suffix, or, as all we have seen so far en-

[10]The restorations are Knudtzon's.

[11]As we shall show elsewhere, two, and possibly three, scribes wrote the letters from Alašia. Both the writing and the language of *EA* 34 are quite similar to what we find at Byblos and on the mainland to the south, and hence the appearance of *berīkunī* in this letter and at Byblos is not surprising.

courages us to do, assume that the determinative is to be disregarded, as is often true in WPA.[12] We should thus understand that the chariots taken and handed over to the ᶜApiru were in fact only two.

Against the case we have been making two objections may be raised. The first is that, except for No. 4, we lack evidence within the same letter for the dual forms *-kunī* and *-šunī* being used in contrast to *-kunu* and *-šunu*. This we must admit and regret, while at the same time stressing the force of the evidence we do have. Anyone denying it must then ascribe to pure coincidence the fact that in eleven of seventeen cases, at the very least, the antecedent is dual.

More serious is the observation that in *EA* 250, from which we have drawn seven of our examples (Nos. 7–12), we also find the barbarism *-šini*: *i̭i-is-sú-uḫ̮-ši-ni*, "he deported them" (line 45, with reference to three cities). Hence it may be argued that just as *-šini* replaces *-šina*, so *-šuni* replaces *-šunu*, and it *is* just a coincidence that that *-šuni* in this letter always refers to a dual.

Unless *-šini* is simply an error occasioned by the frequency of *-šunī* in *EA* 250, an explanation of the form eludes us. But this does not justify the conclusion that *-šunī* is not a dual suffix. Were *EA* 250 the only source for dual forms, the inference might be legitimate. But it is not the only source, and the scribes of Biridiya (Nos. 5–6) and Šuwardata (No. 14), as well as the scribe of *EA* 250, certainly use the suffix in reference to a dual antecedent. Appeal to coincidence in these cases too would in our opinion be mere cavil.

The evidence, then, seems compelling, and we must admit that forms last attested in native Akkadian sources around the middle of the 20th cent. B.C. were preserved for over six hundred years in WPA, in the schools of Egypt, south Palestine, and Ugarit or some other northern center.[13] Though not without parallel (see n. 1), this is surely the most extraordinary example of the tenacity and conservatism of the western scribal traditions.

[12]See Böhl, *LSS* V/2, 10–11; also J. Nougayrol, *PRU* IV 138, n. 1; *Ugar*. V. 146, n. 2. Otiose MEŠ is not confined to the periphery; see W. G. Lambert, *BWL* 152.

[13]A contributing factor may have been the survival of dual pers. pronouns in West Semitic dialects.

17. The Syrian Scribe of the Jerusalem Amarna Letters

This paper draws on the Albright legacy of problems he did not solve but, with characteristic insight, pointed to and left for others to work out.* Almost thirty years ago, in the course of his famous series of articles on western peripheral Akkadian, he mentioned in passing that the Jerusalem Amarna letters should not be included in a description of normal scribal practice in Palestine.[1] He gave no arguments to support this statement, and though both before and since that time others, the writer among them, have noted certain idiosyncrasies of the Jerusalem scribe, no one has offered evidence that could be said to justify the broad implications of his remark.[2] It has remained to this day simply an *obiter dictum*, unchallenged and unproven.

It will be our contention that Albright was right, and in fact more right than he could have known with the sources then available to him. Compared with the scribes in Palestine and along the southern Phoenician littoral, the Jerusalem scribe is indeed constantly *extra chorum*.[3] But

*This paper is a slightly revised version (Jan. 1974) of the one presented to the Albright Colloquium in Jan. 1973. Besides updating the bibliography, it incorporates some of the results of a collation (Aug. 1973–Jan. 1974) of the Amarna tablets in the Ashmolean Museum, British Museum, Musées Royaux d'Art et d'Histoire, Louvre, and Vorderasiatisches Museum. (We gratefully acknowledge the courtesy of the various museum authorities, and the grants of the American Philosophical Society and the American Council of Learned Societies in support of our inquiry.) First-hand study of the Jerusalem letters (four of six; *VAT* 1643 [*EA* 288] and *VAT* 1644 [*EA* 287] missing) and comparison with the other letters have only confirmed, in our opinion, the conclusions we had reached earlier.

[1]*BASOR* 94 (1944) 26.

[2]For various distinctive features of the Jerusalem letters, see H. Zimmern, *ZA* 6 (1891) 246, n. 6; 250, n. 1; F. M. Th. Böhl, *Die Sprache der Amarna Briefe*, LSS V/2, 2; 24; 47, n. 1; O. Schroeder, *OLZ* 18, 295f.; A. Goetze, *Language* 17 (1941) 128, n. 15; W. L. Moran, *The Bible and the Ancient Near East*, ed. G. Ernest Wright (Garden City, N. Y., 1961) 59; 68, n. 42 = Anchor Book 66; 79, n. 42 [see above, Paper 11, p. 205 with n. 42]; A. F. Rainey, *El Amarna Tablets*, AOAT 8, 75; Ichiro Nakata, *JANES* 2 (1969) 19–24. Only the last study, in the style of "friendly amendments" to the present writer's earlier remarks, purports to be a full treatment of the subject.

[3]A frequent exception to this contrast is the scribe from Tyre. Albright's opinion, *JEA* 23 (1937) 190ff., that the scribe was an Egyptian is both very questionable

this is only part of the problem. Compared with other scribes in a wider setting, he is no longer simply an anomaly; he is an alien. For, by and large, what sets him apart in Palestine is paralleled in the writing and language we find as we move northward along the lines of the several Syrian traditions. And what remains unparalleled even there is for the most part more readily understandable in this general area. In short, the Amarna letters from Jerusalem have a large component which we may call northern, and this is their central problem. A description of this component and an explanation of its presence are the subject of this paper.

WRITING

Paleography

Though paleography has never been brought in to the discussion of the Jerusalem scribe's background, it yields perhaps the clearest evidence. In Schroeder's list (*VAS* XII 73–94) there are 120 signs in the Jerusalem column, with a total of 175 different forms.[4] Comparison with the adjacent columns, with no attempt to distinguish or evaluate types

---

and, even if correct, would provide no explanation of the peculiarities of the script. S. Gevirtz, *Or* NS 42 (1973) 176f., has shown how fragile Albright's arguments were, and he might also have pointed to the Egyptian-Akkadian vocabulary (*EA* 368), which Smith and Gadd, *JEA* 11 (1925) 231, on paleographic grounds (note also PI = *pi* 5x), rightly argued could not have been written in Egypt, but rather somewhere in Syria; it is therefore evidence outside of Egypt of the kind of knowledge displayed by the Tyrian scribe's glosses. Certainly the latter was not trained in Egypt. His script exhibits no typically Egyptian features, but in general is that of the scribes from Byblos to Sidon, with its relatively small signs and light impressions. The Tyrian scribe seems, therefore, to reflect a local tradition subject to strong northern influences. P. Artzi, *Bar-Ilan Annual* 1 (1963) 24ff., has already noted the northern "Glossenkeil" notation (like the GAM-sign) at Tyre and Byblos; see chart, 34, and conclusions, 49 (English summary, XV).

[4]This list is not complete and must be used with some caution. To confine ourselves to the major omissions in the Jerusalem column: no. 11 KA, add forms in *VAS* XI 162:2,6; no. 23 LI, add form in *VAS* XI 164:23, and see n. 13, below; no. 77 TUR, add form in *VAS* XI 163:30; 164:66; 165:31; no. 81 LUGAL, add form with three verticals passim; no. 117 AL, add form in *VAS* XI 164:47 (variant of form in *VAS* XI 163:43, which is not, as Schroeder proposes, URU = al_x; note that the alleged URU never appears before city-names but only with a syllabic value); no. 125 GA, add form in *VAS* XI 162:12, 42; no. 128 É, add form in *VAS* XI 162:13; no. 138 MA, add form in *VAS* XI 162:2; no. 171 NIM, add (conventional) form in *VAS* XI 161:7; 162:14, 18; no. 142 ŠA, add form with four horizontals in *VAS* XI 161:27, 163:6,19,31,71; no. 204 KIN, add form in *VAS* XI 161:7. Also, correct copy in *VAS* XI 161:3 of GÌR, and add form to no. 175; both the upper and lower horizontals slant downward and upward, respectively.

or degrees of similarity or difference, reveals the following distribution: 8 Jerusalem forms, the same everywhere; 63, no geographical pattern, identical forms in both north and south;[5] 45, forms either unattested elsewhere or too rare for meaningful comparison;[6] 10, same forms only in Palestine or Phoenicia; 46, same forms only in the north;[7] 3, same forms only in Egypt.[8] Admittedly, this is only a general picture. A more comprehensive list based on more than the Berlin collection would certainly introduce some modifications.[9] It is also true that comparison

[5]By north we mean, roughly, above a line from Ṣumur on the coast to Qatna inland, within which area further distinctions are possible (see J. Nougayrol, *Ugar.* V, 76). This line more or less corresponds to the southern limits of the diffusion of Landsberger's "Reichsakkadisch" (*JCS* 8 [1954] 58; see also 48). The data of paleography are not unrelated to those of language. Note, for example, the contrast in both script and language between the letters of Abdi-Aširta (*VAS* XI 27–29, not included in Schroeder's Amurru column) and Aziru and his sons (*VAS* XI 83–85, 88–93, 95; on 94, see M. Dietrich and O. Loretz, *Beiträge zur Alten Geschichte und deren Nachleben,* Festschrift F. Altheim, ed. R. Stiehl and H. E. Stier [Berlin, 1970] 14ff.). Paleographically and linguistically, the former should be classified with the Byblos letters, whereas the latter are northern in script and typical examples of "Reichsakkadisch."

[6]It should be noted that this relatively high number reflects both the limited range of comparison on which the list is based (e.g., no. 179 "unattested" Ù [second form] is found in *PRU* VI 7, 10, etc., and *AT* 4) and differentiation on the basis of minor details (see, e.g., no. 60 MÁ, which we also list as unattested despite its obvious and very close resemblance to the third and fourth forms in the Byblos column). The only real idiosyncracies are no. 93 IL (to Schroeder's reference add *VAS* XI 164:26; 166:10, 18), concerning which Professor Sachs has suggested to the writer that the excessive number of verticals at the end represents simply a conflation of the wedges in the conventional forms; no. 79 ṢI (second form), actually either UNU or $MURUB_4$, a confusion that is based on the close similarity of ṢI with variant forms of the latter (*BoTU* 1, no. 298, and p. 20, 19); note also the TA+A ligature in TA.ÀM (no. 74).

[7]On the exception Tyre, see n. 3, above.

[8]Despite its location, Egypt is not to be classified with the south, neither in script nor in language. In both respects its closest affinity is with the north. Under the former, see F. Thureau-Dangin, *Le Syllabaire Accadien* (Paris, 1926) v; distinctive logograms such as KAxUD = *šinnu* (see B. Landsberger and H. G. Güterbock, *AfO* 12 [1937–39] 57) and UGU = *elû* (adjective); and in addition to our remarks below on Figure 1, note LA, UŠ, SAL, etc., as paleographical correspondences with northern forms. See also Knudtzon's remarks, *EA* 1 17–18. The language of the letters from Egypt is almost entirely free of the profound Northwest Semitic interference characteristic of the south, and despite certain differences (see R. Labat, *L'akkadien de Boghaz-Köi* [Bordeaux, 1932] 76) closely resembles "Reichsakkadisch"; note, too, lexical rarities like *appūnana* and *mamīnu* (Bog. OB).

[9]The principal modifications based on our collations will be noted below. N.B.: the BM collection now includes both the four "Rostovitz" tablets (purchased in

depends in part on the consideration of minute details, and coincidence and divergence may at times be fortuitous and evidence difference of hands rather than traditions; a larger sampling would require additional adjustments of the distributional pattern. But all this granted, the preponderance of northern forms in the Jerusalem column remains and requires explanation.[10]

Decisive in establishing the northern character of the script is the comparison of signs in which the differences regard more or less sharply defined distinctive features. In such a comparison the correspondences with southern forms virtually disappear, whereas those with northern forms still make up a long list (see Figure 1).[11] It consists, moreover, mostly of signs of high frequency. We may thus rule out chance as a relevant factor.

Figure 1 speaks for itself, and we restrict our comments mainly to supplementary evidence:[12]

No. 23 LI (see n. 4, above), parallels: Mitanni (second form), with variations in Mitanni (first form) and Tyre.[13] Also: Ḫatti (*BoTU* 1 no.

1903) and the eight tablets formerly in the possession of the Egyptian Exploration Society (*EA* 370–377, acquired in 1966, now numbered BM 13864–13871).

[10]It might be objected that the northern corpus is somewhat larger than that of the letters from Phoenicia, and hence the northern character of the Jerusalem sign-forms may only reflect this imbalance. However, the Phoenician forms are, in general, also those of Palestine and southern Syria, and this means that the real imbalance weighs rather heavily on the side of the southern corpus. And this imbalance is only increased if one also includes the pertinent material from Shechem, Taanach (here see the small sign-list of A. E. Glock, *BASOR* 204 [1971] 24–25), and Megiddo (here see the sign-list of A. Goetze-S. Levy, *ʿAtiqot* 2 [1959] 125–27; corrections: no. 213 EL is really no. 93 IL, and the first form of no. 143 ŠA in the Byblos column has an extra horizontal wedge).

[11]Only no. 160 AḪ and no. 162 ḪAR exhibit distinctively southern features, which in this case, as is generally true, means more archaic.

[12]The purpose of the supplement is the very modest one of underscoring the strongly provincial character of the south and thereby the individuality of the Jerusalem scribe. Hence the additional parallels cited are not meant to be exhaustive, nor do they imply that "southern" forms are without correspondence in the north. N.B.: Except for the Babylonian column, which is part of Schroeder's list, we restrict ourselves to the western peripheral sites. Hence we do not adduce Assyrian or Nuzi forms, though they are instructive and an exhaustive paleographical study would have to consider them (see, e.g., the "northern" forms of TUR, IB, MA, ŠEŠ, ŠA, IB, ŠUM in *WA* 9 = *EA* 16, of EN and LI in *KAV* 209, etc.; at Nuzi, EN in *HSS* V/2, 3, 8, etc.; IB ibid. 8, 29, etc.).

[13]The variation should be added to the Jerusalem column; see *VAS* XI 163 = *EA* 287:11. Though we do not cite additional parallels for this form, it could be amply documented. N.B.: Tyre = T in the B(eirut).S(idon).T(yre) column.

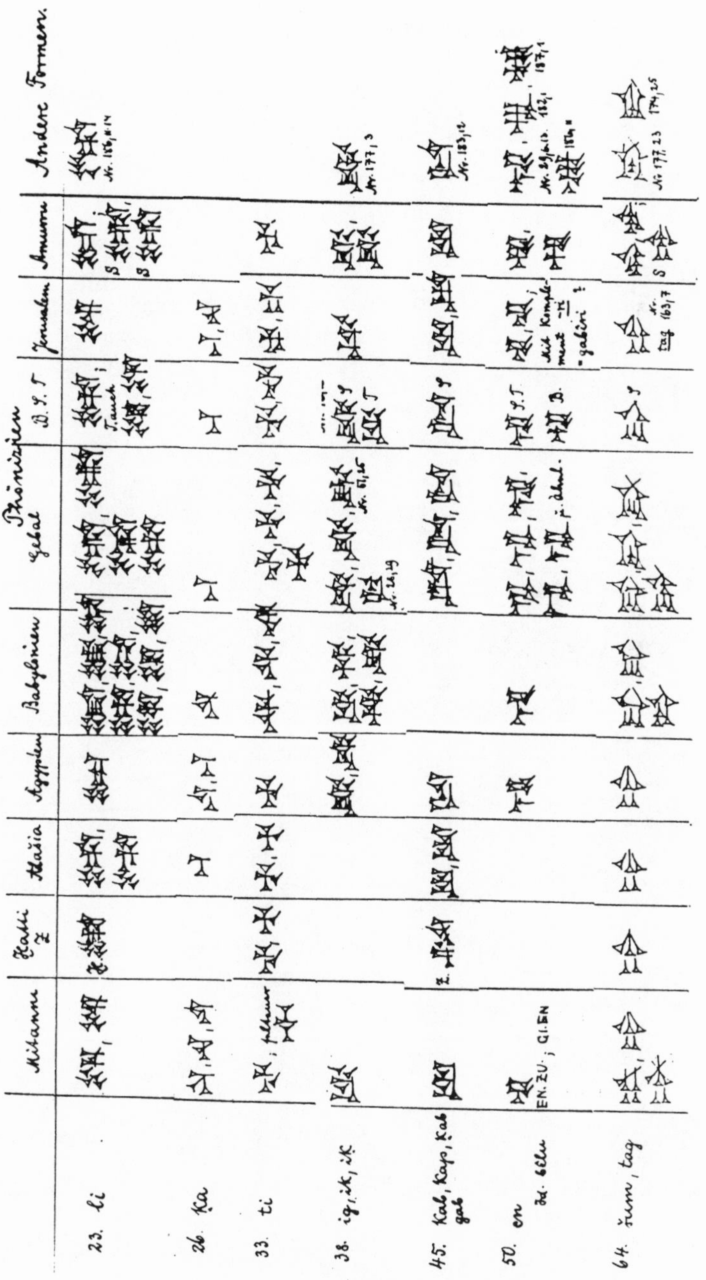
Mitanni
Ägypten
Babylonien
Phönizien
Gebal
Jerusalem
Amurru
Andere Formen
23. li
26. ka
33. ti
45. kab, kap, kab gab
50. en
64. šum, tag

Figure 1

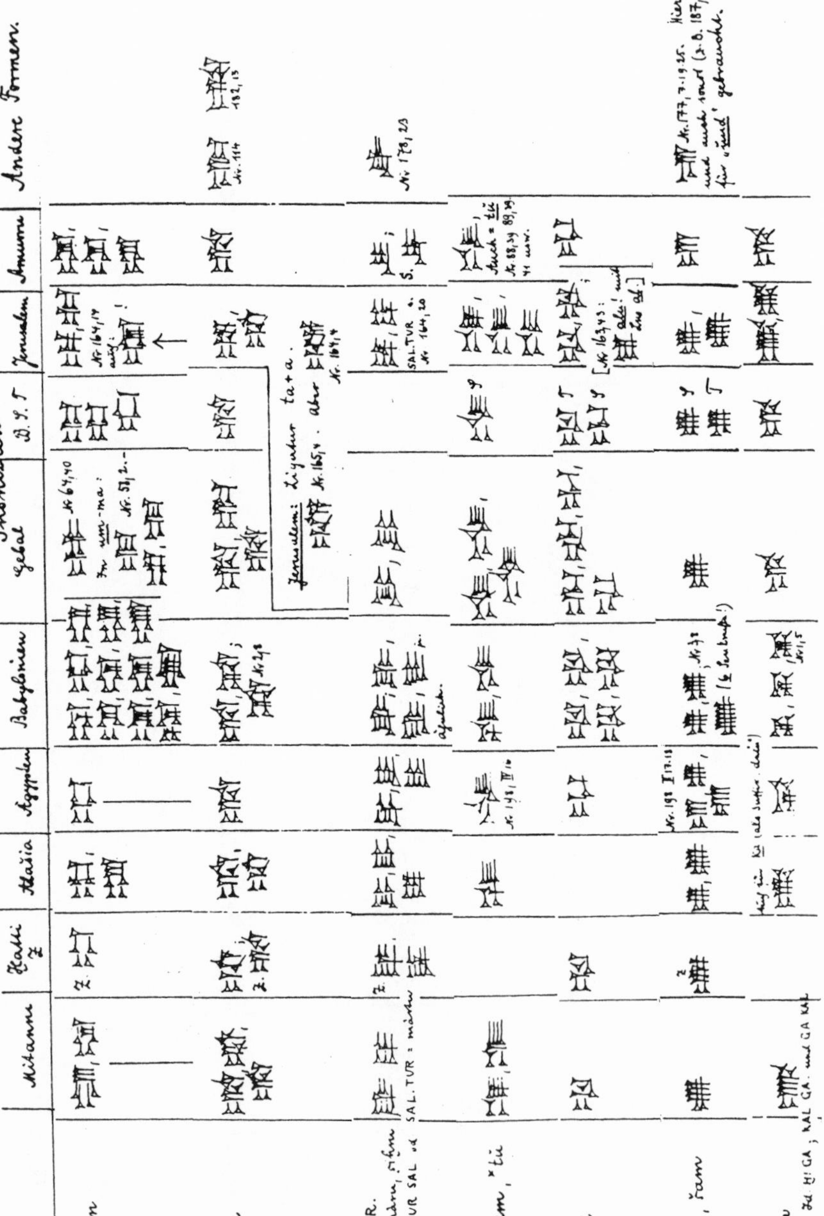

Figure 1 (continued)

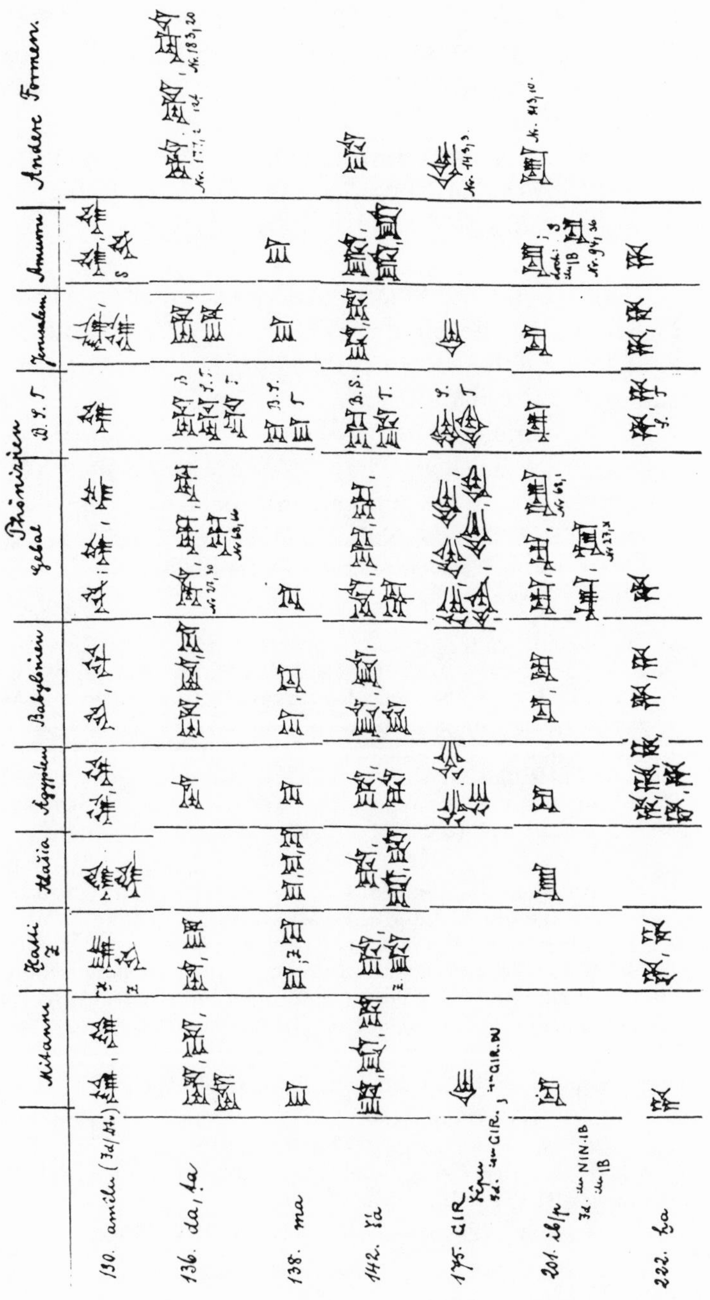

Figure 1 (continued)

158; *Ugar.* V no. 169); Ugarit (*VAS* XI 17 = *EA* 45; *VAS* XI 19 = *EA* 47; *VAS* XI 20 = *EA* 48; *PRU* III, RS 15.14; 15.86; 15.89; 15.Z, and passim);[14] Alalakh (*AT* 70; 447 iv 18–19 [Level II]; rare);[15] Nuḫašše (*VAS* XI 22 = *EA* 51);[16] Qatna (*BB* 37 = *EA* 53; *BB* 36 = *EA* 55; *VAS* XI 23 = *EA* 54).

No. 26 QA (second form), parallels: Mitanni, Egypt, Babylonia. Also: Ḫatti (*BoTU* I no. 219); Ugarit (*PRU* III, RS 15.155; 15.173; 15.A and passim); Qadeš (*VAS* XI 108 = *EA* 189); Ḫazi (*VAS* XI 106 = *EA* 186).[17]

No. 33 TI, parallels: Amurru. Also: Mitanni (*VAS* XII 201: i 21ff. = *EA* 25; *BB* 11 = *EA* 26); Ḫatti (*BoTU* I no. 275; *Ugar.* V no. 169); Ugarit (*VAS* XI 19 = *EA* 45; *PRU* IV, RS 17.42; 17.129; 17.158 and passim); Alalakh region (*AT* 108).[18]

No. 38 IG, parallels: Mitanni,[19] Babylonia, Tyre. Also: Ḫatti (*BoTU* I no. 117; *Ugar.* V no. 169); Ugarit (*VAS* XI 17 = *EA* 45; *PRU* III, RS 15. 109; 16.144; 16.249; 16.368 and passim); Alalakh (*AT* 49, but very rare; see 47, 132, 202, 248, etc.); Nuḫašše (*VAS* XI 22 = *EA* 51); Qatna area (*VAS* XI 24 = *EA* 56; see *BB* 36 = *EA* 55:26, Qatna).[20]

[14]Most of the evidence we possess from Ugarit is later than the Amarna period, but what we do possess from this time (*EA* 45, 47, and probably 46, 48; see Albright, *BASOR* 95 [1944] 30ff.; J. Nougayrol, *PRU* III xxxvii; M. Liverani, *Storia di Ugarit*, 23) suggests that, paleographically, the post-Amarna age at Ugarit was not one of great innovation. (It is to the south, along the Phoenician coast [also in Palestine?], where considerable change seems to have taken place and the writing assumed many features formerly characteristic of the north; see the letters from Beirut [*PRU* III 12] and Sidon [*PRU* III 9].)

[15]Even when allowance is made for the pre-Amarna date of Alalakh Level IV, *AT* gives the impression of a quite conservative tradition and of a surprising independence from the great center at Waššukanni, the contemporary practices of which are illustrated in a few texts at Alalakh and Nuzi (see B. Landsberger, *JCS* 8 [1954] 58, n. 119; 54, n. 95). And again language goes along with the writing; e.g., the absence of *uperris* / *upterris* (contrast *EA* Mitanni and Nuzi, for which see Gernot Wilhelm, *Untersuchungen zum Ḫurro-Akkadischen von Nuzi*, AOAT 9, 25–26).

[16]On the provenience of this letter, see J. Nougayrol, *PRU* IV 32.

[17]The location of Ḫazi is not established (see W. Helck, *Die Beziehungen Ägyptens zu Vorderasien im 3. und 2. Jahrtausend v. Chr.*, 195, n. 67), but along with *VAS* XI 135–136 = *EA* 237–238 (see n. 28 below), it is certainly one of the southernmost sites to exhibit northern forms.

[18]On *AT* 108, see B. Landsberger, *JCS* 8 (1954) 54, n. 95 (contradicted by 58, n. 119).

[19]See also *AT* 13.

[20]On the provenience of this letter, see *EA* II 1121.

No. 45 KAB (first form), parallels: Mitanni, Alašia,[21] Amurru. Also: Ugarit (*VAS* XI 19 = *EA* 47; *PRU* III, RS 16.138; 16.295; *PRU* VI 49, etc.); Amurru (? *VAS* XI 31 = *EA* 67).[22]

No. 50 EN, parallels: Mitanni. Also: Ḫatti (*BoTU* I no. 65); Alašia (*BB* 7 = *EA* 37); Ugarit (*VAS* XI 19 = *EA* 47; *PRU* III, RS 15.85; 15.A; 16.174, etc.); Alalakh (*AT* 70, 132 [but see line 24], 181 [but see lines 9, 14], 440 [Level I], rare); Beirut (*BB* 16 = *EA* 136, Rib-Addi writing from Beirut; *BB* 26 = *EA* 141); Byblos (*BB* 45 = *EA* 139).[23]

No. 64 ŠUM, parallels: Mitanni,[24] Ḫatti, Alašia, Egypt. Also: Ugarit (*VAS* XI 19 = *EA* 47; *PRU* III, RS 16.129; 16.141; 16.200 and passim); region of Alalakh (*AT* 112); Gezer letter.[25]

No. 72 UM (third form, slightly aberrant), parallels: Mitanni, Alašia, Babylonia, Amurru.[26] Also: Ḫatti (*BoTU* I no. 296); Ugarit (*PRU* III, RS 15.139; 16.154, etc.); Tyre (*BB* 28 = *EA* 149; *BB* 30 = *EA* 151); Qadeš (*VAS* XI 108 = *EA* 189).

No. 74 TA, parallels: Mitanni, Ḫatti, Alašia. Also: Ugarit (*VAS* XI 17 = *EA* 45; *VAS* XI 19 = *EA* 47); Alalakh (*AT* 5 = *JCS* 8, 5).

[21]The designation "Alašia" is of itself not a satisfactory term, for the letters of this provenience are, in writing and language, a very heterogeneous group. They deserve special study, and here we can only state our opinion that we must distinguish, certainly two, and probably three, scribes: the first wrote *EA* 33–34; the second, *EA* 35, 38–40; the third, if not the same as the second, *EA* 36–37. Only the latter two scribes exhibit northern forms—C. Kühne, *Die Chronologie der internationalen Korrespondenz von El-Amarna*, AOAT 17, 5, n. 33, refers briefly to the influence in both the Jerusalem and Alašia letters of "eine auswärtige Schultradition." In the case of Alašia, it seems difficult to speak of a *foreign* tradition when there is no evidence for what we might call native.

[22]On the provenience of this letter, see *EA* II 1144f.

[23]These few occurrences of northern forms of EN at Beirut and Byblos should not obscure the striking contrast between Jerusalem and the rest of the south, which is especially noteworthy because of the extremely high frequency of EN as a logogram for *bēlu*. In *VAS* XI 42 = *EA* 85:25, it is difficult to decide whether under the horizontal there are traces of a small vertical or simply a slight break; see Schroeder's copy. The latter seems to us more likely.

[24]Also *AT* 13–14.

[25]R. A. S. Macalister, *The Excavation of Gezer* I, 30. The provenience of this letter is unknown; Albright, *BASOR* 92 (1943) 28ff., suggested Egypt.

[26]The same form appears in *BB* 27 = *EA* 142 (Beirut) but with the value DUB, not UM, from which it is distinguished. At Jerusalem, as in the north in general (except Alalakh) and Egypt (except *EA* 369:2), UM and DUB coalesce, whereas in the south (except Tyre) they are kept distinct (besides Byblos passim, see *EA* 193, 237, 253).

No. 77 TUR (see n. 4, above), parallels: Mitanni, Ḫatti, Alašia. Also: Ugarit (*VAS* XI 19 = *EA* 47; passim in *PRU* III, IV, VI, *Ugar.* V, with variations between Jerusalem first form and Alašia third form); Alalakh (*AT* 49, very rare); Qatna area (*VAS* XI 24 = *EA* 56).

No. 95 TUM (first form), parallels: Mitanni, and for the distinctive feature of the vertical, see Alašia and Babylonia. Also: Ḫatti (*BoTU* I no. 283); Ugarit (*PRU* III, RS 15.86; 15.89; 16.189; 16.287); Alalakh (*AT* 3, 4, but very rare); Qadeš (*VAS* XI 108 = *EA* 189).

No. 117 AL (see n. 4, above), parallels: Mitanni, Ḫatti, Babylonia, Tyre. Also: Ugarit (passim); Alalakh (*AT* 4, etc., but rare).[27]

No. 124 Ú (second form), parallels: Mitanni, Ḫatti, Alašia, Babylonia. Also: Ugarit (*Ugar.* V no. 41; p. 487, RS 15.30+; *PRU* VI 50, etc.); Egypt (C. H. Gordon, *Or* NS 16 [1947] 5 = *EA* 370).

No. 125 GA (see no. 4, above; first form), parallels: Mitanni; (second form), parallels: Alašia. Also: Ugarit (passim); Alalakh (*AT* 361, very rare).

No. 130 LÚ, parallels: Mitanni, Ḫatti, Alašia. Also: Ugarit (*VAS* XI 17 = *EA* 45, etc.); southern Syria (*VAS* XI 113 = *EA* 200).

No. 136 DA (second form), parallels: Mitanni, Ḫatti, and see Tyre.

No. 138 MA, parallels: Mitanni, Ḫatti, Alašia, Tyre, Amurru. Also: Ugarit (passim); Nuḫašše (*VAS* XI 22 = *EA* 51); Qatna (*VAS* XI 23 = *EA* 54); Damascene (*VAS* XI 111-112 = *EA* 196, 194) and in the same general area (*VAS* XI 113 = *EA* 200).

No. 142 ŠA (with four horizontals, see n. 4, above), parallels: Mitanni, Ḫatti, Tyre, and see Amurru. Also: Amurru (? *VAS* XI 136 = *EA* 238),[28] Nuḫašše, Qatna, etc. (as in previous entry).

No. 175 GÌR (see n. 4, above), parallels: Mitanni. Also: Ugarit (*Ugar.* V no. 48; also, *PRU* VI 6 in anše.gìr.nun.na; *Ugar.* V no. 163 iv 14′ in $alim_x$); Amurru (? *VAS* XI 136 = *EA* 238); Syria (*VAS* XI 177 = *EA* 317).[29]

No. 201 IB, parallels: Mitanni, Egypt, Babylonia, Amurru. Also: Ḫatti (*BoTU* I no. 113); Ugarit (*PRU* III, RS 15.132; *PRU* IV, RS 17.334 and passim); Alalakh (*AT* 182, 269, but very rare); Nuḫašše (*VAS* XI 22 = *EA* 51).

[27] *VAS* XI 111 = *EA* 196:16 (Biryawaza of Upe), AL with oblique wedge but preceded by two verticals (see Babylonia, third and fourth forms).

[28] On the provenience of *EA* 237–238, see *EA* II 1304, n. 1.

[29] P. Artzi, *JNES* 27 (1968) 163ff., has demonstrated the Syrian provenience of *EA* 317.

No. 222 Ḫ̮A (first form), parallels: Mitanni, Egypt, Babylonia, Tyre, Amurru. Also: Ḫ̮atti (*BoTU* 1 no. 99); Ugarit (passim); Alalakh (*AT* 435, but very rare); Nuḫ̮ašše (*VAS* XI 22 = *EA* 51); Amurru (? *VAS* XI 135–136 = *EA* 237–238).

To sum up: in the Jerusalem letters the forms of twenty signs—those of LI, IG, KAB, EN, ŠUM, TUR, GÌR, IB are especially important—have no parallels in Palestine, and only occasional, sporadic ones in southern Phoenicia, whereas beginning in southern Syria and northward they have numerous correspondences and are often the rule. From the viewpoint of paleography, it is a northern hand that wrote these letters.[30]

Syllabary

Noteworthy are the following:

*AS*² 104 IA = *a̭a* in URU *a̭a-lu-na*ᵏⁱ (*EA* 287: 57). Reference is to biblical Aijalon, which in *EA* 273:20 appears in a conventional spelling, URU *a-ia-lu-na*. In view of *a̭a-nu-um-ma* (*Ugar*. V 27:49) *a̭a* is established for the northwest periphery.[31]

*AS*² 129 KUM = *qu* in *ḫ̮al-qu-mi* (*EA* 286:51), *ḫ̮al-qu* (*EA* 288:40, 52). Common in MA (note *li-il-qu-ú* and *il-qu-ú-ni*, *EA* 16:34,40) and MB (*AS*²), this value is unattested at Nuzi or Alalakh, but is found, though rarely, in the northwest periphery (*PRU* IV RS 17.252; 17.393; 18.54a—all forms of *ḫ̮alāqu*, provenience of last unknown, language Assyrian or strongly Assyrianizing).[32]

*AS*² 184 SAR = *šir*₉ in *lu-ma-šir*₉ (*EA* 290:20); see *lu-ma-še-er* (*EA* 288:58; 289:42), *lu-ma-še-ra* (*EA* 285:28; 286:45; 287:18). *AS*² restricts this value to a single instance at Nuzi, but R. Biggs, *JNES* 29 (1970) 138 cites a probable MB example (same verb, *ṷuššuru*). Add (all forms of

[30] See also the form of SA (no. 53).

[31] On the values of the PI-sign, see I. J. Gelb, *Or* NS 39 (1970) 537–39; he is reluctant to admit PI = *aia*, but allows that it may turn up in the periphery.

[32] On RS 18.54A see Walter Mayer, *Untersuchungen zur Grammatik des Mittelassyrischen*, AOAT Sonderreihe 2, 3, and note specifically: *-mā* introducing direct discourse; *ētamrū* (Babylonian *ītamrū*), *iṣabbutū* (Babylonian *iṣabbatū*), *iḫ̮ṭiʾuni* (3 singular subjunctive, Babylonian *iḫ̮ṭû*; for the reading see J. Aro, *AfO* 18 [1958] 423); *kunāšunu* (2 plural independent pronoun; see Mayer, *Untersuchungen*, 28); *gab-bu-ru-ti* = *kabburūti* < *kabbarūti*(?). Since the Jerusalem scribe does not confuse stops, *qu* may not be interpreted simply as a graphic variant of *ku*. If one reads *bat-*⌜*qú-ú*⌝ in *EA* 287:36 (so Albright; see *ANET* 488, "they breached"), the restriction of *qu* to forms of *ḫ̮alāqu* is still no difficulty; see below on *šir*₉, and note ṢI = *zé*, *zí* (in the periphery) only in forms of *zêru* (to the references in *AS*² add *Ugar*. V no. 30:30,32′; we thus disagree with Nougayrol, in *Ugar*. V 72, n. 3), etc.

uuššuru): Alalakh (<*ú*>*-wa-šir*$_9$*-šu*, *AT* 15:4); Ugarit (*Ugar.* V no. 44), Amurru (*PRU* IV 180; *EA* 156:13; *EA* 171:5 *ú-wa-aš-šir*$_9$*-an-ni*, see line 13 *ú-wa-aš-ši-ra-an-ni*), Qatna (*EA* 55:20,[49]), Tunip (*EA* 59:33), Tyre (*EA* 149:17,76), Alašia (*EA* 34:14,16), Egypt (*EA* 162:42,51,56), and possibly Byblos (*EA* 131:32). Note also the equation at Boghazköy of *e-sír* = *e-šir*$_9$ (*MSL* XIII 260:5´–8´).[33]

AS^2 218 TE = *de*$_4$ in *li-de*$_4$ (*EA* 289:46), *li-de*$_4$*-mi* (*EA* 286:25; 287:11, 48, 57), *i-de*$_4$*-mi* (*EA* 289:35), *ša-de*$_4$*-e* (*EA* 287:56), *la-ma-de*$_4$*-ka* (*EA* 287:59), *d*[*e*$_4$*-k*]*a* (*EA* 288:41), *de*$_4$*-k*[*a*] (*EA* 288:45), and *de*$_4$*-ka-ti* (*EA* 287:73). In the Amarna archive, with the exception of *ir-de*$_4$*-e* (*EA* 359 rev. 27, Egypt), all occurrences of TE = *de*$_4$ are confined to forms of *idû*, and these are found in letters from Mitanni, Qatna, Amurru, Tyre, Alašia, and two northern sites (*EA* 260, 317).[34]

AS^2 223 PI = *pi* in all thirteen cases of *piṭat(t)u*.[35] In the Amarna archive, this value is confined to texts from Assyria (*EA* 16:10,14), Mitanni (PN in *EA* 27:89,93; 28:12; and passim in the Hurrian letter *EA* 24), Alašia (*EA* 36:15[?], *EA* 37:17), Syria (*EA* 368:1,4,5,14,rev. 5; on provenience, see n. 3), and possibly Byblos (*EA* 138:8, if Edel's reading and explanation, *JNES* 7 [1948] 23, are correct). Aside from occasional occurrences at Boghazköy, these are the only instances we know of for this value in the western periphery.[36]

[33]The list of occurrences of *šir*$_9$ in various forms of *uuššuru* does not claim to be exhaustive, nor do we deny the possibility that the scribes may have confused present, preterite and perfect. We do insist that *šir*$_9$ in *lu-ma-šir*$_9$ is a valid inference from five writings with *-še-er* or *-še-ra*, and if confirmation were needed, *e-sír* = *e-šir*$_9$ would be sufficient.

[34]On the provenience of *EA* 260 and 317, see n. 29, above. It should be noted that TE = *de*$_4$ is not "Hurrian" (*ARM* XV 49; P. Artzi, *JNES* 27 [1968] 167), nor is it a peripheral development from the confusion of voiced and voiceless stops. Rather, it is an archaic survival like *bí* in *qí-bí-ma* and goes back to a syllabary which distinguished between *di* and *de*. The existence of such a syllabary, which Gelb seems to postulate for the OAkk. period (see *MAD* II^2, 97, no. 218), Jacobsen (to whom we express our thanks for making his work available to us) has shown in an unpublished study of the Tell Asmar letters. Thus, in the early Isin-Larsa period, we find *ti-de*$_4$ (AS 31-T 299) "you know," and *lu-úr-de*$_4$ (AS 30-T 399) "I will conduct." The use of *de*$_4$, therefore, and its virtual confinement in the west to forms of *idû* is just one more archaic feature of western peripheral Akkadian.

[35]As noted by Böhl, LSS V/2, 2; see also Rainey, AOAT 8, 75. Note, too, that DA = *ṭa*, not only here, but in all writings of /ṭa/ (9 forms of *paṭāru*); this is the standard MA/MB orthography.

[36]See R. Labat, *L'akkadien de Boghaz-Köi* 7, to which a number of references might be added.

*AS*² 223 PI = *à* in *à-qa-bi* (*EA* 286:22),[37] and perhaps *ú-ša-à-ru* (*EA* 286:21,24),[38] possibly *an-ni-à* (*EA* 289:9).[39] According to *AS*², this value is OB, rare in MA and later, unattested in MB; R. Biggs, *JNES* 29 (1970) 138, adds an occurrence at Boghazköy.

*AS*² 238 ḪAR = *kín* in *li-is-kín* (*EA* 286:38; 287:13, 40; 288:48) and *gin₈* in URU *gin₈-ti-ki-ir-mi-il* (*EA* 288:26; 289:18, +KI) and *gin₈-ti* (*EA* 289:19; 290:28). *AS*² finds this value in the Mari liver models (add PN *Me-kín-nu-um*, *TIM* V 23:2, 9, and seal, Gungunum), MA, Am (= Jerusalem!), Ugarit (see also *Ugar*. V no. 20:18, no. 38:3), and Boghazköy, to which add Egypt (see Goetze *JCS* 1 [1947] 250, n. 7).[40]

[37]The usual reading is with Canaanite verbal preformative {i̯a} or {i̯u}, but one difficulty is that this would be a unique instance in the Jerusalem letters of such a form. Moreover, the one who is quoted in what immediately follows (*ḫalqat māt šarri bēlīi̯a* "Lost is the land of the king, my lord") is certainly Abdi-Ḫeba: (1) *aqabbi ḫalqat māt šarri*, "I say, 'Lost is the land of the king' " (line 49); (2) the "good word" the pharaoh's scribe is to present to his master is *ḫalqat gabbi māt šarri bēlīi̯a* (lines 64–65); (3) in the lines immediately preceding the passage in question (17–21) we have *aqabbi* followed by a direct quotation, and then *u kinanna ušāru ina pānī šarri bēlīi̯a* "and as a result I am lied about before the king, my lord"; in lines 22–24 we have *enūma* (since) PI-*qa-bi* followed by a direct quotation, and then *kinanna ušāru ana šarri bēlīi̯a* "as a result I am lied about to the king, my lord." Hence there is no question that the speaker in lines 22–24 is Abdi-Ḫeba; to credit anyone else with the speech runs counter not only to the clear parallelism with the immediately preceding lines, but also to the tenor of the entire letter—only Abdi-Ḫeba has the courage to tell the pharaoh how parlous the situation around Jerusalem really is. Why, then, assume a periphrastic "it is said" or the like? To which it may be asked, "Why assume such a rare value of the PI-sign?" We suspect the answer to be that we are dealing with a "learned" provincial scribe (see Šarruwa of the Idrimi inscription) who is displaying his learning, probably in the hope of impressing his colleague in Egypt. This would not be the only example of his pedantry.

[38]Favoring *ú-ša-à-ru* is the writing *ú-ša-a-ru* in line 6. Etymology remains a moot point, but for the issue at hand it is not crucial, since the orthography makes it clear that there is question of a hollow root (*šwr* / *šyr*) or possibly a *mediae aleph* verb (*šʾr*). (We interpret the form in question as reflecting a West Semitic qal passive, with indicative present-future {u}; see qal passive perfect *šīrtī* in *EA* 252:14, and *ši-ir*ˡ*-te* in *EA* 180:19.) With either etymology *ú-ša-ia₈-ru* also remains a possibility. For *mediae aleph* verbs, note in the same letter *ta-ra-ia-mu* (18) and *ta-za-ia-ru* (20), and of course hollow verbs may exhibit a similar orthography (*GAG* §22i, §104k–l), with parallels elsewhere in the periphery (see *ta-ba-ia-aš*, *Ugar*. V no. 162:32; *iq-ta-na-ia-al*, *KUB* 37, 210:6).

[39]But *an-ni-ia₈* is more likely (see peripheral *ki-ia-am*, etc.), in view of *an-ni*-PI (*EA* 289:12) = *an-ni-i̯ú* (*u₁₇* in *AT* 2:34, 36 needs collation; *ut-ta-šu*?).

[40]We hesitate to follow Rainey, AOAT 8, 92, and to read URU *gin₈-ti-e-ti* in *EA* 295 rev. 7; the stance of the apparent *gam* is not right for the end of ḪAR.

The Syrian, non-Palestinian cast of the Jerusalem scribe's syllabary is clear. The use of *de*$_4$ in forms of *idû* and of *pi* seems particularly significant.

Orthography

The Jerusalem scribe exhibits a number of orthographic peculiarities pertinent to the problem at hand:

1. /u̯/, initial and intervocalic, is very often written with the *m*-series: (a) all forms (16) of *u̯uššuru*, following the practice in Babylonia, Mitanni, Ugarit, the Alalakh region (*AT* 108), Ḫatti, and Egypt, in contrast with the older spelling with the *u̯*-series maintained at Gezer, Pella, Tyre, Byblos, Qatna, Tunip, Upe, Alalakh, etc.;[41] (b) *mu-ʾì-ru* (*EA* 290:8).[42]

2. In the formulaic *ana* PN *qibīma umma* ..., where it is preserved in the Jerusalem letters, we find *qí-bi-ma* (*EA* 286:1; 287:65; 290:2) rather than the traditional and archaic *qí-bí-ma*.[43] The latter is used exclusively in the Amarna correspondence, with only five or six exceptions: *EA* 132 and 362 (both Byblos), 200, 207 (probably), and 230 (Syrian provenience of all three probable), 28 (Mitanni), and 15

[41]First noted by Böhl, LSS V/2, 47, n. 1. For the classification of these forms under orthography rather than phonology, see A. Goetze, *Language* 14 (1938) 135, n. 3.

[42]From *u̯uʾʾuru*, stative used as West Semitic perfect, imperative form extended to stative (perfect) on analogy *qattil* (imperative) : *qattil*(*a*, perfect) :: *u̯uʾʾir* (imperative) : x = *u̯uʾʾir(a)*. In view of I. Nakata's difficulties, *JANES* 2 (1969) 21 (see n. 1, above), we should perhaps add that many older orthographies survived, in peripheral Akkadian especially, along side the new ones, so that there could be considerable fluctuation between writings with the *u̯*- and *m*- series, even in the same letter (e.g., both writings, *au̯atu* and *amatu*, are found in *EA* 38; for the Nuzi evidence, see Gernot Wilhelm, AOAT 9, 15–16). Thus there is nothing really noteworthy in the Jerusalem scribe's writing *au̯atu* with the *u̯*-series and *u̯uššuru* with the *m*-series. Were the reading *lu-ú a-mi-la-tu-nu* (so *AHw* 90b) in *EA* 289:26 correct, then *au̯īlātunu* should also be listed here. However, it is extremely dubious: (1) as Knudtzon already remarked (*EA* I 874, n. 3), before *mi* there is "ein kleiner Zwischenraum," which does not appear in Schroeder's copy, and this strongly favors *mi* introducing a new word; (2) not only are the two verticals (Knudtzon: *2*; *AHw*: *a*) quite clear (ligature with previous putative *ú*, with Knudtzon, Autogr. no. 156; against Schroeder's copy), but had the scribe intended to write *a*, he would have drawn a smaller first vertical; and (3) it is not clear what, in context, "be ye men" means. Perhaps, with considerable reservation, *lu-ú 2 ṣíl-la-tu-nu*, "The two of you *must* be a protection."

[43]First noted by I. Nakata, *JANES* 2 (1969) 23–24, though his list of *EA* occurrences is incomplete, and no reference is made to extra-Amarna practice.

(Assyria). The Jerusalem spelling is the rule in the letters found at Ugarit,[44] in MA and Nuzi letters, and is well attested in MB.[45]

3. Six times we meet the spelling KUR.URU GN(.KI): *EA* 287:14–15, 25, 46; 289:18; 290:11.[46] In all the Amarna letters, despite their almost innumerable namings of towns and villages, to our knowledge there are only two instances of the sequence KUR.URU: KUR.URU *ḫa-at-ti* (*EA* 44:8) and KUR.URU *ú-g*[*a*]-*r*[*i-it*] (*EA* 45:35). In these letters from Boghazköy and Ugarit, respectively, we meet the practice long known as typical of Hittite scribes and, now with the discoveries of Ugarit, seen to be also quite common elsewhere in the north.[47]

4. In the Amarna archive, in 121 references to the ᶜApiru, with the possible exception of *EA* 207:21, only the Jerusalem letters have a syllabic spelling (8x), and this exclusively. Syllabic spellings elsewhere in roughly contemporary texts: Ḫatti and Ugarit.[48]

5. The use of the *din*-sign, with orthographic doubling of the *n*, in *i-din-nu* (*EA* 287:15; 289:23), is paralleled by *i-na-an-din-nu-nim* (*EA* 155:13, Tyre), *id-din-nu* (*EA* 155:38, Tyre; 171:9, probably Amurru), *i-din-nu-nim* (*EA* 161:22, Amurru) and possibly *i-din-*[*nu*] (*EA* 40:9, Alašia; see Knudtzon's remarks, *EA* p. 296, n. f).[49] Note the cluster:

[44]Exceptions are so rare that they require comment; see J. Nougayrol, *PRU* VI 2, n. 1.

[45]It also appears as an Akkadogram in the Hittite letter *AT* 125 (Levels I-II). Its occasional occurrence in OA and the writing *q*[*ì*]-*bi-ma* in an Ur III letter (David I. Owen, *Or* NS 40 [1971] 398:3) may also be mentioned.

[46]Probably to be included here is KUR.ḪI.A URU *Urusalim*^{ki} (*EA* 287:63), since KUR.ḪI.A seems to be a mere variant of KUR: (1) note the singular suffix in the previous line, *ezābiša* "abandon *it*"; (2) KUR.ḪI.A is always used with singular predicates (*ḫalqat, EA* 286:23, 49, 60, 64–65; *paṭarat*, 286:35; *ibašši*, but see below); (3) see [KU]R.ḪI.A LUGAL EN *gab-<ba>-ša* (*EA* 286:36) and KUR LUGAL-*ri gab-ba-ša* (*EA* 288:24). (The writer is unable to present the distribution of otiose ḪI.A, and can only point to a comparable use of MEŠ. For a further extension of MEŠ, see J. Nougayrol, *PRU* IV 138, n. 1; *Ugar*. V 146, n. 2.) The writings KUR.URU, to which we called attention previously, are dismissed by Nakata, *JANES* 2 (1969) 22, n. 21, as irrelevant in a discussion of the Jerusalem scribe's peculiarities.

[47]For Boghazköy, see Labat, *L'akkadien de Boghaz-Köi* 14f.; for the Ugarit archives, see J. Nougayrol, *PRU* III 2, n. 4. The existence of other writings in the Jerusalem letters—KUR GN$^{(ki)}$ and URU GN$^{(ki)}$—in no way diminishes the significance of the northern parallels; see Nougayrol's remarks, ibid.

[48]See J. Bottéro, *Le problème des ḫabiru à la 4e Rencontre Assyriologique Internationale* (Paris, 1954) 71–129.

[49]Same writing in MA; see Walter Mayer, AOAT Sonderreihe 2, 11. In the south the only writing at all comparable is *ti-id-*[*di-i*]*n-na* (*EA* 244:19, Megiddo).

Amurru, Alašia, Tyre, Jerusalem.

6. The representation of the sibilants in the Jerusalem letters is an old problem, which cannot be discussed here.[50] Suffice it to indicate what seem the two most likely solutions. With Goetze, one may dismiss vacillations (KUR *ka-si*/*ši*, *EA* 287:72, 74) and anomalies (a Jerusalem scribe representing Proto-Semitic /ṯ/ and /ś/ by the same sign: KUR *ša-ak-mi* [*EA* 289:23], *ša-de*$_4$*-e* = Hebrew *śāde* [*EA* 287:56]) as a matter of "syllabary," i.e., an orthographic tradition which does not distinguish the sibilants and which, though to some extent perceptible almost everywhere in western peripheral Akkadian, is typical of "Reichsakkadisch."[51] Or one may take the evidence at face value and accept a binary opposition of /ṯ-ś/ versus /š/, with the support of Egyptian transcriptions of Canaanite. This opposition, however, hardly obtained in the dialect of Jerusalem, for on the evidence of biblical Hebrew, at Jerusalem /ṯ/ and /ś/ never fell together. In either solution we are once again probably confronted with the intrusiveness of the Jerusalem letters in their local setting.[52]

[50]The problem has been thoroughly studied by Dr. Lamia A. Rustam Shehadeh in her dissertation, "The Sibilants in the West Semitic Languages of the Second Millennium B.C." (Harvard University, 1968).

[51]A. Goetze, *Language* 17 (1941) 128, n. 15. We are inclined to this view, but it should be noted that all the problematic cases concern place-names and possibly one or two Canaanite words; there is no confusion of the sibilants in the writing of Akkadian. In other words, the scribe seems to have drawn on a tradition of the spelling of individual *words* (see n. 32 above), and only where such a tradition is lacking do the ambiguities of the syllabary make themselves felt.

[52]A few other idiosyncrasies of the Jerusalem scribe may be mentioned, though they are hard to interpret in terms of background: (1) Formulaic "seven times and seven times (I have fallen)" is always (5x) written 7 TA.ÀM *ù* 7 TA.ÀM, a spelling which in the repetition of TA.ÀM is unparalleled among the many attested for this extremely common phrase. (2) In *EA* 286:7,15,32, the logogram EN (*bēlu*) seems to have a phonetic complement *-ri*, which is still without a convincing explanation; Schroeder, *OLZ* 18, 295f., lists the various solutions, to which we might add that EN.RI could be a Hurrogram reflecting Hurr. *ibri* "lord" (see *Ugar*. V no. 161:20). (3) AD.DA.A.NI "(my) father" (*EA* 287:26, 288:13,15, lit. "his father," see DUMU.MUNUS.A.NI-*ia* "my daughter," *EA* 3:7, Babylonia) is very learned; according to *CAD* A/1, 67, AD.DA is confined to lexical texts, except in É AD.DA (see É AD.DA.NI *BE* 14 40:10, MB). In view of Ugaritic *ʾadn* (*a-da-nu*, *Ugar*. V no. 130:9′) "father," which is perhaps also attested in biblical Hebrew (Joshua Blau–Jonas C. Greenfield, *BASOR* 200 [1970] 16, n. 23; Delbert R. Hillers, ibid., 18), one might consider *ad-da-a-ni* = *addānī* "my father." Against this interpretation are: (1) the syllabic writing *a-da-nu* favors *ʾad*, not *ʾadd;* (2) if, as the Jerusalem writing when taken as West Semitic would suggest, the word is

Punctuation

The "Glossenkeil" is employed quite frequently (19x) by the Jerusalem scribe. Some of its uses are quite normal: (1) West Semitic gloss to Akkadian word or expression (*EA* 286:6 [if *ú-ša-a-ru* is West Semitic]; 287:37,56); (2) West Semitic gloss to Sumerogram (*EA* 287:27 [second "Glossenkeil"], 73, and perhaps 7); and (3) marker of following word as non-Akkadian (*EA* 287:16,41[?]; 290:24[?]). Where it appears at the beginning of a line (*EA* 286:15; 288:53; 290:24[?]), it may serve to mark the line as a run-over of the preceding, with which it constitutes a sense-unit. But this still leaves many instances without explanation. In the latter, the only purpose we can suggest is to punctuate the text and mark major and minor "pauses": major, before new sentences (*EA* 286:47,62; 287:27[first "Glossenkeil"],41[?],75); minor, either before relative clauses (*EA* 287:6, 290:5), or between subject and verb (*EA* 286:10), verb and adverb (*EA* 287:52), verb and object (*EA* 287:58). If this proposal is pertinent, then the occasional use at Boghazköy of the "Glossenkeil" as a punctuation mark seems the relevant comparison.[53]

LANGUAGE

Assyrianisms

Certainly the most striking feature of the Jerusalem scribe's language, though so far it has not been recognized, is its large Assyrian component. The peripheral Akkadian of the west, it is true, exhibits a number of Assyrianisms, some fairly standard, others sporadic and unpatterned.[54] Being neither, those of the Jerusalem letters are unique.

ʾad(d)ān, in the south one expects *ʾad(d)ōn* (at Jerusalem, note *a-nu-ki*, *EA* 287:66, 69).

[53]For the various uses of the "Glossenkeil" at Boghazköy, see B. Schwartz, *ArOr* 10 (1938) 65; on the main thesis of this article we are not competent to judge. C. Kühne and H. Otten, *Der Šaušgamuwa-Vertrag*, *StBoT* 16, 52, n. 1, also point to the "Glossenkeil als Interpunktionszeichen." Before commenting on P. Artzi's study of the Amarna glosses, *Bar-Ilan Annual* 1 (1963) 24ff., we await its completion.

[54]Feminine plural {āte} is very common, as are the demonstrative pronouns (adjective) *šūt* and verbal suffix {šunu} (if indeed these are Assyrianisms and not survivals from OAkk or an early OB dialect). Other Assyrianisms like *abat šarri* "the word of the king" (*EA* 211:19–20; see also 173:15–16), *adi ūmi an-ni-=e* (*PRU* VI 4:10), *išaṭṭurū* (*PRU* III 97:19), *ṣarpu* "silver" (*EA* 161:44), etc., occur here and there.

1. *Demonstrative Pronoun-Adjective*

Nom. *anniʾu* (*anniịu*) — *an-ni-ú epši* PN ..., "This is the deed of PN" (*EA* 287:29).
epšu māti an-ni-ú, "This deed against the *land*" (*EA* 290:25).
epšu ša ēpušū an-ni-ịú, "This is the deed they committed" (*EA* 289:12).

Gen. *anniʾe* — *ina ašri an-ni-e* (*EA* 286:11)

Acc. *anniʾa* (*anniịa*?) — *ḫaziānu ša eppaš epša an-ni-à*, "as for a governor who commits such a deed" (*EA* 289:9).

Uncontracted forms, which are the rule without exception in the Jerusalem letters, have no parallel in the entire Amarna archive.[55] The paradigm is pure MA.[56]

2. *Noun*

The only clear—and correct—Assyrian form is *ú-re-e*, "roof" (*EA* 287:37), which reflects the MA shift /im/ > /e/. In *la-ma-de$_4$-ka* (*EA* 287:59) the bound-form before a pronominal suffix is also, and erroneously, [e] rather than [i].[57]

3. *Verb*

Here Assyrian influence is especially strong:[58]

(a) Where there is a distinction between Babylonian and Assyrian in forms of the precative, the latter is the rule (10x) without exception:

[55]The apparent exception *an-ni-am* (*EA* 369:2) does not exist. Collation shows that the upper slanting horizontal of the alleged *ni* is not on the tablet; instead, there are clear traces which establish the reading *an-na*[!]*-am*, which also occurs in *EA* 45:13, 237:20.

[56]See Mayer, AOAT Sonderreihe 2, 36. It is the absence of contraction that is noteworthy, not the possible allophones.

[57]Despite our "minimalist" approach and the resolution of almost all orthographic ambiguities in favor of Babylonian, we make an exception here and do not read *la-ma-di$_{12}$-ka*, since not only is *di$_{12}$* extremely rare, but the scribe's use of *de$_4$* is otherwise quite consistent. A "hyper-Assyrianism" certainly belongs in this linguistic potpourri.

[58]Elsewhere there are scattered Assyrianisms like *šēzibanni* (*EA* 318:8, 14; see also 62:30) or *lērub* (*EA* 149:19), but they are not only quite sporadic, frequently they are probably due, not to influence of Assyrian, but to ignorance of Babylonian (see after *lērub* in *EA* 149:19, *līmur* in the next line).

1 p. *lāmur*, Babylonian *lūmur* (*la-mur-mi*, *EA* 286:40; *la-mu-ur*, 286:46).
lērub, Babylonian *lūrub* (*le-lu-ub*, *EA* 286:46).[59]

3 p. *lūṣi*, Babylonian *līṣi* (*lu-ṣi-mi*, *EA* 286:56).
lūmaššer / *lūmaššera*, Babylonian *līmaššer* / *līmaššera* (*lu-ma-še-er*, *EA* 288:58; 289:42; *lu-ma-šir*$_9$, 290:20; *lu-ma-še-ra*, 285: 28; 287:18).
lūtirra, Babylonian *līterra* (*lu-ti-ra*, *EA* 290:21).

(b) Verbs primae aleph$_{3-5}$ are consistently (13x) treated as in Assyrian:

G inf., *erāba*, Babylonian *erēba* (*e-ra-ba*, *EA* 286:43); *ezābi*, Babylonian *ezēbi* (*e-za-bi-ša*, *EA* 287:62).[60]

G present, *tippaša* (for *teppaša*), Babylonian *teppuša* (*ti-ip-pa-ša*, *EA* 287:71);[61] *eppaš*, Babylonian *ippuš* (*e-pa-aš*, *EA* 289:9); *eppušū*, Babylonian *ippušū* (*ep-pu-šū*, *EA* 287:19—obviously the writing is ambiguous, but in view of the other forms the assumption of vowel harmony, *eppašū* > *eppušū*, seems legitimate).

G preterite, *ēpušū*, Babylonian *īpušū* (*e-pu-šu*, *EA* 289:12); *ēpušūne*, Babylonian *īpušūni* (*e-pu-šu-né*, *EA* 290:5); prec. *lērub* (see above).

Gt present, *ētelli*, Babylonian *ītelli* (*e-tel-li*, *EA* 287:45).

Š imperative *šērib*, Babylonian *šūrib* (*še-ri-ib*, *EA* 286:62; 287:67; 288:64).

Š present *ušerrubū*, Babylonian *ušerrebū* (*ú-še-ru-bu*, *EA* 287:11, vowel harmony).

Babylonian forms (4x or 2x) of verbs *primae aleph*: *ikkalū*, Assyrian *ekkulū* (*i-ka-lu*, *EA* 286:6); *errub*, Assyrian *errab* (*e-ru-ub*, *EA* 286: 39; perhaps *ērub* with volitive force intended, interference from Canaanite volitive *ʾaqtul*), *erēši*, Assyrian *erāše* (*e-re-š*[*i*], *EA* 289:7); perhaps *eppuš*, Assyrian *eppaš* (*e-pu-uš*, *EA* 286:14), but see above on *errub*.

(c) Verbs *mediae infirmae*. Above, under *Syllabary*, we have already noted the writings *d*[e$_4$-*k*]*a* (*EA* 288:41), *de*$_4$-*k*[*a*] (*EA* 288:45), and

[59]We take *le-lu-ub* simply as a mistake and doubt its relevance for the problem of EN-*ri* (see n. 52, above).

[60]For Böhl, LSS V/2, 63, these two forms of the infinitive were simply errors.

[61]Rather than assume with Albright (*ANET* 488, followed by *CAD* E 209b) two errors (present for preterite, singular for plural) and an omission (*ana muḫ-ḫī*<*i̯a*>), we translate *tippaša epša lamna ana muḫḫi amēlūt māt kāši* "May you treat the crime as the responsibility of (lit. "against") the men of the land of Cush."

de_4-ka-ti (*EA* 287:73). Since all other instances of *de_4* are to be explained in terms of contrast with /di/,[62] and since when the latter is in place the *di*-sign is used (*a-di*, *EA* 287:45,47; 288:60), it follows that we must interpret the forms of *dâku* as reflecting Assyrian *dēk* (plus Canaanite morphs) rather than Babylonian *dīk*.

(d) Verbs *tertiae infirmae*. Only twice do verbs of this class exhibit Babylonian vowel contraction (*i-ba-šu-ú*, *EA* 285:23; *it-ta-ṣú-ú*, *EA* 286:48), whereas lack of contraction characteristic of Assyrian is found five times: *ta-ša-mi-ú* (*EA* 286:50), *te-le-qé-ú* (*EA* 288:38), *i-qa-bi-ú* (*EA* 288:54), *li-il-qé-a-ni* (*EA* 288:59), *i*G-G*i-ú-šu*. To our knowledge, with the exception of the very obscure *i-te-e-i-ú* (*EA* 162:74, Egypt; *īdeʾu* according to *AHw* 321 sub *ḫannipu*), the hardly less obscure *e-ma-e* (*EA* 136:14), and *a-ṣa-i* (*EA* 195:21), nowhere in the Amarna archive are verbs of this class—and it includes some of the most frequently attested, such as *šemû*, *leqû*, *qabû*—written with CV-V that does not represent CV_1-V_1 = $C\hat{V}$.[63]

Under this heading it should perhaps be mentioned that, except in *EA* 285:23, *ibašši* is uninflected and is used with subjects in the plural: KUR.ḪI.A *ù* LÚ *ḫa-zi-a-nu-‹ti›* (*EA* 287:21); LÚ.MEŠ GN (*EA* 289:19).[64] Here again there may be MA influence, but of course with only two examples we cannot be sure.[65]

4. *Lexicon*

(a) *lamnu* (*EA* 287:71), elsewhere in Amarna Babylonian *lemnu* (6x), except *EA* 189:7 (Qadeš, see *i̯í-la-mu-nu-ni*, lines 6, 8) and *EA* 97:5

[62]On the "hyper-Assyrianism" *la-ma-de_4-ka* in *EA* 287:59, see n. 57, above. Besides various forms of *idû*, the only other instance of *de_4* is *ša-de_4-e* (*EA* 287:56), where /de/ rather than /di/ is obviously intended.

[63]Whether Wilhelm, AOAT 9, 46, is justified in denying that comparable forms at Nuzi are to be explained as Assyrianisms since some of them also exhibit Babylonian features (see *te-le-qé-ú*, not *ta-la-qé-ú*, in *EA* 288:38; however, *ta-ša-mi-ú*, not *te-še-mi-ú*, in *EA* 286:50), we need not decide here. In view of all the other Assyrianisms in the Jerusalem letters, we think our explanation of the forms in question the most likely and see no real difficulty in taking *teleqqeʾū* as a hybrid of even three languages: Babylonian assimilation of the vowels, Assyrian lack of contraction, and Canaanite verbal prefix {t(a)} in 3 plural **taqtulū(na)*.

[64]Contrary to *EA* II 1390, *EA* 286:57, 58 are not pertinent, for the subjects in question, LÚ.MEŠ.ERÍN *piṭati* and KUR.ḪI.A, respectively, are treated as singular (*lūṣi*, 54; *ḫalqat*, 60); this also calls into doubt *EA* 287:20. The only other Amarna parallels are in *EA* 1 (Egypt), 35 (Alašia), and possibly 125 (Byblos, but perhaps ŠE.IM.ḪI.A is to be taken as a collective).

[65]For MA, see Mayer, AOAT Sonderreihe 2, 97.

(resembles Byblos tablets; see Knudtzon's observations, *EA* II, 1192, n. 1).

(b) *ḫaziānu* (*EA* 286:52; 287:22; 288:9), plural **ḫaziānūtu* (*EA* 285:19; 286:19; 287:24; 288:56), unparalleled in Amarna despite the frequency of the term.[66] According to *AHw* 338b–339a, *ḫaziānu* MA and NA (PN); add *ARM* XIII 143:5′ (*ḫa-zi-ia-nu-*[*um*]), 18′ (*ḫa-zi-ia-an*); *AHw* 339a, abstract *ḫaziānuttu* MA; add *ARM* XIII 143:8 (*ḫa-zi-ia-nu-tam*).

(c) *a-la-ʾe-e* (*EA* 286:42; 287:58) reflects Assyrian *laʾāʾu* rather than Babylonian *leʾû* (*i-le-ʾe-e*, *EA* 287:62).[67]

(d) *ištu* = *itti* (*EA* 286:43; see line 40). For this there are a number of parallels in the periphery,[68] which are perhaps based on MA usage (see *AHw* 401).

There is, then, no denying a rather strong Assyrian influence on the language of the Jerusalem letters.[69] And, if we look in the west for examples of a comparably Assyrianizing language, we find them at Amurru, Alašia, Ugarit, and Boghazköy, all sources which would seem immediately to furnish an additional argument for the case we have been gradually building up for the northern background of the Jerusa-

[66]This peculiarity was first noted by Nakata, *JANES* 2 (1969) 22–23.

[67]Occasional exceptions to the prevalence of *leʾû* in the Amarna archive are, besides the two passages in the Jerusalem letters: *EA* 137:27 (Byblos), 241:18 (Syria? note also *abat* 10, 19—see n. 54), 326:15 (Ascalon).

[68]See Labat, *L'akkadien de Boghaz-Köi*, 141; Dietrich and Loretz, Festschrift F. Altheim, I, 20. An instrumental meaning is also to be noted in *PRU* IV 36:35 (*ištu kakkīka* "par tes (propres) armes") and several passages of the Byblos letters (*ištu manni* "with what," *EA* 112:10–12; 123:31; 125:11–12. That this is the meaning is clear from: (1) the general context, which makes it obvious *from* whom or what Rib-Addi is to defend Byblos; (2) the parallel passage, *EA* 126:33, where *kī* "how" replaces *ištu manni*; (3) the parallel passage, *EA* 122:11ff., where after quoting the pharaoh's *uṣur* ..., Rib-Addi immediately answers that in the past he had a garrison with which to defend himself, a situation quite different from his present one; (4) *EA* 125:14ff., where after *ištu manni* ..., the days of former strength are again recalled; (5) the question, "Who (what) will protect me?" in *EA* 112:13 and 119:10, in the latter case following immediately upon the citation of the pharaoh's *uṣurme* ..., just as *ištu manni* ... does. In *EA* 112:11–12, *ištu nakrīi̯a û ištu* LÚ.MEŠ *ḫupšīi̯a* "with my enemies or with my *ḫ*" is ironical. On the background of these passages, see the important article of M. Liverani, *OA* 10 [1971] 262–63).

[69]The basic language is still (Canaanitized-)Babylonian. Besides the Babylonian (or hybrid) forms already listed, note especially: *ii̯anu* (not *laššu*), *inanna* (unknown in Assyrian), *šāšunu* (not *šunāšunu*? *šunātunu*?), probably {ūtu} (not {uttu}), lack of vowel harmony (*taraii̯amu*, *tazaii̯aru*, *ušaii̯aru* [?]), *teleqqe* (not *talaqqe*), *u̯uššera* (not *u̯aššera*), etc.

lem letters.[70] Caution, however, is in place. The Assyrian component in these latter documents is understandable and is probably to be explained as ultimately reflecting the expansion of Assyrian political power,[71] whereas at the time of the Jerusalem letters, however late we may date them within the possible limits of the Amarna archive, such an explanation is most improbable.[72] Hence the different political (and cultural) context diminishes somewhat the force of the apparent parallels.

However, if we ask ourselves where—in Syria or in southern Palestine—even prior to the rise of Assyrian political power, the influence of the Assyrian language seems more likely, the answer seems pretty clear; and if other evidence points in the same direction, only one answer is possible: Syria.

Miscellaneous

1. Lexicon

(a) *adi*, "(together) with, besides" (*EA* 287:47; 288:60), is not clearly attested elsewhere in the Amarna archive, in which *qādu* is the rule. However, *adi* is so used in MA and MB, and see *adu* in *PRU* IV 49:17; *adu kinanna* in *EA* 357:88 is a special case which we will discuss elsewhere.

[70] For Amurru, see the very strongly Assyrianizing language of *PRU* IV 141ff.; for Alašia, *Ugar*. V no. 22; for Ugarit (i.e., found there, but provenience not certain), *PRU* IV 228f., 289; F. Thureau-Dangin, *Syria* 16 (1935) 188–93; for Boghazköy, *KBo* 1 14, 20; *KUB* III 73, 75, 77–79. The provenience of the letter published by Thureau-Dangin poses a special problem. In general it is written in Assyrian (with *AHw* 382a, read line 7 *a-na i-ni* "why?" ‹ *ana mīni*), but Thureau-Dangin's opinion that it was written at Assur does not seem to take into sufficient account the following: (1) KUR URU *ú-ga-ri-ta* (5, and see above on KUR URU GN); (2) *inanna anumma* (12, neither word attested in Assyrian); (3) after a temporal clause, *u* introducing main clause (24, "waw of apodosis"); (4) [*m*]*ī-nummê* (24, strictly peripheral; see *AHw* 656); (5) the lapse *du-ub-bu* (20) for *dubub*, and, probably, *šul-ma-ka* (10) for *šulamka*. Though we cannot rule out, especially in view of *EA* 16, the possibility of a scribe at Assur writing a mildly barbarized Assyrian, we must also allow that, as Assyrian political and commercial influence extended westward, (barbarized) Assyrian may have tended in some areas seriously to compete with, or even to replace, the older "Reichsakkadisch."

[71] See A. Goetze, *Kizzuwatna and the Problem of Hittite Geography* (New Haven, 1940) 32.

[72] Abdi-Ḫeba's correspondence is probably to be dated in the early years of Amenophis IV; see Edward Fay Campbell, Jr., *The Chronology of the Amarna Letters* (Baltimore, 1964) 104–5. In other words, Assuruballit had probably not yet begun even to reign.

(b) *an-ni-ka-nu* (*EA* 287:52) is certainly the same word as *an-ni-ka-nu* "here" in *PRU* IV 216:12 and 227:21 (see *AHw* 52, *CAD* A/2, 132 sub *annikīʾam*).[73]

(c) The adjective *banû*, which is attested four times (A.WA.TÚ.MEŠ *ba-na-ta* [*EA* 286:62–63; 287:67; 289:49], A.WA.TÚ.MEŠ [... *b*]*a-na-ti* [*EA* 288:65]), emerges in MB as a replacement for *damqu* (see *CAD* B, sub voce), and is found elsewhere in Amarna in letters from Babylonia, Assyria (*EA* 16), Mitanni, Ḫatti, Amurru, Egypt; to this list we may also add occurrences at Ugarit (see *CAD*). The expression *au̯atu banītu*, *au̯ātu banâtu*, etc., is attested in Babylonia, Mitanni, Ḫatti, Ugarit.

(d) *dāriš* in *ana dāriš* (*EA* 287:61). The only strict parallel in peripheral Akkadian is *ana dārišma* at Nuzi (*JEN* 620:10), but *adi dāriš* (exclusively peripheral: Egypt, Ugarit, Amurru) should also be compared. Standard western peripheral: *ana dārīti* and *adi dārīti*.

(e) *enūma* (12x), which has a number of meanings in the Jerusalem letters, including the extraordinary one of a preposition meaning "like,"[74] is used exclusively, and *inūma* does not occur. The standard MB form is noteworthy in the south, where *inūma* is the rule. Aside from a sporadic occurrence in a letter from Hazor and its consistent use in the letters from Tyre—once more Tyre!—*enūma* belongs in Amurru (? *EA* 237, see n. 28), Mitanni, Nuḫašše, Qatna, Alašia, Alalakh (very rare), Ugarit, and Ḫatti.

(f) *ḫamuttam* "quickly" (*EA* 285:29) is attested once in OB, passim in MB letters, and in the periphery, at Nuzi, Mitanni, Ḫatti, Ugarit, Alašia (see *EA* and *CAD*). It tends to replace *arḫiš*, which is standard in Phoenicia and Palestine.

(g) *maḫru* with *ina* in *ina maḫrīi̯a* (*EA* 289:39). The only parallels in the Amarna archive are *EA* 16:8 (Assyria), *EA* 29:38 (Mitanni).

[73]Why *CAD* A/2 132 considers the Jerusalem occurrence "uncertain" is not clear. In context the meaning "here" makes perfect sense: Abdi-Ḫeba's emphasis ("and send a royal commissioner *here*") reflects his conviction that the crisis he faces is due to the absence of a commissioner in Jerusalem, where he really belongs rather than at Gaza (see lines 46ff.). Note the punctuation mark, before *annikānu*.

[74]*enūma ᶜapiri* "like an ᶜApiru" (*EA* 288:29), *enūma eleppi* "like a ship" (*EA* 288:33), *enūma āl ᶜazzati* "like the city of Gaza" (*EA* 289:16–17), *enūma ‹māri› Labʾayi* "like ‹the sons› of Labʾayu" (*EA* 289:21–22), as seen by Albright (see the translations in *ANET* 488). This meaning probably developed from the lexical overlap of *kīma* and *enūma* as conjunctions, with the former's prepositional meaning then extended to the latter.

2. Typology

A rather unusual feature of the Jerusalem letters is the four postscripts which Abdi-Ḫeba addresses to "the scribe of the king, my lord" (*EA* 286–289). In the Amarna archive, comparable additions to the main text of the letter are found in *EA* 12 (Babylonia), 32 (Egypt), 42 (? Boghazköy), 170 (Amurru), and 316 (southern Palestine).[75] Other parallels are to be found at Boghazköy and Ugarit.[76]

CONCLUSION

So far we have seen various lines of evidence all converge and form a rather consistent pattern.[77] They not only confirm Albright's insight on the individuality of the Jerusalem scribe in a Palestinian setting, but they agree in pointing to its source—a profound influence of northern scribal practices on the exercise of his craft.

However, before speculating on how this might have come about, consideration must be given to two other lines of evidence, the first of which in some sense runs counter to those we have followed so far. This is the absence in the language of the Jerusalem letters of the truly distinctive features of "Reichsakkadisch," and the presence of a large West Semitic component.[78] For this combination there is nothing comparable in the sources from Alašia, Amurru, Ugarit, or Alalakh, not to mention

[75]These postscripts have been studied by A. L. Oppenheim, *Assyriological Studies* 16, 253–56. (To the examples of covering letters which he has pointed out at Mari, the Assyrian letter referred to in n. 70 should be added. On the identity of the addressee, the royal scribe El(i)-milku, see Nougayrol, *Ugar*. V 13, n. 2.) J. J. Finkelstein, *Eretz Israel* 9 (1969) 9, 34, has added the interesting observation that Abdi-Ḫeba's assertion of loyalty "I would die for you" (*mattī ana kāta*) is at the end of the letter, as in the postscript in *EA* 12. The imitation of MA and MB models, as argued by Finkelstein, would be another example of the scribe's learning.

[76]For the evidence, besides Oppenheim's article, see Nougayrol, *Ugar*. V 67, and H. Otten, *MDOG* 87 (1955) 17.

[77]On the modified sense in which this is true of the Assyrianisms, see above.

[78]Missing, besides the typical confusion of stops (on the sibilants, see nn. 50–51, above), are characteristic lexical entries like *kīmê, mannummê, mīnummê*. The number of Canaanitisms is considerable, but a complete list, which would demand long discussion, is unnecessary. Suffice it to note: *a-nu-ki* "I" (*EA* 287:69), *zuruḫ* "arm" (*EA* 286:12; 287:27; 288:14, 34); *ṣaduq* "the right is" (*EA* 287:32), *ḫanpa ša iḫnupū* "what they have done is sacrilegious" (*EA* 288:7–8), **i̯aqtulu* as present-future (*EA* 286:6, 18, 20, 21, 24, 50; 288:61), **qatala* as perfect (*EA* 288:7, 41, 45), 3 plural **taqtulū(na)* (*EA* 288:38; see *JCS* 5, 33ff. [above, Paper 6]), infinitive **qatāli* (*EA* 287:46; see *JCS* 6, 77 [above, Paper 7, p. 166]), etc., etc.

Egypt, Boghazköy, or Mitanni. If we may define the Jerusalem scribe in geographical terms as a "northerner," he is no less a "southerner" too.

The various hypotheses that this curious mélange might suggest must also take into account the evidence on the background of the Jerusalem scribe's master, Abdi-Ḫeba, a question of considerable interest in itself. In *EA* 286:9ff., 287:25ff., and 288:13ff., Abdi-Ḫeba acknowledges that he owes his position in Jerusalem to neither his father nor his mother, but only to the strong arm of his king. With this debt to the pharaoh he also associates the fact that he is not a governor but a soldier (*EA* 288:9–10), a distinction of titles which he makes again at the beginning of another letter (*EA* 285:5–6). Similarly, on another occasion (*EA* 289:69) he reaffirms his membership in the military, with its implications for him of absolute loyalty. In short, running through the correspondence like a theme is a concern for origins of authority, title, and status that is without parallel in the letters of other vassals, and it requires explanation.

In our opinion the main crux is the interpretation of the claim to be a soldier and not a governor.[79] It should not be understood simply as a statement of loyalty. For Abdi-Ḫeba, governors are not synonymous with treachery; rather, he sees in them the faithful and often suffering opposition to the perfidious ᶜApiru (*EA* 288:36–46). Nor may we take his claim to mean that his authority is exclusively military, for example, that of a garrison commander. For not only do the other local princes speak of him simply as one of their number (see *EA* 280), but in taking office he "enters his father's house" (*EA* 286:13; 288:15), a long-established expression for accession to the throne.[80]

What would make sense of this apparent contradiction of a governor who is also not a governor but a soldier, and at the same time explain the unparalleled insistence on the pharaoh's personal intervention in Abdi-Ḫepa's coming to power, would be the assumption that unlike most of his peers he did not come to the throne in an established line of succession, but rather, after belonging to the military, had been brought into Jerusalem by "the strong arm of the king." On this reading of the passages in question, Abdi-Ḫeba would in some sense be a *novus*

[79]Another crux is the title LÚ *ru-ḫi šarri* in *EA* 288. Unfortunately, its significance and its possible implications for the background of Abdi-Ḫeba still escape us; see H. Donner, *ZAW* 73 (1961) 269–77.

[80]See *AHw* 235, 4 j; S. O. Simmons, *JCS* 13 (1959) 82; and the accession years of Sabum and Apil-Sin (*RLA* 2, 176, nos. 51 and 65).

homo on the Jerusalem scene, though perhaps not entirely so, if the reference to his father's house is to be given its full weight. He may have belonged to the old royal house, or a branch of it, which, for reasons we can only guess at, lost Jerusalem but not the pharaoh's favor.

This seems to us the most plausible interpretation, apart from any concern for the scribe's background. However, as is clear, it is also very relevant to this question and, in the light of all the other evidence for the intrusiveness of the writing and language of the letters, gives strong support to the view that the scribe was truly an outsider and not a native Hierosolymitan open to outside influences.

Where, then, did he come from? Since to some extent Egypt belongs under the designation "northern," one could consider looking in that direction, especially when the history of political refugees like his master is recalled. However, there is absolutely nothing in the language of the Egyptian scribes that even remotely resembles the interference-component, both West Semitic and Assyrian, we find in the Jerusalem letters. On the evidence at hand, therefore, we must turn elsewhere, and only Syria, somewhere along the border between "Reichsakkadisch" and "Canaanite-Akkadian," remains as a likely place of origin. And if we may join the scribe's history with that of his master, we would propose that it was in the latter's company, as part of a new royal entourage, that he came south to the Judaean stronghold.

18. Amarna Glosses

I. — The Sin of Labᵓayu

In *EA* 253–254, according to the generally accepted reading of the two letters, Labᵓayu confesses to the Pharaoh that he has sinned and has been guilty of some disloyalty or treachery. Though this is an extraordinary, even unique, act of honesty and frankness, which contrasts so sharply with the self-portraits of perfect innocence drawn by other vassals, no one seems to doubt it.[1] Discussion has turned, not on the fact of sin, but on its nature. For some, it is to be found in Labᵓayu's entry into Gezer, which he admits in both letters.[2] For others, it lies in the speech which, in *EA* 254, he cites as having delivered there after his entry.[3] Some opt for both explanations.[4] But for all, Labᵓayu is a sinner, and he admits it.

Basic to the whole discussion have been Knudtzon's translations of the letters in question. These have never been seriously challenged except in minor details or by an occasional hint at the awareness of other possibilities.[5] And yet they miss an essential fact that to us seems

[1]If one follows W. F. Albright's version of *EA* 252 (*BASOR* 89 [1943] 28–32; *ANET* 496), Labᵓayu was capable of a truculence and contumacy that might suggest a habit of simple, direct speech. However, even if Albright be right (*dato non concesso*), a refusal to submit quietly to the spoliation of one's native town by a hostile third party is, in the context of the vassal correspondence, still something quite different from an open admission of disloyalty.

[2]M. Liverani, *RA* 61 (1967) 10, who understands entry in the sense of occupation; cf. also A. Alt, *Kleine Schriften* I (Munich, 1953) 109, and K. Galling, *Palästinajahrbuch* 1935, 76. Liverani also finds in Labᵓayu's admission evidence for Egyptian policy which, according to him, allowed vassals to attack one another with no concern or interference by the crown, provided they promised, as Labᵓayu does, and maintained their devotion to essential Egyptian interests. We shall argue against this view elsewhere.

[3]J. de Koning, *Studiën over de El-Amarnabrieven en het Oude Testament inzonderheid uit historisch oogpunt* (Delft, 1940) 120; Walter Harrelson, *Biblical Archaeologist* 20 (1957) 6 = *The Biblical Archaeologist Reader* 2 (Garden City, 1964) 262; Edward F. Campbell, *apud* G. Ernest Wright, *Shechem* (New York/Toronto, 1965) 197.

[4]O. Weber, *EA* II 1315–16; J. F. Ross, *Biblical Archaeologist* 30 (1967) 64–65, with different views on the implications of the entry.

[5]In *The Chronology of the Amarna Letters* (Baltimore, 1964) 109, n. 2, Campbell

patent: *EA* 253 also cites Labʾayu's speech in Gezer. This recognized, the affair at Gezer—as reported by Labʾayu—looks completely different, and the confession becomes, not an honest admission of guilt, but, as we should have expected, an exercise in the rhetoric of irony.

The occasion of *EA* 253, as everyone has recognized, was a letter from the Pharaoh charging his vassal with some disloyalty. Immediately after the formulaic introduction and the acknowledgment of having heard his sovereign's message, Labʾayu launches into a declaration of loyalty which he claims equals that of his father and grandfather. He goes on: *ù [l]a-[a] ar-n[a-k]u [ù] la-a ḫa-ṭá-ku an-nu-ú ar-nu-ia ù an-nu-ú [ḫ]i-ṭú-ia i-nu-ma ir-ru-ba-[t]i i-na* URU *gaz-ri um-ma a-[n]a-[k]u-mi i̯e-en-ni-nu-nu-mi* LUGAL-*ru ù a-nu-ma e-na-an-na ia-nu pa-ni ša-nu-ta*$_5$ *iš-tu ur-ru-ud* LUGAL-*ri* ... (15–28). Knudtzon translated: "Und nicht habe ich gefrevelt, und nicht habe ich gesündigt. Dies ist mein Frevel, und dies ist meine Sünde, dass ich eingetreten bin in Gazri. Also (sage) ich: Es möge uns gnädig sein der König! Denn siehe, jetzt gibt es nicht ein anderes Antlitz, davon abgewendet, dem König zu dienen ..." The rest of the letter (29–35) Knudtzon saw as continuing the address to the Pharaoh which began with "Es möge uns gnädig sein der König!"

However, whereas Knudtzon has Labʾayu here confessing as his crime having entered Gezer, but then turning to his master with a plea for mercy, we see Labʾayu saying something quite different: "This is my crime and this is my sin: when I entered Gezer, I said, "The king treats us kindly!" And now, in fact, I have no other purpose than the service of the king ..." In support of this translation are the following considerations:

1. Aside from the question of who exactly is addressed, *i̯enninunu-mi šarru* may not be translated as a plea ("May the king ..."). The form *i̯enninu* is one more example of **i̯aqtulu* in the West-Semitized Akkadian of the Amarna letters.[6] Its use in Labʾayu's letters is as follows:

---

states that *EA* 253:18–24 describes the same event as *EA* 254:25ff., and in *Shechem* (see n. 3) 196, his translation of *umma anākūmi*, with its alternatives "Thus I said (or: say)", suggests in the first instance the possibility that what follows was spoken in Gezer. However, this is not discussed in his commentary.

[6]For a systematic study of the form in the Byblos letters, see the writer's dissertation "A Syntactical Study of the Dialect of Byblos as Reflected in the Amarna Letters" (Johns Hopkins, 1950) [first entry in the present volume]; see also *JCS* 5 (1951) 33–35 [above, Paper 6]; *Or. NS* 29 (1960) 1–19 [above, Paper 10]; *The Bible and the Ancient Near East*, ed. G. Ernest Wright (Garden City, 1961) 63–65 = Anchor Books 72–75 [above, Paper 11]. Anson F. Rainey has verified the Byblos system as obtaining generally in the Phoenician and Palestinian area (see *Israel*

A. Ind. pres.-fut.:

EA 252 :17 *tu-um-ḫa-ṣú*, "it is struck";
:18 *ti-qà-bi-lu*, "does it (not) fight back";
:18 *ta-an-šu-ku*, "(and) bite";
:20 *i-ša-ḫa-tu*, "(how) shall I be timid";[7]
:23 *ti-qa-bu*, "(if) you say";
EA 253 :30 *i̯i-iq-ta-bu*, "(whatever) he says";
:30 [*i*]*š-te-mu*, "I heed";[8]
EA 254 : 9 *i̯i-iḫ-li-qú*, "(what am I that) he should lose";
:40 *a-kal-lu-ši*, "(how) shall I hold her back";
:46 *ip-pu-šu*, "(how) shall I (not) carry out."

B. Past iterative

EA 254 :35 *it-ta-na-la-ku*, "he was consorting"; note Gtn.

Left unclassified are: *i̯ú-sà-an-ni-qú* (254:18), *aq-ta-bu* (254:23), *i̯i-il-te-qú* (254:25). Whereas context permitted little or no doubt about the other forms, these are not unambiguous, and it is to be conceded that they might be translated as preterites. However, in view of the general pattern, which is also well established elsewhere, it seems legitimate and even preferable to assume consistency. The first and third forms, therefore, are to be placed under the pres.-futures, the second under the past iteratives. As will be evident from our translation of the forms below, the assumption of consistency does no violence to the text, and in the case of the past iterative it makes the claim of Labʾayu all the more forceful.

Above all, note well: again in conformity with general usage, *in no instance* is there the slightest possibility of rendering **i̯aqtulu* as a jussive.[9] Therefore, *i̯enninu* may not be so rendered.

Oriental Studies 1 [1971], 86–102; *UF* 5 [1973] 235–262), but a thorough study assembling all the evidence remains a desideratum. The use of **i̯aqtulu* in the letters of Labʾayu is identical with that in the Byblos correspondence.

[7]The analysis of the forms follows Albright's interpretation of the lines in question (*BASOR* 89 [1943] 28–32; *ANET* 486). We differ only in accepting the suggestion of Dr. Avi Hurwitz on the meaning of *ti-qà-bi-lu* (Albright: "accept passively"). In *i-ša-ḫa-tu*, we assume an error for *i-ša-ḫu-tu*. Neither form appears in *AHw*.

[8]General truth; contrast *išteme* in line 7 (also 254:31), with reference to single, past event (hearing the Pharaoh's message). For a similar contrast, see Rainey, *Israel Oriental Studies* 1 (1971) 96–101.

[9]So far as the writer can determine, this is an inviolable rule. The one exception he once conceded (*EA* 92:47) he did not understand, overlooking the obvious plu-

2. If *i̯enninunumi šarru* is addressed to the king, why is it introduced by *umma anākūmi*? The letter is sent to the Pharaoh and so far he is the only one spoken to; nor, *ex hypothesi*, is Labʾayu reporting an earlier message to the king.[10] Why then the marker of direct quotation?[11] The only natural way to understand the phrase is as introducing a speech in Gezer.

3. Consistent with, and almost required by, the usual understanding of *i̯enninunumi šarru* as directed to the king, is the interpretation of the object suffix {nu}, literally "us", as referring simply to Labʾayu himself.[12] If this were correct, it would be the only example of such usage in his three letters. Elsewhere, in at least 50 instances (*EA* 252, 8x; 253, 15x; 254, 27x), he speaks of himself only in the 1 sg. In the letter in question, note especially the vb. suff. in *ištapranni* (line 10, also 254:7), *i̯ipqidni* (line 32). But if Labʾayu is reporting a speech given in Gezer, of course, the difficulty of the plural reference disappears. It is the Gezerites, or their ruler—or both—who are also declared objects of the royal beneficence.

4. And of course in *EA* 254 Labʾayu claims to have spoken in Gezer and reports his speech there. Moreover, at the crucial point note how closely *EA* 253 parallels *EA* 254:

annû arnūi̯a u annû hīṭūi̯a	*šanīta ebašši arnīi̯a*
inūma irrubātī ina āl gazri	*inūma irrubālī ana āl gazri*
umma anākūmi	*u aqtabu.*

—We submit that the evidence is clear and decisive that *EA* 253 also reports what Labʾayu claims to have said in Gezer.

The speech as reported in *EA* 254 must then also be reexamined. For it is clear that in *EA* 253 Labʾayu admits to no disloyalty whatsoever. On the contrary! He went before a presumably hostile audience

---

ral subject, the rulers mentioned in lines 32–34.

[10]A possible exception is Campbell (see above, n. 5).

[11]In the letters of vassals (excluding therefore those from Egypt, Mitanni, etc.), *umma* appears outside the introductory formula only in *EA* 59:5 and 100:7, where it introduces the body of the letter, and in 138:79, where it introduces the speech of someone other than the letter-writer.

[12]Liverani (see above, n. 2) goes so far as to translate "sia benevolo il re verso di *me*" (italics ours). The problem is always ignored. Perhaps some assume Labʾayu includes his family or followers; if he does, this is the only instance. Campbell, *Shechem* (see above, n. 3) 197–198, while considering it "perilous to speculate about Labʾayu's words cited in Letter 253", seems to take the "us" as referring to Labʾayu and Milkilu.

and proclaimed what a truly generous master the Pharaoh was to all of them. No disloyalty here! And so there can be no disloyalty implied by what he says in *EA* 254: *a-nu-ma i̯i-ka-lu ka-ar-ṣí-ia ḫa-ba-lu-ma ù la-a i̯ú-sà-an-ni-qú* LUGAL-*ru* EN-*ia ar-ni-ia ša-ni-ta*$_5$ *e-ba-aš-ši ar-ni-ia i-nu-ma ir-ru-ba-ti a-na* URU *gaz-ri ù aq-ta-bu pu-uḫ-ri-iš-mi i̯i-il-te-qú* LUGAL-*ru mim-mi-ia ù mim-me* ᵖ*mil-ki-li a-ia-ka-am* (16–27), "Though they have slandered me unjustly, the king does not examine my crime.[13] Moreover, my crime was: when I entered Gezer, I said over and over, 'Quite everything of mine the king takes,[14] but where is everything of Milkilu?' "[15]

In another context, this might be understood as a complaint by Lab'ayu that the Egyptian yoke weighs much less heavily on Milkilu. But as the vassal correspondence in general makes clear, such a protest is not likely to be passed on to the king, and it runs completely against the tenor of the speech as reported in *EA* 253. We submit that he merely states a fact, which is in no way resented but rather implies his own ready acceptance of his vassal-status. This lays bare the implications of the obvious answer to his repeated question where the possessions of Milkilu are. The latter, no less an object of the royal largesse, is the real traitor, and an ungrateful one to boot.[16]

[13]*sunnuqu* does not mean "impute" (Albright, *ANET* 486) or "hold against" (Campbell, *Shechem* [see above, n. 3], 197), but, as already argued by Moshe Held, *JCS* 15 (1961) 17, has its usual Akk. meaning. Note also that Held, *ibid.*, 12, provided the West Semitic parallel to *qarṣī qabû* in *EA* 252:13–14; Campbell, *Shechem* 195, n. 7, repeats Albright's erroneous view in *BASOR* 89 (1943) 30, n. 13.

[14]Albright, *BASOR* 89 (1943) 34, n. 9, proposed "publicly" for *puḫriš(mi)* here and in *EA* 333:7, and understood it with the vb. *aqtabu*; see also *ANET* 486. However, there are four or five direct quotations in the Lab'ayu correspondence (*EA* 252:25–27; 253:24–25; 254:24/25–27; 254:43–44; also 252:6–7?), and the text under consideration aside, in all but one (254:43–44) the first word of the quotation is marked by *mi*; hence it seems more likely that in *puḫrišmi* we should understand the enclitic as marker of direct quotation. Favoring "completely" for *puḫriš* (*AHw* 876 "zusammen") is the context (all from Lab'ayu, nothing from Milkilu), with additional support from the use of *puḫru* at Nuzi in connection with property (HSS 5 66:10, 99:6 *mīnummê puḫuršu ša* PN; see E. A. Speiser, *BASOR* 10, 36, 48).

[15]Albright's "and not likewise the property of Milkilu?" must be considered a loose paraphrase.

[16]Thus the two accounts of the speech fit together quite well. What actually happened is of course another question. Against seeing in Lab'ayu's entry into Gezer any kind of real occupation are: (1) he admits it quite openly and without gloss; (2) after his death, his two sons seem to have a loyal ally in Milkilu (*EA* 250:35–

II. — Life from the Pharaoh

In *EA* 369 Milkilu is instructed by the Pharaoh to send forty female cupbearers of faultless beauty.[17] For his obedience he is promised the reward of hearing his master say, "This is excellent" (*ši-ia-tu*$_4$ *ba-an-tu*, line 21). As read by the editor the text goes on: *ka-ši* NAM.TI *iš-pu-ru-ka*, which he translates, "A toi, la vie On t'a envoyé" (lines 22–23). On the authority of an Egyptologist, we are told that the Pharaoh refers to himself by the indefinite 3 pl, a practice attested in Egyptian sources of which this would be the earliest example, and sends the gift of life so cherished by his vassals.[18]

This seems an attractive interpretation and it has won general acceptance.[19] However, it labors under a number of difficulties:

1. Whatever the practice of Egyptian sources, in no letter sent by the Pharaoh to either vassals or independent sources does he refer to himself by the 3 pl. In *EA* 369 alone, seven times he follows the standard usage of the vassal letters and speaks of himself in the 3 sg.[20]

2. *kâši*, masc., is otherwise unknown in the Amarna letters. It

---

39, 53–54; on 35–39, see *BASOR* 211 [1973] 51, nn. 6–7 [above, Paper 16, pp. 244–245, nn. 6–7]), whom we would not expect to cooperate with the successors of the one who ousted him. The fact that Labʾayu quotes his speech in each letter suggests a charge of seditious talk as well as of appropriation of territory (cf. *EA* 254:9–10).

[17]*EA* 369 was published by G. Dossin, *Bull. de l'Académie Royale de Belgique*, Classe des Lettres, 20/5 (1934), 85–92; *RA* 31 (1934) 125–136; re-edited by A. Rainey, AOAT 8, 36–39. With Dossin and Albright (*ANET* 487), and against *CAD* Ṣ 55b ("in whose heart there is no falsehood") and Rainey ("there is no guile in their hearts"), we doubt that the Pharaoh was concerned about the ladies' virtue; see Dossin's comments, *RA* 31 (1934) 135. For *zapurtu* rather than *ṣaburtu* (*CAD*), see W. von Soden, *Or. NS* 20 (1951) 158–162.—Our collation of *EA* 369 resulted in two new readings: 1. in line 2 read *an-n*⌜*a-am*⌝ rather than *an-ni-am* of the editio princeps, and we are thus rid of the curious survival of the OB form and replace it with a form attested in *EA* 45:13 (Ugarit) and 237:20 (cf. also *an-na-a* in *EA* 99:5 [Egypt] and 357:85); 2. in line 8 read *ša-qí-tu*$_4$, as already proposed by *CAD* Ṣ 55b, traces of three horizontals instead of two being visible.

[18]Dossin, *RA* 31 (1934) 135–136, cites M. Capart, *Bull. de l'Académie Royale de Belgique*, Classe des Lettres, 20/5 (1934), 84–85.

[19]See Albright, *ANET* 487 (with minor modification), and Rainey, AOAT 8, 38–39. It is not reflected in the *balāṭu* articles of *AHw* or *CAD*, but the former (462) accepts the reading *ka-ši*.

[20]A rule observed by Knudtzon (*EA* I 16–17) and generally ignored; the exception he granted in *EA* 99:5 was unnecessary, for either his reading (*ublakku*) or the now established correct reading (*uštēbilakku*) may be 3 as well as 1 pers.

occurs only once, and then with fem. referent (*ana kâši, EA* 26:3).[21] In *EA* 369 itself we find *a-na ka-a-ša* (line 4), and similarly in *EA* 99:6, 162:18, 34 (*ga-a-ša*); 367:4; 370:4—all letters from the Pharaoh to vassals.

3. Not less anomalous would be the omission of the preposition, another feature without parallel (see the examples under 2).

4. The usual logograms for *balāṭu* in *EA* are TIL (3x) and TIL.LA (15x).[22] Only TI.LA.MES (*EA* 45:32, Ugarit) and TE.LA (*EA* 94:69, Byblos) reflect the use of TI(.LA) in native Akk. sources. But what makes NAM.TI = *balāṭu* questionable is the NAM. In *EA*, it appears only in NAM.TIL.LA (*EA* 53:66, Qatna), and in general it is virtually unattested as part of the logogram (see *balāṭu*, subst. and vb. in *CAD*).

Such an accumulation of anomalies within three words favors the alternative reading: *pī* (KA) *ši-pir$_6$-ti iš-pu-ru-ka*, "(May the king, your lord, say to you: 'This is excellent') in accord with the message he sent you."

šipirtu is attested elsewhere in *EA*, once in a spelling with *pir$_6$*, and always with reference to the king: (1) *i-nu-ma* ^{lú}MAŠKIM-*ia i-na ši-pir$_6$-ti* LUGAL ^{d}UTU, "when my commissioner is on a mission of the king, the Sun" (*EA* 60:25, Amurru); (2) *a-na* [*š*]*i-pí-ir-ti-šu a-šar i-ba-ša-at ši-pí-ir-ti* LUGAL EN-*ia ša-ri* TIL.LA-*ia ù ú-ba-*[*ú-n*]*a-ši ù uš-ši-ru-na-ši a-na* LUGAL EN-*ia ša-ri* TIL.LA-*ia*, "As to what he ordered, wherever may be what the king, my lord, the breath of my life, ordered, I shall search it out and send it to the king ..." (*EA* 143:12–17, Beirut); (3) *iš-te-mi-me ši-p*[*í-ir-ta*] *š*[*a*] L[UG]AL (*EA* 246:7–8, Megiddo); (4) *ki-e la-a ep-pu-šu ši-pí-ir-ti* LUGAL-*ri*, "How could I not carry out the order of the king" (*EA* 254:45–46, Shechem).

That the king should refer to himself in the 3 sg., as we assume, we have already seen to be the rule without exception in letters to vassals. Even the omission of the relative pro. *ša* and the use of the subj. are not without parallel: *ú-ul ba-na-at ṣú-ḫa-ar-ti id-di-nu-ni*, "The girl he gave me is not beautiful" (*EA* 1:80). Here, it is true, Amenophis III claims to be quoting the Babylonian king, but he certainly does so freely, and it is to his Egyptian scribe that we must credit at least the solecism instead of the correct *iddina*.

Finally, it should also be noted that in the other occurrence of *šiịātu bantu* the Pharaoh's congratulations do not stop there, but continue

[21]The "passim" of *CAD* K 288a for *kâši* in the periphery is quite wrong.

[22]See *EA* II 1388 (read *til-la-ti* in *EA* 91:29; 92:36; 105:30, *til-la-ta* in 91:34; 113:48; 114:60, all from *tillatu*).

with *ša da-ad-din-šu* IGI.DUḪ *a-na* LUGAL EGIR DUMU.MUNUS-*ka*, "what you gave as a present to the king along with your daughter" (*EA* 99:18–20). In other words, what is called excellent is described by a summary of the orders given in lines 10–15. Then follows the formulaic "And you may know that the king ..." From our new reading in *EA* 369, the same structure as in *EA* 99 emerges: 4–18, order of gifts to be sent; 19–23, prospective congratulations of the king, excellence of gifts described by reference to order just given; 24–32, formulaic "And may you know that the king ..."

Only *pī* as a preposition is unparalleled in *EA*, and the omission of *ana* or *kī*, attested according to *AHw* only in Elam, is certainly a difficulty. This admitted, the arguments against the old reading and in favor of the new one still seem decisive.

III. — Baᶜlu-šipṭi of Gezer

The sender of *EA* 292–293, whose concern for Gezer (*EA* 292:43–44) identifies him as its ruler, bears the name ^{pd}IM-DI.KUD. This Knudtzon read as ^{pd}addu-dāni, hesitating about the interpretation of DI.KUD, but appealing to *EA* 294:3, where he believed the traces looked most like [*a*]*d*-[*d*]*a*-[*da*]-*ni*.[23] Here, however, his hesitation ceased, and he was quite convinced that *EA* 292–294 were all sent by the same vassal.

Albright introduced the reading of the logographic spelling as Baᶜlu-šipṭi, and this now seems current and unquestioned.[24] He also made available to Campbell the results of his collation of *EA* 294:3, and the latter concluded that, however the name was to be read, Knudtzon's tentative reading was impossible.[25] But whereas Albright declares the name illegible in *EA* 294 and assumes it was Baᶜlu-šipṭi,[26] Campbell rejects the latter possibility and is thus led to distinguishing the writers of *EA* 292–293 and 294, who, he claims, were one only in their both having troubles with a certain Peya.[27]

[23]*EA* I 884, n. a; II 1344, n. 2.

[24]*BASOR* 87 (1942) 36; *ANET* 484; *CAH*^{2} II, ch. 20, fasc. 51, 9. Albright offers no arguments, but presumably was influenced by the equation Šipṭi-Baᶜlu = DI.KUD-^{d}IM (*EA* II 1568).

[25]*The Chronology of the Amarna Letters*, 101, n. 73; 126, n. 39.

[26]"... assuming that the illegible name of the sender of *EA* 294 ... is a form of *Baᶜlu-shipti*" (*CAH*^{2}, ch. 20, fasc. 51, 9, n. 5). Ross, *Biblical Archaeologist* 30 (1967) 68, must make the same assumption.

[27]*The Chronology of the Amarna Letters*, 126.

Not only this distinction but the entire discussion is wrong, vitiated from the start by the assumption that ^{Pd}IM-DI.KUD can only be read Ba^{c}lu-šipṭi. Consider the evidence:

1. *EA* 292–294 all conclude the introduction identically: *a-na* GÌR. MEŠ LUGAL EN-*ia* DINGIR.MEŠ-*ia* ^{d}UTU-*ia* 7-*šu* 7-*ta-a-an am-qú-ut*.[28] Only in *EA* 297, sent by Yapaḫu of Gezer (!), do we find *exactly* what we have here. Numerous are the instances in which the only difference is 7-*da-a-an* rather than 7-*ta-a-an*,[29] but their very number makes the grouping of *EA* 294 with 292–293, 297, all letters from Gezer, especially significant.

2. Acknowledgment of receipt of the Pharaoh's letter:

EA 292 *iš-te-me a-wa-te*^{meš} *ša iš-pu-ur* LUGAL EN-*ia a-na* ÌR-*šu*;
EA 293 [*iš*]-*te-mi a-wa-at ša iš-pu-ur* LUGAL EN-*ia a-na* ÌR-*šu*;
EA 294 *iš-te-mi a-wa-te*^{meš} *ša* LUGAL EN-*ia ša iš-pu-ur a-na* ÌR-*šu*.

Again, numerous as the parallels are to this form of acknowledgment, the relative clause *ša išpur* appears only in these three letters.

3. Similarly, numerous as the protestations of obedience are in the letters of vassals, the *a-nu-ma iṣ-ṣú-ru* of *EA* 292:22–23; 293:12; 294:11–12 is paralleled only by *EA* 220:15. Common, too, as the verb *naṣāru* is, *iṣṣuru* is confined to these four passages.

4. Another unique expression, again with a commonly used verb, is *u i̯ilmad šarru bēlīi̯a ana ardīšu* (*EA* 292:26–27; 294:14–15).

5. In the expression *ūma u mūša*, *EA* 292–294 are one in the otherwise unparalleled writing of *ūma* by UD.KAM-*ma* (*EA* 292:24–25; 293:13; 294:34).

6. *ù al-lu-ú il*$_5$-*qé* (*EA* 292:33, + -*ši* PN; *EA* 294:23, + -*šu-nu* PN); neither *allū* + form of *leqû*, nor the writing of the frequent 3 sg. pret. with *il*$_5$, is found elsewhere in *EA*.

7. The troubles with Peya: the writers of *EA* 292 and 294 are not only alike in suffering from the attacks of an otherwise unknown Peya, but they introduce them in strikingly similar language:

EA 292:41–44	*EA* 294:16–18
ša-ni-ta$_5$ *a-mur ip-ši*	[*a-m*]*ur ip-ši*
^{P}*pí-e-ia* DUMU ^{munus}*gu-la-t*[*e*]	^{P}*pí-i-ia* DUMU ^{munus}*gu-la-te*
a-na URU *gaz-ri* ^{munus}GEMÉ-*te*	*a-na ia-ši*
ša LUGAL EN-*ia*	

[28]The evidence is that TA.ÀM was pronounced; cf. 7-*ta-na*, 7-*it-ta-na*, 7-*ta-(an)-ni* (see *EA* II 1521).

[29]Cf., e.g., *EA* 266–271, 273–280.

8. To the evidence of language and orthography is to be added that of paleography. Knudtzon, the greatest expert on Amarna paleography and a scholar of the most cautious judgment, asserted without the slightest qualification that the script of *EA* 292–294 was the same. We have found no reason to question that judgment.

A minimal conclusion is evident: the same scribe wrote *EA* 292–294.[30] Hardly less evident is the inference that he wrote them for the same person. The only possible reason for hesitating to draw it would be that ^{pd}IM-DI.KUD must be read Ba^{c}lu-šipṭi or in some way clearly incompatible with the traces in *EA* 294:3. But this is not true. That Knudtzon's Adda-dāni is a possible option and belongs in the onomasticon of the Late Bronze Age is clear from *b^{c}ldn* (*PRU* II No. 32:13), which appears in Akk. texts as $^{\mathrm{[p]d}}$U-DI.KUD (*Ugar.* V 14:3), ^{pd}U-*da-na* = ^{pd}U-*da-na* (*Ugar.* V 86:20, 22). Moreover, Knudtzon's reading is quite compatible with the traces, whereas Ba^{c}lu-šipṭi is definitely excluded (see Fig. 1*a*). One can only agree with Knudtzon's description: the first sign

Fig. 1*a* 

is probably AD or ṢI, the last sign almost certainly NI, and the second and third signs are possibly DA.[31] Given the weight of the evidence that the same person sent *EA* 292–294, the tentative equation ^{pd}IM-DI.KUD = Ad-da-da-ni perhaps errs only in its caution.

There is not the slightest evidence that anyone named Ba^{c}lu-šipṭi ever ruled in Gezer.

IV. — The Investiture of the Commissioner

In *EA* 107:20–24 Knudtzon read: *ù šum-*[*m*]*a da-mi-*[*iq*] *i-na pa-ni-ka ù š*[*u*]*-ku-un i-na* ^{lú}MAŠKIM *ši-mi-rum i-n*[*a*] *pa-ni* $^{\mathrm{lú.meš}}$*ḫa-za-nu-ti* LU[GAL], and translated, "Und wenn es dir gut erscheint, so setze an einen Vorsteher einen Ring in Gegenwart der Regenten des Königs."

This is certainly an unusual request. Rib-Adda has just asked in the

[30]For the same scribe employed by more than one ruler, see *EA* 174–176, 363, virtually identical duplicates of the same letter sent by each of four rulers speaking in the 1 pl. (In *EA* 363:1, Thureau-Dangin failed to copy ^{d}UTU-*ia*, which is written on the reverse; thus even this minor difference between the four letters disappears.) This, however, reflects a special situation, and a town of the size of Gezer would certainly have its own scribe.

[31]For the possible extra vertical in AD, see below, n. 35.

preceding lines (14–19) that the officer in charge of the troops remain in Ṣumur, but that the Pharaoh recall Ḫaʾip to Egypt and subject him and his affairs to close scrutiny.[32] The latter, a high Egyptian official who seems to have been functioning as the commissioner in Ṣumur, is Rib-Adda's enemy. His recall would mean the necessity of a new appointment, but that his successor should be installed in the presence of other local rulers is a strange and unheard-of proposal. What would be the purpose of their presence? According to the literal meaning of the text, we might also ask where the king is to do this. In Egypt, with all the others journeying to the capital? In Ṣumur, with the king making a rare appearance in the provinces just to install a functionary?

Read: *ù š[u]-ku-un i-na* ^{lú}MAŠKIM-*ši* DUGUD *i-n[a] pa-ni* $^{\text{lú.meš}}$*ḫa-za-nu-ti* LU[GAL], "appoint as its (Ṣumur's) commissioner someone respected by the king's mayors." This reading, besides obviating the difficulties just noted, is also supported by the following considerations:

1. If Knudtzon were right, in the Byblos syllabary we should have expected *ši-u̯i-*, and from the generally correct use of case-endings in the Byblos letters, *ši-u̯i-ra(-am)*.

2. There is only the slightest separation between the alleged *mi* and *rum*, and DUGUD (*kabtu*) is a quite legitimate reading.

3. Besides DUGUD glossed *i̯ú-ka-bi-it* in *EA* 245:39, we also have in *EA* 1, as F. Pintore has shown, LÚ-*ka* DUGUD (*EA* 1:15, 33).[33]

4. *EA* 106:35–40: *ša-ni-ta*$_5$ *li-it-ri-iṣ a-na pa-ni be-l[i-ia] ù lu-wa-ši-ra* ^{P}*ia-an-ḫa-ma i-na* ^{lú}MAŠKIM-*ši* ^{P}*ia-an-ḫa-ma mu-ṣa-li-il* LUGAL *be-li-ia i-ši-mi iš-tu* ^{uzu}KA LÚ.MEŠ-*tum* LÚ *em-qú šu-ut ù gab-bi* LÚ.MEŠ *i-ra-ḫa-mu-šu*, "Moreover, may it seem right to my lord, and may he send Yanḥamu as its (Ṣumur's) commissioner—the Yanḥamu who is the fan-bearer of the king, my lord. I have heard from others he is a wise man and everyone loves him."

This passage, written during the same period as *EA* 107, shows Rib-Adda requesting a new commissioner for Ṣumur—*ina rābiṣī-ši* in both *EA* 106 and 107—and his concern for the individual's qualifications. Here they are a practical wisdom and universal popularity. Needless to say, such a candidate might also be described as someone likely to be *kabta ina pānī ḫazānūti šarri* (cf. *gādôl lipnê* in Heb.).

[32]For ^{P}*iḫ-ri-pí-ṭá* = *ḥry pḏt* in *EA* 107:14, see Albright, *JNES* 5 (1946) 14.

[33]*OA* 11 (1972) 37–38. This reading, which rids us of *kamiru*, is confirmed by collation. In both instances, the alleged *rum* is firmly attached to the alleged *mi*; the reproduction in Bezold-Budge is inaccurate.

V. — The Siege of Byblos

In *EA* 88 Rib-Adda writes that Abdi-Aširta has advanced against Byblos itself and day after day has not budged from the city-gate.[34] Knudtzon then read: *ù ú-ul ni-li-ú a-ṣa-am a-na am-ru*^{meš} (20–21). The last word is the crux. Knudtzon's guess ("die Türen") is rejected by both *AHw* and *CAD*. They also agree in assigning the word to *amrummu*, in emending MEŠ to *me*, and in their hesitation to translate (*AHw*, "Poterne?"; *CAD*, " ... ").

The reading is certainly wrong. The two oblique wedges in the putative RU are without a single parallel in the Byblos letters; see Schroeder's list in *VS* 12, No. 21, which is also representative of forms on BM and Cairo tablets. Moreover, the normal form of RU appears in line 41 of the tablet in question.

Collation of the sign (see Fig. 1*b*) also shows that the two oblique

Fig. 1*b* 

wedges are as much a part of the putative AM as they are of the RU, and in fact the impression is of a single sign. It is, we believe, EDIN, and this yields the translation, "(How long has he not budged from the city gate), and so we are unable to go out to the country-side."

Admittedly, we cannot offer other examples of this form, but if allowance is made for provincial deviations, the essential structure is recognizable, the most notable difference being the three verticals instead of two. However, "extra" wedges are not an unknown feature of *EA* forms,[35] and are no more a difficulty than the otiose MEŠ.[36]

This is not the only occurrence of *ṣēru*, "countryside, area outside the city-walls", in the Byblos letters: URU.MEŠ *an-nu-tu* ^{giš}MÁ.MEŠ *ù*

[34] Reading *ma-ni* UD.KAM.MEŠ-*ti la*$^{!}$ *i̯i-na-mu-uš iš-tu* KÁ.GAL (19–20); see the writer's dissertation 159–160 [= p. 110 in the present volume], and now *AHw* 603 (*māni ūmāti*, which probably implies the correction of Knudtzon's *ṣi* to *la*).

[35] Cf. LA with two horizontals in *EA* 88:19 (see above, n. 34), the extra vertical in UN in 107:22, the two verticals in UB in 362:12 (elsewhere in Byblos, always one), GUD probably written as GA in 138:106, UL with three verticals in 118:31 (elsewhere in Byblos, always two; see Knudtzon's remarks, *EA* I 514, n. c), DI written as KI in 96:21, RU with two horizontals in 231:12, the extra vertical in LÚ in 169:12+ (see Knudtzon's note), the form of ŠUM in 150:18, etc.; see also above, n. 30 and discussion of *EA* 101:10 below.

[36] See *BASOR* 211 (1973) 53, n. 12 [above, Paper 16, p. 247, n. 12].

DUMU.MEŠ pÌR-*a-ši-i*[*r*]-*ta i-na ṣe-ri ù* [*i*]*z*-[*z*]*i-za* UGU-‹*ia*› *ù la-a i-li-ú a-ṣa*, "(If they heard I was entering Ṣumur), there would be these cities (with) ships and the sons of Abdi-Aširta in the country-side. They will be lined up against me and I will be unable to get out" (*EA* 104:46–51). This understanding of *ina ṣēri*, dubbed obscure by *CAD* Ṣ 141a, is due to M. Greenberg, who also pointed to the corresponding use of Heb. *baśśāde* (e.g., 2 Sam 10:8).[37] Even clearer is the evidence of *EA* 105:11–13, which describes the same siege of Ṣumur. After comparing the city to a trapped bird, Rib-Adda writes: pDUMU.MEŠ-ÌR-*a-ši-ir-ta iš-tu qa-qa-ri ù* LÚ.MEŠ URU *ar-wa-da iš-tu a-ia-ba ur*-[*r*]*a mu-ša* U[GU-*ši*], "The sons of Abdi-Aširta by land, the men of Arwada by sea, are against it day and night." In *EA* 104:42 Arwada is mentioned as one of the cities that would contribute to the confinement of Rib-Adda within Ṣumur.[38] Both passages refer to his escape being cut off by both land and sea; *ištu qaqqari* (*EA* 105) = *ina ṣēri* (*EA* 104).

VI. — UŠ *ú-ṣa* (*EA* 101:10)

According to Rib-Adda, the reason his fellow-Amorites killed Abdi-Aširta was their own lack of wool and his (their?) inability to furnish Mitanni with certain cloths or garments.[39] The latter are referred to, in Knudtzon's reading, as UŠ *ú-ṣa*, which on the basis of context he translated by "*Bezahlung*."

The three signs, the number of which the reproduction in Bezold-Budge seems to confirm, are in fact two: GÚ.UN (see Fig. 1*c*).[40] As

Fig. 1*c*

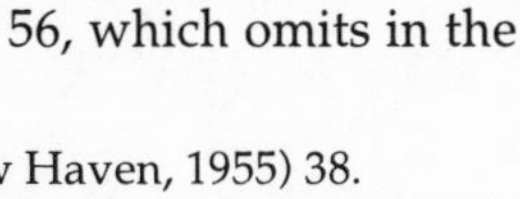

Knudtzon had already remarked, "*ú* scheint nachträglich eingeschaltet zu sein", but this impression is due to the ligature with the previous sign. As is clear, we are again confronted with an unusual form (see Schroeder's list, *VS* 12, No. 56, which omits in the Jerusalem column the

[37]The *Ḫab/piru*, AOS 39 (New Haven, 1955) 38.

[38]With the meaning of *ina ṣēri* established and its correspondence in *EA* 105 recognized, it becomes even more difficult to share Weber's doubts (*EA* II 1202) that URU *er*$_4$-*wa-da* is Arwada.

[39]See *Eretz Israel* 9, 94–99 (above, Paper 14).

[40]The form reproduced, *ibid.*, 99, n. 29 [in the present volume, p. 235, n. 29], reflects our inquiry of Dr. Sollberger; we asked what Knudtzon's UŠ looked like, and he kindly reproduced it for us.

form in *EA* 288:12), but not the only one of GÚ.UN in *EA* (see *EA* 151:47 and pl. 13 in Bezold-Budge). In the UN, there is a small space between the horizontals and the verticals, and there are one (only two tails visible) or two (probably three heads) extra verticals; however, UN with one extra vertical is attested at Byblos (see above, n. 35). In the GÚ, instead of the usual "ḪI" at the end, there is only a single large oblique wedge, but this may be due to the impression of the last wedge obliterating the traces of the first three (cf. ḪI.A in *EA* 228:8 and Bezold-Budge pl. 16, which looks like U.A). There is also the small vertical at the end. But all these peculiarities admitted, the overall "Gestalt" is that of GÚ.UN—and it makes sense.

And so, at least according to Rib-Adda, Amurru was offering some form of tribute to Mitanni, or at least wished to do so.[41] The fact that its inability to make the payments led to Abdi-Aširta's death suggests either a pro-Mitanni faction in Amurru or perhaps fear of reprisals for failure to furnish the required goods. We thus have one more piece to be fitted into the puzzle of the history of this period and the relations between Egypt and Mitanni.[42]

[41]Our translation and commentary, *ibid.*, 98–99, are to be revised accordingly.

[42]See Ph. H. J. Houwink Ten Cate, *BiOr* 22 (1963) 274–275; A. Goetze, *CAH*^{2}, II, ch. 17, fasc. 37, 9–10.—Our collation of the Amarna letters was made possible through grants of the American Council of Learned Societies and the American Philosophical Society. To them and to the authorities of all the museums, who gave us access to the tablets and all possible assistance, we would express our gratitude.

19. Putative Akkadian *šukammu*

AHw 3 1262 has an entry *šukammu*, of unknown meaning and two occurrences: 1. *allūme nadnāku* [*š*]*u-kam-mi šarri* [*bēlī*]*ya*, "I herewith give the ... of the king, my lord" (*EA* 242:9–11, followed by a list of the objects given; from Megiddo); 2. *šanīta* PN *kīma šu-kam-ma nīteriš ištu kāta*, "Moreover, we have requested PN like/as ..." (G. Wilhelm, *ZA* 63 [1971] 71:24–26; found at Kamid el-Loz). Both occurrences, it will be noted, are from the same general area, the southwestern periphery, and from the same period, the Amarna age.[1] Analyzed as Akkadian, *šukammu* would presumably be the accusative plural in the first instance, and an incorrect accusative (singular) in the second.

I propose that the entry should be deleted and the signs read as a logogram: ŠU.KAM.MA/MI = *erištu*, perhaps *mēreštu*/*mēreltu*, "desire, request."[2] On this reading, the ruler of Megiddo would declare that he was handing over what the king had required of him. The expression *erišta nadānu* is used of a vassal's duty to his lord and his lord's representatives, and it also belongs to the jargon of gift-exchange in the international relations of the period.[3] Aziru of Amurru uses it: (PN) *anumma* [*a*]*t*-[*t*]*a-din e*-[*ri-iš*]-*ti šar*[*ri*] *bēlīya* [*u*] *mīnumma e-ri-iš-tù*-⌜*šu*⌝ [*š*]*a šarri bēlīya* ... *a*[*n*]*andin*, "(Tutu), I herewith give the (things) request(ed) by the king, my lord, and I shall (always) give whatever is requested by the king, my lord" (*EA* 158:5–9; also 10–19).[4] The correspondence with the passage from *EA* 242 cited above is obvious. Aziru also uses the variant form, *mēröšta nadānu: u mīnummê mi-ri-iš-ta-š*[*u*] *š*[*a šarri bēlīya*] *anāk*[*u l*]*ū a*[*d-din*]/*a*[*t-ta-din*?] (*EA* 157:17–19; cf. also 156:4–

[1]Besides Wilhelm's thorough commentary, see Anson F. Rainey, *UF* 8 (1976) 337–41, on the language.

[2]The variant form with MI may be simply a provincial corruption; but see, for example, še-kin-gam-ma, var. -me, *MSL* 11 83:170.

[3]C. Zaccagnini, *Lo scambio dei doni nel Vicino Oriente durante i secoli XV–XIII* (Rome, 1973), does not include this expression in his discussion (pp. 195–206) of the terminology associated with gifts.

[4]The readings are based on my collations and those of Edmund Gordon. For the latter I am indebted to the generous cooperation of Professor Albert Glock, Director of the Albright Institute in Jerusalem, who has made Gordon's work available to me. Gordon's collations of the Cairo tablets were especially thorough and are therefore especially valuable.

10). Farther south, at Shechem, knowledge of the expression may be inferred from the use there of its antonym, *erišta kalû*: (I do not hold back my tribute and) *lā akalli erište rābiṣīya* "I do not hold back what my commissioner requests" (*EA* 254:13–15). See, too, in the language of gift-exchange: *mērešta ša ana abīka ērišu abūka ul [i]kla gabbamma lū iddina* (*EA* 41:11–13, cf. 8–11,23–24; Boghazköy); *mērelta banīta ... ul iklû* (*EA* 9:10; Babylonia); *mēreltīya u ṣibūtīya tanaddin-mi* (*PRU* 4 18:20–21, cf. 14–17; Amurru). See also *EA* 27:17; 289:27; *PRU* 4 125:32–35; *PRU* 6 19–20:18–19.

For the other occurrence of the logogram ("we have requested from you PN as (our) request") I know of no exact parallel, but the paronomasia is very reminiscent of *erišta*/*mērešta erēšu* (or relative clause with *erēšu*; *CAD* E 284b; M/2 22).

I am familiar with the logogram elsewhere only in lexical texts:

1. OB: [lú š]u-kam-ma = *ša er-še-tim* (OB Lu Rec. A, *MSL* 12 167:308);

2. MB (periphery): uru-šu-kam-ma.ki = *i-ri-iš-ti* (RS forerunner of Ḫ̮AR-ra XXI, *MSL* 11 45:29; ^{dug}dùg-gan šu-kám-ma (Alalakh forerunner of Ḫ̮AR-ra X, *MSL* 7 116 ii 3; cf. next entry);

3. Canonical Ḫ̮AR-ra: ^{dug}šagan-níg-šu-kam-ma = [*šá e*]-*riš-ti* (Ḫ̮ḫ̮ X, *MSL* 7 82:108); also *MSL* 7 131:182 (^{kuš}šuḫ̮ub, without níg), and cf. *MSL* 7 129:127 (^{kuš}e-sír, níg-šu-kam-ma replaced by níg-ugu-gam-ma; see also *MSL* 10 134:244; *MSL* 8/1 40:275).

That every one of these examples is problematic, or that the pertinence of the meaning "desire, request" may be questionable in almost every instance, is no difficulty for the case being argued here.[5] Even if it should be proved that in native Mesopotamian sources šu-kam-ma never corresponds to *erištu* in the sense defended here, the only legitimate conclusion would be that provincial scribes misunderstood the lexical texts. From the evidence cited it is clear where they found šu-kamma and how they understood it. There is no Akkadian word *šukammu*.

[5]There is no doubt about the *erištu* in the first example, though the precise meaning of "the one of desires/requests" remains obscure. The others are even more difficult, and the variation at times with ugu-gam-ma suggests hesitation in the tradition. See *CAD* A/2 268 (*arištu*) and *AHw* 1 232 (cf. A. Salonen, *Die Fussbekleidung der alten Mesopotamier* [Helsinki, 1969] 18).

20. *duppuru (dubburu)—ṭuppuru*, too?

In *Or.* NS 18 (1949) 393–95, W. von Soden argued that in Akkadian two verbs are to be distinguished, one intransitive, *duppuru*, "to go away," the other transitive, *ṭuppuru*, "to drive away." The distinction has not gained currency; *duppuru* is still generally considered to be transitive as well as intransitive.[1] The Mari specialists, whose corpus contains a large part of the Old Babylonian evidence, have given *ṭuppuru* a respectful nod, but their transliterations and statements on the Mari syllabary make their rejection clear.[2] Nevertheless, as we now see, von Soden still holds to the distinction, which we find canonized and rather emphatically reaffirmed ("nicht *duppuru*!") in *AHw* (3 1980).[3] A brief review of the evidence seems appropriate.

[1]J. Bottéro, *Le problème des Habiru à la 4e Rencontre Assyriologique Internationale*, Cahiers de la Société Asiatique 12 (Paris, 1954) 87 n. 2, accepted transitive *ṭuppuru* in the Amarna letters. For its existence in Old Babylonian, see also the cautious note of R. Kutscher and C. Wilcke, *ZA* 68 (1978) 124 n. 55.

[2]*ARM* 15 42 n. 2, 64f., 275; *ARM* 14 221 ("l'emploi du signe DA avec la valeur *ṭa* n'a pas encore été recontré à Mari"—and see the writings below). See, too, M. Stol, *On Trees, Mountains, and Millstones in the Ancient Near East* (Leiden, 1979) 10, who from writings like *bu-du-ma-tum*, *bu-du-um-ti*, and the like at Mari infers, not *ṭù* in the syllabary, but the byform *budumtum* in the lexicon.

[3]To the references of the *AHw* article, which contains minor revisions of the *Orientalia* article, add Kutscher and Wilcke, *ZA* 68 (1978) 115:60 (OB). The interpretation of some forms as transitive is at times questionable (for example, *UET* 6 391:37), and following *CAD* A/2 474a and K 445a we would delete the reference to *BAM* 401:29f. ("unkl.") and read *šit-pu-ru* rather than *dup-pu-ru* (cf. da-da-ru : *šit-pu-ru* : da-da-ru : *ki-iṣ-ṣ*[*u-ru*], and [da-d]a-ra-ak-ab = *ši-it-pàr*, *MSL* 4 163:1, and other bilingual passages cited *AHw* 3 1171b).—The sorting out of *dbr* and *dpr* roots and determining their meanings are still beset with difficulties. Perhaps only adding to the confusion, I would suggest that in Lambert-Millard *Atrahasis* 94:39, rather than *dapāru*, "to be sated," a verb of questionable existence and not very illuminating here, or an emendation, *it-pé-ša* (von Soden, *Or.* NS 38 [1969] 431), we see a verb *dab/pāru*, related to *dab/pru*, *mundab/pru* // *muddab/pru* (*JCS* 31 [1979] 91), "to become strong," or the like:

> ᵈ*en-líl id-bi-ra ú-ša-aq-bi pí-i-*[*ia*]
> *ki-ma ti-ru-ru šu-a-ti ú-ša-as-ḫi pi-i-i*[*a*]
> Did Enlil prove too strong for me, force my mouth to speak,
> Like Tiruru's in the tale, helpless make my mouth?

(On *šusḫû*, "to make useless," see *AHw* 2 1035a. In view of the rest of Nintu's speech, a rhetorical question stressing her guilt seems more likely than an assertion diminishing it.) Perhaps the forms in Gilg. I ii 40 and II ii 40 (*dapāru*, "to be

Of the transitive verb there are nine occurrences in the Amarna letters: *tu*-Da-Bi-*ir* (*EA* 76:39), [*tu* / *ti*]-Da-Bi-*ra-šu* (*EA* 85:81),[4] *ú*-Da-Bi-*ra* (*EA* 85:68), *nu*-Da-Bir$_5$ (*EA* 74:34), D*u*-B*i*-*ru* (*EA* 104:27), all in letters from Byblos; *yú*-T*a*B-B*i*-*ra*-[*šu-nu*] (*EA* 138:106) and *ti*-[T*a*]B-B*i*-*ru* (*EA* 138:69), in a letter from Rib-Hadda in exile; *ni*-D*u*-B*u*-*ur* (*EA* 279:20), D*u*-*u*B-B*u*-*ru-ni* (*EA* 248:17), in letters from Palestine. It should be observed that the only CV-signs used are either *da* or *du*, for this is clear and important evidence. At Byblos, without exception, /ṭ/ is written with the TA-TI-TE-TU series:[5]

1. always *ṭá*: *ib-lu-ṭá* (twice), *ba-la-ṭá* (four times), TIL.LA-*ṭá* (three times), *ba-al* / *bal-ṭá-at* (twice), *bal-ṭá-ti* (three times), *i-pa-ṭá-ra-ni-mi* (once), *i-pa-ṭá-ra* (once), *pa-ṭá-ri-ma* (twice), *pa-ṭá-ra-ma* (once), *pa-ṭá-ar* (once), *pa-ṭá-ru* (once?), *yú-ḫa-mi-ṭá* (twice), *ši-iḫ-ṭá-at* (once), and passim in *piṭatu*;

2. always *ṭì*: *ba-la-ṭì-ia* (three times), TIL.LA-*ṭì* (three times), *ba-la-ṭì-šu* (once), *ba-la-ṭì-šu-nu* (once?), *ba-al-ṭì* (once), *ip-ṭì-ri* (once), *ip-ṭì-ra* (twice), *ša-ṭì-ir* (once);

or *ṭe*$_4$: *te-pa-ṭe*$_4$*-ru-na* (once);

3. always *ṭú*: *ba-al-ṭú* (once), *tu-ba-li-ṭú-na* (once), *ip-ta-ṭú-ur* (once).

Consistent with this representation of /ṭ/ is the writing of /q/ in the Byblos letters: always *qí* or *qú*. Thus, in forms of *leqû* (ca. ninety-five times), *maqātu* (five times, plus formulaic *am-qú-ut*, passim), *ia-qú-ul* (once), *ri-qí* (once), *ri-qú-tam* (once), SIG$_5$-*qú* (once), *ša-ra-qú-ma* (once).

Such regularity, without a single demonstrable or even probable exception, makes only one conclusion possible: in the Amarna letters, the verb in question is *duppuru* or *dubburu*, not *ṭuppuru*.[6]

sated" *CAD; ṭapāru*, "sich herandrängen an" *AHw*) belong to the same verb, "to push in, become aggressive"(?).

[4]So restored rather than [*ú*] (Knudtzon) because ERÍN.MEŠ *piṭatu* is regularly construed as fem. sg. (*JCS* 6 [1952] 78 [above, Paper 7, p. 168), and in the verb 3 sg. masc. and fem. are distinguished.

[5]For the loci, see *EA* glossaries (VAB 2 and A. Rainey, AOAT 8/2). Note also *ṭám*: *ḫu-mi-ṭám* (*EA* 102:29), *ba-la-ṭám* (*EA* 126:15). The reading *ip-ṭù-ra* in *EA* 84:29 (Rainey, *UF* 7 [1975] 411) is excluded by both syllabary and collation (read *ib-ni* SIG$_4$?). The syllabary of *EA* 137–138, letters of Rib-Hadda not written at Byblos, is somewhat different. Note especially *ḫe-e-ṭí* (*EA* 137:33) and *ti*-[*i*]*m*-[*t*]*a*-[*ṭ*]*í* (*EA* 137:44, rendering 38ff. "May the king heed the words of his servant, and may the king, my lord, grant archers so they may seize Byblos, and traitorous troops and the sons of Abdi-Ashirta not enter it, and then the archers of the king, my lord, be too few (to take it back)").

[6]Perhaps in *EA*, under West Semitic influence (see below), the verb was *dubburu*.

However, as is obvious, evidence from the periphery cannot be decisive in determining the phoneme in native Babylonian usage, for in the periphery we must reckon with the possibility of substrate or adstrate interference, and in the present instance Hebrew **hidbīr* and Aramaic *dᵊbar, dabbar*, "to lead, drive," readily come to mind and suggest a possible source of the unquestionable /d/ of the Amarna lexeme.

The argument for the existence of *ṭuppuru* of course also rested on considerations of syllabary. From the alternation of the surd and sonant series we apparently find in T*u-pí-ra-aš-šu-nu-*[*ti*] (*ARM* 1 39:6′) and *li*T-T*a-ap-pir* (*AMT* 93 3:8), but D*u-pu-ur* (*ARM* 1 120:6,19) and *nu-*D*a-ap-pa-ar-šu* (*ARM* 2 53:25), von Soden concluded that the initial root consonant must be /ṭ/. So, in 1949. However, if I understand correctly the implications of the transliteration in *AHw* 3 1380, *liṭ-ṭa!-ap-pir*, this writing is now taken simply as anomalous, for *ṭá* does not belong to any late syllabary. Thus, unless in the period since 1949 new evidence has turned up—more writings in Old Babylonian with TA or TU, *ṭu* in later periods—the whole case for *ṭuppuru* rests on the one writing with TU in *ARM* 1 39:6′.

To my knowledge, such evidence has not turned up; on the contrary. Post-Old Babylonian writings remain ambiguous CVC's (TAB, DIB, DUB), occasionally DA; the decisive *ṭu* is still missing. Old Babylonian occurrences of the verb have increased considerably, and their writings are consistent: always DA or DU. And since most of these are found in the Mari corpus, the earlier objections based on considerations of syllabary have only gained in force. The emphatic /ṭ/ is regularly represented by *ṭà*(ḪI)-*ṭì-ṭe*$_4$*-ṭú*, facts irreconcilable with an alleged *ṭuppuru*.

Take, for instance, the Yaqqim-Addu correspondence (*ARM* 14), a very homogeneous corpus and ideal for establishing a syllabary. The representation of /ṭ/ is absolutely consistent:[7]

1. always *ṭà*: *i-pa-aṭ-ṭà-ar* (2:28), *i-pa-aṭ-ṭà-ru-ma* (47:43; see also 75:5; 92:18; 103:8′), [*a*]*ṭ-ṭà-a*[*r*]-*d*[*am*] (7:10′; 62:12; 91:14; 123:22), *ṭà-ra-di-im* (16:10; 72:22; 121:18; see also 15:13′; 47:42; 121:12), *mu-ba-al-li-ṭà-tim* (13:25,29,36,40; 15:9′), *ṭà-ba-ḫu-*[*um-ma*] (79:30), *ṭà-ba-tim* (83:27; 118:15), *ši-ip-ṭà-am* (48:5,10; 111:4), *i-na-aṭ-ṭà-al* (121:39), *ḫa-aṭ-ṭà-at* (14:8);[8]

[7]The consistency which I claim is supported by the copies; occasionally the transliterations are inaccurate.

[8]For arguments against admitting a unique exception in 17:9′, see *ARM* 14 p. 221.

2. always *ṭì*: *ḫa-ṭì-šu* (2:9), *ṭì-ri-tam* (14:11), *na-ṭì-il* (15:5′), *ḫi-ṭì-tum* (15:9′; 18:14′; 81:12), [*ú-ša-á*]*š-ṭì-ir* (70:2′; see also 62:30), *ú-pa-aṭ-ṭì-ru-ma* (77:16);

or *ṭe*$_4$: *ṭēmum* (passim), *pa-ṭe*$_4$*-er* (12:7; see also 50:9,11; 82:18), *ša-ṭe*$_4$*-er* (70:4′; see also 61:10; 62:15; 70:10), *uš-ṭe*$_4$*-nu* (74:7; see also 74:18), *ni-ṭe*$_4$*-él* (66:34);

3. always *ṭú*: *ba-al-ṭú-us-sú* (1:9), *ir-ṭú-ub* (2:30), *ip-ṭú-ur* (71:8′; see also 13:7,12,13; 24:8′; 47:36; 70:20′; 103:10′), *na-ṭú-ú* (17:12′), *iš-ṭú-ru-nim* (64:5′; see also 65:11), *iḫ-mu-ṭú-nim-ma* (66:38), *ṭú-bi* (81:27,28,32), *ša-pí-ṭú-um* (81:41; 98:11; 112:5), *iš-ḫi-ṭú-šu-nu-ti-ma* (86:11).

In this syllabary, therefore, the writings *ú-da-ap-pí-ru* (*ARM* 14 2:22) and *du-pu-ra-ku* (*ARM* 14 46:10) are absolutely unambiguous, and /ṭ/ is excluded. The evidence of Babylonian sources, no less than that of the periphery, converges on /d/.

For the writing in *ARM* 1 39:6′, therefore, we must find an explanation other than a putative *ṭuppuru*, and the proposal of J. Kupper to read *tu-‹še›-bi-ra-aš-šu-nu-ti* rids us of the apparent anomaly, fits the context, and is even preferable on other grounds.[9] In this broken passage we read: (3′) ... [... *a-lam*.KI] (4′) *ú-qu-ur bi-ir-ta-šu q*[*ú-lu* ...] (5′) *ù wa-ši-ib a-lim*.KI *šu-zi-*[*ib*] (6′) *an-ni-iš a-na li-ib-bi ma-tim tu-‹še›-bi-ra-aš-šu-nu-t*[*i-ma*] (7′) *a-lam*.KI *ša-a-ti ú-qu-ur qú-lu*, "Destroy [*the city*], *b*[*urn down*] its citadel [...], but save the inhabitants of the city. As soon as you have moved them over this way, into the countryside, destroy the city and burn it down."[10]

[9]Kupper is cited *ARM* 15 275, *ṭapārum*.

[10]Line 4′, *q*[*u-lu*], following Falkenstein, *BiOr* 11 (1954) 114; at the end of the line, perhaps other objects of *šūzib*, besides *wāšib ālim*. At the end of line 6′, the enclitic *-ma* would make the sequence explicit, a clarification the need of which the previous lines might suggest: burn-save-save-burn. The construction in lines 6′ff. could be either "heischendes Präsens" (*GAG* §78d; example from Mari), *tušebberaššunūtī-ma*, "you shall ... and then ...," or preterite *tušēbir* functioning as a future perfect, a very rare use apparently attested only once elsewhere (Mari; see *GAG* §158b), but as here followed by injunctives. This close parallel, in addition to the very similar use of the preterite in a virtual protasis of a conditional sentence, perhaps favors the latter interpretation. (Red-faced clarification file: in *JCS* 31 [1979] 98, I pointed to a number of examples of such virtual protases, among them passages which I knew M. Stol had discussed in his *Studies in Old Babylonian History*, still inaccessible to me at the time of writing. W. Hallo kindly furnished me with the pages I requested, but, unfortunately, I requested too few, and therefore did not see Stol's discussion and longer list of occurrences pp. 107–108. Two more occurrences: *ARM* 8 71:10; 78:14.)

What ill accords in this passage with the use of *duppuru* are the connotations of the latter, which are almost exclusively those of hostility, rejection, disapproval, and the like, in the subject toward the object. One expels or drives away demons, evil, sin, sickness, lions, improperly stationed guards, men from office; one maliciously removes an inscription.[11] The objects are all persons or things one simply wants to be rid of, and since one does not care where they go, so long as they be gone, they are given no goals or destinations.[12] All of which are consonant with neither the concern for the safety of the population nor the express orders on where they were to be led in the passage under discussion.

Conclusion: only one verb, *duppuru*, transitive and intransitive.[13]

[11] *KBo* 10 1 rev. 11–12 is a provincial exception to this rule; Hattusilis removes the hands of female servants from millstones and of male servants from sickles (? see Melchert, *JNES* 37 [1978] 4 n. 9). In normal usage, the millstones and sickle would be removed. *ina bāb anunnakī liddappirū* (*RA* 65 [1971] 134:20) is perhaps another exception, but the text is too fragmentary to decide. That *duppuru* should here mean simply "to send" (so S. Lackenbacher) runs counter to all the evidence.

[12] *ARM* 5 37:9 is taken as an exception to this rule: (*mimma alpū u immerātum ina libbi mātim ul ibaššû*) *ina qaṣêmma duppurū*, which Dossin rendered, "ils ont fui au désert même," and *CAD* D 187b, "they have been removed to the desert (i.e., winter pasture)." But *ina* should not mean "to" (motion towards). On the evidence at hand, "they are gone even from the steppe (or: from the steppe, too)." Similarly (see previous note), *ina bāb anunnakī*, hardly "à la porte des Anunnaki (qu'elles soient envoyées)."

[13] That *duppuru* is a denominative-verb seems likely (so von Soden), but rather than "den Rücken wenden" perhaps "to back-country (someone)," in view of the connotation of disappearance; cf. Heb. **dober*, "pasture land," Aram. *dabrā*, "field, desert," Eth. *dabr*, "mountain" (cf. *bāmtu*, with *AHw* 1 101, R. Frankena, SLB 4 39).

21. A Note on igi-kár, "provisions, supplies"

In *ASJ* 4 (1982) 149–151 P. Steinkeller has argued that igi-kár and gúrum (IGI.GAR) were different words, not simply graphic variants, and in the course of his argument he has also established that the meaning of the former, when used as a noun, in the Ur III period and earlier was "provisions, supplies," or the like. Later, however, as he has also pointed out, the noun igi-kár was equated with Akk. *aširtu*, some kind of offering to a temple, and its earlier, more general meaning was assumed by gúrum-ag, Akk. *piqittu*. The bearing of these observations on a few outstanding problems in the Amarna letters is the subject of this note. If it is as decisive as I think it is, then it is also immediately evident that the older meaning of igi-kár survived in the west, reappearing there more than six centuries after its last attestation in Ur III sources.

In *EA* 337 we read: [7] "The king, my lord, has written [8] to me, *šu-ši-ir-me* [9] IGI.KÁR.MEŠ *ma-a*D*-ni-a* [10] *a-na pa-ni* ERÍN MEŠ GAL.MEŠ [11] : *pí-ṭá-ti* [12] *ša* LUGAL EN-*ia* ...[19] ... *šu-ši-ir-te* [20] IGI.KÁR.MEŠ GAL.MEŠ [21] : *ma-a*D*-ni-a a-na* [22] *pa-ni* ERÍN.MEŠ GAL LUGAL [23] EN-*ia*, 'Prepare ... before the arrival of a large army of the king, my lord' ... I have prepared large ... before the arrival of a large army of the king, my lord."[1] The problems have been the logogram IGI.KÁR and the meaning and reading of its apparent synonym *ma-a*D*-ni-a*. The only solutions that have been proposed are those of O. Schroeder, *OLZ* 1915, Sp. 105f. He challenged the reading *ma-a*D*-ni-a*, which had been Knudtzon's, and read instead *ma-la-ni-a*. This he derived from *malānu*, comparing Heb. *mālôn*, "a place to stay the night," which was also said of military encampments. The latter usage he found relevant for *EA* 337. IGI.KÁR, which he read as IGI.MAL, he left without comment.

[1]The exact provenience of *EA* 337 is unknown. Knudtzon. VAB 2/2, 1348, argued that it was written in southwest Palestine.—In line 11, *piṭati*, lit. "archers," the general term for troops in Egyptian (see A. Rainey, AOAT 8^2, 87), either glosses or, marked as a foreign word, is dependent on, ERÍN.MEŠ; cf. the similar gloss in line 21, where *ma-a*D*-ni-a* goes with IGI.KÁR.MEŠ, not with GAL.MEŠ. The king ordered only IGI.KÁR.MEŠ, but the vassal makes GAL.MEŠ to match the ERÍN.MEŠ GAL(.MEŠ).

The objections to Schroeder's proposals, which *faute de mieux* (I suppose) have won some adherence,[2] are several and serious: 1. the absence of any evidence in support of the assumed meaning of IGI.KÁR, which almost seventy years later, despite the enormous advances in Sumerian lexicography, remains as anomalous as ever; 2. *pace* Schroeder, there is nothing "Hittite" about the sign-forms in *EA* 337—note the very non-Hittite forms of GÌR (line 5) and NI (lines 9, 10, 21)—and even the alleged LA does not have the characteristic TAB+ŠU form; 3. most serious of all, the anomalous writing *-ni-a*, where one expects either *-na* (acc. sg.) or *-ni-ma* (masc. pl.)/*-nu-ti* (fem. pl.), and the failure to reflect the Canaanite *ā* > *ō* shift (*ma-lu-*).

Another and now, after Steinkeller's article, even obvious solution is of course to take IGI.KÁR in the sense of "provisions, supplies." This not only makes perfect sense in context, but it is also confirmed by many parallels, both in *EA* and in other Egyptian sources. Vassals were regularly required to furnish Egyptian troops with supplies as the latter advanced through their territory.[3] A few *EA* examples: Akizzi of Qatna (*EA* 55:11–12) claims to have supplied victuals (NINDA), strong drink (KAŠ), oxen (GUD), *sheep and* goats (ÙZ),[4] honey (LÀL), and oil (Ì.GIŠ); Aziru of Amurru (*EA* 161:21–22), oxen, *sheep and* goats, birds (MUŠEN), victuals, strong drink; Yidya of Ascalon (*EA* 324:12–14; 325:16–17), victuals, strong drink, grain (ŠE), oxen, *sheep and* goats, oil

[2]*CAD* M/1, 161; F. Pintore, *OA* 11 (1972) 102, n. 4, but see D. Edzard, *ZA* 69 (1980) 292, who considers *malania* "unklar" and points to the difficulty of the final *-a* (see our third objection below).

[3]N. Na'aman, *Israel Exploration Journal* 31 (1981) 181.

[4]The reading ÙZ (consultation on the Sumerian word with P. Steinkeller gratefully acknowledged) was also recognized independently by E. Gordon (in notes on the Amarna letters kindly made available to me by Professor Albert Glock of the Albright Institute in Jerusalem) and N. Na'aman, *The Political Disposition and Historical Development of Eretz-Israel According to the Amarna Letters* (Ph. D. dissertation, Tel-Aviv University, 1975, in Hebrew), 54*, n. 47. Since it regularly follows "oxen" (GUD.MEŠ: *EA* 124:50; 125:20; 161:21; 324:14; 325:16), it seems to be a replacive of "sheep and goats" (cf. GUD.MEŠ UDU.MEŠ, *EA* 193:20, and on the meaning of the latter, cf. UDU.UDU.MEŠ : *ṣú-ú-nu*, 263:12). In comparable Egyptian lists the sequence is oxen, goats, sheep, with an alternative "sheep and goats" (*Kleinvieh*); see E. Edel, *Festschrift Alt: Geschichte und Altes Testament. Beiträge zur historischen Theologie* (Tübingen, 1950), 52, n. 1. The terminological lack of differentiation between sheep and goats goes far back in prehistory, as early as the 8th–6th millennia; see I. Diakonoff, *Altorientalische Forschungen* 8 (1981), especially pp. 53, 58f., on *ᶜizz*.

(*EA* 324), and straw (IN, *EA* 325).[5] All of these items would of course be covered by IGI.KÁR as defined and illustrated by Steinkeller, and the archaism would only be one more example of sporadic archaic writings and language in the western periphery of this period.[6]

The interpretation of IGI.KÁR.MEŠ (Akk. *ašrāti? piqdāti?*) as "provisions, supplies," also suggests a very plausible solution to the problem of the gloss. Read *ma-aṭ-ni-a*, and cf. Phoenician (usually yifᶜil)–Punic *ṭn*ʾ, "to erect, install," and Phoenician *mṭn*ʾ, "offering"; cf. also Sabaean *ṭny*, "to erect (a statute)" (Joan C. Biella, *Dictionary of Old South Arabic: Sabaean Dialect*, HSS 25, 220). The formation *maqtil* suggests either a means of standing, a support, or what one stands up, erects (cf. **maḫsiru*, what one needs, *EA* 287:16; Phoen. **mattin*, "gift," and perhaps *mṭn*ʾ, "offering"). In either case the semantic development to "provisions, supplies" would not be difficult; in the former, cf. support, sustenance, maintenance; in the latter, stores, "*collective pl.* Articles (such as food, clothing, arms, etc.) serving for the equipment and maintenance of an army ..." (*OED*), which according to the *OED* goes back, through Old French *estorer*, to Lat. *instaurare*, "to erect, establish," and (not quite as pertinent) Syr. *ʾassānā*, "commeatus," from the verb *ʾesan*, "collegit, coacervavit."

In conclusion, we should note one other occurrence of IGI.KÁR in *EA*, where the king is asked to give fifty men "along with 1 LÚ (or ᵐLÚ).IGI.KÁR EN.[NUN/NU.UN] to guard the city" (*EA* 295 rev. 6–7).[7] Even if the restoration *maṣ*[*ṣarti*] is wrong, the number fifty and the role assigned them argue that there is a question of a garrison-force, and LÚ.IGI.KÁR would seem to be the commanding officer, in Akk. perhaps *āširu* or *pāqidu*.[8] If the restoration is correct, as the Egyptian

[5]See also *EA* 131:42; 226:16; 242:9–13 (line 12: [x ÙZ.MEŠ x *iṣ-ṣú*]-*ra-te*); and more generally, *EA* 141:24–30; 142:25–31; 144:21; 287:16.

[6]See B. Landsberger-H. Güterbock, *AfO* 12 (1937–39) 55ff.; H. Güterbock, *Festschrift Heinrich Otten* (Wiesbaden, 1975) 71ff.; J. Nougayrol, *AS* 16, 29ff.; W. Moran, *BASOR* 211 (1973) 50ff. [above, Paper 16].

[7]N. Na'aman has offered strong arguments that *EA* 295 was written in Tyre; see *UF* 11 (1979) 673ff.

[8]On fifty as the usual number manning a garrison, see *EA* 139:22; 238:11; 289:42. A. Schulman, *Military Rank, Title, and Organization in the Egyptian New Kingdom, Münchener Ägyptologische Studien* 6 (Berlin, 1964), 26ff., has argued that fifty men constituted the basic tactical unit. Following Schroeder, F. Pintore, *OA* 11 (1972) 102, n. 4, restored EN [*ma-la-ni-a*] and proposed that the official was the quartermaster (Eg. *ỉꜣṯw n pꜣ mšᶜ*). The restoration aside, if LÚ.IGI.KÁR could be the "provider," then quartermaster may be right.

name of this officer, *ỉmy-r ỉwʿyt,* "overseer (lit. one-who-is-in-the-mouth) of the garrison," as well as context favors, then LÚ.IGI.KÁR (*āšir* / *pāqid*) is a free but accurate rendering of the Egyptian.[9]

[9]Whether the *ḥry ỉwʿyt,* "the one over the garrison," is a different official and should also be considered as perhaps corresponding to LÚ.IGI.KÁR EN.NUN must be left to the Egyptologists to decide; on the officer, see Schulman, op. cit., 50f.

22. Additions to the Amarna Lexicon

Textum valde ama. Many times—and many years ago—I heard these words from a teacher who was ever quoting (he said) the great classicist Richard Bentley. I recall them now, it seems almost inevitably, as I think of my old friend and colleague Mitchell Dahood, for he was a lover of texts if there ever was one, sitting before the texts of his beloved Hebrew Bible and Ugaritic corpus, pondering and comparing, delighted and absorbed, as only a lover can be. He was especially fond of new words, new entries in the Hebrew lexicon or new occurrences, precious metals mined from the consonantal text. And so I think he would find appropriate and be pleased by this small tribute to his memory, a brief listing of some of the new entries I would propose to make in another lexicon.[1]

aḫātu—(Manya along with his sons) *qadu* NIN.MEŠ-*ti-šu aš-ša-te-e-šu* "along with his sisters (and) his wives" *EA* 162:73 (G. Ries, *RLA* 6, 183b). [Later correction by Moran: Delete entry, retaining Knudtzon's DAM.MEŠ-*ti-šu* (Egypto-Hittite form)—*Eds.*]

amartu—*EA* 13 rev. ^{1}[... *ka*]*m-mu-ša-ak-ku* ^{2}[... ^{giš}*a-ma-r*]*a-tu* X [...] ^{3}[... *kam-m*]*u-ša-ak-ku* x [x x (x)] x KÙ.BABBAR ^{4}[... ^{gi}]^{š}*a-ma-ra-*[*tu a-di ṣú-up*]*-ri* ^{5}[...] ZUR.MEŠ *kam-m*[*u-ša*]*-ak-ku*. *kammušakku*, a type of bed or chair, also read by E. Gordon; double-*m*, otherwise unattested. *amartu*, sideboards or siding, also in *EA* 25 iv 18, 21 (see *CAD* A/1 373, sub *altapipu*).

anniša—*adi an-ni-ša abbaʾūya lā išpurū ūma anāku altaprakku* *EA* 15:9–11. W. von Soden, *Or* 21 (1952) 433 (also *AHw* 14a), proposed

[1] The list is selective. I confine it to reasonably sure readings and to readings that are either unpublished or might easily be overlooked. Among the latter, therefore, I assume that E. Edel's important contributions in *Studien zur Altägyptischen Kultur* 1 (1974) 105ff., 295, and *Der Brief des ägyptischen Wesirs Pašijara an den Hethiterkönig Ḫattušili und verwandte Keilschriftbriefe* (Nachrichten d. Akademie d. Wissenschaften in Göttingen I. Phil.-hist. Kl., 1978/4; Göttingen 1978), are not to be included. For previous additions to the Amarna lexicon, see Anson F. Rainey, AOAT 8^{2}, 61ff. As will be evident, the contribution of Edmund Gordon to our list is not a small one, and again I must thank Professor Albert Glock, who as Director of the Albright Institute in Jerusalem made Gordon's heavily annotated copy of Knudtzon available to me. In some cases I had anticipated Gordon's readings; often, however, I had not.

to read *a-di-an-ni ša ...*, "Verträge, die meine Väter nicht zugesandt hatten ...," as if from *adû*, "oath, (treaty) stipulation," and he has been followed by A. K. Grayson, *Assyrian Royal Inscriptions* I (Wiesbaden 1972) 48. However, *adû* is an Aramaic loanword and, it seems, one that entered the language considerably after the time of Assuruballit I (see P. Artzi, *Bar-Ilan Studies in History* [1978] 27, n. 3; H. Tadmor, in H.-J. Nissen–J. Renger [Hrsg.], *Mesopotamien und seine Nachbarn: Politische und kulturelle Wechselbeziehungen im Alten Vorderasien vom 4. bis 1. Jahrtausend v. Chr.* [Berliner Beiträge zum Vorderen Orient, Band 1; Berlin 1982] 455). Therefore *CAD* A/1 119b, counters with *adi anni*, "until now," and this interpretation has found wider acceptance (G. Wilhelm, *UF* 2 [1970] 279, n. 26; Artzi, loc. cit.). But this proposal has its own difficulties. The translation "whereas until now ..." (*CAD*) glosses over the problem of the assumed relative, and if *ša* does mark a relative clause, then in view of the Ass. subjunctive-marker a few lines below (*aš-pu-ra-ku-ni*, 16) one would expect here *iš-pu-ru-ni*. Hence the suggestion of *adi anniša*: "Hitherto my ancestors have not written; today *I* write to you." In other words, I would assume that *anniša* had a temporal as well as its attested local sense (OA, *ARM* 10 92:6 *annišam*; NA *ana (ḫ)anniša*); cf. *ullānu*, adv. of both time and place, and MA/NA *a(k)kanni*, "now," but NB *akanna*, "here." In Ass., the assumption of the use of *lā* in a main clause is no difficulty, and it should be added that Scheil's copy (*Bulletin de l'Institut français d'archéologie orientale du Caire* 2 [1902] 114) is inaccurate and misleading, for there is no large space between *a-di an-ni* and *ša*, suggesting that *ša* goes with what follows; rather, the lower horizontal of *ni* curves up and stretches out till it almost touches *ša* (see photo in *Bulletin of the Metropolitan Museum of Art* 21 [1926] 170, fig. 1).

aqru—Note the correct understanding of *ana iyāšīma mimma ul aqra u ana kâšāma mimma ul aqarku EA* 10:16–17 in *AHw* 1460b: "Neither for me is there anything scarce nor for you is there anything scarce."

ardūtu—For the abstract, "service," besides the writing ÌR.MEŠ note LÚ.ÌR.MEŠ in *EA* 157:10 and LÚ.MEŠ.ÌR.*TUM* in *EA* 165:11 (cf. LÚ.ÌR. *TUM-ti* in *EA* 171:12), all in letters from Amurru. Cf., too, LÚ.ÌR = *ardu* (*EA* 171:35) in Amurru as well as at Ugarit, Qatna, Tunip and Jerusalem (VAB 2/2, 1378f.; *EA* 288:18). In favor of seeing the abstract in *EA* 157:10 is its use in the closely parallel passage *EA* 171:3ff.; see already N. Na'aman, *The Political Disposition and Historical Develop-*

ment of Eretz-Israel according to the Amarna Letters (dissertation Tel-Aviv University, 1975) 60*, n. 8.

assurri—[*as-s*]*ur*$_x$-*ri EA* 158:22; Amurru-form of ZUR-sign is quite clear, and for the writing of *assurri* in the letters from Aziru see *EA* 165:20; 166:23; 167:25.[2]

aṣû—(When he learned) *ù la-a-me ti-it-*[*ta-ṣ*]*ú-na* ERÍN.MEŠ *pi-ṭá-tu*$_4$, "that the archers were not coming forth" *EA* 244:19–20. This reading, which is due to E. Gordon, accords with the nominative *piṭātu* (as against Knudtzon's *ti-id-*[*di-i*]*n-na*).—[*u l*]*iddin šarru pānīšu* ⌜*ù*⌝ [*lu-ṣi-m*]*i* [50][LÚ.MEŠ] ERÍN.MEŠ *pi-ṭa-ti a-na* KUR-*š*[*u*], "May the king see to it that archers come forth to/for his land" *EA* 288:49–50; cf. *liddin šarru pānīšu a-na* LÚ.MEŠ *pi-ṭa-ti ù lu-ṣi-mi* LÚ.MEŠ ERÍN *pi-ṭa-ti EA* 286: 53–54. The reading [49] ... ⌜*ù*⌝ [*lu-ma-še-e*]*r* [50][LUGAL] ... (Albright, *ANET*^{3} 489) accords with neither the space nor the traces. There is no reason why -*m*]*i* should be read at the end of line 50 (so Knudtzon) rather than line 49.

aširtu—(The king, my lord, wrote to me) *šu-ši-ir-me* [9]IGI.KÁR.MEŠ *ma-aṭ-ni-a*, " 'Prepare the supplies (before the arrival of the archers)' " *EA* 337:8–9 (similarly lines 19–21). On IGI.KÁR, "provisions, supplies", in Ur III documents, and the later equation of IGI.KÁR = *aširtu*, see P. Steinkeller, *Acta Sumerologica* 4 (1982) 149–151. For a fuller discussion of the passage and the reading of the gloss (cf. Phoenician *mṭnʾ*, "offering"), see *Acta Sumerologica* 5 [above, Paper 21].

āširu—This (or *pāqidu*) is the probable reading in *EA* 295 rev. 6, (May the king, my lord, give 50 men along with) 1 LÚ (or ᴵLÚ).IGI. KÁR EN.[NUN/NU.UN], "a *gar*[*rison*]-commander (to guard the city ...)." Cf. *aširtu* above, and see *Acta Sumerologica* 5 [above, Paper 21].

ay—Probably *a-ia*$_8$-*ti*, "where", *EA* 139:36 (Byblos), like the more common *a-ia*$_8$-*mi* elsewhere in the Byblos letters; on the enclitic -*ti*, cf.

[2]On *assurri* in *EA* see M. Held, *JCS* 15 (1961) 20–21. His arguments that it always means something like "God forbid that ..." I find convincing. That it ever means simply "perhaps," as K. Veenhof, *RA* 76 (1982) 126, asserts, restricting the stronger expression with its implications of will to *assurri lā*, is not supported by attested usage. Thus those who favor "perhaps" must make significant additions or paraphrases that in effect reveal the inadequacy of the translation: Finet, *L'accadien des lettres de Mari* (Bruxelles 1956) §51a, to whom Veenhof refers, "peut-être (= il faut espérer que non)"; *AHw* 76a, "vielleicht, hoffentlich nicht," and "ich fürchte" in some of the context passages. "Perhaps" bespeaks only doubt about an assertion; never does it mean, as *assurri*, with or without *lā*, always does, that the speaker hopes the contrary ("il faut espŕer que non," "hoffentlich nicht").

mīya-ti as well as *mīya-mi,* and see C. Krahmalkov, *JSS* 14 (1969) 203–204.

ayyalu—D⌜AR⌝A_3.MAŠ.MEŠ *EA* 25 iv 14 (also E. Gordon).

ballukku—ŠIM.BULÚG (Knudtzon) *EA* 22 iii 33, not ŠIM.BAL (*CAD* B 64).

dabru—ina BA.BAD *ina mu-ta-a-an ina* dáb-*ri,* "by plague," *EA* 244:31–33; cf. Heb. *deber*. Perhaps the scribe had in mind a trilingual lexical text.

išḫunnatu—1 *i*[*š*]-*ḫu-un-na-tu,* "1 bunch of grapes (of gold)" *EA* 25 ii 36 (E. Gordon).

itquru—[X ^{gi}]^{š}DILIM.MEŠ *EA* 25 iv 64 (also E. Gordon). Despite Knudtzon's autograph (VAB 2/1, 1001, No. 43), apparently confirmed by the copy of VS 12, there are traces of only one horizontal followed by only *one* vertical, therefore GI]Š. Note the sequence here in iv 63–64 of ^{giš}BUGÍN.TUR and ^{giš}DILIM as in 22 iv 34–35.

itti—(The king my lord has written me) *urruba du-gu-la-ni* KI *(itti) šarri bēlīya mīya-mi yumaggir urruba it-ti šarri bēlīya,* " 'Come in (and) pay me homage.' Into the presence of the king, my lord! Would that it were possible to enter into the presence of the king, my lord" *EA* 283:8–11 (following *AHw* 576a).

kallû—[^{I}x (x)]-x *ana pā*[*nīk*]*a kī* [*ka-al-li-e*] ^{23}[*a*]*ltapra*[*kk*]*u,* "I have sent PN to you posthaste" *EA* 8:22–23. The assumption that nothing followed *ki-i* in the rather long broken space at the end of line 22 is supported by neither the previous nor the following lines. Nor is the resulting sense, "As soon as I send PN, inquire from him so he can inform you" (so von Soden, *Or.* 21 [1952] 430; J. Aro, *StOr* 20, 148), satisfactory. Burna-Buriaš is complaining about the death of his merchants, and it does not seem likely that he would put off to some future date the despatch of the messenger who was to provide the Pharaoh with additional relevant information. The bearer of the present letter should have a role. For *kī kallê* in letters from Babylonia, see *EA* 10:38; 11 rev. 18.

kanaktu—(1 scent container) Ì ŠIM.GIG *EA* 25 iv 51 (*kanatki,* cf. *EA* 22 iii 32; also E. Gordon). The last sign is neither BAL (*CAD* B 64a) nor any of the BULUG-signs (Knudtzon).

leqû—allû PN *u* PN$_2$ *la-qu a-wa-ta* [*b*]*irīšunu elīya,* "Look, Aziru and Yapaḫ-Adda have made an agreement between them against me" *EA* 116:50–52; cf. *alkamma awatam ina birītīni i nilqe,* "Come so we can reach an agreement between us" (S. Dalley et al., *The Old Babylonian Tablets from Tell al Rimah* no. 15:8–10).

maṣṣartu—See *āširu*.

*maṭni*ʾ*u*—See *aširtu*.

maṭû—(May the king heed the w<o>rds of his servant and may the king, my lord, grant archers that they may seize (*te-eṣ-*[*ba-at*]) Byblos, and that traitorous troops and the sons of ^{c}Abdi-Aširta not enter it) *ù ti-*[*i*]*m-*[*t*]*a-*[*ṭ*]*í* ERÍN.MEŠ *pí-ṭá-at šarri bēlīya ana laqêši*, "and then the archers of the king, my lord, be too few to take it back" *EA* 137:44–45. Knudtzon's reading *ti-*[*i*]*ḫ-*[*š*]*a-*[*ḫ*]*i* is objectionable for several reasons: 1. wrong thematic vowel in Babylonian; 2. overhanging vowel; 3. interpretation (neither A. Leo Oppenheim, *Letters from Mesopotamia* [Chicago 1967] 133, "archers are needed," nor Albright, *ANET*^{3} 483, "archers need to capture it," fits attested usage of *ḫašāḫu*).

minde—(May the king not say) *mi-di lā ṣabtat pa*[*šḫat*], " 'Surely it (Byblos) has not been (cannot be?) taken; it is at peace.' " *EA* 129:53; see *JCS* 31 (1979) 94, n. 46.

mūšu—(Indeed I guard Megiddo, the city of the king, my lord) *urra u* GI$_6$-*ša*, "day and night" *EA* 243:13 (reading the following gloss *l*[*e-l*]*a*, with A. Rainey, *UF* 7 [1975] 405). There is no reason to postulate an otherwise unattested *mīšu*.

nadû—"to pour oil (for divination and other purposes)" (*CAD* N/1 76a), add: ^{17}[DUMU.MUNUS-*ti ki-i*] *ukallimušunūti ana qaqq*[*a*]*d* DU[MU].MUN[US-*ti-ia*] ^{18}⸢Ì⸣.[GIŠ *it-t*]*a-du-ú*, "When I showed them my daughter, they poured oil on my daughter's head" *EA* 11:17–18 (B. Landsberger, *Symbolae iuridicae et historicae Martino David dedicatae*, tomus alter [Leiden 1968] 80, n.). Also *mārat šarri ša šamna* [*ana qaqq*]*adīša* ^{16}[*id-du*]-*ú EA* 11 rev. 15–16.

nalbašu—TÚG.ME.ḪI.A *EA* 1:70.

namsû—10 NÍG.ŠU.L[UḪ.ḪA ZABAR] *EA* 25 iv 60; the apparent third horizontal may be only a scratch, and cf. the same sequence of washbasins and braziers in *EA* 22 iv 22.

qabû—[*ultu aššat*] *abīka qu-ub-ba-tu*$_4$, "After your father's wife had been mourned" *EA* 11:5 (also line 11). Landsberger apud Edward F. Campbell, *The Chronology of the Amarna Letters* (Baltimore, 1964) 46, proposed a noun *qubbâtu*, "mourning".

ruqqu—[... (^{urudu})Š]EN *EA* 13 rev. 20 (E. Gordon). 10 ⸢ŠEN⸣ *EA* 22 iv 24 (E. Gordon).

sakātu—*libbāt aḫīya ul am-la as-s*[*a-k*]*u-*[*ut*], "I was no longer angry with my brother; I fell silent" *EA* 7:32 (E. Gordon). In line 15 *anāku libbāti ša aḫīya am-*[*ta-la*]; the shift from *amtala* to *ul amla* reflects the normal usage of tenses in MB letters.

sinuntu—(the handle) *s*[*i-nu*]-*un-tu*$_4$, "a swallow" *EA* 25 ii 47 (E. Gordon).

sūnu I—[...] DAM.MEŠ-*ia* [28][*ù*] É.GI-*ia ù* [29][*ša-k*]*a-an i-na* ÚR : *su-n*[*i-šu*] [30][*ba*]-*ši-ta*$_5$, "[...] my wives [*and*] my daughter-in-law, and [he *p*]*ut* in his lap (any of the women) [*pre*]*sent*" *EA* 196:27–30; cf. É.GI.A = *kallātu* (Mitanni, Ugarit; *CAD* K 80); *sūni* seems to have been the gloss before the erasure.

sūnu II—*sú-nu-šu*, "its trimming/hem" *EA* 22 iv 14; on *sūnu* = Ugaritic *si*ʾ*n*, see *RA* 73 (1983) 93f.

šarû—(Undoubtedly your neighboring kings) *š*]*a-ru-ti ra-bu-ti*, "are rich (and) mighty" *EA* 1:56–57 (also E. Gordon).

šukūdu—20 GI.MEŠ *šu-ku-ú-*[*du*], "20 arrows, *šukūdu*-type" *EA* 22 iii 53 (E. Gordon).

tabāku—[Ì].GIŠ.MEŠ [*ana q*]*aqqadīša it-tab-k*[*u*], "Oils were poured on her head" *EA* 29:23 (following Landsberger; see *nadû*).

ṭapālu—(As to your saying to me, "He put my chariots among the chariots of the mayors. You did not review them separately.") *tu-ṭe*$_4$*-pí-el-šu-nu ana pānī māti*, "You humiliated them before the (whole) country" *EA* 1:91.

uṭṭatu—(Though I sent my son to the palace of the king) *ištu* 10 ŠE-*ti kašādīya ana* GN, "10 seconds after I arrived in Beirut, (he has not had an audience with the king for four months)" *EA* 138:76. Reference is to a clock, probably a water-clock (*dibdibbu*; F. Thureau-Dangin, *RA* 30 [1933] 51–52; O. Neugebauer, *Isis* 37 [1947] 37ff.) rather than a sand-clock (*maltaktu*). In the Babylonian system of weights (180 grains = 1 shekel, 60 shekels = 1 mina), if 1 mina = 4 hours (see dictionaries, but also Neugebauer, art. cit.), then 10 grains were a little more than 10 seconds.

23. Rib-Hadda: Job at Byblos?

Among the correspondents with the Egyptian court whom we meet in the Amarna letters, none has a sorrier tale, and none tells it more often, than Rib-Hadda of Byblos. He is, as he never tires of assuring the court, the king's loyal servant, Byblos the king's loyal city. However, as he also insists again and again, he and his city are only a small island of fealty in a sea of treason and treachery. The other Egyptian vassals who surround them are not loyal; on the contrary, they are, he constantly claims, ever betraying the king and his interests, ever seeking instead their own. They are, therefore, Rib-Hadda's enemies, united against him, cutting him off, and so he is isolated and suffers for his loyalty. Deserted by his peasantry, whom he cannot feed, he is even, it seems to him, abandoned by his master, the king. Betrayed by his brother, he eventually becomes an exile, and in his last known letter to the king, written from Beirut, he concludes his correspondence of about a decade with the unanswered question, "Why has the king done nothing for me?"[1]

This tale, at least in outline and relieved of repetition, has a certain pathos. But what really happened? *Parti pris* is evident, and no one would accept Rib-Hadda's version of events without question or qualification. But it is the merit of Mario Liverani to have been the first to stress the presence in Rib-Hadda's correspondence of recurring themes and an underlying conceptual pattern that must be recognized and taken into account in any proper assessment of the letters from Byblos as historical sources.[2] This pattern he identifies as one associated with the figure of the "righteous sufferer," one who lives in a tormented present, looks back to a glorious past, and awaits a future that is both imminent and ambiguous, threatening and promising. In the present time Rib-Hadda is a righteous man, that is, loyal to the king—who is innocent but suffering, plotted against and mistreated even by those who

[1]*EA* 138:138. The Amarna letters (*EA*) are cited from the edition of J. A. Knudtzon, *Die El-Amarna-Tafeln*, Vorderasiatische Bibliothek, I (Leipzig: Hinrichs, 1915).

[2]"Rib-Adda, giusto sofferente," *Altorientalische Forschungen* 1 (1974) 175–205 (hereafter cited as Liverani); for an earlier, briefer statement, see *Or.* NS 42 (1973) 184–86.

should be his friends. He appeals to the distant god, the king, who is not only a god in himself but in the role he has in Syro-Palestine—the absolute and final arbiter of all its affairs, who needs only to act and all will be well, the wicked punished, the righteous man saved and rewarded—but who remains remote and indifferent to the latter's plea for intervention. The present is also lived in recollection of the past, in memories of a Golden Age, the good old days when, unlike the present, Byblos housed an Egyptian garrison and was amply supplied, when, if it was attacked, Rib-Hadda could count on Egyptian reinforcements, when indeed at the very sight of an Egyptian the kings of Canaan fled. This present lies, too, at the verge of a future that will bring either total and irrevocable disaster, or a restoration of the peace and security of the past. If the king does not act now, in this final hour, then all will be lost. Rib-Hadda writes in this final hour—for about a decade. But for just as long he also promises the happy alternative, should the king intervene, of a better world, the old world.

Liverani looks for the source of this pattern and considers the possibility of the influence of Mesopotamian wisdom literature. This he does not reject but considers unlikely, even though, as discoveries at Ugarit have shown, the Mesopotamian tradition was certainly familiar in some Syrian courts. Rather, it is the common world of the court—administration, bureaucracy, politics, concern for the king's favor, the envy and calumnies of others, fidelity to one's duty and denunciation of the infidelities of rivals, the experience of life in general in this setting—the world shared by Rib-Hadda, by Byblian and Mesopotamian scribes alike, the world too reflected in the wisdom literature, that Liverani sees as the situation out of which came the conceptual pattern both of Rib-Hadda's correspondence and of the compositions concerned with the problem of the "righteous sufferer."

Such, in brief and inadequate outline, is Liverani's analysis. It is an analysis, it seems to me, that is illuminating and, in its general thesis of the presence in Rib-Hadda's letters of a "schema interpretativo della realtà," convincing. However, I do not think that his description of the pattern is adequate or its identification correct. Here I would like briefly to show why and to propose another "schema interpretativo."

The temporal scheme that Liverani finds cutting across the entire correspondence—a glorious past, a miserable present, an ambiguous future—seems to me neither as extensive nor, where it may exist, as unhistorical as Liverani claims. It is the contrast between the present and the past, the latter allegedly idealized into "una sorta di età dell'oro, di stato paradisiaco ora perduto"[3] that seems especially doubtful. In its support Liverani cites or refers to twenty passages in Rib-Hadda's letters, and in most cases there is no denying that Rib-Hadda looks to the past as a better time.[4] However, what Liverani does not advert to is the fact that of the twenty passages sixteen are found in letters of the time of Amenophis IV, only four in letters of the time of his predecessor.[5] Now, though the correspondence is more extensive, by about a third, in the later period (Amenophis IV), still the imbalance is very striking. Moreover, of the four passages written in the days of Amenophis III, only two really suggest thoughts of a better past, of which neither seems an idealization.[6] In the other two I see no hint of a Golden Age, I detect no "vago sapore paradisiaco" in "May it be pleasing in the sight of the king, my lord, that he give the grain produced in the land of Yarimuta. May what used to be given in Ṣumur now be given in Byblos."[7] This request, which is addressed to the king and then, in essentials, repeated in an accompanying letter to an Egyptian official,[8] suggests nothing more, it seems to me, than reflection on a grave crisis and a certain satisfaction with having found its solution. Grain is available and Rib-Hadda knows where: Yarimuta. In context, therefore, "what used to be given in Ṣumur" is not a sigh for better days, and it savors only of the provincial palace, informed and perhaps contentious, not of paradise. In

[3]Liverani, 192.

[4]*EA* 81:48–50; 85:33–37, 69–73; 86:31–35; 108:28–33; 109:44–46; 112:50–51, 54–56; 114:54–57; 116:61–63; 117:78–82; 118:50–54; 121:11–17; 122:11–19; 125:14–19; 126:18–23; 127:30–33; 129:46–48; 130:21–30; 132:10–18.

[5]*EA* 81, 85–86 (see n. 4) were probably written late in the reign of Amenophis III, though the assignment of *EA* 85–86, it might be noted, is not without its problems; see Edward Fay Campbell, *The Chronology of the Amarna Letters* (Baltimore: Johns Hopkins, 1964) 93–96.

[6]*EA* 81:48–50; 85:69–73. The former passage Liverani mistranslates, "Una volta Ṣumura e i suoi uomini costituivano una fortezza, e davano truppi di guarnigione" (Liverani, 194); render rather, "Formerly Ṣumur and its men were strong (or: there were Ṣumur and its strong men), and there was a garrison with us" (*itti-nu* in line 50 is not a form of *nadānu* but the preposition *itti* plus the [Canaanite] pronominal suffix; cf. the passages referred to below in n. 9). That the latter passage ("Moreover, since your father's return from Sidon, from that time the lands have been joined to the ᶜApiru") reflects simply pattern, without specific historical reference (so Liverani, 193, n. 157) is an inference of the allegedly pervasive temporal scheme: on the problem, see also H. Klengel, *Mitteilungen des Instituts für Orientforschung* 10 (1964) 61, n. 19.

[7]*EA* 85:33–37.

[8]*EA* 86:31–35.

brief, I do not think that there is one consistent temporal scheme that structures the thought of Rib-Hadda throughout his correspondence. It is only in the time of Amenophis IV that he frequently looks to bygone, better days, a restriction that in itself implies an historical, albeit rhetorical, conception of the past rather than its idealization.[9]

Serious doubts must also be raised concerning Rib-Hadda as the "righteous sufferer." There is no doubt that he thought of himself as righteous, that is, perfectly loyal to the king, and there is no doubt that he though of himself as a sufferer. It does not follow, however, that he therefore thought of himself as a "righteous sufferer," whether he be of the Mesopotamian or the biblical variety. The first would be repugnant, the second anachronistic.

The repugnance of the Mesopotamian model resides in the fact that in Mesopotamia the "righteous sufferer" is not righteous at all. "Si je suis sans autre raison apparente dans la peine, c'est que je suis puni; et si je suis puni, c'est que j'ai du enfreindre un ordre souverain des dieux ... Telle est la théologie fondamentale du Mal, qui s'est maintenue durant toute l'interminable histoire de la vieille Mésopotamie."[10] In the Old Babylonian period this theology may find expression in a simple confession of bewilderment and ignorance of what one has done,[11] or in

[9]That the situation in the time of Amenophis III appears less ideal in contemporary letters hardly proves that Rib-Hadda's later, rosier picture of the period is due to "un inserimento delle sue vicende in un quadro precostituito" (Liverani, 195). Contrary to Liverani's claim (192) that all passages introduced by *pānānu*, "formerly," refer uniformly to a kind of Golden Age, and showing that Rib-Hadda thought in terms of a less simplistic conception of the past, *EA* 104:24–26 reads, "Formerly they (the sons of ᶜAbdi-Aširta) would take cities of your mayors, and you (the king) did nothing." If the past here is better, the beginning of an ever deteriorating situation, it is certainly no Golden Age. In general, Rib-Hadda's better past consists of very specific recollections of fact and much repetition; for example, the success of a military expedition he had pleaded for (*EA* 108:28–33; 117:23–28; 132:10–18; see also *Eretz-Israel* 9 [1969] 98 [see above, Paper 14, p. 234]), or the presence in the past, and the absence in the present, of a garrison or guard (*maṣṣāru / maṣṣartu*; see *EA* 117:87–88; 121:11–13; 122:11–14; 125:14–15; 130:23–24; cf. 126:22), facts that the Pharaoh's order, "Guard, be on your guard" (*EA* 112:9; 117:84), or—probably another version of the same message—"Guard yourself" (*EA* 121:9; 122:10; 123:30–31; 125:9; 126:31; 130:16–17), gave Rib-Hadda the occasion to recall *ad nauseam*.

[10]J. Bottéro, *Le Problème du Mal en Mésopotamie ancienne*, Recherches et documents du Centre Thomas More, Document 77/7 (Evaux: Centre Thomas More, 1977) 3; see also W. G. Lambert, *Babylonian Wisdom Literature* (Oxford: Clarendon, 1960) 15–16.

[11]J. Nougayrol, *RB* 59 (1952) 243:14.

the acceptance of one's sinfulness, along with its necessary consequences, as another manifestation of *fragilitas humana* common to all men.[12] Later, one may infer from a clear conscience and a life re-examined and found, according to the known rules, faultless, that the gods hold men to the observance of other rules that he cannot know.[13] To these thoughts one may join a contempt for man as the minion of many moods, a creature that may live gloriously only to die miserably.[14] Or one may make the problem of the mind a problem of the heart, and solve it with reasons of the heart. Instead of wisdom, belief; instead of reflection and argument, a hymn to paradox and contradiction. *Credo quia absurdum.*[15] Attitudes and expressions change; the theology does not.[16]

In his relations with the king and his present sufferings such a conception of evil would hardly appear to Rib-Hadda as either congenial or germane. And as a matter of fact, we have evidence that he shared this common conception. He wrote to the king: "I am old and there is a grievous illness in my body. The king, my lord, knows that the gods of Byblos are *holy*, and the illness is extreme, *as* I have *com<mit>ted* sin(s?) against the gods."[17] Sickness, therefore guilt; nothing could be more conventional. Liverani comments: "(Rib-Hadda) falls into the normal diagnostic procedure of the time, following a deeply rooted conceptual *routine*. But it is not to be transferred to the political situation, which remains without explanation."[18] The assumption that Rib-Hadda

[12] S. N. Kramer, *ANET*^{3}, 590:101–2; see also T. Jacobsen, *Toward the Image of Tammuz*, HSS 21, ed. by William L. Moran (Cambridge: Harvard, 1970) 333, no. 32.

[13] Lambert, *Babylonian Wisdom Literature*, 38–41:23–38 (*Ludlul bēl nēmeqi*, tablet 2).

[14] Ibid., 40–41:39–47.

[15] This is the ultimate position of the author of *Ludlul bēl nēmeqi*, as is evident from the opening hymn now recovered almost entirely (see D. J. Wiseman, *Anatolian Studies* 20 [1980] 102–7); for a revision of the hymn see the writer's remarks in *JAOS* 103.1 (S. N. Kramer Festschrift) (1983) 255–60.

[16] For this reason one must assume that in *Ugaritica* V, No. 162, which Nougayrol saw as an early version of *Ludlul bēl nēmeqi* or as deriving with the latter from a common source, the broken introduction or conclusion contained some reference to the sufferer's guilt. An explicit, unyielding declaration of innocence is not found before the book of Job.

[17] *EA* 137:30–33 (in line 33, in favor of reading *ep-<ša>-ti*, against *epte*, "I confessed," or *epdi*, "I redeemed (by vow)," see our translation of the Amarna letters in *The Amarna Letters* (Baltimore: Hopkins, 1992) 219, n. 4.

[18] Liverani, 203.

was conventional in his religious thought, innovative in the political analogy, I find facile rather than convincing.

Moreover, the figure of the "righteous sufferer," truly righteous or not, ill accords with other recurring features in Rib-Hadda's description of himself. Essential to the latter, it seems, is that he alone is loyal, and that precisely because he is loyal he suffers from the plots and attacks of others.[19] But the "righteous sufferer" never claims that he alone is righteous, nor that he suffers for his righteousness and is isolated for his fidelity to his god.

A truly profound difference between Rib-Hadda and the "righteous sufferer," and again one essential to the figure he describes for the court, is that, unlike the "righteous sufferer," he has a way out of his sufferings that does not depend on the intervention of the "distant god." He can simply go over to the other side. This is always the implication when he contrasts his own suffering as a loyal vassal with the peace and prosperity of his perfidious peers. The possibility of changing allegiance is expressly noted when he reports the tempting pleas of both his family and his fellow-citizens. "Men from Byblos, my own household, and my wife kept saying to me, 'Ally yourself with the son of ᶜAbdi-Aširta so we can have peace between us.' But I refused; I did not listen to them."[20] "The city said, 'Abandon him (the king). Let's join Aziru.' And I said, 'How can I join him and abandon the king, my lord?' "[21]

On one occasion, in separate letters to the king and to an Egyptian official, Rib-Hadda openly threatened rebellion, claiming he could do it with impunity, and also indicating that he was not quite as helpless and cut off as he usually pictured himself, for he had, he claimed, a band of loyal followers. "Moreover, say to Yanḫamu, 'Rib-Hadda is herewith in your charge, and whatever happens to him is your responsibility.' Let not the troops fall upon me. And so I write, 'If you do not tell him this, then I will abandon the city and go off. Moreover, if you do not reply to me, I will abandon the city and go off with the men who are loyal to me.' "[22] Earlier in the same letter: "I have written for a garrison and for horses, and they are not being supplied. Send word to me or I will make a treaty with ᶜAbdi-Aširta just as Yapaḫ-Hadda and Zimredda

[19]See Liverani, 179.

[20]*EA* 136:8–15.

[21]*EA* 138:44–47.

[22]*EA* 83:39–51 (for the readings, see translation referred to in n. 17).

have done, and I will live."[23] To the Egyptian official: "If within two months there are no archers, then I will abandon the city and go off, and my life will be safe."[24]

This is not the language of the "righteous sufferer," who with no alternative can only wail and wait. Life, that good thing that belongs to Liverani's paradise regained, is something Rib-Hadda can have any time he wants. He need only be disloyal and abandon his lord.

But of course he does not. For he is the *arad kitti*, the loyal servant, and it is this figure, I submit, that ideally conceived provides the most comprehensive "schema interpretativo della realtà" in Rib-Hadda's correspondence. In its light he perceived himself; against it he measured himself. Explicit often, implicit at least throughout, the ideal of loyalty unifies the entire correspondence and reveals the nuances and implications of Rib-Hadda's endless claims, requests, and protests.

A detailed examination of this ideal is not necessary here, and a sketch will do. The ideal servant has always been loyal, as has his family.[25] He lives only for his master's interests,[26] and even his ancestral city he protects only because it is the king's, who may be urged to do with it what he please.[27] Whatever is his is the king's, for whom alone he lives.[28] In insisting on his loyalty he in effect abases himself, for as *arad kitti* he is the perfect slave, the pure instrument, renouncing in his relations with his master all autonomy.[29] But if as *arad kitti* he speaks *de profundis*, conscious of his own lowliness and uncertain of royal grace, he also speaks the truth, even the unpleasant truth.[30] And, as we have already seen, just as his loyalty always has been, so it ever shall be, firm and fast, unmoved by blandishment and temptation.[31]

[23]Lines 23–27.

[24]*EA* 82:41–45.

[25]*EA* 74:5–12; 116:55–56; 118:39–41.

[26]See Liverani's penetrating description, *RA* 61 (1967) 12–16, of the mentality of the pure functionary displayed by Rib-Hadda and his fellow-vassals.

[27]*EA* 126:44–46.

[28]*EA* 105:81–83.

[29]"I am a footstool for the feet of the king, my lord. I am his utterly loyal servant" (*EA* 106:6–7); cf. also *EA* 116:55–60, which begins with an assertion of loyalty, then states a problem and a request for its consideration, concluding with "Look, I am the dirt under your feet."

[30]*EA* 107:8–11; 108:20–25.

[31]See nn. 20–21.

He is the *arad kitti*, and the Pharaoh knows this, "knows how long he has been showing me favor because I have no divided allegiance, my only intention being to serve the king, my lord."[32] His role is recognized, appreciated, and at times rewarded; it grounds his confidence, and he lives in hope and expectation.

The figure of the ideal, the perfectly loyal servant is not confined to the letters of Rib-Hadda. The ideal was probably shared by all the royal courts of the time and long before. It is apparent, though fragmentary, in other, less extensive correspondences of other Amarna governors.[33] A most striking illustration, along with related narrative themes, is found in Suppiluliumas' dealings with Ugarit, in which we find the Hittite king writing to Niqmandu, the king of Ugarit, urging him to maintain the peaceful relations of the past between the two kingdoms, now that the neighboring kingdoms of Nuhas and Mukis were in revolt against him. "If you, Niqmandu, heed and observe these words of the Sun, your lord, you will immediately see the favor with which the great king, your lord, will favor you."[34] And Niqmandu did not join the rebellion, and hence the following decree: "The word of the Sun, Suppiluliumas, great king, king of Hatti, the hero. When all the kings of Nuhas and the king of Mukis were at war with the Sun, the great king, their lord, Niqmandu, the king of Ugarit, was at peace and not at war with the Sun, the great king, his lord. And the kings of Nuhas and the king of Mukis urged him, saying, 'Why are you not at war, on our side, against the Sun?' But Niqmandu would not agree to war against the Sun, the great king, his lord. And the Sun ... has seen the *kittu* of Niqmandu and accordingly has drawn up this agreement."[35]

The themes are familiar: long-time royal ally, others disloyal, Niqmandu alone loyal, invitation to join the rebellion rejected, loyalty verified by master. The only real difference between this narrative and what we might call the story of Rib-Hadda's life is in the conclusion: Niqmandu was rewarded, Rib-Hadda was not.

The theme of loyalty demonstrated and/or tested followed by

[32]*EA* 119:39–44.

[33]This statement cannot be elaborated here, but anyone familiar with the Amarna letters can easily recall similar expressions of self-abasement, utter servility, etc., in the letters of other vassals.

[34]J. Nougayrol, *Palais royal d'Ugarit*, IV, Mission de Ras Shamra 9 (Paris: Klincksieck, 1956) 36:14–18.

[35]Ibid., 40–41:1–19.

reward is a narrative scheme that also underlies what Moshe Weinfeld has called a covenant of grant, a type of document that he finds from the second millennium down into Neo-Assyrian times and reflected as well in a number of biblical narratives.[36] He argues that it is such a covenant that is given to Noah, Abraham, Caleb, David, and the priesthood of Aaron. More recently, Jon Levenson has pointed to a theme of these grants that Weinfeld overlooked:

> In most of these instances, if not all, there is a contrast between the vassal and some faithless contemporary(ies). In other words, it is not, as Weinfeld states, simply the loyalty of the donee which wins him his covenant, but rather a loyalty unique in his time, a fidelity unparalleled in his context. This context is explicit in the cases of Noah, the only "righteous and pure man ... of his generation" (Gen 6:9), Caleb, whose confidence contrasts with the faithless cowardice of most of the spies (Numbers 13–14), and Phinehas, whose active zeal stands out against a community paralyzed with grief (Numbers 25).[37]

The relevance of Levenson's observations for Rib-Hadda's self-portrait is evident. It should also be noted that Rib-Hadda is familiar with the argument and the language of reward we saw used by Suppiluliumas. "He (the king) knows my *kittu*. The king (also) knows how long he has been showing me favor because I have no divided allegiance (lit. second heart), my only intention being to serve the king, my lord."[38] Suppiluliumas: to see the *kittu*, and, literally, to favor a favor (*dumqa dummuqu*); Rib-Hadda: to know the *kittu*, and, literally, to do a favor (*dumqa epēšu*).

All of these various themes—loyal service, the enticements and hostility of the disloyal, a unique loyalty, the reward of loyalty—shape and pattern Rib-Hadda's thought of himself and the world about him. With them and through them he sees his life and tells his tale. And so the tale begins to make no sense, to trouble and perplex, to become, as it were, an anti-tale. For though uniquely loyal, Rib-Hadda remains unrewarded. How can this be? "Why has the king done nothing for me?" Rib-Hadda's last words concern an ideal and an ethos. He writes them, not as a Job, but as a puzzled and unrewarded Caleb.

[36] *JAOS* 90 (1970) 184–203.

[37] *CBQ* 38 (1976) 512. See earlier his *Theology of the Program of Restoration of Ezekiel 40–48*, HSM 10 (Missoula: Scholars Press, 1976), esp. 146–47.

[38] See n. 32.

24. Join the ᶜApiru or Become One?

The discussion of the many problems posed by those who in the Amarna letters are called variously GAZ, SA.GAZ, etc., that is, (probably) ᶜApiru, is not over. It extends now even to a basic question of translation. A fairly common expression, especially in the letters of Rib-Hadda of Byblos, is *nenpušu ana* (SA.)GAZ(.MEŠ), etc. It is said of groups or collectives (towns, countries), and it has long been understood more or less in the sense of Knudtzon's "sich anschliesse." However, the correctness of this translation is now challenged. It is argued on the evidence of the Amarna letters themselves that the expression must often mean nothing more than to become an enemy of the crown; the defectors simply become ᶜApiru, they do not join them, as if the ᶜApiru were an already existing group. And in support of this analysis Mario Liverani has recently brought linguistic arguments, claiming that the expression in question is an Egyptianism that reflects Egyptian *ỉrỉ* (Akk. *epēšu*)/*ỉrw* (Akk. *nenpušu*) *m* (Akk. *ana*) 'to make/be made, transformed into', practically 'to become'.[1]

Is this right? What about this Egyptianism? Questions of this sort I have been used to laying before one esteemed colleague, and it seems appropriate to repeat this exercise here. It is one way of thanking him for the many answers in the past.

The first thing that strikes one in the alleged equivalence is the postulated correspondence of Egyptian *m* and Akkadian *ana*. Certainly *ana* is not expected. The basic meanings of *m* 'in', 'from', and 'with', call rather for *ina*.[2] Moreover, in the expression in question we are dealing with one use of the *m* of predication,[3] and one would expect a Canaanite scribe to think of the *beth essentiae*. In Amarna itself we have four comparable cases of such a predicate adjunct, and in all four *ina* is used:

[1]M. Liverani, "Farsi ḫabiru," *Vicino Oriente* 2 (1979) 65–77, especially 70ff., where a review of earlier opinions is also found.

[2]For the meanings of *m*, see Alan H. Gardiner, *Egyptian Grammar* (3rd ed.; Oxford, 1957) 124–25, §162.

[3]Ibid., 65, §84.

a. 'You are a wise man; the king knows (this), and because of your wis<d>om[4] he sent you as commissioner' (*ištaparka ina rābiṣi, EA* 71:7–10).

b. 'Moreover, may it seem right in the sight of my lord, and may he send Yanḫamu as its commissioner' (*luwaššira ... ina rābiṣīši, EA* 106:35–37).

c. 'Then if it pleases you, appoint as its commissioner (*šukun ina rābiṣīši*) someone respected by the king's mayors' (*EA* 107:20–24).[5]

d. 'The king knows whether you appointed me as commissioner (*šaknatani ina rābiṣi*) in Tyre' (*EA* 149:47–48).

These examples as well as general considerations of meaning argue against *m* = *ana*.[6]

Another difficulty with the alleged Egyptianism is that we find *nenpušu ana* followed not only by SA.GAZ.MEŠ, etc., but by an individual identified by name, title, or personal pronoun. For example, 'Send a large archer-host to drive out the king's enemies from his land' *u tinnipšū kale mātāti ana šarri* (*EA* 76:38–43). Obviously the lands are not to be transformed into or become the king, and so *nenpušu ana* now means, not 'diventare', but 'diventare di'. Our unease with such really quite different meanings, which assumptions of an original ambiguity, partial lack of understanding, and inexactness of application do not alleviate, only increases when we find that in the same letter, within only a few lines, we must shift between 'diventare' (*ennepšat māt šarri ... ana* LÚ.GAZ.MEŠ, *EA* 76:34–37) and 'diventare di' (lines 38–43, as just quoted). Nor is this by any means the only example of such a shift; cf. *EA* 73:22 (*ana šâše*, i.e., ERÍN.MEŠ *piṭati*),[7] 28, 32 (*ana* LÚ.MEŠ.GAZ); 79:20, 26 (*ana* LÚ.MEŠ.GAZ.MEŠ), 44 (*ana* ᶜ*Abdi-Aširta*); 88:32 (*ana šâšu*), 34 (*ana* LÚ.MEŠ.SA.GAZ.MEŠ);[8] 129:8 (*ana šarri bēlīya*), 89 (*ana* LÚ.MEŠ.SA.GAZ.MEŠ). In brief, people, towns, or

[4]*ina im-<qú>-ti-ka*, following W. F. Albright, "Cuneiform Material for Egyptian Prosopography, 1500–1200 B.C.," *JNES* 5 (1946) 12, n. 8.

[5]On this passage see my "Amarna Glosses," *RA* 69 (1975) 155f. [above, Paper 18, pp. 284–85].

[6]One could postulate *r* replacing *m* (Gardiner, *Egyptian Grammar*, 65, §84), and this would yield an acceptable equation *r* = *ana*.

[7]Note the grammatical singular but underlying collective reference. Given the assumed meaning of *nenpušu ana* ᶜ*apirī*, one would expect that in this passage the Amorites proposed to *become* soldiers, not to be added to their ranks.

[8]Note the postulated shift particularly in this passage: 'If the king, my lord, does not give heed to the words of his servant, then Byblos will become his (*ennepša ana šâšu*) and all the lands of the king, as far as Egypt, will become ᶜApiru (*tinnipšu ana* LÚ.MEŠ.SA.GAZ.MEŠ)' (*EA* 88:29–34).

countries *nenpušu* to the king, or, on the other side of the ledger, to the ᶜApiru or to an individual enemy of the king. Without absolutely compelling evidence to the contrary,[9] we must assume the same meaning throughout, and the only one that fits is something like the old 'sich anschliessen'.

Rejecting an Egyptian origin for the expression, I would look elsewhere. I might begin by noting that in the probable thirty-eight occurrences of the expression the subject of the action, that which is 'done', is most commonly a city or a land: city-cities, 9x/10x;[10] land-lands-all lands, 15x/17x;[11] 'everything', referring to a territory, 1x.[12] The exceptions may be more apparent than real. Of the remaining ten instances all but two refer to the people as belonging either to a city or to a country; it is as members of such groups that they are 'done' to the ᶜApiru, etc.[13]

This medio-passive construction according to which a geopolitical entity is 'done/made to/for' someone else recalls another idiom of Western Peripheral Akkadian, 'to do a city'. It is attested in the Mari letters[14] and *EA*,[15] and according to the dictionaries it means 'to conquer a city'. *AHw* adds the suggestion that it may be slang. 'To conquer', however, with its implication of force, may not be right. 'To take control of, appropriate', or the like, would also fit, and it seems required by *EA* 148:45, *īpuš māt šarri ana* LÚ.SA.GAZ 'he (the king of Hazor) has taken over/turned over the king's land for/to the ᶜApiru'. To judge from the previous lines, this *epēš māt šarri ana ᶜapirī*[16] was effected by

[9]On ᶜApiru as simply an enemy of the king, see below.

[10]*EA* 74:21; 87:19; 88:31; 89:12; 104:51; 116:38; 117:94; 127:20(?); 144:25, 29. On *EA* 148:45, see below.

[11]*EA* 70:29; 73:32; 74:35; 76:35, 42; 77:28; 79:19, 25(?), 42; 84:9; 85:72; 88:33; 89:31(?); 111:19; 129:80; 362:63.

[12]*EA* 68:17.

[13]*EA* 73:22, 28; 74:27; 81:12; 129:88(?); 138:45, 50, 93. Only in *EA* 138:46 is the subject singular, where to the city's exhortation 'Let's join Aziru', Rib-Hadda replies, 'How can I join him?' (The analysis of forms like *ni-te-pu-uš*, whether N perfect or Gt preterite, need not detain us here.)

[14]*ARM(T)* 1 123:4, 6; 2 131:12, 23, 27; 6 31:24; 14 84:15′. M. Birot, *ARMT* 14 235, has expressed his doubts about the Mari evidence and translates *epēšum* by 'remêttre en état'.

[15]*CAD* E 202a refers to *EA* 174:22; 176:17; 179:17; 363:19, but add (with Knudtzon) 79:24; *AHw* 225b follows *CAD*.

[16]*īpuš* is usually taken as passive, with *māt šarri* as subject (Knudtzon; J.

the king's deserting his family and aligning himself with the ᶜApiru; nothing suggests that he had recourse to arms.

If we may legitimately doubt the implications of force in the expression 'to do a city', then there is another idiomatic use of *epēšu* that also seems relevant. This is *epēšu* in the sense of 'to acquire'. In Akkadian, it is found, broadly speaking, from Old Babylonian–Old Assyrian on, in both G and D conjugations.[17] It is also found in Ugaritic Akkadian, and of course it has good parallels in Biblical Hebrew. One can 'make' any number of things—money, houses, persons, etc.—and 'making' a city or land together with its citizenry in the sense of annexation or some kind of control would be an easy development.[18]

EA 79:18ff. shifts between the active and passive forms of *epēšu*; it illustrates and supports, I think, the main contentions of this article: 'If there are no archers, then all lands will be joined (*ennepšū*) to the ᶜApiru. Listen! Since Bit-Arḫa was seized at the urging of ᶜAbdi-Aširta, they have as a result been striving to take over (*ipēša*) Byblos and Baṭruna, and then all lands would be joined (*ennepšū*) to the ᶜApiru ... Moreover, *if the king* is unable to save me from his enemies, then all lands will be joined to ᶜAbdi-Aširta. What is he, the dog, that he takes the lands of the king for himself?'. 'Making' the last two cities not in ᶜApiru control would mean that all lands were 'made' to the ᶜApiru. Taking the lands for himself means that they are 'made' to ᶜAbdi-Aširta.

'To gain/be gained for the ᶜApiru'—would this imply that the ᶜApiru in some sense already existed? Of course, but if, as seems not infrequently to be the case, ᶜApiru means no more than 'enemy of the crown', then the expression would imply no more than that the king had enemies. And who could or would deny this was so? Certainly not

---

Bottéro, *Le problème des Ḫabiru à la 4ᵉ Rencontre Assyriologique Internationale* [Paris, 1954] 45; Moshe Greenberg, *The Ḫab/piru*, American Oriental Series 39 [New Haven, 1955] 41). But in the Tyrian letters *mātu* is consistently construed as feminine and therefore one would expect *i-pu-ša-at* (*EA* 273:1), *epšat, ennepšat*; see *EA* 147:32; 149:45; 151:55; 153:5. Perhaps LÚ.SA.GAZ refers to the king of Sidon mentioned in line 40 (so Greenberg).

17 See *AHw* 227a, G 5–6; 227b, D 4; *CAD* E 230b, 2.7′; and on the D, see Yochanan Muffs, *Studies in the Aramaic Legal Papyri from Elephantine* (Studia et documenta ad iura orientis antiqui pertinentia, 8; Leiden, 1969) 20, n. 1. For the Ugaritic Akkadian usage, see *PRU* IV 127:10; 231 (RS 17.244):10.

18 Note that the view developed here was long ago anticipated or implied by Knudtzon's translations. Cf. the translations of *epēšu* in *EA* 174, 176, and 179 by 'gewinnen', and in *EA* 79 by 'sich aneignen' (see n. 15).

Rib-Hadda, to whom we owe most of the occurrences of this expression. The world he describes in his letters is one divided and defined by loyalty to the Pharaoh: on one side stands Rib-Hadda, who in some sense stands alone; on the other, a mass of enemies and traitors—ᶜApiru.[19]

[19]For Rib-Hadda's self-perception, see my "Rib-Hadda: Job at Byblos?" pp. 173–81 in *Biblical and Related Studies Presented to Samuel Iwry*, eds. Ann Kort and Scott Morschauser (Winona Lake: Eisenbrauns, 1985) [above, Paper 23].

25. Amarna Texts in the Metropolitan Museum of Art

1.

Royal letter: from Aššur-uballiṭ, king of Assyria, to the king of Egypt (MMA 24.2.11).

Height 77 mm. Width 55 mm. Thickness 25 mm.

Transliteration

Obv.	1.	*a-na* LUGAL KUR *M*[*i-iṣ-(ṣa)-ri*]
	2.	*qí-bi-* [*ma*]
	3.	*um-ma* ^{Id}A-*šur*-TI.L[A LUGAL KUR ^{d}*A*]-*šur-ma*
	4.	*a-na ka-ša* É-*ka a-na* KUR-*ka*
	5.	*a-na* ^{giš}GIGIR.MEŠ-*ka ù* ÉRIN.MEŠ-*ka*
	6.	*lu-ú šul- mu*
	7.	DUMU *ši-ip-ri-ia al-tap-ra-ak-ku*
	8.	*a-na a-ma-ri-ka ù* KUR-*ka a-na a-ma-ri*
	9.	*a-di an-ni-ša ab-ba-ú-ia*
	10.	*la iš- pu- ru*
	11.	u_4-*ma a-na-ku al-tap-ra-ak-ku*
	12.	1 ^{giš}GIGIR SIG_5-*ta* 2 ANŠE.KUR.RA.MEŠ
	13.	⸢*ù*⸣ 1 $^{\text{na}_4}$*ú-ḫi-na ša* $^{\text{na}_4}$ZA.GÌN KUR-*e*
	14.	[*a-n*]*a šul-ma-ni-ka*
	15.	[*ú*]-*še-bi-la-*⸢*ku*⸣
Lo.E.	16.	[DUMU *ši*]-*ip-ri ša aš-pu-ra-ku-ni*
	17.	*a-na a-ma-ri*
Rev.	18.	[*l*]*a* tu_4-*ka-*⸢*as*⸣-*sú*
	19.	[*l*]*i-mu-ur ù li-it-tal-ka*
	20.	[*ṭ*]*é-em-ka ù ṭé-em*
	21.	*ma-ti-ka li-mur*
	22.	*ù li-it-ta-al-ka*

Translation

1–6. Say to the king of the land of E[gypt]: Thus Aššur-uball[liṭ, the king of the land of (the god) A]ššur. For you, your household, for your land, may all be well.

7–15. I have sent my messenger to you to visit you and to visit your land. Up to now, my predecessors have not written; today, I have written to you. [I] send you a splendid chariot, 2 horses, and 1 date-stone of genuine lapis lazuli as your greeting gift.

16–22. Do [no]t delay the messenger whom I have sent to you for a visit. He should visit and then leave for here. He should see what you are like and what your land is like, and then leave for here.

Notes

3: See J. A. Knudtzon, *Die El-Amarna-Tafeln*, Vorderasiatische Bibliothek II/1 (Leipzig, 1915), p. 126, no. 16:3, ^{Id}*A-šur*-TI.LA LUGAL KUR ^{d}[*A-šu*]*r*. Both the use of the title "king" and the designation of Assyria as a land and not simply as a city seem to be innovations of Aššur-uballiṭ. With a new sense of unity and political purpose, Assyria was about to begin its role in Near Eastern history; see R. Borger, *Einleitung in die assyrischen Königsinschriften* I (Leiden, 1961), p. 26.

13: For $^{\text{na}_4}$*uḫīnu* as beads in the shape of (unripe) dates, see P. Artzi, *Bar-Ilan Studies in History* (1978), p. 32, n. 15, and J. Bottéro, *RA* 43 (1949), pp. 14ff.

Remarks

This text (*EA* 15) was previously published in copy in V. Scheil, *Bulletin de l'Institut français d'Archéologie orientale du Caire* 2 (1902), p. 114. For photos, see L. S. Bull, *The Metropolitan Museum of Art Bulletin* 21 (1926), p. 170, fig. 1 (obverse); W. C. Hayes, *The Scepter of Egypt* II (Cambridge, Mass., 1959), p. 296, fig. 182 (obverse). A transliteration and translation of the text is in J. A. Knudtzon, *Die El-Amarna-Tafeln*, Vorderasiatische Bibliothek II/1 (Leipzig, 1915), pp. 124–27, and in P. Artzi, *Bar-Ilan Studies in History* (1978), pp. 27–28. A translation will also be found in A. K. Grayson, *Assyrian Royal Inscriptions* I (Wiesbaden, 1972), pp. 47–48.

2.

Royal letter: from Abi-milku of Tyre to the king of Egypt (MMA 24.2.12).

Height 76 mm. Width 52 mm. Thickness 24 mm.

Transliteration

Obv.	1.	[*a-na*] LUGAL EN-*lí-ia*
	2.	[*u*]*m-ma* ^{I}*Ia-bi*-LUGAL ⸢ÌR⸣-*ka*
	3.	7 *u* 7 *a-na* GÌR.MEŠ-*ka am-qut*
	4.	*ša i*[*q-b*]*i* LUGAL *be-li-ia*
	5.	*šu*-[*ut*] *e-te-pu-uš*
	6.	*pal-ḫa-at gáb-bi*
	7.	KUR-*ti iš-tu pa-ni*
	8.	ÉRIN.MEŠ LUGAL EN-*lí-ia*
	9.	*su-ḫi-iz-ti* LÚ.MEŠ-*ia*
	10.	^{giš}MÁ.MEŠ *a-na pa-ni*
	11.	ÉRIN.MEŠ LUGAL *be-li-ia*
	12.	*ù ša la iš-te-mi*
	13.	*ia-nu* É-*šu ia-nu*
	14.	*bal-ṭá-šu an-nu-ú*
	15.	*a-na-an-ṣ*[*ár* UR]U(?)
	16.	LUGAL *be*-[*li -i*]*a*
Lo. E.	17.	⸢*ù šu-ul*⸣ *-m*[*i*]
	18.	*mu-ḫi* LUGAL *li*-[*de*]
Rev.	19.	*a-na* ÌR-*šu ša*
	20.	*it-ti-šu*

Translation

1–2. [To] the king, my lord: [Mes]sage of Abi-milku, your servant.

3–11. I fall at your feet 7 times and 7 times. What the king, my lord, or[dered], th[at] I have done. The entire land is afraid of the troops of the king, my lord. I have had my men hold(?) ships at the disposition(?) of the troops of the king, my Lord.

12–20. Whoever disobeyed has no family, has nothing alive. Since I gua[rd(?) the cit]y(?) of the king, my lord, [m]y safety(?) is the king's responsibility(?). May [he take cognizance of(?)] his servant who is on his side(?).

Note

2: The name is written Yabi-milku (*Ia-bi*-LUGAL), but certainly Abi-milku, the ruler of Tyre, is meant. The very distinctive writing of the Abi-milku letters is found on this tablet.

Remarks

This text (*EA* 153) was previously published in copy in V. Scheil, *Bulletin de l'Institut français d'Archéologie orientale du Caire* 2 (1902), p. 116. For photos, see L. S. Bull, *The Metropolitan Museum of Art Bulletin* 21 (1926), p. 170, fig. 2 (obverse); J. Pritchard, *The Ancient Near East in Pictures* (Princeton, 1969), no. 245 (obverse). A transliteration and translation of the text is in J. A. Knudtzon, *Die El-Amarna-Tafeln*, Vorderasiatische Bibliothek II/1 (Leipzig, 1915), pp. 630–31.

26. Some Reflections on Amarna Politics

Mario Liverani has argued that the vassal correspondence in the Amarna letters was an exercise in mutual misunderstanding. In his opinion, the Egyptian administration wrote with a conception of suzerain-vassal relations that the vassals had only partially assimilated. Their letters often reflect a quite different conception and one totally alien to Egyptian thinking. Hence the ongoing misunderstanding, which was also fostered by the interference of linguistic substrates. This article offers a different interpretation of the evidence and denies any malentendu.

In 1967 Mario Liverani published an article entitled "Contrasti e confluenze di concezioni politiche nell'età di El-Amarna."[1] Though it appeared in a major Assyriological journal and argued for a radical revision of our thinking about Amarna politics, it was generally ignored by historians of the Amarna period. Perhaps in those "pre-Ebla" days *itala non leguntur* was still too true. Whatever the explanation, in 1983, when he returned to the subject, this time writing in English ("Political Lexicon and Political Ideologies in the Amarna Letters"),[2] Liverani could with good reason complain of the neglect that his work had received. And even now, writing a decade later, I am still unaware of any serious examination of Liverani's position. I wish, therefore, to fill this gap in Amarna studies, to make Liverani's position known and, in the spirit of friendly debate, to argue against it. I wish, too, of course, to salute Jonas Greenfield, no stranger to the Amarna world.

According to Liverani, in the correspondence between Egypt and its vassals in the Amarna period, there are discernible two political concepts or, more exactly, two lines of political behavior, deriving from different political, cultural, and social histories. One he calls Asiatic. Though he sees its diffusion from Anatolia across northern Mesopotamia and down through Syria and Palestine, he finds its classical expression in the Hittite vassal treaties. It is characterized by the presence of obligations that bind suzerain as well as vassal. The latter's oath of loyalty

[1]M. Liverani, "Contrasti e confluenze de concezioni politiche nell'età di El-Amarna," *RA* 61 (1967) 1–18.

[2]M. Liverani, "Political Lexicon and Political Ideologies in the Amarna Letters," *Berytus* 31 (1983) 41–56.

requires of him, inter alia, the acceptance of his master's friends and enemies as his own, and hence his renunciation of all aggression against a fellow vassal. To this the suzerain has a corresponding obligation, also solemnly ratified by oath, that as a reward for his loyalty the vassal be kept on his throne and hence defended from aggression.

Worlds apart is what Liverani calls the Egyptian conception of the vassal relationship. In this view, whereas the vassal has many obligations, the suzerain has none. As a god, the Pharaoh can be bound to no one. The theological absurdity of his being under oath, with its ensuing obligations, is reinforced by Egypt's profound ethnocentrism and consequent contempt for the barbarians abroad. A political arrangement of the Asiatic type is, therefore, unthinkable and completely alien to Egyptian thought and practice. Hence, the Egyptian vassal has no legal claims on his master and, however loyal, he may not, if attacked, demand to be defended. This he could expect only if purely Egyptian interests were at stake, and these—another important difference from Asiatic rule—do not necessarily involve the vassals' maintaining peaceful relations among themselves, provided they continue to serve Egypt.

The originality of Liverani's thesis is in his opinion that, whereas of course the directives and replies of the Pharaoh reflect a purely Egyptian viewpoint, this viewpoint is not completely shared by the vassals themselves, all of whom also betray in their letters the influence of the Asiatic institution. Liverani finds evidence of this anomaly in the numerous instances in which a vassal, in one way or another, insists on his loyalty and then, as if he were addressing an Asiatic overlord, demands help in defending himself against his enemies. The implied argument is naturally quite ineffective, especially since the enemy in question is almost always another Egyptian vassal. Indifferent to such quarrels insofar as the narrow interests of the conflicting parties are concerned, the Pharaoh usually refuses to intervene and tells the vassal to take care of himself. In short, the vassal correspondence is shot through with an intrusive element, a curious survival of a quite alien world of political discourse.

Can this possibly be right? This way of putting the question, even prior to a closer consideration of the evidence, seems legitimate, for to anyone recalling the historical context of the Amarna letters the improbability of such survival is immediately apparent. At the time the letters were written, Egyptian control of the area occupied by the vassals had been more or less firmly established since the reign of Thutmosis III. Experience of Egyptian rule was not something new; it had been a fact of political life for roughly a century. Whatever may have been the initial difficulties in grasping what an Egyptian regime meant and in adjusting to it, they should certainly have been surmounted by four or five generations of Syro-Palestinian princes.

Particularly difficult to understand is how a ruler in Byblos could have failed to see every implication of subjection to Egypt, for in the Amarna age Byblos had already been a center of profound Egyptian influence for over a millennium[3] and, with no exaggeration, its prince could boast that it had served Egypt from the most ancient days.[4] But even elsewhere, at least since the time of Thutmosis III, the sons of many local rulers had been held as hostages in Egypt, educated there and then returned to their native lands to succeed their fathers.[5] After years of such training and, presumably, indoctrination, could anyone have cherished the slightest illusion of enjoying any legal claims on his Egyptian master?

That, in fact, the Egyptian viewpoint was far from being unassimilated, Liverani himself has demonstrated, often with very perceptive observations.[6] Confining ourselves to a brief outline of his remarks, we find:

1. The vassals recognized the futility of arguing their case simply on the basis of their loyalty. Realizing that the Pharaoh was deaf to all but his own concerns, they tried to show that their enemies were really his enemies, and they warned that failure to defend them could only mean the loss of territory for the empire.
2. They adopted a purely Egyptian viewpoint of their duty to defend the city or territory where they were. The true Asiatic vassal saw himself as defending his own city for himself, and he expected to be helped in this by his lord. The vassals in the Amarna letters saw themselves quite differently: they were pure functionaries, defend-

[3]Liverani ("Contrasti," 13 n. 6) acknowledges this dependence but in another context and for a different purpose.

[4]*EA* 75:9; 88:45; 106:4; 116:56.

[5]See, for example, D. B. Redford, *Akhenaten, the Heretic King* (Princeton, 1984), 25–26. The practice is well attested in the Amarna letters; cf. *EA* 59, 156, 180, 198, 296. W. F. Albright, "Cuneiform Material for Egyptian Prosopography 1500–1200 B.C.," *JNES* 5 (1946) 9–10, suggested that Amankhatpi of Tashul(a)tu in South Syria (*EA* 185–186) was a native Syrian who had acquired his Egyptian name while being raised in Egypt.

[6]Liverani "Contrasti," 11–16.

ing city or territory, not for themselves, but for the king, and simply carrying out their duty to him.

3. The mentality of the functionary is also apparent in the resignations and requests for replacements that the vassals submit to the Pharaoh.[7] While such procedures make sense in a bureaucracy, for the holder of a throne with his own territory they are a form of political suicide, profiting no one.
4. The Amarna vassals also manifest a clear understanding and acceptance of their place in a hierarchy of authority. Such a hierarchy would be quite alien to an Asiatic vassal, who enjoyed a personal relationship with his lord and certain equality with other officials. His Egyptian counterpart was subordinated to Egyptian officials no less than to the Pharaoh, and to them, too, he owed a ready and unswerving obedience.

This description of the vassal mind only aggravates our initial doubts about the presence of any Asiatic elements in the thinking of the vassals. What seemed in the historical context of the Amarna letters to be quite unlikely now appears, from a psychological viewpoint, almost incomprehensible. If the vassals recognized the futility of assertions and proofs of loyalty, why did they cling to them? What is even harder to understand is, if they regarded themselves as pure functionaries, how could they return time and again to an argument that had no meaning at all? In fact, if Liverani is right, the self-image may change in the same breath, for a vassal may say not simply, "I am loyal, so protect me" (Asiatic vassal), but immediately add, "that I may guard the city for the king" (Egyptian functionary). This, I submit, is psychologically so implausible that, short of the most compelling evidence to the contrary, we must assume that protestations of loyalty and requests for help were made with an understanding consistent with the legal position of an Egyptian vassal and with the considerable evidence that the implications of such status were neither unfamiliar nor rejected.

One possibility that immediately suggests itself is that behind the assumption that protection is a reasonable reward for loyalty is the logic of enlightening the king with the fact that protecting his vassals is in his own best interests. Utter loyalty is something precious in any polity,

[7]I disagree with Liverani ("Contrasti," 13 n. 4) on the interpretation of *EA* 126: 44–45. I maintain that in this passage the question is of Byblos's being abandoned, not by Rib-Hadda, but by the Pharaoh; for my arguments, see *The Amarna Letters* (Baltimore and London, 1992) *EA* 126 n. 7.

and in a world of dubious allegiances its worth is only the greater. Rib-Hadda knows this and he claims that it has been recognized by his master: "He [the king] knows my loyalty! The king knows how often he has done some kindness to me because I am without duplicity. My only purpose is to serve the king, my lord."[8] Single-minded devotion is recognized and rewarded, and it becomes thereby the grounds of hope and expectations.

Its rarity must also be considered. "Moreover, give thought to me. Who will be loyal were I to die?"[9] "If the desire of the king is to guard his city and his servant, send a garrison to guard the city. [I] will guard it while I am [a]live. When [I] die, who is going to [gu]ard it?"[10] In neither passage may Rib-Hadda be said to be urging any personal claims; the Pharaoh's sovereign liberty to do what he will with Byblos and his servant could not be acknowledged more openly. What the vassal is doing is asking his master to consider the ways he has served him and the difficulty of replacing him with someone of comparable loyalty. This provides some understanding of what underlies the argument, "I am loyal, so protect me."

How far it is removed from the assertion of a legal right may be seen from the connotations of loyalty in some instances of its most formal expression, when a vassal identifies himself as an *arad kitti* 'loyal servant'. It belongs in the realm of expressions characteristic of the greeting formulas, in which the vassal professes his absolute servility and complete self-abasement. Thus Rib-Hadda of Byblos states: "I am a footstool for the feet of the king, my lord, and his loyal servant."[11] Compare this statement with the wording of the following: "Moreover, note that we have been loyal servants of the king from ancient times. Moreover, note that I am your loyal servant, but I have nothing but distress. Note this matter. Note that I am the dirt at your feet, O king."[12] Another example of self-abnegation is found in a letter from South Syria: "(PN), the loyal servant of the king, my lord, and the dirt at the feet of the king, my lord."[13] In the letters of Biridiya of Megiddo, the

[8]*EA* 119:39–44.

[9]*EA* 114:68.

[10]*EA* 130:44–52.

[11]*EA* 106:6–7.

[12]*EA* 116:55–60.

[13]*EA* 192:4–5. In the correspondence of Ammunira of Beirut, "(your, the king's) servant" is frequently followed by "the dirt at (your, the king's feet)," both in the

use of *arad kitti* is even more striking, for there it replaces all other expressions of abject humility and personal worthlessness—footstool, dirt at the feet, mire to be trodden on—and suffices as a declaration of complete submission.[14] The "loyal servant" is, therefore, the perfect slave, the pure instrument, one devoid of all personal autonomy in his relations with his master.

He is also evident in the *arad kitti* who is involved in litigation with a rival ruler. The rival, he claims, is unjustly holding some of his property, and the writer asks the crown to intervene, going on to say: "May *any* property of mine in his possession be taken for the king, and let the loyal servant live for the king."[15] Though maintaining his rights against a fellow vassal, he readily yields whatever is his to his master and asks only that he live for him and his service.

Similar sentiments are expressed elsewhere: "If the king, my lord, loves his loyal servant, then send (back) the three men that I may live and guard the city for the king."[16] He dares not assert his master's devotion to him, but if it exists, then he appeals to it only that he may go on living and carrying out one of his fundamental responsibilities as a vassal. The cautionary clause is important, for it suggests the attitude that must underlie and qualify any apparently forthright "I am loyal, so protect me."

If the *arad kitti* speaks *de profundis*, conscious of his lowliness and uncertain of royal grace, he also speaks the truth, even the unpleasant truth: "Being a loyal servant of the king, the Sun, with my mouth I speak words to the king that are nothing but the truth."[17] This is the introduction to the body of the letter. Rib-Hadda then takes up three topics, each of which is introduced by either "may the king heed the words of his loyal servant" (11–13, first topic; 35–36, third topic) or "may my lord heed my words" (25, second topic). These repetitions, which

---

greeting formula (*EA* 141:4–5; 142:2–4; 143:3–5) and in the body of the letter (*EA* 141:11–12,19–20; 143:11–12). In *EA* 141:39–40, "the servant of the king, (my) lord, and a footstool for his feet."

[14] *EA* 242:5; 243:4; 246:4; 365:4.

[15] *EA* 105:81–83. Cf. "Everything belongs to the king" (*EA* 197:6).

[16] *EA* 123:23–28.

[17] *EA* 107:8–11. Note *arad kitti* and *kitta-ma* 'nothing but the truth'. The courage to report the unpalatable truth seems to be the point of *EA* 149:14–16. It is also claimed by ᶜAbdi-Kheba, who dares inform the court of the dire situation in South Palestine, and as a result he is slandered by his and the crown's enemies; see *EA* 286:22–24,49,63–64.

structure the argument and are so resonant of the opening lines, serve to emphasize the truth and value of what Rib-Hadda asserts or advises. His loyalty, so insisted on, implies not a right to be heard, but the wisdom of doing so.

The same implications of veracity and reliability are stressed again by Rib-Hadda: "Treacherous words are now being spoken in the presence of the king, the Sun. I am your loyal servant, and whatever I know or have heard I write to the king, my lord."[18] Rib-Hadda goes on to discredit the idea that the followers of Aziru in Amurru could possibly resist Egyptian archers, and he recalls how right he proved to be in the past when at his urging the king's father sent archers and Aziru's father was captured. Rib-Hadda's loyalty means that he keeps the king fully informed,[19] with the additional implication that no information is passed on to the king's enemies.[20] It also means that his advice can be trusted, a claim he can bolster with recent history.[21]

In other passages it is difficult to decide among the various connotations of and motivations associated with loyalty: personal value to the king, hope of reward, abasement and denial of personal interest, truthfulness and credibility.[22] When the king is urged to heed his loyal ser-

[18]*EA* 108:20–25.

[19]See also *EA* 145:23–26; 149:14–17, 151:49–51. Furnishing intelligence also appears as a vassal duty in Hittite and Assyrian treaties.

[20]Supplying the enemy with information is treason; cf. *EA* 82:10–12; 147:66–69; 149:68–70.

[21]*EA* 108:28–33 (the capture of ᶜAbdi-Aširta), and see also 117:27–28; 132:16–18; 138:33–34; 362:20.

[22]See *EA* 73:42; 80:17; 85:17,63; 100:32; 101:38; 103:7,24; 108:69; 109:42; 114:43; 116:55; 119:25; 139:30; 155:48; 180:19; 198:10; 241:19; 254:10–11. Occasionally, the stress is on how provocative loyalty is among the king's enemies, who make his servants pay for it. "For what reason is your loyal servant so treated? For service to you!" (*EA* 114:41–43; cf. 114:65–67; 100:15–18).

Cities also have *kittu*. They may be an *amat kitti* 'loyal maidservant' (*EA* 68:11, 74:7), or *āl/ālānī kitti* 'loyal city/cities' (*EA* 74:9,56; 88:8,44; 106:4; 127:25; 132:9; 138:37). According to Z. Kallai and H. Tadmor ("Bit Ninurta = Beth Horon: On the History of the Kingdom of Jerusalem in the Amarna Period," *Eretz-Israel* 9 [1969] 138 n. 2 [Hebrew]), *ālānī kitti šarri* means 'cities under covenant with the king', not 'cities loyal to the king'. Against this view are several reasons: (1) In *EA* 74, *āl kittišu* (9) replaces *Gubla amat kitti ša šarri* (6–8), and the two expressions seem virtually synonymous. But *amat kitti* is obviously the feminine counterpart of *arad kitti*, and the latter does not mean simply 'one under covenant', i.e., 'vassal'. Not only is Yankhamu, the royal commissioner, an *arad kitti* (*EA* 118:56), but this quality is proposed as distinguishing him among the king's servants in general. Moreover, *arad kitti* is obviously a badge of dis-

vant's words and is then asked for help, is the vassal reminding him that the crown's interests are involved? Is he asking to be rewarded for loyalty? Is he implying the purity of his motives? Is he guaranteeing the truth of the need or peril he describes? Often, one may suspect, he was vaguely aware of the whole register and would, if asked, exclude none of the possibilities. Like the poet, he would prefer not to join "that kingdom of single-eyed men to which language (as ordinarily used) aspires." For his purpose, better the richness of ambiguity.

The principal contribution of Liverani's later article in *Berytus*[23] is the discussion of four entries in the "Amarna political lexicon" as illustrative of the misunderstandings and cross-purposes that vitiated the political correspondence between Egypt and her Syro-Palestinian vassals.

The first entry is the verb *naṣāru* 'to protect'. According to Liverani, whereas an Asiatic vassal enjoys with his suzerain a personal relationship of mutual protection, his Egyptian counterpart is simply an impersonal cog in the bureaucratic machinery. When he is told, as he so often is, to protect himself and the place where he is, this is administrative jargon, meaning simply that he should be on the alert, do his job and stay where he has been put. The vassals do not understand this; when told to protect themselves, they think they are to do just that and so, like good Asiatics, under duress, they feel free to ask the Pharaoh for help or "salvific protection" (Liverani's term), in times of crisis.

Aiding and abetting this misapprehension is language interference: on the Egyptian side, because in Egyptian (*sꜣw*) 'to protect' also means 'to pay attention', Akkadian *naṣāru* is given this additional meaning, a plus alien to it in standard Akkadian. On the Canaanite side, on the basis of Canaanite *yšᶜ*, *naṣāru* is given another plus, the meaning not only of 'to protect', but 'to rescue, save'.

---

tinction that a vassal parades before his master; it is not borne by his enemies, even though they are usually vassals like himself. For Rib-Hadda to call ᶜAbdi-Ashirta or Aziru an *arad kitti* is unthinkable, which it would not be if the expression simply meant a vassal under oath to the Pharaoh. (2) Again, in *EA* 74:9–10, the enormity of the scandal of the king's abandoning *āl kittīšu* is emphasized by Rib-Hadda's request, which he immediately urges, that the king should check in the royal archives to find out if there has ever been in Byblos a ruler who was not *arad kitti*. The presence of an *arad kitti* establishes Byblos as an *amat kitti*. (3) In *EA* 88:43–45, despite some question about the end of the passage, Byblos is certainly contrasted with other cities, and Rib-Hadda's argument would certainly be stronger if he could say, not that Byblos was Egypt's most ancient vassal, but that it had the longest record of loyalty.

[23]Liverani, "Political Lexicon," 49–56.

Comments: (1) The linguistic argument, which it must be noted, in its most controversial parts is never supported by the citation of a single text, is quite unconvincing. First of all, it is not true that in standard Akkadian *naṣāru* never means 'to pay attention'.[24] Second, in *EA*, *naṣāru* does not mean 'to rescue, save'.[25] Third, in Canaanite, *yšᶜ* does not mean 'to protect'.[26] (2) That the vassals should so universally and so persistently misunderstand the order to guard the place where they are, with not a word from Egypt to set them straight, seems extremely implausible. (3) If the vassals occasionally read more into the verb *naṣāru* than the Egyptians intend, this does not mean they do not understand their orders. Rather, they play the game of politics, ignore what is said and take the opportunity to state their case and their needs once more.

The second entry, and another source of tension, Liverani asserts, is the word *balāṭu*, both 'life' and 'to live'.[27] In *EA*, 'life' has two referents, one on the ideological level where all life, both now and in the hereafter, comes from the Pharaoh, and the other on the practical day-to-day level of 'victuals', the essentials of staying alive, with their ultimate source again the Pharaoh. Both uses, as Liverani admits, were familiar to the vassals, though naturally they were much more interested in the practical level, especially in times of food shortages. What is not clear is the basis of Liverani's claim that they could legitimately expect only life on the first level, in the form of ideology and propaganda. De

24See J.-M. Durand, *Archives épistolaires de Mari* 1/1 = (ARM 26; Paris, 1988) 391 n. 80 (end). Its appearance at Mari is especially relevant.

25Of the meanings assigned to *naṣāru* in *EA*, Ebeling's glossary ([Vorderasiatische Bibliothek 2/2; Leipzig, 1915] 1483) is representative: *schützen, bewahren, auf der Hut sein, beobachten*. That Liverani is going against *opinio communis* and does not feel required to cite a single passage where the meaning is *(er)retten* is very hard to understand. Note that there are a few passages in which *naṣāru* is construed with *ištu*, but here the preposition is used in the sense of 'with', not 'from'; see the discussion in Moran, *The Amarna Letters EA* 112 n. 1. It might also be remarked that, if *naṣāru* in *EA* means 'to rescue, save', not once, despite its great frequency, is it ever construed with *ištu qāt*, 'from the hand'. Contrast the two verbs that do mean 'rescue, save' in *EA*, *ekēmu* (*EA* 271:13, 274:10) and *šūzubu* (*EA* 62:30–31; 74:33,44; 318:8), and cf. *hôšîaᶜ* / *hiṣṣîl miyyad* in Hebrew.

26Again, a meaning asserted against the dictionaries, with no supporting evidence.

27Among the passages cited by Liverani is *EA* 369:18–23, with reference to my treatment of the text in "Amarna Glosses," *RA* 69 (1975) 151–53 [above, Paper 18, pp. 280–82]. It might be noted, however, that I argue there against any reading of *balāṭu* into the text.

facto, the Pharaoh provided for them in the past, and they appeal to this precedent.[28]

The third entry is the expression *šūšuru ana pānī* 'to prepare before the arrival'. Liverani has identified the underlying Egyptian expression, which, he maintains, though in general understood correctly by the vassals, was misunderstood in a small group of texts.[29] He may be right, but in the overall picture of political relations, such a misunderstanding seems trivial and of no real importance.

The last entry is the verb *qâlu*. According to Liverani, in good Akkadian *qâlu* means simply 'to keep quiet', but in *EA* it acquires a plus, the negative connotation of doing nothing, abstaining from action when the situation cries for it. Liverani traces this plus to Hebrew *dmm*, which means both 'to keep quiet' and 'to be still, inactive'. For the Egyptians, however, on the basis of *gr* in their own language, 'to keep quiet' suggests a different plus, the positive one of self-control. Hence, when Rib-Hadda asks why the Pharaoh keeps silent (and does nothing and neglects his own interests), the Pharaoh understands them to be asking why he exercises such admirable self-control—one more misunderstanding. The Pharaoh does nothing, just to make clear how absurd and useless Rib-Hadda's complaints really are.

Comments: (1) Liverani's description of the use of *qâlu* is very misleading. The negative implications of the verb reappear in Neo-Assyrian,[30] and they are already attested at Nuzi.[31] And given this

[28]See *EA* 112:50–51,54–55; 121:11–17; 122:9–11,24–31; 125:14–18; 130:21–30; cf., too, 68:27–28; 85:34–37; 86:32–35. Liverani himself ("Political Lexicon," 52) points to texts in which the Pharaoh boasts of having supplied foreigners with provisions.

[29]They are *EA* 201–202, 203–206. The phrase *ana pāni*, according to Liverani, was taken in a spatial sense, and this prompted a reinterpretation of the verb to mean 'to make go straight'. Thus, the vassals saw their role to be that of guides. Since in *EA* 203–206 the expression is not 'to go before', but 'to be (at hand, available)', this suggests comparison with Hebrew *hāyâ lipnê* 'to be at the disposition of', and the vassals perhaps saw themselves as providing not so much guidance as assistance in general. It must also be mentioned that Liverani's denial of a temporal sense of *ana pāni* in good Akkadian is wrong. Such a sense is well attested in Old Babylonian (see Moran, *The Amarna Letters*, xxxi n. 100), and its presence in *EA* should be seen as one more provincial archaism (for a selective list, see ibid., xx nn. 40–41).

[30]See CAD Q 73b.

[31]Ernest R. Lacheman, *Excavations at Nuzi V: The Palace and the Temple Archives* (HSS 14; Cambridge, Mass., 1950) no. 12:8–9; and see K. Deller, W. Mayer, and J. Oelsner, "Akkadische Lexikographie: *CAD Q*," *Or.* NS 58 (1989)

earlier evidence, one can make a good case for an even earlier appearance in Old Babylonian.[32] (2) Hebrew *dmm* never connotes culpable or inexcusable negligence. (3) The Pharaoh's failure to act hardly requires recourse to language interference and the influence of an Egyptian verb.

As already noted, another important feature of Liverani's reconstruction of the Amarna age is his opinion that Egyptian policy was one of indifference to peace among vassals, provided they remained faithful to Egypt. To support this view he offers the evidence of two letters and the general consideration that, if intervassal wars were forbidden, we should have to admit Egyptian weakness or inertia and a certain inconsistency between actual practice and political thought.[33]

The first letter is *EA* 162, from Amenophis IV to Aziru in Amurru, and this is interpreted in the light of the latter's letters to the Egyptian court.[34] In these, as he harasses Egyptian vassals, foments sedition, sides with the rebels, and seizes new territory for himself, he goes on writing to the court and pledging his fidelity. He has recognized (says Liverani) what Egypt requires of a vassal and he exploits the limitations of its goals. And when the king writes to him in *EA* 162, he is reproached only for his treatment of Rib-Hadda in exile and for consorting with an enemy of Egypt, and even this is done rather gently. All that is required of him is to conduct himself as a vassal. The Pharaoh's tacit acceptance of Amurru's expansion proves Aziru's assessment of Egyptian policy to be correct.

266. This rules out Canaanite substrate influence.

[32]See M. Stol, *Letters from Yale* (Altbabylonische Briefe 9; Leiden, 1981) no. 20:8, where F. Kraus (note a to translation) is quoted as favoring 'but you keep perfectly silent' (despite the waste just described), which fits the context admirably and was rejected by Stol only because the negative connotations of *qâlu* were otherwise unknown in Old Babylonian. The Nuzi evidence diminishes the force of this argument.

[33]Liverani, "Contrasti," 10–11. Note especially 11 n. 2, where he writes that to hold that vassals were not free to attack one another would be to fall back into the opinion "che il comportamento abituale degli Egiziani nei rispetti di tali episodi fosse in disaccordo con le loro concezioni politiche, il che sembra difficile." The difficulty he does not explain; for a different view, see below.

[34]The most recent translation of Aziru's letters is that of S. Izre'el, *Amurru Akkadian, with an Appendix on the History of Amurru by I. Singer* (HSS 41/1; Atlanta: 1991) 15–64. For a reexamination of the Aziru-Egypt correspondence and the historical context of *EA* 162, see I. Singer, HSS 41/2, 135–95, and in S. Izre'el and I. Singer, *The General's Letter from Ugarit: A Linguistic and Historical Reevaluation of RS 20.33* (*Ugaritica V, No. 20*) (Tel Aviv, 1990) 122–54.

Now there is no denying the conciliatory tone of the letter, and Amenophis IV certainly seems to have acquiesced to Aziru's appropriations. It is questionable, however, whether from this any inference may be made about Egyptian policy in general. Amurru was a very special case. At the time *EA* 162 was written, the Hittite threat was obvious and Aziru was being lured to the Hittite side.[35] Egypt, it is clear, had decided that it needed his loyalty and needed it badly. Under the circumstances, it would have been folly not to connive at a fait accompli or to exercise the gentle art of persuasion towards a very critical ally, tempering threats with promises of reward.[36] But it must also be noted that, aggressive as Aziru undoubtedly was against his neighbors, he never admitted it.[37] Obviously, he did not feel he could make an open mockery of his loyalty by frankly admitting aggression, and his silence in this regard argues against Egyptian indifference to such hostilities.

The other text Liverani cites is a letter from Lab'ayu in Palestine.[38] Here, following Knudtzon's translation, he finds Lab'ayu openly admitting to the Pharaoh that he had occupied nearby Gezer; asking the king's acceptance of the situation, which he seems sure of, he goes on to pledge his loyalty. "Cosa si vuole di più? E in effeti non sembra che il faraone voglia di più."[39]

Since I have elsewhere argued at length against this interpretation, beginning with a radical revision of Knudtzon's translation,[40] I here state only my own opinion: Lab'ayu has been accused by Milkilu, the ruler of Gezer, of treason, and he replies to the accusations with a confession of what his crime really was—before a disloyal and hostile audience he had openly accepted his own vassal status and the obligations that it entails, while suggesting that his colleague Milkilu was himself a traitor. His entering Gezer argues courage and boldness rather than a hostile occupation of the town, but if it looks as though he has occupied it, he has his defence ready: he was there to protect the interests of the crown.

On the other side of the ledger, unless one makes the vassals all hopelessly and blindly Asiatics, there is much evidence that, in principle, Egypt did not permit aggression against other vassals. Thus, Rib-

[35]See especially lines 31–32.

[36]Lines 33–38.

[37]See Singer's remarks, *The General's Letter*, 135.

[38]*EA* 253:11–35.

[39]Liverani, "Contrasti," 10.

[40]See my "Amarna Glosses," 147–51 [above, Paper 18, pp. 275–79].

Hadda frequently denounces ᶜAbdi-Ashirta and his successors for doing as they please;[41] and similar to this accusation is another, namely, that they seem to think that they are like the rulers of Khatti, Mitanni, or Babylonia, that is, rulers independent of the authority of Egypt.[42] A display of aggressive independence seems to constitute a prima facie case of rebellion, a line of argument that is not easily reconciled with an alleged freedom to attack another vassal.

Such freedom is unknown in *EA* 139:11–17, where the killing of vassal kings and a royal commissioner, as well as breaching another's city walls, are declared, simply and without further qualification, as crimes (*arnu*) against the crown. And the murderers of the king of Tyre are eager to deny what they have done, insisting that their alleged victim is still alive.[43] Unless they are guilty of a crime and open to severe reprisals, why do they not simply admit the truth and reassure the king by promises of loyalty?

A ruler in South Palestine reports that the two sons of Labᵓayu have been constantly urging him to support their attack on the citizenry of Gina, who had slain their father. Though they threaten that he will pay for it if he refuses, he does just that, saying: "May the god of the king, my lord, preserve me from waging war against the people of Gina, servants of the king, my lord."[44] The only reason he gives for risking their fury is that the proposed victims are servants of the king. Is this an excess of piety, or is he only doing his duty? That it is the latter seems clear from what immediately follows. The writer requests that the king send an official to another ruler to tell him: "You will march against the two sons of Labᵓayu or you are a rebel against the king."[45] The close association between what he has done and what this ruler should do argues that, in his mind, the only alternative to refusing the sons of Labᵓayu is to become himself guilty of a crime against the crown.

One might cite other passages with the same general thrust,[46] but

[41]*EA* 88:11; 108:12–13; 125:42–43; 126:11–12; 129:6; 139:11; 140:9–10. Note, too, the condemnation of Aziru's having acted, if not disloyally, at least independently (*EA* 162:17ff.).

[42]*EA* 76:12–13; 104:17–24; 116:67–71.

[43]*EA* 89.

[44]*EA* 250:20–22.

[45]Lines 26–27.

[46]For example, in *EA* 280:9–11: "The king, my lord, permitted me to wage war against Qeltu." The writer also promises, despite extreme provocation, to do nothing more until he hears from the king.

what is perhaps most striking and most relevant is the fact, that throughout *EA*, all wars are, in one way or another, wars of defence. A vassal admits only to defending himself and the crown or to carrying out rescue operations for innocent victims.[47] No one ever says, as Liverani thought Labʾayu did, that he has simply expanded his territory at the expense of another vassal. The argument from silence has a special validity here, because it is clear that many vassals were in fact aggressors. If, at least in theory, no special sanctions were attached to aggression, it is hard to see why absolutely no one ever admits the truth.

What, then, was Egyptian policy in this regard? It may be taken as axiomatic that one must distinguish between political ideas and political realities, recognizing that ideas may lag far behind realities. Not less axiomatic is the distinction between what a government says and what it does, between law and its enforcement, between a statement of policy and its implementation, between the power a government wills and the power it actually enjoys.[48]

That these axioms are pertinent to the present discussion was already implied in the consideration of Egypt-Amurru relations. The exigencies of the situation were such that Egypt was faced with a choice between either a much larger commitment of Egyptian forces or letting

[47]It seems a vassal was free to help his colleagues under attack (*EA* 256:21; 366:20–26) but was not obliged to, unless ordered by the king (cf. *EA* 92:30ff.). Noteworthy, too, is the fact that, critical as Rib-Hadda is of his fellow vassals, he never reproaches them for failure to send help. The apparent exception, the complaint against the kings of Beirut, Sidon, and Tyre (*EA* 92:29–40), is based on the fact of the Pharaoh's having ordered them to intervene on Rib-Hadda's behalf. On the other hand, Shuwardata seems to complain of having been abandoned by his brothers, who to judge from context were other vassals (*EA* 366:18–19). The whole question is complicated by the possibility that there were special alliances (cf. *EA* 136) or small leagues permitted by the Egyptians that could create special obligations.

[48]These are commonplaces among observers of contemporary politics and sociologists of law; see, for example, T. W. Arnold, *The Symbols of Government* (New Haven and London, 1935; New York, 1962). Of the gaps between script and performance, two random illustrations: J. K. Hyde (*Society and Politics in Medieval Italy: The Evolution of Civil Life, 1000–1350* [New Studies in Medieval History; New York, 1973]) has shown that the social and political ideology of the Italian communes first found expression in the 15th century, approximately 300 years after it had taken form in the realities of social and political life and as it was in the course of disappearing; J. Hurstfield (*Freedom, Corruption and Government in Elizabethan England* [London, 1973]) has shown, inter alia, how far in Tudor England the working of a government could be from the way it would like to work, indeed from how it even thought it worked. Hence I do not agree with Liverani's "il che sembra difficile" (n. 33).

Amurru grow into a considerable power. In opting for the latter, it did not abolish its claims to absolute obedience, as [c]Abdi-Ashirta and his successors acknowledged by paying them lip service. The political idea remained intact, though it no longer reflected the political reality.

In general, war and rebellion were chronic evils of the political order, and on the day-to-day level of administration Egyptian policy was probably about as tolerant as Liverani claims. But again we must question the legitimacy of inferences from what a government does or allows to what it says or claims. All that we may conclude is that the arrangement probably assured certain, perhaps short-sighted, Egyptian interests in the area, and that the limits of control, at least with the expenditure of resources Egypt was willing to make, had been reached. This does not mean that more far-reaching claims of control had been renounced in principle. Such a renunciation can be established only from statements of principle by either the governing or the governed. For the Amarna period, no such statements exist. On the contrary, from what the vassals say (and do not say) we can see what Egypt required them to say, that is, to acknowledge an absolute power that no longer existed, if indeed it ever did.

27. Amarna Letters

AMARNA LETTERS. In 1887, Egyptian peasants rummaging in ruins on the plain of Amarna found inscribed clay tablets. The script was Near Eastern cuneiform—at the time, a startling and unprecedented discovery. The site was the city of Akhetaten, founded by Amenhotpe IV (Akhenaten) of the eighteenth dynasty, and the find-spot proved to be the "Place of the Letters of the Pharaoh," the storehouse of Egypt's diplomatic correspondence with its Near Eastern neighbors along the Fertile Crescent—another startling discovery. Eventually, the corpus of letters, with four attached inventories, would number 350. Discovered elsewhere on the site were thirty-two more tablets in a miscellany of genres.

The language of the Amarna Letters, with a few exceptions in Assyrian, Hurrian, and Hittite, is Babylonian, but not the standard language of contemporary Babylonia. It is, rather, a provincial language that had become a lingua franca, a language of international diplomacy and trade. Within this language are two principal traditions. One is called "Hurro-Akkadian," a name that reflects the role of the Hurrians in the formation and diffusion of the language. This was the usual language of correspondence of the major powers. The other tradition is confined to the Levant, southern Syria, and Palestine, and it is radically different. The transforming influence of the underlying Canaanite speech of the area is everywhere, manifest and profound, especially in morphology and syntax. The Babylonian component is mainly lexical and therefore relatively superficial, whereas the grammar is radically Canaanitized. These Amarna Letters are therefore an important source for the reconstruction of early Canaanite dialects such as Proto-Hebrew.

Correspondence with independent powers to the north is attested from late (about the thirtieth year) in the reign of Amenhotpe III to early in the reign of Tutankhamun, a period of about twenty-five years. It should be read in the light of a central and pervasive metaphor that goes back about a millennium: the household. Allies were members of the same household and were therefore "brothers," hence the dominance of the themes of love and friendship that bind the "brothers," and of gifts, the visible expression of this bond. "Send me much gold, and you, for your part, whatever you want from my country, write me so that it may be taken to you" (the king of Babylonia to the pharaoh). The notion that they hold all in common is the ideal; the reality includes squabbles, misunderstandings, and disappointments with gifts, all frankly expressed.

The correspondence with vassals in Syria and Palestine, about three hundred letters, tells us much about the Egyptian administration, but a number of major problems remain. How many provinces were there—two, three, or four? What was the pharaoh's role and the nature and frequency of his intervention? Were these troops in transit, on an annual tour, or on their way to a great campaign in the north? Answers to these questions are fundamental to the interpretation of a large part of the vassal correspondence.

This much is clear, however: Egypt's claims of service were total and absolute, denying the vassal all autonomy and receiving his ready acknowledgment. Just as clearly, vassals pursued their own goals of expansion and self-interest. A healthy pragmatism provided a *modus vivendi*. Practically, Egypt accepted limits to its power, and the vassals continued to acknowledge an absolute power that no longer existed, if indeed it ever had.

Bibliography

Knudtzon, J. A. *Die El-Amarna-Tafeln*. Vorderasiatische Bibliothek, 2. Leipzig, 1908–1915; reprint, Aalen, 1964. A classic, still the only reliable version of the cuneiform text.

Moran, William L. *The Amarna Letters*. Baltimore, 1992. The only up-to-date translation of the entire corpus.

Rainey, Anson F. *El Amarna Tablets 359–379*, 2d ed. Alter Orient und Altes Testament, 8. Kevelaer und Neukirchen–Vluyn. A careful edition and translation of the post-Knudtzon Amarna tablets.

Indexes of Text Citations

1. Amarna Texts

1 *268n64*
1–5 *224*
1:15 *42n100, 285*
1:33 *285*
1:56–57 *306*
1:70 *305*
1:72–73 *246*
1:80 *281*
1:86 *243*
1:86–88 *246bis*
1:91 *306*
3:7 *264n52*
6–11 *224*
7:15 *305*
7:32 *305*
8:22–23 *304*
9 *238bis*
9:10 *290*
9:31–35 *238*
10:16–17 *302*
10:38 *304*
11:5 *305*
11:11 *305*
11:17–18 *305*
11:rev. 15–16 *305*
11:rev. 18 *304*
12 *272*
13:rev. 1–5 *301*
13:rev. 20 *305*
15 *224, 262, 323–24*
15–16 *224, 238*
15:9–11 *301*
15:16 *302*
16 *270n70, 271*
16:3 *324*
16:8 *271*
16:10 *260*
16:14 *260*
16:34 *259*
16:40 *259*
17 *224, 238*
17–29 *224*
22:i 46 *113, 235*
22:ii 38 *113, 235*
22:iii 32 *304*
22:iii 33 *304*
22:iii 53 *306*
22:iv 14 *306*
22:iv 22 *305*
22:iv 24 *305*
22:iv 34–35 *304*
24 *223, 237, 260*
25:ii 36 *304*
25:ii 47 *306*
25:iv 14 *304*
25:iv 18 *301*
25:iv 21 *301*
25:iv 51 *304*
25:iv 60 *305*
25:iv 63–64 *304*
25:iv 64 *304*
26 *238*
26:3 *281*
27:17 *290*
27:89 *260*
27:93 *260*
28 *262*
28:12 *260*
29:23 *306*
29:38 *271*
31–32 *223, 237*
32 *272*
32:21 *13*
34 *246n11*
34:8 *193n57*
34:14 *260*
34:16 *260*
34:19 *176*
34:33 *243*
34:39 *246*
34:52 *17n30, 176*
35 *268n64*
35:13 *173+n2, 176bis*
35:22 *176n10*
35:37 *173n2*
35:48 *176n10*
35:52 *176n10*
35:53 *176n10*
36:15 *260*
37:17 *260*
38 *262n42*
40:9 *263*
41:8–11 *290*
41:11–13 *290*
41:23–24 *290*
42 *272*
44:8 *263*
45:13 *266n55, 280n17*
45:32 *281*
45:35 *263*
53:66 *281*
55:11–12 *298*
55:12 *118*
55:20 *260*
55:49 *260*
59 *329n5*
59:5 *278n11*
59:33 *260*
60–64 *224*
60:25 *281*
62:30 *266n58*
62:30–31 *335n25*
68–95 *7, 225*
68–96 *227n1*
68:9 *152n7*
68:9–10 *64*
68:10 *28, 99*
68:11 *333n22*
68:12 *100*
68:14 *17, 81n223, 99–100, 100*
68:14–17 *188*
68:15 *152n7*
68:17 *78, 319n12*
68:19–20 *9*
68:21 *34, 58n149, 219n1*
68:22 *99*
68:25 *99bis*
68:27–28 *336n28*
68:29 *100*
68:30 *81n223*

2. Other Akkadian Texts

3. Biblical Texts

4. Ugaritic Texts

5. Other Northwest Semitic Texts